Decent
Interval

Decent Interval

An Insider's Account of
Saigon's Indecent End
Told by the CIA's Chief
Strategy Analyst in Vietnam

Frank Snepp

RANDOM HOUSE NEW YORK

Part-title drawings by Nancy Goodwin

ISBN: 0-394-40743-1
Manufactured in the United States of America
4 6 8 9 7 5 3

To Sep and Mai Ly
In Memory

Contents

Part 3: Collapse

MAPS

Foreword

In the summer of 1975 hundreds of schoolchildren crowded into a museum in Hanoi to marvel at an exhibit that had already assumed mystical significance for many Vietnamese. It was a simple affair: a white rectangular box with portholes painted on the sides and a tiny wooden figure stuck on top. Every half-hour or so—or as spectator interest demanded—a small toy helicopter would be lowered on a string, and the wooden figure pushed inside. Then, to the resounding applause of the onlookers, the helicopter would be yanked away into the dimness of an imaginary dawn.

No one who watched this ritual hour after hour needed to be told what it depicted. The white box was a replica of the now-abandoned American Embassy in Saigon; the wooden figure represented the last U.S. Ambassador, Graham Martin, and the helicopter was the one that had carried him away from Saigon forever in the early morning hours of 30 April 1975.

By the time the exhibit was opened to Hanoi's public, most Vietnamese were steeped in the lore of what had led to Martin's humiliating departure and Saigon's defeat. But few Americans knew any more about it than what was reflected in sketchy news accounts. Indeed, in the months following Saigon's collapse the State Department, the CIA and the Pentagon made a determined effort to keep the truth under classified wraps.

This book attempts to strip away some of that camouflage. It does not pretend to be a definitive history. That can come only with time and the lowering of political temperatures. But it does offer at least one perspective from the bull's-eye.

In preparing this book I have relied on "sources and methods" almost as diverse as those that contributed to the CIA's operations in Vietnam. My own experiences were, of course, my primary reference. During my four and a half years in Vietnam, I ran one of the CIA's most productive informant networks, interrogated its best agents and became the agency's principal briefer and political-strategic analyst at the Embassy. These myriad activities kept me

close to the center of decision-making, and in the following pages I have tried
to convey some sense of what it was like to be there.

To buttress my recollections, I have drawn heavily from a briefing notebook which I kept during the last two years of the war. Reading over its
contents—which included everything from notable ambassadorial quotes to
excerpts from my own briefings—I have been able to reconstruct much of the
thinking of the time.

A personal diary also provided useful documentation. Dating back to my
first Vietnam assignment in 1969, it was conceived initially as a verbal snapshot
file, but as time went on, I began inserting snippets of social conversation and
cocktail banter out of a vague impulse to "write a novel about all this one day."
These jottings—sprinkled here and there in the text—provide a glimpse of a
world, now extinct, that was seldom penetrated by anyone outside the company.

In addition to my own conjurings, the book is based on hundreds of
interviews with former colleagues. Because most of them still have careers to
protect in the State Department or the CIA, I have generally avoided direct
quotes.

One exception is Ambassador Graham Martin. Sitting with me hours on
end, he provided a great many highly quotable if not always dispassionate
observations about those with whom he worked during his nearly two years
in Saigon. To supplement this material, I have drawn liberally from his
recorded testimony before several Congressional committees in 1974 and
1976.*

Since many of the actors in this story still belong to the shadowy world
of espionage, I was confronted with the problem of how to identify them in
the text without endangering their lives or careers. I finally opted for a technique favored in the intelligence business: except where the officer in question
has given permission, or has previously been "blown" by the press, I have used
aliases to refer to my former CIA colleagues. (Quotation marks around the
name as first cited in the text and in the index denote an alias.)

I have also made a special effort not to betray the identities of Vietnamese
agents whom the CIA abandoned in Vietnam. The last thing I would want
to do is to cause further pain to those who made the mistake of trusting in
us.

During my CIA career I became fairly well versed on North Vietnam, and
some of what I learned is woven into the text. Yet because probing Hanoi's
thought was always as much an art as a science, a few shortcuts have been
necessary. The reader will discover, for instance, that while much is made of
the struggle between "hawks" and "doves" in the North Vietnamese leader-

*Hearings before the Committee on Foreign Relations, U.S. Senate, on S. 3394 (June 7,21,26, July
24 and 25, 1974); Hearing before the Subcommittee on Asian and Pacific Affairs, Committee on
Foreign Affairs, House of Representatives (July 31, 1974); Hearing before the Special Subcommittee on Investigations, Committee on International Relations, House of Representatives (January
27, 1976).

ship, only a few of the principals are identified. Unfortunately, this was una-voidable. Although most of us who worked on North Vietnamese affairs during the war agreed that factionalism played a part in Hanoi's decision-making—and were able to pinpoint its effects—there was never any consensus on precisely who belonged in which pigeonhole. I happen to believe that many of those who were admitted to the Politburo a year after Saigon's collapse were former "moderates"—that is, technicians or ideological purists who had been reluctant during the final phases of war to gamble the socialist experiment in the North on the vagaries of a policy of military escalation.

One other point should be made about my treatment of the North Viet-namese. Throughout much of the book my unsung collaborator is General Van Tien Dung, the North Vietnamese general who led the final offensive against Saigon and whose extraordinarily candid memoirs on the campaign were published by Hanoi in the spring of 1976. Where appropriate, I have included excerpts from them to amplify my own version of what took place.

There is (I hope) little in this book that will touch anyone's ideological nerve. By now most Americans have made up their minds about the rightness or wrongness of the Vietnam war, and the aptness of its ending. Instead of rehashing old arguments, I have attempted to set out the evidence as fairly and as objectively as I can, without malice, or favoritism, toward any of the principal actors. This in itself was perhaps the most difficult part of the writing, for many of those who figured prominently in the story were close personal friends whose mistakes and shortcomings might have been forgotten, except for Saigon's final tragedy.

F.S.
Arlington, Va.
September 1977

ACKNOWLEDGMENTS

This book simply would not have been possible without the untiring support of Bernadette Longford, who typed and retyped the manuscript—often from dictation—and assisted me in countless other ways during the arduous eighteen months of writing.

Also instrumental in keeping the project afloat was Carla Christiansen, who drew on her own expertise on Vietnam to help me refine parts of the text.

Beyond this first line of support, there were numerous others who pro-vided invaluable assistance, most notably Laura Palmer, who kept me supplied with news clippings and other data vital to my research. In addition, I owe a belated debt of gratitude to those with whom I worked most closely in the Embassy and whose expertise was always my own best teacher: among them, Frank Scotton, Jim Nach, Jim Haley and Dave Walker.

Special thanks must also go to my chief editor at Random House, Robert Loomis, and my diligent and tolerant copyeditor, Bertha Krantz, who made the best of my jumbled manuscript.

Mr. Loomis, I am afraid, learned more about the spy business on my account than he had bargained for. Out of concern for possible CIA interference, we conducted all of our business in secret, exchanging ideas during clandestine rendezvous in New York City parks. Even the publication and distribution of the book were conducted secretly, without the knowledge of any more than a handful of Random House executives.

Finally, I would like to express thanks to my old friend Hal Emerson, whose interest in international politics gave rise to my own during the years we worked together at Columbia University.

Part 1

First Rites

Homecoming

When I returned to Saigon in October 1972 after a year's absence, the North Vietnamese offensive was beginning to sputter out, the country was awash with rumors of imminent peace and the Vietnamese for the first time in decades were allowing themselves the luxury of hoping against hope it would all end soon. As the big Cathay Pacific jet began its final approach to Tan Son Nhut air base, I had an immediate sense of how far we and our allies had come since I had first set foot on Vietnamese soil back in June 1969. On that sweltering summer's day three years before, the plane had corkscrewed in for a landing to avoid Communist ground fire on the outskirts of the airfield. This time the final descent was a long, slow glide over rows of corrugated roof shanties that had grown up around the city with the continuing influx of refugees, and the green and brown patchwork terrain stretching away into the distance looked as pacific as the Louisiana countryside.

As I jogged across the tarmac to beat the crowds to immigration I remembered my seat companion on that first flight in '69, a colonel's wife who was paying a surprise call on her husband to check into rumors he had taken up with a Vietnamese bar girl. By the time we rolled to a stop in front of the arrival terminal, she had rehearsed her worst fears to me a dozen times, over nearly as many martinis, and when she stepped out on the tarmac in the blazing sun she had collapsed on the spot, sending the marines on duty at the front gate into gales of laughter.

Now there were no army wives among my fellow passengers. The only westerner besides myself was a potbellied Australian construction worker with a scruffy Chinese girl on his arm, and if there were any M.P.s backboning the scattering of Vietnamese sentries, they were keeping themselves well out of sight, in deference to Vietnamization.

The ramshackle barn of a building that served as the arrival terminal was in its perennial state of disarray, with broken crates and abandoned luggage strewn across the cement floor—and still without a money changer's window to accommodate new arrivals. At the immigration counter the same rumpled functionaries who had tested patience and endurance during my first tour of duty still took an eternity picking through passports and shot records, and the Vietnamese who had arrived with me, mostly bejeweled old mama-sans and their shriveled husbands, all seemed quite typically oblivious of the carefully stenciled signs admonishing everyone to line up and wait his turn.

The Vietnamese chauffeur whom the Embassy had sent to pick me up apologized for the chaos, said he remembered me from before, and quickly guided me through the crowds of cabbies and cyclo drivers out front to his air-conditioned Chevrolet. As we pulled out of the main gate of the sprawling air base I caught a glimpse of the small monument the South Vietnamese had recently erected to commemorate U.S. war dead. "The Noble Sacrifice of the Allied Soldiers Will Never Be Forgotten" read the inscription. It was all but overgrown with elephant grass. Three years hence, after the fall of Saigon, the Communists would repaint it yellow and substitute a quote from Ho Chi Minh.

Like all new arrivals I was bedded and boarded in the Duc Hotel, a heavily fortified CIA residential complex only a few blocks away from the South Vietnamese Presidential Palace and the U.S. Embassy. In the late 1960s, during my first tour in Saigon, the Duc had been run like an enlisted men's barracks, with a carnival atmosphere and T-shirt informality. There had always been a poker game in progress in one of the bedrooms downstairs, and although house rules strictly forbade Vietnamese guests after curfew, few of the foot-loose CIA men had slept alone. The old Vietnamese gentleman who ran the restaurant on the ground floor had never learned to cook hot dogs or hamburgers, and the French bread he bought on the local market had always had a weevil or two baked inside.

In the past year, however, somebody at CIA headquarters in Langley, Virginia, had decided that the boys on the front deserved better, particularly now that consideration was being given to opening Saigon to the families of Embassy personnel, and the Duc was in the process of being Americanized and sanitized. The restaurant had been moved upstairs and remodeled in Howard Johnson's modern; a bar, swimming pool and sun deck had been built alongside so you could sunbathe and sip Bloody Marys simultaneously; and the menu was all staple American and fresh-frozen besides. Even the bread was now imported (bugless) from stateside. The Vietnamese waitresses had all been rung through CIA security investigations to make sure none had Communist connections and the tuniclike *ao dai* dresses that had once made them so provocative had been replaced by neat little uniforms straight out of a kindergarten graduation.

Every evening at eight o'clock you could catch a first-run movie in the new screening room just off the downstairs lobby, and a fully equipped photographic darkroom, recording studio and library were open at all hours. CIA shuttle buses made the run to the Embassy each morning so you didn't have to fight rush-hour traffic, and there were always chauffeured cars available to take you to the PX or to the commissary or to the CIA's ultramodern infirmary down the street, where two reasonably qualified doctors were on duty around-the-clock to tend to the ravages of your overindulgence. Eventually almost every CIA officer was issued an automobile of his own, together with a free gas ration, although usually only after he had also been assigned a permanent residence, an apartment or villa depending on rank, elsewhere in the city. Curiously enough, Ford Pintos were the Station's automotive preference, and whoever drove one might as well have been wearing a sign "I work for the CIA," for we were the only "official Americans" in Vietnam who used them.

For the 300 men and women who now made up the CIA Station, life had been wrapped up in a neat little package, complete with one stateside vacation each year to break the routine. Nowhere in the world, in no other hot spot did CIA personnel live so well or so expensively, courtesy of the American tax-payer.

A day or so after settling in at the Duc, I made a foray into downtown Saigon, only a few blocks away. It was midday when I managed to break away, and the hands of the big clock on the face of the Post, Telephone and Telegraph building had just gone upright as I maneuvered my borrowed Pinto in among the milling Vietnamese out front, many of whom were dispersing for home or heading across the street to vie for sleeping space in the shadowed porticoes of the Catholic cathedral. As I repeatedly applied my brakes to avoid running down an oblivious pedestrian, I remembered a similarly lazy day in the summer of 1969, when the Viet Cong had tied wires and a charge of plastique to the hands of the clock and had blown out the entire façade of the PTT offices. Scores of dozers and passers-by had been wounded or killed outright and the local diocese had kept day laborers working for weeks picking shards of glass out of the cathedral's clay columns.

Now the prospect of such violence seemed almost whimsical. No doubt you could still go to the roof of the Caravelle Hotel at night and watch Vietnamese helicopter gunships rivet parachute flares out along the skyline like studs in black velvet, and the crump of artillery and distant B-52 strikes still shook the bed at night. But there had been no spectacular Communist sabotage for months and the last native to immolate himself in the bizarre tradition of the Buddhist radicals of the early and mid-1960s had been a one-armed disabled veteran who had dropped a Bastos cigarette in his lap three weeks before as he dozed under the eaves of a flower vendor's kiosk on Nguyen Hue Boulevard.

When I returned to the Duc Hotel at dusk, one of the old-timers who had done several tours in Vietnam had his elbows on the bar and was reminiscing about Saigon as he had known it in the early 1960s, when it was still the Paris of the Orient, with wide tree-lined boulevards, the best Chinese restaurants in Southeast Asia and equally superior brothels, one of which—the "House of a Thousand Mirrors"—had reputedly offered as many diversions as its name implied.

But as I listened, his memories ran out around the year 1965, for it was then that the explosion of easy money touched off by the influx of U.S. combat forces had reduced the best of the city to debris. By the time the great Communist offensive of 1968 had done its worst, Saigon had become a grimy imitation of frontier Dodge City. American GIs with bandoliers over their shoulders and a month's salary in their fatigues had the run of the place, and the local citizenry had either withdrawn into their own quiet lives to wait out the storm or begun working up schemes to turn a profit from it. Even the brothels had turned low-quality, as inexperienced peasant girls flocked in from the countryside, determined to make up in fast service and easy availability what they lacked in finesse. The cleverer and prettier ones eventually settled in at the 147 Club on Vo Thanh Street or the Dragon Bar off Le Loi Boulevard or the incomparable Mimi's Flamboyant, a grubby niche in a wall on Nguyen Hue, where a generation of American GIs lost both their shirts and their innocence.

Doing a tour of duty in Saigon in those earlier days was like being locked up in an overcrowded sweatbox for a year and a half. None of the saner Americans who had worked in the Embassy in 1969 and '70 had wanted to be there; and those who did were tottering drunks, old maids or fuzzy-headed romantics who were too intoxicated with their own illusions to realize where they were. The Vietnamese, of course, had wished a plague on all our houses and would have preferred being left totally alone. But since the war in those days still washed around the edges of the city, there had been no margin for anyone's solitude. We were all in it together, elbow to elbow, with no headroom and no diversions except the bars or massage parlors on Tu Do Street or the waterfront rattraps that passed for nightclubs, where hyped local bands like the CBC could lay down Jimi Hendrix or "American Woman" with a mocking vengeance.

Not all of that had disappeared by the time I returned to Saigon in October 1972. Some of the old shabbiness still clung to the city like a scab. The stubby apartment houses and hotels in the center of town near Lam Son Square all wore the flaking gray façades that had always betrayed their age, and the gutters even along the major thoroughfares still reeked of urine and garbage, despite periodic rounds by trash-sweeping trucks provided to Saigon municipal authorities under U.S. aid programs. The traffic itself was as lethal and improvisatory as ever, and invariably at rush hour the air over the city turned gray and spongy from the exhausts of the countless Hondas and Japanese automobiles the Vietnamese managed to keep running despite the rising price of gas. The last of the surviving tamarind trees along lower Tu Do Street seemed finally to be succumbing to the pall, although wits in the local French community continued to blame their passing on the residual effects of U.S. military defoliants.

From what I could see and touch, there had been no improvement in the esthetic or hygienic qualities of the city's night life. A few weeks before, the government in a paroxysm of energy had shut down all the junkier bars and massage parlors along Tu Do and Nguyen Hue to celebrate the shrinkage of the American market and to staunch the resulting inflation. But like most efforts at reform in this city, this one turned out to be mere shadow play. The toughest hookers had decamped to the veranda of the colonial Continental Hotel, where Graham Greene had sat at a corner table in the early 1950s and scrawled out a first draft of *The Quiet American,* and most of the "restaurants" that had sprung up in place of the bars offered the same attractions, except now the girls all wore white "waitress" smocks and offered you a salad and a hamburger of water-buffalo meat before lapsing into the usual hard sell.

For all the shabbiness, though, there was an air of accomplished and impending change about the city that perhaps only a Vietnamese could fully appreciate. The people I brushed up against in the streets or in the marketplace or in the course of business seemed more generous, less driven than before. The beggars and street urchins along Nguyen Hue Boulevard were more polite and deferential in their ancestral manner, as if they realized that the American bonanza was ending and hoped through some small act of diplomacy to keep a few of the big spenders on. And the Vietnamese GIs who still crowded into the shops and cafés on weekends were holding hands again, as they had ceased doing at the height of the American involvement only a few years before, when U.S. GIs—not knowing the custom to be an old and venerated one among Vietnamese men—had dubbed them a nation of queers.

An old Chinese merchant who had bought up one of the better massage parlors on Tu Do and turned it into a noodle stand told me with a great show of candor that it was the disappearance of the American GIs that had made all the difference, just as their arrival, he insisted, had caused the war. "Because of the riches you brought us," he said, "we were forced to acknowledge our own poverty and to compete among ourselves to change as you wanted us to do. But now that you Americans are going home, we can again feel safe and comfortable with our illusions."

The same old merchant would be among the first of my Saigon friends to leave Vietnam in April 1975, as the Communists, Vietnamese all, began their final drive on the city.

Except for the dwindling numbers of American GIs, Saigon's principal cast of characters remained as I had remembered it: a menagerie of innocents and rogues and variations on the two that might have sprung from the imagination of Hieronymus Bosch.

Over there, at the corner of Le Loi and Nguyen Hue—surely you remember him—that aging cyclo driver perched vulture-like on the seat of his cab, the very portrait of the city's resiliency and indifference, as familiar as yesterday, pith helmet pressed down over the ears, sunglasses vainly seeking purchase on an archless nose. And there, at the corner of Tu Do: tough, vacant, hips swinging in imitation leather, breasts silicone-stretched to centerfold proportions, the hooker maybe seventeen or eighteen, hopped up on coke or bennies, babbling half-understood obscenities in barroom Americanese at the cabbies, who ignore her.

Or the peasant girl: feline, timid, the conical hat tipped to one side, the rubber-tire sandals slapping the pavement as she moves just ahead of you from stall to stall in the Central Market, the black silk trousers billowing around thin legs. Or her counterpart: the young South Vietnamese soldier, eyes extinguished beneath steel visor, the M-16 rifle almost as big as he, the unappreciated, undermotivated fall guy forced to eke out a living for his wife and expanding family on the equivalent of twelve dollars a month, with no hope of escape or respite until he is carried out on a stretcher or turns thirty-seven, too old to become anything else.

And remember, too, the elite, the central players. By noon on an average day they've already gathered at the ramshackle French colonial sports club, Le Cercle Sportif, for their two-hour lunch break at poolside. On one side of the sun deck: expatriates from the underside of French society, old *colons* and young pretenders, lean, bronzed mixed-bloods in rubber-band bikinis, their talk careening from plastic intellectualism to drugs to fast cars, to swapping lovers to shady deals and contraband. And there, just beyond them, in a claque of their own: quiet men gone to flab, each balancing himself on a lounge chair with care and a certain flourish, to give maximum girth to an already considerable paunch, the mark of prosperity and distinction in this strange land. Vietnamese or Chinese doyens all, whispering business or politics over their *citrons presses,* with the wealth to buy their way out if the latest plot fails.

Later, maybe at three or four, you drive over to Tu Do Street and stop by Givral's café for a French coffee, black as ink. And here, too, the elite holds court—but young faces these, bonnets of black hair, the two sexes indistinguishable in their tie-dye shirts and bell bottoms: the student set in Saigon, detesting the Americans they imitate.

And should you wander down the street to browse through some of the more expensive shops in the Eden Arcade, sooner or later another of the city's privileged brushes past, head up, unnoticing, a gilded copy of the latest vogue, nose and eyes surgically reshaped to western proportions, the Thai silk dress and Cambodian amulets radiating wealth, all advertisements for a discreet affair, pitched to gentlemen of means. Second wife or concubine to a prominent Vietnamese general or politician: speaking French, patronizing the French, condescending to flirt with an American only when it might prove more profitable.

At last cocktail hour rolls around, and you drop by Mimi's for a quick beer, and inevitably, at the center of the courtesans, he is already granting audience, another lord in this domain. Florid, bull-necked, checkered shirt hanging loose over the barrel gut, he hardly looks the part. But lord he is, for here, in all his glory, is the American homesteader, the former truckdriver or factory foreman, who hangs on from year to year bossing Vietnamese road gangs or construction teams on behalf of the American firms contracted out to pick up after every skirmish. Master to a cringing Vietnamese wife or mistress, keeper of the American superiority complex, the last of us they will see when the Americans go home.

•   •   •

The United States Embassy on Thong Nhut Street had not changed much in the year I had been away. Someone at last had planted flowers in the urns in the courtyard, where the Viet Cong had set up machine-gun nests during their attack on the compound in the opening days of their offensive in 1968, but the concrete artillery shield covering the façade of the building, with its rows of rectangular portholes, still had no more esthetic appeal than the underside of a waffle iron, and the plastic-paned windows just behind it rattled and shimmied as they always had with each burst of artillery fire on the city's outskirts. Looking out from inside, you could not see much of the surrounding grounds, for the portholes transformed the vista into a series of disjointed triptyches that seemed to bear little relation to each other. But perhaps that was a fitting metaphor for the way Americans had seen Vietnam all along—disconnected images, never the whole.

Architecturally there was something about the Embassy that had always seemed a mockery of our pretenses here. I suppose that if you have to build the seat of your diplomatic Mission in the image of a self-sustaining fortress, that says a little about the efficacy of your diplomacy. And fortress it was, with its own sixty-man Marine guard force, its artillery shield, a rooftop helicopter landing pad and a ten-foot-high wall to keep locals and tourists out of the compound.

Ambassador Ellsworth Bunker and his State Department staff still occupied the first three floors of the building, while the top three were given over to the CIA Station. Initially I was assigned a desk in the office of the CIA's counterintelligence staff, which to my delight was located on the fifth floor, one removed from the top. Those who worked above me, in the Station Chief's office or the "situation room," not only had to contend with the rattle of incoming helicopters and the vibration of the rooftop incinerators that were constantly gnawing away at classified trash, but were also that much more exposed to the direct impact of an incoming artillery round—not the least of one's considerations in Vietnam.

Just to the side of the main Embassy building, a series of makeshift Quonset huts known as the "Norodom complex" housed additional CIA personnel. During the Communist attack on the Embassy in 1968, a Viet Cong commando had got inside Norodom, only to be machine-gunned to death by a Marine guard in what was now the CIA map-storage room. Since then an army of termites had accomplished what the Viet Cong had been unable to do, subduing the place and reducing it to a veritable tinderbox that would burn merrily on the last day of the war.

A new three-story consular building was going up next door to Norodom, and out back, just beyond the parking lot where helicopters would set down to rescue us on the final day, there was a new recreation compound, with an American-style restaurant and a large swimming pool, which like the pool at the Duc was closed to locals.

Completed in 1967, the Embassy was meant to provide home and haven for the entire American diplomatic establishment in Vietnam, which by then had already outgrown the original chancery near the river. But the architects apparently had never been made privy to high-level U.S. policy planning, for the structure they designed turned out to be too small to accommodate the ever-expanding Embassy staff, and a number of overflow agencies continued to operate out of makeshift quarters scattered around the city. The hybrid agency dedicated to Civil Operations and Rural Development Support (CORDS), which was supposed to orchestrate Vietnamese and American pacification efforts, had two separate headquarters some distance from the Embassy, and officials of the Agency for International Development (USAID) dispensed economic assistance from an imposing set of buildings not far from Le Cercle Sportif. And if it was propaganda you wanted, you had to fight your way through the traffic on Le Qui Don Street to the tree-shrouded "Lincoln Library" where the United States Information Agency (known as USIS overseas) made its home.

The most important of the Embassy annexes was five miles away, at Tan Son Nhut air base, accross the street from the arrival terminal. There in the bowels of a sprawling bunkerlike complex known as "Pentagon East," the American generals who made up the United States Military Assistance Command for Vietnam (MACV) had plotted the course of the war since the mid-1960s with the help of the South Vietnamese Joint General Staff, headquartered nearby. In the halcyon days of America's full-time involvement in the hostilities, MACV had always been a dynamo of activity, with rumpled, disenchanted enlisted men pumping heroin in the dressing rooms at the bowling alley or alongside the Olympic-sized swimming pool as earnest young officers scurried along the sidewalks pretending not to notice. But if anything was testimony to the change that had overtaken South Vietnam by the time I returned in October 1972, it was the slowed tempo of life at MACV. With the American military now playing second fiddle to our Vietnamese allies, in the best spirit of Vietnamization, some desk officers didn't even bother to answer their telephones.

Eventually, following the cease-fire, the far-flung Embassy community would alter and contract. CORDS would discard its counterterrorist functions and re-emerge as the more benign pacification-oriented "Office of the Special Assistant for Field Operations." MACV would be replaced by a much smaller Defense Attaché's Office (DAO) and U.S. diplomatic and military personnel spread throughout the rest of South Vietnam would retreat into modest consular establishments in a few major cities, including Danang, Nha Trang, Bien Hoa and Can Tho. Yet for all of this shrinkage, the various Embassy components on the last day of the war would seem to be at a hundred different places at once, at countless disparate addresses, and except for providence and the bravery of a few American helicopter pilots, some of the Embassy's staffers might have been left behind, just as were so many of their Vietnamese employees.

•   •   •

In theory, the Ambassador was the axis of the official American community in Vietnam, but in fact, the center of political gravity had shifted radically and often in the past twelve years. As the role of the military expanded in the early 1960s, Ambassadors Henry Cabot Lodge and Maxwell Taylor were gradually upstaged by the planners at MACV. Ellsworth Bunker did nothing to alter the balance when he moved into the Ambassador's third-floor suite in the Embassy in 1967, but once Vietnamization became the basis of U.S. policy two years later, the priorities and epicenter shifted again, and gradually Bunker became the central player on the American stage in Vietnam as he and General Creighton Abrams, by then chief of MACV, began carefully passing the initiative to the South Vietnamese.

Since a stable regime was vital to this transfer of responsibility—and essential to Henry Kissinger's negotiating strategies—Bunker took on the additional job of coddling South Vietnam's power elite, in particular, President Nguyen Van Thieu. It was a job he did with relish and imagination. In 1971, during my first tour of duty, when all other contenders had dropped out of South Vietnam's presidential race in deference to Thieu's invulnerability, Bunker devised an ingenious scheme for broadening the field so no one in the American peace gallery could say Thieu had won without a fight. Bunker decided to bribe the moderate opposition figure, General Duong Van "Big" Minh, to stay on the slate for the sake of appearances. The caper would have worked—Bunker made his overture with typical diplomacy—had not Minh ultimately concluded that the three million dollars offered him for his campaign were less compelling than the prospect of assured defeat.

On my return to Saigon in the fall of 1972 my own bureaucratic chrysalis, the CIA Station, was under increasing criticism from the American press for alleged abuses in Vietnam, including the notorious Phoenix Program. No doubt we would have been a less tempting target if we had been concentrating on our primary job for the past few years—gathering intelligence. But ever since the early 1960s the CIA had been dabbling increasingly in other millponds and (as the press gleefully pointed out) had gotten embarrassingly diverted.

Not that we had been operating much beyond our legal charter. There is a neat little catch-all phrase in the National Security Act which authorizes the CIA and its overseas stations "to perform such functions and duties related to intelligence affecting the national security as the National Security Council may from time to time direct." In the early 1960s the White House took advantage of this loophole to move the CIA into areas of activity—such as the recruiting and training of counterterrorist teams—where no other American expertise was available. Later, as the military began digging in for a hot war, President Johnson decided to let the CIA continue its extracurricular activities lest the Pentagon steal the whole show.

With his acquiescence, the Station in Vietnam gradually expanded in the mid-sixties to over 600 assorted bodies, including secretaries, intelligence analysts and spy handlers, known as "case officers" in the trade. It was the largest concentration of CIA personnel anywhere in the world outside agency headquarters in Virginia, and as time passed, the pressure for continuous augmentation and replacement became so intense, each component of the agency was forced to cough up a quota of Vietnam volunteers each year regardless of their past experience. Many of the "case officers" who ended up in Vietnam were old German or Latin-American hands with no knowledge of the country and no interest in developing any. Yet in a month or so of their arrival and without any language training whatsoever, they often found themselves exiled to a godforsaken outpost in Vietnam's western highlands or in the delta, responsible for recruiting agents, gathering intelligence, and administering an amorphous new program for saving the country, known as "Rural Development."

Robert Komer, a former CIA intelligence analyst, had devised the rural development concept in 1967 while he was serving as a White House advisor. What he envisaged was a coordinated approach to "rooting out" the Viet Cong political apparatus (through counterterrorism) and "rooting in" the government (through various public works projects in the countryside). The Vietnamese responded to his plan by setting up a special ministry for the purpose while the Americans created CORDS to guide the effort on the spot. In late 1967 Komer's deputy, William Colby, who had been chief of the CIA's East Asia Division for covert operations, was appointed to replace him as head of CORDS.

Conceptually, CORDS was to be a model of bureaucratic ecumenism, drawing upon various elements of the Saigon Mission for its executive personnel. At most there would never be more than a hundred CIA officers attached to its 800-man staff, but since the CIA Station had always been the best organized and best funded of the Embassy's civilian components, it would end up administering many of CORDS' most highly publicized projects, including the Phoenix.

As Colby continually pointed out, the object of the Phoenix Program was to capture Communist cadres and bring them in alive so they could be interrogated and exploited for intelligence purposes. But as had so often happened in the past, the American game plan was more than our Vietnamese allies could handle. Bureaucratically, the problem was definition. No one, neither Vietnamese nor American, had ever decided who was to be considered a Viet Cong cadreman. Was he a local village chief who served the North Vietnamese part time? Or did the definition extend only to hard-core Communists with full party membership? For lack of finite guidance the Phoenix strike teams opted for a scattershot approach, picking up anyone who might be a suspect, and eventually when the jails were filled to overflowing they began simply taking the law, such as it was, into their own hands.

Even before the press corps got wind of the Phoenix excesses, however, the CIA was running for cover. With the onset of Vietnamization in 1969, Station Chief Theodore Shackley had decided to begin phasing CIA personnel out of CORDS and its "nation-building" programs and to concentrate on more traditional intelligence functions, such as stealing secrets from the Communists and from the South Vietnamese government. As it happened, the Station was already well equipped to deal with the first "target," for we had long been blessed with several productive spies inside the Communist high command. One of them, who was to predict the end of the war in 1975 just the way it happened, had provided us with some spectacular strategic intelligence over the years, including advance warning of the Communist offensive in 1968, which analysts in Washington unfortunately had ignored.

But Shackley, an ambitious technocrat, was not satisfied with Station accomplishments, and throughout his tenure, from 1969 to 1972, he continually pushed Station personnel to "recruit, recruit, recruit"—that is, bribe, inveigle and hire anyone and everyone to work for us as agents. By the time he was through, the Station's spy roster had swollen impressively and the stream of intelligence reports flowing back to Washington had reached a record 500 per month. Only some time later, in 1974, as the CIA was frantically trying to clarify Hanoi's cease-fire strategy, were we to realize what havoc Shackley's zeal had visited upon us: over a hundred of the VC "agents" who had been recruited during his reign were discovered to be fabricators, clever Vietnamese entrepreneurs who knew nothing of Communist plans but who had been able to patch together enough information from newspaper stories and soup-kitchen gossip to keep us supplied with what looked like valid intelligence— at great cost to the U.S. government.

With respect to the "friendly target," as the Thieu regime was called, the difficulty was as much the thrust of our policy itself as the quality of the agents we used to implement it.

In the years immediately following the overthrow of President Ngo Dinh Diem in 1963, South Vietnam was rocked by a succession of coups and counter-coups as one ambitious general after another tried to exploit the country's political instability for his own gain. By 1967, partly at the suggestion of a bright (and as yet unreconstructed) young military analyst in Saigon named Daniel Ellsberg, the U.S. government had decided to throw its support behind yet another contender—a modest, supposedly non-political southern general named Nguyen Van Thieu—in a last effort to tamp down the chaos.* When Thieu was elected to the presidency later in the year, the main power broker in the country was still Nguyen Cao Ky, the flamboyant northerner who had previously been Premier and was now Vice-President. But Ambassador Bunker was not impressed with Ky or his entourage and managed gradually to nudge them aside by addressing all policy questions to Thieu alone. The *coup de grâce* for Ky came during the Communist offensive of 1968 when a number of his most powerful allies were killed off.

From that point on, the Embassy's primary objective was to strengthen

---

*Ellsberg's study, though far from an endorsement of Thieu, paid him the indirect compliment of suggesting that among the military candidates he was somewhat more attractive than Nguyen Cao Ky.

Thieu's government at all costs so that the United States could begin withdrawing its troops from Vietnam without fear of precipitating a new political
crisis. By October 1972, in pursuit of this goal, we had bought, bribed and sold
so many South Vietnamese military and political figures that our spies and
collaborators inside the government were mere extensions of ourselves. Shackley himself had drawn General Dang Van Quang, Thieu's ebullient security
advisor (his Kissinger, if you will), into an informal collaborative relationship
with the Station and had developed close ties with General Nguyen Khac
Binh, who rose to become the powerful chief of South Vietnam's National
Police on the strength of CIA backing. Neither Quang nor Binh was ever
formally "recruited," in the sense of regularly accepting money for his services,
but both were so indebted to us professionally, they became frequent collaborators and sources of information.

Up until the final days of the Republic, Binh and Quang were touted as
perhaps our most important properties in Vietnam, but in fact their worth was
grossly overstated. Neither provided us with much information that could not
have been obtained otherwise, through the bugs and telephone taps we had
planted in the Presidential Palace (the Prime Minister's office was completely
wired), and what intelligence they did supply was often misleading, for both
soon realized they could serve their own interests, and Thieu's, by giving us
precisely what we wanted to hear. On top of this, the Station remained so
dependent on them politically, as spokesmen for American policies and interests inside the government, that we could never approach their reporting
objectively or critically. Even when it became apparent in Saigon's final days
that they were holding out on us, we continued to pamper and humor them
lest we lose our last levers on the regime.

Our reliance on these two men had terrible consequences. Not only was
our intelligence adversely affected, but so too was our moral and political
position among the Vietnamese. By virtue of the wealth and prominence we
bestowed on them, both Quang and Binh became symbols of the American-
inflicted corruption and decadence that ultimately provided the Communists
with their best propaganda weapon.

In attempting to strengthen the Thieu government we did not of course
limit ourselves to planting collaborators in its ranks. "Neutralizing" the non-
Communist opposition was also part of our strategy. In fairness to the CIA
personnel who handled this delicate task, the tactics they employed usually
stopped well short of "termination with extreme prejudice." Indeed, the pride
of the Station in the fall of 1972 was the quite benign case of Tran Quoc Buu,
a decidedly pro-American politician who headed South Vietnam's powerful
labor union federation. A year or so earlier Station personnel had succeeded
in turning Buu into a "collaborator," and since then we had been able to use
him quite profitably, as an instrument for keeping the unions loyal to Thieu
and for channeling pro-government propaganda to labor organizations around
the world. From time to time Station personnel had even helped Buu draft

letters to labor leaders in the United States, soliciting their support. No one in the Station's front office seemed bothered by the fact that this was a violation of the CIA charter, which prohibits the agency from dabbling in U.S. domestic politics.*

Not all of Thieu's rivals were as malleable as Buu, and in the more difficult cases where persuasion, bribery or blackmail failed to have the desired effect, the Station reluctantly resorted to more forceful measures. When Tran Ngoc Chau, a prominent South Vietnamese nationalist and legislator, became a political threat to Thieu in 1970, Shackley and Colby cooperated with the South Vietnamese police to paint him as a subversive and a Communist agent. Since Chau's brother was in fact a Communist, and since Chau himself had once contacted him on behalf of the Station, it was relatively easy to build a case against him simply by dressing up certain parts of his official police dossier and by de-emphasizing others. Shackley did not actually design the frame-up —it was the brainchild of the CIA confidant General Quang—but he did nothing to avert it, even though he knew the truth. And when the South Vietnamese government surfaced its allegations against Chau in the local press, both Shackley and Ambassador Bunker supported them. A few days later Chau was dragged out of the National Assembly building in downtown Saigon and thrown into jail to await trial, in violation of all legal process in South Vietnam.†

Once convicted, Chau would remain imprisoned for four years, only to be released in early 1975. A few days before the Communist takeover in April, several sympathetic CIA officers cabled agency headquarters in Langley, Virginia, asking permission to put him on one of the evacuation flights. But Shackley, who by then had become chief of the CIA's East Asia Division, cabled back vetoing the request on the grounds that Chau had never contributed to American interests in Vietnam. Chau was duly left behind.

One other facet of Station operations, our reporting on the South Vietnamese military, remained crucial to American perceptions and misperceptions up until the end. Bureaucratically, we were interlopers in the field. The U.S. military, in all its permutations, had always had chief responsibility for keeping book on Thieu's army and its capabilities (and if blame were ever to be levied for our miscalculations concerning South Vietnamese resiliency in the

---

*As became public after the fall of Saigon, the CIA also had lavished large sums of money on the Thieu government to be used in cowing and "neutralizing" its opposition. The primary CIA subsidy, amounting to millions of dollars, was for the creation of a pro-government coalition of political parties in the early 1970s. Thieu's cousin Hoang Duc Nha was the primary conduit for the funds. As Nha once explained to me, only a small portion of the money was ever applied toward its intended purpose. The rest was pocketed by members of the Thieu regime.
†Former colleagues of Daniel Ellsberg claim that the Chau case was instrumental in turning the young analyst against the Vietnam war, since he and Chau had long been close friends. It may not be too much to say that in persecuting Chau the CIA gave impetus to the most spectacular intelligence leak in the history of the war—the surfacing of the *Pentagon Papers,* for which Ellsberg was responsible.

last year of the war, the lion's share would belong to our Defense Attaché and his lieutenants). Yet because of the Station's resources, its money and wide-ranging contacts, it too remained a major contributor of data on the subject.

Our principal pipeline to the South Vietnamese high command was a kindly old soldier named Charles Timmes, who had been a battalion commander in the heroic 82nd Airborne Division when it spearheaded the Normandy invasion in 1944. A Hollywood muscleman played Timmes' role in the film *The Longest Day*—a curious piece of casting, since Timmes himself was a short, stringy fellow with a jaunty step who looked more like a Fred Astaire than a John Wayne.

From 1962 to 1964 Timmes had served as the chief of the U.S. advisory command in Vietnam, which eventually gave way to MACV. His position put him daily in contact with up-and-coming young soldiers in the South Vietnamese army, and some of them, including Nguyen Van Thieu, became his fast friends. By the time his tour of duty ended, however, he had wearied of Vietnam and was ready to retire, and he would have spent the next few years playing world traveler had not the CIA interceded. But in 1967 the agency offered him a deal he could not turn down. He was invited to hire on as a contract employee, return to Vietnam and reopen contacts with his old South Vietnamese military friends.

Timmes accepted immediately, and throughout the remainder of his CIA career, which lasted till the day Saigon fell, he did his job with surpassing skill and sensitivity. He became a regular tennis partner of "Big" Minh, leader of the 1963 coup against Diem and the target of Bunker's bribery attempt, and between sets managed to glean valuable information on Saigon's "loyal opposition," including Minh himself. Through periodic flying visits to the provinces, Timmes also stayed in touch with various South Vietnamese field commanders, many of whom had been no more than first lieutenants when he had met them years before. They all loved and respected him, as one fellow officer to another, and were always willing to assist him in drafting summaries of their conversations to give them a ring of authenticity. As a result, Timmes' reports from the field were invariably deadly accurate accounts of what the top men in the South Vietnamese military wanted him to convey back to the Embassy.

Working-level CIA analysts in Washington and Saigon remained wary of Timmes' reports and treated them as but one perspective on a highly complex subject. But as other sources of information on the South Vietnamese army gradually dried up with the cutback (in 1970 and '71), and finally the removal of our military advisory teams in the countryside, top-level bureaucrats in Washington and Saigon were increasingly inclined to accept his findings at face value. In the last days of the war the Ambassador and the Station Chief in Saigon would be quoting Timmes to each other as proof for their own wishful thinking.

Timmes himself never made any great claims about the honesty of his Vietnamese friends. In reporting what they told him as accurately as he could, he was simply doing what comes naturally to a good intelligence officer, which he was. If the policy-makers read more into his reports than they should have, they had no one to blame but themselves.

A Great Day

The autumn I returned to Vietnam, I was a four-year veteran of the CIA with a proven expertise in North Vietnamese affairs. My status and reputation within the agency never ceased to amaze me. I had joined the CIA back in 1968 precisely to avoid the Vietnam war, and that I should now be part of the government's war-making machinery there was a token of both my utter lack of conniving and the weakness of the system.

The professor who had first suggested a CIA career to me had insisted that the man and the organization were perfectly matched. After two years at Columbia University's School of International Affairs, I had a fairly good grounding in strategic studies, and my professor-advisor assured me upon graduation that I was well qualified to become a CIA analyst. I was intrigued by the prospect, though not for the professional or patriotic reasons he supposed. Back in the spring of 1968 my draft board was breathing hot on my neck and I figured the best way to avoid recruitment and a stint with the U.S. Army on Vietnam's battlefronts was to cast my lot with a major government agency.

The CIA was most accommodating. I was quickly inducted, indoctrinated and farmed out to the European Division as an "expert" on NATO affairs. For months I prospered. The Soviet invasion of Czechoslovakia had just brought an end to Alexander Dubček's gentle Communism, our NATO allies in Europe were in near-hysteria over it, and the new President's national security advisor, Henry Kissinger, who had built his academic reputation on turgid books about the Atlantic Alliance and nuclear deterrence, was constantly badgering the agency for news and views on the crisis. Inundated with his requests, I stayed perpetually in motion throughout the winter and my draft board gave me up as a lost cause.

Yet eventually, because of my somewhat humorless devotion to work, some of my colleagues grew concerned about me and decided to try to lighten my spirits through a harmless practical joke. One Monday morning when a job application form for a Vietnam assignment circulated through the office, they filled in my name without consulting me and sent it in to CIA management, with an impassioned appeal for consideration. A few days later I received notice that I had been accepted. I was to be sent to Saigon the following June as a "Communist strategy" analyst for the agency.

My pleadings and demurrals were to no avail. I was told that if I did not take the job I would probably never be "invited" to go overseas again, and that of course would mean the end of my CIA career. Faced with the choice between no protection at all from the U.S. Army and two years at the Embassy in Saigon, I reluctantly opted for the latter.

By the time I completed my outprocessing I was so inured to my worst imaginings, I could almost shrug off the black humor my colleagues threw up at me. I was also beginning to take some comfort in the way the political winds were blowing. Several months before, in late January 1969, semi-public peace talks at last had gotten under way in Paris after much bickering among the four participants over the shape of the table, and in early June, on the eve of my departure, President Nixon met with South Vietnamese President Nguyen Van Thieu on Midway Island to announce that he was withdrawing 25,000 men from South Vietnam as a fillip to negotiations and as an expression of confidence in the South Vietnamese army. It was the first practical step in what would become known as the Vietnamization program, which in essence meant handing most of the dirty work over to the South Vietnamese themselves.

Those first two years in Saigon, from 1969 to 1971, were not as harrowing as I had expected, since my job kept me largely walled off from the outside world. For the most part I saw the war only secondhand, through the steady stream of intelligence reports that flowed across my desk, and perhaps typically, the closest shave I had in those years was in a barroom shoot-up in the Saigon suburb of Dakau.

Despite the accelerating Vietnamization program, the Americans in those days were still controlling the "show." While Bunker and my own boss, Ted Shackley, manipulated and penetrated Thieu's government and vanquished his political opponents, General Creighton Abrams attended to the other enemy. The strategy he adopted, known as "accelerated pacification," was essentially a reaction against General William Westmoreland's massive and costly sweep-and-destroy operations of the mid-sixties and was aimed principally at destroying the enemy's base camps and supply lines from North Vietnam. It reached its apotheosis in early 1970 with a joint United States–South Vietnamese drive into Communist sanctuaries in eastern Cambodia, on the heels of the overthrow of Prince Norodom Sihanouk, who had always opposed direct U.S. intervention. The new Cambodian head of state, Prince Lon Nol, did not oppose it, no doubt to his everlasting regret, for as American involvement increased in his country, the North Vietnamese and Chinese felt perfectly justified in stoking the Communist insurgency there.

The Cambodian operation did have one beneficial side effect. Through captured documents and continuing collaboration with Lon Nol, the CIA and the Pentagon soon discovered they had been dead wrong for years about the flow patterns of supplies arriving from North Vietnam. Senior CIA and military analysts had long been convinced that the majority of the supplies destined for Communist forces in Cambodia and the southern half of South Vietnam were funneled in via the "Ho Chi Minh" trail system in southern Laos. (Hence, the heavy U.S. bombing there.) But the intelligence gathered in Cambodia in 1970 revealed that in fact nearly eighty percent of this matériel was shipped in by boat from North Vietnam, and unloaded at the Cambodian port of Sihanoukville. The revelation was a shock to everyone, not the least of all to those who had built their careers in the CIA by pushing the countervailing theory. Yet their apprehensions turned out to be misplaced. None was penalized for his error, and two of those who had championed the mistaken view most vigorously soon became Chief and Deputy Chief of all of the CIA's analytical services.

In February 1971, nearly a year after the Cambodia invasion, the South Vietnamese tried to duplicate Abram's success by mounting a foray of their own against Communist supply lines in southern Laos. The campaign, known as Lam Son 719, stalled at the outset, as the North Vietnamese, fighting on familiar terrain, massed four divisions against the attackers, surrounded them and destroyed them piecemeal, despite heavy U.S. bombing.

In the final analysis, therefore, neither the Vietnamese nor the American variety of accelerated pacification was an unqualified success. The Lam Son operation raised serious doubts, in both Washington and Hanoi, about the ability of the South Vietnamese to cope on their own, and even though Abrams through his own initiatives did manage to extend government control into some previously disputed areas, both inside South Vietnam and along its borders, his accomplishments were the beginning of Thieu's final undoing, for they left the South Vietnamese dangerously overextended at the very moment the Americans were preparing to go home.

In addition to Lam Son, the Cambodia incursion and accelerated pacification, my first two years in Saigon saw the start of the secret negotiations that would eventually lead to Vietnam's illusory peace. The original premise of the U.S. negotiating position was not exactly a paradigm of flexibility. In early 1969, during the first days of the Nixon Administration, Kissinger secretly advised the Soviets that the United States was willing to obliterate Hanoi to achieve a non-Communist South Vietnam. A few weeks later, as if to underscore the threat, Nixon launched his secret bombing campaign against Communist base camps in eastern Cambodia.

Despite this somewhat inauspicious beginning, Kissinger and Le Duc Tho, Hanoi's chief negotiator, did manage to get together the following August to begin secret talks. Initially the discussions did not yield much. The North Vietnamese insisted on the removal of Nguyen Van Thieu as a precondition for everything else. The U.S. position envisaged a cease-fire in place throughout Indochina, followed by the withdrawal of United States and North Vietnamese troops from all battlefronts, the release of U.S. prisoners of war and an Indochina peace conference to wrap up loose ends—all in that order.

By the spring of 1971, however, as I was winding up my first tour in Saigon, the international climate surrounding the negotiations had begun to alter. Kissinger had achieved a breakthrough in his discussions with the Soviets on strategic arms limitation, the arrangements for his first secret visit to Peking had been completed, and U.S. troop strength in South Vietnam had dropped from 500,000, the peak in 1969, to less than 300,000 as part of the ongoing Vietnamization program. In view of these developments, Kissinger felt there was a chance the North Vietnamese would be less hard-line at the conference table, and throughout the fall and winter he began relaxing our negotiating position in hopes of drawing them into a deal. Glossing over the previous demand for a North Vietnamese troop withdrawal from the south, he offered to set a deadline for a total U.S. pullout provided the North Vietnamese agreed to support an Indochina cease-fire and the release of our prisoners.

Le Duc Tho sat and listened, but was not impressed, at least not in the way Kissinger hoped. The softening of our negotiating position was seen as a softening of U.S. will, and the North Vietnamese Politburo resolved to test it one last time by mounting another major offensive against Saigon. Crucial to its decision was the failure of the South Vietnamese incursion into southern Laos earlier in the year, which the war lobby in Hanoi depicted as proof of the failure of Vietnamization itself.

During the fall and winter of 1971 Le Duc Tho merely bided his time with Kissinger, giving no sign of flexibility. Kissinger in turn directed Bunker in Saigon to do all he could to secure Thieu's position—including his reelection in October—for together with the bombing of Cambodia, Thieu was now Washington's most valuable bargaining counter.

In the meantime, I had ended my first tour in Vietnam and had returned home to CIA headquarters to become the principal analyst responsible for determining political trends in Hanoi. Despite my august title, I was not made privy to Kissinger's secret negotiations. Almost no one in the CIA was. Yet I was able to draw some useful inferences from the continued intelligence reporting from Saigon.

By late fall the tone and content of the reporting were becoming increasingly ominous, and several colleagues and I concluded that a major North Vietnamese offensive was in the offing. Our ever-cautious superiors at the CIA, however, were not so sure and decided to check our conclusions with Kissinger before officially committing the agency to them. Kissinger was preoccupied with negotiations and could not imagine the North Vietnamese might be preparing to revert to their old bad habits. Throughout the fall and early winter our superiors therefore dutifully blocked, qualified or modified any analyses that tended to suggest they were.

Meanwhile, Kissinger requested contingency studies from the intelligence community to determine if there might be some way to jog the North Vietnamese off dead center. One proposal drawn up jointly by the CIA and the Pentagon called for the assassination and/or kidnapping of one or more of

North Vietnam's leaders, on the theory this might precipitate such turmoil in Hanoi the survivors would be obliged to bow to U.S. demands. When my colleagues and I were asked to evaluate the scheme we could hardly contain our amusement. As the American raid on the Son Tay prison camp outside Hanoi had proved so painfully in 1970, our intelligence on the life and times of the North Vietnamese was something less than perfect. If we couldn't even accurately pinpoint the whereabouts of a large group of American prisoners in the North Vietnamese capital, how could we possibly expect to locate and snatch select members of the party leadership?

On 17 February 1972, as President Nixon was packing up to leave for Peking, Kissinger sent a message to Hanoi, proposing a resumption of secret talks within a month's time. He was gambling that the prospect of the historic first meeting of American and Chinese heads of state might inspire some moderation in the North Vietnamese Politburo. But true to form, the North Vietnamese equivocated and then asked for postponement of the proposed talks until mid-April.

In Saigon, Thieu by this point was growing increasingly uneasy. Unlike his American mentors he had no trouble envisioning another large-scale NVA offensive, and in late winter he and his staff drew up an assessment predicting a massive North Vietnamese drive across the demilitarized zone into the northernmost provinces of the country. By the time the study was completed, U.S. intelligence officials in both Saigon and Washington were beginning to have some doubts about their own benign forecasts. Yet even as they came to accept the notion that Hanoi might be planning another military push, they could not quite bring themselves to accept Thieu's scenario for it. They argued quite confidently that if there was going to be another NVA drive, its main focus would be in the western highlands and the delta.

On Good Friday, 31 March 1972, four NVA divisions charged across the demilitarized zone precisely as Thieu had predicted. Senior U.S. officials promptly congratulated themselves on having installed such a perspicacious client in Saigon. Their own strategic miscalculations were conveniently forgotten.

The Communist offensive broke across South Vietnam only weeks after Nixon's return from Peking and just as the White House was wrapping up preparations for the upcoming Moscow summit conference in May. The timing raised some agonizing questions in the White House about the value of great-power détente both to the Soviets and the Chinese and as a deterrent to Hanoi.

Throughout the first few weeks of their campaign NVA forces made spectacular gains, particularly in the northern part of South Vietnam, and the Administration was soon faced with the delicate problem of how to intervene to shore up the Saigon government without pulling the plug on the prospective Moscow summit. Ultimately, Kissinger opted for a two-track approach. He ordered planners in the Pentagon to begin drawing up a blueprint for massive air strikes against military targets north of the 20th parallel, coupled with the mining of the port of Haiphong in North Vietnam. He also decided to take the issue to the Soviets.

On a secrecy-shrouded trip to Moscow on 20 April, he put part of his strategy into effect. Unveiling a dramatic new plank in the U.S. negotiating platform, he told party boss Leonid Brezhnev that the United States would not insist on a total NVA withdrawal from the south as a prelude to a settlement, provided the North Vietnamese dropped their demands for Thieu's removal.

None of this, of course, was made known to CIA analysts or to more than a handful of Washington policy-makers. Nor was Thieu informed, for Kissinger did not, and would not, keep him apprised of the secret exchanges destined to decide the fate of his country.

On 2 May, at Soviet prodding, Le Duc Tho met with Kissinger secretly in Paris. The discussions did not break the political impasse, since NVA forces were still riding high on the battlefield, and Kissinger left the meetings convinced that some spectacular new U.S. initiative would be required to nudge the North Vietnamese into a more conciliatory stance.

President Nixon favored the more extreme mining-and-bombing option the Pentagon had put forward, and at a series of National Security Council sessions, representatives of various Washington bureaucracies were asked to comment on the possible effectiveness of such a move and its likely impact on United States–Soviet relations. The discussions were heated and emotional, and within the CIA itself a schism developed on the question. Working-level analysts like myself were unable to see how the proposed blockade of Haiphong, for instance, could have any impact on Hanoi's war-making capability, since the vast majority of foreign aid to North Vietnam was delivered overland, by rail lines through China. But a number of higher-ranking CIA officials, whose antennae were more attuned to the political atmospherics in Washington, saw which way Nixon himself was tending and tacked accordingly.

Nixon of course made the final decision—on the basis of typically Nixonian logic. He could not go to Moscow, he explained to aides, without first showing the Soviets that the United States would not be buffaloed. Thus, on 8 May he announced publicly that our bombers were going north again, flying missions above the 20th parallel for the first time since late 1968.

His declaration exploded on the nation like a bombshell, setting off a wave of public protest, but significantly, the indignation did not seem to extend to the most important of the interested parties, the Soviets themselves. The summit meeting in Moscow was held on schedule, and during the final sessions Kissinger decided the atmosphere was right for mounting a new peace initiative on Vietnam. The United States, he told the Soviets, was now prepared to halt the bombing of North Vietnam, even before the release of all our prisoners, if Hanoi would only back off its anti-Thieu plank.

As Kissinger had hoped, the Soviets were impressed and offered to serve as messenger to Hanoi. On 15 June, Soviet President Podgorny flew to the North Vietnamese capital with the new proposal in hand. Almost simultaneously Communist troops in South Vietnam began to receive detailed secret briefings on the prospects for a settlement. Since the CIA had agents plugged deep into the Communist high command, our intelligence reports soon began registering the shift in tone and emphasis.

By mid-July the intelligence indicators pointing to a real change in Hanoi's negotiating line had reached seismic proportions. According to agent reports, Communist troops in the south were already discussing plans for an imminent cessation of hostilities—possibly without Thieu's prior removal. CIA circuitry also revealed that the Chinese had just advised Hanoi to soften its political demands to facilitate an accommodation. In addition, the Communist offensive itself had begun to stall, thanks largely to U.S. bombing, especially in the northern areas of the country.

Against this backdrop Kissinger accelerated his secret diplomacy, meeting again with Le Duc Tho in Paris on 19 July to discuss the new U.S. negotiating package. A few days later he flew to Saigon to brief Thieu, although as usual he was far less candid with him than he had been with the Communists, making no mention of our willingness to leave NVA troops in the south after a cease-fire.

At CIA headquarters my colleagues and I remained innocent of these machinations. But as the summer wore on and the intelligence from inside the Communist command itself continued to suggest a change in Hanoi's political stand, some of us became convinced a breakthrough on the negotiating front was a real possibility.

Senior CIA officials, however, once again knew better. Though as ignorant as we were of Kissinger's activities, they interpreted the apparent lack of movement in the public negotiations in Paris as the definitive barometer. "But what about the cadre briefings in South Vietnam?" I asked. "They're only for morale purposes," my immediate boss assured me. "The Communists are not doing as well as they had hoped on the battlefield; so they're playing up the prospects for an early peace to bolster the spirits of their troops."

Kissinger undoubtedly would have been surprised and amused at this explanation. By early August he and Le Duc Tho had in fact made such progress in their secret talks that he was resolved to start leveling with Thieu about them, so as to prepare him for the inevitable. General Alexander Haig, Kissinger's deputy, was sent to Saigon to do the honors.

According to several who participated in those Saigon meetings, Thieu was flabbergasted and enraged at what he was told. Although Haig did not broach the topic of the continued North Vietnamese troop presence in South Vietnam, he said quite enough to convince Thieu that he was being stampeded.

When Haig returned to Washington he advised Kissinger that Thieu would not be budged. But Kissinger was in no mood for such pessimism. He evidently was convinced that the increasingly cordial relations between the United States and the Soviets and the Chinese provided him with the unique opportunity to bring the war to a satisfactory conclusion, and he was not about to let Thieu spoil it. He therefore shrugged off Haig's warnings and scheduled a trip to Moscow for 10 September, to be followed by another secret session with Le Duc Tho in Paris.

The North Vietnamese for their part had just reached a critical decision. In late August the members of the party Politburo concluded that in view of the stalemate on the battlefield, they might as well give Kissinger's diplomacy a chance, particularly since they were unlikely to be offered better terms after Nixon's reelection in November, which they considered a certainty. Thus, on 1 September, North Vietnam's National Day, Hanoi gave an explicit public signal that it was willing to meet Kissinger's primary demand. Addressing the nation by radio, Premier Pham Van Dong did precisely what Communist briefers in South Vietnam had been doing since mid-June—he studiously avoided any mention of President Thieu in his rundown of the usual catalogue of Communist negotiating demands.

As luck would have it, the translation of Dong's speech reached CIA headquarters on a weekend, and I was the only member of the Vietnam Task Force on duty in the office at the time. Once I had read it through several times, I called my immediate boss at home and told him I thought it was the sign we had been waiting for. He said he would be right in.

Working together, he and I completed a full analysis of the speech in time for the 6 P.M. deadline of the "President's Daily Brief." In our conclusion we stated clearly that the omission of Thieu's name in Dong's recitation of the standard Communist negotiating demands could well represent a shift in Hanoi's political position.

The next morning the ceiling fell in. Senior agency officials called my office every hour on the hour, accusing me of having played foul by releasing such a controversial item over the weekend when none of them was around to "coordinate" it. Although my boss emphasized that he had had a hand in preparing the piece, no one seemed mollified. Since I had been pushing the breakthrough theory for so many weeks, I was held responsible for what had been written.

Within twenty-four hours the Chief of the CIA's Vietnam Task Force informed me that effective immediately, I was barred from writing any more analyses. I would have to find another job elsewhere in the agency.

Several days later, on 10 September, Kissinger traveled to Moscow, as he had planned. On the third day Brezhnev confirmed to him that the Pham Van Dong address and a subsequent, similarly worded Viet Cong pronouncement indeed signaled a shift in Communist negotiating demands. Thieu's removal was no longer a precondition for achieving a cease-fire and the release of U.S. prisoners of war.

Buoyed by these assurances, Kissinger pressed ahead in his efforts to work out a settlement prior to the U.S. elections, now less than two months away. During the next two weeks he met secretly with Le Duc Tho in Paris on numerous occasions.

As for myself, once released from the Vietnam Task Force, I was no longer authorized to review the flow of intelligence from the battlefront. I therefore spent most of September reading spy novels in the CIA library or watching the groundhogs gambol on the hill just behind the large cafeteria.

Toward the end of the month a friend of mine who was involved in running espionage operations in Vietnam took pity on me. "How'd you like to go back to Saigon on temporary assignment to debrief a couple of prisoners of war?" he asked.

It took me exactly four days to complete all the necessary medical and bureaucratic processing and to check out of my old office. On 2 October, I was airborne, heading across the Pacific to begin my second and last tour of duty in the U.S. Embassy in Saigon.

As I settled into my new assignment the Paris peace agreement took final shape. On 8 October, Le Duc Tho tabled a new negotiating formula that made no mention at all of Thieu's removal, and within four days almost all outstanding issues had been tentatively resolved. Despite minor snags, Tho and Kissinger were optimistic that the remaining details could be worked out expeditiously, and as the meeting broke up, Tho proposed 31 October as a date for formal signing ceremonies and inauguration of the cease-fire—evidently in hopes of ringing in the peace before the U.S. presidential elections. Kissinger agreed to fly out to Hanoi on 24 October to initial the draft as certification of U.S. intent.

Within the next few days he passed a memo to CIA headquarters requesting an assessment of Thieu's probable reactions to a cease-fire. My old colleagues in the Vietnam Task Force, who by now had some inkling of what was afoot, quickly provided him one. Thieu, they said, would never support any cease-fire agreement that demanded a political accommodation with the Communists or left NVA forces in the south. Kissinger read over the assessment and impatiently tossed it aside. Too much gloom, he declared. Then he went home and packed his bags for a trip to Saigon, where he intended to get his answer firsthand.

If Kissinger was not much taken with the CIA's views, there was one man in the White House who was—Nixon himself. Moreover, as he contemplated the tentative agreement Kissinger had worked out with Le Duc Tho, he became increasingly convinced America's more conservative voters would consider it a sellout. He saw no need to go into the elections with such a shadow hanging over him, and therefore decided to make Thieu's anticipated resistance a pretext for holding off a settlement until a more opportune moment.

In Saigon, meanwhile, Thieu gave his American patrons all the resistance they could have imagined. In his first meetings with Kissinger in mid-October he rejected the entire negotiating package as it was written. He was particularly critical of the provision permitting North Vietnamese forces to remain in the south after a cease-fire, a concession on which he had never before been consulted. For days Kissinger threatened and cajoled, trying to change Thieu's mind.* But at last, on 23 October, he conceded to his staff there was no chance he could swing the South Vietnamese into line in time for Hanoi's proposed cease-fire deadline eight days later. He sent a message to the North Vietnamese capital, canceling his scheduled trip, and then, in hopes of preserving the political bridges he had so carefully built, he cabled Nixon, recommending a suspension of bombing above the 20th parallel as a signal to Hanoi that the United States was still interested in peace.

Shortly before Kissinger's departure from Saigon one of the CIA's most reliable agents provided us with a verbatim text of the negotiating document Le Duc Tho had tabled in Paris on 8 October. He had transcribed it from a briefing at a Communist field headquarters in the delta. When Tom Polgar, the newly arrived CIA Station Chief, showed it to Kissinger, the presidential advisor was flabbergasted. "How did you get that!" he exclaimed. Polgar told him about our source and asked if the information was accurate. Kissinger conceded it was "just about right."

It was through that document that most of us in the CIA and State Department bureaucracies in Saigon and Washington first became fully aware of the progress Kissinger had made in his secret negotiations. We were not alone. Throughout their own stormy sessions with Kissinger in late October the South Vietnamese were able to stay one step ahead of him only because one of their own agents had also managed to turn up a copy of Tho's platform. Drawing on it, Thieu and his staff could tell immediately when Kissinger was lying to them and when he was not, and were able to anticipate him at every turn.

When the North Vietnamese received Kissinger's advisory that the October cease-fire was off, they immediately expected trickery and decided to make the whole record of the negotiations public so the United States at least would have to bear the onus for it. On 26 October, Radio Hanoi and the Viet Cong's clandestine Liberation Radio broadcast the full text of the 8 October negotiating document, together with some uncomplimentary remarks about Washington's lack of good faith. Kissinger realized at once that the North Vietnamese had misunderstood, and in a press conference in Washington the following morning he tried to signal indirectly to them that their suspicions were unfounded. "Peace is at hand," he assured the startled newsmen present, and then he went on to insist that only a few more negotiating sessions were needed to nail down a final accord.

---

*Kissinger's tactics of persuasion did not always conform to traditional diplomatic lines. When he discovered that Hoang Duc Nha, Thieu's cousin and the principal intransigent on the South Vietnamese side, was something of a ladies' man, he decided to play his own hand accordingly. Taking Nha aside, he pulled out a little black book, opened it to a page with the names and addresses of several American movie starlets, and offered to introduce Nha to some of the choicest ones if the two of them could be "friends." Nha retaliated by whipping out a massive address book of his own and offering to extend similar favors to Kissinger. That prospect apparently cowed the President's security advisor. The matter was never raised again.

At the same time he and Nixon agreed to give Thieu himself some new incentive toward compromise. A massive supply lift, code-named "Enhance Plus," was mounted to refurbish his army—and to buy his cooperation. On 9 November, only two days after Nixon's landslide victory, General Haig arrived back in Saigon to exact Washington's price. He told Thieu that the Administration now expected him to close ranks with it at once on the proposed agreement, and warned that Nixon would sign the draft, with or without his support, as soon as Kissinger and Le Duc Tho wrapped up the final details, perhaps as early as 15 December.

Two days later Nixon himself sent a long letter to Thieu, reaffirming and sharpening much of what Haig had said. He also added a sweetener. "You have my absolute assurance," he wrote, "that if Hanoi fails to abide by the terms of the agreement, it is my intention to take swift and retaliatory action." It was the opening flourish in Washington's postwar commitment to South Vietnam, one on which the U.S. Congress would never be consulted.

When Kissinger met again with Le Duc Tho in late November he made a careful effort—clearly for Thieu's benefit—to convey a new sense of resolve. He tabled over sixty new demands on behalf of the South Vietnamese and forty-four textual changes of his own. Le Duc Tho questioned him on several of them but was not receptive to any. Indeed, with each new emendation, he became increasingly suspicious of Kissinger's motives. Were the Americans deliberately playing for time so they could finish resupplying the South Vietnamese before the cease-fire? By 25 November he was convinced the answer was yes, and asked for a temporary adjournment so he could return to Hanoi for consultations.

In South Vietnam, government forces immediately took advantage of the stalemate to intensify their land-grabbing operations. Kissinger, meanwhile, returned to Washington and began reviewing various proposals aimed at bringing the negotiations to a swift conclusion. One of the contingency papers submitted to him by his National Security Council staff envisioned renewed military pressure against Hanoi—bombing of the capital itself—to prod the North Vietnamese toward a settlement. It was an old solution to an old problem. But under current circumstances it had a special new appeal, particularly since it might coincidentally help to ease Thieu's own concerns about a U.S. sellout.

When Le Duc Tho returned to Paris in early December to resume private talks with Kissinger, he was decidedly cooler toward the draft accord than before, and Kissinger was strengthened in his belief that Hanoi was now deliberately dragging its feet so its forces could counter recent South Vietnamese military gains. On 14 December, after considerable debate and no progress, Tho again asked for a leave of absence, and several hours later Kissinger, too, departed Paris, leaving his deputy, William Sullivan, to continue discussing the draft protocols with lower-ranking North Vietnamese officials.

The following day Sullivan cabled Washington, indicating that his so-called "technical talks" were stalemated. At this point Nixon and Kissinger decided that the time had come to get tough. That afternoon Hanoi received a chilling message from the President of the United States. Unless the North Vietnamese agreed to "serious" negotiations within seventy-two hours, the message read, the United States would resume bombing above the 20th parallel. On 18 December, Nixon's deadline ran out and waves of B-52s swept north to hit military installations inside Hanoi and Haiphong, which till then had remained off-limits.

Simultaneously, General Haig was sent to Saigon with a new ultimatum: If Thieu should still refuse to sign the draft accord more or less as it was written, the United States would cut off all assistance to South Vietnam and would sign a separate agreement with the North Vietnamese. Concurrently, in a personal letter to Thieu, Nixon warned that further intransigence would be "an invitation to disaster," and "would be inexcusable, above all because we will have lost a just and honorable alternative."

Thieu was offended and unmoved by these pressure tactics, but the North Vietnamese proved more responsive. After twelve days of the blitz they called for a halt, promising to resume "serious negotiations" at once. On 30 December, Nixon publicly announced that air operations above the 20th parallel would be terminated.

Seven days later, at Hanoi's request, Kissinger resumed his meetings in Paris with Le Duc Tho. Although the North Vietnamese negotiator was hardly the congenial figure he had been before the bombing, he was polite and correct, and most important, his negotiating position was again what it had been in October.

As the talks progressed, the Administration continued to bombard Thieu with threats and promises in a relentless effort to bring him to heel. Finally, on 20 January, Nixon made it patently clear that he would conclude a separate peace with the North Vietnamese at once if Saigon refused to bend. His message to Thieu was blunt and to the point: "As I have told you, we will initial the agreement on 23 January. I must know whether you are prepared to go along with us in this cause and I must have your answer by twelve hundred Washington time 21 January 1973."

Staring total isolation in the face, Thieu capitulated.

Three days later, on schedule, Kissinger and Le Duc Tho initialed the agreement on behalf of the two other "parties"—the Saigon regime and the Communist Provisional Revolutionary Government. The next morning a white-suited Ambassador Bunker strode into the conference room on the third floor of the U.S. Embassy in Saigon and proclaimed, with tears in his eyes, "This is a great day for us all. There is to be a cease-fire." That afternoon the briefing officers at MACV flashed a cartoon onto the viewing screen they had so often used to display body counts and territorial gains. One caricatured Viet Cong soldier was shown asking another, "What is a cease-fire, after all?" The reply: "Damned if I know."

On 27 January the formal signing ceremonies took place in Paris. It was a curious affair; four separate copies of the agreement—two in Vietnamese, two in English—were laid out on the table before the foreign ministers of the four "parties," but only Secretary of State William Rogers and his North Vietnamese counterpart, Nguyen Duy Trinh, signed all of them. The Foreign Ministers of the Republic of South Vietnam and the Provisional Revolutionary Government merely countersigned one each, under the signatures of their respective allies, so their names would not appear together on any single copy, for that would have implied mutual recognition.

At eight in the morning Saigon time, 28 January 1973, the cease-fire went into effect, to the melancholy wail of the city's air-raid system. I stood on the roof of the Duc Hotel and toasted the new era with a Bloody Mary.

For all its solemnity and import, the advent of peace was not without its lighter side. In his haste to conclude the agreement, Kissinger had forgotten to cable to Saigon all the changes he had made in the text during the last few days of the negotiations. Thus the document Thieu read out to his cabinet on the first day of the cease-fire was not the one Kissinger and the North Vietnamese had actually agreed upon.

The normally reticent Ellsworth Bunker had only one comment when he learned of the oversight: "I'll be goddamned!" It was a fitting prologue to all that was to follow.

In Good Faith

During the fall and winter months that bracketed the signing of the Paris peace agreement, my overriding concern was not the coming peace at all, but a small man in a snow-white room, a North Vietnamese prisoner of war who had been in solitary confinement for the past year and a half. His name was Nguyen Van Tai.

A former deputy minister of "public security" in North Vietnam, Tai had come south in 1962 to take charge of the Communist counterespionage and terrorist network in Saigon and had helped engineer the spectacular attack on the U.S. Embassy in 1968. During his long career he had been responsible for numerous assassinations and terrorist acts, and when in December 1970 he was captured in mufti during a government dragnet south of Saigon, he had not been treated kindly. With American help the South Vietnamese had built him his own prison cell and interrogation room, both totally white, totally bare except for a table, a chair, an open hole for a toilet—and ubiquitous hidden television cameras and microphones to record his every waking and sleeping moment. His jailers had soon discovered one essential psychic-physical flaw in him. Like many Vietnamese, he believed his blood vessels contracted when he was exposed to frigid air. His quarters and interrogation room had thus been outfitted with heavy-duty air conditioners and been kept thoroughly chilled.

South Vietnamese interrogators had spent over eight months with him after his capture, trying to break him. They were unsuccessful. He told one of his tormentors, "I'll shoot you down in the street if I ever get out." In early 1972 an American specialist had been called in. He had made some progress by confronting Tai with former subordinates who had either defected to the government or had likewise been captured. Their testimony and face-to-face confrontations with him forced him to surrender part of the false identity and cover story, but once having been exposed to these accusers, he also knew just how much incriminating evidence the government had on him, how much he had to admit and how much he could continue to conceal.

•   •   •

In the meantime, unknown to Tai himself, he had become the focus of one of the most delicate U.S. intelligence operations ever mounted in South Vietnam, one that seemed to hold the key to the release of countless American prisoners of war. The case dated back to 1967, three years before his capture. In August of that year the head of the secret Communist party organization in Saigon, a man named Tran Bach Dang, had contacted our Embassy through an emissary in Cambodia and offered to open negotiations on a possible prisoner exchange and on other "political issues." A subsequent contact revealed that Dang was angling for the release of ten high-level Communist operatives.

Despite the significance of the overture, not everyone in Saigon and Washington was receptive. President Nguyen Van Thieu was reluctant to release the ten prisoners on Dang's list because all were dedicated Communists and foes of his regime. CIA officials in Washington sympathized with his view. Only after considerable debate was a deal arranged. In December 1967 the South Vietnamese handed two low-ranking prisoners over to the Communists, one of them Dang's own wife, and Dang in turn promptly freed two Americans, Marine Corporal José Agosto-Santos and Army Private Luis Ortiz-Rivera. Thieu then released two of Dang's original nominees and two substitutes. At the same time the Embassy passed a list to the Communists of ten Americans for whom it wanted an accounting.

That ended the bargaining for the time being. Dang responded to neither Thieu's gesture nor our request. Instead, two weeks afterward, in late February 1968, Communist forces throughout South Vietnam launched the first phase of their Tet "general offensive." There were no further private exchanges on the prisoner issue until the offensive had run its course.

Finally, a year later, contacts were reopened at the Communists' initiative. In mid-January 1969 a French-speaking female who claimed to represent Dang telephoned the Embassy and proposed renewed discussions. Fearing another communications blackout, Embassy officials decided to try to make the most of the opening. They told the caller they wished to "identify" the prisoners available for release; in other words, they wanted a list of Americans in Communist prison camps. The request evidently did not impress Dang. The emissary did not call back.

The circuits remained silent for another year and a half, then abruptly came alive again in July 1971. Quite unexpectedly the Communist Provisional Revolutionary Government sent a letter to the Embassy requesting a special telephone number that could be used for continued discussions of the prisoner issue. The Embassy duly supplied one, publishing it in a bogus newspaper ad in one of the Saigon dailies, as suggested in the letter.

For the next three months CIA operatives sat by an Embassy phone specially keyed to the number, but no one ever called. At last, in early October 1971, there was a surprise breakthrough. With almost no prior arrangement, the Communists released Army Sergeant John Sexton, who had been a prisoner of theirs for over a year. When the American trudged out of the jungle several miles south of the small town of Snoul, Cambodia, he carried with him a Communist request for reciprocity. In return for his freedom, Dang was demanding the release of two of his senior operatives within the next three days. One of them was a Communist labor agitator named Le Van Hoai. The other was Nguyen Van Tai, the denizen of the government's snow-white cell who had been captured the previous December.

Working against the short deadline, U.S. and South Vietnamese officials weighed every aspect of the proposal, the potential advantages and disadvantages. Ultimately Thieu, seconded by the CIA, rejected it. Sexton was a mere "sergeant"; the two prisoners the Communists wanted for him were among the highest-ranking enemy agents ever to fall into government hands.

The deadline was thus allowed to pass. For days the Communists seemed to have lost interest. Then, on 27 October 1971, Dang's emissary again contacted the Embassy. In exchange for Hoai and Tai, the caller said, the Communists were willing to offer a "high-ranking" American, Douglas K. Ramsey, a Foreign Service officer whom they had seized north of Saigon in 1966.

The proposal set off a frantic debate in the Embassy and in Washington. Clearly the Communists were raising the stakes, but if they were so anxious to get back both Hoai and Tai, then possibly the entire deal could be parlayed into something even more advantageous to "our side." Operating on this logic, United States and South Vietnamese officials decided to offer only Hoai, the labor agitator, for Ramsey. Nguyen Van Tai would remain in his exclusive white cell.

The CIA was particularly adamant against surrendering Tai. As a senior agency official later explained to me, Tai was a top Communist intelligence operative; Ramsey was "no more than a Foreign Service officer." Thus, to have exchanged one for the other would have been no act of reciprocity at all. The Communists would have gotten the better side of the deal. Besides, the agency was hoping to trade Tai for a CIA officer who had been captured during the 1968 offensive.

When Dang's emissary telephoned on 27 November 1971, Embassy officials put forward their counterproposal: Hoai alone for Ramsey. Tai's status was non-negotiable. In addition, they asked for a list of all prisoners of every nationality who were being held by the Communists. What had begun as a cautious, albeit extraordinary, series of contacts between the two sides had now escalated into a bid for the release of all prisoners of war.

Seven days later the Communists gave their answer. Dang's representative informed the Embassy that the counterproposal was unacceptable. Both Hoai and Tai would have to be traded for Ramsey. Otherwise: no deal.

Incredibly, the CIA operative on the Embassy end of the line had no fall-back option to propose. He simply hung up—and that was that. In effect, our government had just squandered a chance to obtain the release of an American who had been a captive of the Communists for six years.

For the next few days American officials from Saigon to Washington nervously tried to convince themselves they had done the right thing. Vietnam-watchers at the CIA were particularly defensive, since they had been chiefly responsible for taking Tai's name out of the bargaining. At their urging, Kissinger and the National Security Council agreed on 17 December 1971 to stick by the counterproposal if the Communists should call again. It would be Hoai for Ramsey, or nothing.

Days, then weeks, passed with no word from the other side. The Embassy tried to provoke a response through cryptically worded advertisements in the Saigon press, but the designated telephone line remained silent.

On Easter weekend 1972 North Vietnamese forces plunged across the demilitarized zone between North and South Vietnam in the most ambitious Communist offensive since Tet 1968. The Embassy and the Thieu government concluded that any further dealing on the prisoner issue was now out of the question.

In May, however, something happened to revive the prospects for Ramsey's release. Government troops captured an old and battered Communist party member—Nam Quyet, one of Dang's right-hand men and chief of the "propaganda and training" section of the Communist party in Saigon. Under interrogation, Quyet admitted that he knew of the earlier negotiations concerning Ramsey and said he himself could now be traded for the American.

Inexplicably, South Vietnamese authorities did not inform the Embassy of Quyet's proposal until mid-September. By then the Communist offensive was winding down and the Kissinger–Le Duc Tho negotiations in Paris were moving into a decisive stage. Against this backdrop, the idea of trading the old Communist operative for Ramsey did not seem as attractive as it might have earlier. While delighted to have a new line on the American prisoner, U.S. officials also saw in the proposed deal the danger of acute political embarrassment to the Administration, at the very moment Kissinger least needed one. What if the Communists had briefed Ramsey on the earlier proposal and on Washington's refusal to go through with it? Once released, he might well go to the press with the story, and the result undoubtedly would be a massive popular backlash in the United States that would only add to the pressure for an immediate Vietnam peace.

There were also parochial concerns. The CIA had a special reason to fear a full public disclosure. Since it had been instrumental in persuading Kissinger and the White House not to accept the original two-for-one proposal for Ramsey's release, any public reaction would inevitably find its way to the agency's doorstep. The impact on the CIA's "public image" would be devastating.

Hastily, Administration and CIA officials devised a plan to protect themselves. Before taking action on Quyet's suggestion, they moved to build an airtight excuse for having bungled Ramsey's release in the first place. Nguyen Van Tai, the man whom they had considered "too important" to be exchanged for him in 1971, must now be shown to be the hottest property in Saigon's hands, as they claimed he was. His worth as an "intelligence source" would have to be demonstrated in the form of immediate and concrete intelligence "production" so no one could possibly object to the earlier decision not to trade him for the Foreign Service officer if the story should ever become public.

It was at this juncture I was brought into the case. Having just been fired from the CIA's Vietnam Task Force, I was both available and qualified. Since I was a "specialist" on North Vietnamese affairs, it was thought I might be able to prod sufficient information from Tai to establish his "strategic value." No one else had been able to do so.

Just before I departed Washington for Saigon in October 1972, a senior CIA official briefed me on the case, stressing the need for immediate progress. It was the first I had heard of Tai or the proposed prisoner exchanges, even though much of the initial dickering between Dang and the Embassy had taken place during my first tour in Saigon.

Ordinarily an interrogator would be given weeks to read into a case and prepare his assault. I was thrust into Tai's frigid white chamber almost immediately upon my arrival in Saigon.

He was a small, though powerfully built, man who had kept himself in fair physical trim by doing hours of calisthenics each day in his thirty-by-thirty-foot cell. Only his face showed the ravages of his prolonged isolation—a gaunt, drawn mask, ashen-hued for lack of sunlight, the beard far heavier than most Vietnamese's, since he was allowed tweezers only twice a week to keep it pared. Disciplined to an extreme, he awoke automatically each morning at six, went through his exercises, read for half an hour from one of the French or Vietnamese books his jailers provided him, and then awaited breakfast. Afterward he repeated the routine, again and again throughout the day, until he put himself to bed, automatically, at ten o'clock in the evening, never once having seen the rising or setting of the sun.

According to the record of the case, he had only two discernibly exploitable flaws, aside from his aversion to cold air. As a rising young party member in Hanoi in the early 1950s he had tried to prove himself to his superiors by helping to prosecute and imprison his own father, a distinguished North Vietnamese writer with a bleak view of the Communist utopia. Since the Vietnamese are powerfully family-oriented, such an act, no matter what the rationale, could only have been traumatic. In addition, Tai was made in the mold of many of our own intelligence operatives. Having sacrificed so much of himself to his mission, he had been obliged to convince himself of its righteousness and of his own superior sense of duty and morality. Persuade him of the falseness of any one of these premises and the whole personality would begin to crumble.

Relying both on my rusty French and a Vietnamese interpreter, I insulted and cajoled, playing the insolent American with no respect for age or experience. He counterattacked, clinging to what remained of his cover story, but all the while attempting to shield his ego with half-truths about his exploits that always told me more, always added to his dossier. I volunteered the story of a man who had betrayed his father, and he flashed back "Don't try to trick me with such claptrap"—while denying the story was relevant to him in any case. "I'm a simple farmer who came south to support the liberation forces," he insisted, but he could not bring himself to turn down books of French poetry I brought him—heavy fare for a simple farmer—or the Vietnamese histories of the United States. I also gave him an English grammar and he tried to teach himself some phrases between sessions.

As the weeks passed, the going got rougher—for both of us. Each day I scheduled two or three bouts with him, two or three hours each, varying their times so as to throw off his internal clock. Then, some six weeks into the case, during a morning session, I accidentally discovered a small fracture in his façade. I had been trying to spark some nostalgia by raising questions about his wife and children, whom he had not seen since he left North Vietnam in 1962. Suddenly he grew very still. "I cannot think about my wife and children," he said. "The only way I can survive this is by putting all such hope aside. Then there are no illusions or disappointments."

I spent the next few weeks trying to drive the wedge deeper. What about your wife? How old is she? Are your children still going to school? What will you do if peace ever comes to Vietnam? There was a prisoner exchange at the end of the Korean War, after all. Perhaps you will be released.

His dossier began to grow as he inadvertently let slip one detail after another in his helpless grasping after the one hope he knew he could not afford. I reported the progress to Washington. My superiors seemed satisfied.

Since I was becoming such an expert on the case, my duties were expanded. In November 1972 I was invited to take on two additional sources, Le Van Hoai and Nam Quyet, the two other prisoners who had figured in the proposals concerning Ramsey. Hoai, the labor agitator, turned out to be a sniveling and easy subject who would betray top secrets for a cigarette or a candy bar. Nam Quyet was more difficult. Whenever I prodded him with leading questions he would lapse into a fit of coughing, thereby tearing open tubercular scars in his lungs and throat. As the interrogation continued, blood would begin oozing from his nose and mouth. He couldn't resist spitting mouthfuls at me.

Nonetheless, by early January 1973 I was beginning to generate usable intelligence from all three sources. Tai seemed on the verge of collapse. Washington urged me on; the South Vietnamese advised that I apply strong-arm tactics. Then, abruptly, the cease-fire brought all these interrogations to a full stop.

In keeping with understandings reached in Paris, all prisoners of war held by the government and the Communists were to be informed of the terms of the agreement, including the provision for prisoner exchange, within several days of the signing. On 1 February 1973 I briefed Hoai and Nam Quyet. Two days later I informed Nguyen Van Tai.

He sat for a moment, trembling in the draft of the air conditioning. "If what you tell me is true," he said in French, "then this is the happiest day of my life." His face betrayed no emotion. His hands remained folded in his lap, the sleeves of the gray pajama shirt hanging limp from his shoulders. "I have only one question," he said at last. "Will the 'liberation forces' be permitted to participate in the great-power conference in Geneva. We must not be sold out again." I said I did not know. The seasoned revolutionary, in his forty-fifth year, on the eve of peace, was wary of surrendering himself to the ultimate hope.

That was the last I saw of Nguyen Van Tai. South Vietnamese authorities were furious that I had informed him of the Paris accord. They grumbled that I had squandered the only leverage they still had with him and had betrayed their good faith in me. They insisted the terms of the prisoner exchange did not apply to him, since he had never acknowledged his full identity.

The Embassy took me off the case. Other American personnel likewise were withdrawn from interrogation centers around the country, and the responsibility for disposing of all Communist prisoners was turned over to the South Vietnamese, in accordance with the U.S. government's desire to end its active role in Vietnam.

A year and a half later, as analyst and briefer for the Embassy, I lectured a group of special visitors from Washington on the status of the cease-fire. The audience was unique—ten or twelve American military officers and civilian officials, all of whom had once been prisoners of the Communists, either in Hanoi or in South Vietnam. Among them was the man whose fate had been so intimately intertwined with that of Nguyen Van Tai and my other sources —Douglas K. Ramsey. He had been released in early 1973, just after the cease-fire, pursuant to the terms of the accord. When I saw him he was still walking with a cane. His legs were partially disabled as a result of malnutrition he had suffered while a guest of Tran Bach Dang. He had spent most of those seven years in a small bamboo cage, just large enough for him to stand, in a Communist prison camp near the Cambodian border. During my briefing he asked me one question, which held unintended irony. "How good is the Communist underground subversive apparatus?"

"Not as effective as it was before Tet 1968," I replied. "Most of their primary operatives have been killed or captured."

A year after the collapse of South Vietnam, I visited Ramsey in Washington and revealed to him the details of the intelligence operation that had very nearly brought his release in 1971. It was the first time he had heard of it. His superiors in the State Department had not seen fit to inform him that he had spent an extra year in a Communist prison camp because the CIA had not considered him important or valuable enough to be exchanged for Nguyen Van Tai.

As for Tai himself, there was no salutary ending to his ordeal. While both Hoai and Nam Quyet survived the Communist takeover in April 1975, he did not. Just before North Vietnamese tanks rolled into Saigon a senior CIA official suggested to South Vietnamese authorities that it would be useful if he "disappeared." Since Tai was a trained terrorist, he could hardly be expected to be a maganimous victor. The South Vietnamese agreed. Tai was loaded onto an airplane and thrown out at ten thousand feet over the South China Sea. At that point he had spent over four years in solitary confinement, in a snow-white room, without ever having fully admitted who he was.

This story is not unique. On several occasions during the last years of the Vietnam war, the Communists secretly offered to release various American prisoners, only to be held off by the U.S. government as it angled for "better terms." The CIA was particularly inflexible, usually insisting on strict reciprocity, an intelligence operative for an intelligence operative, as if agency personnel deserved first consideration over any other Americans who might be prisoners of the Communists. Douglas Ramsey was lucky. He lost only one additional year of freedom as a result of such "gaming." Others were not so lucky. They lost their lives or their health, to disease, malnutrition and Communist abuse, as the haggling dragged on.*

*One other "player" in this prisoner-exchange story apparently also came to grief. A short while before the cease-fire, Tran Bach Dang was summarily removed from his post as Communist party chief in Saigon. One of the charges brought against him by his superiors was "subjectivism," a tendency to want to run the show in his own way, without due attention to mandates from above.

Leaves from a Pocket Notebook

January 29, 1973: Long live the Vietnam peace, but keep your head down. Twenty-four hours after the cease-fire the outgoing's still rattling Saigon's windows.

Reports have it that the PRG delegates to the Joint Military Commission have refused to disembark at Tan Son Nhut air base in protest over government customs regulations (to submit to them, they claim, would imply recognition of Thieu and his "clique"). To add to the confusion, the Hungarian and Polish representatives to the International Commission of Control and Supervision apparently are put out over their living accommodations at Tan Son Nhut. Thieu has offered them billets usually reserved for South Vietnamese army dependents, but the proletarians from Eastern Europe feel they deserve better.

Group of Poles downtown yesterday: they nearly broke their necks craning after the local beauties. A bunch of them apparently got thoroughly Sanforized in the "Golden Hands" Steam and Massage Parlor.

The first wave of prisoner exchanges went off like clockwork yesterday. But no one in the Embassy seems interested. Despite the general elation about peace and all that, some of us are suffering a kind of lover's letdown. The passion's all spent. No great storm and strife to justify further self-indulgence. Even the pleasures are becoming dully routinized. Each evening the same group of lard-bound colleagues gather at the rooftop bar on the restaurant behind the Embassy for a few laughs and some booze. The jokes are as stale as the popcorn, and promptly at 7 P.M. the usual swarm of bats materializes in a funnel of activity over the swimming pool in the courtyard.

"It's hard to accept," the Vietnamese girl I had known during my previous tour mused this afternoon over tea on the veranda of the Continental Hotel, "but the soothsayers around town say the Americans' time has come. Whatever you touch you now leave tainted and broken." She's an educated and reasonably sophisticated girl, with the equivalent of a graduate degree in law, but she had spent the morning waiting in line at the French Grall Hospital to catch a glimpse of a terribly deformed baby the local press has dubbed the "snake thing." Government authorities decided to put it on display, for they thought it would teach an important lesson. While the mother was Vietnamese, the father was American, undoubtedly (according to the Vietnamese press) the wellspring of its deformities.

This morning, three hours with a new source: a swarthy province cadre from Binh Dinh, a southpaw with a missing index finger. The nose and jaw are something out of a Joe Palooka cartoon, but the spirit is gentle, simplistic. They say he's got no more than a fourth-grade education and has been completely "turned around." The Viet Cong apparently let his wife die in child-birth, and we're exploiting the aftershock. He's ready to betray all his former comrades.

You watch him across the chipped black enamel of the interrogation table and wonder what hopelessness feels like. But there he is, meticulously charting Communist plans, exposing his friends, taking some apparent pride when you recite his dissertation back to him to check for errors. And when the session's over he grasps your hand with both of his. Grateful for something, maybe only for having nothing at all to do, nothing more to rationalize.

Quick trip upcountry for a firsthand look at Kissinger's "peace": the wait at the Air America terminal drags out long and hot as they gas up the C-47. A Vietnamese family shows, clutching tickets, two badly scarred children at the mother's elbow. Victims of whose aggression? Whose mistake? No smiles among them. Finally we are aboard and away, the grind of the motors as jarring as the screech of chalk on a blackboard. Across the aisle one of the kids stares at me, unblinking. I pretend not to notice, but finally force a faint smile. The edges of her mouth contort, stretching the scars, flattening them, her idea of reciprocity.

The plane lurches. The GI on my right, hunched over his dog-eared paperback, seems unaware. I fight the nerves by playing sightseer. To no avail. As the shadow of the plane ripples over the burnt-green scrub of the mountains below, I instinctively scan the horizon for the puff of smoke and corkscrew trajectory that marks the unique signature of an SA-7 missile. It's about as relaxing as watching for a dorsal fin in the surf.

Two-day stopover in Nha Trang: the weather steely gray, a low ceiling with a chill. Clouds have settled on one of the abrupt hills just beyond the airfield, socking in the Communist artillery spotters. In the dry season Nha Trang is a picturesque strand—somebody once called it Nice in beggar's clothing—with rows of palm and faded French villas scattered out along the main beachfront thoroughfare. The surf runs strong, but out beyond the breakers the water is crystal-clear, right down to the slugs and starfish.

I walk along the beachfront, ignoring the soliciting cyclo drivers and trying to avoid the loops of barbed wire that curl up suddenly here and there in the sand. Two or three years ago old ladies with Viet Cong sympathies used to trudge along this beach selling fresh coconuts to unwary GIs—with hand grenades buried inside.

From Nha Trang the flight westward to Pleiku City in the central highlands is a short shot over tree-covered humps and ground haze. On the starboard, a bank of clouds explodes straight up like a tripped Claymore, with crests of blinding neon-white.

Within two hours of arrival in Pleiku, I'm done with formal business, and after lunch, to kill time, a colleague and I drive out to the crest of a weather-beaten knoll overlooking the city. An old French barracks still stands there, a block of moldering cheese pocked with rounds from who knows how many passing armies. The rolling terrain reaches out almost furtively toward NVA base camps in the low mountains to the west, the "third Vietnam."

We take the jeep through rows of ramshackle huts, corrugated tin roofs, a street the American GIs used to call the Valley of the Dolls: the red-light district. No montagnard maids did service here, for the montagnards took care of the widow or orphaned daughter. The market belonged to the less-pampered Vietnamese girls.

The remnants of a national banner droop sadly from a radio antenna atop a neighborhood soup shanty on the corner. Sun and weather have bleached its yellow folds an off-color white, and except for the faded red stripes down the center, you might take it for an emblem of surrender. Suddenly a chill breeze sets it fluttering like a coquette's handkerchief. An off-duty ARVN, pedaling by, pulls his raincoat more tightly around him. He's wearing it backward, hind part before, as they all do—to cut the wind.

Rust or dirt, the dull red of dried blood, seems to cling to every surface. Even the denizens are steeped in it, for many of the montagnards bleach their black hair a rust-colored ocher and their clothes are inevitably fringed with mud.

A church at the end of the rutted street off to the left pokes an unfinished skeletal spire toward heavy rain clouds, low-slung and wallowing. The spire's frame is white, but the preferred color scheme takes over in the body of the building, a red flange running its edges.

You drive on, jeep wheels struggling for purchase in the bog of the road. Red-flecked children, shirts torn, light a match, put it to a rat's carcass near the street's edge, watch, mesmerized, as the center of the small pyre goes from black to grizzly, sizzling white. Pass on.

We come to Route 19, a slash of broken tar across the center of the region to Qui Nhon City on the coast. A convoy is forming at the first intersection, armored personnel carriers squeezing into place between lumbering deuce-and-a-half's, Vietnamese soldiers barking orders. No one seems in command: business as usual.

Out beyond the convoy the highway empties, a few buses coming our way from Qui Nhon. Somebody said a culvert was blown the other side of the Mang Yang Pass, but apparently it's been patched over.

You don't open up on this road. Potholes materialize as quickly as dimes in a cheap crap game, and here and there without warning a row of artillery duds sprouts along the faded center line to form a makeshift jeep trap. You keep your eye on that line, catching the countryside only in sidelong snatches. Rolling red-mud hills, patches of moss-grass, and rows of the lollipop trees that would seem more at home in southern Italy. In the distance: weathered mountains and heavier forests interspersed with green pasture, accidental splashes of paint on an aging canvas. Every few miles a hamlet springs up, shacks with wrinkled metal roofs going from glistening silver to gun-gray as the rain clouds heave their shadows along the landscape. A few montagnards shuffle forward, the muddy footpaths they follow slippery and shining like a just-healed scar. They're a handsome and rugged people, the women with heavy bared breasts, sarong-like skirts, hair swept back in a careless bun, often a pipe clenched in their teeth.

Finally we come to the pass, the notorious Mang Yang. The road narrows, slicing through the sheer slopes as abruptly as a river through a deep canyon. Scattered along the roadside: the carcass of a bus or jeep riddled with bullet holes. And off on the left, a small plateau, with a few gnarled trees, leafless and bone-white from U.S. defoliants. Far off on one slope you can see the vague obelisks of a small cemetery, final resting place of a company of French soldiers ambushed in the pass in the early 1950s. The wind rattles a piece of tin, the siding of a bus, a few hundred yards away. All too much like gunfire. We swing the jeep around and head back toward Pleiku as fast as we dare.

Later, at cocktail hour, we sidle bravely up to the bar at the CIA compound and exchange shop gossip. Someone asks: Did you hear about the female agent undergoing a lie-detector test? She bit off her tongue and spit it at the interrogator. And that was that. You counter with your favorite: Female agent hanged by her captors. Evidently she knew too much about corruption and drug-trafficking at the highest levels of the South Vietnamese government. So the authorities did away with her before she could talk. Her American interrogator (not me, thank God) found her the next day, swinging from the light cord in her cell, her four-year-old son—also arrested—sitting quietly in a corner, playing with her sandals.

Back in Saigon again: Last night, to regain my bearings, I dropped in on Mimi's Flamboyant. Over a beer "Thirty-Three"* I heard for the millionth time a bar girl drone on about her long-lost American GI. He's gone. She's a mother. But now, unlike 1969 or '70, she who tells the tale is no more than

---

*A Vietnamese beer manufactured under French license, its most distinctive quality was its formaldehyde-like preservative which packed a wallop that equaled or surpassed that of Carolina white lightning. As the GIs used to say, it killed you and pickled you in one stroke.

thirteen or fourteen, only beginning to discover what so many others before her are trying to forget. "I'm no animal," she says, "but the Americans make love to me as if I was." And she pounds her fist in her hand to demonstrate. But then one of her favorite customers comes in and she is all smiles and sweetness. Soon she is gone for the night.

I noticed this morning that the dog who usually sits in the middle of the intersection of Duy Tan and Chien Si Circle outside my apartment building has abandoned his post. He used to plump himself down there, in the center of traffic, oblivious of the risk, and scornfully survey the motorists' dance of death. Then one day last week I saw him limping down the sidewalk. Obviously his luck had run out. Now he's disappeared altogether. Sort of sad: he was somehow a symbol of Vietnam's mad resiliency.

There's a celebrated tale (they were telling it around the Embassy this afternoon) about a much-disputed piece of real estate in the northernmost province of the country. The Communists occupy it, so the story goes, and government forces surround it. Finally the ARVN troops call on their adversaries to withdraw and offer them safe conduct. Otherwise: a long siege, and starvation. The Communists reject the proposal. So the waiting begins and the weather starts to change, dry season giving way to the monsoons. The government troops wile away their time eating and drinking in their trenches. The Communists build rafts. When the floods come, the government forces pull out because of the high water. But the Communists merely float their rafts to the top of their trenches, paddle over the ARVN positions and occupy them. The government charges a blatant "cease-fire violation."

I was called to the front office just after lunch today to brief an old journalist who writes for a British magazine. He's been a conduit for CIA handouts for years and I knew at once this was all going to be friendly fire. He winked at me, wrinkled his nose, and asked me to go as slowly as I could so he could get down every word verbatim.

Trouble in the trenches several days ago. The chief of Vietnamese counterintelligence called and asked how I was faring with three of the "sources" I had under interrogation. Okay, I said and hoped he would leave it at that, since I had yet to maneuver even the meekest of them into a candid dialogue. "So you won't take my advice and apply a little pressure," he laughed, and hung up.

I would have forgotten the comment, since it was so much in character, had I not gone down to the National Interrogation Center later in the day and discovered that someone *had* taken his advice. I didn't immediately notice anything was wrong. The source, the meekest one, just seemed more subdued than usual, though perhaps more willing to answer questions than he had been the day before. But after an hour or so he began to waver in his chair and finally slipped to the floor. As my interpreter and I pulled him to his feet I accidentally brushed his shirt open. His chest and stomach were covered with bruises. I got him to admit that his Vietnamese interrogators had worked him over, though he pleaded with me not to report it, since they had threatened to beat him again if he told me what had happened.

I made a full report to the CIA officer responsible for coordinating the Station's dealings with the Interrogation Center. I had always been against strong-arm tactics and said so. Apart from the moral aspects, such techniques made it impossible to develop any rapport with a source, which is the key to effective interrogation. I suggested to the CIA officer that we send one of our own doctors over to the Center to look at the man. That at least would discourage further beatings, since the Vietnamese never like to have their indiscretions exposed to the Americans. The officer, an old Asia hand who always sported a jaunty bow tie, listened to me in silence and then laughed. "Well now, don't get so excited. The boys over there are just having a little fun. Anyway, we can't rock the boat. The Viets would lock us out of the Interrogation Center if we did. We'll just have to overlook this one and go on."

I remember yelling at him, something about his cowardice and the Station's moral responsibilities, and storming out of his office. I wrote a letter of resignation and sent it to the Station Chief. He called me in just before the end of the day and promised he would set things right.

This morning I was taken off the case. Now I have only two sources on my hands.

On the road again, this time to the delta to brief government commanders on what we believe they should know about Communist plans. First stop, My Tho: not the Wild West town I remember from two years ago, but civilization is still elusive.

According to the CIA hands here, corruption has gotten so bad, wounded government soldiers have to pay to be medevacked. One chopper hovered for nearly an hour last Monday as the pilot bickered with a hamlet chief by radio over the price of lifting out a bleeding militiaman. They finally settled on six ducks from the hamlet pond.

The chief CIA officer in My Tho took time out over lunch to give me some pointers on an interrogation technique he insists will break a prisoner in less than forty-eight hours, without any need for violence. The "Arabic method," he calls it. Simply undress the subject, bandage his eyes, tie him to an armless, straight-backed chair, then let him sit—and sit. Eventually, after three or four hours, he loses all sense of orientation ("returns to the womb"). Then you begin questioning him, softly and soothingly at half-hour intervals, a voice out of the gloom. Guaranteed: he'll be eating out of your hand by the following morning.

The half-hour flight from My Tho to Chuong Thien Province in the lower delta is a lurch and a rattle over cobblestones at ten thousand feet. Vi Thanh, the province capital, is no better than a patch of rust and barbed wire in a quilt-work of rice paddies, most of which are controlled by the Viet Cong. The handful of State, USAID and CIA men who make up the Embassy outpost here live out their one-year tours amid piles of dirty clothes and plates of half-eaten food. "Sure, we could hire maids full time," one of the guys told me, "but if the compound was spick and span, we'd die of boredom."

After dinner one of the CIA men and I wander across the road for cocktails with the local ICCS personalities. A Pole named George has caught VD from a local lovely and is playing up to the CIA team in hopes of wrangling a vial of tetracycline. Needless to say, our boys are playing hard to get. The going price of a curative: Polish state secrets.

Saigon again: Jottings at Josette's Beauty Salon, the only place in town where you can escape the tyranny of the Vietnamese bowl-cut. I always try to get in early, before the female clientele, who pretend not to notice I'm not one of them. But the girls who work the shop notice and they kid and joke at the expense of the guy with the hot comb in his forelock.

Long day—two briefings, plus the first draft of an intelligence appraisal —and at the end of it I'm ready for a few tranquilizing martinis. As the way of least resistance I opt for the rooftop bar at the Duc Hotel. The clatter of plates from the kitchen competes with the low murmur as I walk in. I dig into a bowl of oily peanuts and try to avoid hearing anything too clearly. An inevitable leak-through: somebody talks up the scruffy golf course out near the former American military headquarters at Tan Son Nhut. "Is there really grass on that goddamn course?"

"Some mud," comes the reply, "especially now the rainy season's setting in." The conversation struggles briefly, then surrenders to the too-loud refrain of a cheap recording of "The Things We Did Last Summer" as someone turns up the stereo in the corner. The quilted mirror behind the bar breaks reflected faces into a thousand mosaics, jaws drawn out too long, eyes translated into crawling amoebas. I stare absently down the bar: anonymous hands gripping chilled glasses, bouncing cigarette butts on heavy black ashtrays. "You got a haircut?" a voice drifts in. "Cleaned your neck up." A flash of the green of an upturned bottle as a familiar face—who is that guy?—puts away the dregs. Suddenly the two fellows next to me drop into a low whisper. Very secret stuff, apparently too secret even for a member of the family.

Vung Tau, dilapidated resort city on the coast, southeast of Saigon. I take a Sunday off and drive down, an hour and a half on a modern two-lane highway, as secure from the Viet Cong as the center of Saigon. Cocktails on the open-air veranda of Les Roches Noires as I wind down. Across the road: a fisherman, his conical hat stained by salt water, stops his bicycle at the edge of an embankment leading down to the surf. Black rocks stab up through foam and eddies. He removes his shirt, revealing a torso as seamed and sinewed as polished cyprus. He picks his way down the slope and into the surf, unraveling a small baglike net with attached buoys. The net disappears; swells roll up under his arms as he moves after it, pawing it up slowly like a cat on a bedspread. Small wriggling flashes of silver are caught in the folds. On the beach he picks each one out, dropping it into a small sack. The last you see of him, he is pedaling off in the direction of the rockier promontory up the road, the bag over his shoulder.

Soon a small Lambretta ice truck pulls up to the doorstep, water trickling through the floorboard. The iceman hawks and spits as he gets out, then reaches through the tailgate and shoulders a large opaque chunk. The edges brush his pockmarked cheek as he stumbles up the steps of the restaurant. He heaves his load into an ice chest, then smashes it with a meat cleaver. The owner grovels in his pocket, producing the equivalent of a dollar; the iceman bows, walks out and climbs back into the cab. The motor grinds as he pulls off, a thin line of melt marking his path.

Another weekend, another trip to Vung Tau. This time I pulled a Vietnamese couple out of the surf. I spent an hour alternately giving artificial respiration to each of them as a crowd of Vietnamese bathers watched, fascinated but useless. The young male swimmer revived at once, and now, two weeks later, he seems fit enough, but the doctors say his wife suffered brain damage in the accident. Shuffling through the intelligence reports on my desk yesterday I discovered that the young man is actually a high-ranking employee of the South Vietnamese Information Ministry. Since the Station has long been interested in planting an agent in the Ministry, my boss wants me to try to recruit him by playing on his blood debt to me. I'm not much taken with the scheme. It just doesn't seem right to save a man's life, then make him pay for it by turning spy. But I guess I'm too soft. Business before charity, after all.

Nights later: a fine rain drives me and my companion off the patio of the Club Nautique, the French sailing club on the Saigon River, and we finish dinner inside. After a few minutes a small black rat scuttles to the center of the vacated patio and begins nosing about for food crumbs. Two resident cats lounge under a nearby table, legs intertwined, indifferent to the intruder. A waiter watches the rat for a while, then drags one of the cats from under the table and carries him by a foreleg onto the patio and flings him at the rat. The two animals dart off in different directions. The perfect paradigm of the cease-fire. Nobody at the patio level wants to mix it up, but there's always somebody higher up who insists on precipitating a fight.

As the rain comes harder, the rat moves cautiously back to the center of his liberated area on the patio and the two cats resume their lazy vigil under the table. Yes, it is an imperfect peace.

"The trouble with the Vietnamese," one of my colleagues harrumphed the other day, in his best colonialist's pique, "is that they don't share even our most basic values. I was talking to a Vietnamese general recently and I happened to mention that a counterattack the ARVN had launched against a retreating NVA unit was like 'kicking a man when he's down.' The general looked at me, and said as seriously as you please, 'Why, that's the best time to kick him, isn't it? Then he can't fight back.' "

Several members of the Hungarian ICCS team apparently suspect I'm an intelligence operative. Two of them took me to dinner last night at the "Viet My" (Vietnamese-American) restaurant and plied me with steak and French wine. "But who's your boss?" they asked. "What's your position in the Embassy?" I laughed and played tipsy, tossing off a plaint now and then about how badly young diplomats are paid, as if to suggest a well-placed dollar or two might earn them a secret. They slapped me on the back, poured more wine, and proceeded to get rip-roaring drunk (or apparently so) in an effort to keep up with me. Finally, over dessert, I dropped the act, turned cold sober, and lectured them briefly on the virtues of détente and the hazards of overdrinking in the tropics. Then I stalked out. The last I saw of them they were tussling with each other at the table over which of them would pay the massive bill I'd run up. So much for the romance of espionage.

Unpleasant incident yesterday: everybody in the Embassy is upset over it. An American wife ran over a Vietnamese picket outside our commissary on the edge of the city. The workers were out in the parking lot with their signs, protesting recent pay cuts. And she was impatient to get inside. One of them made the mistake of stepping in front of her bumper; she killed him, by accident.

Reprehensible of course. But the terrible thing is you can understand. She's from Peoria or Milwaukee, wants desperately to be there and hates Saigon, had a hell of a time driving out to the commissary anyway, the little beasties veering all over the highway as if it were their country. Then, these pickets outside the commissary gates. Something snapped, as at My Lai.

The police kept her in the clink till eleven o'clock last night. Station management had to intervene to secure her release. She left this afternoon for Bangkok. The Embassy's administrative staff worked all morning to get her household effects packed out in time.

Son of Cease-Fire

"It was an exceptionally untidy war," my boss, Tom Polgar, used to say. "So the peace has got to be untidy too." That quip neatly described it all. Since neither the North nor the South Vietnamese had been able to win a clear-cut victory in their twenty-year bloodletting, neither could accept to lose; and by the time the 1972 offensive came to an end the United States was so weary of the whole affair, it was unwilling to hold out for definitive concessions from either of them.

The Paris agreement was thus a cop-out of sorts, an American one. The only thing it definitely guaranteed was an American withdrawal from Vietnam, for that depended on American action alone. The rest of the issues that had sparked the war and kept it alive were left essentially unresolved—and unresolvable.

The breakthrough in the negotiations the previous summer had come when Kissinger managed to persuade the North Vietnamese to accept a cease-fire without the prior removal of Nguyen Van Thieu. It was his greatest diplomatic triumph. Yet in this so-called "de-coupling" of political and military issues also lay the greatest weakness of the Paris agreement. For what had happened in the process was a deferral of the very question that had kept the two sides fighting for so long: the problem of who would rule postwar South Vietnam. The Paris agreement not only ignored this issue; it provided for a process of political evolution that could not work. There was no mention in the text of the kind of government that might or should emerge in Saigon after the cease-fire (the word coalition never appeared); instead, under the agreed terms representatives of the Thieu regime and the Communist Provisional Revolutionary Government were merely to get together with neutralists of their choice, once peace was declared, to set up a nebulous negotiating body known as the National Council of National Reconciliation and Concord. This group in turn was to agree—by unanimous vote—on the shape of Saigon's future government and was to supervise elections leading to it.

Given the abiding differences of the two sides, it is a wonder anyone ever took this formula seriously at all. Even if Saigon and the PRG had been able to put together a neutralist "third segment" acceptable to them both, the unanimity principle would have prevented any real progress toward accommodation. Either the PRG or Saigon could have vetoed anything that did not suit its interests. The concept of the National Council thus died aborning; the body was never formed and the issue of Saigon's future remained a smoldering ember that would in the end ignite the final Communist offensive in April 1975.

Militarily, the agreement was also a failure. Not only had grandiose political issues been left hanging; so had more technical ones, vital to the enforcement of the cease-fire itself. There was no attempt in the text, for instance, to spell out who controlled what piece of real estate in the south or to pinpoint where the two sides were to pick up the replacement matériel both were permitted to receive on a one-for-one basis. These and many other equally critical questions were also "deferred"—left to be resolved by the two sides in further negotiations after the cease-fire. Two "truce teams" were created for this purpose. One, the Joint Military Commission (JMC), was made up of representatives of the major combatants. The other, the International Commission of Control and Supervision (ICCS), was composed of Hungarians, Poles, Indonesians and Canadians. In a sense the two organizations were duplicative. The ICCS was to arbitrate any disputes concerning enforcement or violation of the cease-fire that the JMC could not. Yet in fact neither of them was of much use at all, for under the terms of the agreement they, too, were to be governed by the unanimity principle. Neither could take any action without the full consent of all its members. Under the circumstances this was a prescription for perpetual stalemate.

Realizing the imperfections of the draft accord, Kissinger had tried in the final stages of the Paris negotiations to incorporate some safety catches into it. Since he had not been able to persuade the North Vietnamese to withdraw their forces from the south, he attempted to create obstacles to a further build-up once the agreement became effective. Hence both the Communists and the Saigon authorities were prohibited under the terms he forced on them from "accepting" any additional troops into South Vietnam after the cease-fire. They were also obliged to withdraw all their forces from Laos and Cambodia —a provision that was meant to shut down NVA supply lines and sanctuaries there.

In his haste to conclude the agreement, however, Kissinger had allowed himself to be outmaneuvered on both these important points. According to the precise language of the text, the restriction on the introduction of additional manpower and matériel into South Vietnam was to take effect only "from enforcement of the cease-fire"; in other words, only at the moment the two sides stopped fighting. Up to then, Communist troops were legally quite free to go on "accepting" additional supplies and reinforcements from Hanoi— which they did.

Kissinger also slipped up on the wording of the provision dealing with Laos and Cambodia. Inexplicably, he neglected to include in the text a specific deadline for the withdrawal of NVA troops from either country. In later public testimony he insisted he had reached a secret "unconditional understanding" with Le Duc Tho that ensured an immediate pullout. But the North Vietnamese denied this, claiming that the understanding had been no more than a U.S. ultimatum, which they had rejected. From their standpoint, nothing in the agreement pertaining to Laos and Cambodia was legally binding until settlements were reached there as well.

In sum, then, the peace of Paris was no peace at all. It imposed no limitation, or obligation, on either side that could not be nullified through the unanimity principle, and apart from the withdrawal of U.S. forces, all major provisions were subject to reinterpretation and further debate.

Furthermore, in his rush to complete the negotiations, Kissinger had made commitments to each of the combatants, which if known to the other —or to the American people—would have given all of them second thoughts about the wisdom and practicality of his diplomacy. On the one hand, he had assured Thieu of continued U.S. support—and had threatened to withdraw it if he did not sign the accord. On the other, he had promised Le Duc Tho that all U.S. reconnaissance flights over North Vietnam would be suspended and all American technicians withdrawn from South Vietnam within a year in return for Hanoi's acceptance of the draft. If Thieu had known of these pledges, he might well have stood his ground even longer.

Kissinger made these commitments, and kept them secret, for quite pragmatic reasons, but in doing so, he raised false hopes and expectations that could only lead both Vietnamese sides to overplay their hand in the aftermath. Like the agreement itself, the secret underpinnings were a political minefield, waiting to explode on anyone who ventured within range.

As the Vietnam cease-fire gave way to renewed warfare, some of Kissinger's critics charged that he had never meant for the agreement to work anyway, but was merely trying through its convolutions and vagaries to assure a "decent interval" between the American withdrawal and a final fight to the death between the two Vietnamese sides. This judgment, however, hardly did justice to Kissinger himself. While he may not have put together a truly workable peace, he was most certainly concerned about preserving a non-Communist government in South Vietnam and the semblance of accommodation between Saigon and Hanoi.

The essence of his "postwar" strategy was equilibrium. A rough parity, economic and military, he felt, must be established between the North and the South so that neither could impose a military solution on the other, and each would have an incentive to settle remaining differences peacefully. In part, this meant keeping Thieu strong enough to fend off the North Vietnamese troops on his doorstep. At the same time Kissinger hoped to moderate the aggressive tendencies of the North Vietnamese through various pressures and plums—

by providing them with reconstruction aid, as called for in the Paris agreement, and by persuading the Soviets and the Chinese to reduce their support for the "revolution." Ideally, under these conditions Hanoi would be influenced to turn inward, eventually abandoning its crusade in the south.

This was the vision behind Kissinger's strategy: equilibrium leading to stalemate and finally to a live-and-let-live attitude on both sides. At no point did he seriously consider the alternative of promoting a genuine coalition arrangement. To have done so would have meant abandoning the ideal of a non-Communist South Vietnam to which he and Nixon remained committed.

On the heels of the formal signing ceremonies in Paris, Kissinger and Nixon moved quickly to turn their concept of equilibrium into reality. While Nixon publicly reaffirmed our support for Thieu, Kissinger made a quick trip to Hanoi in early February 1973 to assure the North Vietnamese that we were indeed prepared to help with their reconstruction.* He also made it clear that the United States would not be overly squeamish about occasional breaches of the peace if a more stable balance seemed likely to result. When a reporter asked if he was troubled by a series of flare-ups immediately following the cease-fire, he said no: "After all, how are the two sides going to establish areas of control except by testing each other."

Kissinger also emphasized, however, that American tolerance did have its limits. And within a few days of the cease-fire, as it became apparent the North Vietnamese had no intention of withdrawing their forces from Laos or Cambodia, the Administration reverted to its ultimate bargaining chip. B-52 raids were resumed against NVA base camps and Khmer Communist units in Cambodia, with some occasional spillover into Laos, and a new military headquarters, the U.S. Special Advisory Group (USSAG), was set up at Nakom Phanom air base in northern Thailand to coordinate the bombing. By the end of the month the 7th Air Force, operating under USSAG's guidance, was flying over sixty B-52 missions per day against Cambodian targets.†

The American Congress, of course, did not understand the logic behind the renewed bombing—how could Kissinger explain it without acknowledging

---

*The letter Kissinger carried with him promised $4.25 billion in economic aid to Hanoi and made only the most cursory mention of the need for Congressional approval, as if the Administration could guarantee such a gratuity on its own. Hanoi would later refer to the letter to justify its claim that the United States had committed itself to provide postwar assistance.

†That Kissinger should have expected a cease-fire in Cambodia remains a curiosity. By early 1973 one-half of Cambodia's 7,000,000 people and two-thirds of its territory were under some kind of Khmer Communist control. The government of Premier Lon Nol, which the United States had supported since the overthrow of Sihanouk in 1970, was floundering, and the Communist movement itself was speaking with several voices. Most "KC" forces were under the immediate command of Khieu Samphan, a long-time but highly independent revolutionary. But politically the insurgency was overshadowed by the deposed leader Norodom Sihanouk, whom the Chinese in effect had adopted and set up as the Cambodian ruler in exile in Peking. To complicate matters, the Soviets were seeking to counter Chinese influence by continuing to maintain an embassy in Phnom Penh and by supporting Khieu Samphan as well. Considering all of these crosscurrents, the prospects for peace and accommodation could hardly have been more elusive.

his shortcomings in Paris?—and immediately dug in its heels. Administration officials countered by offering all sorts of trumped-up rationalizations, claiming (falsely) that NVA troop infiltration through Laos and Cambodia was increasing and that Hanoi was almost solely responsible for the continuing cease-fire violations in South Vietnam. The White House also began casting about for other means of bludgeoning the North Vietnamese into quiescence. In mid-March, Nixon publicly warned Hanoi not to "take lightly" his expressions of concern over the infiltration question, and a week later he suspended the secret negotiations in Paris on proposed reconstruction aid to North Vietnam.

By early April, Kissinger was suffering deep reservations about the very practicality of the cease-fire. The Administration had already overturned parts of the Paris agreement in its effort to enforce the rest, and the Communists for their part were becoming increasingly inflexible. The PRG delegates to the Joint Military Commission were now stubbornly refusing to delegate "points of entry" for replacement arms and matériel destined to their side, and without that, because of the tyranny of the unanimity principle, no other member of the JMC could enforce the one-for-one resupply restriction. Meanwhile, several Congressmen were busy drawing up legislation to end all U.S. military activity in Indochina, including the bombing of Cambodia. Worst of all, the Administration was sinking ever deeper into the mire of Watergate.

For Kissinger, this disarray was unsettling for a number of reasons, not the least of all for its impact on his most important diplomatic project: détente with the Soviet Union and China. Soviet party leader Brezhnev was due in Washington in June as part of the continuing series of summits that had begun in 1971, and Kissinger had hoped to have the docket cleared of all extraneous items, such as Vietnam, so Nixon and the Soviet leader could concentrate on more vital business. But it was now apparent the Indochina irritant would not go away, at least not without some dramatic new antidote. Given the outcry against the bombing, there was only one possibility left—token political concessions to Hanoi as an inducement to restraint.

In a face-to-face meeting with President Thieu at San Clemente, California, in early April, Nixon and Kissinger outlined what they had in mind. It would be necessary, they told him, to begin making preparations to establish the National Council, the tripartite electoral commission called for in the Paris agreement.

To sweeten the pill, they also made new commitments to him. Nixon assured Thieu unequivocally that Saigon could count on continued military aid at the "one-billion-dollar level" and "economic aid in the eight-hundred-million range" for several years. Kissinger promised that if "Hanoi's lack of good faith in the agreement could be demonstrated," American retaliation would be "massive and brutal."

Thieu, quite understandably, was delighted by these reassurances. For the first time the United States was giving him an explicit pledge of economic and military aid at precise levels and a very nearly explicit promise to bomb Hanoi into submission if necessary. That Nixon and Kissinger were essentially talking out of turn, offering far more than they could deliver without Congressional approval, did not trouble him. Being an accomplished manipulator himself, he assumed they would find a way.

In Hanoi, meanwhile, the party leaders who had led the Democratic Republic of Vietnam through so many years of war had already settled on a new strategy of survival and conquest. As with Kissinger, their initial objective was "equilibrium." Yet within the scope of their new policies, equilibrium was not merely a means to an enduring stalemate, as it was for Washington, but a stepping stone to something more. By achieving military equality with Saigon, they were hopeful of keeping Thieu so far off balance that he would succumb eventually to the internal "contradictions" of his regime.

In their propaganda and planning papers the North Vietnamese turned their notion of equilibrium into an easily digestible slogan, claiming the Paris accord had certified the existence of "two governments [the Saigon regime and PRG], two zones of control and three political groupings in South Vietnam [Communist, neutralist and rightist]." The first principle of Hanoi's postwar strategy was to make this slogan a reality.*

By the time the 1972 offensive came to an end the Communists were about as far from being Saigon's "equal" as they ever had been. By their own account their holdings in the south amounted to little more than "rubber trees and bricks"—underpopulated, mountainous territory along the western fringes of the country, plus a scattering of isolated "leopard spots" in the delta. Their political-agent network, particularly in the cities, had been decimated, and their perennial allies, the students and the radical Buddhist groups, had been broken and intimidated by Thieu's universalized military draft and by mounting economic pressures.

Within a month of the cease-fire two high-ranking North Vietnamese officials, Central Committee member To Huu and General Van Tien Dung, army chief of staff, toured the battlefront to assess the "balance of forces." They visited all the principal military commands—Military Region Tri-Thien Hué in the northernmost provinces; "the B-3 Front" and Military Region 5, which jointly controlled operations in the western highlands and along the central coast; and finally COSVN, the Central Office for South Vietnam, which was responsible for the Saigon area and the Mekong Delta. After talking with various field commanders they reached a depressing conclusion. As To Huu

---

*The North Vietnamese actually had begun planning for a cease-fire two years before, in 1971. As a high-ranking defector explained to me, North Vietnamese logisticians had been directed at that time to draw up plans for a series of interlocking enclaves along the western border of South Vietnam—a "third Vietnam"—that would give their forces a base from which to harass the government during the postwar "political struggle." Hanoi's strategists also devised a scheme for winning an anticipated constituent assembly election: over three million "voters" were to be moved to South Vietnam to assure the Communists and their "neutralist" allies a majority at the polls.

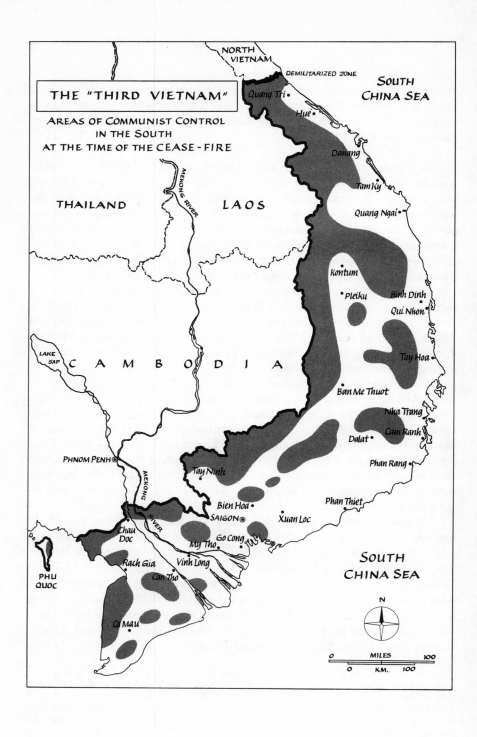

THE "THIRD VIETNAM"

AREAS OF COMMUNIST CONTROL
IN THE SOUTH
AT THE TIME OF THE CEASE-FIRE

NORTH
VIETNAM

DEMILITARIZED ZONE

SOUTH
CHINA SEA

Quang Tri

Hué

Danang

Tam Ky

Quang Ngai

THAILAND

LAOS

Kontum

Pleiku

Binh Dinh

Qui Nhon

Tuy Hoa

CAMBODIA

LAKE
SAP

Ban Me Thuot

Nha Trang

Cam Ranh

Dalat

PHNOM PENH

Tay Ninh

Phan Rang

Bien Hoa

Phan Thiet

SAIGON

Xuan Loc

Chau
Doc

My Tho

Go Cong

Rach Gia

Vinh Long

Can Tho

SOUTH
CHINA SEA

PHU
QUOC

Ca Mau

MEKONG RIVER

MEKONG
RIVER

N

MILES

0   100

KM.

0   100

told cadres at COSVN's headquarters in northern Tay Ninh Province, no new large-scale offensive could be attempted for three to five years because of the "international situation" (read: great-power détente) and the evident weakness of the army.

Although To Huu did not broach the matter, the North Vietnamese also were facing formidable constraints at home. Their economy was all but nonexistent after years of U.S. bombing and a constant siphoning off of able-bodied manpower (over a million lives had been lost in the war since 1965), and the party leadership itself was racked by disagreements over the proper "balance" of its main priorities: revolution and reconstruction. In the final stages of the Paris negotiations, Party First Secretary Le Duan, the spindly jug-eared hardliner who had effectively ruled the country since the early 1960s, had held out for maximum concessions, only to precipitate the devastating U.S. bombing attacks against Hanoi in December. Thus, his wisdom and prestige were now in question, and many of his colleagues were insisting the time had come to devote more resources to domestic development.

All of these problems figured in the Politburo's deliberations immediately following the cease-fire. Ultimately its eleven Old Men opted for a compromise policy of "no war, no peace," a careful balancing act that would enable them to husband resources at home while slowly building toward military parity in the south, behind the "shield" of the Paris agreement.

As an initial step, NVA forces labored long and hard during the first few months of the year to forge their border enclaves in South Vietnam into a fortress "third Vietnam" where they could rest and refit themselves without interference. Over 30,000 civilians and top managerial cadres were sent south to populate this thin wedge of real estate; logisticians began building a fully paved highway down its center from the demilitarized zone to a base camp just north of Saigon; and port facilities at the small town of Dong Ha just below the DMZ, which they had captured in 1972, were rapidly expanded. Within twelve months over twenty percent of the war matériel destined for Communist units on the front line was flowing through Dong Ha, and NVA road networks, both inside the "third Vietnam" and through Laos and Cambodia, had been so effectively streamlined, reinforcements could move from bases in North Vietnam to the Saigon area in less than twenty-five days, one-third of the previous travel time.

Despite American claims to the contrary, the North Vietnamese did not engage in much offensive military activity during the first year of "peace." Immediately before and after the cease-fire there was a so-called "war of the flags" during which their forces attempted to snatch disputed territory on the fringes of their enclaves, both along the western border and on the central coast. Government forces retaliated immediately, however, and within three weeks the Communists had lost most of what they had gained. For the next half year they concentrated largely on tending their wounds and building up their supply caches inside the "third Vietnam." By early summer they had already replaced most of the arms and matériel they had lost in 1972 and had studded the "third Vietnam" with sophisticated antiaircraft artillery to ward off marauding South Vietnamese warplanes.*

Since parity, not superiority, was the initial strategic aim of the North Vietnamese, there was no immediate expansion of their army in the south even though Washington insisted there was. While nearly 70,000 NVA troops were funneled into the "third Vietnam" during the first year of the cease-fire, nearly an equal number returned home for rest and relaxation or died in battle, leaving no more than 170,000 regular infantrymen (plus about 30,000 indigenous Viet Cong) on the front line at the end of 1973. They were far outmatched by the 300,000 combat troops and 500,000 support personnel Thieu's government kept under arms.

While the United States and the North Vietnamese sought to realize their separate visions of "equilibrium," the third party to the cease-fire endeavored to achieve something quite different. Convinced that his own salvation lay in the preservation of the status quo, Nguyen Van Thieu did everything he could to ensure that the "superiority" he enjoyed on the eve of "peace" was reinforced and amplified in the aftermath.

By the time the Paris negotiations were concluded, Thieu had made himself indisputably master of his own house. The foundations had been laid a year and a half before with his unchallenged reelection to the presidency. Since then he had carefully and meticulously consolidated his position. He had eliminated the unpredictable institution of hamlet elections (once the pride of American nation-builders); created a military bureaucracy to rule in the countryside; and had managed to isolate, fragment and finally outlaw almost all political groupings except his own Democracy party. Most important of all, he had transformed himself into something of a respected (if not altogether loved) figure in the eyes of his public. By holding his own against the Americans in the final stages of the negotiations, he had won the applause and respect of many of his xenophobic countrymen; and by casting himself as the only sure claimant on U.S. support, he had succeeded in keeping the generals squarely behind him.

Yet for all his power and Machiavellian skill, Thieu also remained critically vulnerable as the war drew to a close—and for precisely the reason he was so strong. For if he had succeeded in enhancing his prestige by twitting the Americans, his regime nonetheless remained balanced on the knife edge of American generosity. The support of the army and the acquiescence of the

---

*The United States, needless to say, vigorously protested the NVA supply build-up. Yet we were hardly in the strongest position to object. In the months directly preceding the cease-fire we had set a provocative example for Hanoi by ramming huge quantities of war matériel into the south as part of our last-minute Enhance Plus logistics program. Unable to match us in timing, the North Vietnamese had no choice (if they were to maintain their foothold in the south) but to mount their own Enhance Plus program as the cease-fire went into effect and afterward. Inasmuch as neither of the truce teams could impose limitations on them without their consent, they remained "legally" free to do pretty much as they pleased.

people were to some extent conditioned on American support for him. Should it diminish, or appear to, he would lose part of his claim to the "mandate of heaven," the mystical right to rule.

Moreover, despite four years of Vietnamization, his army had yet to prove it could survive on its own. The high command itself was still slavishly dependent on American advice, and its logisticians and strategists remained convinced that the only way to wage war was the American way, with fleets of helicopters, massive interdiction fire and plenty of trucks and air transports to haul the army from one brush fire to another.

Worse still, the country as a whole remained an economic invalid. The war, of course, was primarily responsible for this. In the past ten years over 3,000,000 people had fled the countryside and retreated into the relative security of the cities. Rice production and employment patterns had declined and altered accordingly. In the late 1960s the American presence itself had helped to take up the slack, but even this had proved a mixed blessing. The easy dollar of the free-spending GI had created a level of prosperity—and corruption— which the economy on its own could not support.

To add to the malaise, the basic source of income for millions of Vietnamese—the American army—had all but disappeared by the time the cease-fire materialized, and rising prices in the world market were already cutting into the value of the economic aid that was available. Consequently, the country was perhaps more dependent on handouts from Washington than ever before.

Some members of Thieu's inner circle were repelled by the country's dependent's status. While under no illusions about the necessity of continued American support, particularly economic aid, they were convinced the regime could chart its own course politically, with a little wisdom and cunning. One of those who argued this point most convincingly at the time of the cease-fire was Hoang Duc Nha, Thieu's thirty-two-year-old cousin, who had risen to become Commissioner General for Information. Young and exceedingly brash, Nha was unburdened by the sentimentality that blinded so many of his elders to American faults. He had trained as an engineer in the United States and had seen many of these faults firsthand, and he tended to base his policy judgments and recommendations on a cool, dispassionate appraisal of what he thought the American character to be. During the Paris negotiations it was he, among Thieu's closest advisors, who had realized Kissinger was about to sacrifice Vietnamese interests for American ones and who had persuaded Thieu to press for further concessions. Now, as Kissinger sought to impose his imperfect peace on the country, Nha again urged his cousin not to rely excessively on American good will. "The Americans are traders," he warned Thieu at one point. "They'll sell you out if you can no longer assure them profit."

But Nha was waging an uphill fight. His youth and pretensions immediately aroused the enmity of the older bureaucrats and generals, who owed their status to French education and American support. Moreover, to counter his influence, the Embassy and the CIA carefully promoted the fortunes of their own closest allies in the government, making Prime Minister Tran Thien Khiem and General Dang Van Quang, Thieu's security assistant, their primary contact points at the Palace and by-passing Nha at every turn. As Nha once complained to Thieu, the CIA had come to treat the entire government like a band of "cheap Latin-American desperadoes," to be bought and sold at will.

By wit, talent and sheer ruthlessness Nha almost succeeded in out-maneuvering his American-made opponents. Through the Information Ministry he set up a network of informants in every major South Vietnamese embassy in the world, and was able to keep Thieu better apprised of political trends abroad, particularly in the United States, than anyone else in the government. He also sought to wean visiting Congressmen and other American officials, particularly senior CIA officers, away from their traditional policies and prejudices by showering them with favors, including girl friends and free nights-on-the-town. Yet in the end Nha lost out—to tradition, vested interest and American money.

Thieu himself was intrigued by Nha's unflattering vision of the United States. He personally hated Kissinger and mistrusted him, particularly in the wake of the Paris "sellout," as he called it, and what Nha told him about American callousness and pragmatism seemed to ring only too familiar.

Yet like most of Saigon's elite, Thieu simply could not bring himself to turn his back on his benefactors, as Nha advised. Indeed, there was something fundamental in the Vietnamese mentality that made this impossible. If the Vietnamese were xenophobic, they were also slavishly imitative, in part because of their colonialist past. Every major political movement in the country owed its inspiration to an outside influence. Even the Communist party of North Vietnam was an import, modeled after the Chinese Kuomintang, which had in turn been fashioned by the great Russian intelligence operative Mikhail Borodin. It was therefore simply beyond Thieu's habit or capacity to try to "go it alone."

And perhaps, after all, Nha was wrong; perhaps the Americans were as anti-Communist and as committed to Saigon's survival as they professed to be. In considering this possibility, Thieu was particularly encouraged by the expressions of support Nixon and Kissinger continued to heap on him in the wake of the cease-fire, seeing them as an endorsement of his own hard line. It never occurred to him that the reason they were pumping him up was to make him more amenable to compromise.

Thieu's attitude toward compromise found expression in a simple slogan —"the Four No's": no territorial and no political concessions to the Communists, no recognition of their party, no commercial dealings with them. Committed to this ideal at the time of the cease-fire, he built his subsequent policies around it. The obstinacy it reflected was in a sense an articulation of an old oriental concern, the fear of losing "face"; to give up anything would mean a sacrifice of prestige and self-respect that would be all but intolerable to any Vietnamese. But Thieu also attempted to rationalize it in American terms, advising friends and subordinates that the United States would cease supporting him if he showed himself soft on Communism. The argument and the policies based on it amounted to a closed loop, trapping him and his allies in a continuum of resistance to any form of modus vivendi with the other side.

It was no accident of rhetoric that the first of the Four No's was the proscription against territorial concessions, for territory was the basis of Thieu's rule, the proof of his legitimacy, and if he gave up one inch of it, he feared, the Communists would be strengthened in their claim that two "administrations and two zones of control" existed side by side in the country. So he clung to the first "No" like an article of faith, at least through the first year of the cease-fire, and perhaps inevitably it was the motivation for his initial assault on the peace agreement once it was in effect.

In early February, soon after the Joint Military Commission had set up its headquarters at Tan Son Nhut, the South Vietnamese and PRG delegates got together to discuss the still unresolved problem of areas of control. The South Vietnamese insisted that proprietorship be determined by the location of army units alone, while the Communists argued that since their own units never stayed in one place, the country would have to be carved up arbitrarily. The discussions ended inconclusively and thereafter each side began hunting for alternate means of staking out real estate. The Communists opted for manipulation of the Paris agreement itself. Once the prisoner exchanges got under way they were careful to schedule all pickups and deliveries in areas where they wanted to show the flag, and whenever PRG representatives gathered at the edge of the jungle to be ferried to Tan Son Nhut on American helicopters, they always managed to locate the landing zones in previously disputed territory, in hopes of conveying the impression they had been in control there all along. Their most potent weapon, however, was the Joint Military Commission itself, since one of its primary responsibilities was to delineate the territorial holdings of the two sides. Once the JMC deployed inspection teams to the field, the Communists felt, Thieu would be unable to deny them access to large parts of the country.

Thieu immediately realized what the Communists were up to and took steps to frustrate them. During the first few months of the cease-fire, whenever the PRG nominated a disputed area as the site for a prisoner exchange, he would bomb or shell the place beforehand. He also attempted to limit the movements of PRG and North Vietnamese delegates to the JMC by bottling them up at Camp Davis, their headquarters at Tan Son Nhut. In addition, to discourage them from deploying their JMC field teams, he organized anti-Communist demonstrations in a number of major cities.

In early March the PRG responded as he had wanted, refusing to cooperate any further in setting up JMC field sites. The North Vietnamese reacted

less satisfactorily, however, warning the United States that unless their delegates were assured the "privileges and immunities" guaranteed under the Paris
accord, they would suspend the exchange of American prisoners.

That, needless to say, had an immediate effect. Under heavy American
pressure Saigon agreed to assure the safety of the two Communist delegations.

From Hanoi's standpoint these concessions came too late, however. By
early March the "war of the flags" which had begun with the cease-fire had
been resolved largely in Saigon's favor, and in some areas, particularly in the
northernmost provinces of the country, the two opposing armies had already
accepted a de facto standstill cease-fire. In view of all this, the Communists
decided the JMC would no longer be of much use in their land-grabbing
strategy and essentially gave up on it. At the end of the month the PRG's chief
delegate, the ever-smiling General Tran Van Tra, flew off to Hanoi, never to
return. He would soon take up his old post as the principal military commander at COSVN, and from there would help coordinate the cease-fire war
against Saigon for the next year and a half.

From the moment Tra departed, the Communist JMC delegations made
no further effort to deploy their field teams, thus rendering the entire body
useless as an instrument for policing the cease-fire. Within the next few weeks
the other supervisory mechanism, the ICCS, likewise ground to a halt.

The issue that led to its paralysis was ostensibly the same that had
crippled the JMC—privileges and immunities. In early April a chopper with
ICCS markings strayed off course in the northernmost province of South
Vietnam and was shot down by Communist ground fire. The Polish and
Hungarian representatives seized on the episode as a pretext for suspending
their participation in ICCS field investigations, pending written guarantees
from each side assuring safe passage to various areas of the country. Because
of the unanimity principle, their refusal to cooperate effectively stymied all
other ICCS members.

During the winter and spring of 1973 the Canadian ICCS delegation tried
vainly to break the hammer lock of the unanimity principle. Choosing their
test cases carefully, they attempted to establish a precedent for conducting
unilateral investigations into breaches of the peace. But the North Vietnamese
would have none of it, and operating on their behalf the Poles and Hungarians
refused to allow the Canadians' reports to be issued as "official" ICCS findings.
After six months of frustration the Canadians bowed out of the truce team and
were replaced by a delegation from Iran.*

•   •   •

*In the meantime, Hanoi had thrown another clinker into the ICCS machinery. Under the terms
of the Paris agreement, each of the four signatories was to pay nearly a quarter of the ICCS budget
and was to have an equal voice in determining its size. Since the North Vietnamese had never been
interested in a strong ICCS, they took advantage of this loophole to weaken it, insisting in early
1973 that the budget be cut back. A year later both the PRG and the North Vietnamese would
refuse to pay any of their share, on the somewhat irrelevant grounds that the United States had
never paid "war reparations" to Hanoi. From that point on, the United States would foot the ICCS
bill almost on its own.

While the North and the South Vietnamese brooded and bickered over the cease-fire and the enforcement mechanisms, they also squared off on the most volatile issue before them: the political future of the country. On 19 March representatives of the Thieu government and the PRG met at a private villa in the suburbs of La Celle–St. Cloud outside Paris to discuss the matter. According to the Paris agreement, they were obliged to reach a basic understanding within ninety days; but it quickly became apparent that even if they had had ninety years, they wouldn't have been able to do so.

The proposals and the counterproposals they exchanged were so at odds, it is a miracle they could carry on any discussion at all.* But because Henry Kissinger was now hoping to placate the North Vietnamese through some show of reasonableness—particularly since Congress was threatening to suspend the bombing of Cambodia—he insisted that Thieu act as if he might be willing to bargain. Thieu reluctantly obliged him, and during late spring and early summer the two sides indulged in some exquisite haggling over such issues as how the neutralist "third segment" of the proposed National Council of National Reconciliation and Concord was to be chosen.

There was also considerable debate over something else close to each side's heart—the release of civilian prisoners of war.

By 25 March the exchange of military prisoners, both Vietnamese and American, had been completed, Saigon handing over nearly 27,000 NVA and Viet Cong troops, the PRG turning over 5,000 government ones. But Thieu was still dragging his feet on another part of the bargain, the release of civilian cadres, for he knew his adversaries would simply fold any releasees into their agent networks and use them against him. He was not willing to risk that, particularly since his own police and intelligence agents had been extraordinarily successful in the past two years in rooting out the Communists' political apparatus. During 1972 alone, over 14,000 Vietnamese civilians had been sentenced or detained under the country's somewhat improvisatory legal system, and to speed up the process Thieu had recently modified the proce-

---

*Procedurally, the differences between the two sides boiled down to the question of which of several steps toward accommodation should come first. In his own "platform" statement Thieu made it clear that his *sine qua non* was the withdrawal of NVA forces in the south. Within thirty days of the pullout, he said, he would be willing to legalize "opposition" activity, and within sixty days he would agree to a popular referendum to elect a new President and the National Council envisioned in the Paris agreement. Afterward the new President (presumably Thieu himself) would treat with the Council to decide the shape of Saigon's future government.

The Communists in their counterproposal essentially reversed this process to their own advantage. Long before any elections they wanted Thieu to legalize the Communist party, free all Communist political cadres under detention and agree to the establishment of the National Council. Only then would elections be held—but not the kind Thieu proposed. What they envisaged was the election of a constituent assembly to write a new charter for the country, which would wipe out all vestiges of the old order. Furthermore, during the elections and the transition phase, the National Council would function as a de facto government, supplanting Thieu and his entourage and thus giving substance to their claim that three independent political forces— neutralist, rightist and Communist—coexisted as equals in the country. Only after a new government was formed would North Vietnamese forces go home.

dures under which an individual could be detained for "suspected" subversive activities. Previously it had taken the accusations of three separate witnesses to justify an arrest; now only one was necessary.

Officially, at the time of the cease-fire the government had a total of 32,000 civilians behind bars. The actual number was undoubtedly much larger, although how much larger no one, not even Thieu, could be sure, since the meticulous accounting procedures the Americans had devised at the height of the war had fallen into hopeless disarray with the onset and the economies of Vietnamization.

Some of the inmates in Thieu's jails were no more than common criminals; others were recent Communist defectors who were undergoing interrogation. Still another percentage were genuine "political prisoners" who owed their confinement to known or suspected connections with the Communists, or simply to anti-government behavior. It was these Thieu was determined to keep under lock and key at all costs.

To accomplish this, he initially played innocent, claiming that he held no more than 5,000 Communist cadres. The figure was absurdly low, though no more so than the one the Communists were using for the number of government operatives under their care (637 in total, they insisted). Later, in April, Thieu resorted to another ploy, announcing that he would release a much larger number of civilian detainees if they could all provide proof they had been working for the Communists all along. (This of course would have given him a pretext to rearrest them immediately after their release.) Finally, in an effort to clamp off the dispute altogether, Thieu declared that most of his 5,000 Communist prisoners had elected not to be exchanged. When a group of them was flown to a designated release site near Loc Ninh, a Communist headquarters north of Saigon, government agents planted among them staged a demonstration as they disembarked. The PRG promptly called off all further exchanges.

In an immediate sense Thieu thus won the round, but in broader terms he lost far more than he gained, for his critics and detractors around the world quickly locked on to his handling of the prisoner issue as a pretext for pummeling him. Peace groups in the United States soon began complaining about 100,000 to 200,000 political prisoners in Saigon's jails and blaming Thieu for all the ills of the cease-fire. Their arithmetic was as impressionistic as Thieu's own, but because it was tossed about so often in public, many commentators and Congressmen in the United States came to accept it as fact. What's more, as temperatures rose and emotions became engaged, the equal cynicism and perfidy of the North Vietnamese were lost to view. During the mid-1960s Le Duan, Hanoi's Party First Secretary, had imprisoned or otherwise eliminated hundreds of his comrades in an effort to consolidate support for himself and for his hard line on the war, but because the foreign press corps had never had a free run of Hanoi's prisons, word of the "Hoang Minh Chinh" affair, as the purge was called in honor of its first victim, seldom leaked out. Instead, the public spotlight remained focused on Thieu, for he obviously was far more accessible, and as the cease-fire took effect he suffered mightily for it. For as his faults and excesses were exposed and debated, Congress became ever more convinced he was not worthy of U.S. support.

By early May, Congressional opposition to the centerpiece of Kissinger's cease-fire strategy, the bombing of Cambodia, was coming to a head. The House Democratic Policy Committee voted on the fourth to recommend a cutoff of all supporting funds for the operation, and six days later the entire House reached a similar decision. With Nixon's strength and prestige continuing to slide as a result of Watergate, Kissinger had few hopes of reversing the trend. His only choice was to try to engineer a Cambodian settlement, or at least an NVA withdrawal from Cambodia, before the Congressional ax fell. With this in mind, he met with Le Duc Tho in Paris in mid-May.

As a fillip to North Vietnamese cooperation, he offered to resume the recently suspended aid talks and to discontinue reconnaissance flights over the north. He also promised to push the South Vietnamese toward concessions on such issues as territorial demarcation and establishment of the National Council, which had already been discussed with Thieu at San Clemente a month before.

While Tho, and the South Vietnamese, considered these proposals, Kissinger also made it clear to the Soviets that it would be a "useful" corollary to Brezhnev's upcoming visit to Washington if they would guarantee a cutback in military aid to North Vietnam, as he had been urging since the cease-fire. He also used what influence the United States had in Laos to nudge the rightist, neutralist and Pathet Lao factions toward accommodation. By the end of the month the three sides had been persuaded to address a plan for coalition that would give the Communist Pathet Lao two-thirds of the territory and one-third of the population.

As the talks continued in Paris, Kissinger invited a colleague with a personal stake in the outcome to sit in as an observer. Graham Anderson Martin, sixty-one-year-old career diplomat, had just been designated our next Ambassador to Saigon and wanted to get a "feel" for the Communists. As Martin subsequently told a Congressional committee, Le Duc Tho did not appear to have changed much since their first meeting during the Geneva negotiations of 1954; he was still a "true believer" in the Eric Hoffer sense, convinced of the utter righteousness of both his means and his ends. Martin was more favorably impressed, however, by some of the younger North Vietnamese technocrats who took part in the talks. He considered them more malleable and more inclined toward moderation. It was one of his first fatal miscalculations.

The communiqué that was finally hammered out at the meeting was not the breakthrough Kissinger had been looking for. Its only significant ingredient was an appeal for a new cease-fire within twenty-four hours—"son of cease-fire" we quickly dubbed it in Saigon. Beyond that, it offered no new hope for peace or reconciliation. Although it committed the United States to several positive gestures, including a revival of the aid talks and resumption of the recently suspended mine-clearing operations along North Vietnam's coastal waterways, it skirted the most difficult issues confronting the two sides, precisely because Kissinger had been unable to bridge the differences between them.

It quickly became apparent, moreover, that Kissinger had failed in his primary purpose. On 14 June, the day after the communiqué was made public, Le Duc Tho told reporters in Paris that there was "no tacit agreement on Cambodia."

Hoping to recoup that loss, Kissinger attempted to project the Cambodia issue into the aid talks once they got under way in Paris several days later. A final deal, the American negotiators made clear, hinged on withdrawal of all NVA troops from Laos and Cambodia. The North Vietnamese, however, refused to be bought off, and on 23 July, in the face of their continuing intransigence, the United States broke off the aid negotiations for good, thus destroying one of the main elements of Kissinger's strategy of equilibrium, the plum he had hoped to use to nourish a spirit of moderation in Hanoi. The North Vietnamese and the PRG retaliated by declining to cooperate any further in the search for American servicemen still missing in action.

As the aid talks stalled, the North Vietnamese called for a cessation of the mine-clearing operations out of concern the United States might use them as a cover for espionage activities. President Thieu, for his part, took advantage of the new freeze in United States–North Vietnamese relations to pull back from the few commitments imposed on him during the May-June negotiations. He refused to move the JMC headquarters to the center of Saigon, as he had guaranteed, and when a final effort was made to put the civilian prisoner exchanges on track, his agents staged another demonstration at the release point, leading the PRG once again to rule out any further dealings on the matter.

In the meantime, Congress finally turned the screw, voting on 31 July to cut off all funds for the bombing of Cambodia, effective in two weeks, and to prohibit any further U.S. military action in Indochina without its explicit approval. Since the ban was appended as a rider to a crucial appropriations measure, Nixon could not afford to veto it.

Not all was lost, however. Eventually Kissinger achieved at least one of his main objectives. Under Soviet pressure the North Vietnamese grudgingly and gradually reduced their military presence in Laos and Cambodia; as the summer wore on, the number of NVA troops operating with Khmer Communist forces dropped from 45,000 to 3,000 "unofficial advisors," and by the time the three factions in Laos agreed to a coalition arrangement in September, the North Vietnamese were in the process of withdrawing a full division from the Plain of Jars north of Vientiane. These "adjustments" did not, however, end the flow of North Vietnamese supplies into South Vietnam, for by the time they occurred Hanoi had already developed alternate road networks down the spine of the "third Vietnam" and had opened the small port at Dong Ha to sea traffic.

Nor did the Soviets and the Chinese impose the kind of constraints on Hanoi that Kissinger had hoped for. Although they did cut their military aid to North Vietnam by fifty percent during the first year and a half of the cease-fire, they more than doubled their economic assistance, thus enabling Hanoi to muddle through economically without demobilizing its army in the south.

Like the war itself, the peace Kissinger had wrought thus remained untidy in the extreme. Having negotiated an extraordinarily poor agreement, he was obliged in the aftermath to apply political and military salves that could only weaken it further. Like the legendary American GI who called air strikes in on a disputed Vietnamese town, he was forced, finally, to destroy his objective in order to save it.

Even before the June cease-fire communiqué was issued I had moved out of the interrogation chambers of Saigon's primary detention center and had been installed on the sixth floor of the Embassy as the CIA's resident specialist on government and Communist strategy, with responsibility for drafting our primary estimates on the subject, which were known in the trade as "field appraisals." There were three or four other analysts in my office who were responsible for watching over various parts of the "big picture"—economics, logistics questions, and so on—but my job was to bring their findings together and make sense of them for the distracted policy-maker both in the Embassy and in Washington.

As I threw myself into the task, I could hardly draw much comfort from it. "Both the Communists and the government," I wrote in an estimate on 13 July, "are interpreting the new cease-fire agreement selectively, emphasizing in their public statements those parts of it which favor their respective interests and ignoring those that do not. Therefore, negotiations between the two sides over the next few months are not likely to bring the country any closer to genuine stability or concord. The Communists, in fact, have a special stake in ensuring that this does not happen. Since they have almost no population base in the country, their interests are best served by keeping conditions as unstable as possible. This would enable them to make maximum use of their subversive assets and their military strength. It would also put them in a position to thwart the government's plans for economic recovery, which is essential to its long-term survival."

Martin's Embassy

On 24 June 1973, five months after the cease-fire, Graham Martin was sworn in as Ambassador to Saigon, replacing Charles Whitehouse, who had been serving as "acting" Chief of Mission since Bunker's departure several weeks before. Few of the secretaries who gossiped about the new appointee around the Embassy swimming pool knew very much about him. All of us would soon learn as much as we needed to know.

The first brush I had with Martin's Embassy was through a thirty-one-year-old former infantry officer named Moorefield. At the end of the second week in July he burst into my office. "Hi!" he shouted exuberantly, extending a hand. "I'm the new Ambassador's aide. Just trying to sort out who's who. They tell me you're the power behind the throne up here. So you're the man I need to know."

Brash, blond, bespectacled, Ken Moorefield was not immediately loved. His State Department colleagues considered him "shallow." The secretaries around the Embassy felt he needed cutting down to size. But Moorefield, as Martin's hand-picked administrative assistant, knew better: if anyone would have to make adjustments in style and personality, it certainly would not be an "insider" like himself. In his arrogance and self-confidence he was the best advertisement for Martin's Embassy that I could have conceived.

Unlike many others the Ambassador brought with him, Moorefield was no stranger to Vietnam. A West Point graduate, he had distinguished himself as a battalion advisor in the southern delta in the mid-1960s and had been badly wounded the very year I was first assigned to Saigon. In recognition of his meritorious service he was later appointed to the presidential honor "battalion" in Washington, D.C. But then his awakening began, for as the peace movement steadily gained momentum he found himself time and again holding a cordon against young men and women like himself who reviled everything he stood for. Embittered and disillusioned, he left the Army in 1971 and spent the year drifting, finally taking a job as a lifeguard at a neighborhood swimming pool. There he met and befriended a young man named Martin. His new acquaintance turned out to be the only surviving son of the next Ambassador to Saigon.

As Moorefield soon discovered, the Martin household had seen more than its share of tragedy. The Ambassador's eldest son had died in an automobile accident several years before, and an adopted boy, Glen, had been shot down and killed in 1966 while serving as a helicopter pilot in Vietnam. Perhaps because of Moorefield's own Vietnam experience, the new Ambassador took an instant liking to him, and after several casual meetings, invited him to accompany him to Saigon as his personal aide.

In selecting the young veteran for the job, Martin was displaying a typical disregard for bureaucratic form. The position of ambassadorial assistant, particularly in a major post like Saigon, had always been a plum, usually reserved for rising stars in the Foreign Service. Moorefield was not only no rising star; he wasn't even a Foreign Service officer. But perhaps that, too, appealed to Martin. As a self-styled maverick himself, he had little patience for the strait-jacket mentality the Foreign Service produced. He wanted an activist, not a bureaucrat, as his principal fetch-and-carry man.

Moorefield clearly fit that role, and relished it. To his regret, however, he would never be as close to the Ambassador in the next year and a half as he had hoped. Martin would remain aloof and inaccessible. His protégé was not cerebral enough for him—nor perhaps loyal enough. Yet despite the distance between them, the two would share experiences that would leave Moorefield with a special empathy for the older man. On the day Martin arrived in Saigon it was he who took the Ambassador's arm and helped him down the plane's ramp onto Vietnamese soil. On 30 April 1975, Moorefield was again at the Ambassador's side, this time lifting him aboard *Lady Bird 9*, the helicopter that would carry him away from Saigon forever.

To all appearances Graham Martin was a self-sufficient man who needed no one's help in anything. The son of a Baptist minister, he had been raised in the rigorous tradition of southern evangelism in the small town of Mars Hill, North Carolina, and he spoke in the biblical cadences and the absolutes of one fully confident of his own divine mission. As he often reminded friends and colleagues, he owed much of what he was to his father, whose stern sense of values, he insisted, was the basis of his own. "I've always been saved from trouble," he once commented to a Congressional committee, "by my father's advice, who told me I was too lazy to lie. He said if you tell the truth, you never have to remember what you said."

Young Martin graduated from Wake Forest College in 1932, and spent the next year working as Washington correspondent for a string of small southern newspapers. "I was regarded as a good reporter," he later remarked. "I often wonder what would have happened had I accepted to do a column for the *Washington Post*. Perhaps today it might be my by-line rather than Scotty Reston's [actually, of the *New York Times*] to which you would turn over your morning coffee."

His brief career in journalism left him with a confident appreciation of its foibles and potential, and in later years he would frequently draw upon this "expertise" to judge and measure its practitioners, most of whom, particularly those who criticized his policies in Vietnam, he found wanting. "Perhaps as some of my journalistic friends have observed, I left the profession so young that I still regarded it as a profession, not a trade," he recalled. "I thought then and now that those who were fortunate enough to enjoy the protection of the First Amendment had a corollary professional responsibility to inform the American people of the whole truth as clearly and impartially as one might perceive it after persistent digging, cross-checking and making every attempt to ensure all facts were accurate. Under no circumstances would one slant a story either to conform to an editor's known prejudices or to push one's own personal point of view. Those who did were not regarded as journalists but as propagandists—the word we used was flaks."

In 1933 Graham Martin left journalism and cast his lot with the New Deal, taking a job as assistant to Averell Harriman, who was then deputy administrator of the National Recovery Administration. The cool but tough-minded young North Carolinian impressed his boss and through him was soon introduced to many of Washington's elite. In the meantime, he enlisted in the Army Reserve as an intelligence officer, an assignment that prepared him for his future in more ways than one. "They assigned you areas of responsibility and made you work at it in those days," he said later, "and mine was Southeast Asia. When the war came I found myself getting up and reporting to Secretary [of State Henry L.] Stimson and General [George] Marshall each morning on the conduct of the fighting during the past twenty-four hours in the Pacific." From this not entirely inauspicious beginning Martin developed an enduring love of intelligence work and of Asia and a sense of expertise in both. He also became a past master in the art of briefing—"I used to memorize my lines so I could sound spontaneous," he remarked to me—a skill he would apply to great effect throughout his later diplomatic career.

After the war, as the nation turned its sights from fascism to "international Communism," Martin's friends in Washington remembered his skill and quickly enlisted him in the new struggle. With the help of Harriman and others he was brought directly into the Foreign Service in 1947 and was immediately appointed administrative counselor to the U.S. Embassy in Paris, where he soon became an "expert" in manipulating the State Department's own bureaucracies.

His precipitous entry into the Foreign Service was not without its price. As one almost religiously committed to "earning" his way, Martin was haunted by the thought that he owed his advancement solely to patronage, and years later, in the summer of 1973, he would succumb to his sensitivity on the point. Soon after his arrival in Saigon, an American journalist reported quite accurately that the new Ambassador had never passed the Foreign Service exam. Martin flew into a rage over the story and promptly banished the offending newsman, George McArthur of the *Los Angeles Times,* from his presence, denying him any official contact with the Embassy for many months. It was the beginning of Martin's grudge match with the American press corps in Saigon.

During his eight years in Paris, Martin refined not only his administrative skills but also his knowledge of the "enemy." "From 1947 to 1955 in France," he recalled, "I watched the marvelously subtle implementation of an increasingly effective propaganda campaign waged by the North Vietnamese and their ideological allies in France and Europe. In 1954 I saw it succeed in France." Deeply affected by the experience, Martin became in succeeding years almost obsessed by the danger posed by Communist propaganda, from whatever source, and devoted himself to defeating it.

From his vantage point in Paris he also perceived another danger that few other Americans recognized at the time. He saw that colonialism and its surrogates were dead in Indochina and that if the United States tried to intervene directly to preserve them, the result would be disaster. "I watched the evolution of General [Vo Nguyen] Giap's perfection of the techniques of guerrilla operations," he told a Congressional committee years later. "I thought it would be a grave mistake, in fact impossible, given the wave of nationalism that was obviously apparent, particularly in the Far East, for the French colonial control to ever be successfully reasserted. I thought it would be a mistake for us to help, and I so said."

Martin returned to Washington in the mid-fifties and was promptly awarded a sabbatical at the Air War College, where "I tried to get cranked into the seminar discussions some kind of consideration of what kind of war this was [in Indochina], not really thinking that we would ourselves become very soon very deeply involved." Later he was shifted from one choice assignment to another, serving in several advisory positions at the United Nations. Finally, in 1963, he was promoted to the rank of career "minister" and named Ambassador to Thailand. It was a crucial appointment and in many ways an enviable one, for while tangentially involved in America's growing crisis in Indochina, he was not in the direct line of fire and enjoyed a flexibility his counterpart in Saigon did not.

Martin made the most of both the flexibility and the prestige of the job, carving out a reputation for himself as one of the most effective crisis managers in the State Department. He also showed himself to be incredibly lucky. When a beaten and disgruntled presidential candidate named Richard Nixon passed through Bangkok, Martin rolled out the red carpet for him, treating this particular "private citizen" like visiting royalty. Nixon never forgot the courtesy, and when he later became President he repaid Martin handsomely.

The posting in Bangkok was not all pomp and political good fortune, however. Throughout his four years there Martin waged a vigorous battle with the American military, which was then trying to turn Thailand into another Vietnam, complete with American ground forces. Remembering the lessons of the first Indochina war, Martin resisted the trend—as it turned out, successfully—even to the point of kicking his hawkish military aide, General Joseph Stillwell, Jr., out of Bangkok. It was an accomplishment he remained duly proud of—so proud, in fact, he could hardly conceal his disappointment when he discovered years later that David Halberstam had overlooked him in his monumental study of the architects of American policy in Indochina, *The Best and the Brightest*. "I am not even mentioned in the book," Martin groused to a Congressional committee in the summer of 1974. "I am told that when asked how I could possibly be omitted, he [Halberstam] replied that the thrust of the book was to demonstrate that when the military machine started rolling no one could stand in its way. Since I had fought so bitterly and successfully to keep the Americans totally out of any direct involvement in the Thai insurgency, it would have disproved his thesis to have mentioned me."

For all his opposition to a direct U.S. role in Thailand, Martin had no qualms about supporting our commitment in Vietnam once it had been cast in concrete. "When I was assigned to Bangkok," he noted in a Congressional hearing in 1974, "I think at one period I was asked whether or not Vietnam should be allowed to crumble. Not being in a position to make an independent analysis of my own, I said I did not think it would be in the interest of the United States to have that happen if it could be avoided without great cost . . . I thought and still think our best course of action would have been, if we decided it was in our best interest to keep this new kind of aggression from succeeding, to have confined ourselves to the provision of military aid, perhaps training, but not to introduce forces of our own."

As his own contribution to the burgeoning anti-Communist struggle in Indochina, Martin managed to persuade the Thais in the mid-1960s to lease several large air bases to the U.S. Air Force for bombing raids against Communist supply lines in Laos, Cambodia and Vietnam. Even as he continued insisting publicly that no such arrangements had been made, the majority of the American bombing missions against the Ho Chi Minh trail in southern Laos were being flown from the airfields he had "borrowed" from the Thais.

It was during Martin's third year in Bangkok that his adopted son, Glen, was killed in the western highlands of South Vietnam, and from that point on, the Ambassador's mood and perspectives seemed to change. He lost what small tolerance he had for the bureaucracy, and in 1967, during his continuing fight to keep the American military out of Thailand, he turned his impatience on the U.S. Secretary of State himself, urging Dean Rusk in a particularly sharp cable to rally to his support. "For expressing these opinions within the privacy of proper channels, but with some pungency of expression that was perhaps too tart," Martin noted dryly some years later, "I was relieved of my post in Bangkok."

The firing was not the end of the splenetic Ambassador, however. A year later his friend Richard Nixon was elected to the White House and in return for past courtesies rehabilitated him and appointed him Ambassador to Rome.

It was one of the most spectacular cases of political recovery in the recent annals of the Foreign Service.

During his three years in Italy, Martin became an Ambassador truly suited to an imperial presidency. Building a staff of loyalists around him, he ruled the Embassy with an iron hand and brooked no criticism either of himself or of the Foreign Service. When several State Department officers cabled him asking that a special fund be set up in the memory of a colleague who had killed himself after being fired, Martin refused to allow the message to be distributed among his staffers, claiming it "reflected the techniques of propaganda which in other contexts the whole civilized world has found to be revolting. The purpose of this communication is not to improve but to destroy."

As in Bangkok, Martin also uncovered an enemy in his midst. This time it was not the U.S. military but the local CIA Station. Convinced he was a better intelligence operative than all the CIA officers combined, he insisted on controlling personally and directly the secret funds which Washington had allocated for the manipulation of Italian politics.

Just before the end of his Rome assignment Martin pulled off a significant political coup. By pouring thousands of dollars into the faltering Christian Democratic party on the eve of the 1972 parliamentary elections, he snatched victory from the hands of the Italian Communists. It was an ephemeral victory —the Communists continued to gain strength in the aftermath—but for Martin it was symbolic. He could leave Rome with his own credentials intact; he had managed to thwart a Communist assault on one of America's closest allies.

Martin had intended to retire after the Rome tour and had even bought a farm in Tuscany, where, as he later recalled with ponderous humor, he had planned to do some writing and to "experiment with grafting an olive to a juniper tree to produce an instant martini—one that needed no gin." But in mid-1972 Kissinger asked him to assume yet another challenging assignment. Veteran diplomat William Sullivan, who had been slated to replace Bunker in Saigon, had just turned down the job. Would Martin consider taking it? "Although I love Asia and treasure my friends there," Martin later noted, "I spent eight months after the question was raised, saying, 'Hell no! I won't go!' I had absolutely no illusions about what lay ahead of us. But when the highest officials of your country say, 'I thought the Foreign Service took the tough posts as well as the nice ones,' you respond, 'Yes, we do,' and then wonder how to tell your wife that we are going to Saigon and not to a Tuscan farm." He advised Kissinger he would accept the posting for one year only, and no longer.

Dorothy Martin resisted decision till the end. Having lost a son in Vietnam she had a natural antipathy to the place, and as Martin later remarked, she realized that the assignment would be both thankless and debilitating, particularly since it would involve defending policies and "truths" most Americans now rejected. "My wife reminded me of that old fable of the magic cloth that only the pure of heart can see," Martin recalled. "You remember the story with everyone saying, 'Oh yes, isn't that cloth marvelous.' For no one would admit that his heart was not pure. And the king bought a robe for the parade. A little boy said, 'Look, Mama, the emperor is naked.' My wife said, 'If you want to play that role, you ought to think about the sequel.' I said, 'I don't remember the sequel.' 'Well,' she said, 'what happened to the little boy —for the next fifteen years he was absolutely bound to be the most unpopular brat in the entire kingdom.' "

When I first saw Graham Martin he was hunched over the edge of a long oblong table in the briefing room at the Defense Attaché's Office at Tan Son Nhut air base. Stoop-shouldered in his pin-stripes, the hair iron-gray, the face as lined and angular as a wood-block portrait, he looked like Hollywood's perfect image of an ambassador, and he spoke of "commitment" and of "the need to get the job done" in terms that set the adrenaline running after the six months of drift that had followed the cease-fire. As he glanced around the room I was struck by his eyes, a stone-gray. To some of the more imaginative among us they recalled the death stare of a cobra ready to strike.

When he was not "on stage" Martin was a quiet and unassuming man, almost shy. He had a graciousness and a dignity in the old southern manner, and the combination apparently made him quite attractive to women. "He was a real charmer," his Defense Attaché, General John Murray, once said of him. "My wife thought he was tops."

But beneath that exterior there were beams of Calvinist steel in the man that seemed tempered against normal stress. Staffers who had long worked with him used to recall with awe that terrible day when he had learned his son Glen had been killed. He and Mrs. Martin were about to attend a reception for the King of Thailand. The initial reports had been garbled and misleading: "Yes, Glen had been wounded but not seriously." Then he had learned the truth, but had refused to succumb to it. Withholding the news from his wife, he ushered her through the King's reception, comporting himself with all the reserve and dignity befitting an Ambassador of the United States.

Physically Martin was a frail and broken man. He was still tormented by injuries he had suffered in an automobile accident several years before and could hardly turn his head from left to right. His disabilities inevitably limited his effectiveness in Vietnam, making it impossible for him to travel around the country for a firsthand look at the problems. Only once in fact did he journey outside Saigon.

Yet if Martin remained reclusive, he was hardly inactive. A chain-smoker and incurable insomniac, he pushed himself to the limits of endurance, working late into the night in the private study of the Ambassadorial Residence, poring over intelligence reports and other raw data.

A secretary who apparently was put off by his devotion to solitude and hard labor once described him half jokingly as "God": "I know he exists but I haven't seen him." But that characterization, like so many others of Martin, was unfair. While he was self-sufficient and demanding, he was far more accessible to his lower-ranking staffers than Bunker or his predecessors had ever been. He was perfectly capable of sitting around and casually discussing a problem right in the middle of things—provided you had your facts lined up.

And at times he even allowed himself a moment to relax. He particularly enjoyed movies, and each night after dinner at the Residence he would wander into his living room and sit there in the dark as his Marine bodyguards screened a reel or two of one of the first-run American films that regularly made the Embassy circuits in Saigon. I remember sitting with him one evening, toward the middle of his second year in Vietnam, when he was under fire from Congress and the press. We were watching *Hitler's Last Days,* a saga of the Führer's death watch in the Berlin bunker, and as the lights came up after the first reel, Martin looked at me and sighed, "You know, I'm beginning to realize what that son-of-a-bitch felt like." He then pulled himself out of his chair and went upstairs to his study, to begin culling through the intelligence reports he had brought home with him.

As a personality, Graham Martin was a kaleidoscopic man, a hundred changing images at once, none of them adequately defining the whole. By his own admission this elusiveness was quite deliberate and contrived. He once told a Congressional committee that stagecraft was part of a diplomat's standard "luggage." If so, then he was the quintessential diplomat, the consummate actor with the uncanny ability to appear all things to all people. Yet ultimately he paid a price for this skill, for nothing about him ever seemed quite constant, nothing altogether credible. And as time went on he seemed to lose sight of the distinction between his stagecraft and the reality. Thinking he could remake reality to his own vision, he was overcome by both.

"In the beginning," said a colleague, "he seemed a romantic character embarked on a crusade, and if you were the least bit romantic you could identify with him." Others found his zeal, and his changeableness, considerably less attractive. "Merely a culmination of the megalomania that has marked all U.S. ambassadors in Vietnam," one associate observed of him. "He's a born conspirator," remarked another. "He habitually schemes, has a conspiratorial and clandestine mentality, and immediately tries to put you under his control. He's always searching for weakness, like a shark going for blood. When he's mad, for instance, his voice drops to a hardly audible whisper. His object is to make you strain so as to get your undivided attention. The CIA Station Chief in Rome managed to foil him, though, by pointing out time and again that he was wearing a hearing aid so Martin would have to speak up."

For yet another aide, the epithet Martin contemptuously attached to Le Duc Tho during their meeting in Paris in June 1973 seemed to fit him only too well: "He's a 'true believer' in the sense that his goals are transcendental and anything that works to their fulfillment seems justified. But one must ask: a true believer in what? He speaks of national interests, but in fact his own interests lie solely in manipulating foreign policy. The game itself is his candle."

To U.S. military officers in Saigon, Martin at first seemed made in their own image. "The next best thing to a B-52," an old Pentagon hand said of him. "A super American patriot," asserted another. "He didn't give a goddamn about the Vietnamese. All he cared about was the United States. And if he had his way, I'm sure the flag of the United States would not be the Stars and Stripes but that flag with the coiled snake and the legend 'Don't tread on me.' "

General Murray, who had served under both Bunker and his deputy, Whitehouse, felt that neither of them could approach Martin for sheer hawkishness. "If [General] Curtis LeMay had invented an ambassador," Murray once commented to me, "he would have invented Martin. You know: 'Bomb them back to the Stone Age.' When Martin came [to Saigon] he didn't ask me about the money situation or the logistics picture, the morale of the troops or anything like that. He wanted to know what our authorities were to bomb within the [Communist] sanctuaries along the [Cambodian] border." Murray explained to him that the "sanctuaries" had recently been declared off-limits to B-52s because of civilian concentrations there, and he and Air Force General John Vogt reminded the new Ambassador that the Pentagon had consistently refused to lift the ban. But Martin told them, "I'll get you the bombing authority." As Murray later recalled, "Vogt looked at me, I looked at Vogt —and we both thought this guy is an idiot. But you know, he got the authority, thirty days before the bombing halt in Cambodia.

"But then, when we were going over to hit the targets—and we got some good secondary explosions—there were one or two areas we didn't hit. I remember one of them; it was a little village that had an ammunition factory. Martin wanted to know why we didn't hit it. I told him, 'Well, there's people there, and we don't want to hurt the population and we want to concentrate on military targets.' Martin said to me, 'Tell Vogt I don't care if they spill over and hit the civilians.' So I told this to Vogt, and Vogt says, 'Maybe he doesn't care, but for chrissake, I do!' He didn't hit 'em."

In a sense Martin was a perfect extension of the Nixon White House. He had an almost instinctive appreciation of power and how to parlay it into certain objectives, and like the President himself, he was a dedicated anti-Communist, almost religious in his fervor. "To him," said a friend, "there was nothing so loathsome as being a Communist. His attitudes were formed at a time when Communism was the nemesis of all that was good, and Vietnam was a psychological battleground for him."

Martin's outlook, however, was not purely ideological. Like Kissinger, he also saw the Vietnam conflict in pragmatic global terms, as a crucial ingredient in the balance of power and perceptions around the world that comprised America's best security. "I strongly believe," Martin told many a Congressional committee in this memorized cant, "that we should end American involvement in Vietnam and we should end it as quickly as possible. How we end it, however, is of crucial importance. I believe our objective must be to end it, leaving a South Vietnam economically viable, militarily capable of defending itself, free to choose its own government and its own leaders, and able to work out its own eventual reconciliation with its enemies in the north . . . I believe our successfully completing the job has an enormous effect on the perception of the United States, on the will of the United States, on the value of the commitment of the United States in Peking and Moscow."

Not merely an admirer of Kissinger's world view, Martin also had a profound respect for the man himself, at least until the fall of Vietnam, and he once told me a story to illustrate the personal affinity he felt existed between them. He and Kissinger were standing at the washbasins in the executive men's room on the top floor of the State Department. "You're a genius, Henry," Martin murmured over his shoulder. "Well, Graham," Kissinger purportedly replied, "you're a genius in your own way."

Whether Kissinger was actually as fond of Martin as the Ambassador supposed remains a source of debate among their former associates. According to one of Kissinger's closest aides, the Secretary viewed Martin simply as a useful instrument, "the meanest son-of-a-bitch around," who could get a tough job done and who could also serve as a lightning rod for criticism that might otherwise be directed at him and the White House. In addition, the policy he foisted on Martin seemed to demand someone of the Ambassador's special talents. It was not, after all, a policy in the truest sense, but merely the appearance of one. The United States was obliged to crawl out of Vietnam standing up, and to foster that illusion required the kind of conjuring and stagecraft at which Martin was so adept. Then, too, since Kissinger's main subsidiary objective was to keep Thieu both stable and responsive to American dictates, he needed a man in Saigon who had the savvy and force of character to dominate the South Vietnamese. Martin had already proven he had such qualities in abundance.

From the beginning Martin approached his task as Kissinger wanted, as a kind of conjurer and Madison Avenue pitchman, for only in this way, he felt, could he rally a reluctant Congress tó Saigon's support and restore Thieu's faith in the Americans. He also promptly declared war on Hanoi's own image makers and propagandists, for he considered them the only real obstacle to his own goals. Just as they had destroyed French will power in the first Indochina war, so, he believed, they were trying to weaken the remaining American commitment in Indochina with their "lies" and "distortions." In his effort to alert Congress and the American public to the danger, he attributed to Hanoi's propaganda machine powers and influence that might have surprised even the North Vietnamese. It was not merely the propaganda itself that posed the threat, he warned, but a whole "conspiracy out there," a network of leftists and sympathizers around the world who echoed Hanoi in their own forums for their own reasons. In the quarter of a century he had been watching events in Indochina, he once told a group in Saigon, he had become "utterly fascinated by the success of Hanoi in fashioning a propaganda apparatus which in its efficiency, in its pervasiveness and its sheer perfection of techniques has no parallel in recorded history. Herr Goebbels [the Nazi propaganda chief] would whirl in his grave," he remarked, "in complete frustration at the realization that he was the most callow, unsophisticated neophyte in comparison."

Throughout his year and a half in Saigon, Martin remained convinced that various peace groups in the United States were actively serving the "great conspiracy." He was hard-pressed to demonstrate any direct connection between them and Communist organizations abroad—the CIA in Saigon vainly searched its files for shreds of evidence—but he remained adamant in his contention that there existed a spiritual bond between the two, a desire to see Saigon defeated.

He also considered the American press corps an active contributor to this "plot." As he explained to *Time* magazine a few weeks before Saigon's collapse, he held the practitioners of his old profession partly responsible for the "distortions that have turned America inward" over the past few years.

The Watergate scandal strengthened him in these sentiments. As leaks and counterleaks proliferated in Washington throughout 1973 and '74 Martin began to look upon the American press as a rogue elephant on the loose, and his colleagues in the State Department and the Executive Branch as quavering fainthearts without the courage to oppose it. Even before he reached Saigon he had persuaded himself that no one in Washington could keep a secret, and once he took up residence in the Embassy he immediately set out to reduce the currency of those secrets that might do his own new client harm. Any information that tended to impute imperfections or shortcomings to the South Vietnamese he carefully overclassified to restrict its circulation in Washington, or he simply refused to put it out at all. He also insisted on a rigidity and precision in Embassy reporting that ultimately served to filter out much of the information he considered objectionable. If you wanted to report on a corrupt South Vietnamese official, for instance, you had to have an impeccable source, and the more highly placed the official the more "impeccable" your source had to be—to the point we seldom confused Washington with data on the peccadilloes of Thieu's own entourage.

Martin also attempted to turn his staff away from the "negativism" that he felt had done such harm to the American cause in the past. In a typically straightforward cable soon after his arrival he warned us all, and his colleagues in Washington, not to overindulge in "proctological examinations" of the South Vietnamese body politic and to accept the society "warts and all." A short time later he attempted in another message to Washington to play down the threat posed by the venality of South Vietnamese officials and military officers. "The level of corruption currently existing in South Vietnam," he wrote in the cable, "corresponds roughly to that in the state of Massachusetts and the city of Boston during the first decades of the century. That problem was eliminated and . . . perhaps even more rapid progress may be made in

Vietnam." With that kind of optimism in the Ambassador's office, few of the rest of us felt comfortable or justified in nurturing our own worst suspicions.

As the Embassy's perspectives narrowed to Martin's own, the weaknesses of our ally were lost to view. Martin himself believed he could compensate. With all his years of experience in Asian affairs he felt he knew the Vietnamese and could identify what was important in their character to U.S. interests. But in fact he hardly knew them at all. While he did do considerable homework on them in those long hours alone in his study each night, his focus was always tactical. He was always looking for some angle to pursue in his effort to make Administration policies work and he seldom seemed to glimpse the people themselves. He saw Thieu himself no more than once or twice a month, although he professed to consider him an expert politician, and after his own first year in Saigon he spent so much time shuttling between Saigon and Washington, he hardly had a chance to get to know any Vietnamese outside Thieu's inner circle. "Under the best of circumstances," remarked a friend, "Graham was never people-oriented and he tended merely to treat the Vietnamese like pawns to be moved about on a board."

"You know, I consider myself a Jeffersonian," Martin once said to me. "And I believe in treating the Vietnamese the way Jefferson taught us to treat our own citizenry. We should interfere in their affairs as little as possible. But if they should do something contrary to their own best interests, we should stand ready to rein them in and point the way."

In the end he would find himself both confounded and surprised by those for whom he assumed such a responsibility in Vietnam. After Saigon's collapse he confided to a State Department colleague that he had never "trusted those Vietnamese anyway," as if they had betrayed him by losing.

As a presidential appointee and favorite, Martin took full advantage of his position to cow and influence. He refused to fly out to Saigon until the White House had provided him with a special plane, and during his confirmation hearings, and later in frequent discussions with his staff, he left no doubt he considered the President, nôt Kissinger, his immediate and only superior. "I was hoping Kissinger would come to town so we could put that to the test," General Murray remarked. "But he said Kissinger would sit on his left."

Martin's fixation with protocol quickly set him against other prima donnas in the diplomatic and military community. Even before he reached Saigon he managed to have a falling-out with Admiral Noel Gayler, commander in chief in the Pacific, precisely because the old Navy man did not seem deferential enough. "When Martin talked to me," Murray later noted, "he always referred to Gayler as your 'polo-playing friend.' The story of what happened I got from the staff at CINCPAC [Gayler's headquarters in Honolulu] and from Martin, and I think it's authentic because when Martin wasn't playing to an audience and we just talked back and forth, he was honest, though Machiavellian, and he revealed the devious workings of his mind.

"The reason he was so upset with Gayler was that Gayler wanted to see him on his way out to Saigon. So there was a stopover at the airport in Honolulu. Martin got out of the plane, but Gayler was not there. They had a car to take Martin to CINCPAC headquarters. But when they got there Gayler wasn't there either. So Martin had to sit around cooling his heels. Finally Gayler came in in his polo-playing clothes and sweating up as if he had just had great exercise while the Ambassador was waiting.

"Martin thought he was going to talk about something important, about the situation in Southeast Asia. But they just talked about trivialities and exchanged niceties. And you know Martin; he was always all business. He didn't like 'How are you? What are you doing?' 'Good morning' wasn't even part of his vocabulary. And, doggone, he was just upset with Gayler. I can understand it. In the military we are trained to defer to the ambassadors. So they never did get along."

Murray himself also had protocol problems with Martin. One day each month he and his staff would prepare an intelligence briefing for senior Embassy officials to supplement what the CIA provided them on a more regular basis. As Murray later reminded me: "Martin came to the first meeting, but he never came to another one. The reason—I found out from his aide Al Francis—was that I sat in the head chair and Martin sat on my right. I told Al Francis, 'For chrissake! I'll put him up on a golden throne. I think the man ought to come to these briefings.' But Martin never came again."

Part of Martin's attachment to protocol clearly was tactical. He had a nervous ally on his hands who needed reassurance that American strength and prestige were still behind him, and with U.S. monetary support and military backing fast disappearing, Martin had no choice but to make his own prestige and stature proof of that commitment.

The Embassy itself also seemed to demand a strong and visibly uncompromising helmsman. There were still over 9,000 "official Americans" in Vietnam at the time Martin took charge, and bringing such a vast and motley cast of characters under control no doubt required every bit of will power and prestige he could muster.

Of all the components of the Embassy, the most cumbersome and challenging was the Defense Attaché's Office itself (formerly MACV), with its 400 civilian employees, 50 American military officers and 2,500 American civilian contract workers. By the summer of 1973 the White House was already considering plans to reduce it to more manageable proportions; indeed, Kissinger had given Le Duc Tho secret assurances that if Hanoi abided by the Paris peace agreement, the United States would withdraw the civilian technicians who were helping to maintain and service the South Vietnamese army. Yet as the cease-fire war continued, Martin urged against any such cutback. He considered the DAO's logistical expertise critical to Saigon's survival, and its intelligence apparatus an important supplement and counterweight to the CIA Station. He also felt a strong DAO was essential to his own efforts to control the South Vietnamese. While he had no doubt he could handle Thieu and the politicians, he knew soldiers respected soldiers and he therefore looked to Murray and his staff to keep the South Vietnamese military in line.

Under Martin's tutelage the DAO thus remained massive and redundant, at least for the first year and a half of the cease-fire. The Ambassador believed his own interests, and those of the Vietnamese, would be served, but actually there were unfortunate side effects that seemed to cancel out the advantages. The generals who made up the South Vietnamese high command remained so dependent on the advice of Murray and his staff, they were unable to act on their own instincts even when simple prudence demanded it. Moreover, the monetary impact of the continuing U.S. military presence was anything but beneficial to the South Vietnamese. Because of fiscal constraints imposed by Congress after the cease-fire, the $30-million-a-year upkeep of DAO, including the costs of the American commissary system and the care and cleaning of the DAO swimming pool, had to be drawn from the aid funds allocated to support the South Vietnamese army. As the one ARVN officer commented bitterly to me after the fall of his country, money that could have been applied toward the purchase of arms and matériel was being used to keep the Americans supplied with cognac.

By the time Martin arrived in Saigon the top command at DAO was well entrenched. General Frederick Weyand, MACV's last commander in chief, had departed in late spring to become Vice Army Chief of Staff in Washington, and Murray had already begun shaping the vestigial U.S. military establishment to his wants and needs.

During his own first weeks in Vietnam, Martin spent considerable time sizing Murray up. Because of his problems with Stillwell in Thailand, he was acutely sensitive to the kind of general he had on his hands. At last he decided Murray was acceptable.

From a professional standpoint Murray seemed precisely what he needed. Short and wiry, with the Ambassador's own devotion to hard work, he had proven himself an accomplished logistician during a previous tour of duty in Vietnam. In the words of a subordinate, he was essentially a "hardware man," an expert in ensuring the prompt delivery of the right American equipment to the right Vietnamese unit in the field. It was this particular quality that recommended him to the Ambassador, for if anything was crucial to Saigon's survival, Martin reasoned, it was the continuing flow of supplies from the United States. In the waning days of the cease-fire war Murray would be replaced by a "maintenance man," General Homer Smith, a specialist in making do with meager resources. The changing character of the Defense Attaché was a token of the declining fortunes of the South Vietnamese as Kissinger's peace fell apart.

Temperamentally John Murray was not the Ambassador's ideal. He was "not a patient man," declared one of his subordinates; "considerate of others, thoroughly professional, perceptive, and highly skilled in the use of colorful language, but not patient." That last trait naturally made Martin wary of him, but once he had managed to throw his own coils around Murray's staff, he was willing to overlook the general's faults for his usefulness.

To keep his Defense Attaché mindful of who was Chief of Mission, Martin resorted to countless tricks and stratagems he had developed to perfection in Bangkok. Soon after his own arrival he planted one of his most loyal subordinates at the general's headquarters at Tan Son Nhut to keep watch over him. ("Martin thought I was doing some reporting on my own he was not aware of," Murray commented.) A short time later, when a problem developed over the weekly U.S. liaison flights to Hanoi, which were provided for under the Paris agreement, the Ambassador took advantage of the incident to give Murray an object lesson in humility. "I had gotten a call from General O'Keefe [of the 7th Air Force in Thailand] to halt the C-130 [flights]," Murray recounted to me, "because the local commander in Hanoi said if they didn't come down over a certain route, he was going to shoot them down. So I stopped the flights. Martin called me up and said, 'By what right did you do this? I'm the boss.' I said, 'I got the orders from General O'Keefe. I think your problem's with him.' Martin called up O'Keefe and Gayler.

"Martin later told me he'd won that fight. O'Keefe and Gayler said they'd won it. So I don't know who did. I felt a little like Curtis LeMay when he used to talk about the Army/Navy game: he said he hoped they'd both lose."

In a further effort to discipline DAO and the rest of the Embassy, Martin played the old conspirator's game of divide and conquer to devastating effect. He continually played one agency off against another and attempted to keep each of them in the dark about his own plans and policies so none could challenge him. "He always liked to talk to you alone," Murray noted. "He never coordinated with anybody else and you never knew what was going on in the Embassy, except what you told Martin and he told you. This was his method of control. It was quite different from the way things were in Bunker's Embassy, where everything was fully coordinated."

Since Murray's office and the CIA Station were the Embassy's two most powerful components, Martin quickly set them at each other's throats so neither could dominate. "In my first meeting with Martin," Murray acknowledged, "I was very high on the guy. But then a couple of weeks later I got a CIA report across my desk. One of the CIA guys had gone into one of the ARVN units in MR [Military Region] 1 and had talked about the logistics being in poor shape. They didn't have enough fuel or ammunition. [His report] was really a gripe list. So I put a little note on it and sent it over to the Ambassador and said, 'Gee, I thought the purpose of the CIA was to look at the enemy and not at our own people.'

"The next time I was in talking to Martin he looked at me with that eye that resembled a peeled grape and said, 'You know, I had the CIA looking into those things myself, because if I can't get the information from you, I want to get it from the CIA.' I said, 'Sir, any information you want to get on the

ARVN, I'll be glad to get it for you.' But he would have no part of it and said he was going to continue to have the CIA investigate the ARVN units. I later asked the Deputy Chief of Station if Martin had asked the CIA to go out and get that report. He said, 'Hell no!' That's when I first became suspicious of Martin."

As final insurance of his control over Murray, the Ambassador "recruited" several ardent supporters within the general's own staff. One of them was Murray's principal intelligence officer, Colonel Bill Legro, who ultimately became chief of all plans and operations at DAO. An infantryman with combat experience in Vietnam, the quiet, crew-cut and unassuming Legro was essentially a good soldier who respected authority and followed orders to the letter. Slowly but surely Martin drew him into his confidence, using him to influence and monitor the Defense Attaché himself.

As DAO's intelligence chief, Legro was also ideally suited to help keep the CIA in check, as Martin clearly was determined to do. When the CIA Station seemed to be veering too far away from the Ambassador's viewpoint, Legro would always weigh in with a caveat in his own briefings or communications to Washington. His perspectives, moreover, seemed to square neatly with the Ambassador's own goals. As a combat veteran who had seen the worst the North Vietnamese could do, Legro was naturally inclined to give them every bit their due, and then some, and to the extent he overplayed their strengths and potential, his analyses served to reinforce the Ambassador's appeals to Congress for additional military aid. Within several weeks of Martin's arrival, Legro was already predicting a massive North Vietnamese assault in the next few months, much to Martin's delight.

In addition to Legro's analytical shop, Martin insisted that DAO retain a network of civilian intelligence operatives around the countryside to keep track of the South Vietnamese army. The group, commanded by Colonel Al Weidhas, received little support from the Pentagon and essentially duplicated much of the CIA's work. But that, of course, was exactly what Martin wanted. Weidhas, like Legro, was meant to offset the CIA's Chief of Station.

Martin shaped his civilian staff as he did DAO's with the same ulterior motives in mind. He wanted no one around him who could effectively challenge or obstruct him; his subordinates were to be mere extensions of himself, neither advisors nor collaborators.

One of the holdovers from Bunker's staff who served him most faithfully was sixty-two-year-old George Jacobson. An accomplished bureaucrat who had survived four different Ambassadors in Vietnam, "Jake" in his garrulous way was the Embassy's residual memory. He had helped set up the pacification program during his decade and a half in Saigon and knew nearly every important Vietnamese in the government. He had made only one apparent mistake in his career. Back in the late 1960s, when he was being considered as a replacement for Colby as chief of CORDS, the pacification advisory group, he had misjudged Henry Kissinger. Believing Kissinger optimistic about pacification, he had sounded appropriately optimistic when being interviewed for the job. Unfortunately for him, Kissinger considered pacification a failure and promptly ruled Jacobson out as Colby's successor. By the summer of '73 Jacobson was therefore clinging to his post as acting chief of CORDS by his professional fingertips.

For reasons of his own, Martin rescued him, keeping him on even as the CORDS apparatus was dismantled. In due time Jacobson became the Ambassador's special assistant for field operations, and he and a small staff were put in charge of a handful of agricultural specialists spread around the country. It was not much of a job—the four U.S. consulates outside Saigon shared supervisory responsibilities with him—but eventually his value to the Ambassador became manifest. Since he owed his salvation to Martin, he became the utterly loyal lieutenant, always doing Martin's bidding, always deferring to his judgment. In countless staff meetings and briefings I watched Jacobson sit mum and unprotesting as the Ambassador rambled on naïvely about the "improved" security in the countryside. As our reigning pacification expert, Jacobson knew better. But he also apparently knew the price of survival in Martin's Embassy.

Josiah Bennett, a thin, almost wispy man who had proven his mettle as a province advisor during the 1968 offensive, was another old Vietnam "hand" who won Martin's favor. Some who knew and worked with him claimed he never ranked very high in the Ambassador's estimation, but that judgment failed to recognize Martin's own sense of utility. During the Communist takeover in China in the late 1940s, Bennett had been a young Foreign Service officer in Chungking, and as a result of his experiences, had become a fervent anti-Communist. Martin not only respected this bias, but also was quite obviously determined to make the most of it, for he kept Bennett on as his political counselor, the third-ranking member of his staff, with responsibility for monitoring the tone and content of Embassy reporting.

During the next year and a half Bennett performed his job just as Martin wanted. He spent much of his time assembling atrocity reports for Martin to present to unwary Congressmen, and scuttling up the street to the Foreign Ministry with directives to the South Vietnamese government. He also developed a keen awareness of the Ambassador's own wants and prejudices. In early 1974 when a young Foreign Service officer tried to clear a report with him on corruption in the Thieu government, Bennett vetoed its dissemination because —as he explained in his covering note—"I don't know what Washington would do with it and it could so easily be slipped to [newspaper columnist] Jack Anderson and be reported all out of context."

Besides retaining the most responsive members of Bunker's staff, Martin quickly began plugging loyalists of his own making into key positions. John Robinson, an old friend and associate, took over the local office of the Agency for International Development. Paul Popple, who had worked for Martin in Italy, became Consul General in Danang. Moncrieff Spear, his special assistant in Bangkok, was named to head the consulate in Nha Trang. Dick Peters, who was on the State Department's Far Eastern desk during Martin's Bangkok tenure, became the Embassy's chief political-military officer, and was finally assigned to the consulate in Bien Hoa. Lannon Walker, a close friend of the Martin family, was appointed the Embassy's administrative counselor. Al Jazynka, deputy budget officer in Rome, became Walker's assistant, and Harry Hinderer, who had gotten to know the Ambassador when both were working for the Alliance for Progress in Washington, was brought in as a special administrative troubleshooter.

Martin even attempted to provide his own secretary. Al Jazynka's wife, Janie, who had served as the Ambassador's Girl Friday in Rome, was slated for the same job in Saigon, and would have gotten it had not Bunker interceded at the last minute to ensure that his own trustworthy Eva Kim was retained. Eva became Martin's secretary and Janie was palmed off on his principal deputy.

Predictably, the men who formed the Ambassador's innermost circle were all specially hand-picked for their proven loyalty. By far the most influential was Albert A. Francis, a bearded forty-one-year-old Foreign Service officer who had first worked for him in Bangkok and had caught his eye there by compiling detailed biographical dossiers on key Thai leaders. Martin found Francis' information useful in manipulating the Thai government and duly repaid his subordinate by assuring him steady promotion.

After a brief stint in Vietnam in the mid-1960s, Francis was assigned to Okinawa, where he taught himself Japanese. He would have been posted to Japan itself had not the "Nippon clique" in the State Department objected to his close and enduring relationship with Martin. Just as he was preparing to resign from the State Department in protest, his old patron rescued him, inviting him to accept a job in Saigon.

Francis was the very model of the Martinesque bureaucrat. Intelligent, hard-working, he put loyalty to the chief above all else. During his year in Saigon he emerged as Martin's principal aide, confidant and hatchet man. He monitored the ebb and flow of sentiment in the lower echelons, reported the malcontents to the Ambassador and helped to discipline them when necessary. For his devotion and service he was amply rewarded, soon becoming Dick Peters' replacement as chief of the political-military section and, finally, successor to Paul Popple as Consul General in Danang, where with typical resourcefulness he performed heroically in Vietnam's final days.

Second only to Francis in influence was Jim Devine, a plumpish, chain-smoking former Pentagon official who showed up in Saigon in the summer of 1974. Devine had begun his career as an auditor at the Pentagon, had met Martin in that capacity and had impressed him, particularly with his knowledge of the Pentagon's myriad bureaucracies and how to manipulate them. When Martin went to Rome he invited Devine to join him as his political-military counselor. The same job was offered him in Saigon.

The third member of Martin's ruling triumvirate was Wolfgang Lehmann, a fifty-two-year-old German-affairs expert with a lean, hatchetlike face and a subtlety of mind to match. He had first come to Martin's attention as the State Department's political advisor to the NATO commander in Europe and was very much a man in the Ambassador's image—crusty, irascible and unimpressed by rank or position. In the fall of 1973 Martin invited him to become Consul General in the delta town of Can Tho, and the following spring appointed him Deputy Chief of Mission, the second highest-ranking post in the Embassy.

Lehmann proved himself Martin's perfect alter ego, the master mime, capable of matching the Ambassador in zeal and argumentativeness. He also boasted one quality even the Ambassador couldn't claim. Having served six months in "the field," he could present himself to any unknowing Congressman or newsman as an expert on pacification. His credentials helped to give an aura of credibility to the optimistic assessments he peddled on the Ambassador's behalf.

Not all of Martin's appointees found it so easy to follow his lead. In Danang, Consul General Paul Popple soon discovered that pacification and the morale of South Vietnamese forces were somewhat less impressive than Martin was claiming in cables to Washington, and he urged the Ambassador to change his line. Similarly, as administrative counselor, Lannon Walker quickly found that Martin's whims were not always the best and most economical approach to management. When Martin asked that a private swimming pool be built at the Ambassadorial Residence, Walker vetoed the project as too expensive. He also resisted pressure from the "front office" to keep various fiscal shell games within the Embassy hidden from State Department auditors, particularly the Ambassador's penchant for preserving defunct programs by merging them with solvent ones.

In offering Martin their advice and their objections, Popple and Walker were simply comporting themselves as professional Foreign Service officers. Yet the price they paid for their integrity was brutally high. When Popple fell ill in the spring of '74 Martin immediately "offered" to replace him with Al Francis. In the meantime, while holding off an inspection tour by State Department auditors, the Ambassador arranged a plush assignment for young Walker in Kinshasha and replaced him with someone more to his liking—sandy-haired, fiftyish Henry Boudreau, who had been his administrative counselor in Rome.

Perhaps the most "troublesome" of the Embassy's components was the one responsible for handling Martin's principal *bête noire,* the press. Since the United States Information Agency wielded enough power to name its own staff in Saigon, the man who eventually headed up its office there, Alan Carter, was not a hand-picked Martin man. Nor, as it happened, did he share the Ambassador's low opinion of the press. Ebullient, outspoken, Carter favored an open and candid press policy and refused to treat journalists as the "enemy," as Martin preferred. For his trouble he soon found himself shunted into bureaucratic limbo, without access either to the Ambassador's inner councils or to the Embassy's most important cable traffic. So total was his isolation, he was obliged to rely on tips from lower-ranking officers like myself to keep abreast of Embassy policy. Meanwhile, the Ambassador insisted that all press inquiries be channeled through John Hogan, a veteran of Bunker's Embassy who had been retained because of his obvious devotion to Martin's ideals. It was Hogan —a songwriter by avocation—who drafted the Ambassador's most scathing attacks on the press.

Of all the principals in Martin's Embassy, my own boss, Tom Polgar, was potentially the most threatening to him. Not only did he command independent sources of information and a strong self-contained bureaucracy, but he also had no fear of the Ambassador himself. He felt the Station was producing such useful intelligence, Martin was in his debt, rather than the other way round.

Even so, Polgar remained one of the most responsive, if not the most admiring, of Martin's senior staffers. He believed in the Ambassador's objectives, was equally anti-Communist, and shared his devotion to the manipulative use of intelligence. Despite all their dissimilarities, and occasional antagonisms, the two turned out to be the perfect odd couple.

My first impressions of Polgar remain vividly fixed in memory. "Physically he is not one to put the Ambassador's grandeur to shame," I wrote in a pocket notebook soon after we met. "Short and squat, with a butcher's build and a sagging barrel chest, he looks more like an overgrown gnome than 'Special Assistant to the Ambassador,' as his cover title proclaims him to be. The face is round and fleshy, dominated by a bulbous nose and thick square-framed glasses, and what is left of his hair (not much) bristles above the ear line like a row of blunt thistles.

"The first thing you notice when you enter his office is the huge oak desk that dominates the end of the room like a sleeping terrapin. There are also other accouterments of executive privilege—a sofa and a few straight-backed chairs scattered about haphazardly—and a particularly noteworthy picture on the side wall shows a Viet Cong soldier in cartoon loading a spear into an elephant's trunk while another prepares to belabor the poor animal's testicles with a huge hammer. The inscription reads 'The Last VC Offensive—Heavy Artillery.' It is a token of Polgar's brand of humor.

"The 'Old Man' never greets a staffer at the door. I've been told that occasionally, depending on the rank of the visitor, he'll trundle across the room and extend a hand wordlessly, but that is merely gossip, never seen, never proven. For the rest of us, the reception is carefully choreographed to impart a clear sense of hierarchy. After an interminable wait in the anteroom, where the two crack secretaries invariably kid you about your nerves, you are ushered into his presence, to a point a respectful distance from the terrapin. At last the Old Man raises his eyes from an impressively lean manila folder in front of him and surveys you suspiciously, the back of his chair looming over his round shoulders like folded leather wings. After another wait—the scenario never alters—he snorts or clears his throat, rubbing his nose vigorously with the back of his right hand. 'What do you vant?' The words, swathed in an East European accent (as good an imitation of Kissinger's as any around), sail at you like an accusation. As you try to explain, he interrupts, 'Oh yes, I know; oh yes, I remember.' Then there is another pause, more unhurried glances at the folder, more snorts and massages, and finally he gets up clutching a sheaf of papers, eyes focused on it, and moves to the sofa. Once nestled in, he gestures idly for you to take one of the straight-backed chairs, and the interview begins."

Tom Polgar was born of peasant stock in southern Hungary in the early 1920s, and like many others of his vintage, became passionately attached to the land. But being Jewish and defiantly outspoken, he quickly decided, as the shadow of Hitler's Germany loomed eastward, that his own fortunes lay elsewhere. In the early 1930s he fled across Eastern Europe, toward the west, finally making his way to the United States. In the course of his travels he picked up a smattering of various languages, French, Greek, Spanish, English and German. He spoke none of them very well, his thick Hungarian accent always clearly discernible. Yet as World War II broke out and the U.S. military began casting about for potential intelligence operatives, his facility for languages earned him a commission. Drafted into the army, he was co-opted by the Office of Strategic Services, trained as a counterespionage agent and dropped behind German lines with no more than a false Nazi party identity card to protect him. Miraculously, he survived the ordeal, operating in and out of Berlin as the war drew to a close—no mean accomplishment for a Hungarian Jew whose German was only passable.

After the war the energetic young operative rose quickly in the new and expanding Central Intelligence Agency. Because of his capacity for language he was soon engaged as a principal assistant to General Lucian Truscett, the World War II hero who in the early 1950s became Chief of the CIA's then-massive 1,600-man Station in West Germany. Under Truscett, Polgar developed managerial skills that became hallmarks of his later career. From Germany he moved on to a variety of other assignments, always impressing his superiors with his diligence, and finally in the late 1960s he ended up as the CIA's Station Chief in Argentina. There his career took a sudden and unexpected turn. One morning a group of American dissidents hijacked an airliner and put down at Buenos Aires airport for refueling. Polgar was called in to try to talk them into releasing their hostages. As he recounted the incident to me: "It was really a rather simple affair. The hijackers were getting pretty hot in the cabin with no air conditioner. I offered to send some Cokes in to them. I drugged the Cokes and then, when the fellows were feeling relaxed, I walked in and took their guns away." For all of his modesty about the accomplishment, Polgar was immediately declared a hero by his CIA colleagues and mentors. Shortly thereafter he was offered one of the agency's most important and prestigious overseas assignments—the position of Chief of Station in Saigon—even though he had never before set foot in Asia.

Because of his accent and his past Polgar always considered himself an outsider in the CIA's ivy-covered bureaucracy, and as an outsider he felt obliged continually to demonstrate his knowledge and astuteness. The role of pontificator came easily to him, as he quickly proved in Saigon, for with it he apparently felt would come acceptance and respect among his colleagues. In a sense, Henry Kissinger's personality was as important to him as his policies, for Kissinger's own accent and past were proof to Polgar that outsiders could triumph in the elite world of American diplomacy.

Personally Polgar was stand-offish. He refused to overcommit himself in dealings with others, perhaps because the outsider in him was never quite sure of acceptance. He obviously felt comfortable only with those colleagues who were not powerful enough to undermine him; the rest he held at arm's length.

His personal insecurities no doubt helped to shape his relationship with the Vietnamese. In Saigon's mercurial society generals and politicians with imposing titles were a dime a dozen, and Polgar clearly enjoyed hobnobbing with them, as if he expected to gain through the association the status that seemed to elude him among his American peers. The Vietnamese themselves were flattered by his attentions, but whether U.S. interests were well served is yet another question. For in dealing with Saigon's high and mighty, Polgar tended to suspend critical judgment, accepting what they told him even when he knew it to be self-serving. The image he projected of them in his reporting to Washington was never quite as discerning as it might have been.

Polgar's manners and sense of humor were as rough-hewn as his past. He could turn a cocktail party cold with an innocent off-color joke, and if someone dared to criticize him or his views, his rejoinders often seemed drawn from the idiom of the barnyard. "Never wrestle with pigs," he often counseled us in reference to the liberals in Congress. "They enjoy it and you get dirty."

According to one of Polgar's oldest associates, he and Martin secretly loathed each other, and for precisely the same reasons. Polgar, the Hungarian émigré, evidently detested Martin's background and all that went with it. Martin, the would-be southern patrician, appeared equally contemptuous of Polgar's past and his pretensions. "Polgar's one great fault," Martin once remarked to me, "is his overweening vanity." Undoubtedly Polgar would have leveled the same criticism at the Ambassador.

Despite his reservations about Martin, however, Polgar was fascinated by his many talents, particularly his rhetorical skills. As one who had often used language as a shield and a weapon, the CIA Station Chief could appreciate, as few of the rest of us could, the Ambassador's ability to wield language manipulatively, to score rhetorical points. During our Thursday-afternoon staff meetings Polgar would frequently entertain us by reading out loud from the Ambassador's cables, exclaiming after each sizzling phrase, "What a pistol this man is! What a pistol!"

In approaching his own job Polgar was a man true to his background. Trained in counterespionage he viewed "political action," the manipulation of both information and individuals, as part of the natural order of business. But like so many other professionals in his trade, he seemed to have learned his skills almost too well. They had become instinctual, and under the pressures of Martin's Embassy he tended from time to time to apply them without due regard for the target, turning them against Washington as well as Hanoi and Saigon. "He saw his job in terms of a balancing act," observed a friend. "He felt he was straddling a fence between forces on the one side that demanded a scientific description of the world around him and those on the other that required that he put it into language that would have a desired effect."

A few months before the collapse of Saigon, when the Embassy was heavily engaged in trying to wring additional aid out of Congress, one of Polgar's subordinates complained to him about the increasingly polemical tone of CIA reporting to Washington and our willingness to supply Martin with whatever propagandistic data he needed to influence Congressional votes. Polgar wrote a reply that spoke directly to his own concept of his responsibilities: "I have read your remarks and wish to make the following points, to avoid any possible misunderstanding of my position as Chief of Station. I represent one segment of the U.S. Mission in Vietnam. The Ambassador is the Chief of the Mission, and by direction of President Kennedy and reaffirmed by every President since then, the Ambassador is responsible for all U.S. activities in the country. If the Ambassador, be it Martin or anyone else, asks me to provide, I will try to comply with his request, provided that such a request is not illegal and would not interfere with my basic responsibilities.

"All of us must act according to our own perceptions as to the limits imposed by policy, integrity, wisdom and if you wish—a sense of caution. I for my part do not propose to withhold the truth because the truth may offend some of our critics. The fact that at times the truth may have a polemic effect does not relieve us from the responsibility to provide the truth."

In that brief note Polgar summed up his professional philosophy and that of many other senior CIA officers like him. He was an advocate and activist, as well as an intelligence collector, with an obligation to try to influence those with the power to achieve results, be they the eleven members of Hanoi's Politburo or Congressional leaders in Washington. It was a logical extension of his experience in the hot and cold wars of the past three decades and a philosophy with which Martin totally agreed.

Beyond defining his outlook and tactics, Polgar's background had another profound effect on the way he performed his job in Vietnam. Despite his staunch anti-Communism, he was in taste and disposition a man of his home-land, and once the Hungarian ICCS delegation established itself in Saigon, he was drawn to it as if by an affinity of blood.

Initially the relationship was foisted on him. Because of a protocol prob-lem the Thieu regime never accredited the Hungarian Ambassador to the ICCS. Consequently, Martin refused to deal with the delegation himself and left it to Polgar to establish working contacts to bridge the gap.

The Hungarians for their part were delighted. They knew Polgar was the CIA Station Chief and were determined to make the most of their unique liaison with U.S. intelligence. A year after the cease-fire they brought several special operatives to Saigon, led by Anton Tolgyes, to orchestrate the affair. Ostensibly political counselor to the delegation, the fifty-year-old Tolgyes in fact was a brilliant and accomplished intelligence officer, a Hungarian Jew who had been converted to Communism during a stint in a Soviet prison camp in World War II. His prime mission in Saigon was to trick and mislead the CIA's Chief of Station.

It is an old and trusted axiom of the intelligence business that East European émigrés are the most nostalgic people in the world, particularly vulnerable to the blandishments of heritage and homeland. Tolgyes must have believed this himself, for he played heavily on Polgar's own nostalgia, inviting him out from time to time to drink barach and to exchange non-political anecdotes about old Hungary. He also found another chord in Polgar's makeup, his vanity, that could be played to effect, and as time went on he did so diligently and expertly, encouraging Polgar in the belief that the two of them, with Kissinger, in their similarity and shared interests, could somehow work together to liquidate this unpleasantness of Vietnam.

Soviet-bloc specialists at CIA headquarters remained deeply skeptical of Tolgyes and warned Polgar to be on his guard. But Polgar's own skepticism seemingly remained in abeyance. Perhaps he could not believe a fellow Hun-garian would deceive him, or perhaps he felt he could best Tolgyes at his own game. In any case, with each passing month he allowed the Hungarian to draw him ever more deeply into a relationship of openness and intimacy that would ultimately cloud his own vision of what lay ahead.

My own relationship with Polgar likewise hinged on his personality and his past. Rightly or wrongly, he decided I had an aptitude for manipulating language in the manner he so admired in the Ambassador. Perhaps, too, he saw me as a useful buffer in his dealings with Martin. I was, after all, a southerner, a North Carolinian like the Ambassador, with the same accent. I was also close to Martin's daughter and amply endowed with Martin's own brand of opportunism. Janet Martin once told me I reminded her of her father. I took the remark as a supreme compliment.

My position with Polgar was cemented in early August 1973. Ted Shack-ley, his predecessor as Chief of Station and now his superior as head of the agency's East Asia Division, showed up on an inspection tour. Shackley had long been both feared and revered by subordinates because of his penchant for computerlike rhetoric and convoluted reasoning that always seemed more profound than it was. Since I had worked for him during my previous Saigon tour, I was well acquainted with these idiosyncrasies and simply mimicked them, with charts and pointers and statistics-studded rhetoric, when I was called upon to brief him during his trip. Polgar was so impressed he resolved to use me from then on as his principal briefing officer.

In the final year and a half of the cease-fire I also wrote virtually all of Polgar's "field appraisals" (the only two he wrote himself were rejected by CIA headquarters) and many of his personal communications to Washington as well. I was assigned to run one of the CIA's most sensitive intelligence operations in North Vietnam, and was given carte blanche to interrogate whatever prisoners, defectors or intelligence agents I felt might contribute to our understanding of North Vietnamese intentions. I was Polgar's mouthpiece, shadow and front man, and probably one of the three or four staffers with whom he maintained a truly close relation. Some of my colleagues thought he had adopted me as a surrogate son.

As my own job altered and expanded, so did the small analytical staff of which I was a part. Some of my less-productive colleagues were sent home and Polgar began selecting replacements with a view to his own professional ideals. One of his first appointees was blond, vivacious Pat Johnson, wife of a senior Station official. Neither an analyst nor a Vietnam "expert," Pat nonetheless had a "specialty" that made her attractive to Polgar. In her twenty years as a CIA operative she had become thoroughly steeped in the lore of counterespionage. To Polgar she seemed a kindred spirit.

Pat and I didn't get along at first. She was too ideological, too conservative for my tastes, and too anxious to cop my job. But despite her abrasiveness she had a quality that eventually benefited us both: an unerring sense of integrity. Her chidings and her criticism became a compelling reminder to me where truth and honesty lay as I was drawn ever deeper into the vortex of Martin's Embassy.

Nibblers and Anti-Nibblers

When the United States ended its bombing of Cambodia on 15 August 1973, in accord with Congressional dictates, President Thieu was in the midst of battening down his military and political defenses. An "administrative revolution," aimed at securing his control over the French-trained civil bureaucracy, was now several weeks old, and with the country's biannual Senate elections only a few days away, he was busily manipulating the electoral laws to assure his supporters a majority at the polls.

None of this was idle muscle-flexing. The B-52s had been Thieu's major life insurance. Now he had to find something else.

The bombing halt puzzled him, however. As master in his own domain, he could not imagine Nixon might not be master in his, and several days after the B-52s made their final run, a well-meaning visitor helped to compound his confusion. Sir Robert Thompson, a retired British counterinsurgency expert who had come out to Saigon as a White House emissary, assured him unequivocally that Nixon would find a way around the Congressional bombing ban.

Believing this, Thieu decided the best thing he could do was to demonstrate to the Americans once again that he was worthy of their support. To his mind this meant, in part, simply averting embarrassments at home (hence, the systematic tightening of his hold on the society). He was also convinced a modest display of military prowess was in order, since the Americans always seemed to be impressed by assertiveness on the battlefield.

As the summer of 1973 came to an end he therefore launched several large-scale military operations, ostensibly to clear NVA units out of base camps in the delta and along the Cambodian border north of Saigon, but in fact to eliminate any lingering American doubts about his capabilities. Within the next four months he scored impressively. A traditional Communist enclave at the western tip of the delta was captured, and over 700 previously disputed hamlets were added to the list of those in which the government exercised "dominant influence."

•   •   •

As the pressure mounted, Hanoi's military leaders, General Giap and his chief of staff, General Dung, began clamoring for a response-in-kind. For the past five months NVA forces had been marking time, building their supply caches in the south and occasionally snatching territory where they could do it on the cheap. Their objective was to confront Thieu with such a threat-in-being, he would feel obliged to compromise. But clearly this tactic wasn't working. By early fall COSVN's field commanders were readily admitting to subordinates that no more than twelve percent of the population and one-fifth the land mass of South Vietnam were even accessible to them.*

Given these "realities," the hawks in the Politburo concluded a return to "revolutionary violence" was unavoidable, and General Giap, writing anonymously in the army newspaper, made this point again and again with chilling eloquence.

But against his well-wrought arguments, there were strong countervailing ones. Most compelling were the attitudes of the Soviets and the Chinese. Immediately following the Brezhnev-Nixon summit in June, Party First Secretary Le Duan had flown to Moscow and Peking, hat in hand, to ask for additional aid to carry on the war. To his surprise, he received little more than a cold shoulder. Neither the Soviets nor the Chinese were willing to promise massive new military aid, and though both agreed to increase economic assistance, they insisted on attaching all sorts of strings to ensure it was used wisely, even to the point of demanding that the North Vietnamese actually let them help supervise how the aid was applied.

None of their stipulations sat well with Hanoi, but the Politburo felt it had no choice but to accede to them. Recent flooding had very nearly wiped out the fall rice crop and the country was in dire need of immediate food imports. For the first time, moreover, the North Vietnamese were beginning to grasp the immensity of the economic problems confronting them. A property survey, undertaken at the Soviets' behest, revealed that waste, inefficiency and even corruption were far more widespread than the leadership had ever imagined, and a population census, the first since the early 1960s, carried an even greater shock: despite the war, the population of North Vietnam had grown by nearly fifty percent in the past fifteen years, thus posing far greater burdens for the economy than had been estimated.

In early October, several weeks after Le Duan returned from Moscow and Peking, the Party Central Committee convened a plenary session, the twenty-first in its history, to consider its next move. The generals argued strenuously for a step-up in the fighting, insisting that the morale and discipline of the army would more than compensate for the loss of Soviet and Chinese support. But

---

*These points were spelled out explicitly and in some detail in COSVN Resolution 12 and a Politburo Resolution 21. Excerpts from both documents fell into CIA hands literally within a week or two of their being issued.

Premier Pham Van Dong, a curious and mercurial old revolutionary with a well-honed pragmatic sense, was not so certain. Without the backing of their traditional allies, he warned, there would be nothing to keep Nixon from sending the B-52s back to Hanoi, and that would mean an end to all prospects for both victory and reconstruction.

This argument swung the debate. While reasserting their faith in "revolutionary violence," the conferees chose to peg their objectives far short of all-out warfare. Instead of striking at Saigon's army in the months ahead, they elected to target its weakest spot, its pocketbook, launching a series of hit-and-run attacks—"strategic raids" they called them—against roads, airfields and fuel storage facilities to further weaken the economy and to frighten off foreign investors.

Few of the grizzled old party members who sat through the long discussions were confident that any of this would produce immediate success, and in their directives to the field they made no effort to suggest it would, for fear of raising false expectations and undermining troop morale. The closing paragraphs of their main policy resolution explicitly cautioned troops and party members not to expect ultimate victory before 1979 at the earliest, and General Giap himself publicly acknowledged that the "struggle had become protracted and complex"—a struggle between "anti-nibbling forces and the nibblers."

On 6 November, only days after the plenum ended, the equivalent of a full NVA division carried out the first "strategic raid," overrunning three border outposts in Quang Duc Province northeast of Saigon, where ARVN forces had recently been conducting probes of their own. That night Le Duan and his Politburo colleagues held their breath. Would Nixon respond with B-52s? Within the next twenty-four hours they got their answer.

Quite coincidentally, the drive in Congress to limit the President's war-making authority had just come to a head, and on 7 November the House and the Senate overrode a presidential veto and passed special legislation formally setting forth the restrictions. The monumental War Powers Act made it illegal for the President to introduce American forces into "hostile" situations for more than sixty days without Congressional approval. Actually, the bill was irrelevant for Indochina, for the Cambodia bombing ban of August had already ruled out any further military involvement there for any length of time. But as confirmation of American intent, and of Nixon's political impotence, it duly impressed the North Vietnamese.

The hawks in the Politburo responded predictably, again demanding escalation, and a week later Khmer Communist forces in Cambodia launched a direct ground assault on Phnom Penh to test Lon Nol's staying power in the wake of the bombing halt.

During the first week in December the moderates in Hanoi wavered and nearly succumbed to the war sentiment now sweeping through the upper echelons of the party. Only by invoking the priorities of reconstruction and the uncertainties of Soviet and Chinese support were they able to hold the line.

Still, their margin of victory was a slim one, and lest they be faced with continuing debate, they insisted that another policy conference be called at once to formalize the regime's commitment to economic development. A few days later the Central Committee's Twenty-second Plenum was convened to do just that. The hawks had no choice but to bide their time.

From the standpoint of American intelligence the North Vietnamese might as well have been living in a glass house during all this. Within a week or so of the two plenums we were inundated with agent reports about them, and soon after the strategic raid in Quang Duc, our most "sensitive" intelligence source picked up a top-priority North Vietnamese directive which revealed that NVA forces in the south would not be significantly expanded during the next half year—certainly not enough to permit them to mount a countrywide "general offensive."

To all appearances, General Giap and his hawkish allies had been soundly defeated in Hanoi's latest political infighting. The strategic-raids campaign was not the ambitious initiative they felt was needed. From a practical standpoint, however, they had fared far better than they realized. For in making the South Vietnamese economy their primary target, the eleven Old Men of the Politburo had zeroed in on the enemy's Achilles' heel.

Economically, the first year of the cease-fire had been the worst for the South Vietnamese since 1966. Prices had increased by a staggering sixty-five percent; unemployment had skyrocketed with the departure of the last American GIs (only 17,000 Vietnamese were now making their living off the "U.S. presence," as compared to 160,000 only seven years before); and the value of economic aid from Washington had continued to decline as a result of worldwide inflation and in particular the doubling of the price of such key imports as fertilizer and petroleum. And the worst, of course, was still to come. Thanks to the Arab oil embargo in the wake of the recent Middle East war, petroleum prices around the world would soon quadruple. Nor had other much-needed sources of income materialized. Foreign investors were still staying away out of concern for the uncertainties of the battlefield.

On top of all this, Thieu had so far been unwilling to move against the corruption in the army and in the upper levels of the government that was draining off valuable revenue. To have done so would only have alienated the generals and leading politicians whose backing was essential to his survival.

Apart from economic ills, South Vietnam was facing another fiscal crisis as the first year of "peace" drew to a close. Because of Congress' unwillingness to go on supporting Thieu's war-making effort, the flow of American arms and supplies was beginning to taper off.

Ever since the cease-fire the Pentagon and Congress had been trying to work out a new military aid program for Saigon. In the past several months, pending a decision, the Pentagon had begun drawing stop-gap funds under a "continuing Congressional resolution authority." Essentially this meant writing checks in advance against the appropriation requested of Congress. It was a risky business, to be sure, for if Congress ultimately voted less money than had been anticipated, many of the checks and commitments could not be made good.*

By the end of 1973 the prospect of such an aid squeeze was looming very large. On 20 December, General Murray, the Defense Attaché in Saigon, was advised by the Pentagon that various Congressional committees had pared the Administration's current aid proposal to roughly $1 billion. The revelation came as a shock to him, since he had been expecting far more and had already written checks nearly equaling this amount. If the new, more modest proposal was enacted, only about $40 million in "uncommitted funds" would be left to meet any unforeseen expenses before the end of the current fiscal year (and the next annual aid appropriation) in June.

Sadly enough, just such an "unforeseen expense" soon materialized. Incredible as it might seem, logisticians for the U.S. Army had recently made some grave bookkeeping errors in their efforts to keep track of Saigon's ammunition expenditures. As a result, no one in Washington could now say for certain how much money had already been spent for this vital commodity or how much ammunition had actually been delivered to South Vietnam in the past few months.

Frantically Murray queried Saigon's high command on the next most important question: the size of existing ammunition stockpiles. But this only compounded his troubles. Since the South Vietnamese wanted to get all they could from the Americans, they took advantage of his confusion to expand their shopping lists. They told Murray that their ammunition expenditures during the past year had been much larger than previously disclosed, that their army had been firing eighteen shells for each one the Communists lobbed at them. Consequently, they said, their stockpiles were now well below "prudent levels." At least $221 million worth of additional ammunition would be needed to bring them up to what they were at the time of the cease-fire.

For the next few weeks, throughout late December and early January, Murray and his staff worked night and day to try to make ends meet. But each time they thought they had found a way to stretch resources, another problem arose to send the trend lines plunging back into the red.

---

*The technicalities of the aid program would take pages to explain. Suffice it to say that during the cease-fire period there was always a large gap between what Congress authorized and what it actually appropriated in military aid. During the fiscal year 1973–74 (lasting from June of one calendar year to June of the next) the "continuing Congressional resolution authority" was used to justify Pentagon outlays for Saigon even as Congress debated the amount of aid to be appropriated for the same twelve-month period. Once it became apparent that more had been spent under the "authority" than Congress ultimately intended to be paid out, then supplemental appropriations were sought and the Administration attempted to persuade Congress to raise the ceiling on its original authorization so "loose change" from the Pentagon's coffers could be applied to the Vietnam account. During the next fiscal year roughly the same act was replayed, with only slight variations. Consequently, the Administration and Congress seemed constantly to be juggling scores of aid proposals at once. To further complicate matters, the economic aid program was handled separately.

Then, too, as the aid debate continued, certain industrial lobbyists in Washington began pushing Murray, and the South Vietnamese, to accept expensive equipment whose sales might benefit American business. Representatives of the Northrup Aviation Company, for example, insisted that sophisticated F-5E jet bombers be bought to replace worn-out F-5As already in Saigon's inventory. When the North Vietnamese learned of the substitution they complained, quite rightly, that it violated a provision of the Paris agreement stipulating that all matériel replacements be made on a one-for-one *facsimile* basis. But the Northrup lobbyists and their allies in Congress and the Pentagon did not seem troubled by such legalisms and rammed the F-5Es down Saigon's throat. "It was extravagant and cruel political taxidermy— stuffing, so to speak, a dying bird," Murray later commented. "But challenging the sale of the F-5Es was as ineffectual as a Greek's cry in the night inside a Turkish prison. I was told that Senator [James] Pearson of Kansas, viciously pork-barreling, backed Northrup, and if we didn't take the F-5Es, then we wouldn't get anything for the RVNAF [the South Vietnamese army] in '75."*

In his own desperation Murray pleaded with Martin to allow him to brief the South Vietnamese on the aid picture. But Martin was unwilling to let him go this far. He was afraid that a display of candor might demoralize Thieu and his commanders and diminish his own political leverage with them. He therefore advised his Defense Attaché to say nothing to Saigon's high command about the continuing erosion of the aid bill in Congress.

As the Embassy officials agonized over the fiscal crisis, their colleagues in Washington remained curiously unperturbed. During the past half year, despite the traumas of the aid debate, top officials in the State Department and the White House had in fact allowed the cease-fire and its failings to drift into memory. A psychology of almost manic indifference—a "gone with the wind" syndrome, one State Department official called it—had replaced the obsession Vietnam once was.

Henry Kissinger was no exception. In recent months he had given far less attention to Saigon than Martin felt was warranted. Outside pressures and Kissinger's own style of personalized diplomacy were primarily to blame. In September, amid the turbulence of Watergate, he had finally triumphed over

---

*Several of the Pentagon's own fiscal wizards also heartily endorsed the aircraft sales. During the Enhance Plus program in late 1972 the Pentagon had moved a large number of jet fighters to South Vietnam from Iran, Israel, Taiwan and South Korea. The purpose was to create the impression that the South Vietnamese had a great many aircraft in their inventory at the time of the cease-fire so that they could continue receiving parts and replacements for a comparable number. (The Paris agreement allowed for this, since it authorized replacement of any "worn-out" military equipment after the cease-fire on a one-for-one basis.) The aid squeeze in late 1973, however, put a damper on these plans. Taiwan, South Korea and all the rest now wanted their aircraft back, but there was not enough money in the Vietnam aid budget to cover replacements for them, so Saigon was in danger of having its air force cannibalized. The only way the Pentagon could wriggle out of this dilemma was to press for higher aid allocations. Also, there was hope among Pentagon planners that as part of the replacement and transfer process, some of the new and more sophisticated F-5Es could be slipped to allies like Israel and South Korea.

and replaced William Rogers as Secretary of State. The following month the outbreak of hostilities in the Middle East had confronted him and the embattled Administration with a crisis of the first order, and although he had managed to arrange a cease-fire among the combatants, he was now facing the challenge of follow-up negotiations under the shadow of the Arab oil embargo. Against this backdrop the continuing unpleasantness of Vietnam seemed small beer indeed, particularly since, to all appearances, the war was dying away.*

But Graham Martin was not one to be easily upstaged. Early in the winter he began pushing the Administration toward a more active role in the aid debate, urging that plans be made to seek a supplemental appropriation should Congress finally emasculate the currently proposed budget. In addition, he began lobbying for a new economic aid program of sufficient magnitude to make South Vietnam self-reliant—or at least far less dependent on American support—within three years.

Throughout the winter Martin also attempted to turn diplomacy into a palliative for Saigon's ills. For the past several months French officials had been quietly working behind the scenes to try to arrange, through Chinese mediation, a cease-fire in Cambodia and the restoration of Norodom Sihanouk, who was still living in exile in Peking. In early December, Martin latched onto the idea and tried to adapt it to his own purposes. As he explained to me one night over cocktails, Cambodia in his opinion had always been a drain on American resources that could be better applied in Vietnam. Therefore, he was hopeful of persuading Kissinger to agree to the resurrection of Sihanouk, as the French proposed. If that happened and Sihanouk was returned to power, the burden of Cambodia's support, Martin predicted, would shift to the Chinese.

When Martin broached his idea to Kissinger, however, he found little enthusiasm for it. Kissinger detested Sihanouk and felt that withdrawal of U.S. backing for the Lon Nol regime would be seen in Peking and other foreign capitals as a sign of American weakness. Accordingly, although he made a perfunctory overture to the Chinese Foreign Minister several weeks later, in early April, he made no real effort to realize Martin's plan. "I don't want to hear about Laos-type compromises," he told John Dean, the U.S. Ambassador in Phnom Penh, who likewise saw Sihanouk as the key to peace. "Your job is to strengthen the military position so we can negotiate from strength." That would remain Kissinger's attitude toward a Cambodian settlement for the next half year.

Of all Martin's schemes for warding off the rigors of Congressional parsimony, perhaps the most sensible was the one that dealt most directly with the

---

*The number of weekly incidents was now roughly half of what it was in January 1973, at the time of the cease-fire, and far below the extremes of 1972. Casualties on both sides were also declining, as was evident from the table showing "allied killed and wounded per day," which I often displayed in my briefings at the time: 1969 — 78; 1970 — 70; 1971 — 64; 1972 — 128; 1973—39.

war itself. Even before the aid debate came to a head, he had worked out the basic outlines: since Congress seemed unlikely to vote sufficient money for Saigon's defense, then the obvious answer was to make its defense unnecessary. In mid-December, Martin proposed a specific line of march to Kissinger. The result was another round of secret negotiations with Le Duc Tho.

The meeting took place in Paris on 20 December. Kissinger flew in to conduct the discussions himself. He did not bother to invite the South Vietnamese, but he did ask Martin to sit in so that he could brief Thieu on the proceedings later on.

Throughout the session Kissinger played heavily on the immutability of the status quo in South Vietnam. The war was now stalemated, he told his old North Vietnamese debating partner; Thieu was unbeatable; and the Communists might as well try to reach an accommodation with him.

As an initial step, he urged a stand-down in the fighting in the Saigon area and the Mekong Delta and offered to see to it that Thieu recognized de facto lines of control in the central highlands and along the central coast. He also promised to nudge the South Vietnamese leader toward establishment of the National Council of National Reconciliation and Concord, the negotiating body that was to give the Communists some role in Saigon's political future.

Tho listened politely but would make no commitment. He could not. The Twenty-first Plenum, with its endorsement of the strategic-raids campaign, had already prejudged negotiations a dead end, at least for the moment.

Tho's inflexibility did not, however, dampen Martin's own enthusiasm. He was absolutely convinced, he later remarked to me, that some pretense toward political accommodation was vital to Saigon's survival in the face of the aid cuts. Therefore, when he returned to Saigon the day after the Paris meeting he began carefully pressing for concessions from the South Vietnamese themselves. He advised Thieu of the need to appear forthcoming on the issue of the National Council and urged him to consider a de facto delineation of the two sides' territories. As time passed, he also made a determined effort to keep both proposals before Le Duc Tho and his comrades in the Politburo. With White House approval, he passed a message to Hanoi through Polish intermediaries, calling on the North Vietnamese to reconsider. He also began cultivating the Polish and Hungarian ICCS delegations with a view to winning them over to his schemes. Since Polgar was already on friendly terms with the Hungarians, he became a primary conduit for the Ambassador's message—which was always the same: there was indeed a stalemate in the south; Thieu was strong and getting stronger; therefore, the only reasonable option for the Communists was to turn down the pressure.

While belaboring the Poles and Hungarians on Saigon's resiliency, Martin also attempted throughout the winter to translate what we knew of Hanoi's strength and intentions into an argument against further aid cuts. In a cable to Washington shortly after Christmas he set out his main themes: The North Vietnamese, he argued, were even now in a state of indecision and were weighing their options. Under these conditions, any further reduction in American support for Saigon would only galvanize their aggressive tendencies.

To give urgency to his pronouncements, Martin reminded Washington repeatedly of the belligerent side to Hanoi's planning, and coaxed both Polgar and Murray to highlight it in their own cables and intelligence appraisals. As it turned out, this was no easy task, for the latest agent reports made it clear that the strategic-raids campaign was to be a relatively modest undertaking, at least in terms of actual offensive military activity. The ever-hawkish analysts at DAO, however, chose to overlook this fact and did as the Ambassador wanted, playing on every grunt and growl from Radio Hanoi—and anything else that might tend to impute extreme aggressiveness to the "enemy" ("analysis by billingsgate," we called it in my shop).

For a while Polgar seemed tempted in the same direction. But finally he drew back, largely on the advice of friends and contacts in the Hungarian ICCS delegation, who assured him time and again during the winter that no major offensive activity was likely in 1974. Taking them at their word, he decided to accept our reports on the Twenty-first Plenum at face value and directed me to draft my field appraisals accordingly—with the emphasis on the modesty of Hanoi's immediate plans.

Because the Station's estimates did not quite suit his own aims, Martin quickly walled Polgar and the rest of us off from the American press. Previously, Station analysts, myself included, had been routinely called upon to provide "backgrounders" to journalists of the Ambassador's choice. But by mid-January, Al Francis, his favorite protégé, had assumed this role.

He performed it with considerable aplomb. Drawing his inspiration from the Ambassador and Murray's staff, he managed to convince a great many journalists that the North Vietnamese were preparing to launch a formidable new offensive in the weeks ahead. He also attempted (with less success) to intimidate those of us who disagreed. At one point he called me to his office and advised me Martin did not like the "tone" of the briefings I provided each Tuesday morning to the Mission Council, the Ambassador's senior staff. If I didn't change my tune, he intimated, Martin could always find another principal briefer. I nodded—but went on casting my briefings as I saw fit.

Francis' responsibilities expanded almost as rapidly as the Ambassador's stratagems, and from his vantage point as chief of the Embassy's political-military section he was able to put his, and Martin's, stamp on much of what the Mission produced. While he made no effort to interfere with CIA reporting, he saw to it that the Embassy's own regular intelligence publication—the Weekly Wrap-up—conformed to the Ambassador's purposes and point of view. Reports from State Department officers in the provinces, which portrayed the Communists as too benign, or the South Vietnamese as too aggressive, were systematically summarized and synthesized into oblivion. Staff investigators for the Senate Foreign Relations Committee later described the process in a report to Congress: "The Embassy is also known to make substantial deletions in reports from its Consulates General before relaying them to Washington. Earlier this year [1974], one of these posts reported to Saigon a serious deterioration in security within its military region. The message in question included five specific references to declining security conditions or poor performances on the part of government forces. In this instance, the text of the Consulate General's report was relayed to Washington, but only after the passages in question had been deleted, thereby eliminating significant aspects of the field assessment."

Despite the Ambassador's efforts to keep his staff in rein, "truths" prejudicial to his (and Saigon's) position in the aid debate continued to seep into the public media. In early January, for instance, an unknown source in the Embassy generated a series of newspaper reports which challenged his assessment of the security situation and South Vietnam's supply requirements. Almost at once he launched an investigation throughout the Mission to determine who the culprit was. His first suspect was the CIA Station.

Colonel Al Weidhas, one of Murray's intelligence officers, was put in charge of the inquiry. Because Weidhas and his subordinates were not equipped to handle sophisticated surveillance, they were obliged to borrow their telephone taps and their electronic bugs from the Station. We thus found ourselves in the curious position of contributing to the investigation that was being directed against us.

As the Station's principal strategy analyst, I was a prime target for Weidhas and his team. Ironically, it was through the press itself that I became aware of this. In the course of his dragnet Weidhas called George McArthur, correspondent for the *Los Angeles Times,* and asked him point-blank if I was the source of some of his recent news dispatches. McArthur (quite rightly) denied that I was and then phoned the Ambassador's office to protest. My friend Ken Moorefield, Martin's aide, took the call, and then, without informing anyone else, alerted me. When Martin learned what Moorefield had done he was apoplectic. Soon afterward Moorefield was shifted to another job in the Embassy and would never again enjoy the Ambassador's confidence.

That I should have been the focus of Martin's suspicions was quite a surprise to me. For the past few months I had been seeing his daughter Janet socially and had been a frequent guest at the Residence. Martin and I, in fact, had become fairly close, so much so that he would sit with me in his living room late into the evening, talking over ideas and theories and providing me with directives to pass on to Polgar. (It was during one of these after-hours séances that I learned of the latest Kissinger-Le Duc Tho talks in Paris. I was the first CIA officer in Saigon to be fully briefed on them.)

Eventually, Martin and Weidhas narrowed their list of suspects to an unfortunate few. Because Martin's own secretary, Eva Kim, was an old friend of McArthur's, the Ambassador felt she ought to be included in the number, and directed Weidhas to watch her house and bug her telephone. No incriminating evidence (aside from a few indiscreet remarks about the boss) was ever uncovered.

At last, after days of snooping, Weidhas managed to nail his man. He discovered that one of Martin's own trusted aides, Dick Peters, tended to talk too much during casual golf games with McArthur out on the soggy links at the DAO compound. To substantiate his suspicions, Weidhas planted one of his own men, armed with a directional microphone, in Peters' foursome. Peters' idle banter was duly recorded and the findings handed over to Martin. Several weeks later Peters was transferred to the consulate in Bien Hoa, far from the center of decision-making.

Not content to deal with troublesome leaks at their source, Martin also began taking swipes at the press itself. In early February, when a story in the *New York Times* accused the United States of violating the spirit of the Paris agreement by providing sophisticated technical aid to Saigon, he sent a long cable to Washington intimating that the reporter was a mouthpiece of Hanoi, and barred any further Embassy contacts with the *Times* or the *Washington Post*. In a letter to the Senate Foreign Relations Committee, he explained why: "I feel no compulsion at all to grant interviews to reporters from papers whose emotional involvement in a North Vietnamese victory is transparently clear and whose reporting, features and editorials combine to present gross and blatant distortions to the public. To do so would permit my own reputation for integrity to be used as a platform to deceive the American people, and this I simply will not do, no matter what the personal cost."*

Nor did Martin limit his jibes to the press. He had no qualms about taking on some of the most powerful members of Congress, if it might serve his purposes. One of his primary targets during the winter months was Senator Edward Kennedy, who was fast becoming an outspoken opponent of additional support for Saigon. When Kennedy asked the State Department in February if an increase in aid would amount to a new commitment to Thieu, Martin advised his colleagues in Washington that "it would be the height of folly to give an honest and detailed answer" to him. The cable was immediately leaked by a Kennedy sympathizer, to Martin's own discredit.

One of the Ambassador's most celebrated assaults on the "opposition," however, was directed not at Congressman, colleague or newsman, but at a theologian—Reverend William Webber of the New York Theological Seminary, who visited Saigon in February with a group dominated by anti-Thieu activists. During the first week and a half of his tour Webber studiously

---

*Martin's suspicions of the press were not altogether unjustified. When North Vietnamese troops entered Saigon a year later, reporters who had stayed behind to cover the takeover for the Associated Press discovered that one of their primary Vietnamese photographers had long been a covert Communist party member. In addition, a reporter for the *Washington Post* informed Martin after Saigon's collapse that one of the newspaper's Vietnamese "stringers" apparently had been working secretly for the Communists for years.

avoided the Embassy, but just before leaving he dropped in on Martin for a chat. In the course of their discussions, which Martin had taped, the Ambassador asked Webber to contact his "friends" on the Communist side and plead with them to stop the bloodshed. He even gave Webber the number of the PRG delegation to the Joint Military Commission at Tan Son Nhut. Webber, already suspicious of Martin and resentful of the suggestion he had influence with the Communists, declined to make the call, advising the Ambassador the next day that the number he had given him was a wrong one.

Weeks later, when incoming artillery rounds killed nearly a hundred children in a town in the Mekong Delta, Martin sent photographs of the maimed and dying victims to Webber, now back in the United States. "No one can be certain your intervention would have saved these children," the Ambassador remarked in a covering note. "It is my judgment that it might well have had a determining influence. But for the rest of your life you will have to live with the unresolvable doubt that but for your decision not to call, these dead children might still be alive, and these horribly maimed children might still be whole. As an American, I cringe inwardly when local representatives of some of the great humanitarian American volunteer agencies bitterly refer to these children as 'Doctor Webber's wrong numbers.' "

As time went on, such antics as these naturally gained Martin a great deal of public attention. But whether he accomplished anything more than a publicity coup remained very much in doubt. There were, in fact, some of us who considered his tactics counterproductive. His insistence on the criticalness of additional aid as a salve for South Vietnamese morale, for example, quickly became self-fulfilling, and the virulence of his attacks on his critics in the press and elsewhere seemed only to polarize feelings in Congress itself.*

By early February it was clear that Congress' mind was made up. The Pentagon advised Murray in Saigon that although a final effort would be made to restore what had been cut from the aid budget, it had little chance of success.

The news cemented Murray's thinking on an important matter. Despite Martin's reluctance to alert the Vietnamese to the bleak aid prospects, he decided the time had come at least to urge them to tighten their belts. Meeting quietly with Saigon's top commanders, he began preaching conservation.

---

*Realizing how difficult Congress could be, Martin developed yet another plan for influencing its attitudes during a brief trip to Washington early in 1974. In a meeting with Tran Kim Phuong, Saigon's Ambassador to the United States, he outlined his ideas for a Vietnamese-sponsored "public relations" campaign on Capitol Hill to reinforce the Administration's aid drive. When Phuong protested that such an effort might be beyond the budget of his own Embassy, Martin replied, "If you need money, perhaps we can provide it." Phuong rejected the offer, however. In his view, the use of American funds to support a lobbying effort directed at Congress by a foreign government was both unethical and politically dangerous. Nonetheless, he did ask Martin to suggest to Thieu that funds be made available for this purpose from Saigon's own budget. As it turned out, the proposal never got very far. Hoang Duc Nha demanded that the funds be channeled through his Information Ministry, while officials of the Foreign Ministry insisted the prerogative was theirs. The controversy was never resolved, and Congress was spared the ministrations of a Saigon lobby.

His advice and entreaties must have come as a surprise to some of them. Most of Saigon's military elite knew that their supply needs were not as severe as Murray supposed. But rather than admit this to him—or attempt to eliminate the corruption that was still siphoning off vital supplies—they agreed to do exactly as he proposed. As one high-ranking South Vietnamese official later told me, they were convinced that by showing themselves agreeable to the Americans, they could retain their support.

Accordingly, they moved at once to impose strict new quotas on the amount of matériel and equipment issued to troops in the field. So arbitrary were the restrictions, and so hastily applied, they finally did far more damage to the army's capabilities than was necessary. Each of the four military regions in the country was saddled with roughly the same ammunition and matériel quotas, regardless of the widely varying level of combat from one area to another. Previously, the average foot soldier had gone into battle with ten hand grenades on his belt; now he was to be limited to two, whether he was fighting guerrillas in the delta or North Vietnamese regulars in the northernmost provinces. Over half of the available armored vehicles were taken out of commission to conserve petroleum; bombing missions and harassing artillery fire against all but clearly identified targets were cut back; and nearly one-fifth of the South Vietnamese air force was grounded.

In the final analysis, Murray could not have asked for more. It was as if Saigon's top commanders were determined to be as ruthless in their plans and calculations as he. The trouble was that their devotion to the American way did not take account of the Vietnamese foot soldier. It was he who ended up on the short end of the supply line as Murray's quotas were imposed; it was he who was abandoned to an indefensible outpost without air or artillery support while the generals wallowed in American esteem.*

---

*The irrationality and, indeed, the criminality of Saigon's approach to the supply problem were later highlighted in a report by the General Accounting Office, Congress' auditing arm. In a study released in April 1975 GAO reported that major pieces of equipment had actually been sitting ignored and unused in Saigon's warehouses throughout the past two years, even as the Defense Attaché's Office continued to request delivery of the same items from stockpiles in the United States. In addition, according to the report, over $200 million worth of matériel had been lost or squandered by the South Vietnamese during the same period (excluding what had been abandoned to the Communists as a result of military setbacks). Large amounts of equipment, it said, had been stolen or sold illegally to the Communists. Among the items listed as "missing" or "unaccounted for": 143 small warships valued at $37 million; $2 million worth of ammunition, rendered unusable because of poor storage; and $10 million in small arms which had simply disappeared from supply depots. GAO also pointed out that American and South Vietnamese auditors had never kept complete or continuous records of South Vietnam's stockpiles. At the time of the Paris agreement, for instance, there had been no comprehensive accounting of the amount of American equipment assigned to the South Vietnamese air force or navy, and although American auditors did have a record of what was assigned to the army, their accountings differed substantially from South Vietnam's own. As a result, noted GAO, the Pentagon and the Defense Attaché's Office, in an effort to reconcile the separate balance sheets, simply wrote off $44 million in military aid—four percent of the total recorded value of U.S. assistance—during the two years following the cease-fire. The American taxpayer, in short, was asked to subsidize Saigon's corruption, and the Vietnamese foot soldier was obliged to die for it.

As Saigon's top command strained to do Murray's bidding, the politicians downtown in the Presidential Palace struggled with another piece of American advice. From the moment Martin returned from his meeting with Le Duc Tho in late December, Thieu's closest advisors had been worrying and debating the two proposals put forward there: the possible creation of the National Council and the de facto delineation of areas of control in the western highlands and in the borderland north of Saigon.

The demarcation concept proved particularly controversial. Hoang Duc Nha, Thieu's powerful cousin, was totally opposed to it, on the grounds that any kind of retrenchment, territorial or otherwise, could lead to an unraveling no one could stop. But General Cao Van Vien, chairman of the South Vietnamese Joint General Staff, was more favorably disposed; so was Prime Minister Tran Thien Khiem, who as a long-time friend of the Embassy was only too willing to bend with the American winds. As Khiem later explained to an associate, he was convinced by early February that the country had only two options: "It could continue to fight and suffer defeat or it could negotiate and cede part of its territory to the Communists to gain time."

Thieu himself stood somewhere in the middle of the debate. Still committed to his "Four No's"—including "no territorial concessions"—he could not believe that the Americans would force him to back off from them. Nor did he appreciate the constraints under which the Administration in Washington was operating. He was still convinced the Americans would come to his assistance with bombers if necessary, in spite of the Cambodia bombing ban and the War Powers Act. Indeed, during a year-end review Hoang Duc Nha was horrified to discover that only he among Thieu's closest advisors had ever seen a copy of either piece of legislation.

For all his confidence in the Americans, however, Thieu remained chronically suspicious and cautious, and as Martin continued to preach to him on the virtues of demarcation and the National Council, he decided he had better take some steps to strengthen his position, just in case he was forced to agree to the American proposals. Consequently, in mid-February, even as Murray's quotas went into effect, he ordered the high command to launch a new and costly land-grabbing campaign to shore up the government's holdings in the southern half of the country.

The drive kicked off almost immediately. One ARVN division pushed into a promontory of Cambodian territory, known as the "Parrot's Beak," northwest of Saigon, while another lunged into a contested area in the northern delta, "Tri Phap," long a Communist supply base. In the most daring maneuver of all, two full ARVN divisions mounted a massive search-and-destroy operation into the so-called "Iron Triangle," a heavily forested area due north of Saigon.

To ward off criticism abroad, Thieu borrowed some of Martin's hyperbole, warning that the North Vietnamese were preparing to launch a "major offensive" and had to be preempted. In a speech before the Vietnamese Council on Foreign Relations in March, Hoang Duc Nha made the government's essential case, arguing that the leaders in Hanoi were reassessing their policies and would probably go on the attack in the fall of 1974. Although his remarks echoed Martin's own line, the Ambassador was not pleased with them. He feared the young Information Minister was becoming too independent. From that point on, Nha's days were numbered.

While the South Vietnamese pursued their new "grand strategy," Congress rendered judgment on Martin's own. On 3 April the Senate Armed Services Committee voted not to increase the current Vietnam aid budget at all, and within twenty-four hours the full House followed suit.

When Thieu himself learned of the action he was dumfounded. For the first time, according to several of his closest advisors, he seemed to realize that what Martin had been telling him about the resiliency of American support was overdrawn. But how to be sure? To satisfy himself, he decided to put American sympathies, and tolerance, to a final test—by withdrawing from the bilateral talks with the PRG in Paris. He knew he would need a strong pretext for such a drastic move, lest he be condemned at home and abroad for bad faith. And together he, Nha and several other officials devised a scheme to provide one. Their plan had only one drawback: it involved overstepping Thieu's own cardinal rule against surrendering territory to the Communists.

For over a year the small outpost of Tong Le Chan, north of Saigon, had been under siege by NVA forces. Despite its negligible military value, Thieu had held on to it to underscore his commitment to the "Four No's." Now he decided to make it serve a more useful purpose. By letting it fall to the Communists, he reasoned, he could generate enough sympathy in the United States and elsewhere to justify the "countermeasures" he planned to take against the PRG—and perhaps to catalyze support for himself in the American Congress. The beleaguered 200-man garrison was duly informed of his decision by radio, and on 11 April all of its defenders, including sixty-two wounded, slipped away into the bush, with the tacit acquiescence of the surrounding NVA units, which were delighted to be handed such a bloodless victory.

The following day the government charged publicly that Tong Le Chan had been "overrun" in a "massive North Vietnamese ground attack" and that the entire garrison had been lost. Thieu then "reacted politically," in the words of the State Department announcement, by refusing to participate any longer in the bilateral talks in Paris and by withdrawing once again the "privileges and immunities" guaranteed to the PRG delegates at Tan Son Nhut under the Paris agreement. Telephone lines to their compound were cut off; their press conferences were canceled; and the weekly liaison flights to the PRG headquarters at Loc Ninh, north of Saigon, were suspended indefinitely.

The Embassy was well aware of the charade from the beginning. Intelligence reports revealed that not one member of Tong Le Chan's garrison had fallen in battle on the day it was supposedly "overrun." But like Thieu, Martin saw the episode as an opportunity to tweak the conscience of Congress, and he therefore skirted the truth in all but the most highly classified Embassy reporting to Washington. Kissinger, for his part, though unhappy about the collapse of the bilateral talks, was equally indulgent of Thieu's public claims, presumably because he, too, believed the "tragedy" could be turned to political profit in Congress.*

As it happened, Thieu achieved more than he had bargained for. In protest over his actions, the PRG walked out of the Joint Military Commission in Saigon, and along with Hanoi, ended its participation in ongoing discussions over the status of servicemen missing in action. These boycotts remained in effect till the last day of the war.

The abandonment of Tong Le Chan and the breakdown of the JMC and the bilateral negotiations in Paris marked the end of the last vestiges of Kissinger's peace in Vietnam. By early summer none of the organs established to implement or enforce the Paris agreement was functioning, and all exchanges on the issue that still linked Americans emotionally to Vietnam—the MIA question—had come to an end. Moreover, the South Vietnamese, out of reaction to American political initiatives, were back on the offensive.

---

*So complete was the secrecy surrounding the events at Tong Le Chan that Saigon's own Ambassador to Washington, Tran Kim Phuong, was not informed of what had actually happened. Only later, during a trip to Saigon, did he learn that the outpost had been abandoned, not overrun as the government claimed. The discovery infuriated him, since he had put his own prestige on the line in Washington in defending the "official version." He pressured Thieu to keep him better informed of military developments in the future so he could more effectively represent the government's position to the Americans. Thieu virtually ignored this request, and before long Phuong was relying on CIA friends for information on the military situation in his own country. Theodore Shackley, head of the agency's East Asia Division, became Phuong's primary contact and frequently briefed him in his own office at CIA headquarters in Langley, Virginia. This must surely be one of the few instances in which the CIA has become directly involved in running a foreign mission in Washington.

Fiscal Whores

As Thieu tried to adapt to the quirks and turns of American policy in the late winter and early spring of 1974, the North Vietnamese did likewise. Like Thieu, they found the Americans' renewed interest in territorial demarcation deeply unsettling—but for somewhat different reasons. Because of the meagerness of their holdings in the south, any partitioning of territory, de facto or otherwise, would have left them in a decidedly unfavorable position vis-à-vis the government. They would have preferred to ignore the proposal altogether. But they could not. With the Poles and Hungarians serving as messengers for the U.S. Embassy, pressure obviously was building toward some kind of deal, and they knew that if they were to make the best of it, they would have to grab as much territory as possible beforehand. That meant escalating the strategic-raids campaign beyond what they had intended.

Shifting course was not going to be easy, particularly since the Central Committee's Twenty-second Plenum had already set the regime on the path toward reconstruction. The hawks, however, had recently been handed new political ammunition. The Communist victories in Quang Duc in November and December had proven that NVA forces could play aggressor without provoking immediate American retaliation, and with Thieu himself now clearly on the offensive, the logic of a response in kind was almost irresistible.

In early March the party's top military experts, meeting in an old French villa at number 33 Pham Ngu Lao Street in Hanoi, decided to push the strategic raids to new limits. Not only would Communist forces continue to strike at the foundations of the South Vietnamese economy—roads, storage facilities and airfields—but from now through the summer they would also seek to regain territory lost since the cease-fire.

A few weeks later, as Thieu was preparing to abandon Tong Le Chan, the North Vietnamese set their plan in motion. One NVA division stabbed into the western border areas northwest of Saigon, while other Communist units moved to tie down the 18th ARVN Division, east of the capital. Several weeks later yet another division thrust deep into the "Iron Triangle" north of Saigon to counter ARVN clearing operations there. Once again the war was in full bloom.

In the meantime, the Nixon Administration girded itself for another round with Congress on the aid question. Even as Senator Kennedy and the anti-aid lobby voted down additional money for the current fiscal year, Martin and his allies in the State Department and the Pentagon were conjuring up a proposal for the next one. Assuming that Congress would again prove parsimonious, they deliberately inflated their recommendations so that once the inevitable cuts were made, there would still be enough meat left on the bone to sustain the South Vietnamese. Martin himself suggested the target figure for military aid: $1.45 billion.

Throughout April and May all of us in the Embassy pitched in to promote the new proposal. General Murray and several other senior Mission officials even flew to Washington to coax and persuade the recalcitrants in Congress. But by the time the first roll call was taken, it was obvious they might as well have saved the air fare. On 22 May the House trimmed the Administration's proposal by $300 million, and clearly the fight was only beginning.

When Murray returned to Saigon at the end of the month he was deeply depressed. Convinced that Congress was bent on turning Saigon into a military invalid, he resolved to do all he could to prevent it.

A cable from the Pentagon soon gave him an opportunity. Essentially it was a request for an "impact" assessment of the likely consequences of further aid cuts. Murray decided to turn his reply into a mind-bending exercise, calculated to reshape Washington's perspectives. He filed his message to the Pentagon on 1 June.

Given the level of aid under consideration for the next fiscal year, he asserted, the South Vietnamese would not be "capable of defending against a sustained major offensive." Any further reductions, in his view, would mean surrendering territory: "You can roughly equate cuts in support to a loss of real estate. As the cutting edge of the RVNAF is blunted and the enemy continues to improve its combat position and logistical base, what will occur is a retreat to the Saigon-delta area as a redoubt."

In particular, he went on, if the upcoming appropriation dropped much below the $1 billion mark—to $750 million, for example—the South Vietnamese would be in a position to "defend only select areas of the country." If donations slipped even further, "write off the Republic of Vietnam as a bad investment and a broken promise. The government would do well to hang on to Saigon and the delta."

It was an extraordinary prognosis—a logistician's answer to historical determinism—and tendentious in the extreme, since no one, either on Murray's own staff or in Washington, was sure how much equipment the South Vietnamese still had tucked away in the nooks and crannies of their supply system. Even so, Murray was ready to insist that without at least $1 billion in military aid South Vietnam would literally shrivel to a shadow of its former self.

This projection became a primary weapon in the general's own assault on Congress, and he did everything he could to make its cold edge felt in Washington. During June and July he and several officers from Admiral Gayler's Pacific Command headquarters in Honolulu whipped up a briefing, complete with maps and charts, to illustrate its central thesis—namely, that anything less than $1 billion in aid would mean the end of South Vietnam as we now knew it.

When Martin heard of the briefing he was delighted. Although he did not share Murray's extreme sense of pessimism, he was hopeful that by playing on the dangers he might be able to rally Congress to Saigon's support. He therefore directed Murray to turn his maps, charts and his briefer over to him. The presentation, he insisted, would have far greater impact in Washington if it appeared to have originated with him.

Martin's decision to adopt the briefing and the underlying thesis was the "death knell" of both, Murray later commented. In a cable to the Pentagon, explaining the need and indeed the logic of truncation in the face of further aid cuts, the Ambassador managed to set Defense Secretary James Schlesinger and most of his principal staffers against the concept by suggesting they had been remiss in not thinking of it themselves. "The message," Murray noted, "sent Schlesinger through the roof because the insinuation was that Schlesinger's people didn't know what they were doing, the whole Pentagon didn't know what it was doing, and only Graham Martin had the solutions."

Although Murray and Martin did not succeed in sensitizing the Pentagon to the possibility of truncation, they had somewhat better luck with the Vietnamese. On the basis of projections Murray fed to them, Saigon's top commanders drew up a study of their own in midsummer showing that they would indeed have to give up territory if Congress cut the aid budget any further. Some of them considered the exercise merely a propaganda ploy, to influence Congress, but the majority took its basic premise—if not the practicality of an actual retrenchment—to heart. Prime Minister Khiem, ever trustful of the Americans, repeatedly emphasized to Thieu and the cabinet the interrelationship between high aid levels and maintenance of their current defense lines, and in early August, during a trip to the country's northernmost provinces, he warned the regional commander that it might be necessary to surrender real estate there to buy time. Meanwhile, Hoang Duc Nha conducted a contingency study of his own to determine how all 3,000,000 people in the northern quarter of the country might be efficiently moved to the Saigon area and the delta if truncation became necessary.

As the prospect of discarding "marginal" territory continued to be debated inside the government, those who favored it received a boost from an unexpected quarter. Several months before, a retired Australian brigadier general named Ted Sarong had come to Saigon to look for a job as an unofficial military advisor to Thieu. Sarong had first met the South Vietnamese leader in the early 1960s and now he was hopeful of trading on that friendship to win

a seat at court. Realizing that truncation was a live consideration, he quickly
latched onto it as an entrée.

Neither Thieu nor the Americans ever took Sarong very seriously. Murray considered him a "fake" and the rest of us in the Embassy were advised
explicitly to stay away from "that kook." But through unofficial contacts with
Thieu's security advisor, General Quang, Sarong did manage from time to time
to put in a word on behalf of the truncation concept, and in so doing, helped
to keep it alive within Thieu's inner circle.

Thieu himself was as opposed to truncation as he was to Martin's demarcation scheme. Under no circumstances was he ready to give up large chunks
of territory, as Murray (and Sarong) contemplated. He did not feel this was
necessary for any reason, political, fiscal, or otherwise. But he was convinced,
as Martin was, that if Congress could be made to believe that a drastic retrenchment was a possibility, it might respond more sympathetically to the
plea for additional aid. He therefore asked General Vien for a copy of the JCS
truncation plan, and for the next month or so, whenever American Congressmen passed through Saigon, he would unfurl it and proclaim sadly that "this
is what will happen if Congress is not more forthcoming."

Some of Thieu's subordinates were annoyed by his cynicism. They felt he
did not fully appreciate the problems facing him and should take the truncation prospect more seriously. In a sense they were right, at least about his
failure to grasp the problems. Despite the shock of the latest aid cuts, Thieu
still did not sense how fragile the American umbilical cord had become. Nor
was he altogether to blame for this. In a deliberate effort to keep him calm and
collected, Martin and other Embassy officials had continued to nurture the
illusion that Congress could be turned around, and had done their utmost to
minimize Nixon's political travails. In early June, at a cocktail party marking
South Vietnam's Armed Forces Day, Polgar emphatically assured a group of
top government officials that "the worst is over" in the Watergate affair.

Thieu later repeated this assessment in a cabinet meeting. Indeed, he
remained so confident of Nixon's staying power he couldn't accept the truth
even when it was staring him in the face. On 24 July, when news reached
Saigon that the tapes of certain White House conversations had been sub-
poenaed, Nha told Thieu that Nixon was finished and that they had better
begin charting a new political course for themselves. Thieu retorted, "Such
pessimism is crazy."

Martin himself spent much of the summer in Washington, stumping for
the Administration's aid requests. In June and July he appeared before several
key Congressional committees to make his case, which he now had down like
a religious litany. "It is now crystal-clear," he told one group, "that the North
Vietnamese cannot conquer the South militarily." Instead, "what they are
counting on is that their propaganda campaign, which has been mounted with
some success in Europe and with great success here will erode [American]

economic support to the Republic of Vietnam to the extent that it will affect both [Saigon's] political unity and military morale." Martin's predictable antidote for all this was a resounding show of American confidence in South Vietnam through yet another massive dose of aid.

In setting forth his arguments, the Ambassador did some exquisite waffling on the question of Soviet and Chinese aid to Hanoi, claiming that while their military assistance had dropped in the past few months, their economic donations made American aid to Saigon look like a starvation diet by comparison. To underscore this judgment, he declassified and handed out to his Congressional audiences a memorandum I had recently prepared for him on the subject. The study was based on intelligence I had obtained from informants I myself was running in North Vietnam. Martin's precipitous disclosures very nearly led to their exposure. But apparently winning votes in Congress was more important to him than protecting a few intelligence operatives.

While the Ambassador waged his battle on Capitol Hill, Polgar and several State Department colleagues devoted much of their time during the summer to trying to convince the Polish and Hungarian ICCS teams that territorial demarcation really was in everybody's interest. In the course of the exercise the CIA Station resorted to a ploy that may be unique in the annals of American intelligence. On Kissinger's authority I was directed to provide a full intelligence briefing to the Hungarian ICCS delegates in Saigon. The object: to convince them—and through them, Hanoi—that we were fully aware of North Vietnamese plans and that the military stalemate was here to stay.

The briefing was as candid and straightforward as I dared make it. While avoiding any reference to our intelligence-gathering techniques, I outlined what we knew of the latest North Vietnamese policy decisions, including those of the Twenty-first Plenum, and provided my astounded audience with a fairly complete rundown on the relative strengths of the two sides. It was the kind of intelligence the North Vietnamese would have squandered a great deal of blood and treasure to obtain.

Yet the briefing was only the beginning. During the next several months Polgar continued to feed sensitive data to contacts in the Hungarian delegation in the belief they would be prompted to nudge Hanoi to the conference table. In his zeal to appear forthcoming he occasionally became careless. In one session he unveiled a chart I had prepared for him for other purposes which revealed not only what we knew of NVA force dispositions but also how we had secured the information—"our sources and methods." I had warned him to review the chart beforehand, but he had forgotten. His oversight resulted in the exposure of several of our most closely guarded secrets.

As Martin had hoped, our message to the ICCS did not fall on deaf ears. By the end of July both the Polish and Hungarian team members had informed their own capitals that the South Vietnamese had the military initiative. The

North Vietnamese in turn had begun altering their own policies to fit this fact. Toward the end of the month the Politburo sent a new directive to troops in the south, advising them for the first time that demarcation of areas of control and the establishment of the National Council might occur in the near future —and warning them to prepare for hard last-minute fighting.

At the same time Hanoi took steps to ensure its maneuverability in this new political environment. During the summer Le Duc Tho was sent off to Paris to recruit supporters among Vietnamese exile groups who might be called upon to provide nominees for the neutralist "third segment" of the National Council. In addition, four new "corps commands" were created to control the movement and garrisoning of troops throughout South Vietnam. Although they were all well suited to coordinating major offensive operations—and would be adapted to this purpose in the spring of 1975—their initial purpose was to facilitate the care and feeding of large infantry units once the two sides agreed on areas of control.

Through agents and other intelligence sources the Embassy immediately became aware of these new elements in Hanoi's planning. Yet because so few of us had been briefed on the Ambassador's specific plans concerning demarcation, it was difficult to put the intelligence in perspective. Throughout August my colleagues and I, in our ignorance, continually debated the significance of Hanoi's sudden interest in the issue.

If Martin managed to swing Hanoi around to his viewpoint, Congress continued to be far less malleable. In spite of his impassioned testimony in June and July, one Congressional committee after another took a bite out of the Administration's latest aid proposals. Watergate was partly responsible. President Nixon's prestige had slipped to such depths, he was now almost powerless to influence Congress on anything. Another source of the Administration's troubles was Martin himself. He and Murray had made so many grandiose and often dubious claims about Saigon's needs and potential, Congress did not know what to believe. In a belated effort to resolve the confusion Senator John Stennis, head of the powerful Senate Armed Services Committee, proposed in midsummer that the Pentagon appoint a single individual to nail down what Saigon actually needed. Defense Secretary Schlesinger gave the job to Erich Von Marbod, one of the most experienced civilian logisticians on his staff.

On the basis of his own surveys Von Marbod quickly concluded Martin and his Defense Attaché had overshot the mark in their latest aid recommendations. While the $1.4 billion they had proposed would obviously be a comfortable nest egg, he felt the South Vietnamese could get by with less.

Congress took him at his word and in late July a Senate-House conference voted to impose a ceiling of $1 billion on all military spending for Vietnam during the next eleven months. On 5 August, Nixon signed the legislation into law. It was one of his last acts as President. Four days later he resigned.

But the aid debate was far from over. The $1 billion ceiling was no more than that—a ceiling on spending. Congress still had to appropriate funds to cover the actual allocation, and what it had given with one hand it could take with the other. Within a day or two of Nixon's departure it became clear it was prepared to do just that. The House voted to cut the annual appropriation to $700 million.

In the meantime, as Von Marbod tried to tidy up the Vietnam account he found himself increasingly at loggerheads with Murray. During the past month, in his own efforts to make the latest allocations go further, the Defense Attaché had been trying to slip some of DAO's overhead costs into other Pentagon budgets. But Von Marbod would have none of this, and in early August informed Murray that all such costs would be applied against the Vietnam aid account. Some quick arithmetic revealed that if this was done, the effective value of the prospective $700 million allocation would slip to less than $450 million.

In the midst of all this budgetary confusion the new President of the United States, Gerald Ford, sent a personal letter to Thieu assuring him of continued support. Drafted by Martin with Kissinger's approval, it was an explicit reassertion of American commitments to Vietnam at a time when Congress was giving every indication it opposed strengthening them. "I know you must be concerned by the initial steps taken by Congress on the current fiscal year appropriations for both economic and military assistance to the Republic of Vietnam," Ford stated in the letter. "Our legislative process is a complicated one and it is not yet completed. Although it may take a little time I do want to assure you of my confidence that in the end our support will be adequate on both counts.

"In these important endeavors I shall look to Dr. Kissinger, whom I have asked to remain as Secretary of State, for guidance and support. He has my fullest confidence, as does Ambassador Martin."

Thieu reacted to the letter as Martin had hoped, interpreting it as a sign, however tenuous, of continued U.S. backing. For Murray, however, the missive seemed a cruel and ugly mockery. "It was a stupid letter and a commitment," he later remarked. "And citing Kissinger for support—the Benedict Arnold of diplomats to the Vietnamese—is like telling the Israelis we look to [Egyptian President Anwar] Sadat for guidance."

But what most concerned the Defense Attaché was the intimation that American aid to Saigon would be "adequate." In view of Von Marbod's strictures and the latest Congressional budgetary action, he had persuaded himself it would be anything but that. In his "impact" study at the beginning of the summer he had concluded that if American aid slipped below the $700 million mark Saigon might as well be written off as a "bad investment." Now, with the effective value of the pending aid package reduced to $450 million, he was staring his own worst nightmare in the face.

A decent and sensitive man, Murray reacted from the heart. By mid-August he had become "bitter and disillusioned," in his own words. To one of his staffers he looked like "the bottom of hell." He had already decided to retire from the Army because his name had not appeared on the most recent promotion list, and knowing he had nothing to lose, he resolved to let Von Marbod and the Pentagon know exactly how he felt about their economies and the latest reductions in the aid budget. In a series of unauthorized press interviews he charged that the South Vietnamese were being forced to substitute "bodies, bone and blood for bullets" and he bitterly described the budget-makers in the Pentagon as "fiscal whores."

"We set one standard for ourselves and another for the Vietnamese," he told a reporter. "If an American officer began to take casualties, he would stop and call in the air and artillery and generally blast the hell out of the enemy positions. Today the South Vietnamese are forced to hoard their air power and artillery, and so they get more people killed and wounded. It's not only sadistic, it's racist."

Martin, who was still in Washington trying to patch things up, was enraged by Murray's remarks, and the Pentagon's chief public relations officer let the general know by fast cable that his candor had not been appreciated.

But Murray was undeterred. Having leveled with the press, he was now determined to do the same with the Vietnamese, and he called Martin long distance to ask permission. As he noted in his record of the conversation, "the Ambassador was somewhat irritated. He told me to tell General [Cao Van] Vien and [Dang Van] Khuyen [the army chief of staff] that all was not lost. When the votes came on the Senate floor, it will be a new ball game with a new President. He told me to tell them that. I told him I would, but in my own mind I have never really bought this business of a honeymoon euphoria for Ford. That Ambassador would be an optimist with a blowtorch up his butt."

In the end Murray did not follow Martin's orders; instead he spread his gloom to the Vietnamese. In a final meeting with Saigon's top commanders on 16 August he and other American officers pleaded with them to give up territory and adopt an enclave-type strategy to conserve their resources. Vien and Khuyen agreed that the idea was militarily sound, but politically, they said, it was still out of the question.

Murray left the meeting convinced that the South Vietnamese were doomed, and a day or so later, in a tearful farewell to his Embassy colleagues, he bade all of us to do what we could to help them, "for they're going to need all the help they can get."

On his way back to the United States, Murray stopped off in Honolulu for a brief chat with Admiral Gayler. He made no effort to conceal his despondency. When Gayler asked him what changes he would make in U.S. policy in Vietnam, he replied without hesitation, "First, fire the Ambassador; second, cut the [South Vietnamese] air force down to the number of planes they can maintain . . . and make sure the Congress understands the [adverse] effect."

Murray also warned Gayler flatly that without proper support the South Vietnamese were going to lose—"maybe not next week or next month, but after the year they are going to go through." The key to Hanoi's intentions, he added, was the status of the six reserve divisions that were being built up in North Vietnam. If one or more of them were sent south, the prospect for major military activity would increase proportionately. "Watch those six enemy divisions," he repeated as he shook Gayler's hand. "Watch them like a flute player watches a cobra."

As Murray was about to leave Gayler's headquarters he received a call from General Homer Smith, the jut-jawed, soft-spoken logistician who was to replace him as Defense Attaché in Saigon. Smith was in Honolulu boning up on his new job, and he was beginning to realize what horrors were in store for him. "I've just finished two days of briefings," he exclaimed to Murray, "and Jesus Christ, I feel like I've been shot at and hit."

"It is the usual syndrome," Murray replied gloomily. "The further you get away from Washington, the closer you get to reality."

Murray's outlook at the time of his departure had a deep and subtle effect on the South Vietnamese. Although they could not bring themselves to give up territory, as he advised, his recommendations and contingency studies to this effect produced a mind-set among them, a kind of fatalism that would help condition their responses to the trials ahead. The American military command-er had said they could not survive if U.S. aid slipped far below the $700 million level. With the worst now a reality, they became ever more convinced their future was out of their hands and that all depended on direct American support and intervention. Their morale took on the very fragility of the Ameri-can commitment itself.

Within hours of Nixon's resignation the coffeehouses along Tu Do Street in downtown Saigon were buzzing with a chilling rumor. Earlier that morning, so the story went, a huge rock perched atop a grotto in President Thieu's native village of Tri Thuy on the central coast had miraculously split in two. The way the local soothsayers told it, the event was clearly an ill omen.

No doubt Thieu himself viewed Nixon's passing with some trepidation, despite the reassuring letter from the new President. Nixon had been a pro-vider and protector, and had he not received poor advice from Kissinger, Thieu believed, South Vietnam would have fared far better in the past year and a half.

But the political turmoil in Washington was scarcely Thieu's only worry as the summer drew to a close. The war itself was now very much with him. In the nineteen months since the cease-fire over 26,000 of his troops had died in battle (NVA casualties were reportedly five times that number), and the Communists' strategic-raids campaign had accomplished part of its objective, weakening the South Vietnamese economy and producing new pressures within the society. In the western highlands NVA units had expanded their supply lines eastward toward the coast, whipsawing two ARVN divisions in the process, and had looped Kontum and Pleiku Cities with interlocking road networks that were like a hangman's noose waiting to be drawn tight. Although NVA probes in the immediate Saigon area, to the north and east of the capital, had recently been blunted, the 5th and the 18th ARVN Divisions had suffered heavy casualties, particularly in the "Iron Triangle," and were now exhausted and overextended. In the Mekong Delta security had recently plummeted as Communist units tried to recapture base camps lost to the government earlier in the year. They had yet to recover any of the principal ones, but they had driven deep into contested territory, particularly in the central and southern parts of the region, where they now controlled just about everything but the province and district capitals.

During the pivotal month of August the level of fighting throughout the country continued to climb, reaching a new high for the cease-fire, as the Communists moved to test President Ford's reflexes and to prepare for territorial demarcation. By early September NVA initiatives near Hué and Danang in the northernmost provinces of the country had displaced over 700,000 villagers, thus completely reversing the gains the government had made in its refugee resettlement program since the cease-fire.

These setbacks immediately touched the morale of the population. According to a public-opinion survey conducted by the government at the end of the summer, popular confidence in its performance and in its ability to defend the population was now at its lowest ebb since 1968.

Morale within the army also was wearing thin. With the ever-tightening quotas on the use of supplies and ammunition, the Vietnamese foot soldier was beginning to feel the hard edge of war as never before. To add to his miseries, life away from the front was becoming crushingly expensive. Prices of many vital commodities had risen over a hundred percent since the cease-fire, while the salary of the average infantryman had increased by only twenty-five percent. Under these conditions, desertions, petty thievery and corruption were bound to increase as well.

In late August, as tension continued to build within both the army and the population, several opposition groups took to the streets to exploit it. Father Tran Huu Thanh, a fifty-nine-year-old Catholic militant devoted to conservative politics but radical tactics, organized a movement "to eliminate corruption" in the government. In a daring public manifesto he accused Thieu of masterminding the country's heroin traffic, of illegally amassing a fortune in public property and of turning the lucrative rice-distribution system in central Vietnam over to a favorite aunt.

Initially Thieu tried to placate his critics by promising reform, offering in early September to loosen restrictions on political activity and to root out corruption. But it soon became apparent that all this was empty talk. Not even his closest advisors could persuade him to act. For weeks Thieu had had a report on his desk, prepared by the military command itself, which verified that corruption among militia units in the delta had become ruinous to their performance and that the regional commander, General Nguyen Vinh Nghi, was implicated in it. Yet despite the impeccable authorship of these charges, Thieu had refused even to issue a reprimand. Nghi was an old friend and crony.

To move against him could prompt a backlash among other corrupt field commanders, which Thieu feared even more than the debilitating effect of their venality on the army's capabilities.

As the demonstrations continued, however, Ambassador Martin's own tolerance began wearing thin. It was not so much the corruption that worried him as the agitation itself. Fearful it would work to Thieu's discredit back in the United States, he urged the South Vietnamese leader to take steps to diffuse it, even including genuine reforms.

Finally, in late October, Thieu bowed to demand. He fired four members of his cabinet, demoted nearly 400 field-grade officers who were suspected of corruption and removed three of his four regional commanders, including General Nghi and General Nguyen Van Toan, commander in Military Region 2, whose reputation was just as tarnished as Nghi's.

Having made his concessions, however, Thieu then exacted his price, slapping new controls on the press and warning opposition groups that they continued to agitate at their peril. The Embassy tried to rationalize the crackdown to American reporters as "something essential to the country's security," but privately Martin agonized about it. Such extremism in pursuit of order, he realized, was simply bad public relations.

Yet for all this, the Ambassador did have one consolation. As part of his own push for reform, he had managed to persuade the South Vietnamese leader to fire Hoang Duc Nha. Although Nha's name had appeared on nobody's "most corrupt" list, Martin considered the young Information Minister an obstacle to his efforts to impose his own will—and his desire for concessions—on the South Vietnamese. He therefore insisted that Nha be removed, warning in a letter to Thieu in September that Nha's brashness and negativism diminished the chances of squeezing additional aid out of Congress. That was enough for Thieu, and as part of the housecleaning in October he forced his cousin out of the cabinet. Nha's departure left Prime Minister Khiem and the government's slavishly pro-American faction unopposed. There was now no one in Thieu's inner circle to caution him against overreliance on American advice and support.

As Martin moved deftly to eliminate his only formidable opponent inside the Saigon regime, he also attempted once again to bring Congress to heel. By the time the House and the Senate voted definitively at the end of September to reduce the Administration's military aid bill to $700 million, he had already proposed to the State Department that it seek a supplemental appropriation. Although the White House decided to hold off for a while before making such a pitch to Congress, Martin started preparing for it at once. Since the South Vietnamese seemed determined to put their worst face forward, the first order of business, in his opinion, was to camouflage their blemishes.

In the coldest and most calculating terms, this meant (once again) playing down Saigon's faults and weaknesses both in briefings to the American press and in Embassy reporting to Washington. Thus, throughout the fall and early winter the decline in the army's morale, the slippage of security in the country-side and the now intolerable level of corruption in the government—the very problems that were setting Saigon up for the kill—were all systematically glossed over in the Embassy's public and private reflections on the situation. The Defense Attaché's Office contributed more than its share to the obfusca-tion, but the sleight of hand that most troubled me was that which I witnessed in my own front office.

Fully committed to the Ambassador's aims, Polgar soon began carefully altering the Station's reporting to enhance their appeal and salability in Wash-ington. The technique he adopted was fully within his prerogatives as Station Chief. There was no heavy-handed distortion of the intelligence; it was more a matter of excessive quality control—"creative intelligence gathering," as one of his senior colleagues described it. When the CIA Base Chief in the Mekong Delta, for example, tried to issue a series of reports on the security and corruption problems there, Polgar insisted on reviewing them all beforehand. He then applied such rigid quality standards, few of them were ever cleared for release. Some he pigeonholed for semantic reasons, claiming that the term "security" was too loosely defined. Others he delayed or sidelined for "im-proper sourcing."

Polgar also made a meticulous effort during the fall and winter to keep the gripes and plaints of opposition figures out of reporting channels. He refused to authorize any Station contacts whatsoever with Father Thanh, the anti-corruption agitator, on the excuse that Thanh would misconstrue them as a sign of support. And whenever, by some fluke, facts or observations unfavorable to the government or to the Ambassador's cause did slip through his sieve, he was usually quick to file a disparaging follow-up cable to discredit them in the eyes of consumers in Washington.

At the start of the anti-corruption drive in August, for example, one of the Station's most experienced and knowledgeable operatives wangled an inter-view with several respected South Vietnamese politicians who had long been Thieu's supporters but who were now disturbed about his policies and con-vinced concessions to the Communists were mandatory. One of them, Nguyen Ngoc Huy, who had represented the government at the bilateral talks with the PRG in Paris, delivered a devastating critique of corruption in the military. "Except for a few special cases, in which officers look after their troops and help them surmount financial difficulties," he remarked, "the soldiers are unable to feed their families and no longer have the will to fight. They are demoralized because of shameless exploitation by their superiors . . . Generally speaking, the army has become a vast enterprise for corruption; even artillery support must be paid for . . .

"As long as security was good and living standards decent the people tolerated corruption and inefficiency in government. These defects are becom-ing less and less tolerable as security and living standards decline and numer-ous large-scale scandals bring into the open the rotten character of the leaders of the regime. If Thieu continues to govern with the support of corrupt and incompetent men while rejecting any true dialogue with other non-Communists, it will be difficult for South Vietnam to win the struggle against the Communists, whether it is fought militarily or politically."

All of this was sensational stuff, particularly coming from a government official, and despite Polgar's "quality" standards, the CIA officer who conducted the interview made sure his report reached Washington. When analysts at CIA headquarters read it over they were both shocked and impressed and gave it high marks for political import.

Polgar's reaction was somewhat different. When he learned the report had slipped out and had been well received at home he was furious and immediately dispatched a protesting cable to CIA headquarters. "The important thing to remember," he wrote, "is that the type of comment reflected in REF [the referenced report] can be had by the barrel. It is the type of comment that can be readily obtained by the international press and which has contributed to the consistent and continuing misrepresentation of events in South Vietnam . . . The fact that the REF got a [high value rating] while soberer and therefore less sensational reports get [lower ones] does raise suspicion that headquarters analysts may have seen something unusual in the report. [My] view is that there was nothing of unusual significance. Specifically I do not believe that the view reflected in the REF will have any particular direct bearing on the way things will evolve here in the foreseeable future."

But Polgar was not content to air his dissent merely in an informal cable to CIA headquarters. He wanted to make certain it got a wider hearing in Washington. So he asked me to draft a field appraisal showing that the morale of the army and population was holding steady. I neither accepted this view nor wanted to defend it. Luckily for me, I had an excuse not to do so. I was already spending night and day simply trying to figure out Hanoi's next military move; so I shunted the assignment off on my office colleague, Pat Johnson.

She in turn wrote an honest and fair study, demonstrating that morale was anything but good. Predictably enough, Polgar didn't like it at all. He shelved her version and wrote one of his own. The document was one of the most extraordinary ever produced by the CIA in Saigon.

Insisting at the outset that no foreigner could possibly understand the psychology of the Vietnamese, he proceeded to offer an analysis of it himself, arguing that it was one of their national characteristics to overdraw their problems to outsiders. "Against the backdrop of a culture where begging is an accepted and indeed an honored way of life," he wrote, "no responsible Vietnamese would eschew an opportunity to present his views in such a way that the necessity of continuing foreign assistance would not emerge as an obvious and essential conclusion . . ."

From this turgid beginning Polgar moved on to attack the prevailing assumptions about morale in the military. "There is no strong evidence," he insisted (totally ignoring the government's own recent findings in the delta), "that the morale factor has at this stage significantly affected ARVN's combat performance." In any case, he went on, fluctuations in the mood of the people and the army really didn't matter, since the government still had an iron grip on the society. "Not withstanding the [press's] pessimistic appraisals," he observed, "the essential functions of government continue to be carried out. Rice and other foodstuffs reach the markets. There is ample gasoline; the national police do a good job of maintaining public order; and the performance of the security forces during the demonstrations in September and October has been excellent in effectiveness as well as discipline. There has been no interruption of basic public services. There have been no strikes. The mail gets delivered routinely, which cannot be said in some more advanced countries . . .

"The people clearly have not risen against the government in recent demonstrations. Equally clearly, the vast majority of the population goes about its business, trying to make ends meet, coping with the cruel world and making the most of it while they are doing it. They demonstrate daily the Vietnamese virtues of stoicism, flexibility, resourcefulness and resiliency. The three percent per annum population increase suggests both physical prowess and a hopeful view of the future. It is not only the poor and ignorant who have babies in Vietnam."

As a piece of political analysis, Polgar's handiwork was so extreme and ludicrous his superiors at CIA headquarters refused to pass it on to any of our regular intelligence customers, to Kissinger, the President or anybody else. It was the first time in my experience that an analysis from the field had ever been allowed to die on the vine.

But neither Polgar nor Ambassador Martin was discouraged. They quickly declassified the study, issued it as a State Department cable and handed copies out to every visiting Congressman or journalist who had the misfortune of being within briefing range. Martin even sent a copy to our Embassy in Moscow, to be passed to Soviet officials, in hopes of convincing them that Saigon and its army were still solid as a rock.

As Martin and Polgar labored to conceal Saigon's ills the North Vietnamese continued to try to turn them to their own profit. During August the hawks in the Politburo again raised a cry for all-out war, describing the latest U.S. aid cutbacks as both a repudiation of Thieu and a blow to Saigon's military potential. The bleats and moans of the Embassy in Saigon did nothing to disabuse them of these ideas. General Dung commented to his comrades during one meeting that Thieu was being forced to wage a "poor man's war." It was a phrase Ambassador Martin had begun using in his own efforts to swing public opinion in Saigon's favor.

The resignation of President Nixon broke like a shock wave on Hanoi, but initially the principals of the Politburo did not quite know what to make of it. On the one hand, there was definitely reason for elation. Nixon had been their archenemy, the man whose unpredictability had been a major influence for moderation among them. Even so, the question remained: Would Ford be any different? The more cautious among them said no.

The generals and militants, however, remained impatient of such easy logic. While Ford might try to imitate Nixon, they argued, the turmoil in Washington could not help but benefit their cause, if only to the extent of frightening and confusing the South Vietnamese. This argument apparently prevailed, for Radio Hanoi was soon proclaiming triumphantly that the Nixon resignation had created "new opportunities" for "liberation forces" to deliver decisive blows against the enemy.

Another consideration also weighed in the hawks' favor. With the United States now insisting on territorial demarcation, they could argue with considerable justification that there had to be some improvement in the Communist position on the battlefield. In addressing themselves to this point the proponents of escalation invariably hearkened back to a remark Henry Kissinger had made to Le Duc Tho during their secret meeting in Paris the previous December. In the course of that session Kissinger had commented offhandedly that the North Vietnamese could not make too many demands at the negotiating table, since they commanded so little on the battlefield. That observation had haunted Hanoi's policy-makers ever since, for they knew it to be true, and by now the prospect of negotiations had become tightly linked in their thinking with the necessity for a new round of offensive activity.

As the hawks pressed their case the moderates fought back, and as at so many crucial junctures since the cease-fire, it was the Soviets and the Chinese who provided them with their strongest counterarguments. In the past few months Hanoi's annual aid talks with the two Communist powers had dragged on interminably as both continued to urge their Vietnamese ally to spruce up its economic planning. Although economic-aid agreements had finally been concluded, the Soviets were still playing cagey on the issue of military assistance, and the moderates made this their primary debating point as they sought to hold the generals and the war lobby in check. For one brief moment it looked as though they had succeeded. In his annual National Day speech on 1 September, Premier Pham Van Dong advised his countrymen that the priorities of the regime must remain "balanced" between revolution and reconstruction.

Yet no sooner had he uttered this standard paean to moderation than the tone of Hanoi's public commentary shifted again. The lead editorial in the September issue of the party journal warned of "a current of evil thoughts" throughout the society, and other press articles complained of a new "strain of humanism" in the arts and national literature, a typically euphemistic warning to the more dovish elements of the party that their views were not in favor.

The turning point in the policy debate was the explosion of demonstrations that ripped through South Vietnam in early September as Father Thanh pressed his anti-corruption crusade. The North Vietnamese saw the unrest, coming on top of everything else, as final proof of the growing fragility of the Thieu regime—and as a symptom of a widening breach between Saigon and its American ally. Some North Vietnamese officials even went so far as to interpret the demonstrations as an extension of political infighting in the United States, claiming that the Democratic party was secretly sponsoring Father Thanh's protest group in an effort to discredit the new Ford Administration.

Ultimately it was Party First Secretary Le Duan who turned the vision of a Washington-Saigon split into an unassailable argument for renewed war. The United States and the South Vietnamese were now at such loggerheads, he insisted, Washington would never intervene massively to save Thieu from defeat. Although the Americans might reintroduce air power in the wake of initial government setbacks, any bombing, in his opinion, would be limited in time and scope, posing no real danger to North Vietnam's long-term economic potential. That last point effectively disarmed the moderates, demolishing their claim that war and reconstruction were incompatible.

In early October, Le Duan and the rest of the Politburo finally settled on a plan. Falling back on their traditional hard line, they publicly announced the PRG would no longer negotiate with President Thieu at all. (Obviously they were hoping to catalyze the supposed domestic and American hostility to him by casting him as the sole obstacle to peace.) They then concocted an ambiguous military strategy that was tailored to please both doves and hawks. Rather than commit themselves to specific objectives, they drew up a list of options, ranging from "liberation of one-half" of the South Vietnamese countryside to seizure of "two-thirds" of the rice harvest in the Mekong Delta and the isolation of Saigon. Lest the moderates balk at all this, the leadership made it clear in its policy guidance that the practicality of each option would be carefully tested before a plan of action was built around it. Hence the first phase of the upcoming offensive, to begin in mid-December, would be aimed at "identifying" South Vietnamese vulnerabilities; the next, at exploiting them; and each phase would be predicated on the success of the previous one. The overall aim, party officials explained to subordinates, was to foment such turmoil inside South Vietnam and between Washington and Saigon that Thieu would be overthrown and a new cease-fire agreement forced on his successors.

The Politburo's conclusions and recommendations were enshrined in a policy document known as the "Resolution for 1975," and distillations of it were quickly distributed to the military commands in South Vietnam. Within two weeks CIA agents were providing the Embassy with meticulously detailed information on its contents and ambiguities.

As the data accumulated I began drafting a field appraisal to explain what it all meant to policy-makers in Washington. Almost immediately I found myself in irresolvable conflict with Polgar. In his desperation to convince whoever would listen at home of Saigon's needs, he insisted on painting Hanoi's intentions in the most menacing terms imaginable. By contrast, I was determined to interpret the Resolution for 1975 as it was written, emphasizing Hanoi's stated intention to move cautiously and gradually on the battlefield, with negotiations as its interim objective.

In hopes of substantiating my forecast, I scheduled a meeting with our top agent in early November to question him directly about the Resolution. The source confirmed my views, stressing that much of the bellicose rhetoric in the document was aimed merely at stiffening troop morale. He also acknowledged that the principal motivation for the upcoming campaign had not been cutbacks in U.S. aid (as Polgar and Martin would have had Congress believe) but, rather, Henry Kissinger's allusions the previous December to the sparseness of the PRG's territorial holdings.

When I turned my findings over to Polgar he immediately discounted them, insisting that the source was "obviously not up to date" on Hanoi's plans. Although CIA headquarters did eventually disseminate my notes as a bona-fide intelligence report, the references to Kissinger's ill-considered remarks to Le Duc Tho were carefully deleted, lest the Secretary be offended.

The field appraisal I finally prepared on the Resolution for 1975 was a feeble attempt to bridge Polgar's views and my own. Completed in late November and issued soon after, it merely repeated all we knew about Communist plans without offering any speculation on Hanoi's next move. Polgar made only one concession to my viewpoint, allowing me to include a line to the effect that "further evidence is needed before the scope and intensity of the 1975 campaign can be predicted with any accuracy, particularly since the Resolution itself is not precise on this point."

With all the intelligence now pointing toward some kind of offensive activity, Kissinger made a final attempt in November to head off the worst. During a meeting between President Ford and party leader Brezhnev at Vladivostok he saw to it the problem of Vietnam was once again cast up to the Soviets as an implicit adjunct to détente, and a few days later during a brief stopover in Peking he asked the Chinese to intercede with the Cambodian Communists to bring about a halt to the fighting around Phnom Penh.

These last-minute ministrations were pointless, however. The Chinese were particularly adamant in their refusal to intervene in Cambodia. Instead they again urged the United States, as they had previously through French intermediaries, to abandon the Lon Nol regime and to support the restoration of Sihanouk. It was the same proposal Martin had tried to sell to Kissinger the previous spring, and recently our Ambassador in Cambodia, John Dean, had rallied behind it. But Kissinger remained opposed. He wanted Sihanouk to negotiate a cease-fire directly with Lon Nol and was unwilling to by-pass our Cambodian client to work out a settlement with the Chinese and Sihanouk.

The Khmer Communists, meanwhile, were making final preparations for a new "dry season" offensive against Phnom Penh. By November they had closed off all overland arteries to the capital, except for the Mekong River, which extended to the South Vietnamese border. To offset the blockade, the Pentagon immediately mounted a massive airlift with chartered civilian aircraft to ferry in rice and military supplies from South Vietnam and Thailand.

The Chinese took umbrage at this and reacted by providing additional aid to the Khmer Communists, including newly designed water mines and heavy artillery for use against the Mekong River traffic. The North Vietnamese in turn promised to expedite the shipment of Chinese supplies across their own turf and to provide the Khmer Communists with surplus equipment from their own stockpiles.

By early December 1974, therefore, the stage was set for intensified fighting on both Indochina fronts.

Part 2

The Unraveling

Polgar

Martin

Van Tien Dung

Thieu

Improvisatory Offensive

Militarily the Republic of Vietnam had long been a checkerboard of conflicting fiefdoms. The Joint General Staff in Saigon was supposed to be the supreme military authority in the land, but because Thieu feared concentrating so much power in the hands of so few, he had made his four regional commanders near-sovereigns in their own domains.

The Military Regions themselves varied widely in climate and geography. Perhaps the only truly unifying feature among them was National Highway 1, which ran along the coast (though not always unbroken) from Hué to Saigon.

The five provinces that made up Military Region 1 in the northern quarter of the country were rugged and inhospitable. The majority of their 3,000,000 inhabitants lived clustered around the major cities of Hué and Danang, and government "control" was limited largely to the lowlands along the coast. The "important" war in the region had always been a conventional one, waged by main-force units along fixed battlelines. Up until the fall of 1974 the two sides had recognized a de facto cease-fire boundary along the Thach Han River north of Hué, but with the recent Communist drive into the lowlands west of the city, the stand-off had begun breaking down.

Even more than MR 1, Military Region 2, in the center of South Vietnam, was a collection of contrasts. From the hot white sands of the central coast the land swept westward in ever-increasing folds and terraces to culminate in the rugged mountains of the western highlands along the Cambodian border. The ramshackle city of Qui Nhon dominated the northern reaches of the coastal area; Nha Trang, the central portion; and Phan Thiet, the south. In the highlands Pleiku and Kontum Cities marked the northern boundary of government control and Ban Me Thuot the southern. In between were scattered small montagnard settlements inhabited by the brown-skinned mountain tribesmen much reviled by all Vietnamese.

The war in MR 2 generally shaped itself to the rigors of the terrain. Around Qui Nhon the Communists had long pursued a combination of conventional and guerrilla-style tactics, imposing their control on large portions

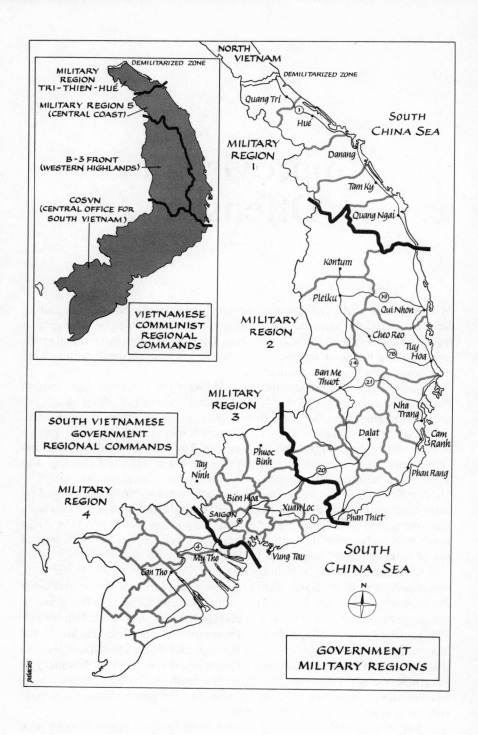

VIETNAMESE
COMMUNIST
REGIONAL
COMMANDS

MILITARY
REGION
TRI-THIEN-HUÉ

MILITARY REGION 5
(CENTRAL COAST)

B-3 FRONT
(WESTERN HIGHLANDS)

COSVN
(CENTRAL OFFICE FOR
SOUTH VIETNAM)

SOUTH VIETNAMESE
GOVERNMENT
REGIONAL COMMANDS

MILITARY
REGION
4

MILITARY
REGION
3

MILITARY
REGION
2

MILITARY
REGION
1

DEMILITARIZED ZONE

NORTH
VIETNAM

DEMILITARIZED ZONE

Quang Tri

Hué

Danang

Tam Ky

Quang Ngai

Kontum

Pleiku

Qui Nhon

Cheo Reo

Tuy
Hoa

Ban Me
Thuot

Nha
Trang

Cam
Ranh

Dalat

Phan Rang

Phuoc
Binh

Tay
Ninh

Bien Hoa

SAIGON

Xuan Loc

Phan Thiet

Vung Tau

My Tho

Can Tho

SOUTH
CHINA SEA

SOUTH
CHINA SEA

N

GOVERNMENT
MILITARY REGIONS

palacios

of the surrounding province, but further south in the vicinity of Nha Trang and Phan Thiet, far from NVA supply lines from the north, Communist guerrillas fought largely alone, and ineffectually. To the west, in the highlands, NVA main-force units, drawing their strength directly from the supply caches of the "third Vietnam," hovered on the wooded slopes surrounding the major towns and cities, ready to wreak havoc with artillery and ground assault whenever the overextended government units let down their guard.

In Military Region 3, the zone surrounding Saigon, the opposites of the highlands and the delta melded together in a confusion of foothills, jungles and rice paddies. North of the capital, NVA main forces had for years had free run of large stretches of forest. There they periodically taxed and proselytized scattered hamlets while building the supply stocks they needed for occasional thrusts toward Saigon. To the south and east of the capital, American and South Vietnamese clearing operations in the late 1960s and early '70s had driven the Communist guerrillas into the swamps.

Next to Saigon, the most strategically important city in MR 3 was Tay Ninh, tucked away in the northwestern corner of the region near the Cambodian border. Long a target for NVA harassment and attack, this bustling metropolis of 40,000 sat athwart key Communist supply lines running south toward Saigon, and whoever controlled it and the surrounding alluvial plain controlled the gateway from Cambodia. No more than twenty miles northwest of the city the Communists maintained the headquarters of COSVN, their primary command post in the southern half of the country.

South of Saigon, the last of the government's military command zones, MR 4, embraced the richest and most populous area of the country, the Mekong Delta. Home of over a third of South Vietnam's population and producer of eighty percent of its rice, the delta had always been the ultimate prize for each side. Yet because of its humid climate and soggy terrain, it was not suited to the kind of main-force confrontations that would decide the war. Communist troops had long operated in dispersed battalion or company-sized units without heavy artillery or armor and relying largely on hit-and-run attacks to advance their objectives. Government forces, meanwhile, had waged an increasingly ineffectual defense from a few large towns and cities and a series of far-flung outposts, many of which were now untenable without American helicopters, air and artillery support. In the southern half of the region the anchor of the government presence was the city of Can Tho; in the north, My Tho. In recent months Communist influence and control had seeped to the very threshold of these and other principal urban centers, and for the first time in over a year the chief north-south artery in the region, National Highway 4, was being interdicted for long intervals by marauding Communist sabotage squads.

This, then, was the Vietnam that Hanoi's military strategists contemplated as they planned the offensive outlined in their Resolution for 1975. Inevitably, the campaign they devised was not one campaign at all, but a series of highly individualized military operations, each keyed to the peculiar topography and climate of the target area.

Preparations for this last Communist offensive of the war proceeded by fits and starts. Few NVA reinforcements entered the trail systems in southern Laos en route to the front until mid-November, two weeks before the launch date, and recruitment and training cycles in North Vietnam idled along until the end of the month. None of this was typical of the North Vietnamese. Normally they took months—and considerable care—in preparing for an offensive. This time they seemed to be literally stumbling into battle.

In a sense, they could not have done otherwise. Having waited until October to decide on a course of action, they simply did not have the time for detailed preparations. Nor did they have the ideal weather. The fall monsoons in the North Vietnamese panhandle and southern Laos had been particularly heavy, and the movement of manpower and supplies south had already become a 500-mile slog through knee-deep mud.

In briefings and analyses for Polgar, I also posited another reason for Hanoi's bumbling. There was a possibility, I argued, the North Vietnamese were deliberately playing it low-key, to mislead us and their own dovish factions into believing nothing special was in the offing.

But if this was their intent, they did not quite succeed. Captured documents and agent reports reflecting their general aims, if not their precise objectives, continued to rain in on us throughout the month.

Given this torrent of information, both the Embassy and the South Vietnamese government should have been prepared for what finally took place. Sadly, we were not. What was lacking was solid interpretation. From the moment Polgar and I parted company over the meaning of the Resolution for 1975, no one seemed to be able to agree on the implications of the available intelligence, and as time passed and more data piled up, divergent lines of analysis only multiplied.

Polgar remained the consummate alarmist, arguing that the Communists would key their initiatives in the next few months to the more ambitious objectives set out in the Resolution. I remained convinced we were facing something more modest: sharp, though selective, attacks to pave the way for renewed negotiations.

The ambiguities in the intelligence accounted for some of our analytical differences, but not all. The continuing debate over aid to Saigon also played a part. By early December the Administration was preparing to beard Congress on the "supplemental" aid appropriation Martin had proposed several weeks before, and inevitably this new priority affected the way we looked at, and analyzed, the intelligence. Alarmist interpretations were obviously to the Administration's advantage, since they gave a note of urgency to the "supplemental" request; more cautious ones were not.

Our reports on the Resolution for 1975 lent themselves particularly well to the Ambassador's purposes. Since they reflected a willingness on Hanoi's part to push the fighting to the limits if necessary, they could be read as proof for the darkest military forecasts. Martin realized this possibility at once and was soon pontificating to one and all about the "grave new threat" foreshadowed in the document. He encouraged others to do likewise. As the Embassy's principal intelligence officer, Polgar could hardly avoid being caught up in the gambit. Nor did he try. During the next few weeks he eagerly nudged me toward hand-wringing appraisals of what lay ahead, and began leaking our most bearish data to reporter friends. By the end of the month an average subscriber to the *Washington Post* or the *New York Times* would have had every reason to believe Saigon was facing the apocalypse.

In spite of my respect for Polgar, I didn't like this shell game at all. It seemed to me that in overplaying the upper end of Hanoi's option scale we were running the risk of losing sight of the other end, including the possibility of negotiations. I therefore made some effort to restore the balance. During the second week in December, I began spending an hour or two each day debriefing prisoners and Communist defectors at the National Interrogation Center, in hopes of dredging up enough additional data to cause Polgar to moderate his views. I succeeded only to a point. One knowledgeable defector assured me unequivocally that the upcoming NVA campaign would be more modest than the 1972 affair. But when I submitted these findings to Polgar, he shrugged them off. The only point he would concede was that the term "general offensive," implying a coordinated countrywide drive against numerous cities and towns, might not be appropriate to describe what Hanoi was planning—though he also insisted that such definitions were no longer applicable. Because of the latest aid cutbacks, he asserted, the South Vietnamese were so weak and vulnerable, anything the Communists might throw at them would have the *impact* of a general offensive. End of argument.

Colonel Bill Legro and his hawkish intelligence analysts at DAO were only too willing to support Polgar in this position. Since they had been predicting a general offensive every month since the first day of the cease-fire, his alarms were like music to their ears.

Of all the outsiders looking in on the Vietnam scene, perhaps the least alarmist in the winter of 1974–75 were the CIA analysts in Washington. Tucked away in their prefab niches and cubbyholes, they were, at least initially, far less susceptible to the pressures of the aid debate than those of us on the front line. In a year-end National Intelligence Estimate they set out their projections in such temperate hues, you had to wonder if we were all contemplating the same war. While conceding that the North Vietnamese were stronger than ever before, the authors insisted that the South Vietnamese army itself was still "strong and resilient," despite leadership problems, corruption and a recent decline in the quality of militia units. And although they were willing to allow for some kind of Communist initiative in the near future, they felt nothing "significant"—by which they meant a countrywide campaign

based on the introduction of the now seven strategic divisions in North Vietnam—would occur before 1976, an election year in the United States.*

When the estimate was cabled out to Saigon, Legro and Polgar reacted
almost indignantly. "Overall, the estimate too narrowly defines the scope of
the threat," Legro remarked archly in a return message to Washington. "We
feel the estimate is out of focus because of its faulty definition of what consti-
tutes a 'major military offensive,' " Polgar added in a retort of his own. "The
North Vietnamese could conceivably take a number of province capitals such
as An Loc, Tay Ninh, Kontum, conceivably one or two in the delta, without
moving any strategic reserve divisions as such into the south. Such a victory
would not be decisive in the sense that it would topple the government, but
would be an ominous overture for 1976 or later."

Our colleagues in Washington were not particularly chastened by these
arguments. Throughout the next few weeks—at least until the aid debate
forced a change in their tone—they and several kindred spirits at the Pentagon
(the Defense Secretary included) would continue to err on the side of excessive
optimism.

Part of their problem was simply vested interest. Most of the officers who
had drawn up the National Intelligence Estimate had built their careers on
Vietnam and could not imagine that their stepping stone might abruptly
become a pile of sand. CIA Director William Colby, whose experience as the
architect of the pacification program had left him with an overriding confidence in ARVN's capabilities, confided to me after the fall of Saigon that it
was he who had set the upbeat tone of the year-end estimate. "Yes," he said
sadly, "I was responsible for the judgment nothing significant would happen
until 1976."

For the South Vietnamese themselves the future, like the past, was a
borrowed vision. Having long relied on the Americans for just about everything, they continued to depend on us for their understanding of what was in
store for them. To some extent they had no other choice. The analysts who
worked for the military intelligence apparatus and the civilian Central Intelligence Organization were notoriously timid, with a strong attachment to the
accepted wisdom of their superiors. Also, since knowledge was power, Thieu
usually kept the most important intelligence data so tightly held, his analysts
could not have developed an independent line even if they had been so inclined.

Because of their close working relationship with the CIA, Thieu and his
senior staff drew heavily on the Station's estimates in framing their own, and
in early December their basic reference was the field appraisal I had written
a week before on the Resolution for 1975. Reflecting all my waffles and
generalities—the results of my differences with Polgar—they ended up with

*Like all National Intelligence Estimates, this one, NIE 53/14-3-'74, was a collaborative effort,
produced jointly by all members of the American intelligence community. However, the CIA, and
in particular an analyst who had previously served as my boss, had chief drafting responsibility.

an even more confused picture of NVA intentions than we had, if that was possible.

In an effort to bring their vision into line with his own, Polgar did some heavy lobbying for Armageddon among his closest Vietnamese contacts. As usual, he used me as his mouthpiece, and repeatedly dispatched me into the countryside during the month to brief senior South Vietnamese field staffs on what "we" felt the other side would do.

In mid-December, precisely on schedule, the North Vietnamese launched the first phase of their winter-spring campaign. Predictably, their sharpest attacks were focused in the southern half of the country, in Military Regions 3 and 4, where the seasonal monsoons had just come to an end. In the north, where the rainy season was only beginning, the two sides remained fairly inactive.

Between 14 and 16 December two district towns just northeast of Saigon were overrun, and to the south, in the upper Mekong Delta, NVA units seized several outposts near National Highway 4. The broad purpose of these initiatives was scarcely in doubt. The Communists clearly were aiming to turn Saigon into an island by severing all major access routes from the north and south, as they had often attempted to do in the past.

If the Communists' overall objective was understood, however, there was considerable debate in the Embassy over their precise local ones. Ambassador Martin quickly concluded that the main enemy thrust in Military Region 3 would come in Tay Ninh Province, and he soon managed to persuade Thieu likewise. Polgar and I were less convinced. In view of continuing pressure in Phuoc Long Province, northeast of Saigon, we felt there was an even chance *it* would be the main target.

Unbeknownst to us, the North Vietnamese themselves were even then debating the same question. As General Van Tien Dung, the man who would eventually lead the NVA to victory, pointed out in his postwar account, another policy review was initiated in Hanoi in early December, just as phase one of the NVA offensive was grinding forward. During the first few days Dung and his colleagues simply ruminated on the prospects for implementing the Resolution for 1975. But on the fourth day something happened to shift their attention abruptly.

A spy in President Thieu's inner circle sent a top-secret report to them on government plans and perspectives. By his account an important strategy session had been held in Saigon on 9 and 10 December to sort out *Hanoi's* intentions. In the course of it, he said, Thieu and his commanders had agreed that the Communists would "fight on a larger scale" in the coming months than they had in 1974, but "would not push their campaign to the level of the 1968 offensive." (It was precisely the waffling estimate Polgar and I had foisted on the South Vietnamese two weeks before.) In addition, so the agent maintained, Thieu had concluded that the NVA were incapable of attacking and holding major cities; that their main thrust would be in Military Region 3 and

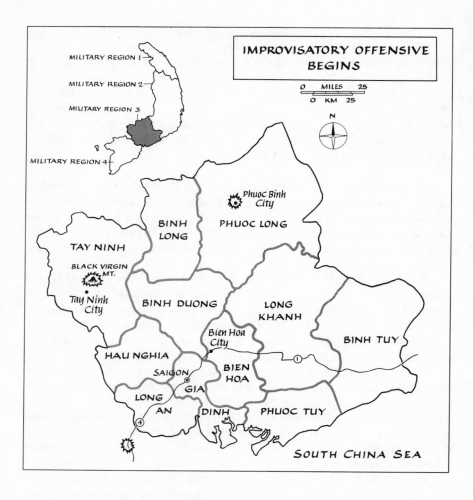

MILITARY REGION 1

MILITARY REGION 2

MILITARY REGION 3

MILITARY REGION 4

Phuoc Binh
City

BINH
LONG

PHUOC LONG

TAY NINH

BLACK VIRGIN
MT.

Tay Ninh
City

BINH DUONG

LONG
KHANH

BINH TUY

Bien Hoa
City

HAU NGHIA

SAIGON

BIEN
HOA

GIA

LONG
AN

DINH

PHUOC TUY

SOUTH CHINA SEA

would be aimed at Tay Ninh (Martin's guess); and that they would pursue
their offensive in earnest only through the end of the dry season in June,
whereupon they would stop to rest and refit. According to the agent, Thieu
had also decided, on the basis of this estimate, not to reinforce the western
highlands of MR 2, but to concentrate his reserves in the southern half of the
country.

It is not hard to imagine the excitement Hanoi's leaders must have felt
when the report was deciphered and handed to them. By any measure it was
priceless. In their Resolution for 1975 they had set out a potpourri of options
for themselves. Now, with full knowledge of what Thieu expected of them,
they could narrow and refine their plans accordingly, to outmaneuver him.
Since he anticipated an attack in Tay Ninh, they would strike first in Phuoc
Long; since he did not expect a push in the highlands, that was where they
would make their major play; and because he doubted their ability to take and
hold province capitals, they would do just that, first targeting the capital of
Phuoc Long Province and then Ban Me Thuot in the highlands of MR 2.

Among those responsible for the ultimate North Vietnamese victory, the spy in Thieu's entourage clearly must rank high on the credit list. To this day his identity remains a secret, known only to the North Vietnamese, but at the time he provided his spectacular intelligence to Hanoi four members of Thieu's inner circle were on the CIA's list of possible Communist collaborators and could have duplicated his accomplishment. Among them was the chief of the counterespionage section of the army's Military Security Service (MSS), a man whose family had close ties to Thieu's secretarial staff.

Despite long-standing suspicions, the CIA Station, unfortunately, had never seen fit to take action against the MSS officer or any of the other suspects. All four were among Thieu's closest confidants and two of them, including the MSS man, had been actively supported in the earlier phases of their careers by the CIA. To have found them guilty of espionage would thus have been an acute embarrassment for all of us. Rather than risk that, the Station had preferred to give the suspects the benefit of the doubt.

On 18 December the North Vietnamese Politburo met again to consider the implications of the agent's extraordinary disclosures. The deliberations dragged on for another two weeks as NVA forces in the south scored one success after another. Toward the end of the month, with the tide clearly running in their favor, the Politburo secretly dispatched the 316th NVA Division, renowned as the vanguard unit at the battle of Dien Bien Phu in 1954, to the central highlands to prepare for the attack against Ban Me Thuot. A few days later Le Duan and his colleagues authorized an immediate and all-out assault on the capital of Phuoc Long Province in MR 3.*

The decision for escalation was not arrived at easily. The doves and moderates remained concerned about American intervention and the hazards to reconstruction. But Le Duan managed to fend off their objections with the same arguments he had used the previous fall to win support for the Resolution for 1975. The Congressional aid debate, he insisted, proved that there was only a slim possibility of U.S. intervention. Consequently, escalation carried little danger. In a slight nod to his more cautious colleagues, he did agree to make the battle for Phuoc Long a test case for his convictions. If the Americans did not intervene to try to save the province, he argued, then it could be assumed he was right about their reticence to come to Saigon's defense. If they did, there would still be time to pull back from the brink.

By the end of December three district towns in Phuoc Long had fallen to the Communists; all roads to the province capital, Phuoc Binh, had been

---

*As General Dung points out in his memoirs, he and his Politburo colleagues were spurred on both by the NVA's rapid military gains and by the apparent confusion in the United States over their plans. Particularly encouraging to them, he says, was a series of public comments by Secretary of Defense James Schlesinger to the effect that no major Communist offensive was in the offing. In their view, if Washington actually believed this, then obviously they could go on escalating with impunity.

cut; its airfield was bracketed by enemy mortar and artillery, and over 8,000 NVA regulars had arrived to do battle with its 3,000 defenders, most of whom were undertrained militiamen.

On New Year's Day, Communist forces opened their assault, pouring 300 rounds of artillery and rocket fire into the city and seizing a strategic hilltop position overlooking its southeastern suburbs. From that moment forward, Phuoc Binh was theirs, for the hilltop gave them a clear field of fire against the key government positions.

Three days later, as the first NVA ground attacks smashed into the city, Thieu ordered the Foreign Ministry to prepare a public statement conceding all of Phuoc Long Province to the enemy. But a few hours later he changed his mind and dispatched 200 rangers to reinforce Phuoc Binh. According to a CIA agent in his cabinet, he was hoping to buy time so Congress would "reconsider" its ban on American combat operations in Vietnam. For him, as for the Communists, the battle had become a test of American reflexes.

The city, meanwhile, continued to die its agonizing death. In the face of the intense shelling, many of its 26,000 residents and more and more of the militiamen quietly slipped away into the bush, leaving only the rangers and a few army regulars to hold the line. The air force was called in to support them, but NVA antiaircraft artillery fire kept the planes at 10,000 feet, or above, too high for effective targeting, and time and again the frightened pilots released their bombs on "friendly" troop positions.

By 6 January the city's outer defenses had been breached and the defenders reduced to a handful of demoralized rangers. During the morning Thieu met with his top military advisors to consider sending more reinforcements, but ultimately decided against it. Since the United States had yet to give any indication it would come to his rescue, further muscle-flexing was pointless. Phuoc Binh might as well be abandoned. The following day NVA forces planted their flag in the city's marketplace.

Militarily Phuoc Binh had always been of marginal value, an island in the heart of hotly disputed territory, but psychologically its loss was a devastating blow to the government. Not since the surrender of Quang Tri City in the opening phases of the 1972 offensive had a province capital been given up to the enemy (and even then Quang Tri had been regained). Nor had the United States seemed so passive.

As the bad news circulated through the capital, government forces suffered another reversal, this one in Tay Ninh. After five days without food or water a garrison of eighty ARVN troopers gave up their besieged position atop Black Virgin Mountain north of the city. The loss not only eliminated a crucial lookout station on the city's flanks, but was also deeply unnerving for the local population, since the mountain had long had sacred value for the eclectic Cao Dai religious sect, which made its home in Tay Ninh. Many of the city's residents soon began pulling up stakes and heading for Saigon.

•   •   •

The Communists' multiple victories in northern MR 3 tipped the political scales in Hanoi toward escalation, for in effect they confirmed that the United States would not intervene to stave off a major defeat for its ally. The hawks in the Politburo wasted no time turning this revelation to advantage. On 8 January, the day after the capture of Phuoc Long, Le Duan went before his colleagues to press for a bolder military strategy and to urge them to adopt officially and formally a two-year timetable for victory—"widespread attacks in 1975, to create conditions for a general uprising in 1976 to liberate all of South Vietnam." He also recommended that a slip-clause be written into their plans. "If opportunities present themselves early or late in 1975," he said, "South Vietnam should be liberated this year."

Because of the breadth of his proposals the moderates held their ground till the last moment. Only by promising to keep an eye cocked for American intervention was Le Duan finally able to win them over. He also assured them that no move would be made toward a costly "general offensive" or commitment of all the army's reserves unless total victory was clearly within grasp, and pledged to leave the way open to negotiations, at least with the United States. Since the Americans had not intervened to save Phuoc Long, perhaps they were indeed prepared, he reasoned, to bargain Thieu out of existence, or to force him to compromise on key issues. Negotiations for that purpose would be perfectly acceptable.

To help bring the naysayers around, Le Duan had a special editorial prepared for the January issue of the party journal. The article spelled out succinctly and explicitly the logic behind his views and Hanoi's current planning, and if we had had immediate access to it in Saigon, we might have been in a better position to anticipate what was in the offing. But through a foul-up in the international mails the Embassy's copy of the party journal did not arrive until early March. By then it was too late.

In addition to Le Duan's arguments, the hawks in the Politburo came armed to the crucial deliberations in January with yet another weapon—the support of the one party whose attitude could spell success or failure. For the first time since the cease-fire Hanoi's most important ally, the Soviet Union, seemed ready to endorse a more aggressive policy in the south.

In late December, just before the attack on Phuoc Long, General Viktor Kulikov, chief of the Soviet armed forces, flew to Hanoi to take part in the Politburo's deliberations. Polgar and I immediately alerted CIA headquarters. Although we had no way of knowing what Kulikov meant to discuss with his hosts, it seemed significant to us (as I pointed out in my cable) that the last time such a high-ranking Soviet military officer had paid a visit on the North Vietnamese was back in the fall of 1971, just before they launched their last major offensive. Needless to say, Polgar felt obliged to remind Washington it could happen again.

But the overcautious analysts at the CIA and State Department were unpersuaded and assured us the Kulikov visit was merely routine. If any of us had known that the Politburo was then in session, that point might have been arguable, but since none of us had any inkling of this, Polgar let the matter drop.

Only later would it become apparent that our concern about Kulikov had been wholly justified. In the weeks following the general's visit, seaborne shipments of Soviet war matériel to North Vietnam increased fourfold in volume, as Moscow gave full aid and comfort to Hanoi in its final offensive.

The renewal of Soviet support for the "revolution" should have come as no surprise. Despite the amicableness of the November summit in Vladivostok, relations between the two great powers had recently taken a turn for the worse. The main irritant was the rising concern in the United States over the mistreatment of Soviet Jews—and an aggressive effort by Congress to punish Moscow for it. The moving force on the issue was Senator Henry Jackson, a presidential hopeful, long-time hawk, and perennial critic of Kissinger. For months he had been clamoring for the Administration to do something to force Moscow to liberalize restrictions on the emigration of Soviet Jews. He and other sympathetic Congressmen had finally found a sounding board for their views in the draft of a landmark trade bill worked out by Kissinger and Soviet representatives two and a half years before.

In late fall Jackson and his supporters drew up an amendment to the bill, making extension of its benefits contingent on a loosening of the Soviet emigration rules. Moscow protested and Kissinger warned Congress that such an intrusion on Soviet national prerogatives could prove counterproductive. But by mid-December it was apparent the Congress would not be deterred. The bill was passed with the controversial amendment included, and Ford signed it into law on 3 January.

The Soviet's response was swift and predictable. Rejecting the agreement out of hand, they protested that linkage of trade and emigration issues violated their original understandings with Kissinger. Tass, the Soviet press agency, warned of unspecified "retaliation," and a week or so later the Soviet Ambassador to Washington was called home for "consultations." In the meantime, Kulikov had been sent to Hanoi and Soviet military aid to North Vietnam was on the upswing.

Moscow's decision to register its displeasure with the Jackson amendment by way of Vietnam was all but inevitable. Back in the fall of 1972, as part of his desperate, last-minute search for a Vietnam peace, Kissinger had led the Soviets to believe that they could expect "most favored nation" trade status from the United States if they in turn would help to promote a settlement. The Soviets had taken the bait and had urged the North Vietnamese to drop their demand for Thieu's removal as a precondition to a solution. In September— at the same meeting in Moscow where Brezhnev had announced Hanoi was ready to deal—Kissinger had offered the Soviets his quid pro quo, a menu of commercial concessions. These were later translated into the trade agreement.

From the outset the Vietnam peace and the trade issue were thus implicitly linked, though neither Kissinger nor the Soviets ever acknowledged it publicly. When Congress attached its emigration rider to the trade bill in the winter of 1974, it therefore kicked over many more traces than it realized, and from that point on, the Soviets had reason to complain that their original understandings with Kissinger had broken down. Since he had failed to deliver in the commercial sphere, were they obliged to go on supporting the Vietnam peace? Evidently they thought not. Months after Saigon's collapse, Washington learned that the Soviets indeed had actively encouraged the North Vietnamese in their final offensive, advising them that since Congress was now unlikely to grant any additional economic or military assistance to Saigon, their chances for decisive gains were better than ever.

On 9 January, General Giap and Hanoi's top military commanders met to discuss the new goals the Politburo had set for them. During the session Le Duc Tho dropped by to underscore the importance of one of them—the capture of Ban Me Thuot, an operation which Giap and his colleagues had already code-named "Campaign 275."

A few days later the Politburo made a final adjustment in the tactical blueprint for it. Because of the criticalness and delicacy of "Campaign 275," Le Duan and Le Duc Tho insisted that one of their own number be put directly in charge. General Giap, decrepit and ravaged by Parkinson's disease, was obviously not up to the task. The next most logical candidate was the man who had been running the Defense Ministry for the past four years, General Van Tien Dung.

Gruff, square-faced, Dung at fifty-eight was the youngest member of the Politburo—and the only one who could honestly lay claim to the sacred title of "worker," having risen from humble peasant beginnings in Ha Tay Province to become foreman of a French textile factory in Hanoi in the mid-1930s. Somewhere between Ha Tay and Hanoi he had joined the Indochinese Communist party, and like other members in good standing, had been imprisoned by the French during their anti-Communist crackdown in 1939. After a daring breakout four years later he divided his time between the front lines and revolutionary training camps in the Soviet Union and gained enough practical military experience to qualify for a top political commissar's post in the newly formed army of the Viet Minh. In 1950, after a few more battles and another promotion, this one to the rank of major general, he took command of one of the first divisions ever organized by the Viet Minh, the 320th. It was one of three units he would lead into battle at Ban Me Thuot in the spring of 1975.

Throughout the early phases of his career Dung labored constantly in the shadow of his more flamboyant patron, General Giap. Although Giap took credit for the Viet Minh victory at Dien Bien Phu in 1954, it was Dung who as army chief of staff actually orchestrated the thing, marshaling supplies and resources for the month-long siege that finally brought the French garrison to its knees. And while Giap and his Politburo colleague Truong Chinh busied themselves during the next several years writing theoretical tracts on guerrilla tactics and "people's war," Dung passed his time in Saigon as a member of the North Vietnamese delegation to the first International Control Commission, studying the enemy firsthand, looking for practical ways to defeat him.

When he returned to Hanoi in the late 1950s he had a basic formula in mind—an escalating guerrilla-style war waged by regular forces—and it was on the basis of his recommendations and those of Giap and Le Duan that the Politburo began building its long-range strategy for victory.

During the pivotal party conferences of 1959 and 1960, at which the strategy and basic goals were established, Dung was awarded another star and elected to the Politburo as an "alternate" member. Ho Chi Minh had already taken a special liking to him, in part because of their shared peasant origins, and he went out of his way to assure the general's advancement. Dung also profited from a controversy between Giap and a rival officer over the seemingly mundane question of whether professionalism or party status should be given top priority as a ticket to promotion in the army. Giap favored professionalism and so did the pragmatic Dung, and when Giap finally won his point he generously rewarded those who had sided with him.

Dung repaid Giap with utter loyalty, shouldering the military's toughest assignments and making himself a lightning rod for criticism of the high command. When Giap and his colleagues made their gravest miscalculation of the war, deciding in 1964 to up the ante in the south and to send in regular North Vietnamese divisions on the theory the United States would not retaliate, it was Dung who provided a public apologia, writing in the party's theoretical journal that the Politburo had known all along that the Americans would unleash their B-52s against the "homeland." Afterward, through the years of massive U.S. involvement and the great NVA counteroffensives, he continued to do what he had always done best, operating as Hanoi's de facto commander in chief, planning and running the campaigns in the field while Giap copped all the glory.

Eventually he received his due. Some six months after the 1972 offensive came to an end, Dung was raised to full membership in the Politburo, along with the chief of Hanoi's secret police, Tran Quoc Hoan.

In view of Dung's daring and experience, it was therefore logical that the Politburo should now turn to him in its last great gamble of the war. He was a fighting man's general, a kind of North Vietnamese Ulysses S. Grant, practical-minded and unfettered by doctrine, and if the job could be done, he would do it, as quickly and efficiently as possible, with all due attention to the wishes of his seniors in the Politburo.

As Dung notes in his memoirs, he was "elated" at his new assignment. Soon after being informed of it, he told his old friend General Tran Van Tra, commander in the Saigon area and the delta, "I will fight in the highlands to the rainy season [in June]; then I will go to the Nam Bo [the region around Saigon] to prepare for the 1975–76 dry-season campaign." Dung's optimism was somewhat misplaced. He would actually join Tra in the Nam Bo within three months.

•　　　　　•　　　　　•

By the end of the first week of January the North Vietnamese were thus embarked on a strategy of escalation and improvisation whose ultimate objective and potential even they could not foresee. Furthermore, any similarity between their actual planning and what American (or South Vietnamese) intelligence analysts expected of them was largely coincidental. While Polgar and the DAO staff continued to warn of Armageddon, the North Vietnamese themselves were busily refining their objectives and preparing for the kind of limited military campaign I had been predicting for weeks, though on the basis of intelligence that was now out of date (the Resolution for 1975—the linchpin of my analysis—had in effect been superseded by the latest Politburo decisions, about which we still knew nothing). Although Polgar would eventually get his Armageddon, the shifts in North Vietnamese strategy that would lead to it were still several weeks—and several victories—away.

A Thousand Cuts

As the North Vietnamese unleashed their dry-season campaign, the Khmer Communists did the same in Cambodia. Having already shut off all roads to Phnom Penh, they moved at once to sever the city's only other overland link to the outside world—the Mekong River running to the South Vietnamese border. The water mines the Chinese had recently given them soon accomplished the job.

In the meantime, KC forces north of Phnom Penh maneuvered mortars and artillery to within striking range of Pochentong airfield, to preempt the American airlift. In the first nine weeks of the bombardment over 1,000 rockets and artillery rounds plummeted in on the city, killing 150 people and wounding six times that number.

On 7 January, Kissinger called an emergency meeting of his crisis management team, the Washington Special Action Group (WSAG), to consider ways of stanching the fires in Indochina. CIA Director Colby opened his briefing on Vietnam with an ambiguous forecast. While noting that increased fighting was likely in the "next six months," he reminded his listeners that the latest National Intelligence Estimate ruled out a "general offensive this year."

One possible solution to the Cambodia crisis was dismissed at the outset of the meeting. Although the French had recently resurrected their proposal for the return of Sihanouk, and negotiations between him and the United States, Kissinger still opposed it, out of concern for preserving America's reputation as a steadfast ally to Lon Nol. As a feeble alternative, WSAG decided a little saber-rattling was in order, just to remind the Khmer Communists, and the North Vietnamese, that the American military was still to be reckoned with. Word was leaked to the press that several warships just departing Subic Bay in the Philippines would swing past North Vietnam to dramatize Washington's concern over Communist "cease-fire violations." Unfortunately, in all the hurly-burly no one thought to alert the Navy itself, and before the orders could be amended, the fleet in question put in at the Strait of Malacca without even so much as a brief tack toward Vietnam. Kissinger was furious, blaming Defense Secretary Schlesinger for the oversight.

The following day the Administration set another phase of its Indochina strategy in motion, announcing that it would ask Congress for additional military aid for our Indochina clients to tide them over till the end of the fiscal year in June—$300 million for Vietnam and over $200 million for Cambodia.

From the moment the proposals were surfaced, it was obvious they faced rough going. The newly elected Congress was young and reform-minded and hardly a friend of Indochina's autocracies. Inflation and unemployment in the United States, moreover, were running at stunningly high levels and the idea of siphoning off tax money to feed far-off conflicts that were supposed to be over seemed almost laughable to many Congressmen and news commentators.

The Administration also had the backlash from Watergate to contend with. Having toppled a President, Congress was now determined to assert itself in the making of foreign and domestic policy. Senator Jackson's assault on the Soviet trade bill was one symptom of the trend. Yet another had been provided by the recent Cyprus crisis. When Turkish forces had invaded the island the previous summer to counter a Greek-Cypriot uprising, many in Congress and the Executive Branch had cried foul, particularly since the use of American arms in the operation clearly violated U.S. aid laws. Now Congress was determined to make its complaints stick by cutting off all military assistance to Turkey. The move, however justified, had bleak implications for a whole gamut of Administration policies, including Kissinger's approach to Indochina's problems. If Congress was willing to short-change a NATO ally like Turkey, how could he rationalize continued support for Cambodia and South Vietnam, whose niche in the American security picture had always been far more questionable?

There was also another force moving in Congress—equally the legacy of Watergate—that had a direct bearing on the aid debate. Over a year before, Kissinger himself had been almost untouchable in his glory and in his achievements. Now he was the object of a growing antipathy in Congress that exceeded all rational bounds. His style and his approach to diplomacy—the chronic secrecy, the propensity for executive agreements secretly arrived at—seemed to many legislators all too reminiscent of what had been wrong with Nixon himself. Then, too, he was the last real bulwark against a reassertion of their own prerogatives in the foreign policy sphere. If he could be circumvented, Congress would be that much stronger. Like the Soviet trade deal and the Cyprus affair, the Indochina aid debate thus became a philosophical and political battleground, a contest between Kissinger and the Legislative Branch over their proper roles in the conduct of foreign affairs.

To Kissinger himself the aid debate also represented a crucible for something he considered vital to American security—the resiliency of America's image around the world as a defender of friends in need. Sustaining this image had always been a central ingredient in his formula for international diplomacy, but recently it had taken on a new and special significance. By January

1975, after weeks of careful spadework, his search for a Middle East settlement seemed to have reached a turning point, and now, as perhaps never before, the decisive element in it was the reliability of U.S. support for Israel. It was this that would determine how far both the Israelis and the Arabs would go to achieve accommodation. Currently, Israel was resisting proposals for a pullback in the Sinai desert out of uncertainty over the extent of our backing for its latest negotiating position, and the Syrians and the Egyptians were withholding substantive concessions of their own for the same reason. Considering the sensitivities of each side, Kissinger and his staff felt it would be grossly "destabilizing" if at the very moment he was trying to lever Israel toward compromise, Congress should turn its back on friends in need in Indochina.

Ambassador Martin knew and appreciated the geopolitical reasons behind the new aid drive, but he also favored a supplemental appropriation for the good he felt it might do for the South Vietnamese themselves. He had long believed high levels of aid were psychologically vital for them as a morale stiffener, and had repeatedly emphasized this point to newsmen and Congressmen. If he had failed to win many converts among them, he had clearly done better with the leaders of both North and South Vietnam, most of whom now took it as an article of faith that the morale of Saigon's army would collapse without some new gesture of U.S. support.

But there was more to Martin's crusade than simply the salvation of Saigon, for he had also come to view the aid debate as another round in his ongoing struggle against the great "conspiracy out there," that anarchy of "alienated intellectuals" in the hinterlands of American politics who he supposed were serving as propagandists for Hanoi. By now his demonology had become fairly well defined—Tom Hayden, Jane Fonda, Fred Branfman and Don Luce of the non-profit Indochina Resource Center were the names he mentioned most often—and as he prepared for what in fact would be his final battle on Saigon's behalf, he was determined to make them, as well as additional aid, the issue.

It was not an arbitrary decision, but in effect, had been forced on him. In mid-December, just as the North Vietnamese were preparing to launch their dry-season campaign, a group of prominent American churchmen had issued a "pastoral" letter on Vietnam to various religious communities around the United States. Drawing on information supplied by the Indochina Resource Center, they had chosen to interpret the continued bloodletting in Vietnam as largely an American responsibility. "There is no peace, the war goes on," they wrote. "American funds and American prestige support a dictatorship in South Vietnam that arrests and tortures dissidents. Why is this so? As we approach the anniversary of the signing of the Paris peace agreements, the unpalatable truth we choose to ignore is that we have failed to honor the agreements we pledged to honor. Our slogan was 'peace with honor.' Our reality is 'no honor, therefore no peace.' This is our abomination. This is why the war goes on."

The tone and content of the letter so nettled Martin he felt obliged to respond, particularly since the State Department seemed unwilling to. In a cable to Washington on Christmas Day, in which he included a copy of the letter, he summoned his colleagues to the battlements: "It is perhaps a desecration of all this day should mean for this [letter] to be received in the Department on Christmas Day. However, to borrow a word from its text, it is such an 'abomination' that we believe no time should be lost in the careful consideration of the nature and extent of the Department's responsibility for a response.

"[This cable] was sent in the increasingly forlorn hope that the Department would come to share our deeply held belief . . . that distortions so gross that they approach the dimension of caricature ought not to go without corrective action . . . and that failure to [respond] becomes a positive albeit tacit contribution to a cleverly orchestrated campaign to deceive the American people, a campaign of which this 'pastoral letter' is only a part.

"We fully share the Department's evident distaste to become soiled by the attacks which inevitably will be made on anyone who dares to observe that the interfaith group's statement is a tissue of lies from beginning to end . . . Although we share the distaste, we cannot share the rationalizations that would permit the Department to evade its moral responsibilities to provide the whole truth to the American people. The memories of Pontius Pilate washing his hands are too fresh in our minds this Christmas season."

With that, Martin seized the initiative, goading his colleagues into one last tilt against the conspiracy "out there," with the aid proposals as both their pretext and their weapon. He was truly dismayed at the State Department's reticence—"I was then convinced," he told me over a year later, "that Vietnam was finished, that I could do no more than wage a holding action"—but he was hardly loath to shoulder the burden himself.

Given the atmosphere, it would have been nothing short of miraculous if the debate over the supplemental aid proposals had remained low-key and dispassionate. It did not. Up and down Pennsylvania Avenue, and from Washington to Saigon, tempers flared, egos became engaged and, as usual, truth and candor were among the first casualties.

The Administration itself was perhaps the worst offender, cynically skewing the facts to suit its case. Yet in a sense, it probably could not have done otherwise, for the facts by themselves were anything but helpful. As CIA analysts in Washington now realized, Cambodia was already too far gone to be able to profit from any additional aid. And as for Saigon, the proposed $300 million supplemental was far less urgent in terms of its immediate needs than the Administration insisted.

Administration officials could hardly claim to be unaware of this. In a recent field survey a Pentagon logistics team had finally uncovered some of those untapped stockpiles in South Vietnam that had eluded General Murray in the first year and a half of the cease-fire. According to its findings, if ammunition continued to be expended at the December rate—18,000 tons per month—the stocks would last for a year or more. Even if expenditures rose to 1972 levels, the army would be able to hold its own through August. The CIA essentially confirmed these views.

Furthermore, as an additional hedge against Saigon's future, there was still money and matériel in the U.S. aid pipeline to be drawn upon. As the Pentagon itself later admitted, only a fraction of the current aid budget had so far been disposed of—$158.4 million out of the total $700 million allocation. The rest had yet to be spent or was committed to matériel awaiting delivery.

None of these considerations, of course, affected the Administration's calculations concerning the urgency of the supplemental aid requests. Since the proposals were keyed to Kissinger's geopolitical priorities, the actual needs and deserts of the recipients were almost beside the point. Yet the Administration could not admit this to Congress without weakening its hand. So in the end it chose to distort and equivocate, arguing that the supplementals were necessary to save South Vietnam and Cambodia from fiscal and psychological collapse, pending the next annual appropriation in June.

In hopes of winning support for this view, public relations experts at the Pentagon drew up a memo in late December, calling for a massive propaganda effort to convince Congress and the public that Saigon would run out of ammunition in thirty days without additional aid. A week later State Department officials urged the White House to make the loss of Phuoc Long Province the centerpiece of a sympathy drive on Saigon's behalf. "Military aid to Indochina remains one of the least popular issues in Congress," the Assistant Secretary of State for Congressional Affairs wrote to Kissinger in a memo on 13 January. "However, we are slightly heartened by the recent reactions to stories of North Vietnamese tanks overrunning South Vietnamese soldiers in embattled province capitals . . . We look for less [Congressional] attention to Thieu's domestic political behavior and greater focus on North Vietnamese aggression, which inevitably will lead to questioning as to how we can abandon a country where 55,000 Americans gave their lives."

In Saigon, meanwhile, the Embassy continued to do its part. My briefing schedule was expanded to two or three performances per day to accommodate the Congressmen and Congressional aides who suddenly crowded into the city to be enlightened, and my field appraisals were carefully retooled and revised to put the North Vietnamese in the worst possible light. "The Communists' strategy for 1975," read a heavily edited estimate in early January, "is aimed at winning a significant victory through military means while continuing to pay lip service to the Paris agreement. Militarily they may do better this year than in 1972, since in the meantime the United States has reduced its assistance to South Vietnam, leaving the government with uncertainties and problems it has not faced before . . . Under these circumstances the South Vietnamese are limited merely to reacting to Communist initiatives and, as the *Economist* magazine recently put it, are confronted with the prospect of 'death by a thousand cuts.' "

That cute turn of phrase may have impressed some of the Congressmen to whom the appraisal was discreetly leaked in Washington, but it did nothing to help pinpoint North Vietnamese intentions. But that, of course, was no longer the primary purpose of my estimates. Now I was in the advertising business.

As in the fall, the priorities of the aid debate also affected our perspectives on the South Vietnamese themselves. While it was perfectly all right to play devil's advocate in dealing with NVA intentions, it was unacceptable when you were addressing the problems and potential of our ally. Saigon's vulnerabilities, we were now careful to point out, were principally the result of aid cutbacks. Thieu himself bore little responsibility for them. If anything, his capacity for leadership was at a premium.

In mid-January, Polgar wrote an estimate to underscore this point, arguing that Thieu was so firmly ensconced in power he would probably run for reelection in October without any significant domestic opposition. He also proposed that we begin cultivating a token opposition candidate—CIA client Tran Quoc Buu—so Thieu would not have to face the embarrassment of a one-man contest as he had in 1971. Even for the myopics in CIA headquarters this was a little much, and in a return message they advised Polgar as politely as they could that they had thrown both his proposal and his analysis in the shredder. It was too early in the year, they explained, to make any confident predictions about Thieu's political future.

Although Polgar continued actively to support the Administration's overall aid strategy, he did balk at several individual schemes, including Martin's recurring proposal for an economic aid appropriation of adequate size to make Saigon self-sufficient in three years. In mid-January, the Ambassador again surfaced the idea, as a corollary to the proposed military aid supplemental, and Polgar challenged him on it. Their relationship was never quite the same again.

The showdown came during an interview with Senator Sam Nunn of Georgia, who had come out to Saigon to review the "situation." The Ambassador had been arguing for the past half-hour that there was a good chance the South Vietnamese could become economically and militarily independent of the United States after another three years of massive aid transfusions. Nunn listened but obviously was not convinced. Finally he looked across the table at Polgar and asked his opinion. For a moment Polgar hesitated, his eyes pinwheeling behind the Coke-bottle glasses as if he were searching for some place to hide. But there wasn't any. "No, sir," he said at last, "I don't believe the South Vietnamese can ever expect to be militarily or economically independent of us as long as the Soviets and the Chinese go on supplying the North Vietnamese. If they could be persuaded to cut back on their aid, we perhaps could make parallel reductions in our own. But that would be the precondition."

Martin turned white. "What Mr. Polgar meant to say was . . . " But Nunn cut him off. "Would you mind repeating your answer, Mr. Polgar?" he said casually. At that, the other members of Martin's staff who were seated around the oblong table in the conference room began bobbing and weaving as if fearful of being hit with the same question.

But Polgar was unperturbed. He repeated what he had said: it all depended on the Soviets and the Chinese. Otherwise we were in Vietnam for good.

By the end of January, Congressional opposition to the aid proposals was stiffening, but the Administration continued to lobby hard for them. In a note to Congress on the twenty-eighth, Ford insisted melodramatically that the $300 million was needed "as a minimum" to prevent "serious reversals" in South Vietnam, and Vice-President Rockefeller warned that further aid reductions would lead to the loss of the country and a bloodbath there, the responsibility for which, he said, would have to be borne by Congress.

Finally, on the thirtieth, a group of high-ranking State Department and Pentagon officials went up to Capitol Hill to lay the Administration's case before the crucial House Appropriations Subcommittee. Taking their cue from the Embassy, they advertised and oversimplified the available intelligence to underline the prospects for significant fighting in the months ahead. General Daniel O. Graham, chief of the Pentagon's Defense Intelligence Agency, disclosed that the North Vietnamese were preparing to send two additional divisions into South Vietnam and had recently moved another out of southern Laos into the western highlands. Erich Von Marbod, Deputy Assistant Secretary of Defense, quoted selectively and explicitly from Hanoi's Resolution for 1975, in an effort to portray recent aid cutbacks as the principal motivation for Communist aggressiveness.

Von Marbod claimed that the excerpts he cited were drawn from a version of the Resolution that had been picked up in North Vietnamese radio traffic. This was false. Hanoi seldom committed such high-level directives to the airwaves. Actually, Von Marbod was quoting verbatim from a report provided by one of our top agents.

When I learned what he had done I was shocked and discouraged. For the sake of impressing a single Congressional committee, the Administration was once again putting an important operative in jeopardy. If it was willing to go that far in its effort to win support for the aid proposals, the chances for a reasoned judgment of any kind on Saigon's future were all but nil.

There were, to be sure, a few stalwarts in Washington who tried to address the issues sensibly in the last winter of the war. In late December the Vietnam desk officer at the State Department made a quick tour of the battle zone and returned home convinced South Vietnam was in grave danger, not so much because of supply shortages as because of skyrocketing inflation and declining morale within the army and population. His findings, reasoned as they were, were generally ignored in the front offices at the State Department, since they did not square with the Administration's strategy in the aid debate. It was one thing to emphasize Saigon's needs and vulnerabilities; it was quite another to count the South Vietnamese out even before Congress had voted.

At about the same time the deputy chief of estimates for the Defense Intelligence Agency came out to Saigon for an independent assessment of his own. The conclusions he reached were equally bleak, and few of his colleagues in the Pentagon wanted to go on record as supporting them. His final report was therefore quickly sidetracked down one of those long corridors in the Pentagon that had served as the burial ground for so many Vietnam truths in the past.

In mid-January still another of Washington's skeptics had his worst suspicions confirmed. On a two-week field trip a prominent USIA official who had previously served in Vietnam discovered that security in the countryside, particularly in the delta, had seriously eroded in the past few months—far more than the Embassy admitted—and that morale in the army was on the verge of collapse. Through an old friend on Thieu's staff he also obtained "accountability" records proving that Saigon was facing no immediate short-age of supplies or matériel. What was needed, his friend told him, was merely a token of continued American support for Saigon. The proposed $300 million supplemental would of course serve nicely, but so would a far lesser amount.

The USIA officer explained this to Martin's number-two man, Wolfgang Lehmann, and urged him to recommend a shift in objectives to Washington. In place of the $300 million proposal the Administration should seek a more modest package, he said, one that was more likely to be approved by Congress. That would meet Saigon's immediate need, the psychological one, with a minimum of controversy.

But Lehmann shook his head. "You're too late," he explained. "The Administration has already decided to go for broke."

And so it had. At no point did Kissinger or his staff seriously consider the low-road approach to the aid question. Instead they would continue plumping for maximum aid allocations that far exceeded Saigon's immediate wants or Congress' generosity, while rejecting compromises that would have assured the minimum "gesture of support" Saigon needed above all else.

They did so for reasons quite unrelated to Indochina. How could you hope to purchase a new lease on American credibility around the world, in the Middle East or the Soviet Union, at bargain-basement prices? Saigon would get that $300 million, whether it needed it or not.

Realizing that the Administration was locked on this ill-considered course, the USIA man returned to Washington in despair over Saigon's pros-pects. Once again, it seemed to him, the South Vietnamese were to be sacrificed on the altar of American self-interest. He was right.

Hail-Fellow

The capture of Phuoc Long Province was like the crack of a starting pistol. Scarcely had the reverberations died away than North Vietnamese forces were bearing in on other priority targets. In MR 1, the northernmost region of the country, three NVA divisions slid into position west of Hué and Danang Cities as several unattached regiments from North Vietnam filtered across the demilitarized zone to back them up. In the meantime, the flow of NVA reinforcements into the western highlands of MR 2 accelerated dramatically, and further south, in the Saigon area, one of the divisions that had taken part in the Phuoc Long campaign edged across the top of the region toward Tay Ninh Province to join other units poised for attack. By early February, Communist forces were arrayed in an arc all across the northern frontiers of MR 3.

With so much territory to protect, the opposing government units throughout the country found themselves overextended and hamstrung. Their only choice, aside from surrendering huge chunks of territory, was to hug their positions, lie low and wait for the next blow.

As the backing and filling continued on both sides, General Van Tien Dung prepared to depart for South Vietnam. During the last week in January he paid a farewell call on Le Duan at his home in Hanoi. As they clinked cognac snifters and wished each other good luck, Le Duan reminded his commander of the slip-clause in their strategic plan. "If we win great victories," he told Dung, "we might be able to liberate the south this year."

On 5 February, Dung took a plane from Hanoi to Dong Hoi in the North Vietnamese panhandle and then drove across the border into Quang Tri Province in northern MR 1 to begin his journey south. From there he traveled by boat and car along the NVA logistics network through western South Vietnam and southern Laos. All along the way he was hailed and applauded by NVA forces as they, too, groped toward the front. It is doubtful many of them recognized the stocky, square-jowled figure in the back seat of the freshly painted field car, but there was no question, in view of the license number—"TS 50," a top-priority designation—that the passenger was a high-ranking military officer.

From the outset the campaign remained shrouded in secrecy. "Even my movements had to be kept under wraps," Dung notes in his own account, "and everything was done to confuse the enemy's intelligence. Accordingly, after my departure the press in Hanoi carried a number of reports on my 'activities' as if I was still there. Daily my Volga sedan would make the trips from my house to the general headquarters . . . [and] late in the afternoon troops would come to the courtyard of my house to play volleyball as usual, because I have a habit of playing volleyball after the afternoon working hours."

The subterfuge paid off handsomely. Not until Dung published his memoirs a year after the fall of Vietnam did any of us on the other side of the lines realize he had joined the army in the field for the final offensive.

With so much riding on Dung's mission, Le Duan made a final effort to shore up support for it in the party, particularly among the "reconstruction-firsters" who were still complaining about the dangers and potential costs. In a speech on 3 February, marking the anniversary of the party, he belabored them with both carrot and stick, on the one hand, threatening reprisals if they persisted in their objections, on the other, promising continued moderation and "balance" in decision-making. As proof of his own reasonableness he reemphasized the primacy of political over military objectives, offering a provocative new formula for negotiations. In outlining "the most important conditions" for a settlement, he carefully omitted the demand for Thieu's removal, which he and his colleagues had resurrected the previous October, and instead called only for "an end to U.S. involvement and interference, and the formation in Saigon of a new administration that will implement the Paris agreement." The formulation, in its vagueness, was reminiscent of the one Hanoi had used to signal the breakthrough in the Paris negotiations of 1972, and as a subliminal declaration of caution and flexibility, it could hardly fail to impress those in the leadership who were now worried about Dung and his fellow hawks pushing the military option to its limits.

When I read over a translation of the speech I was strengthened in my own conviction that a new round of negotiations, not military victory, was the Communists' immediate objective. A few days later a high-level agent filed a report that seemed to confirm this. Predicting new and intense initiatives north of Saigon (Ban Me Thuot was not mentioned specifically), he noted that once the fighting was done, the PRG would call for resumption of the now suspended bilateral talks, as well as a shift in venue for them, from Paris to some city in South Vietnam.

In light of the report, Le Duan's speech seemed doubly significant, and I wrote an analysis of it for Polgar, setting out what I saw as the political and military implications. Polgar was so intrigued he decided to test my ideas on his contacts in the Hungarian ICCS delegation. He passed my memorandum to them and asked for comment. A few days later they gave him one, assuring him my conclusions were "about right." In other words, there was still a chance for a negotiated settlement, though the level of activity was likely to increase in the weeks ahead.

Polgar immediately cabled a summary of the Hungarians' remarks to Washington. The Hungarians in turn alerted Hanoi to our thinking so that the Politburo could adjust its plans and strategy accordingly. In effect, out of the best of motives Polgar had just handed the North Vietnamese another intelligence coup, one that provided an invaluable insight into what we expected of them.

The newly highlighted prospects for a political solution did not still Polgar's drumfire about the military threat. Congress had yet to be persuaded of the need for additional aid, and he was determined to do his part. Consequently, we declassified and leaked to the press two recently captured Communist planning documents—with a commentary I had written—that seemed likely to convince any reader in Washington the North Vietnamese were coming over the hill. I also kept my briefings to visitors and other Embassy personnel simplistically alarmist in line with Polgar's specifications, skirting the difficult and perplexing issue of Hanoi's political intentions.*

After one of my particularly vivid dissertations on the Communist threat, a CIA colleague threw up his hands in dismay. "Good Christ!" he exclaimed. "You were telling us only a few weeks ago everything was secure. Now it looks as though we're facing the final reckoning."

Such sentiments soon became widespread in the Embassy, and a number of my colleagues began planning for the worst. The Station's administration section proceeded to store up additional supplies of C-rations and drinking water, and several senior CIA officers ordered their subordinates to put together caches of arms and ammunition just in case they had to defend themselves against the onslaught.

At the same time the Defense Attaché's Office and the Embassy's administrative component took an even more drastic precaution. They began updating the Embassy's standing 400-page evacuation plan. (Each U.S. Embassy in the world has one, as a matter of routine.) Colonel Garvin McCurdy and Captain Cornelius Carmody, the Air Force and Navy Attachés, were put in charge of the project. Working with a small staff, they refined parts of the

---

*The two planning papers—COSVN Directive 08 and a Binh Dinh Province Resolution—together with my commentary were issued as a single package through the auspices of the USIA office in Saigon, as part of its continuing series "Vietnam: Documents and Research Notes." Since the USIA, by charter, is supposed to be a vehicle for projecting America's best image abroad, its involvement in disseminating intelligence to the western press on Communist strategy was something of an anomaly. In fact, however, throughout the cease-fire period the USIA's Saigon office frequently provided journalists through its "Documents" series intelligence which the CIA had generated and commentaries I had produced. My good friend Jim Haley of USIA protested the CIA's intrusion into the affairs of his agency, but was ignored.

massive blueprint, developing a separate scenario for the evacuation of Americans in each of the four military regions and, finally, Saigon. Most of their emendations were procedural, rather than substantive, and among the elements of the original plan they retained was its arbitrary ceiling on the number of allowable evacuees: no more than 6,800 in total, the majority of whom were to be American.

In early February, as the exercise continued, a DAO representative dropped in on Polgar and asked him if he wanted to participate. As one of its own contributions, DAO was drawing up a contingency plan for secretly evacuating intelligence agents and high-ranking government officials. The Station naturally faced a similar requirement.

But Polgar said no; he saw no reason to become involved. Despite his concern about the military situation, he could not bring himself to believe the country would ever have to be abandoned or that a full evacuation might be necessary.

While the majority of us in the Embassy labored over our evacuation schemes and our alarmist propaganda, Ambassador Martin tried to use his own time more profitably. In early February he packed up and headed back to Washington to help buck up the Administration's position in the aid debate.

Immediately on arrival he began agitating among Administration colleagues and Congressional contacts for a scheme close to his heart—his plan for a massive aid program sufficient to leave Saigon "economically independent" in three years.

On 8 February, President Ford formally endorsed the overall concept, but others in Washington remained unimpressed. Schlesinger considered the proposal disingenuous. If the United States was prepared to cut Saigon adrift in three years, he commented to a reporter, why not now? Congress seemed equally skeptical, and several of the more cynical legislators complained that the three-year plan was meant simply to win the Administration a reprieve from Vietnam until after the next presidential election.

Martin took such sniping in stride. The trouble, he assured Kissinger's staff, lay not in the aid proposal itself, but in Congress' perspectives. If the House and the Senate could be persuaded to send an official fact-finding team to Saigon to look into the situation, the opposition would melt away.

The Administration in fact had long been in favor of such a Congressional tour, and in early February it offered to postpone all hearings on the proposed aid bills for several weeks so a team could be put together and sent out to Saigon. Within a few days, however, a flap developed over the makeup of the delegation. Representative Tom Harkin, a young Democrat from Iowa who had served as a Navy pilot in Vietnam, announced that his interpreter for the trip would be none other than Don Luce, constant critic of American policies in Vietnam and one of Martin's pet demons. Representative Bella Abzug, the aggressive dove from Manhattan, disclosed she was planning to use a former

South Vietnamese "political prisoner" as her guide so she could get an "unbiased" view of the situation. The more conservative members of the delegation threatened to bow out in protest.

Just as these problems seemed about to be resolved, another intruded to put a freeze on the entire project. This one had nothing to do with Vietnam itself. For days a feud had been brewing between the White House and Congress over controversial legislation that would have suspended President Ford's oil tariff program, and like most of their colleagues, the twenty or so Congressmen who were to make up the Indochina fact-finding group finally decided to postpone all outstanding business, including the trip, pending a showdown. With that, the Administration's Indochina strategy threatened to come to a full stop. Martin returned to Saigon discouraged and embittered.

Other Administration officials, meanwhile, made a last effort to restore the momentum. Reverting to an old trick, they again began crying wolf, this time making Cambodia the object of their alarms. The Lon Nol government would fall in a few weeks, they warned Congress, unless the proposed supplemental for Cambodia was approved at once.

None of this was very persuasive, however. The CIA had just completed a National Intelligence Estimate which showed that even with additional aid, the Phnom Penh government would be unable to regain the military initiative in the foreseeable future. CIA Director Colby spelled out these conclusions candidly and in detail to a Congressional committee, and from that point on, Administration aid lobbyists were in something of a dilemma. Kissinger and Schlesinger, both realizing the hazards of overplaying the aid-as-salvation line, soon began pulling back from it, conceding privately to newsmen that Cambodia might be doomed in any case.

From Saigon, President Nguyen Van Thieu watched this spectacle with growing concern and bewilderment. The Administration's loud talk about the importance of additional aid as a surety for his survival cut deeply into his self-confidence, all the more so since his enemies in Hanoi seemed to be drawing encouragement from it.

In addition, he was now facing new problems at home. Encouraged by his dwindling credit in Washington, his domestic critics were becoming active again. On 3 February, Father Tran Huu Thanh, the conservative Catholic priest who had played gadfly to the government in early fall, issued yet another public indictment of Thieu himself, accusing him of "high treason" and of "undermining the nationalist cause for his own financial gain."

Although Thanh himself remained untouchable because of his church affiliations, Thieu wasted no time in moving against the priest's confederates. Five oppositionist newspapers that had dared to publish the indictment were shut down and eighteen journalists who had made the mistake of writing similarly uncomplimentary things about the government were arrested on charges of pro-Communist activity.

•   •   •

As Thieu brooded over the rumblings on the political front he also tried to come to grips with the enemy and his works. In his most decisive response to the loss of Phuoc Long he ordered a shake-up in the MR 3 command and appointed a new regional commander, General Nguyen Van Toan, who had been removed from the top post in MR 2 the previous fall for corruption and inefficiency. Explaining Toan's reinstatement to the press, Thieu said it was aimed simply at improving Saigon's defenses in light of the recent setbacks. Actually, he had another motive as well. Toan was one of the few ARVN commanders he felt he could trust in a position of power so close to the flagpole.

Since Toan's reputation for corruption still clung to him like a bad odor, his elevation caused considerable grumbling among Saigon's already disgruntled reformers. Perhaps the only satisfied witness to the event, outside Thieu's own entourage, was the American Embassy. It was, in fact, Ambassador Martin who had initially urged Toan's candidacy on Thieu. Despite the reverses Toan had suffered in MR 2 the previous summer, the Ambassador had got it into his head the general was an effective field commander. "But what about all those rumors of Toan's corruption?" Thieu asked incredulously when Martin first suggested the appointment. "Won't that make for bad publicity?" Martin, as he later told the story, merely shrugged. "You've heard of General Ulysses S. Grant?" he replied. "He, too, had a bad reputation. The newspapers said he was a drunk and a no-account. But he won the American Civil War for Mr. Lincoln, didn't he? That's what Toan will do for you." Which of the implied analogies more impressed Thieu was never clear. In any case, he decided to act on Martin's recommendation.*

In addition to the personnel changes, Thieu instituted a (slightly) "new look" in strategy in the wake of the Phuoc Long debacle. For the past month his chief military advisor, General Cao Van Vien, the ever-smiling, bush-haired chairman of the Joint General Staff, had been urging him to adopt a variation of the truncated-Vietnam concept that he, Prime Minister Khiem and, from time to time, the Americans had been advocating for almost a year. The government's decisions of 9 and 10 December—the ones the North Vietnamese spy had so fully described to his masters in Hanoi—had been a first, faltering step in this direction: a concentration of all available reserves, such

---

*General Toan had long been a popular figure among American generals and diplomats in Vietnam. His size may have been partly responsible. Nearly six feet tall, with barrel paunch, he had the "aggressive look" of an American football pro. In the late 1960s he strengthened his claim on American esteem while serving as commander of the 2nd ARVN Division in southern MR 1. It was during his tenure there that an American unit massacred three hundred and forty-seven civilians in My Lai, a village in his operational zone. Although Toan and his staff knew what had happened, they remained silent out of deference to American sensitivities. The Embassy and MACV, needless to say, were grateful. Later, during the NVA offensive of 1972, Toan bolstered his image as an "aggressive" field commander with the successful defense of Kontum Province —an operation which in fact had been planned largely by his legendary American advisor, John Paul Vann.

as they were, in MR 3, with no effort to reinforce the highlands or MR 1.

But now Khiem and Vien wanted Thieu to go one step further, actually forfeiting territory in the northern half of the country to facilitate a conservation of ammunition and other resources.* To buttress their case, Vien handed Thieu a broad strategic outline that had recently been drawn up by that eager entrepreneur Ted Sarong, the retired Australian brigadier general who still had visions of serving as Thieu's private military advisor. Sparse in detail, but long on pretensions, the plan envisaged a pullback of forces in the highlands and in northern Military Region 1 prior to the next wave of Communist attacks, which Sarong predicted for 15 February.

Thieu looked over the document, weighed its implications, and rejected it. But even as he was trying to convince Vien and Khiem of the rightness of this decision, the news from Washington turned depressingly bleak. According to Thieu's own envoys there, the prospects for additional appropriations were growing slimmer by the day.

In this light, Vien's recommendations became somewhat more appealing, and Thieu decided to give them closer scrutiny. In early February he put together a study group under Vien and Khiem to think out the full range of their strategic alternatives, and directed his MR 1 commander to prepare to withdraw the crack Airborne Division from the contact line north of Hué and hold it in reserve for possible transfer to Saigon.

Vien and Khiem were not satisfied. They considered the pullback of the Airborne "inadequate" in view of what they felt was required. Others in Thieu's entourage were put off for precisely the opposite reason, feeling the decision went much too far. One of those who objected most strenuously was the MR 1 commander himself, General Ngo Quang Truong. In his view the trimming of his forces was nothing short of madness.

Tall and even-tempered, Truong had long been an American favorite. He was a man an American could look in the eye without looking down, and that undoubtedly had helped his reputation. As a commander in the delta in the early 1970s, he had been fairly successful in promoting pacification, the Americans' favorite game, and in May 1972, at the height of the NVA offensive, he had been hastily appointed to the MR 1 command on American advice, largely because MACV believed he was the only field commander who could rally ARVN forces there. Guided by his American advisors, he had done precisely that, and probably had saved the country. Since then, he had frequently been mentioned by Embassy officials as the most appealing of the potential replacements for Thieu—a fact Thieu himself had duly noted, much to the detriment

---

*Vien's new interest in truncation stemmed in part from a kind of pack-rat mentality, according to subordinates. Since the first days of the cease-fire, even before matériel shortages were dreamed of, he and his principal commanders had been insistent on keeping the government's supply stocks close to major urban centers where they could be hoarded and protected with ease, and had seldom been willing to parcel matériel out in great bulk to troops in less secure areas. By early 1975 the uncertainties of the aid debate had strengthened these tendencies and had made stockpiling in the provinces—and hence the defense of far-flung outposts—unthinkable to them. The surrender of some territory thus became inevitable.

of his own personal relations with Truong. Indeed, Thieu's abiding suspicion of his MR I commander had probably figured in his decision on the Airborne. With one less division at his disposal, Truong would be that much less dangerous.

It was not the political ramifications of the pullback that bothered Truong himself, however, but the military ones. His five divisions were already overextended, and without the Airborne he would never be able to defend against the four NVA divisions and numerous other units opposing him.

In mid-February, General Charles Timmes, the CIA's principal liaison with the South Vietnamese command, dropped in on Truong's headquarters in Danang for a routine situation briefing. During their discussion Truong surprised him by unveiling a new strategic plan for the region, though without confiding to him why it had become necessary. It provided for the defense of four major enclaves: the cities of Hué and Danang; Tam Ky, capital of Quang Tin Province; and the Chu Lai Peninsula just to the south, site of a large airfield and the headquarters of the 2nd ARVN Division. If the Communists sent reinforcements across the demilitarized zone, Truong explained, he would withdraw into these enclaves and make his stand there. Timmes (as he later confided to me) was taken with the concept; he assumed it would enable Truong to make better use of his five divisions. Undoubtedly he would have been less impressed if he had known the MR I commander was to have only four divisions to make it work.

Several days later Truong traveled to Saigon to clear his plan with the high command. To his dismay Thieu himself was unreceptive, and attempted to stall off any final decision by quibbling over details.

So what was to be done? Truong demanded bitterly after an hour or so of useless banter. Well, Thieu replied, while it was necessary to defend Danang at all costs, it would also be useful to hold on to anything else that could be defended without heavy loss of manpower and supplies. In effect, he wanted no real change at all in the government's defense lines, even though he freely acknowledged that the withdrawal of the Airborne Division would leave Truong's forces dangerously outnumbered. To give up territory, he feared, would adversely impress the Americans.

Thieu's decision to pull the Airborne out of MR I was an extension of the strategic logic that had led to the abandonment of Tong Le Chan in April 1974 and Phuoc Binh one month before. Born of an impulse to save supplies, impress Congress and bolster the defenses around Saigon, it signaled a deliberate sloughing off of secondary commitments, such as Murray had urged the previous summer. But even as Thieu edged, reluctantly and in his own fashion, in this fateful direction, the majority of us on Martin's staff remained too diverted by the aid debate itself to take much notice. By the third week in February my own briefing schedule had become very nearly a round-the-clock marathon, thanks to the continuing influx of Congressional visitors and Administration officials, and this, coupled with the expanding requirement for propagandistic position papers, left me little time to contemplate the subtler side of government or Communist strategy.

To make matters worse, my office had been short of one valued member for the past several weeks. Early in the month Pat Johnson had wolfed down a bad shrimp-salad sandwich at a Sunday brunch alongside the pool of the Duc Hotel and had ended up flat on her back. By the time she fought her way back to health I was worn to a frazzle and looking forward to a more relaxed routine. But it was not to be. The third member of our little staff decided he, too, had had enough and was due a vacation. A few days later he took Pan Am back to the States, where he would spend the next four weeks watching South Vietnam disintegrate through the lenses of the Cronkite news.

Luckily, Polgar had the foresight to provide us a stand-in. His name for the purposes of this narrative was "Joe Kingsley." A CIA operative with no analytical experience whatsoever, he had caught Polgar's eye because he knew MR 1 like the back of his hand. He had served there as a Special Forces officer in the early 1960s and had taken a piece of shrapnel in his leg for his trouble, and he still walked with a dancing limp that always became more pronounced after the first martini.

When Joe and I first met he didn't impress me. The shock of black hair, arched eyebrows and perennially puckish smile combined to give him a look of boyish innocence, even naïveté , that neatly disguised his thirty-eight years and all too worldly wisdom. Worse, he seemed far more impressed with the trinkets of espionage—the radios, the weapons and secret codes—than with the substance. He was, in a word, the last man I would have chosen to share the analytical trenches with me as Saigon faced the final onslaught.

But I soon discovered that first impressions did not do justice to Joe Kingsley. He turned out to be one of the finest (and most enthusiastic) intelligence analysts I had ever known, and the hail-fellow-well-met air he affected so naturally would eventually prove a godsend to us both. In the last few weeks of the war he would laugh, joke and wheedle his way through countless checkpoints at Tan Son Nhut air base to ensure the evacuation of his best Vietnamese friends and my own.

Pyrrhic Victories

Graham Martin now wanted to have it out once and for all. Since Congress was still playing coy with the Administration over the supplemental aid requests, he was convinced, as he later explained to me, that the only way to force a decision was to subject the skeptics to some direct heat. He therefore was delighted when Congress decided at the end of February to send its much-delayed fact-finding team to Indochina.

The delegation seemed somewhat more manageable from Martin's viewpoint than the originally proposed one. There were only six members, instead of twenty-one, and young Congressman Harkin and his controversial aid Don Luce were not among them. Still, the group did pose a challenge. Among its more liberal constituents were Donald Fraser of Minnesota and the irrepressible Bella Abzug. The powerful and articulate "Pete" McCloskey of California also had chosen to schedule a fact-finding tour of his own to coincide with the delegation's. With so many skeptics on his hands, Martin knew he would have to do some hard and fast persuading.

Typically, he left nothing to chance. He whipped up a Barnum and Bailey extravaganza that was meant to impress through sheer spectacle. Each agency in the Embassy was called upon to contribute an act or two, in the form of briefings or position papers. My own office was slated to carry much of the show. Several of my field appraisals were declassified and mimeographed, to be handed out like programs on first night, even though the sources and information on which they were based were among our most sensitive.

I was also directed to produce several special memoranda for the occasion. One of them dealt lengthily with what Polgar liked to describe as the "strategic realities." The line it spun out could have been lifted verbatim from the Ambassador's own briefing book. The current balance of forces, I argued, should not be viewed as a measure of the strength of the two sides. Although the South Vietnamese had 300,000 combat troops (and a total of 1.1 million men under arms)—against nearly 200,000 Communist regulars in the field—

they also had more population and territory to protect. Therefore, they could hardly be expected to wage war so frugally.

The argument was sensible enough. The way we set it forth was not. The document contained a complete survey of the balance of forces between the two sides, the most valuable intelligence the North Vietnamese could have obtained. Yet nothing in the memorandum bore any kind of classification. It was all to be made freely available to the visiting Congressmen, and to accompanying journalists, with no caveats whatsoever about its use or publication.

The trifling way we handled intelligence throughout this period troubled me deeply. Seldom had the Ambassador or Polgar had any qualms about declassifying and publicizing agent reports that might win support for additional aid, but now, with the military situation so fluid and confused, this continued outpouring of confidences did our allies a considerable disservice. Not only was the average newspaper reader being treated to a running commentary on the strengths and weaknesses of the two sides, but he was also being handed large slices of our latest data on North Vietnamese intentions. And the irony was we actually thought we were helping the South Vietnamese by being so forthcoming.

Beyond the wisdom of these excesses there was also a question of their legality. Under the National Security Acts the CIA is expressly enjoined from involving itself in domestic politics in the United States. And yet every memo and briefing I prepared for the delegation was a feint in this direction—an effort to change Congressional minds on a matter of domestic concern.

As the Embassy prepared for the Congressional visit, so did Thieu and his cabinet. General Vien had subordinates put together a canned briefing on the military situation designed to convince the delegation the country was on the verge of disaster. Even Martin found it a little extreme and asked Vien to tone it down. Too much gloom, he warned, could be as harmful as too little.

Other members of the cabinet concentrated on tidying up the government's dirty laundry. Since the recent arrest of the eighteen journalists in Saigon had prompted such a hue and cry in the western news media, it was one of the items that got a thorough going-over. The Ministry of the Interior was instructed to compile a batch of dossiers proving that all eighteen were "positively" Communist agents. This turned out to be no easy task, for there was an embarrassing dearth of evidence against them. Police investigators, therefore, immediately went to work on the suspects, extracting confessions from a respectable number of them and building variously defensible cases against the rest. The Station was fully aware of this rush to judgment, and the frame-ups. An agent provided us a detailed report on them. But we quickly put a classified lid on his disclosures to keep them from falling into the hands of our Congressional guests.

In Washington, meanwhile, colleagues in the State Department and the CIA were struggling through last-minute exertions of their own. For days, ever since learning of the Congressional visit, Martin had been plaguing them for documents and position papers to strengthen his hand with his guests, and the pressure for instant wisdom on a variety of topics was now reaching a crescendo.

One of the baubles Martin requested of them demanded all the ingenuity they could muster: a fully updated study of Soviet and Chinese aid to North Vietnam. He had long believed that if he could convince the doubters in Congress of the generosity of Hanoi's allies, he could persuade them to respond to Saigon in kind.

When his request was transmitted to CIA headquarters, however, analysts in the economic intelligence section let out howls of protest. For weeks they had been resisting White House pressure for such a study, for the very good reason that it was beyond their capabilities. While they could quite accurately pinpoint the kind and quantity of imports into North Vietnam, it was something else again to put a price tag on them in U.S. dollar terms.

But the impracticality of the exercise did not trouble Martin. On the contrary, he was determined to wring all he could from it. Not only did he want a value estimate for aid to North Vietnam during the past year; he wanted one for every year dating back to 1967 so he could calculate and chart the trend against concurrent aid deliveries to South Vietnam.

The study the analysts produced was a travesty, not only on the intelligence but also on their integrity. For one thing, it was so heavily qualified, as it had to be, its findings were all but meaningless. But far worse from Martin's perspective: it failed to prove his point. The final tabulation showed that while total foreign assistance to North Vietnam had risen to unprecedented levels in 1974, the jump had been in economic rather than military aid categories. If you were trying to prove Hanoi's "aggressive" intent, as Martin was, that was an embarrassing fact indeed, particularly since the trends for South Vietnam were precisely the reverse. The South Vietnamese, in fact, had received far more military aid than economic in the past year, and roughly twice the amount of military assistance (in dollar terms) that had gone to Hanoi.*

When the study was cabled out to Saigon, it was as if we had been handed a hot potato. Polgar read it, saw it did nothing for the Ambassador's case, and quickly declared that such estimates were irrelevent to determining Hanoi's military capabilities or intent. Martin was similarly put off, but rather than reject the study out of hand, he decided to draw on it selectively, citing only the most "helpful" findings and statistics while ignoring the others.

For sheer sleight of hand the aid study surpassed anything I had ever seen CIA analysts produce. Few of my colleagues back in Langley, moreover, were under any illusions about what it was. Indeed, the two top men in the analytical directorate had both made their careers as economic intelligence specialists

---

*The value of total economic and military aid to the two Vietnams in the past year had been roughly the same: $1.2 billion for Saigon, $1.7 billion for Hanoi. However, the latest military aid appropriation for Saigon had amounted to $700 million, while Hanoi had received only about $300 million in military assistance from its allies.

and were well acquainted with the difficulties of putting together such an estimate. Yet rather than risk Kissinger's ire by warning him off the project, they both had preferred to proceed with it as if there were no difficulties at all.

After all the excitement of the warm-up, the arrival of the Congressional delegation seemed almost anticlimactic, at least for the first hour or so. It soon became apparent, however, that the real ordeal was still ahead of us.

From the outset not only were our visitors suspicious of the Embassy, they were downright hostile. They had brought along several "Vietnam specialists" from the USIA and the State Department to handle introductions for them around Saigon, and they were clearly determined to rely as little as possible on Martin and his staff for help and guidance. Their independence was inspired in part by Assistant Secretary of State Philip Habib, who was accompanying the group as a kind of de facto advisor. Habib was no admirer of Martin's. He had grown impatient of the Ambassador's annoying habit of by-passing him in his dealings with Kissinger, and considered Martin's enthusiastic espousal of the Thieu government bad politics (if not necessarily bad policy). A little less passion, he once told an associate, could win far more points with Congress. Thus, as the delegates settled into their whirlwind schedule, Habib went to some lengths to retain control, carefully guiding them through their paces so none would be exposed to Martin's fire for any longer than necessary.

Normally, whenever high-ranking visitors turned up at the Embassy, I would be called upon to deliver the inaugural "situation briefing." This time Martin decided to do the honors himself, with only the help of the senior Mission Council members. Apparently he did not want to bore his visitors with a lengthy recitation of the facts.

His presentation, as it happened, was a disaster. The outcome was apparent from the moment Representative Abzug came bounding into the conference room, calling out at the top of her voice, "Which one is Polgar? I wanna see Polgar." After that it was all downhill.

During the two-hour session Polgar and the Ambassador succeeded in offending even their most sympathetic listeners by dodging most of their questions. When Abzug demanded to know how the Embassy could go on talking about political stability in Saigon in the face of so much unrest, Polgar flatly denied there was any unrest at all. The question, he said, revealed a misunderstanding of the "realities." None of the opposition groups demonstrating against the Thieu government amounted to much of anything, he insisted. Only the "loyal" oppositionists had any political clout, and they were as placid as ever.

The discussion turned next to the most sensitive issue of all, the question of political prisoners, and here again Polgar equivocated. When Representative Fraser invited his views on the subject, Polgar replied that the question was ill-phrased. Better ask about the jailing of dissenters in North Vietnam, he said, for there the practice had been raised to a high art. Whereupon he slid one of my memos on the subject across the table to the Congressman. Fraser didn't bother to look at it. "Why do you insist on throwing North Vietnam up to us?" he snapped. "Do you think some of us are pro-Communist and in need of reforming?" Polgar smiled angelically, but said nothing.

Martin then thrust himself into the exchange, hammering away at a point he always managed to inject into any public forum. "I've been in public service for forty years," he said, "and consistently I've been proven right. So you can take my word there are no political prisoners here." He went on to explain as he always did when the issue was raised that he had recently sent investigating teams into South Vietnam's jails and had determined without the "slightest doubt" that the inmates were all proven criminals—and no more than 35,000 of them at that, despite the claims of Amnesty International and other members of the conspiracy "out there."

Some of the younger Embassy officers in attendance couldn't help wincing at that statement, for they knew what the "investigations" amounted to. A year before, two or three of Martin's staffers had been sent to each of the major prisons around the country to inquire who was inside. Needless to say, the answer the Vietnamese had always given them was the one we wanted to hear: "Common criminals only. There are no political prisoners here."

As the session dragged on, Martin relied increasingly on rhetoric over facts to bludgeon his listeners into quiescence. Asked about the objectivity of Embassy reporting, he adverted once again to his proven integrity in forty years of government service. On the question of security in the countryside, he denied there had been any significant slippage at all. As he told it, the eleven towns in the Saigon area and in the delta that had been lost in the past two months were all "marginal" to the country's economic and political life.

Later, when someone pressed him on the topic of NVA intentions, he tossed off a *non sequitur* I had heard him use in so many briefings before, I knew it by heart: "All I can say is I wish the North Vietnamese *would* mount a major offensive in the next month or so. No doubt the ARVN would give ground at first; they always do. But after that they would surely go on to defeat the NVA decisively, as they did in 1972."

That opening get-together was the last time the Congressmen consented to sit still for one of Martin's lectures. Afterward each went his own way, pursuing his own favorite will-o'-the wisp. McCloskey, the former marine, journeyed by helicopter to the northernmost region of the country. Discovering he could fly unimperiled into previously disputed areas he quickly concluded that maybe the South Vietnamese were not doing so badly after all. Representative Abzug, meanwhile, sought out the leftist agitator Madame Ngo Ba Thanh, and presumably shared feminist thoughts with her. The following evening she and Fraser managed to offend the Ambassador royally by refusing on "political grounds" to attend a special dinner he had arranged for the delegation at the Residence. Later, when the entire group met with President Thieu, several of them behaved so undiplomatically, pummeling him with insulting questions as if they, not he, were sovereign in the country, that Martin felt obliged to apologize to him afterward.

But what irrevocably soured relations between the delegates and their Vietnamese hosts was a contretemps that took place far from the Palace, at a prison on the outskirts of Saigon. During a tour of the place one afternoon Representative McCloskey and his traveling companion, Senator Dewey Bartlett of Oklahoma, asked to interview several of the Vietnamese journalists who had recently been arrested. General Binh, the National Police chief, reluctantly consented. When three of the prisoners were finally brought out, each of them admitted under Binh's pointed questioning to being a VC agent. But McCloskey wasn't satisfied. He and Bartlett wanted to talk to the prisoners alone, without benefit of Binh's presence, he explained. Could it be arranged? At last, after much debate, Binh agreed. No sooner was he out of earshot than Miss Phuong Thi Thao whispered to the two Americans, "They've beaten us very much." Afterward McCloskey brought the matter up with Thieu. "Yes, Communists would say they'd been tortured," Thieu replied somewhat irrelevantly. The Embassy, of course, had no comment.

By the third day of the visit several of the less rambunctious Congressmen had run out of pet projects, and with time on their hands, decided to see if there was any wisdom in the Embassy beside Martin and Polgar's. They had brought a list with them from Washington of some of the reputedly more knowledgeable and candid members of the Ambassador's staff and asked to speak with several of them. My name, justifiably or not, was included.

With Martin's approval, McCloskey and Bartlett set up what was supposed to be a private interview with me and one of my CIA colleagues. When Polgar told me about it, I had that sudden sinking sensation I used to get at the sound of incoming rocket fire. The arrangements for it were just about as benign. The meeting was to take place at Polgar's house that very evening, with Polgar "moderating." Quite obviously the Ambassador's idea of a "private session" was something a little different from the Congressmen's. I saw little potential profit in it for anybody.

My apprehensions, it turned out, were more than justified. McCloskey set the tone of the discussion, intimating to Polgar at the start that he suspected him of being the Ambassador's toady—hence the need to cross-check facts with subordinates. Naturally, Polgar had a few things to say about that. He was, and always had been, his own man, he insisted vigorously, and on issues of conviction he would readily stand up to anyone, the Ambassador or the honorable Representative from California included. McCloskey let that pass (Bartlett sat quietly, if somewhat uneasily, through most of this) and moved on to something more substantive. "Is the delta still as secure as the Ambassador claims?" he asked, turning to me. I opened my mouth to respond, but Polgar interrupted. "Yes, just about," he said. "Roads and lines of communication remain open and the rice still flows to Saigon."

McCloskey continued gazing at me. "Well?" he asked. "What do you think?"

Maybe I was tired and off guard, or perhaps he was merely a compelling inquisitor. In any case, I found myself reeling off an answer without any real premeditation—hardly wise for a burgeoning young bureaucrat. "As we've pointed out in our recent estimates," I said, trying to leave an opening for Polgar, "the South Vietnamese are in a contraction process. For the past year they've been pulling out of marginal areas we bequeathed to them, giving up outposts in the highlands and the delta which they no longer have the air power or artillery to defend. The other side, of course, is trying to exploit this and to bring about a new 'equilibrium' that can be turned to political advantage." I wound up by predicting some heavy fighting in areas like Tay Ninh Province in the next few months as the Communists tried to consolidate their border enclaves. That, as events would prove, was the understatement of the year.

All this seemed to please McCloskey immensely, and as I sat back I couldn't for the life of me figure why Polgar and the Ambassador were having such problems with these fellows. But Polgar obviously was not satisfied with what I had said and spent the rest of the evening trying to explain it away.

The next day, as word of our discussion seeped through the delegation, Frank Scotton, one of the accompanying staff aides, called me and asked if I would consider a return engagement, this one slightly more exclusive. He and several "friends" were breakfasting together the following morning. Would I join them? I said I would.

When I showed up at daybreak at the delegates' billet a few blocks from the Embassy, Scotton and the same CIA man who had been with me at the McCloskey session were already on their second cup of coffee. Seated across from them were Representative Fraser and Representative Millicent Fenwick of New Jersey, plus several aides. For the next three hours my colleague and I fielded questions on everything from Communist intentions to Thieu's survivability. Mrs. Fenwick, a lady of surpassing grace, was smoking a pipe, and throughout the session some perverse imp in my psychological bottle caused me to address her repeatedly as "sir."

"Is there any chance," she asked me at one point, "the North Vietnamese might agree to a new cease-fire?"

"Well, sir," I said, "they are facing pressures and constraints that could nudge them that way. North Vietnam's man-on-the-street, for example, was told the Paris agreement was a great victory and life would get better. Both claims have fallen flat. So the population is restless. By itself, that wouldn't amount to much. Government control is still more than adequate. But other things have happened to change the context, and the regime's tolerance level. Most important, of course, is détente. The Soviets and the Chinese are becoming increasingly unpredictable for Hanoi, and that could give the North Vietnamese fresh pause about all of their chronic problems.

"None of this, mind you, is going to cause them to quit the war tomorrow. But given, say, two or three more years of the same—stalemate in the south, stagnation at home—plus a few deaths and retirements in the Politburo, they just might end up refocusing their energies."

Both legislators listened intently and took notes. As I paused to catch my breath I felt a twinge of guilt. My comments and prognostications were hardly as spontaneous or original as I tried to make them sound. In one way or another they had all been carefully rehearsed in Administration position papers during the past year and were the basis of Kissinger's fondest hopes for Vietnam.

The discussion continued for another hour or so. Then, just as my colleague and I were preparing to wrap it up, the door was flung open and Representative Abzug stomped into the room, a broad-brimmed Panama flapping about her ears like an awning in a monsoon. "What's going on here!" she boomed. I hardly needed to be reminded of her views on the CIA, her distaste for its "pervasive" influence in the world, so I decided to introduce myself at once and get the worst over with. "I'm a CIA officer," I said as I stood up, and then, in an ill-advised attempt at humor, added mirthfully, "So watch out what you say." She turned on me as if I had tossed a gauntlet at her feet, riveted me in the eye and rumbled (with no trace of amusement), "You'd better watch out what *you* say, sonny!" On that disconcerting note the meeting broke up.

Ms. Abzug notwithstanding, the morning had not been wasted. By the time the delegates began winding up their tour, several of them had come to accept that there were a few free agents in Martin's otherwise closed society.

That premise would stand me—and Polgar—in good stead, as I discovered shortly after the session, when one of the Congressmen's aides dropped by my office to clarify some odds and ends. Was Polgar really the Ambassador's dupe? he asked. If so, Fraser and several of the others would call for his removal, as well as Martin's, in their final recommendations to Congress. I repeated more or less what Polgar himself had told McCloskey the night before. By about any standard, I said, Polgar was his own man—a cold warrior perhaps, one who shared Martin's antipathy for the devil and Communism and his confusion over the same, but still, his own man. If he seemed to cleave to the Ambassador's point of view, it was only because they were so much alike philosophically.

The aide thanked me and left. A week or two later he sent me an interesting follow-up note. On the basis of what I had told him, as well as several other considerations, he said, Fraser and company had decided not to make an issue of Polgar's continued presence in Saigon. In effect, I had helped to save my boss's job.

As the Congressional tour drew to a close most of us in the Embassy were gloomily convinced we had won few converts, and perhaps made new enemies. Two of the State Department aides declared flatly the aid proposal was dead. Given the mood of the delegates, I would have been inclined to agree, but then, as if by providence, something happened on the final afternoon of their stay to change some perspectives, and the odds. Ironically, the North Vietnamese themselves were the instrument of the turnabout.

A few hours before their departure, several of the Congressmen drove out to Camp Davis at Tan Son Nhut to meet with the resident North Vietnamese and PRG delegates to the moribund Joint Military Team.* As they had made clear to their hosts in advance, they were looking for an open discussion, free from propaganda and acrimony, of the 1,300 American servicemen still missing in action. During the past year 107 dossiers on these MIAs had been forwarded to the Communist team members, but so far there had been no response. A week before, in a personal letter to Senator Edward Kennedy, North Vietnamese officials had acknowledged there was information available on the MIA but emphasized that the only way the United States could get it was by renouncing its support for the Thieu regime. This was not exactly the kind of forthrightness the State Department had been hoping for, and the Congressional delegates were determined to see if something more might be done.

When they arrived at Camp Davis, however, the deck had already been stacked against them. Some seventy-six newsmen were on hand, all guests of the North Vietnamese; the conference hall was festooned with VC flags and there was a bust of Ho Chi Minh—hardly the setting for a dispassionate discussion. The chairman of the Congressional group, Representative John Flynt, tried to protest, but the North Vietnamese delegates merely turned their backs on him and ushered the reporters into the hall.

Lieutenant Colonel Bao, the deputy chairman of the North Vietnamese team, refused to answer questions as the meeting was called to order. Instead he insisted on reading a twenty-minute prepared statement accusing the United States of "illegal" interference in Vietnamese affairs. There were groans and shuffling among the legislators, some of whom under other circumstances might have been inclined to agree.

When Bao had finished, Senator Bartlett removed a bracelet from his wrist and passed it down the table to him, explaining that it was an MIA amulet inscribed with the name of Captain Richard Feizel, lost over North Vietnam on 30 June 1968. Under the terms of the Paris agreement and the Geneva Convention, he observed, the North Vietnamese were obliged to provide information on Feizel's fate—and he added, for good measure, that Bao's statement had not really been to the point. "In fact, in Oklahoma, where I come from," Bartlett continued in his Will Rogers twang, "they have a word for your remarks—and that word is hogwash." Bao stiffened.

Representative Fenwick then demanded to know if Hanoi had any intention of settling outstanding problems with the United States. Bao shuffled through some papers and attempted to launch into another diatribe, but Bartlett interrupted. "Excuse me," he said, pointing again at the bracelet, "but your remarks have nothing to do with our specific questions. What about Captain Feizel? What do I tell his wife? Do I tell her that you won't help? Or do I tell her that you have refused to answer?" (No response from the North Viet-

---

*The Joint Military Team, not to be confused with the Joint Military Commission also headquartered at Tan Son Nhut, was concerned exclusively with accounting for prisoners and missing-in-action on all sides. The United States and North Vietnam were both represented on the Team, whereas only Saigon and the PRG now sat on the equally paralyzed Commission.

namese end of the table.) "All right, I take it by your silence that you want
me to tell her that you have refused to answer. I will do just that."

After a half-hour of such fencing, the legislators moved to a conference
hall a few doors away to meet with the PRG's delegates. Their chief spokesman, Major General Hoang Anh Tuan, tried to lead off with a prepared lecture
of his own, but this time the Americans were forewarned, and forearmed. After
a minute or so Bartlett interrupted, declared himself chairman pro tem, and
gave the floor to Representative Flynt. "If as you say you are interested in
seriously implementing the Paris agreement," Flynt growled, "then why has
your government refused to repatriate the bodies of forty-one U.S. servicemen
whose names were on the list which your government passed to us in Paris
when the agreement was signed? Those men died while prisoners of war in
PRG camps."

Tuan: "I was explaining this systematically by showing the overall problem of the Paris agreement and the continued intervention of your government,
but regretfully, I was interrupted. Allow me to continue, since we only have
five minutes of time remaining. The real problem is the U.S. continuation of
the war . . ."

Representative Flynt (impatiently): "No, I want to know why you have
not returned the forty-one bodies. Where are they?"

Tuan (ignoring the question): "After the signing of the Paris agreement
the United States illegally continued to perpetuate the war, making it impossible for the treaty to be implemented while hundreds and thousands of Vietnamese are miserable and dying each week . . . "

Flynt: "I'm sorry but I don't want to hear this. I want to know where the
forty-one bodies are. Where are the forty-one bodies?"

Tuan (visibly shaken): "I thought you came to exchange views, to try and
understand more clearly the situation in Vietnam. I will not be forced to
answer such a question, and I believe the American people will understand.
(Glancing at his watch.) It is 1200 hours, fifteen minutes since the agreed
thirty-minute session began. I see the time is up."

Senator Bartlett (vehemently): "Good!"

As the legislators stalked out, Representative Fenwick rummaged in her
purse for a handkerchief. It was then she noticed that her wallet with four
hundred dollars was missing. Apparently, during all the excitement, one of her
Communist hosts had managed to liberate it.*

The North Vietnamese and the PRG team members had been hoping to
win some propaganda points with their afternoon spectacular, but the scheme

---

*Throughout the session at Tan Son Nhut, Representative Abzug, normally one of the most
outspoken of the Congressional delegates, remained conspicuously subdued. She had neglected to
attend an earlier briefing on the MIA issue provided by the American representatives to the Joint
Military Team and showed little willingness to pursue the matter with the Communist delegates
themselves. To some of us, her reticence was surprising, particularly since she had displayed
exemplary zeal in rooting out the evils of the Thieu regime.

obviously had backfired. Several of the fence-sitters in the Congressional group came away fully determined to vote some additional aid to South Vietnam.

Their conversion, of course, was to prove a Pyrrhic victory for the Administration, for within a few weeks the rapid deterioration of the South Vietnamese army would render all aid proposals virtually irrelevant. The Embassy, moreover, had paid a price for its own antics during the Congressional visit. By championing Saigon's "cause" so vigorously, we had succeeded only in convincing our guests we were not really fit to judge anything very well. This slippage in credibility would make it all the more difficult for us in the weeks ahead to persuade Congressional friends in Washington of the seriousness of the military situation.

At the focus of all the doubts and criticism was Martin himself. Representative Flynt told reporters in Saigon the Ambassador was a "disaster," and both Abzug and Fraser vowed to push for his removal.

But if Martin was discouraged by any of this, he did not show it. From all appearances he still seemed serenely confident of the righteousness of his position and of his standing with Kissinger. Indeed, on the evening of 2 March, as the legislators gathered at Tan Son Nhut to board their plane back to the United States, he embarked on a last grandstand play. Just before flight time he pulled up at the VIP lounge in his black limousine, strode in and announced to the group he wanted to accompany them back to Washington. He had some final lobbying to do for the aid bill, he said, and would be much obliged if they would spare him a seat on their plane. Few of the Congressmen were enthusiastic—they had spent just about as much time with Martin as they wanted and the prospect of a long plane ride with him was hardly their idea of an easy comedown after a grueling week-long trek through Indochina. But Martin persisted, and out of courtesy Flynt, the delegation chief, agreed.

Throughout most of the long flight the Ambassador sat alone, picking through briefing notes and classified documents. In one brief lapse into social intercourse, he buttonholed Frank Scotton and lambasted him for putting members of the delegation in touch with middle-level Embassy officials like myself.

Blossoming Lotus

During the turmoil of the Congressional visit the battlefield suddenly turned quiet. Polgar interpreted the lull as a political ruse. The Communists, he insisted, were deliberately pulling their punches to convince our high-level visitors the war was over and further aid to Saigon was unnecessary.

He may have been right, but only partly. For if the lull was a ruse, it was also a necessity. North Vietnamese strategists had changed course so abruptly in the wake of the Phuoc Long battle, their logisticians needed the breathing spell to prepare for the next round—the drive on Ban Me Thuot City in the western highlands.

The South Vietnamese high command was not unaware of the enemy's maneuverings. In the past few days ARVN intelligence officers in MR 2 had uncovered several telltale clues, including a diary, found on the body of an NVA soldier, with explicit references to a planned campaign against Ban Me Thuot. In addition, a North Vietnamese defector had confided under interrogation that the 320th NVA Division had recently slipped down out of Pleiku Province and was now targeted against the city. Almost coincidentally, government informants in Quang Duc Province just to the south of the town reported heavy NVA troop concentrations across the border in Cambodia.

General Pham Van Phu, the MR 2 commander, became extremely agitated at these revelations, and with good cause: he did not have enough forces in the highlands to cover all the potential targets equally. The 23rd ARVN Division, the best in his command, was already stretched dangerously thin, with two regiments dispersed through Kontum and Pleiku and part of another detached to the Ban Me Thuot–Quang Duc front. To meet a frontal assault on Ban Me Thuot, he knew he would have to fold in two more regiments and perhaps even more, depending on the size of the opposing force. But his dilemma was that he could only release extra units by stripping his defenses in Kontum and Pleiku to the north, and that, in his view, was out of the question. The two provinces were too important strategically. Not only did they lie astride key NVA infiltration routes from Laos and Cambodia, but they also provided a springboard to the coast. The major east-west highway in MR 2, Route 19, ran from Pleiku to Qui Nhon City, and if the Communists should make another attempt to cut the country in two, as they had so often tried and failed to do in the past, Route 19 would be the logical line of march. So both the highway and its western nexus in Pleiku must remain securely in government hands.

Against all this, the prisoner report and the flaky intelligence from Quang Duc Province seemed slim justification for a major redeployment of forces. If the 320th NVA Division was indeed edging south from Pleiku to Ban Me Thuot, then a parallel shift in Phu's army was imperative. But if the defector was wrong—and Phu shifted his forces anyway—Pleiku and Kontum were as good as lost.

No, Phu advised his staff, he simply could not take the chance. He would leave his units where they were, keeping the bulk of them, including most of the 23rd Division, concentrated in the northern highlands. In defending his decision he cited recent intercepts of Communist radio communications which seemed to indicate that the headquarters of the 320th Division was still in its normal area of operations, at Duc Co in western Pleiku. If that was so, then clearly the defector was lying: the 320th Division was not targeted against Ban Me Thuot at all.

As it turned out, Phu had misplaced his trust, and his skepticism. It was not the defector report that was counterfeit, but the radio intercepts themselves. As part of an elaborate charade to cover their true objectives in the highlands, the NVA had recently established a bogus command post at Duc Co and were now beaming radio signals from it to mislead local ARVN commanders into believing the 320th was still in the area. The ruse fooled all of us, with ultimately fatal consequences for the government.

As Phu was trying to make up his mind about enemy intentions, the Station's peripatetic military liaison officer, General Timmes, paid him a visit in Pleiku. The MR 2 commander made no effort to conceal his confusion. Despite the reported enemy build-up at Ban Me Thuot, he said, he still believed the main enemy thrust would be toward Kontum and Pleiku. And yet there was no way to be sure. Could Timmes advise him?

Timmes shook his head sadly. He could listen, he said, but could offer no advice. The Paris agreement, with its proscription against American military involvement in Vietnam, had made that impossible.

A few days later Phu turned to his own superiors for help. What he needed most, he told the Joint General Staff in Saigon, was additional fuel and ammunition. Given the uncertainty of enemy plans, he felt he should have sufficient stockpiles on hand in Kontum and Pleiku to support his army for at least ninety days of hard fighting.

But the generals at JGS were no more forthcoming than Timmes. While acknowledging the possibility of multiple attacks in the highlands, they refused to grant Phu additional supplies. Many considered him listless and unimaginative, anyway, and were convinced that if he was given surplus, he would have little incentive to keep open Route 19 to the coast, now his primary lifeline.

While Phu agonized over North Vietnamese objectives, the principals themselves continued to prepare for battle. By the end of February, General Dung had completed his circuitous journey from Hanoi and was busily organizing a field headquarters—the Central Highlands Front Command—west of Ban Me Thuot itself. "Our command post was in a green forest whose dry leaves covered the ground like a yellow carpet," he commented lyrically months later. "Whenever someone walked on them they crackled like crisp griddle cakes."

Hoping to keep his presence a secret, Dung cut back on all radio transmissions and insisted on communicating with Hanoi exclusively by telephone. This minimized the danger of detection but posed another special risk all its own. Because of the primitive equipment, his telephone circuits constituted an acute fire hazard in the tinderbox dryness of the highlands. Consequently, "signal and communications officers had to work hardest here," he acknowledged in his memoirs. "Whenever a small fire broke out and destroyed the communications wires they had to fight the flames and often returned with their bodies as black as coal miners'."

Soon after his arrival Dung and his principal deputy, Lieutenant General Hoang Minh Thoa, sat down with their unit commanders to review the balance of forces. In overall terms, they decided, the two sides in the highlands were evenly matched, but because the NVA had no specific real estate to protect, they were free to shift and maneuver to achieve superiority in any given target area. This was to be the key to their strategy at Ban Me Thuot, as it had so often been in other crucial battles. The essential corollary of course was subterfuge and surprise: only as long as they could keep Phu convinced the main attacks would come in the northern highlands, could they prevent him from reinforcing Ban Me Thuot and matching them man for man.

The campaign, as Dung outlined it to his staff, was to be carried out in phases, starting with the interdiction of all major highways into and through the highlands and ending with the capture of Ban Me Thuot. As one of his options, he was willing to consider a direct frontal assault on the town, but his preferred mode of attack was a tactic he called the "blossoming lotus"— a deep sudden thrust into the very center of the objective, followed by an explosive, multi-directional drive outward to destroy enemy units on the outskirts.

From spies and radio intercepts Dung soon became aware of Phu's confusion over the location of NVA units. According to these sources, the South Vietnamese commander not only had lost track of the 320th NVA Division, but was also now frantically searching for another, the 10th NVA Division, which likewise was normally targeted against Kontum and Pleiku. In fact, the 10th was even now creeping south to join the 320th at Ban Me Thuot, but Phu did not realize this and Dung was determined to keep him guessing. He

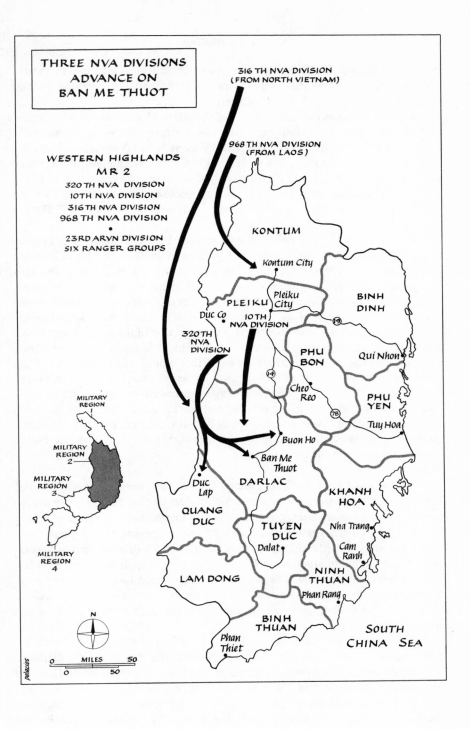

THREE NVA DIVISIONS
ADVANCE ON
BAN ME THUOT

316 TH NVA DIVISION
(FROM NORTH VIETNAM)

968 TH NVA DIVISION
(FROM LAOS)

WESTERN HIGHLANDS
MR 2

320 TH NVA DIVISION
10TH NVA DIVISION
316 TH NVA DIVISION
968 TH NVA DIVISION

23RD ARVN DIVISION
SIX RANGER GROUPS

KONTUM

Kontum City

PLEIKU
Pleiku
City
Duc Co
10TH
NVA DIVISION

BINH
DINH

320TH
NVA
DIVISION

PHU
BON

Qui Nhon

Cheo
Reo

PHU
YEN

Tuy Hoa

Buon Ho

Ban Me
Thuot

Duc
Lap

DARLAC

KHANH
HOA

QUANG
DUC

TUYEN
DUC

Dalat

Nha Trang

Cam
Ranh

LAM DONG

NINH
THUAN

Phan Rang

BINH
THUAN

SOUTH
CHINA SEA

Phan
Thiet

MILITARY
REGION
1

MILITARY
REGION
2

MILITARY
REGION
3

MILITARY
REGION
4

N

MILES   '50

0   50

Palacios

therefore ordered remaining NVA units in Pleiku and Kontum to mount diversionary attacks in the areas where the 10th normally operated so Phu would be led to believe it was still there.

In the meantime, the last elements of the 316th NVA Division arrived west of Ban Me Thuot to round out Dung's strike force. Like the commander himself, the division had made the journey from North Vietnam in less than three weeks, maintaining radio silence all the way. By the end of February there were thus three NVA divisions poised to attack the city—giving Dung a manpower advantage of five to one—with another division, the 968th from southern Laos, handling the diversionary maneuvers in Kontum and Pleiku.

At the Embassy in Saigon we had no idea Van Tien Dung was even in South Vietnam, much less that he had set up a headquarters west of Ban Me Thuot and was preparing to attack the town. The NVA build-up in the area had gone undetected, except for those few intelligence reports no one believed, and while it was obvious a new phase in the Communist dry-season campaign was in the offing, none of us was certain where its main focus would be.

Nor were we any better informed of the direction of the government's own planning. Thieu still had not seen fit to alert us to his decision to withdraw the Airborne Division from MR 1—a move that would affect the course of the war in the next two months every bit as much as the attack on Ban Me Thuot. As Joe Kingsley, my new office colleague, burrowed into his assignment as "MR 1 analyst," the prevailing assumption on the sixth floor of the Embassy was that the next few weeks would see only minor changes in otherwise stable government defense lines in the northern part of the country as the North Vietnamese stepped up their pressure.

As Joe and I took turns reinforcing each other's views on this point, Pat Johnson, the third member of our little analyst clique, turned increasingly somber, not so much about Vietnam as about Cambodia, her primary area of concern, for the crisis there now seemed to be deepening by the hour.

With all river and road access shut off, Phnom Penh continued to depend on the U.S. airlift for life-giving food and military supplies. In the past few days, however, the Khmer Communists had intensified their rocket and mortar attacks on the airfield and finally had brought their ultimate weapons into play: captured U.S. 105-mm howitzers that were undoubtedly a gift of the North Vietnamese.

The State Department in Washington immediately responded with expressions of "grave concern" and announced that the aircraft carrier *Okinawa* with marines and helicopters on board was moving into the Gulf of Thailand in case the evacuation of the 400 American civilians in Cambodia might become necessary. Soon afterward, as the Khmer Communists continued to shell Phnom Penh airfield, a charter DC-6 was hit by shrapnel; it was the first American plane to be damaged by ground fire since the start of the airlift months before.

Within hours of the incident Defense Secretary Schlesinger advised newsmen the airlift would be terminated unless the Lon Nol government could do a better job of securing the landing zones. He also conceded that marines might have to be sent to Phnom Penh to rescue the Americans if there turned out to be no other way to assure their safety. Other government spokesmen quickly issued qualifying statements, emphasizing that the marines would be used only in a "fallback plan" to protect Phnom Penh airfield. Such caveats were well advised. Although President Ford had authority under the Constitution to take steps to protect American lives abroad, it was questionable how far he could actually go in Cambodia or Vietnam, for the War Powers Act and the Cambodia bombing ban legislation of 1973 had expressly enjoined him from reengaging the military in Indochina without the prior approval of Congress.

In the meantime, as the KC tightened their cordon around Phnom Penh, a half-hearted effort was made to shift the conflict to the diplomatic arena. On 3 March, Lon Nol volunteered to step down to "ensure peace," as he had offered to do the previous July and November. But now as before, the gesture was fruitless. The Khmer Communists were too close to total victory to be willing to settle for anything less.

In Washington an increasing number of self-proclaimed experts on Indochina, particularly in Congress, felt the Administration was looking for salvation in the wrong places. Instead of dealing with the combatants themselves, they wanted Kissinger to seek Soviet and Chinese help in turning off the fighting in both Cambodia and Vietnam. When the Congressional fact-finding team returned to Washington several of its members made just such a proposal to the White House. State Department officials let it be known, however, they did not consider this practical, particularly in Cambodia's case. "The situation on the ground is not conducive to negotiations," one of them declared in a press briefing, meaning that the Lon Nol government had nothing to bargain with. Embassy officials in Phnom Penh were even more candid; Ambassador John Gunther Dean quietly informed newsmen the best that could be hoped for was a negotiated surrender.

Kissinger for his part seemed determined to ignore such pessimism. It was not that he disagreed with Dean, but having glimpsed the prospect of total defeat, he was now resolved to limit the damage it might do to American interests elsewhere in the world. In his view, this implied one last act of pretense and generosity by the U.S. government.

In secret briefings to the Senate Foreign Relations Committee during the first week of March, he set out his case. If as seemed likely, he said, the Lon Nol government was on the brink of collapse, it was essential to keep open the aid pipeline so no one could later blame the United States for the disaster. President Ford made the same point publicly, advising newsmen that a suspension of aid to Cambodia or Vietnam at this juncture "would draw into question the reliability of the United States and encourage the belief that aggression pays."

Some Congressmen and newsmen dismissed these statements as an em-

barrassing throwback to the discredited domino theory of the Johnson Administration, but in fact Kissinger and the President had a dynamic of far
greater immediacy in mind. During the past few days President Anwar Sadat
of Egypt had secretly informed them he was ready to try again for a Middle
East settlement. Since the credibility of American guarantees and assurances
were critical to this enterprise, the Administration could hardly hope to make
the most of Sadat's flexibility if at the same time it appeared to the world the
United States was preparing to abandon its two Indochina allies.

As Kissinger flew off to the Middle East on 7 March to begin a new round
of shuttle diplomacy, he therefore left instructions with his aides and subordinates: Do everything possible to ensure that Congress lived up to our aid
commitments to Cambodia and Vietnam—not because the two countries were
necessarily salvageable, but precisely because they might not be.

The irony of the Administration's dilemma was hardly lost on those of
us on the firing line. At the very moment Cambodia and Vietnam were teetering on the brink, the White House could least afford to admit it.

Even as Kissinger turned his attention elsewhere, the storm clouds over
Vietnam continued to gather thick and fast. By the end of the first week in
March recruitment and training cycles for the army in North Vietnam were
rapidly accelerating, and NVA dry-season infiltration into the south had risen
to over 63,000 men in the last six months—more than double the total for the
comparable period in 1973–74. The largest spurt had come in the past four
weeks, along with a significant increase in the flow of supplies into the south.

According to the available intelligence, over half of the reinforcements we
had detected had ended up in the Saigon area and the delta, with the remainder
distributing themselves between the highlands and the coast. Joe Kingsley and
I and our colleagues at DAO took this as an indication the main enemy
offensive in the next few weeks would center on the lower half of the country.
What we did not know, of course, was that in addition to the 63,000 individual
troops, a full division, the 316th, had secretly slipped into the country, to take
part in the drive on Ban Me Thuot.*

Besides the troop and supply movements, there were other ominous blips
on the intelligence screen. In the past four weeks the North Vietnamese air

---

*Actually, the movement of the 316th had not gone wholly unnoticed. As early as 25 January,
CIA analysts in Langley had remarked in their daily intelligence bulletin for the President that
the "316th or at least part of it may be moving to South Vietnam from its normal area of operations
in North Vietnam . . . it would be the first North Vietnam division to do so since the cease-fire
agreement." In subsequent weeks, however, such speculation on the whereabouts and mission of
the 316th became increasingly infrequent, since there was simply no intelligence to support it.
There were signs that another reserve division—the 341st—might also be preparing to move south,
but none of us, in either Saigon or Washington, was quite willing to go on the line as saying so,
since the data on its activities were extremely sketchy. The consensus of the intelligence community was that part of the 341st was sent to MR 1 as reinforcement in late February. In fact, as we
would discover after the offensive was well along, the 341st had been expanded to the size of almost
two divisions, and parts of it had been parceled out to both MR 1 and MR 3. Hanoi's evasion and
deception tactics thus succeeded splendidly.

force had begun shifting planes to airfields in the North Vietnamese panhandle, within striking distance of targets in MR 1, and several additional MIGs had arrived from China—the first such deliveries in nearly a year. Also, at least eight NVA helicopters had recently made round trips from North Vietnam to Quang Tri Province. They were the first North Vietnamese aircraft ever firmly identified inside South Vietnam.

In addition, there were indications of increasingly active collaboration between Hanoi and its two primary allies. In the past few days a deputy Soviet Foreign Minister had showed up in the North Vietnamese capital for consultations and a Chinese army delegation had conducted a discreet tour of several of the country's military installations. What the Soviets discussed with their hosts remained a matter of conjecture for us in Saigon, but given the recent aircraft deliveries from China and the upsurge in Soviet military shipments to Hanoi, it hardly seemed likely they had put in an appearance simply to urge sweetness and light on the Politburo.

NVA forces in the highlands formally opened their campaign against Ban Me Thuot on 1 March, seizing the small crossroads village of Duc Lap, the only government outpost on the southern approaches to the city from Cambodia. Other NVA units overran several outposts along Route 19 between Pleiku and the coast, clamping off this vital artery. By 4 March the only other step in the initial phase of Dung's strategy that remained to be accomplished was the interdiction of Route 14 between Pleiku and Ban Me Thuot. Dung wanted to postpone this till the last possible moment so as to avoid exposing the size or location of his forces. But on the morning of the following day overanxious troops of the 320th NVA Division attacked a small South Vietnamese convoy on the highway and thus tipped their hand to the enemy.

At General Phu's headquarters at Pleiku, the chief intelligence officer made a quick review of the intelligence and concluded Ban Me Thuot was about to be attacked. Phu himself remained skeptical, but was finally persuaded to send an additional regiment to the village of Buon Ho, twenty-five miles north of the city, to provide a backstop for the other ARVN regiment already on the scene.

This prompted General Dung to rethink his own tactics. If the newly arrived ARVN unit should launch extended reconnaissance operations, he knew he would risk losing the advantage of surprise and would have to strike Ban Me Thuot at once. The next day or so would tell.

In Saigon, meanwhile, I was just finishing up a new strategic appraisal for Washington which attempted to put all we knew of NVA intentions into perspective. After reviewing the recent manpower and supply build-up ("unprecedented") and phase one of the Communist offensive in December and January ("exceeded in scope and intensity anything we had seen since the cease-fire"), I took a bead on the near-term prospects. At least four NVA divisions would attempt to isolate Hué and Danang in the next few weeks, I predicted, with other NVA units slicing into the coastal lowlands of southern MR 1. Concerted attacks also could be expected in MR 2, particularly against road networks south and east of Kontum and Pleiku Cities and around Ban Me Thuot. In addition, I forecast renewed NVA initiatives in the Saigon area, including a major drive against Tay Ninh City to the northwest as a possible prelude to a new North Vietnamese negotiating initiative. In the delta, Can Tho and My Tho Cities were likely to come under heavy pressure.

As a hodgepodge of guesswork and cautious prediction the estimate was respectable enough. Despite the lack of firm intelligence on a great many crucial questions, I had managed to anticipate much of·what the North Vietnamese would do in the next few weeks. There was one blind spot, however, and it was critical, for what I had failed to foresee was where the Communists would strike first.

While taking note of the indications of unusual NVA troop movements west and north of Ban Me Thuot, I chose fatally not to read the worst into them. Instead of an outright assault on the town, I predicted the Communists would simply try to isolate it by cutting the highways in the area. It was, of course, a monumental error, but one which I like to think stemmed more from ignorance than from outright stupidity.

When I sat down to write the estimate, there was perhaps less intelligence available on NVA intentions in the highlands than on anything else. One of the main reasons for the shortage was corruption—within the ranks of the CIA itself. A year and a half before, auditors for the Station in Saigon had discovered that one of the principal officers at the CIA base in Nha Trang had misused and mislaid operational funds that should have been applied toward the development of agent networks in the highlands and elsewhere in MR 2. The officer had been summarily yanked out of his job and sent home, but the effects of his "mismanagement" had never been overcome: the agent networks had remained only a glint in the eye of his successors.*

On top of this, the CIA Base Chief in MR 2 had decided in the summer of 1974 to shut down the agency's outpost in Ban Me Thuot as part of a cost-cutting exercise. Since then we had been obliged to depend on local ARVN and police sources for most of our intelligence. This was hardly an ideal arrangement, since many of the police and army officers in the area had long been involved in across-the-lines trading with the VC and were not about to provide us with information that might hurt business. To complicate matters, the montagnard hills tribesmen who lived in and around Ban Me Thuot (the very name of the city means "daughter of Thuot" in the local montagnard

---

*Once the officer in question returned to CIA headquarters in Langley, he was forced to retire. Yet because his superiors wanted no embarrassing publicity, they decided not to take him to court and even allowed him to leave the agency with full retirement pensions and benefits. Their attitudes remained unchanged even after the fall of South Vietnam. Although the man's misconduct had contributed directly to one of our most critical intelligence failures in Vietnam, the CIA remained unwilling to take any further action against him, lest its own public image suffer in the process.

dialect) detested their Vietnamese overlords and seldom shared the kind of information with them that might have helped pinpoint Communist intentions. Nor was the CIA itself now anxious to deal with the montagnards directly (as we had so often done in the past), lest our friends in the government be offended. As a result, when I began sifting through the intelligence during the first weeks of March, I found the files on the highlands depressingly bare.

In the midst of my labors General Timmes dropped by my office and reminded me of the recent report from the defector pointing to the shift of the 320th NVA Division from Pleiku to Ban Me Thuot. I was, of course, intrigued and troubled by it, but like General Phu and his analysts, I finally dismissed it as false, principally because of the recurring radio intercepts that seemed to place the 320th in its normal operating area in Pleiku to the north. Unfortunately, all of us in the analytical business in Saigon had come to rely excessively on such electronically obtained intelligence, in lieu of human-source data, in fast-moving crisis situations. As I drew up my conclusions I thus ignored the one real clue to North Vietnamese plans. I then did what an intelligence analyst can do only at great hazard: I guessed at the adversary's intentions—and was dead wrong.

I was not alone, however. Assessments prepared by DAO and by my CIA colleagues back home also continued to focus on the traditional "threat areas" of Kontum and Pleiku Provinces, while glossing over Ban Me Thuot altogether.

On 7 March, a few hours after my appraisal was cabled to Washington, I flew off to Bangkok to meet with several other "specialists" on North Vietnam. That night we all got into a friendly row over Thieu's options in the face of the emerging threat. One of my companions wanted to know why Thieu couldn't give up territory to buy time and consolidate his forces. "His troops would never be able to stand the stress of a strategic withdrawal," I remarked almost offhandedly. "They're just too undisciplined for it and would disintegrate in the process."

Little did I know.

During my two-day sabbatical General Dung closed the ring. By the afternoon of 8 March, ARVN troops operating out of Buon Ho, north of Ban Me Thuot, were still conducting reconnaissance operations and Dung decided he could no longer risk their stumbling across his own units. Therefore, he ordered the 320th NVA Division to move at once against the section of Route 14 between Buon Ho and Pleiku. Within a few hours the road was cut and ARVN troops in the southern highlands found themselves isolated from the rest of Phu's army to the north.

It was then Phu saw the light. He immediately ordered yet another regiment to be airlifted from Pleiku to the Buon Ho–Ban Me Thuot sector. But on surveying his helicopter fleet he discovered that only one of his four giant CH-47s was in flyable condition. He anxiously petitioned Saigon for replacements, but none was available. The Embassy briefly considered mobilizing several Air America choppers on his behalf, but gave up the idea out of deference to the provisions of the Paris agreement ruling out renewed U.S. involvement in the war.

On the morning of the ninth Dung sent a message to his comrades in Hanoi, outlining for the first time his complete tactical plan for the attack on Ban Me Thuot. "We will attack Ban Me Thuot on 10 March," he told them. "All requirements have been met . . . Wish you all in the Central Military Party Committee and the Politburo good health. Tuan [Dung's code name]."

Later that day the American consulate in Nha Trang contacted Walt Martindale, its representative in Quang Duc Province, south of Ban Me Thuot, and directed him to prepare to evacuate his post. In view of the recent scattered fighting between Quang Duc and Ban Me Thuot, consulate officials were concerned that Martindale might be bottled up. But the young officer refused to pull out, arguing that his departure might precipitate a government withdrawal from Quang Duc. Since the consulate was not prepared to assume responsibility for that, it agreed to let Martindale stay put for the time being.

Further north, in Ban Me Thuot itself, Paul Struharick, the local consulate representative, had just returned from vacation and was trying to acquaint himself with the military situation. Late in the afternoon of the ninth he called the consulate in Nha Trang and announced he was just heading off to see the province chief a few blocks away to check on the latest reports on NVA troop moves. It was Struharick's last communication with the consulate before the North Vietnamese sprang their attack.

Ban Me Thuot and the surrounding hill country might have been lifted out of a Henri Rousseau painting. The setting and color scheme were strictly nineteenth-century exotic, from the dull rust-red of the highlands clay to the lush green of the neighboring coffee plantations and jungle. Even the wildlife seemed an extension of fantasy, for despite the years of B-52 strikes and generations of western hunters, a few tigers and elephants still roamed the undergrowth.

There was also an aura of structure and discipline about the place that had long seemed to me untypical of Vietnam. Part of it no doubt stemmed from the contrived symmetries of the plantations, with their rows upon rows of coffee trees, all set out in closed rank like an army frozen in a snapshot. But beyond this, there was something insubstantial that rounded out the impression, perhaps the calm of the city itself. Not since 1968 had the war touched Ban Me Thuot directly, and since then the majority of its 150,000 inhabitants —Vietnamese, Chinese, French and Italian planters—had struck their own accommodations with the local Communists, if not with each other, to make sure it would not happen again.

One of the city's most celebrated scenic attractions was the old hunting lodge of the last Emperor of Vietnam, Bao Dai—a huge wooden building with peaked roofs and pinewood rafters, all vaguely reminiscent of a Viking drinking hall. In recent years local Catholics had added stained-glass windows and a confessional and had converted it into a church, and in its potpourri effect it was surely one of Vietnam's wrier comments on the ecumenical spirit.

Another favorite reference point for residents and visitors alike was a dilapidated old bar in the center of town, known as the "White Rat," where planters gathered each Saturday and Sunday morning for a glass of beer while their wives went shopping in the city's central market. If you had been in the "White Rat" on 9 March, you undoubtedly would have heard rumors of Communist troop movements on the edge of the city, but since the planters stayed to themselves, sharing nothing with the local Vietnamese authorities for fear of Viet Cong retribution, what they knew or suspected did not go beyond the huddle at the bar.

Shortly before dawn on 10 March the Communists struck, moving directly against the town from the north and west, focusing their initial thrusts at the two airfields and the ammunition depot on the outskirts of the city. "Long-range artillery immediately zeroed in on military targets," Dung recounted. "At a point forty kilometers from Ban Me Thuot our tank units started their engines, crept through the trees and headed for town. Modern ferryboats were rapidly assembled, while tanks, armored vehicles and antiaircraft guns were queued up for fast boarding. The mountains and forests of the central highlands were shaken by a storm of artillery fire.

"No sooner had the artillery opened up than the lights of the city went off. Sappers soon occupied the main airfield . . . At 7:30 A.M., the first of our tank columns, advancing from the north and west, arrived at the Mai Hac De armored-car depot. Vanguard units had already passed the broadcasting station and were advancing on the 23rd ARVN Division's communications center. At 7:45 our tanks infiltrated the headquarters compound and one began firing point-blank at the Division's local command post."

When the attack came, there were only two ARVN battalions, less than 1,200 men, actually inside the city, plus two more just to the north, backed by part of another regiment and a few ranger and militia units. Arrayed against them were Dung's three crack divisions, totaling 25,000 men, with an assortment of armor and heavy artillery. During the first few hours of the offensive South Vietnamese aircraft were called in to support the defenders, but as in the battle of Phuoc Long several weeks before, their strafing and bombing attacks proved more hazardous to friendly units than to enemy ones. Operating at their customary 10,000 feet, well out of range of Communist AAA, the pilots splattered their objectives haphazardly and at one point accidentally bombed an ARVN command post in the city. Thereupon government command and control began breaking down, ARVN troops and militia abandoning their positions piecemeal.

"By 1700 hours on 10 March," Dung continued in his account, "we had occupied the major part of the city and attacked the local 23rd Division headquarters and the local sector command, though we had not yet seized these objectives entirely. The enemy's artillery had been paralyzed at the beginning and the support provided by his tactical air force was not very effective. But enemy forces in the area of the main airfield and rear elements of the 53rd [ARVN] regiment counterattacked rather fiercely. I ordered the front to hold occupied areas . . . and to organize attacks to knock out the remaining elements of the 23rd ARVN Division there . . .

"After seizing the 23rd Division's command post and the armored-car area, our troops overran the 45th Regiment's rear base and occupied the military police's communications areas and the regional force training school. Partisan [montagnard] units then met at the 23rd Division headquarters and an armed action [secret police] unit entered Ban Me Thuot City. Basically, the battle was over by 10:30 on 11 March 1975.

" 'Basically, the battle is over'—these words were jotted down on the incoming message recorded by an operations cadre at our command post. Our men's elation cannot be described. I told those with me: the fact that it took us only a little more than a day and a night to attack and occupy so large a city proves that the enemy can find no means to resist our strength . . ."

Despite the capture of Ban Me Thuot itself, elements of two ARVN battalions would cling to the smaller airstrip on the edge of the town for the next six days, waging a gallant holding action against impossible odds. At last they were forced to withdraw, retreating into the jungles to the south, never to be heard from again.

As the battle entered its final hours the government in Saigon still had no clear idea what was taking place. Not until 14 March did any of us realize the city had been lost. The only available intelligence came from high-altitude photographs taken from Air America and South Vietnamese aircraft, and they told us next to nothing. I remember looking over a batch of them a day or so after the initial NVA push. Smoke and air bursts were discernible at one of the airstrips but the rest of the city seemed tranquil. A few tanks were parked in the central market, near the "White Rat," and several bicyclers could be seen pedaling lazily around them. We concluded from this slim evidence that government forces had driven the attackers off (we still did not know there were three NVA divisions in the area). But of course, the opposite was true: the city was already in NVA hands.

Our inability to keep track of the battle as it unfolded led to the fumbling of a crucial priority—the rescue of the westerners trapped inside the city: eight American missionaries, an Australian and Paul Struharick, the consulate representative.

When Dung sent the first of his tank columns rumbling toward Ban Me Thuot, all of the westerners immediately fled to the USAID compound and the province chief's headquarters, where emergency provisions had been stored. At approximately 8 A.M., the same morning, Struharick radioed the consulate in Nha Trang to say that he and his companions were surrounded by NVA armor. Consulate officials immediately dispatched a helicopter to the rescue, but Communist ground fire prevented it from landing. For the next several hours Struharick continued to communicate with the pilot, assuring him everyone was safe, but eventually, as the batteries feeding his small radio weakened, he dropped off the air.

Hoping he could still receive messages, the pilot continued to beam instructions to him on behalf of the consulate, directing him to set out a small flag if he could hear. Several other Air America choppers tried to land, but they too were driven off by sniper fire. When Dung's forces finally completed their sweep of the town Struharick and the rest were placed in custody.

For the next eight months they were held prisoners of war, some at Ban Me Thuot, others further north in Pleiku. Struharick, whom the Communists suspected of being a CIA officer, was kept in solitary confinement but otherwise treated well. The food was poor, though no worse than what the average NVA trooper received. At last, in the early fall of 1975, the NVA apparently concluded all ten were what they claimed to be—innocent bystanders—and decided to release them.

During their long ordeal several members of the group had developed curious yearnings. After Saigon's collapse, as I was wrapping up an interim assignment in Bangkok, an American newsman who had come out of Vietnam on 5 May let me read a letter from one of the detainees, which the Communists had asked him to mail. The writer, a missionary, had complained to his parents of his overwhelming longing for a chocolate candy bar.

By the time the loss of Ban Me Thuot was confirmed, Kissinger was on a flight from Cairo to Tel Aviv, in the midst of his continuing diplomatic shuttle, and he was both surprised and puzzled at the news. Yet according to staffers who were with him, he did not feel that this unfortunate turn of events betokened any real crisis for South Vietnam. In his view, Ban Me Thuot had been "marginal" to the country's security and probably had been given up deliberately, as part of a painful but systematic effort by the government to adjust its commitments to its resources.

Meanwhile, as the political reverberations of the setback continued to shake Saigon, Pat, Joe and I were beginning to feel a little like holdouts in a bunker under fire. Tactical intelligence reports were now raining in on us in a never-ending barrage, and each of us was spending long hours after closing time updating battle maps and trying to absorb the data. Nor were the grid coordinates for Ban Me Thuot the only ones we learned by heart, for even as Dung and his legions made short work of this crucial objective, there was a sudden upsurge in fighting throughout the rest of the country, in the various target areas I had managed to pinpoint in my estimate a few days before.

On 8 March, VC guerrillas struck at fifteen hamlets scattered between Quang Tri and Hué in MR 1. During the next few days NVA units in the southern part of the region isolated two district towns in central Quang Tin Province, sealed off all roads to the coast and then tacked toward the province capital of Tam Ky. The predicted offensive against Tay Ninh Province, just northwest of Saigon, also suddenly burst on us as Communist units overran the town of Tri Tam on the eastern approaches to the province capital and a sliver of territory to the west.

Within a day or two of the Ban Me Thuot offensive, government forces thus were giving ground all across the country, and the high command in Saigon was already frantically rummaging about in its collective imagination for possible antidotes. General Vien, the chairman of the Joint General Staff, conferred endlessly with his principal subordinates. Unfortunately, however, the one officer whose counsel he most needed was not on hand to give it. On 11 March, General Dang Van Khuyen, the army's chief of staff and its senior logistician—and a man particularly close to the Americans—had flown off to Japan to be with his father, who was undergoing surgery for cancer. Khuyen would be gone for a full week, during which time his logistical expertise and his contacts with the Americans would be sorely missed.*

But Khuyen's absence was not the only handicap the government had to contend with. Thieu posed a few of them himself. Infuriated by the surprise attack on Ban Me Thuot, he soon began snubbing all his senior intelligence officers, on grounds they had failed him. One of those who felt the chill of his wrath was Colonel Le Van Luong, chief of the intelligence section of the Joint General Staff. Luong was no more guilty than the rest of us who had misread the signals, but Thieu marked him down as an incompetent, criticized him to his face, and thereafter ignored him. Morale in Luong's office plummeted, and as a result, the army's military intelligence apparatus was already in tatters as the war entered its final weeks.

---

*Khuyen, second-in-command of the army, was another of its American-made officers. He had become a particular favorite of General Murray in the wake of the cease-fire, since both were logisticians by training and outlook. So high was his credit with the Americans that the Embassy conveniently forgot that his "blood uncle" was a three-star NVA general.

Light at the Top

For all his tactical faux pas, President Thieu was no man's fool. He had read *People's War* and commanded troops in the field, and he knew with a veteran's instinct that the ultimate objective of the ongoing Communist attacks, dispersed as they were, was the isolation of Saigon itself and the overextension of his army.

Only three front-line divisions were currently deployed in the Saigon area to defend the capital, with two newly formed and untested marine and airborne brigades and a ranger group in reserve—hardly a match for the local NVA presence, which was now the equivalent of six divisions. On 12 March, Thieu therefore sent an urgent cable to General Truong in Danang, instructing him to revise his plans and send the Airborne Division to Saigon at once.

The following morning he met with his Security Council to announce an even more dramatic decision. After months of debate and stonewalling he had finally resolved to do as so many of his colleagues had been urging: he would shuck off the "unproductive" areas of the country, vast portions of MR 1 and 2, and concentrate his forces where they would do the most good: around Saigon. He called the new strategic concept "Light at the Top, Heavy at the Bottom."

For the past two weeks Prime Minister Khiem and a team of experts had been studying the plan. Originally the exercise had been strictly contingency, a general review of the long-term options, with no specific purpose. Thieu himself had insisted on this approach. He had no desire to give his commanders the impression he was considering a humiliating retreat from certain key areas until it was absolutely necessary. Out of deference to his wishes, and despite the urgings of Ted Sarong and others, Khiem and his team had therefore scrupulously avoided digging into details or querying their subordinates for recommendations. Aside the gradual contraction of General Truong's battlelines in MR 1, the practical implications of a general retrenchment—precisely what territory ought to be given up and when—had scarcely been considered.

A few days before the fall of Ban Me Thuot, Thieu's Economics Minister had called his counterpart at the American Embassy, the newly arrived economics counselor Dan Ellerman, and bounced some of the ideas under consideration around with him. Was Martin in favor of truncation? Had the concept been discussed in Washington? On 11 March, with Ban Me Thuot in its final hours, Ellerman sent back a reply which he had prepared with the acting Chargé, Wolfgang Lehmann. Whether or not any part of the country was to be abandoned, he said, was a decision only the Vietnamese could make. "And whatever you do, the world will respect that which is executed successfully."

That message, noncommittal, almost flippant, finally made up Thieu's mind for him. If the Americans could approach a problem of such magnitude so casually, he concluded, they would hardly be influenced by anything he did. There was no sense in his trying to hold on to every piece of territory simply to impress them.

It was on this basis he decided to alter his entire strategy, sliding abruptly and irrevocably into "Light at the Top, Heavy at the Bottom."

In retrospect the sudden shift seems all too rational, for the essence of Thieu's strategic policies had always been the manipulation of the Americans for the national good as he saw it. And once the Americans no longer seemed manipulatable, then it was simply time to change—quickly, and yes, even abruptly, particularly if the nation's survival depended upon it. That was what had brought him to the landmark decisions he put before his colleagues over breakfast on 13 March.

But having shifted course so quickly, he had had little time to think through the practicalities, no more than Khiem or General Vien or any of the others who had been involved in the contingency planning of the past two weeks. Thus, as he sipped his morning tea and mulled over the concept, there were long pauses, embarrassing blank spaces that left many of his listeners wondering what exactly was to be done.

Khiem and Vien would have liked to pose some practical questions, but both were so relieved that Thieu had finally swung over to their viewpoint, they decided—fatally—to leave well enough alone for the moment.

No questions? Well then, Thieu went on, they might as well consider the next item on the agenda: their immediate response to the attacks at Ban Me Thuot. On this topic the President seemed to have his ideas sorted out. First, it would be necessary to determine if the city had actually been lost (none of his intelligence officers was yet sure). Secondly, if it had indeed fallen, every effort must be made to retake it. Here Thieu launched into an historical digression. Ban Me Thuot had always been the key to the highlands. The French had used it as their primary base of operations there, and having been trained as a French officer, he could fully appreciate their point of view. Whoever controlled Ban Me Thuot controlled the western access routes to Saigon.

Vien shifted uneasily in his chair. Indeed, Ban Me Thuot was critical, he conceded. But how was General Phu to secure it? His one full division in the highlands, the 23rd, was already overextended. More than one regiment had already been dispersed and presumably was lost at Ban Me Thuot, and two others were being flown in to reinforce. That left Pleiku and Kontum undermanned. And there were no reserves to fill the void.

Thieu sat for a moment, fingers templed, chin resting on them. Vien was right of course: no reserves. And Phu's units were stretched tight as a drum.

He looked around the table, searching the faces for an answer. There was none. They were all the perfect courtesans, all deferring to him. He fumbled in his pockets, cleared his throat, then gave them his decision, almost in a whisper, a turning point in the history of the war. Kontum and Pleiku would have to be abandoned, he said. The strategic withdrawals, "Light at the Top, Heavy at the Bottom," would begin there.

The room went dead silent. He continued: such a pullback was logical, necessary; it would release forces to move on Ban Me Thuot. And Ban Me Thuot was the key, after all, as French tacticians had proved twenty years before.

His colleagues may have been too stunned or simply too afraid of him to object. In any case, there was no discussion, and in closing, Thieu ordered them to keep their silence. Tell no one of the plan, he said, not even the Americans. They had had their chance to help, and had failed him.

Later that afternoon Thieu met with Truong, who had just flown in from Danang. He greeted him coolly, for he knew his MR 1 commander had come for only one reason, to ask him to reverse his decision on the Airborne Division. But there was no chance now. The new strategy would not permit it. "Light at the Top, Heavy at the Bottom": the Airborne would have to come to Saigon at once.

But Truong was unusually persistent, explaining for the hundredth time that his forces were already dangerously overcommitted. To withdraw the ·Airborne precipitously, before he had time to adjust, would tear great holes in his defenses, would force him to make drastic and sudden changes in them. In bluntest terms, Quang Tri City, bloody battleground in 1968, lost and won again in 1972, would have to be given up. For he could no longer afford to keep his Marine Division deployed to defend it. The marines would have to fall back to Hué and to Danang to fill the void left by the Airborne.

Thieu nodded and sympathized—but would agree to only one small concession. He would stagger the withdrawal of the Airborne, he said, to give Truong time to rearrange his defenses. The first of its brigades would be pulled out on 17 March; the next one, eight days later, while the third could remain in MR 1 until the end of the month. Meanwhile, some of the raw marine units outside Saigon would be sent to help fill the gaps.

When Truong returned to Danang later in the day he was hardly appeased. He told several of his staffers privately he would resign or perhaps even mount a coup if the President changed signals on him again. For the normally reticent MR 1 commander this was serious talk indeed, and Thieu's own informants quickly passed word of it on to him, strengthening him in his conviction that Truong was not only a rival but an enemy. A few hours later he issued an executive decree lowering Saigon's curfew from midnight to ten o'clock as precaution against any coup attempt after hours.

Actually, Thieu's apprehensions were misplaced. During the next few days Truong proved himself first and foremost a disciplined soldier. Almost immediately he ordered one of the marine brigades north of Hué to prepare to shift to the Danang front as he began dutifully altering his defenses to Thieu's specifications.

At General Dung's headquarters in the western highlands, officers and men were now working around the clock to keep the NVA commander abreast of developments across the country. "The operation map was covered with circles and red crosses marking the places where our troops had annihilated the enemy and taken full control of targets," Dung later recalled. "There were red arrows showing the advance of our units, and overlapping blue arrows indicating the direction of enemy withdrawals to adjacent forests. Telephone calls flowed in constantly . . . Comrades serving in the command post worked and walked quietly and handed around cigarettes which had just been delivered from the rear."

Only two weeks before, Dung had been sent to South Vietnam for one purpose and one purpose only—to mastermind the campaign against Ban Me Thuot. But now that cracks were appearing in government defenses elsewhere, he quickly resolved to broaden his objectives. As with so many of his decisions in the final months of the war, it was an intelligence coup that provided the initial inspiration. In the final hours of the Ban Me Thuot battle Dung's men had captured the deputy commander of the 23rd ARVN Division. The officer turned out to be both talkative and well informed. Although he had no direct knowledge of "Light at the Top, Heavy at the Bottom," he was well acquainted with the logic that had given rise to it. Under interrogation he confided that Nha Trang and Cam Ranh Bay on the central coast were now the most important government holdings in MR 2 and that Thieu would probably choose in a crunch to abandon Pleiku and Kontum in the highlands, as well as the coastal city of Qui Nhon. The air force was broken and demoralized, he said; if the Marine and Airborne Divisions in MR 1 were defeated, the entire South Vietnamese army would fall apart.

In effect, the officer was anticipating precisely what would happen in the next few weeks, and Dung, even at this early date, was impressed. On 11 and 12 March he therefore cabled some startling recommendations to his comrades in Hanoi. Not only did he plan to hold Ban Me Thuot at all costs, but he also wanted to extend operations into Phu Bon Province just to the northeast as a first step toward isolating Pleiku and Kontum and capturing all of the western highlands. He also called for new initiatives north of Hué in MR 1 so Thieu would be unable to divert marine or airborne units to the highlands front.

Undoubtedly his proposals rekindled debate in the Politburo. Party First Secretary Le Duan had won his colleagues over to the idea of a major offensive in the first place by guaranteeing it would be held within bounds—for the next year at least—so reconstruction could go forward. Now the commander in chief was advocating dramatic new initiatives.

The Central Military Party Committee was called into session to weigh his recommendations. As Dung later pointed out in his memoirs, the final decision—reached within two days—was presented to him as a collective one, both the Politburo and the party's military experts giving their imprimatur to it. Clearly, no one wanted to assume sole responsibility for turning the offensive into a potentially open-ended proposition.

Under the new plan Dung was to complete mopping-up operations around Ban Me Thuot and strike northward, into the center and the remaining western portions of the region, severing all the major highways and capturing other key towns. The government's response, the Politburo predicted, would be to regroup its forces in Pleiku or it "might be forced to make a strategic retreat and abandon the highlands altogether." In light of this perspicacious assessment, Dung was instructed "to encircle Pleiku immediately."

In an effort to reassure the Politburo, Dung sent a message to Hanoi on the fourteenth suggesting that his forces might in fact be able to "overfulfill" their current objectives in the next few weeks and "even meet the plan forecast for 1976." To some of his more cautious comrades, however, that last projection must have been anything but consoling. The plan for 1976, after all, envisaged the liberation of the entire country.

The controversy Dung's proposals fomented within the leadership was wholly predictable, for the decisions he was urging on them pointed clearly toward a monumental shift in strategy. What had begun only weeks before as a limited military campaign, focused on the highlands and carefully calibrated not to overprovoke the United States or detract from reconstruction at home, was now being expanded toward the threshold of a multi-front "general offensive," with all the uncertainties and hazards that implied. And what if the highlands were brought under control? Would Dung then insist on "overfulfilling" his plan for 1975, as he indicated he could do? The moderates in the party's Central Committee were afraid so.

As both Dung and his critics were aware, there was, in the planning and execution of any offensive, a kind of momentum that fed on success. In the case of the current campaign, however, the pressure for continued escalation and risk-taking was heightened by a factor totally divorced from Dung's own optimism. This additional stimulus was the weather. In Dung's primary target area (as well as in MR 3 and the delta), the rainy season was only two months away. If NVA forces were to achieve any kind of decisive breakthrough, they would have to push hard and fast, making every battle count—or else risk getting bogged down on disparate, mud-clogged battlefields far from their main lines of supply. The necessity of beating the rainy season put an urgency on everything Dung meant to accomplish, and added to the impulse toward immediate, all-out war.

Perhaps fittingly, it was the Communists' preoccupation with the limits and imperatives posed by the weather that first broke the web of secrecy surrounding their plans. At one point, shortly after the capture of Ban Me Thuot, one of our intelligence sources overheard a conversation between two NVA field commanders that bore directly on this crucial concern. "Shall we continue pushing toward the coast or hold up for the rainy season?" one officer inquired of the other. "Continue pushing toward the coast" was the reply. "We can't stop for anything." This was among the first clues that the North Vietnamese were on the verge of a massive new offensive.

It was not the only one, however. Soon after the Politburo decisions of mid-March, there was an abrupt escalation of Hanoi's negotiating demands, almost as dramatic as its swing in strategy. Back in January and February, when Le Duan had wrought his initial strategic compromise, he had eased away from the previously standard demand for Thieu's resignation in hopes of convincing the doves at his elbow (and us) that the next round of fighting would not go all the way. Now, suddenly, the old intransigence resurfaced. North Vietnamese propagandists not only demanded Thieu's removal once again, but also insisted that the entire Thieu "clique" bow out as the price for peace. When I first spotted the change in the propaganda from Radio Hanoi, I drew up a memorandum for Polgar, reminding him that it was just such a grandiose demand that had heralded the North Vietnamese "general offensive" of 1972.

While the Embassy tried to make sense of the new and ominous tone of Hanoi's pronouncements, the American officials who lived and worked in the highlands, in the direct line of fire, began scrambling for cover. On 12 March, two days after the attack on Ban Me Thuot, Walt Martindale, the consulate representative in Quang Duc Province to the south, was ordered unequivocally to drop everything and leave. Driving southeast along little-used back roads, he made his way to Lam Dong Province and then to Nha Trang, on the coast, home of the American consulate for MR 2.

Consular officials in Pleiku City, meanwhile, were preparing for their own departure. By the time word reached them that Ban Me Thuot was under massive attack, Earl Thieme, the fifty-year-old USAID official who doubled as the senior American province representative, had dusted off his standing evacuation plan and was reviewing its provisions. But the more he studied it, the more he realized it simply was not adequate. Its most glaring shortcoming was the basic premise itself, namely, that in the event of an American evacuation the local citizenry would remain docile. Pleiku City, with its mixed Vietnamese-montagnard population of 60,000, was already a smoldering fuse. The Ban Me Thuot offensive had sent shock waves of panic reverberating through the labyrinthine byways and shantytowns that made up its heart, and local Vietnamese air force officers were even now smuggling their own families out as fast as they could.

Thieme sat down with several other staffers on the twelfth to work out a new evacuation drill, one better suited to the explosive conditions they faced. Later that day his senior CIA colleague took a plane to Nha Trang to clear the plan with the consulate.

The next morning the officer briefed his own boss, the CIA Base Chief for MR 2, "Howard Archer." Pleiku was fast becoming a ghost town, he explained, food markets were closing and the population was as jittery as he had ever seen it. It was time to pull out the Americans. Archer suggested they talk with the "Congen" himself.

Consul General Moncrieff Spear, a thin, high-strung man with Brahmin pretensions and a Romanesque profile, was not exactly the kind of paramilitary bureaucrat the emerging crisis in MR 2 required. He had no love for Vietnam or its never-ending war, and in fact had not wanted to come here at all. Although Nha Trang, with its azure waters and resort-city ambiance, was at least the most elegant consular outpost in the country, he would have much preferred serving his time in real luxury elsewhere, as he had in Nassau, his previous posting. Moreover, in his eighteen months on the job in Nha Trang he had yet to develop any real "feel" for command. The Ambassador had not let him. Shortly after his arrival Spear had made the mistake of alerting the Embassy to deteriorating security conditions in the highlands—and had been roundly chastised by Martin for being too "alarmist." Since then, he had been marching scrupulously to the Ambassador's drum.

The assault on Ban Me Thuot, however, left Spear in a quandary, and once the loss of Struharick and the rest of the westerners there was confirmed, he began mulling over some tough questions. Should he continue to play his hand coolly and cautiously, as Martin wanted? Or had the time come to seize the initiative and accelerate his own contingency planning?

As he listened to Archer and the CIA man from Pleiku on the morning of the thirteenth he decided that prudence lay in the second direction, and by the time the briefing was over, he had resolved to begin pulling "non-essential" American staffers out of Pleiku.

The following morning Spear and his staff learned from ARVN sources that a village just north of Ban Me Thuot which General Phu had been hoping to use as the jumping-off point for a counteroffensive had been lost to the Communists. They were also informed that the main west-east artery out of the southern highlands had been interdicted and that thousands of refugees were now strewn out along parallel secondary roads running to the coast.

A few hours later Archer advised the Embassy in Saigon he was sending a crew and helicopter to the town of Phuoc An, east of Ban Me Thuot, to get the story of the rout firsthand. Some of the Station's paramilitary sports gave a hurrah of approval, for in their eyes such derring-do was very much in the good old "company" tradition. But when "John Pittman," Polgar's deputy, asked me what I thought of the idea I could hardly conceal my dismay. NVA forces were moving so fast and intelligence was so spotty, I warned him, we couldn't be sure if Phuoc An was even in ARVN hands. Pittman ultimately took my caution to heart, and vetoed the mission—none too soon, for within hours Phuoc An was under heavy bombardment and isolated.

The morning of the fourteenth was parched and heat-ridden, quite typical of the dry season. The flight to Cam Ranh Bay on the central coast took approximately one hour. There was little air turbulence to buffet the stripped down C-47, and out beyond the starboard window the sun glistened off the South China Sea like so many flecks of mica in gray granite. President Thieu sat alone during most of the trip, picking through the latest intelligence from the front. Prime Minister Khiem, General Quang and General Vien talked quietly among themselves on the other side of the aisle. Thieu had called the meeting in Cam Ranh this auspicious morning to brief General Phu, his MR 2 commander, on a matter of grave concern to them both—"Light at the Top, Heavy at the Bottom."

As Thieu put the documents aside and leaned back to ease the chronic stiffness in his right shoulder, he seemed, to one of his companions, to be lapsing into a daydream. Perhaps he was only musing on the odds. Were they truly as unpropitious as they appeared? The night before, Thieu had consulted both his family astrologer and Ted Sarong about his plans for truncating the country (though without tipping his hand on the details). The astrologer had been dubious. Sarong had told him time was running out. Maybe both of them had read the omens correctly. But what else was there to do? Thieu could only hope that his old friend General Phu would have an answer of sorts to that question. The fate of the highlands and perhaps that of the entire country would soon be in his hands.

Major General Pham Van Phu had long been one of Thieu's favorite field commanders. Like the President, he had first distinguished himself as a soldier under French command, fighting the Communists in the first Indochina war. Captured with the French garrison at Dien Bien Phu, he had spent the next several years in a Viet Minh prison camp, where according to associates he had lost his health (to tuberculosis) and his nerve. Years later he had served shoulder-to-shoulder with Thieu as both rose through the ranks of the French-trained, American-supported nationalist army. Once Thieu became President, Phu's own career blossomed as well, for his old friend rewarded him generously with one choice assignment after another, finally appointing him successor to the MR 2 commander, General Nguyen Van Toan, in the fall of 1974.

As Phu admitted at the time, he considered himself underqualified for the job. He had had little experience as a "headquarters man" and felt more at home with day-to-day tactical planning than with the ambiguities of grand strategy. Some of those who had known him for years insisted he also suffered from a far more serious handicap—an almost pathological fear of being pinned down on the battlefield and captured by his adversary. It was the legacy, they said, of the years he had spent as a prisoner after Dien Bien Phu.

During his own tenure in MR 2, Phu's predecessor, General Toan, had turned the command into a petty fiefdom, parceling out provincial posts and other assignments on the basis of various personal gratuities. Now Toan was MR 3 commander, appointed on Martin's recommendation, and Phu had been left with the vestiges of Toan's style of command—an inept staff with almost no feeling for the troops and an ill-concealed contempt for the montagnard irregulars who made up much of the army in the highlands. The inadequacies of his staff, plus Phu's own shortcomings, would inevitably make for a lethal combination.

As the conference at Cam Ranh got under way shortly before noon, Phu attempted to put the military picture in perspective for his old comrade in arms. Enemy forces equal to four divisions were now deployed from Pleiku to Ban Me Thuot, he told Thieu, and all major roads to the coast were shut down. With the forces available to him, he continued, he would be able to defend the highlands for no more than a month or so, and only if he got additional air support, munitions and reinforcements.

When Thieu heard that, his eyes seemed to glaze over. Again one of his subordinates thought he was daydreaming. Finally he looked over at Phu and shook his head. None of this, neither reinforcements nor additional equipment, could be provided, he emphasized. The army was already stretched perilously thin all across the country and stockpiles had to be kept close to easily defensible areas. Thus there was no way to shore up the defenses of Kontum and Pleiku. The only course open to them was to abandon both provinces and use the forces there to reinforce the coast and to support a counteroffensive against Ban Me Thuot.

Despite the stunning import of these words, Phu showed no reaction. He may have nodded briefly in agreement, but that was all. Nor did he raise any questions or pose objections. Now as always he was the utterly obliging, completely deferential friend.

Seeing he had made his point, Thieu turned next to an all-important specific, the selection of a withdrawal route. Although Route 19 across the center of the region, and Route 14 running south toward MR 3, were both interdicted, there was a chance the army could punch through. Which road would Phu prefer to gamble on? Here General Vien interrupted, insisting that neither could be adequately secured by the forces Phu had available. That left only Route 7B, an old logger's road extending eastward across the belly of the region through Phu Bon Province. While parts of it had not been used in years, Vien observed, there were two advantages to using it. First, it was clear of enemy forces, as far as anyone knew. Secondly, the Communists would not be expecting any movement along it. When Vien asked Phu what he thought of this option, the MR 2 commander once again merely nodded.

As the conference was about to wind up, Phu bestirred himself to ask about a vital point: timing. When should the pullout begin? Thieu brushed the question aside. That would be left to Phu's discretion, he said. His only stipulation was that the final decision, whatever it was, be kept absolutely secret. Not even the territorial forces or the montagnards in Kontum and Pleiku were to be informed of it. To include them in the initial planning, he asserted, would only cause complications and increase the risk of betrayal. Besides, they would undoubtedly make their way out once they realized that a withdrawal was in progress.

For callous and slipshod planning, this almost casual exchange of questions and instructions must surely mark some kind of watershed in the history of the Vietnam war. Thieu himself set the tone for the proceedings, with his glancing treatment of such issues as the timing of the withdrawal and his utter disregard for the fate of the montagnard irregulars, the backbone of Phu's army. General Vien must also bear responsibility for what transpired, if only for acquiescing so readily to Thieu's ommissions and misjudgments. It was Vien, moreover, who dealt the final blow to the chances for success by proposing Route 7B as the avenue of escape without bothering to determine which parts of it were usable and which were not. Without such advance planning, Phu's army was set, literally, on the path to its own destruction.

Before returning to Pleiku, Phu conferred briefly with Vien's chief of operations. As a basic tactical guide they decided to rely on a little-known contingency plan for a logistics drawdown in the highlands, which had been lying around the headquarters of the Joint General Staff in Saigon for months. The document seemed adaptable and adequate to Phu's new mission, except in one particular: it allowed for six months of preparation prior to the start of the operation.

Phu did not feel he had that long.

Despite Thieu's own indifference to the question, the timing of the withdrawal was all but a foregone conclusion even as the conference at Cam Ranh came to an end. On the same morning Phu's senior staff in Pleiku met to discuss the possibility of shifting part of their operations to an alternate headquarters in Nha Trang so they could better coordinate the planned counter-offensive against Ban Me Thuot. It was not to be a full-scale pullout, as they envisioned it. Part of the headquarters staff was to remain in Pleiku. Yet coming within an hour or two of the Cam Ranh meeting, the decision established a momentum, a kind of evacuation-now psychology that would inform all the tasks and responsibilities Thieu thrust on them. The abandonment of the highlands indeed might have been less reckless if Phu's staffers had not already opted for an immediate change in their own venue.

The consular officers who attended that morning session in Pleiku considered the headquarters shift one more ill omen, and when Spear cabled them from Nha Trang an hour or so later, directing them to trim their own ranks, they were more than ready to oblige.

Besides the ten U.S. officials spread between Kontum and Pleiku, there were twenty or more individuals of various nationalities for whom Earl Thieme felt responsible, including American and Filipino contractors who worked at the Pleiku airfield, several French businessmen and a team of medical specialists from New Zealand. Moreover, each of the U.S. agencies that made up the "official" community in the highlands had numerous Vietnamese employees with families—about 500 people in total—who would have to be evacuated if and when the Americans left.

Just before lunch Thieme radioed Nha Trang and asked if he could use a regularly scheduled courier flight to begin funneling people out. Spear agreed immediately.

In Saigon, General Homer Smith, the Defense Attaché, paid his usual Friday-afternoon call on General Vien, who was just back from Cam Ranh. Vien, all smiles and optimism, said nothing about the monumental change in plans that had just been put into effect.

When General Phu returned to Pleiku after dusk he held a short meeting with his field commanders to brief them on their new mission. He seemed highly agitated and touched only cursorily on operational details. In his most decisive act of the evening he appointed his ranger commander, Brigadier General Pham Duy Tat, to coordinate the withdrawal and instructed him to advise all regular units (though not the irregulars) to prepare to move at once. He cautioned his logistics chief, however, not to destroy any fuel stores "till the last minute" lest the local population realize what was coming. Nor should the Americans be informed, he emphasized. With that, he went home to pack.

In Saigon my colleague, Joe Kingsley, spent the earlier part of the evening closeted over drinks with some old friends from the U.S. Special Forces who had returned to Vietnam after their discharge. They called themselves the "Special Forces Association of Saigon," and their raison d'être was to be ready to give their all if the United States should ever decide to come back in. They had assembled a small arsenal and discussed battle plans and had a hell of a good time doing it.

When Joe showed up at this particular meeting, however, he was not his usual free-guzzling self, and the others noticed right away. "What's wrong, Joe? Your wife catch you at one of the bars downtown?" someone bellowed and there were guffaws all around, for in his premarital days Joe had been famous for his womanizing. "No," he said sadly, "we've all got real problems. The place is going down the drain." He then briefly outlined the arguments —the loss of Ban Me Thuot, the government's apparent inability to rally its forces. He may have laid it on a bit heavy; of all of us in the analytical shop, he had suddenly become the gloomiest, so gloomy, Pat had nicknamed him "Armageddon." But his Special Forces chums listened with great interest and sympathy, for this was something they all understood. When he finished, someone suggested they step up their own preparations and plan to reconvene for strategy talks several weeks hence, on 30 April. Joe shook his head. "We don't have that much time," he said. "We won't be here on 30 April." He was right, of course.

For the Embassy the following morning was a normal one for a Saturday. We all showed up early for the obligatory half-day in the office while hoping against hope the sun would hold so we could spend a leisurely afternoon at poolside. Chargé Lehmann, who was still substituting for Martin, spent part of the morning with Thieu at the Palace, discussing nothing in particular. Then he went off to the dentist.

Polgar, meanwhile, had a brief meeting with another Palace contact, General Quang. The exchange was routine. Quang expressed his now-familiar concerns about the situation at Ban Me Thuot, but neglected to mention the government's plans for the rest of the highlands. Polgar had no reason to suspect the general was holding out on him. At about nine-thirty he returned to the Embassy, satisfied he had had his excitement for the day.

In Pleiku the standard morning briefing at Phu's headquarters went off like clockwork. One of the local CIA staffers sat in as usual and took notes for the record. At no point did the Vietnamese briefer say anything that might have led him to suspect that a full-scale withdrawal of the army was only hours away.

Soon afterward Thieme himself arrived at the headquarters to inform Phu of the impending withdrawal of his own non-essentials. Phu, nervous and haggard-looking, endorsed the move, but said nothing about his somewhat more grandiose evacuation plans.

Less than an hour later the MR 2 commander dropped by his villa near the center of Pleiku to pick up his suitcase, and then, with a few close aides, flew off to Nha Trang without alerting anyone else on his staff. He told one of those who accompanied him that he was moving to the coast so he could better direct the withdrawal. But when the rest of his subordinates, those who had been left behind, found out he was gone, they were in no mood to take any further orders from him. It was now every man for himself.

Meanwhile, the awful truth about the decisions taken at Cam Ranh the day before was beginning to leak out. Shortly after the morning staff meeting, a CIA agent on Phu's staff alerted his local American case officer that a total abandonment of the highlands was imminent. The case officer was so stunned by the news, and so incredulous of it, he neglected to apprise Thieme or any of his other colleagues. Instead he sent an immediate, top-priority message to Archer in Nha Trang, setting out the details and asking for clarification.

At approximately 10 A.M. I joined Polgar in his office to assist in briefing a newly arrived State Department officer. I was ten minutes into my usual show-and-tell when one of the front-office secretaries suddenly burst in and shoved an intelligence report under Polgar's nose. It was a copy of the dispatch from the CIA officer in Pleiku. The first paragraph alone was enough to cause Polgar to blanch through his tan: all ARVN forces in the northern highlands,

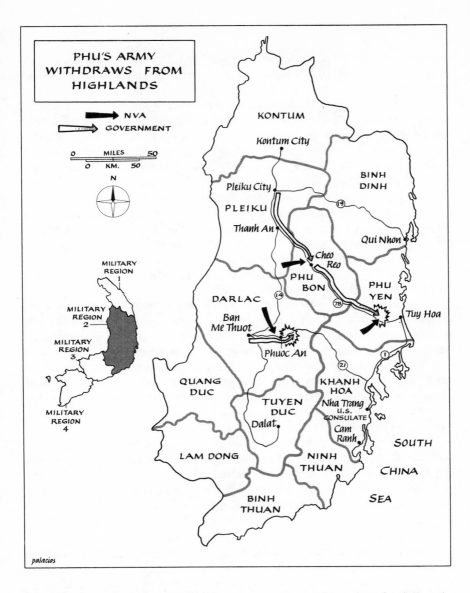

PHU'S ARMY
WITHDRAWS FROM
HIGHLANDS

the equivalent of nearly two divisions, were now on the verge of a full-scale withdrawal.

Polgar jumped up and rushed down to the Ambassador's suite on the third floor to inform Lehmann, but the Chargé was still out. He then put in a call to Nha Trang for confirmation. Archer, however, had nothing more to offer. Polgar then asked to speak to the Consul General himself.

When Spear got on the line, Polgar assured him of the reliability of the agent in Pleiku and advised him to evacuate the remaining Americans at once.

"Is that an order?" Spear asked cautiously, for he knew only Lehmann could authorize evacuation of a full province staff.

"No, of course not," Polgar snapped, "but I'm telling you: unless you move those men out right now, you'll risk losing them. If panic breaks out up there, the airstrip will be out of business in a few hours."

A short while later Lehmann returned to the Embassy. But he was no more inclined than Spear to order a total pullout. He doubted the validity of the intelligence report, particularly since he had met with Thieu only a few hours before and nothing had been said about any withdrawal. Besides, to shut down the last of the American field posts in the highlands would be political dynamite. It could precipitate panic among the locals and the army and might even lead to the loss of Kontum and Pleiku.

Finally, around noon, Polgar lost what was left of his patience. He personally ordered up Air America aircraft, instructed Archer to pull all CIA officers out of Pleiku, and again recommended a complete shutout to Lehmann. The Chargé stalled a bit longer but at last agreed to the course Polgar suggested. He called in his secretary and dictated a message to Spear, instructing him to close out all highlands operations at once.

Grudging as the decision was, it represented a landmark. Not since the consular team in Tay Ninh Province had been evacuated (briefly) in October 1973 had the Embassy deliberately given up a major outpost under pressure. There was something else about the move that also seemed noteworthy, at least to a few of us. Despite clear and accurate intelligence that left no doubt of the need for urgent action, senior Embassy officers had taken their time following through on it, insisting that an overhasty response could panic our allies. The same scene, with identical dialogue, would be replayed again and again during the next few weeks.

Soon after alerting Spear, Lehmann summoned Polgar and another CIA officer and asked what ought to be done about the ICCS team in Pleiku. Should the Hungarians and the Poles be advised of the pullout? Polgar said yes, emphatically, even though he knew both teams would immediately alert the North Vietnamese. But Lehmann had another idea. The Embassy would inform only the Indonesians in their capacity as current chairman of the ICCS, he said. They could tell the rest what they wanted.

This was precisely what was done. The Indonesians in turn chose to warn only their own team and the Iranian representatives in Pleiku, leaving the Poles and Hungarians to fend for themselves. If this was meant to confuse the two Communist delegations, however, it was pointless. As the Indonesians and Iranians started packing, their East European colleagues immediately realized something was up. The Hungarians promptly contacted the ICCS headquarters in Saigon and demanded an additional plane to pull them out. Air America, which was serving the ICCS under contract, readied a transport with special markings, then at the last minute canceled the flight because of "mechanical difficulties," offering to send a regularly marked plane instead. But the Hungarian team balked at that. They were not about to fly out of Pleiku in an American aircraft—not with all the NVA antiaircraft artillery in the vicinity. They told ICCS headquarters they would wait until Air America could provide a properly marked transport.

And so they did, spending the next twenty-four hours in a ditch alongside their compound as the North Vietnamese lobbed rockets into Pleiku City. An American civilian, who handled contracting for the ICCS, stayed with them throughout, to assure their safety. The Hungarian government later commended him for bravery.

When news of Phu's pullout first reached Washington, officials at the Pentagon and the State Department began frantically phoning around town, trying to locate the itinerant Ambassador Martin in hopes he could shed some light on this startling development. But Martin was too far out of circulation to be of much help. A few days before, he had undergone minor dental surgery and was now convalescing at his family home in North Carolina. Finally, Secretary of Defense Schlesinger, with the help of his assistant, Erich Von Marbod, managed to reach the Ambassador by long-distance phone. "Why, I know all about that," Martin drawled after the Secretary had given him the details. "Phu has long been planning to withdraw part of his headquarters from the highlands. That's all it is." Try as he might, Schlesinger could not convince him there was more to the pullout than that. Nor would Martin consent to return to Washington at once to deal with "such a minor problem."

By early afternoon on the fifteenth, Pleiku City was slipping rapidly into the full throes of panic. NVA reconnaissance squads were halting traffic on the northern and western outskirts, rockets were dropping in periodically near the airfield, and as Phu's army began preparing for withdrawal, the local citizenry, without the slightest prompting or hesitation, did likewise.

When Thieme left Phu's headquarters and returned to his own compound around noontime he immediately contacted the three DAO representatives on his staff—Mike Chilton, John Good and Nelson Kief—and asked them to come around to his office. Since all three had had some combat experience, he was confident they would be able to keep their nerve and their wits about them in the grueling hours ahead. He then set up a makeshift "command post" in his living room with special radios and telephones, and proceeded to call his Vietnamese employees, directing them to prepare to leave at once. By the time he reached the third or fourth one on his list, the three DAO men had arrived and were putting together several convoys of jeeps and small vans. Shortly thereafter, they began their hazardous run through the city, stopping at designated assembly points to pick up their first passengers. Because the airfield had already been closed to Vietnamese civilians, Thieme, or one of the DAO men, had to escort each convoy to the front gate and bribe and humor the guards to make certain it was allowed to pass.

Like all official Americans in Pleiku, the three young operatives who made up the local CIA contingent (a fourth was still in Nha Trang with

Archer) were technically responsible to Thieme as the senior U.S. representative on the scene. But as soon as the pullout commenced, Archer directed them by radio to leave immediately, in accordance with Polgar's urgent instructions from Saigon. They were intelligence operatives, not consular officers, he reminded them; they were under no obligation to help Thieme evacuate Vietnamese employed by USAID or anyone else.

A few minutes later the CIA men dropped by Thieme's compound to alert him to this. They were so nervous and overwrought that they forgot to advise him of the agent report earlier in the day indicating Phu's army was in full retreat. He would not learn of this crucial piece of intelligence until he himself had reached Nha Trang much later in the afternoon.

After leaving Thieme's office the CIA officers drove back to their own compound, informed their Vietnamese employees they were evacuating, and urged them to make their way to the coast as best they could, on whatever roads were still open. Then they skittered out to the airfield with the last of their top-secret radio gear and caught the next Air America flight out.

Unfortunately, in their haste to save themselves, they committed a host of sins for which any intelligence operative should be drawn and quartered. In addition to abandoning their American colleagues and their own Vietnamese employees, they neglected to provide for the safety of the long-time agent on Phu's staff, or to dispose of all their classified files. At the last minute they did think to instruct one of their local employees to make a final survey of the CIA compound, but whether he in turn located and destroyed the remaining documents was never confirmed. The papers included information that would have been of interest to NVA intelligence officers, and to their Soviet and Chinese brethren.

Throughout the afternoon twin-motor Air America C-46 and C-47 transports streamed into Pleiku airfield, and each time one landed, sixty or seventy passengers were already lined up and ready to board, thanks to the industry of Thieme and the three officers from DAO. In the meantime, an Air America chopper spun north to Kontum City to pull out the handful of Americans and other foreign nationals who made their home there.

At around four-thirty Spear, nervous to the point of irascibility, radioed from Nha Trang to order Thieme to bring the airlift to a close. One more flight would be scheduled, he said, and Thieme himself was to be on it. But as Thieme looked over his list of Vietnamese still to be evacuated, he realized that one more plane would never be able to accommodate them all, and he advised Spear that under no circumstances would he leave until at least two more planes had been provided. Spear, though furious at his insubordination, had no choice but to oblige him.

By the time Thieme boarded the last of the air transports an hour later, the front gate of the airfield was creaking under the weight of the crowds outside, and sporadic fighting had broken out among the soldiers on the edge of the tarmac. But as his own plane arched up over the chaos he and his DAO assistants had some reason to feel satisfied. In the past four and a half hours they had managed to rescue and dispatch to the (relative) safety of Nha Trang over 450 people, many of them Vietnamese employees of USAID. Thieme himself deserved much of the credit. A former Army colonel with battlefield experience, he had kept his cool under the most incredible pressures and had seen to it the American government paid its debt to many of the Vietnamese and montagnards who had served it loyally over the years.

During the same long afternoon, in which Thieme labored so valiantly, the withdrawal of Phu's army from Pleiku and Kontum began as it had been conceived, in utter confusion. The basic operational concept was childishly simple: evacuating units were to follow National Highway 14 south to the town of Thanh An and there jog east along Route 7B to Phu Bon and the coast. But General Tat, the coordinator, managed to turn simplicity on its head by failing to make even the most fundamental preparations. Neither he nor anyone on his staff bothered to survey Route 7B or to provide for the thousands of civilians who were bound to follow the units out. Troops and civilians soon became hopelessly intermingled, tank commanders and battle-hardened rangers bullied their way to the head of the column, and as the heavy armor and caissons pulled out in front, the road broke and rutted under their weight. The 2,000 cars, jeeps and trucks strung out behind quickly became mired in a river of mud. Field commanders haggled over rank and privilege, and the air force, ever jealous of its independence, refused to heed calls for medical evacuation or tight air support from army captains and lieutenants on the ground.

Polgar and several of us remained in the CIA situation room on the top floor of the Embassy throughout the afternoon, monitoring the chaos through radio pickups and reports from reconnaissance aircraft. "Why, it's like a goddamn circus parade gone haywire!" Polgar exclaimed. "The elephants have moved out in front and everybody else is stumbling through their shit." It was an apt description.

By evening Thieu, exhausted and pessimistic, was already casting about for scapegoats. Phu had misunderstood him, he complained to subordinates, and he ranted bitterly about the montagnards, particularly those at Ban Me Thuot, who, he insisted, had likewise betrayed him. His suspicions sprang from a report he had received a few hours earlier, disclosing that the montagnard militia at Ban Me Thuot had abandoned their posts on the first day of the battle there to defend their homes against rampaging ARVN deserters. It was this, Thieu asserted, that had led to the collapse of the city's defenses and to the current crisis throughout the highlands. As he left the Palace later that evening he ordered his staff to get to the bottom of the montagnards' treachery if it was the last thing they did.

Not long afterward police officers pulled in a French journalist, Paul Leandri, who had reported in a recent news dispatch that montagnards had actually led the attack on Ban Me Thuot. Leandri, a splenetic Corsican, refused to answer any questions, even after he was hauled downtown to National Police headquarters. Instead he became embroiled in a shouting match with his captors, insulting and taunting them. Then he made an even graver mistake. He turned his back on them and dashed out of the building and into the courtyard. As he was grappling with the door to his car, a police guard shot him through the head.

The French Ambassador flew into a rage when he learned of the incident, and shortly after midnight Polgar was called back to the Embassy to mediate between him and police authorities.

By the following morning Leandri's death and the French Embassy's protest, however, were the least of Thieu's own concerns. The evacuation column from Pleiku and Kontum had already stalled in western Phu Bon, and pressure was mounting elsewhere in the country. In western Binh Dinh Province, on the central coast, government defenses were breaking up under steady pounding. Fighting had flared overnight in Tay Ninh, northwest of Saigon, and other NVA forces were threatening road networks running northeast from the capital to the resort city of Dalat in southern MR 2.

To relieve the pressure in the immediate Saigon area, Thieu ordered the air force to bomb NVA troop and armor concentrations in the Cambodian borderlands due north of the capital. He also sent an urgent cable to General Truong in MR 1, canceling the agreement to stagger the pullout of the Airborne and directing that the entire division be shifted to Saigon at once.

Soon after daybreak on the sixteenth Earl Thieme sloshed down another cup of black coffee and ordered up a chopper to take him back to Pleiku. He had been up all night at the Air America terminal in Nha Trang, trying to reach stay-behinds by long-distance telephone.

As the chopper came in low over the edge of Pleiku City, Thieme and his pilot could hardly believe what they saw. Overnight the main thoroughfares had become rivers of struggling, panic-stricken humanity, and now, as the small Air America UH-1 bore off toward the center of town, a thousand eyes seemed riveted on it.

Over two hundred Vietnamese were waiting at Thieme's compound when the chopper landed in the courtyard. Quickly winnowing out his own employees, he drove the rest away at the point of his .45 automatic, and also radioed for a plane from Nha Trang. Then he trucked his passengers through the refugee-clogged streets to the airfield. Soon an Air America C-46 transport lumbered in, picking its way carefully along the tarmac through throngs of soldiers and civilians. Thinking this was the plane he had just summoned, Thieme dashed over to it and grabbed for the hatch-lock. But as he did, the pilot gunned his motors and pulled off down the runway, to a parking area reserved for military planes. Thieme, at once frightened and furious, put in a radio call to Nha Trang to demand an explanation. He was told that the C-46 was a specially scheduled CIA plane sent in to rescue "a high-ranking Vietnamese military officer" (actually, the CIA agent on Phu's staff who had been abandoned the day before).

A short while later another Air America transport arrived to pick up Thieme's group. But no sooner had it rolled to a stop than it was mobbed by armed Vietnamese troopers. The pilot radioed Nha Trang that he was being forced to take on passengers at gunpoint, and Thieme, realizing he would be unable to get aboard, raced to a waiting Air America chopper. He and the pilot were able to pull only a few of his select passengers through the hatchway before the press of the crowds forced them off. As the helicopter veered east toward Nha Trang, Thieme gave silent thanks that somebody at the Embassy in Saigon had had the foresight to order the evacuation of Americans the day before. Otherwise, he and the rest would still be there, possibly locked in Pleiku for good.*

Sunday was normally a day of rest, even for the Embassy, but given the grim turn of events all across the country, Polgar ordered his staff on the sixteenth to put in at least a half-day in the office. One item in the overnight cable traffic particularly amused him. According to press playback from Washington, Secretary of Defense Schlesinger was publicly proclaiming there was no "crisis" in South Vietnam. Polgar wondered—in somewhat unquotable terms—what would have qualified as a "crisis" in the Secretary's view.

But the most troubling news was not from Washington or even from South Vietnam, but from across the border in Cambodia. According to a message from the Embassy there, Ambassador Dean had decided to begin moving out non-essential staffers. More than anything else, that seemed to bring the precariousness of our own situation—and of U.S. policy—home to me.

I spent the afternoon writing an appraisal for Polgar on the implications of the highlands withdrawal. Historically, the pullback boded no good. It was the evacuation of French forces from Kontum in January 1954 that had marked the beginning of the end of French domination in the southern half of Vietnam, just as the Communist victory at Dien Bien Phu a few months later would write a finish to it in the north. General Giap, the Viet Minh's master strategist, had once written that he who controls the northern highlands controls the key to Indochina. That still seemed true enough, since the road

---

*Actually, this was not Thieme's last flight to Pleiku. He returned the next day by chopper to pick up several Vietnamese employees on the road to Phu Bon. Meanwhile, other consular officers in the highlands and the border areas also acquitted themselves heroically. Ed Sprague, the consular representative in Phu Bon, succeeded in evacuating most of his Vietnamese employees before the chaos of Phu's retreat forced him to abandon his post. In addition, young Walt Martindale from Quang Duc Province flew back into the province capital on the fourteenth, two days after he had been ordered out by Spear, to rescue those Vietnamese and montagnards he had been obliged to leave behind. Unable to cram all of his intended evacuees aboard the aircraft provided to him, he gathered the rest together, formed a convoy and led them out himself, by way of back roads and logging trails, to Lam Dong Province to the southeast and finally to Dalat City. At one point along the way he actually fought off an attack by ARVN deserters, holding one of the troopers hostage until the convoy was safely past.

networks there provided ideal communication lines between North and South
Vietnam and a perfect jumping-off point for a blitzkrieg to the coast.

The highlands were also important in their own right. Kontum, Pleiku,
Darlac and Quang Duc Provinces encompassed sixteen percent of the territory
of South Vietnam, with a population of 500,000, not an inconsiderable bonus
for either side.

Yet like everybody else in the Embassy, I wanted to believe there was still
a chance, and in my assessment I argued that if part of the six ranger groups
now en route from Kontum and Pleiku could reach the coast safely, the
government might be able to turn the withdrawal into a Dunkirk-type "victory."

But Polgar merely shook his head when he read that. "You're trying to
make lemonade out of a lemon," he said. "Let's wait and see what happens
to those units before we weigh in on the side of optimism." His caution was
well advised.*

---

*Within hours of my assessment, the intelligence community in Washington, in a joint memoran-
dum, rendered an equally guarded verdict on the withdrawal from the highlands: "Although
President Thieu's decision [to give up Kontum and Pleiku] can be explained in terms of military
expedience, it nonetheless risks a psychological unraveling within ARVN that could seriously
complicate an orderly consolidation of the GVN's [government's] military position."

Glass Mountain

The revelation came slowly. Only toward the end of the day did General Dung realize what was happening just to the north of him in Pleiku and Kontum, and even then his forces weren't quite ready to exploit it.

On the morning of the sixteenth the radio monitoring staff at his headquarters outside Ban Me Thuot intercepted several messages indicating heavy air traffic at Pleiku airfield. A few hours later the Politburo alerted him by telephone that General Phu had shifted his own headquarters from Pleiku to Nha Trang. Soon afterward a forward NVA patrol spotted a large convoy of military and civilian vehicles heading east into Phu Bon Province in the center of the region.

Dung hurriedly assembled his staff to review these developments. Some officers saw them as heralding a counterattack against Ban Me Thuot. Others felt government units were pulling out of Kontum and Pleiku, as the Politburo had predicted two days before. Finally, at 7 P.M., Dung received definitive word from Hanoi. The Hungarian ICCS delegation in South Vietnam had just sent a flash message: the highlands were indeed being abandoned.

Dung's first response was unbridled anger. Relieved as he was to know what the enemy was doing, he was furious his field commanders had been so slow in anticipating it. He was particularly critical of General Kim Tuan of the 320th NVA Division. Several days before, when he had asked Tuan about the condition of Route 7B through Phu Bon Province, he had been told the road was impassable. "Now, upon learning that the enemy was retreating along Route 7 and that the 320th had no concrete information about it, I severely criticized the unit commander," Dung wrote later. "I told Comrade Kim Tuan emphatically, 'This is a shortcoming, a reproachable mistake. The slightest hesitation, mistake, fear of hardship or delay could now mean failure. If the enemy escapes, you will be responsible.' "

The dressing down apparently had the desired effect. Tuan immediately swung two of his regiments north into Phu Bon to intercept the column. The South Vietnamese commander, General Tat, who was soon to be captured in the melee, subsequently explained to NVA interrogators what it was like to be on the receiving end: "On 16 April, Communist forces began attacking part of the 23rd Ranger Group in Ban Bleik Pass [just west of Cheo Reo City], inflicting heavy casualties. The following day they shelled our command post in the city itself. Regional force [militia] units then deserted and fled.

"The 7th [ARVN] Ranger Group on 17 March called for air support. A formation of A-37 aircraft launched a bombing run but struck our own units, annihilating almost a full battalion. The following morning the Rangers were attacked once again and sustained serious losses. Only a few troops escaped. [Communist] forces then advanced and occupied [Cheo Reo] City itself."

With the fall of Cheo Reo, the evacuating column was effectively cut in half, part of it trapped west of the town, the rest strung out along Route 7B to the coast. Its destruction was now only a matter of time.

In MR 1, meanwhile, General Ngo Quang Truong was wrestling with a deepening crisis of his own. That last directive from Saigon had brought it to a head—Thieu's instructions to him to send the Airborne Division to MR 3 at once. He would have liked to ignore the message altogether, but there was nothing in its language that gave him any choice: either he complied, or threw the whole thing back in Thieu's teeth, and that would mean resignation or a coup. And bitter and disgruntled as he was, Truong still could not bring himself to embrace either extreme. Wearily, reluctantly, he therefore opted once again to play by the rules.

On the afternoon of the seventeenth, as the first of the airborne troops filed aboard transports at Phu Bai air base just south of Hué, Truong began hurriedly repositioning his forces for the second time in two weeks. Inevitably, the center of gravity would have to shift, from Hué to Danang, for he no longer had sufficient forces to defend the two equally and Danang was still where his main priorities lay. Another marine brigade therefore was ordered to pull out of the lines north of Hué and prepare to shift to the rugged hill country just below it to help secure the Hai Van Pass and the stretch of National Highway 1 extending south to Danang.

Only one part of the northern perimeter was left untouched. A third marine brigade was held in position on its northwestern rim, near a section of National Highway 1 that had so long been a focus of fierce fighting; its French nickname—"Street Without Joy"—still seemed apropos. If the North Vietnamese should mount a blitzkrieg south out of Quang Tri along this route, as they had in 1972, the marines were to act as a shield for the 1st ARVN Division, still deployed around Hué itself. Truong had no doubt the marines would eventually have to give ground in the face of such an assault, but he hoped they might at least buy him time to evacuate the 1st Division and part of the population of the city.

The adjustment of Truong's northern defenses was accompanied by a shift in his battlelines to the south. In accordance with the enclave plan he had discussed with President Thieu a week before, the 2nd ARVN Division was

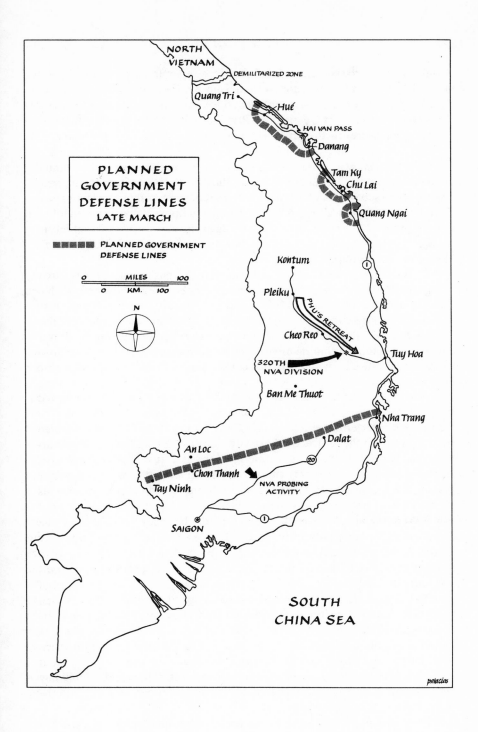

PLANNED
GOVERNMENT
DEFENSE LINES
LATE MARCH

▨▨▨▨▨ PLANNED GOVERNMENT
         DEFENSE LINES

0   MILES   100
0   KM.   100

N

NORTH
VIETNAM
DEMILITARIZED ZONE
Quang Tri
Hué
HAI VAN PASS
Danang
Tam Ky
Chu Lai
Quang Ngai
Kontum
Pleiku
PHU'S RETREAT
Cheo Reo
Tuy Hoa
320TH
NVA DIVISION
Ban Me Thuot
Nha Trang
An Loc
Dalat
20
Chon Thanh
Tay Ninh
NVA PROBING
ACTIVITY
1
SAIGON
1

SOUTH
CHINA SEA

palacios

withdrawn from its ragged forward positions in central Quang Tin Province
and pulled up in a tight cordon around Tam Ky City and its headquarters at
Chu Lai air base on the coast. Further south, four or five battalions scattered
through the lowlands of Quang Ngai Province fell back (in the face of continuing NVA pressure) to the provincial capital to make their stand there.

For the past several days a number of us in the Embassy had been laying
bets on what the government was up to. Phu's withdrawal from the highlands
and the shake-up in MR 1 obviously were part of some comprehensive strategic
plan, but how the pieces fitted together remained pure conjecture. Finally, on
the afternoon of the seventeenth, a CIA agent inside Thieu's cabinet let us in
on the secret, providing us with our first real insight into "Light at the Top,
Heavy at the Bottom."

From what he told us, it was clear that the basic concept was already
being modified to fit fast-changing circumstances. Three days before, Thieu
had envisaged a pullback in MR 1 and the abandonment of the northern
highlands to release forces for the protection of Saigon and a counteroffensive
against Ban Me Thuot. Now it seemed he was ready to give up much more.
The report intimated that he might even be prepared to abandon his plans for
retaking Ban Me Thuot and was also considering the surrender of a large slice
of central MR 2.

Not everything he meant to do, however, apparently involved such back-
tracking. According to the agent, Thieu was also aiming to establish a new
forward defense perimeter north of Saigon, running from Tay Ninh in the west
to Nha Trang on the central coast. In addition, a series of interlocking enclaves
was to be hammered out in MR 1, along Highway 1 from Hué to Quang Ngai.
In the event of intense enemy pressure, Truong was to give up the southern
part of the region and to focus his strength on defending Hué and Danang,
and finally—if necessary—Danang alone.

When Polgar read over the agent's report he made no effort to conceal
his alarm. "We got plenty of withdrawals," he remarked grimly to me, "but
there's nothing strategic about them. The forces Thieu had hoped to salvage
in the process, particularly from the highlands, are being torn to pieces on the
way out."

Later that afternoon General Smith dropped in on General Vien, to
express his own reservations. The pullout from Kontum and Pleiku had been
badly planned, he said testily, and was threatened with disaster. And why
hadn't Vien told him about it during their conversation the previous Friday?
At least he might have helped with the logistics.

Vien shuffled his feet and looked a little sheepish. Thieu had wanted it that
way, he said. But he admitted that maybe he had been remiss in not informing
the Embassy of the most important policy decision since the cease-fire.

That evening Polgar invited me and several Vietnamese officials to his
home to discuss the crisis. General Binh, the National Police chief, was the
first to arrive; then Colonel Le Van Luong, the intelligence chief for the Joint

General Staff whom Thieu was now ignoring out of pique over the intelligence failures concerning Ban Me Thuot. Finally, General Quang, Thieu's security advisor, showed up in his chauffeur-driven Mercedes. He spent the next half-hour thumbing through mail-order catalogues as Polgar tried to focus his attention on the problems at hand.

Finally, a cocktail or two later, I took the floor, opening with a detailed military briefing. I then asked Quang point-blank if the government had any hope of retaking Ban Me Thuot. As usual, he could not think of a straight answer and bounced around the point like a plump rubber ball.

At dinner I pressed him again about government plans. Finally, after a little wine and roast beef, he rose to the bait. What Thieu was doing, he said gloomily, was taking a leaf out of history. Just as the Russians had destroyed Napoleon's armies in 1812 by trading land for time, so the South Vietnamese would defeat the NVA aggressors. I couldn't resist reminding him that the Russians had had two advantages the ARVN didn't—a lot of territory and plenty of snow. He nodded, ignoring my sarcasm. "Well, perhaps the monsoons will do for us what the winter did for the Russians," he said in his French-accented English. "The rains begin in a few weeks. They should slow the NVA down."

For the next two days government forces seemed to be trapped on the sheer face of a glass mountain, and slipping badly. On 18 March, An Loc, the small outpost in northern MR 3 which had been the scene of a massive bloodletting in 1972, was quietly abandoned, leaving NVA forces in the area free to throw all their strength against Tay Ninh Province.

Elsewhere, NVA units seized a crossroads village seventy miles east of Saigon and severed the main highway to the resort city of Dalat in southern MR 2. The Joint General Staff was particularly troubled by this setback, since Dalat lay across the proposed new northern defense line for Saigon.

By the following morning the first glimmerings of disaster also were apparent in the reporting from MR 1. Nearly 150,000 inhabitants of Quang Tri City and the surrounding hamlets were now stumbling south toward Hué , army stragglers and provincial militia strong-arming their way to the front of the column. As the first of them streamed through Hué itself, many of the city's own population were caught up in their frenzy and soon a monstrous tidal wave of honking jeeps, Honda riders and overloaded buses was rolling south toward Danang, along Route 1.

From the outset, the flight of the civilians had a devastating impact on the morale and effectiveness of the army. Not only did the surging masses on each road and airfield hopelessly disrupt troop movements and supply lifts, but their mood, the panic itself, soon became infectious. Thanks to an old army tradition, many of the refugees from Quang Tri and Hué in fact were military dependents. Years before, the high command in Saigon had decided the troops would fight better with their wives and children at their side and had chosen to base dependents wherever the army itself made its home, be it Hué, Danang,

Phu Bai or an even more remote outpost. The only exceptions were the Marine and Airborne Divisions. Since these units had been conceived many years back as mobile reserves, their dependents remained tucked away in Saigon, far from the immediate battlelines.

The difference would tell dramatically in the next few days, for as Hué, then Quang Ngai and finally Danang came under direct Communist attack, the ARVN troopers in each of these cities would fall prey to family commitments—the "family syndrome," we described it in Saigon—spending more and more time away from the trenches, looking after their next of kin, many of whom were only a few miles behind the front lines. Only the marines, with their dependents safely in Saigon, would finally be left to fend off the attackers.

The South Vietnamese command realized at once that the family syndrome would be a terrible handicap, and soon after the withdrawal from Quang Tri, Vice-Admiral Chung Tan Cang, the new chief of naval operations, moved every available vessel to MR 1 to help pull out both troops and their next-of-kin. Up until recently he had been governor of the Saigon military district and by his own admission was not "up to date" on naval matters. But in the next few weeks he would prove himself an able commander, turning the navy into the only real bulwark against instant defeat. Without his leadership and initiative, even the small portion of the army that was finally salvaged from MR 1 and 2 would have perished on the beaches.

But Cang's ingenuity was not the only reason for the navy's efficiency. Like their marine and airborne counterparts, the sailors enjoyed an advantage the regular troops did not. Since the navy's principal headquarters was in Saigon, the wives and children of its personnel were based there too. The family syndrome would thus have little effect on Cang's men until the war reached the capital's very doorstep.

On the morning of the nineteenth Prime Minister Khiem and several other cabinet members flew up to MR 1 and 2 for a firsthand look at the crises. Ostensibly they were to take stock of the massive refugee problem, but Khiem, a five-star general, was also to provide a progress report on "Light at the Top, Heavy at the Bottom."

In Nha Trang he found nothing that remotely resembled "progress." Phu himself was on the verge of incoherence. He had been cringing in his office ever since his flight from Pleiku three days before and could hardly carry on a polite conversation with the Prime Minister.

The stopover in Danang proved equally discouraging. Truong told his visitors that a coordinated attack against both Hué and Danang was imminent. Three NVA divisions were already committed against the two cities and possibly a fourth had recently moved across the demilitarized zone into Quang Tri Province. Khiem was so alarmed he asked Truong to fly to Saigon as soon as possible to brief the President.

When Khiem returned to the capital just before nightfall, he sought out Thieu to discuss his findings. Explaining Truong's dilemma, he suggested that

Hué be given up at once to release forces to defend Danang. He also recommended that Phu be replaced by someone who could do the job.

Thieu would hardly hear him out. There was no one to take Phu's place, he insisted. And as for surrendering Hué, that, too, was out of the question. In fact, during the past few hours he had decided the city must be held at all costs. He would advise Truong directly.

Khiem was shocked. Although he could half understand Thieu's attachment to Phu, the decision concerning Hué seemed to him nothing short of madness. Only a few days before, Thieu had assured his MR I commander that Hué was strategically less important than Danang, and Truong, accepting the President at his word, had begun trimming his defenses there. Now suddenly Thieu wanted the clock turned back.

Khiem did not press his objections, however. He could see the President had made up his mind. And for all of his own doubts about the defensibility of Hué, he knew that the matter was, for Thieu himself, beyond rational debate. Militarily the city had long been of marginal value, even a liability, but culturally, historically and, hence, politically it remained a prize for both sides.* For this reason, the Communists had made it a primary objective in their great offensive of 1968, seizing it in the first month of the campaign. American and South Vietnamese troops had later retaken it, in twenty-six days of bloody door-to-door fighting—though not before the Communists had massacred some 2,700 of the residents as an act of "political purification." Hué was thus bathed in blood: an emblem of revolution and counterrevolution to both sides. To give it up without a fight would seem to many of Thieu's supporters a sacrilege.

But there was something else—something far more of the moment—that had also figured in the President's decision to defend the city at all costs. This Khiem did not fully understand. During the past few days Bui Diem, the former Ambassador to the United States, and Tran Van Do, another old associate, had visited Thieu and told him flatly he would have to step down for the good of the country or do something spectacular to rally the army and population. Thieu could think of nothing more spectacular than a gallant defense of the old imperial capital.

Later that evening NVA forces threw pontoon bridges across the Thach Han River, north of Quang Tri, and sent the first of several tank columns rumbling across. It was a significant initiative, an appropriate beginning to the NVA drive in MR I, for the Thach Han had served as a kind of de facto demarcation line between the two sides ever since the first months of the cease-fire. The withdrawal of the last of the government's militia and ranger

---

*Founded in 1792, Hué had emerged ten years later as the capital of the first unified Vietnam under the Nguyen dynasty, and from then till the French incursions in the 1880s it had been the political and cultural center of the country. At the end of the first Indochina war, it also had become the home of thousands of refugees from the north, many of whom were now among the government's staunchest allies.

units in Quang Tri City began just after dusk, and NVA tank commanders helpfully switched on their headlights so the evacuees could find their way in the dark.

Almost simultaneously two NVA divisions launched probing attacks along National Highway I twelve miles south of Hué. Marine and ARVN units managed to blunt the initial thrust, but the clatter of artillery and small-arms fire in the near distance fed the fear and confusion that were already building among the long columns of refugees on the highway.

When General Truong showed up in Saigon the following morning he was still an innocent, thinking he had been called in simply to provide Thieu with a firsthand situation report. He soon discovered otherwise. Five minutes into the interview, Thieu dropped his bombshell. Hué, he told the startled MR I commander, must be defended to the last man; he would go on television the next day to announce the decision to the nation.

For once Truong lost his cool. He could not go on waging the war by fits and starts, he thundered. His forward lines at Hué were even now being dismantled, much of the artillery there had been shipped out, and the remaining marines and ARVN troopers were already dispirited over the earlier shifts in strategy. What would another one do to their morale? Thieu listened patiently and finally acknowledged that perhaps he was demanding too much. The defense of Hué was still less important than the survival of the division defending it—the 1st ARVN, which if worse came to worst, would be needed to reinforce Danang. Therefore, he was willing to grant Truong some latitude. Hué should be held, he said, only as long as it was possible to guarantee an escape route for the 1st, either overland along Highway I or by sea. The moment the division was in danger of being bottled up, Hué should be abandoned. He would leave it to Truong to determine when that moment had arrived.

When the disheartened MR I commander returned to Danang later that afternoon he immediately called a halt to the withdrawal of heavy equipment from Hué that had been in progress for several days. He then sat down at his desk to study the pile of intelligence reports that had accumulated in his absence. All of them seemed to point to one conclusion: the anticipated offensive against Hué and Danang was only hours away.

That night Thieu delivered a four-minute speech on national television. He did not mention Hué—he was saving that for the following evening—but he did acknowledge for the first time that Ban Me Thuot had been lost. Blaming U.S. parsimony for recent setbacks, he warned his countrymen of worse times ahead. At least five fresh NVA divisions, he said, had recently moved into South Vietnam to reinforce the thirteen others already committed.

At daybreak the next day Truong cabled Thieu from Danang, asking him to postpone his defend-to-the-death speech on Hué until the military situation had clarified, lest he have his hands tied at the very outset of a major offensive. Thieu agreed, but several hours later recorded the speech on videotape so it could be broadcast on a moment's notice. By the following evening the offensive still had not materialized and Thieu decided to delay no longer. The videotape was aired at 8 P.M., publicly committing him and his army to defend Hué to the last man.

As Thieu forced his MR 1 commander into a tactical strait jacket, what remained of Phu's army in MR 2 continued to disintegrate under the hammer blows of the 320th NVA Division. By the evening of the nineteenth the 200,000 troops and refugees from Kontum and Pleiku were backed up behind the Tu Na Pass and a river crossing, less than twenty miles from Tuy Hoa City on the central coast. In the meantime, on the basis of his recent conversation with Khiem, General Phu had managed to make up his mind about one thing. As his field commander, General Tat, later explained to NVA captors, he "ordered us to abandon all heavy weapons and war matériel and flee from Phu Bon Province. I then directed my troops to leave their vehicles and artillery pieces on the road and advance through the woods, skipping the Tu Na Pass altogether . . . Since officers and soldiers had brought their families with them, hundreds of thousands of people clung to their flanks, exposing their whereabouts.

"On the morning of the twentieth [communist] forces launched a surprise attack against the first detachment of the 6th Ranger Group [at the rear of the evacuating column], causing fairly heavy losses. During the next few days the remaining units broke and ran but were pursued and repeatedly attacked. Only a small number of them were finally able to reach Tuy Hoa."

Further south, in Military Region 3, government fortunes were also continuing to slide—less dramatically perhaps—but the effect was the same: a loss of territory and tactical flexibility Thieu could now ill afford. By 20 March two ARVN divisions were effectively tied up in the defense of Tay Ninh and the northwestern portion of the region. Some government commanders wanted to give ground there or, alternately, to pull in an extra division out of the delta to serve as a mobile reserve. But Thieu would have none of it. The abandonment of Tay Ninh would shatter the morale of troops and civilians in the rest of the country, he insisted, and the removal of any of the forces from the delta would mean ceding vast amounts of territory to the enemy, since the three ARVN divisions there were already stretched to the limit.

If it had been no more than a chess game, Thieu would already have lost; he was effectively checkmated on every front. Had he been able to salvage some of the units from the highlands, he might have been able to consolidate his defenses along the coast and around Saigon as he had hoped. But without that, "Light at the Top, Heavy at the Bottom" became a pointless and fatal exercise; he was trading land for nothing.

His losses, moreover, were the enemy's clear gain. The pullbacks of the past two weeks, both in MR 1 and 2, had left the North Vietnamese with vast sections of territory where they could rest and refit without fear of their

adversary. Politically the landscape had changed as well. Back in the fall of
1974 when Hanoi's strategists had first devised their "dry season" campaign,
a major objective had been to give continuity and political structure to their
scattered enclaves along the western border of South Vietnam so in the event
of a new round of negotiations to formalize "lines of control" they could
bargain effectively. In the past two weeks Thieu had ceded them all the
bargaining power they could possibly have imagined, for what had been a
harlequin's coat of Viet Cong pockets and base areas was now indeed a "third
Vietnam," with all the accepted attributes of a nation-state—continuity, population and definable borders.

Apart from the military and political implications, there was another
consequence of Thieu's abrupt and mismanaged change in strategy. In less
than ten days hundreds of thousands of people, most of them military dependents, had been uprooted and thrown back on the government for shelter and
support. Besides the 200,000 refugees on the road from Pleiku and Kontum,
there were some 60,000 more trying to make their way to the coast from Ban
Me Thuot, and in MR 1 the number of displaced persons had already topped
2,000,000. But because of aid cutbacks and uncertainty over additional appropriations, Thieu was unwilling and unable to release resources to feed, clothe
and house them.

By the third week of March, I was churning out an appraisal per day to
help keep Washington abreast of these nightmares-in-progress. The tone of my
estimates was entirely appropriate to the theme. For the first time ever, I
broached and explored the possibility of decisive defeat for the government.

Since the appraisals all went out over Polgar's signature as the "views of
the senior officer on the scene," they in effect committed him to my bleak vision
of the future. Polgar had no qualms about that. If the worst should befall the
country, he told me, he wanted the record to show that he and the Station had
delivered fair warning.

He also had another reason for endorsing such pessimism. He was still
hoping to shock Congress into coming to Saigon's rescue. Accordingly, he
insisted on weaving into each of the appraisals a thread or two of the old line
on U.S. aid we had so often played out in the past. More American money and
equipment, he emphasized again and again, just might save the day for the
government.

Whether he still believed this, I cannot say. In any case, I did not. But
because of the incredible pressures of those days I did not attempt to debate
him on the point. I merely amended the analyses as he wanted. In doing so,
I helped him defeat one of our primary objectives. Instead of convincing
colleagues in Washington of the gravity of the military situation, we succeeded
only in persuading them there was still an out. For the optimists back in the

State Department and the CIA could always assure themselves after reading our analyses, "Well, yes, things are going badly out there, but Polgar and his boys say aid is still the answer." It was the beginning of a last fatal illusion.

To add to the confusion in Washington, another crisis was beginning to flicker to full flame. By 20 March there seemed no doubt the war in Cambodia was nearing its climax. The U.S. Mission was now the only foreign legation still conducting business in Phnom Penh. American aircraft were evacuating hundreds of westerners each day, and the Pentagon had just finished updating plans for securing the airfield and other landing zones in the event of a total pullout. In view of these very immediate problems, the loss of the western highlands in South Vietnam attracted less attention at the State Department than it might have otherwise.

At the far end of Pennsylvania Avenue, meanwhile, Congress was creating a diversion of its own. In the past few days a bipartisan move had developed in the Senate to terminate all military assistance to South Vietnam by 30 June. Part of the inspiration was simply public sentiment. A recent Gallup poll showed eight out of every ten Americans favoring an immediate aid cutoff, for fear of renewed involvement in the war. But there was also a good deal of practicality and common sense to the Congressional backlash. Better than the experts at the State Department or the CIA, the Congressmen seemed to realize Thieu was done for.

Nor was their skepticism reserved for South Vietnam alone. During the past week, through a variety of stratagems, Senate and House leaders also had effectively written an end to hopes for additional aid for Cambodia, on the grounds that no allocation, however substantial, could save the Lon Nol regime.

Halfway around the world the Congressional action brought a cry of anguish from the itinerant Secretary of State. By now Kissinger's latest round of shuttle diplomacy in the Middle East had run aground, and during a stopover in Saudi Arabia he confided to newsmen he was deeply distressed, not only about events in the Middle East, but also about the dual crises in Washington and Indochina. As he explained it, there were connections among all three. Egypt and Israel could not agree on mutual concessions precisely because they were uncertain how valid and binding any U.S. guarantees might be, in light of the way we had treated our allies in Indochina.

For the past few weeks Kissinger had been following developments in Vietnam only cursorily, through the CIA's finished analyses and Ambassador Martin's back-channel cables. But now he wanted some raw data so he could draw conclusions of his own. Among the items cabled out to him was the long article that had appeared in North Vietnam's theoretical journal in January, the exegesis of Le Duan's views. Only recently had it been acquired and translated. Kissinger was deeply troubled by it, particularly by its emphasis on revolutionary violence, and together with indications of accelerated troop recruitment and training in North Vietnam, it convinced him Hanoi was preparing for renewed heavy fighting.

Just as Kissinger was preparing to leave Saudi Arabia, however, an unexpected light broke over the horizon. King Faisal, a long and ardent admirer of his, took him aside and offered to do him an extraordinary personal favor. He respected what the South Vietnamese people were trying to do for themselves, he said. Therefore, out of his feelings for them, and for Kissinger, he was willing to guarantee a huge grant-in-aid to the Saigon government to help compensate for U.S. aid cuts. Kissinger was stunned and overjoyed. Here was the *deus ex machina* he had been looking for to help him make good on his Indochina strategy.

But like all his other antidotes to the thirty-year war, this one was destined to be short-lived and ephemeral. Only three days after making his offer to Kissinger, King Faisal of Saudi Arabia was shot dead by a jealous nephew. With him died this strange scheme for Saigon's salvation.*

---

*In dealings with Kissinger several weeks before, Martin had himself broached the idea of seeking a grant-in-aid from Saudi Arabia. It was King Faisal himself, however, who finally set the project in motion. Even after Faisal's death Martin continued to press Kissinger to keep the plan alive, but to no avail.

Black Box

When Al Francis, Martin's protégé, took over as Consul General in Danang in the fall of 1974, one of his first command decisions was to update the consulate's standing evacuation plan. The officer to whom he assigned the task eventually produced a thirty-page catalogue of options. One of them, the most extreme, envisaged a helo-lift out of the main airfield under U.S. Marine protection. Francis considered this an "improbable" contingency. As he explained to me after Saigon's collapse, he had always believed the Americans could count on the cooperation of the locals, even if a total evacuation became necessary.

The plan was revised at least twice in the next few months. Francis was never satisfied—"you can't anticipate everything"—but he considered the exercise a useful way of "sensitizing" his staff to the problems. In January, when he returned to Washington for a vacation, he never dreamed he might soon have to put his contingencies to a test. As he told one and all, he was convinced the Saigon government could weather the current offensive despite aid cutbacks.

During his leave he tried to stay abreast of developments by dropping by the State Department every few days to read incoming cable traffic. On his return to Saigon in early February he felt he had missed nothing and was anxious to plunge back into the job. But within a day of his arrival he fell dangerously ill with thyroiditis and had to be medevacked back to Washington. By the time he was declared fit a month later, the highlands had been abandoned, airborne units were pulling out of MR 1 and Hué's defenses were in shambles.

In the meantime, Terry Tull, Francis' deputy in Danang and the only senior female Foreign Service officer in the country, had begun dismantling several of the consular outposts around MR 1. With NVA units inching toward the major cities, she was not about to risk losing any of the Americans or Vietnamese for whom she was responsible.

Politically, however, she was caught in a dilemma. Lehmann, who was still substituting for Martin in Saigon, had instructed her to do nothing that might convey a sense of faltering resolve to the Vietnamese. She knew a wholesale cutback in the provinces would do just that, so she opted for half a decision. Rather than close out the provincial outposts altogether, she authorized a gradual reduction of their staffs so that if and when the crunch came no more than one or two choppers would be needed to finish the job. In mid-March she also ordered CIA and State Department personnel assigned to Hué to begin spending their nights in Danang fifty miles south.

None of her decisions was earth-shaking, but some of her colleagues found fault. The local CIA Base Chief, a middle-aged China hand whom I shall call "Philip Custer," complained she was "overreacting."

Ever since his arrival the previous summer Custer had been a fervent apologist for the South Vietnamese army—so fervent, his ego was now engaged. When Tull argued for a trimming of the consular staff, he therefore felt obliged to disagree. "General Truong will hold; the region is secure," he assured his own subordinates. Three days before the collapse of Danang he offered the same opinion to the Iranian representatives to the local ICCS team, thus causing them to delay their departure till the last minute. Relations between the Embassy and the Iranian delegation would never quite recover.

To be fair to Custer, the intelligence on which he was basing his judgments was hardly definitive. None of us was fully aware of the changing and conflicting orders Truong was receiving from Saigon, and even a confirmed pessimist would have been hard-pressed to anticipate the collapse of the entire army in MR 1 within the next two weeks. For an optimist like Custer, it was all but impossible.

When Francis arrived back in Danang at the end of the third week in March, he summoned six of his officers and directed them to revise the consulate's evacuation plan once again. He dubbed the group his little "black box" ("black" for secret) and promised them carte blanche. Each of the six had been chosen for his expertise, without regard to rank or agency affiliation, and Francis warned the more senior officers among them that if there was a subordinate around who could handle a specific job, he would not hesitate to put him in charge. As if to prove his point, he gave a relatively junior CIA man responsibility for boiling the evacuation guidebook down to manageable proportions.

The CIA officer clearly had his work cut out for him. Besides the fifty Americans attached to the consulate—half of them CIA officers—there were hundreds of other Americans in Danang, ranging from contract workers to U.S. Army deserters who would have to be included in any pullout. Over a thousand "local" employees also were listed on the consulate's manning tables, and with families, close friends and their relatives, the number of potential Vietnamese evacuees rose to ten thousand or more.

Despite the magnitude of the target group, the CIA officer succeeded in reducing the standing plan to two and a half pages in a single afternoon. What he envisioned was a phased evacuation by air and over the beaches. Barges and motorboats would be sent up the Han River to pick up evacuees at designated spots while larger vessels loaded up at the deepwater pier outside the city. Other evacuees would be flown out by Air America or other charter aircraft operating out of the main airport on the west edge of the city or from the military airstrip near Marble Mountain. The pullout was to be low-key and gradual, spanning a week or more, so none of the citizenry would be alerted. It was also to be integrated. Francis was determined to move Americans and Vietnamese together so if the citizenry did realize the Americans were leaving, they would have a strong incentive to cooperate.

In principle the "black box" seemed a stroke of inspiration: the focusing of all available expertise on an incredibly complex problem. Yet the evacuation of an entire consulate under wartime conditions would hardly fit easily into any bureaucratic formula, and methodical as Francis was, the systems he devised quickly began breaking down.

For one thing, every old Army hand on his staff wanted to become involved, and overnight the exclusive little knot of experts who made up the "black box" swelled to an unwieldy twenty-five. Francis' own assessment of the situation also posed an obstacle. Hopelessly out of date after his long convalescence, he was more inclined than ever to defer to the Ambassador on key issues. If Martin was convinced the South Vietnamese still had a chance, he would be the last to disagree.

Then, too, there was the matter of tactics. Lehmann had advised him only a few days before: Do nothing to panic the Vietnamese; American tenacity must be an example to them. Francis accepted this as axiomatic and resolved to put up a good show. Therefore, after making his gesture to contingency planning in the form of the "black box," he was ready to let the matter lie.

Nor was he the only one. Custer never completed a prospectus for the evacuation of his own Vietnamese staffers and was nearly as slow in preparing for the departure of his American ones. Even the destruction of classified files was held off till the enemy was at the gates, and as a consequence, many younger officers spent considerable time in the final days crumpling and burning while their Vietnamese friends and associates searched vainly for a way out.

Moreover, what few preparations Custer did authorize were generally cast in deep secret. "We can't risk stampeding the wives or the younger officers," he told his senior subordinates, in an echo of Lehmann. "So keep the wraps on." Accordingly, many of his younger officers were never fully aware of the evacuation planning or of the seriousness of the military crisis—until they were obliged to abandon Vietnamese they might otherwise have provided for.

Besides the carelessness and wishful thinking of those at the top, there was another drag on the consulate's contingency planning: overconfidence in the U.S. military. Earlier in the month a team from the 7th Fleet had paid a visit to Danang to survey existing evacuation plans and facilities, and subsequently the U.S. Navy had promised to provide a sortie of helicopters if any sort of pullout became necessary. When Francis returned to Danang he was confident this promise still held. Only several days later, after an exchange of messages with the Navy, did he realize differently: he would have to do it all on his own.

His first day back, Francis toured the hinterlands, touching down briefly in the cities of Hué, Tam Ky and Quang Ngai. As he reported to Saigon, most of the Vietnamese commanders he met were "in the center of the emotional spectrum," obviously in control of their nerves but uncertain of Communist intentions. General Truong seemed particularly perplexed: although the latest intelligence heralded imminent attacks throughout the region, there had been a sudden slackening of Communist pressure along Hué's northern defenses. He had no idea what it meant.

The uncertainty over Hanoi's plans was wholly justifiable. The North Vietnamese suffered from it too. Only a few days before, their spy inside Thieu's senior staff had provided them with another spectacular piece of intelligence, a full report on the government's new strategy, "Light at the Top, Heavy at the Bottom." Now they were debating what to do about it.

On 20 March the Politburo transmitted a gist of the intelligence to General Dung at his headquarters outside Ban Me Thuot. As he recounts in his memoirs, he and the rest of the leadership spent the next two days frantically discussing possible responses to it by long-distance telephone. One decision was quickly arrived at: an immediate effort would be made to prevent the regrouping of South Vietnamese forces in select enclaves in Military Region 1, as envisioned in Thieu's strategy. Before the 1st ARVN Division could withdraw toward Danang, its home base, Hué, must be taken.

The decision came within twenty-four hours of Thieu's own advisory to Truong to defend Hué at all costs.

On 22 March, Polgar, surveying the chaos in MR 1 from Saigon, decided to undertake some contingency measures of his own. During the morning he dispatched a special Air America plane to Danang with crates and packing materials in hopes Custer might be coaxed into moving out some of his staff's household belongings. He succeeded only to a degree. Custer immediately had his own clothes and furniture crated up and carted off to a warehouse. But there they were to remain. The end would come so fast in the next few days, neither he nor almost anyone on his staff would have time to ship out personal effects.

Francis for his part continued to try to soothe Vietnamese nerves by assuring local politicians and military figures the army could hold. He also attempted to convince the American press of the same. On the afternoon of the twenty-second he personally hosted a helicopter trip to Hué for the dozen or so journalists who had gathered in Danang for the great last bloodletting.

Hué was still secure and defensible, he told them confidently, despite all the rumors to the contrary.

The North Vietnamese struck early the following morning, immediately severing National Highway 1 south of Hué near the district capital of Phu Loc. In this one stroke they accomplished their initial objective: the 1st ARVN Division was now left with no direct escape route to Danang. As the fighting intensified, panic erupted among the masses of refugees strewn out along the highway north of the roadblock, and within hours thousands of them were pouring eastward toward the small port of Tan My, which Truong had hoped to use as an alternate egress point for the 1st. Soon all roads leading to the port were brimming with traffic, and the Vietnamese naval vessels that had been lying offshore to remove troops and matériel began taking on distraught civilians instead.

With the main highway cut and the port all but inaccessible, the population of Hué was now at the mercy of North Vietnamese artillery. Shortly after daybreak the shelling began in earnest, and as South Vietnamese helicopters tried to shuttle in to pick up evacuees NVA artillery riveted on the airfield itself.

An hour or two later rioting broke out in the central market as panic-stricken civilians battled each other for space in the taxis and Lambretta buses headed for the coast. In the residential areas of the city rumors of an impending NVA bloodbath swept from home to home like a gathering fire storm, fanned by the incandescent memories of '68, the great Hué massacre that had left over 2,000 of the residents dead and moldering in the lime pits in a nearby swamp.

Only a few of the citizens were untouched by the horror: the long-time Viet Cong spies and collaborators who knew they had nothing to fear from tomorrow's victors, and the old and decrepit who were too close to death to care. Tu Cuong, the eighty-six-year-old mother of South Vietnam's last Nguyen Emperor, Bao Dai, refused to board an ARVN chopper that had braved the artillery fire to rescue her. She preferred to await her fate, she explained, in the familiar surroundings of her beloved city.

In the lower half of the region, south of Danang, NVA forces also were on the attack, closing in on Quang Ngai and Chu Lai air base behind a shield of rocket and artillery fire. The locals responded like those at Hué and Tan My, pushing and clawing their way to the beaches. In a few hours the entire 2nd Division had been reduced to an unruly mob of ten thousand, officers and troops all bent on a single objective: saving themselves and their relatives. The commander of the 2nd, General Tran Van Nhut, was so demoralized by the spectacle, he retreated to an island offshore, there to pray and meditate as his division suffered its death throes.

Sometime during the morning General Truong contacted President Thieu by radio to brief him on the catastrophe. Hué was bottled up and the 1st Division in extreme peril, he said. There was no way to clear the roadblock on Highway 1 south of Hué, since the North Vietnamese had possibly two divisions in the area. He would, therefore, have to begin withdrawing what was left of the 1st over the beaches. Hué could be held for a short while longer, though only at great cost. Part of the 1st Division would have to be sacrificed in a delaying action west and northwest of the city simply to buy time.

Thieu did not object. He knew he had an alternative open to him: he could send the Airborne Division back to MR 1 as reinforcement. But he felt he could not do that without jeopardizing Saigon's security. So he gave Truong authority to proceed as he wanted.

Even as Truong outlined his plan to Thieu, the forces he needed to put it into effect were disintegrating. He was partly to blame. A few days before, he had given the troops of the 1st Division permission to look to the safety of their families. He had done so out of compassion, a commander's concern for his men, but once Highway 1 was closed down, the directive quickly became a prescription for bedlam, for officers and men were now abandoning their posts in droves to help relatives find other ways to escape.

By midafternoon only a single unit—the 147th Marine Brigade—remained in position north of Hué. Truong was reluctant to sacrifice it, since it was one of the best units in his command. He therefore did the only thing he felt he could: he ordered a pullback of all front-line elements around the city, the marines as well as the scattered troops of the 1st.

The marines on the city's perimeters were stunned by this abrupt reversal of plan. They had been prepared to wage a fight to the last man, as Thieu had ordered. Their spirits were up for it; they were dug in and ready. Now suddenly they were being directed to pull out, to abandon their equipment and retreat to the beaches. Their morale and discipline broke under the shame.

Because of the congestion at Tan My, Truong decided to move the marines and other stragglers southward along the Vinh Loc Peninsula, a spit of sand running parallel to the mainland. The route would take them around the Communist roadblock at Phu Loc to a point where they could link up with National Highway 1 just above the Hai Van Pass. From there they would have a clear road to Danang. The only natural obstacle was an inland waterway lying between the tip of the peninsula and the mainland. Navy engineers had already been sent to throw a bridge across it.

Fifty miles south of Hué, tensions continued to mount in Danang itself as thousands of refugees surged in from all fronts. Air Vietnam, the government-owned airline, immediately scheduled additional flights into the city to help siphon off some of the new arrivals, and the Embassy in Saigon reached into its own coffers to charter still more passenger space from a private contractor, World Airways, whose flamboyant owner, millionaire Ed Daly, had made considerable profit off the U.S. government in the past year by hiring his planes out to ferry arms and rice to Cambodia.

Just before noon on the twenty-third, Francis finally put his staff on a siege footing. If Danang was to become an enclave, the consulate might well have to operate on a self-sustaining basis, and he wanted to be ready if that happened. One of the officers he put in charge of the emergency planning was a burly young CIA man whom I shall call "Ron Howard." A logistics specialist on his first overseas assignment, he was determined to prove himself to his superiors, so he threw himself into the work with relish, scurrying around the consulate, stashing C-rations in every conceivable nook and cranny, including the pile of spare tires in the parking lot. And when he uncovered a stock of rusting food tins he promptly handed them out to some of the consulate's Vietnamese employees, on the theory they would be less likely to panic, once the city came under siege, if they had a little extra food in hand. He also broke out tents and sleeping bags and spread them around the CIA logistics compound, which was a few blocks from the consulate itself. The compound had been designated a bivouac for local employees recently evacuated from Hué and other outlying areas, and he wanted them all to be as comfortable as possible. He knew his own safety might depend on it.

Early the following morning General Vien met with Thieu at the Presidential Palace to brief him on the latest developments at Hué. The 1st Division was in total disarray, he said. Thousands of soldiers had thrown away their arms and were streaming toward the beaches with their families. An hour later Truong provided confirmation by radio, adding that Hué probably could not be held for more than a day. To avert further bloodshed he wanted permission to abandon the city at once.

When Thieu was informed of Truong's request he gave vent to a rage few of his subordinates had ever seen him display before. Pacing his office amid a clutch of advisors, he accused his MR 1 commander of defeatism, blamed him for the disintegration of the 1st Division and vowed to make him pay for it. But all of this of course was wasted spleen. Thieu was stuck with Truong's dilemma and his solution, and much as he might have wished otherwise, Hué would have to be abandoned immediately.

By the morning of the twenty-fourth North Vietnamese gunners had found their range. The outskirts of Hué were under constant artillery fire. As the shelling increased, more and more of the city's residents fled eastward toward the coast. For want of any other means of escape, some pushed out into the surf in small sampans or rowboats. But the tide was running strong and many of the overloaded vessels capsized fifty or a hundred yards from shore. Soon bodies littered the whitecaps like pieces of gnarled driftwood.

Initially the 147th Marine Brigade and the stragglers of the 1st Division made good progress as they moved out onto the Vinh Loc Peninsula shortly after daybreak to begin their trek southward, as Truong had ordered. They had managed to elude the thousands of refugees on the eastern fringes of Hué, and some of the troopers took off their boots and waded through the surf like Saturday-afternoon bathers. Within an hour or so, however, news of their departure had spread through the city, and by midmorning hordes of bedrag-

gled civilians were gathering at their flanks. In the meantime, NVA forces to
the south moved to intercept them, and by the time the marines and the
survivors of the 1st reached the port town of Tan An near the tip of the
peninsula, NVA artillery was hammering away at the still-incomplete bridge
across the waterway just ahead. Within an hour it was reduced to debris,
leaving them trapped, unable to move forward or backward, with no shelter
and no means of escape as the NVA artillery stabbed at them with ever-
increasing accuracy.

At their first distress calls, General Truong diverted every available ship
to the area to pull them off the beaches. But as the smaller vessels maneuvered
in through the breakers, panic seized the masses spread out along the shoreline,
and marines and troopers began shooting and clubbing each other and the
civilians among them to clear a path to the surf.

In the southern part of the region the same nightmarish act was being
played out on the beaches east of Quang Ngai City and Chu Lai as troops from
the 2nd Division battled with civilians for space on the last available fishing
boats. By early afternoon the city and the air base were virtually defenseless.

As news of the multiple disasters flowed into Danang, Francis' studied
confidence gave way. Tension was still building dangerously among the city's
populace. Obviously something would have to be done to damp it down, if only
to keep Truong's remaining forces from being infected by it. Around midmorning Francis sent a message to Saigon, requesting an airlift sufficient for forty
thousand refugees. Surely that would take some of the pressure off.

An hour or so later the first of the chartered World Airways 727s landed
at the main airfield. Over a hundred passengers were crammed aboard and
ferried to Cam Ranh Bay on the central coast, which had been tentatively
designated as a refugee "regroupment point." Shortly after lunch Custer advised the four secretaries in his office to prepare to pack out and relocate to
Saigon. When they protested, he assured them they would all be returning
soon. None of them, therefore, bothered to put anything of real value in her
overnight kit.

In Saigon, meanwhile, General Smith and his staff were busily rounding
up tugs and barges to send to MR 1 to help pull out South Vietnamese troops
and matériel. There was considerable debate in the Embassy—and in Washington—over whether the Defense Attaché's Office actually had the legal right to
participate in the rescue of the beleagured army at Hué. Such an operation
obviously would come perilously close to violating Congressional mandates
against the reinvolvement of the U.S. military in Indochina's hostilities. For
the moment the problem was circumvented as it had been in Cambodia. Only
civilian vessels and aircraft would be utilized, albeit under charter to the
Pentagon's Military Airlift and Sealift Commands. It was a shell game, to be
sure, but one that conformed at least to the spirit of the law. Perhaps fittingly,
many of the vessels Smith commandeered had previously been committed to
the American supply lift in Cambodia.

As Smith assembled his flotilla, other Embassy officials flailed about aimlessly. Unused to crises of this magnitude, Lehmann and his colleagues wasted hours of precious conference time on minutiae that could have been left to subordinates. One question particularly troubled them: the choice of a refugee relocation center. Lehmann himself favored Cam Ranh, with its huge deepwater port, its airfield and Quonset hut complex—all legacies of the earlier U.S. involvement. But one member of the Mission Council considered the selection premature. "What makes you think Cam Ranh is so secure?" Polgar asked his colleagues. "Sooner or later we may have to evacuate the evacuees there."

Lehmann and the Mission Council were not the only parties to the storm who were busy with contingency planning. For the past few days, as Hué's defenses disintegrated, the North Vietnamese leadership had continued to debate its own options. General Dung, among others, was wholly in favor of accelerating the timetable of conquest. As he later pointed out in his memoirs, it seemed clear from the available intelligence that the South Vietnamese were trying to rally their strength, through their strategic withdrawals, in preparation for a "political settlement, either the establishment of a coalition government or the partition of South Vietnam." He was not intrigued by either prospect. NVA forces had the initiative, he emphasized repeatedly in his messages to Hanoi. Why not strike out for a quick and total victory?

Evidently his views finally won the support of the majority of his comrades. "During its historic 24 March meeting," he later wrote, "the Politburo made clear its intention to concentrate forces, weapons and technical and material means to liberate Saigon before the rainy season—that is, in early May—and to take advantage of the enemy's strategic retreat to annihilate and destroy the enemy's 1st Corps [MR 1] and the bulk of his 2nd Corps [MR 2] to prevent his troops from withdrawing and regrouping around Saigon."

A top-secret policy resolution to this effect was drawn up the following day and transmitted to Dung at his headquarters outside Ban Me Thuot. With that, the Hanoi leadership committed itself to the most important policy decision of the war. The North Vietnamese army was to race the clock, the oncoming monsoons, to forestall the regroupment of South Vietnamese forces around Saigon and to "liberate" the entire country in the coming weeks. What had been glimpsed as only a remote possibility in the Politburo's deliberations of December and January—total victory in 1975—was now a concrete objective.

The decision had immediate and momentous implications for the offensive in MR 1. If the "enemy's 1st Corps" was to be destroyed, then Danang, as well as Hué, must be brought under attack and captured immediately.*

*The CIA's vision of what might happen at Danang altered almost as abruptly as Hanoi's. A memorandum which the CIA prepared jointly with the State and Defense Departments on the seventeenth predicted: "The North Vietnamese will probably choose to by-pass Danang" (while targeting Hué and southern MR 1). Three days later Colby told WSAG confidently, "Danang will

•   •   •

When Kissinger arrived back in Washington on 24 March his mood was Wagnerian dour. His Middle East shuttle had stalled, the Indochina crisis was worsening, and his hand-picked man-on-the-spot, Graham Martin, was not on the spot at all, but still in the United States, recuperating from his dental surgery. Even more disturbing, Martin did not seem to appreciate fully the problems that had overtaken Vietnam in his absence. He had consented to fly back to Washington from his home in North Carolina only a few days before, and no sooner had he arrived in the capital than he had set about disparaging the alarmist reporting from the front. He had told a television interviewer that South Vietnamese forces were making an orderly withdrawal from the highlands despite all the reports to the contrary, and when the deputy chief of the State Department's Vietnam desk had protested his optimism, he had countered by promising to take the officer and his wife on a tour of Ban Me Thuot "a year from now." He even seemed to have grown impatient with his own protégé, Al Francis. After looking over a particularly bleak cable from Danang, Martin commented somewhat uncharitably that "Francis' thyroid must be acting up again."

Martin's confidence stemmed not merely from a failure to comprehend the facts. As he persisted in telling one pessimist after another in Washington, he considered the northern half of South Vietnam good riddance. It had never been economically productive and had always been a drain on the government's resources, he insisted. What was left was far richer, far more politically vital, and since it was considerably more compact than the country as a whole, it could be defended that much more effectively.

Some of Washington's bureaucrats were shocked by what Martin said, but he was not without allies. The high command at CIA headquarters continued to reject the grim assessments of the Saigon Station in favor of its own worn-out hopes and prejudices. Indeed, CIA and Pentagon analysts had just completed a National Intelligence Estimate on Vietnam that might have been authored by Martin himself. While acknowledging that the loss of large parts of MR 1 and 2 might be permanent, they argued that government forces elsewhere in the country were strong enough to hold the new defense line north of Saigon which the South Vietnamese high command envisioned for itself, at least through the beginning of the rainy season in May. After that the North Vietnamese offensive would almost surely run afoul of the weather, they asserted, and the government might have time to refit and rally its forces and perhaps reopen negotiations from a position of relative strength. Some of the younger CIA analysts had wanted to qualify this upbeat projection, but Colby had refused, penciling in the final paragraphs on the government's survivability himself.*

---

hold." But on the twenty-fifth, shortly after Hanoi had opted for an all-out assault on the city, CIA analysts advised President Ford in their daily intelligence bulletin: "The government's ability to make a strong defense of Danang appears to be increasingly questionable."

*The estimate (SNIE 53/14.3-75), ambiguous to the point of incomprehensibility, showed all the

At the Pentagon, Secretary Schlesinger had already concluded that such optimism, guarded though it was, was "crap," as he put it succinctly to one colleague, and he wanted to start planning at once for a "drawdown" of the American community in Vietnam, similar to the one that was already under way in Cambodia. But he and Kissinger had crossed swords so often before, his ability to influence White House decisions was hardly at a premium.

Others in the military establishment were somewhat less disconsolate. Top officials at the Defense Intelligence Agency were generally in agreement with Martin on the viability of a truncated Vietnam. Meanwhile, across the Potomac in the State Department, simple bureaucratic inertia played into the Ambassador's hands. Since no one had been given authority to act in Kissinger's stead during his Middle East trip, much of the planning and analytical machinery had been left idling. Those officers who had devoted attention to Vietnam had concentrated largely on the aid debate or on inconsequentials. Earlier in the month a State Department inspection team had returned from Saigon with a long list of recommendations for a routine reorganization of the Embassy. Since then senior Department officials had spent endless hours debating it, even as Saigon's very survival came into question.

Cambodia also presented a distraction. With typical efficiency Ambassador Dean in Phnom Penh had continued bombarding Washington with details of each turn of the screw. Even the most apocalyptic reporting from Saigon paled by comparison. Each morning, up until the fall of Phnom Penh, Assistant Secretary of State Habib would open his staff meetings in the East Asia Division with a briefing on Cambodian developments. The news from Saigon always placed second or third on the agenda.

There were a few Indochina "specialists" in the Department who felt the Vietnam imbroglio was being dangerously underrated. But they were either too low in the bureaucratic pecking order to have much impact on policy, or too confused about the sudden setbacks of Thieu's army to be able to make a convincing case for disaster. Among those in the latter category was Douglas Pike, the resident Vietnam specialist on the Policy Planning Staff, the State Department's think tank. A USIA official and author of several books on the

---

earmarks of countless revisions and analytical compromises. Predicting the loss of Danang "within two weeks" or "a few days if the GVN Marine Division is removed," it also forecast that the "South Vietnamese will be unable to defend their enclaves" in MR 2. Yet—it went on—even if the North Vietnamese were to commit their remaining six strategic reserve divisions (several more had recently been created), "we believe that the GVN's military strength in the southern part of the country will enable it to survive the dry season (through early summer), although additional losses were certain." There was a parting note of pessimism: "The GVN will probably be left with control over little more than the delta and Saigon and surrounding populated areas. The result is likely to be defeat by early 1976." On 28 March, the day after the estimate was formally issued, Colby in a briefing for WSAG reemphasized its more positive aspects, those for which he had been responsible, although he warned that the collapse of Cambodia could bring "added psychological pressure" on Saigon and that "the continuing debate in the United States on the question of aid to South Vietnam is also an unsettling factor." With so many caveats, so much ambiguity in its analytical diet, it is small wonder the White House had difficulty figuring out what was in the offing.

Viet Cong, Pike had served in Saigon for many years and knew the "enemy" like the back of his hand. But that was his problem now. While he was well acquainted with Communist plans and capabilities, he had almost no appreciation at all of those of the South Vietnamese government. The briefings and analytical papers he prepared for Kissinger and the White House reflected this skewed perspective, and as a result they tended to obscure, rather than clarify, the real causes of the crisis.

As Kissinger settled back into his Washington routine he thus had a major challenge before him. Not only did he have to mobilize the bureaucracy to meet the problems of Vietnam and Cambodia; he also had to determine just how serious those problems were. Within hours of his arrival his dynamism was already being felt. The Pentagon announced that an additional aircraft carrier would soon join the USS *Okinawa,* which was already on station off Indochina, just in case the evacuation of Americans in various embattled areas might become necessary.

On the morning of 25 March the South Vietnamese government announced Hué had fallen. Within twenty-four hours Communist forces hoisted the flag of the Provisional Revolutionary Government over the famed inner citadel, site of the old imperial capital.

During the city's final hours thousands of panicked civilians crowded onto the beaches ten miles away. Many plunged into the surf and tried to swim to the evacuation fleet offshore, only to be dragged down by the treacherous undertow. By now the 1st Division had simply ceased to exist.

Further south, Chu Lai and Quang Ngai City were given up the same morning. As the last Air America helicopter pulled out of Chu Lai with several consulate employees on board, it was machine-gunned by South Vietnamese troops and just managed to limp to Danang. Over 6,000 stragglers from the 2nd Division somehow escaped before the end came, but their discipline and morale were destroyed. The division could no longer be considered an effective fighting force.

When General Dung, the supreme North Vietnamese commander, heard the news from MR 1 he could hardly control his emotions. "My eyes were filled with tears," he wrote. "I then lit a cigarette. I had quit smoking long ago, but each time we succeeded in solving a thorny problem, won a victory or achieved a particular success I smoked a cigarette with particular satisfaction."

Despite his elation he wasted no time in planning for the next blow, the drive on Danang. Although he was too far from the MR 1 battlefront to take direct command, he had definite ideas on how the campaign should be run. On the afternoon of the twenty-fifth he telephoned his recommendations to Hanoi. Among other things, he urged that one of his own protégés, General Le Trong Tan, deputy chief of the NVA General Staff, be put in charge of the Danang front. The Politburo agreed, and within the next few days created a new command in MR 1. General Tan immediately left Hanoi by chopper to set up a field headquarters west of Danang.

In the meantime, government defenses elsewhere continued to crumple under NVA pressure. Only hours after the collapse of Hué, Joe Kingsley drafted a cable on NVA advances west of Nha Trang in MR 2, asserting that the city was in "grave peril." Closer to Saigon, South Vietnamese troops abandoned a district town thirty-five miles to the northwest, just off the main highway to Tay Ninh City, and in neighboring Binh Long Province, NVA tanks converged on the isolated town of Chon Tanh, now the government's northernmost outpost in central Military Region 3.

A few hours later President Thieu unveiled several cabinet changes which he claimed would strengthen his hand. Actually, they represented no change at all. Most of his cronies, including Prime Minister Khiem and General Vien, retained their jobs—and their handle on power.

At Tan Son Nhut air base, meanwhile, the North Vietnamese and PRG delegates to the Joint Military Team were paying a price for their comrades' successes. When they went to their shower rooms that evening they found the tap dry. Thieu, in perhaps his most pathetic response to the North Vietnamese offensive, had shut off all water mains to their compound.

Cannonball to Papa Lima

Danang, the second largest city in South Vietnam, now stood isolated and condemned 370 miles northeast of Saigon. On the morning of 25 March the pounding began, fourteen Soviet-made 122-mm rockets slamming into the center of the city, killing six civilians, wounding fourteen others. Shudders of panic rippled through the long lines of refugees streaming in from Hué and Quang Ngai.

The destruction of the 1st Division in the past two days had cost Truong his reserves. Twenty-five thousand troops were still left to him to defend Danang, but they were already outmatched by the two NVA divisions and countless independent regiments arrayed against them, and two additional divisions would soon jog south from Hué to join in the attack.

Below Danang, the collapse of Quang Ngai and Chu Lai had released other NVA units for operations against his southern flanks. Truong had only one division to deploy against them, the 3rd, the worst in his command.*

During the past week and a half over 500,000 stragglers and other fugitives of defeat had converged on Danang from all directions, swelling its population to nearly 2,000,000, undermining morale, draining off supplies, and finally driving a wedge between the army and its duty. At what point would the discipline snap? When would the "family syndrome" steal away officers and men needed for the last desperate stand? Truong could not know, but he could hope, with some justification, that the worst could be avoided this time. Danang was different from Hué, after all. There was a deepwater port nearby and the navy could help ease the pressures by hauling out some of the populace before the blow fell. But time was the key, and clearly, the North Vietnamese were determined to deprive him of it. Even now the piers along the Han River

*Specifically, the Communist "order of battle," as we perceived it at the time, was as follows: in the Quang Tri–Hué sector, the NVA 324B and 325th Divisions, plus elements of the 341st and possibly one other division, were now free to move south against Danang. The 304th Division was already in position there, backed by the 2nd Division and the 52nd Brigade, which had been operating in Quang Tin and Quang Ngai Provinces.

were swarming with civilians looking for a ride south, some offering the equivalent of $1,200 to the inevitable profiteers. If the North Vietnamese began shelling the waterfront, the outflow would be choked off and then, unavoidably, the city would turn on itself.

Time was the key. Some of us in Saigon realized this too, and on the morning of the twenty-fifth General Smith sent five additional tugs, six barges and three cargo vessels up to Danang to help pull out equipment and refugees.

Meanwhile, at his morning staff meeting Al Francis made a concession of his own to the crisis, issuing the order everyone had been waiting for. Remaining consulate dependents were to be flown to Saigon at once; then, American contract employees and their families. All other Americans in the city were to be advised to leave immediately.

When someone asked what the evacuation plan was, Francis had one comment: "Improvisation." The blueprint the CIA man had drawn up had already been rendered impractical by the scarcity of aircraft. Only Air America and World Airways could be counted on, plus whatever Air Vietnam and the Vietnamese air force might commit.

"I wheeled and dealed with everyone and anybody to assure the optimum lift possible," Francis later confided. "I would have moved out everybody in the city if I'd been able to, but of course that wasn't remotely feasible.

"My decision to press forward was cinched by the realization the Communists were using the refugees as a shield. They were hoping to bulldoze thousands of them in on us, and thus demoralize and cripple the army, as they had at Hué."

Francis claimed that he had known by the twenty-fifth that the end was near. "I simply looked at the arithmetic and the chaos in the city and decided it would all have to come to a head fairly soon. I picked midnight, 29 March. I was right."

Not all of his colleagues agreed. Chargé Lehmann called him from Saigon to reprimand him for making "alarmist noises" in radio messages to Okinawa and other U.S. military control points. Danang had at least ten more days, Lehmann insisted, and perhaps would not fall at all. But Francis held to his new-found pessimism. "I'm the man on the spot," he replied, "and I say time is running out. Where do you get your information?" Lehmann for once did not have an answer.

As the morning staff meeting broke up, Custer called the Station in Saigon and asked for additional Air America planes to help fly out Americans and dependents. But amazingly, Air America could not provide them. There were no planes to spare, the controllers explained. Danang would have to make do with those already on the circuit.

Other CIA officers spent the afternoon drawing up tickets for the regular Air America run—the "Freedom Train," they called it—and handing them out to Vietnamese friends and employees. They deliberately overbooked, parceling out far more space than was available, in hopes the controllers in Saigon would eventually change their minds.

•   •   •

Most of the Vietnamese who gathered at Danang's main air terminal during the next several hours comported themselves with unaccustomed patience and discipline, for they knew their lives might depend on it. But to some of the American and foreign journalists who also showed up, this display of good sense was a keen disappointment. They had been expecting some dramatic action, some real head-bashing, to spice up their dispatches back home, and without it were hard-pressed to justify their own continued presence on the battle line to their worried editors. Finally a handful of correspondents for a British broadcasting firm took it upon themselves to manufacture what the circumstances seemed unlikely to provide. Just as a weary CIA officer was maneuvering a dozen or more Vietnamese up to the front gate the reporters began pushing and shoving them, trying to prod the crowd into charging the American. What spectacular viewing that would make back home on the telly: an American official beating off innocent Vietnamese as they tried to clamber aboard an evacuation flight!

Later in the day the family of General Truong's operations chief was evacuated on a special DAO plane, together with Custer's wife and Terry Tull, the Deputy Consul so recently criticized for "moving too fast." Brunson McKinley, the newest member of the consulate staff, stayed on to become Francis' second-in-command.*

That evening Mrs. Custer, haggard and distraught after the long journey, dropped by the Embassy to see Polgar. "Forget the household effects," she pleaded, "just get our people out of Danang."

Polgar nodded and assured her he would. But in fact he had no intention of taking a more active hand. "I was determined not to try to second-guess the men on the spot," he subsequently explained. "The staff in Danang had to be allowed to set their own pace and priorities, since only they knew what they were contending with." This would remain his attitude throughout, in the face of each new crisis, and the result would be perilously close calls for more than one CIA officer in the field. For what Polgar forgot was that only he had the total strategic picture at his fingertips; the men on the spot saw only one piece of it and could not know that the larger reality was often far more precarious than what they saw just beyond their front gates.

On 25 March, I drew up an assessment for Polgar that attempted to put the strategic picture in starkly comprehensible terms. "The military situation is rapidly deteriorating," I wrote. "Eight provinces have been lost in the past

---

*McKinley was one of Martin's "Rome Mafia," having served as the Ambassador's aide there in the late sixties. Young, tall and exceedingly correct, he became an ardent spokesman for Martin's optimism immediately upon arriving in Danang, assuring his colleagues—many of whom were long-time veterans of the place—that Truong's army could hold. Together, he and Francis managed to shield much of their staff from the truth till the last minute, presumably on the theory they were also shielding them from panic.

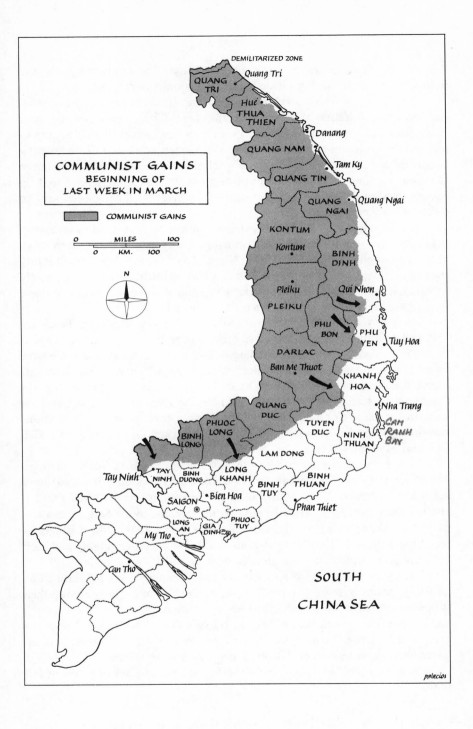

DEMILITARIZED ZONE

QUANG TRI
Quang Tri

Hué
THUA
THIEN

Danang

QUANG NAM

Tam Ky

COMMUNIST GAINS
BEGINNING OF
LAST WEEK IN MARCH

COMMUNIST GAINS

QUANG TIN

QUANG
NGAI
Quang Ngai

KONTUM

Kontum

BINH
DINH

MILES
0   100

KM.
0   100

N

PLEIKU

Pleiku

Qui Nhon

PHU
BON

PHU
YEN
Tuy Hoa

DARLAC

Ban Me Thuot

KHANH
HOA

Nha Trang

QUANG
DUC

TUYEN
DUC

CAM
RANH
BAY

PHUOC
LONG

NINH
THUAN

BINH
LONG

LAM DONG

Tay Ninh

TAY
NINH

BINH
DUONG

LONG
KHANH

BINH
TUY

BINH
THUAN

SAIGON

Bien Hoa

Phan Thiet

LONG
AN

GIA
DINH

PHUOC
TUY

My Tho

Can Tho

SOUTH

CHINA SEA

palacios

three weeks, four more are in imminent danger, and over a million people have been left homeless, placing incalculable strains on the economy.

"The strategic withdrawals in the western highlands and northern MR 1 have been so precipitous and haphazard they are unlikely to yield any benefits. Huge stocks of ammunition and hardware have been abandoned. The surviving units from Kontum and Pleiku are still pinned down at a river crossing twenty miles inland and are unlikely to reach the coast intact, and the Airborne Division, withdrawn from MR 1 to protect Saigon, has already been split up between Military Regions 2 and 3, one of its brigades having been sent to defend Nha Trang.

"In the north the only remaining government enclave is Danang, and in MR 2 four or five NVA divisions are moving rapidly toward the coast to strike at the key population centers of Qui Nhon, Tuy Hoa and Nha Trang. Only the recently deployed airborne brigade and two regiments of the 22nd ARVN Division stand in their path. All other government forces in the region have been obliterated or are pinned down on Route 7B.

"In MR 3, three or four NVA divisions are fast converging on Tay Ninh City and its immediate environs. Two others are trying to establish a foothold in the 'Iron Triangle' due north of Saigon, and east of the city two more have swept across Long Khanh Province, eliminating all government holdings, except for the province capital of Xuan Loc, now the only obstacle on the Communists' traditional attack route to Saigon's military complex at Bien Hoa. In the delta, Communist forces have locked three government divisions into defensive positions by posing and maintaining serious threats to both Can Tho and My Tho Cities.

"Given the near-total collapse of government defenses in the northern half of the country, Communist forces enjoy a degree of flexibility they have never known before. They control most of the key highways in MR 1 and 2, and are therefore in a position to send reinforcements to the Saigon area and the delta more quickly and efficiently than ever before. One of the distinguishing characteristics of their campaign up to now has been their ability and their willingness to exploit such advantages with lightning speed.

"In the face of recent supply losses and continuing NVA pressure on all fronts, government forces are not likely to regain the initiative or recoup their strength in the near future, since the very factors that sparked the current crisis are still operating unchecked in Saigon, Hanoi and in Washington. The entire complexion of the Vietnam war has altered in a matter of weeks, and the government is in imminent danger of decisive military defeat."

Such were the warning signals the Station sent to Washington in late March.*

*The excerpts of the estimate quoted here are lifted from my briefing notebook, which I brought out of Saigon on the day of the evacuation. The final paragraph is virtually as it appeared in the estimate, although the discussion of the tactical situation varies rhetorically, by a word or two (though not in substance), from the draft sent to CIA headquarters.

•　　　　　•　　　　　•

The meeting had been hastily organized. Kissinger had been back in the country only twenty-four hours, and staff aides had been working around the clock, putting together option papers and briefs to set the stage. But by the morning of the twenty-fifth, as he and other key officials gathered at the White House for a major strategy session, his own policy preferences, and those of the Administration, seemed fairly well defined.

The attendance list for the meeting was strictly top level. In addition to Kissinger and the President, it included Ambassador Martin, General Frederick Weyand, Army Chief of Staff, and Brent Scowcroft, Kissinger's deputy on the National Security Council staff. Only one ranking Administration official was absent (conspicuously so). In keeping with their long-standing rivalry, Kissinger had managed to have Secretary of Defense Schlesinger excluded from the deliberations.*

Much of the discussion centered on recent intelligence reports and appraisals from Saigon. Martin was frankly unhappy about their doomsday tenor, and Kissinger, not quite sure how far to credit Martin's reservations, had already decided to send Weyand to Saigon to make an independent assessment of his own. He also wanted Martin himself to get back to the front, if only (as he noted sardonically to the group) so Assistant Secretary of State Habib would have someone to blame if the worst came to pass.

Since so much hinged on the rescue and restoration of battered forces from MR 1 and 2, Kissinger and his colleagues spent much of their time mulling over what the United States could do to help. Their range of options was, of course, severely circumscribed. The War Powers Act and the Cambodia bombing-ban legislation made it illegal to commit American forces to Indochina's hostilities for any purpose, including (by any reasonable interpretation of the law) the rescue of Thieu's army. Yet one way of overcoming these obstacles had already been found to be workable, and acceptable to Congress. As long as the Pentagon continued to rely on civilian aircraft and ships under charter to move Vietnamese forces and equipment out of war-torn areas, none of the doves or liberals in Congress could claim that the military was again becoming directly involved in the war.

Yet was it really necessary to stop there? Martin interposed. If the job was

---

*Throughout late March and early April, Schlesinger in fact was kept on the periphery of a great deal of high-level decision-making concerning Vietnam. Kissinger (according to his own associates) had become greatly annoyed by Schlesinger's apparent reticence to "get out in front" of the Vietnam problem with recommendations of his own. Schlesinger's defenders say that the trouble stemmed from the Defense Secretary's refusal to embrace the Kissinger-Martin thesis that Vietnam was still salvageable. In any case, the tension between the two men seriously complicated the development of a concerted Administration line on the crisis, and was also a source of discomfort for their associates. One of those who found it particularly embarrassing was General Weyand. As Army Chief of Staff he was technically Schlesinger's subordinate. Yet as he was drawn ever more deeply into the Administration's final strategy for Vietnam, he was obliged increasingly to act behind the Defense Secretary's back.

worth doing, it was worth doing to the fullest, with all the assets available. Apparently Ford and Kissinger agreed, for they ultimately decided to commit American naval vessels as well to the sealift out of MR 1 and 2. The ships were to stay away from the shoreline, and the hostilities, in deference to the War Powers Act, but they were to be given authority to hover outside Vietnam's three-mile limit and pick up any evacuees, civilian or military, who might happen by. Presumably such limited action would be legally permissible, provided Congress was kept informed.

Given the tremendous matériel losses the South Vietnamese had suffered in the past few weeks, it seemed obvious to Kissinger and the rest that the United States would have to do something extraordinary to compensate. General Smith in Saigon had already asked that arms and supplies on order be delivered as quickly as possible. Kissinger heartily endorsed the proposal and Ford approved it. In addition, Weyand suggested that the Pentagon's leading expert on Vietnam's logistics problems, Erich Von Marbod, be allowed to accompany him to Saigon to update Thieu's shopping lists.

There was also extensive discussion during the meeting of a possible new approach to the smoldering aid debate. As a concession to the realities on the battlefield and on Capitol Hill, Kissinger and the President had already made up their minds to scuttle the Administration's proposal for additional military aid for Cambodia.

As for the Vietnam aid problem, two solutions were held up for perusal. On the one hand, Kissinger pointed out, the Administration could simply continue peddling its current proposal for over $300 million in supplementary military assistance. On the other, it could use the Weyand mission as a pretext for seeking a much larger emergency allocation. Kissinger himself favored the second option. He felt it had a better chance of bolstering the capabilities and morale of the South Vietnamese army, and also was a surer guarantee for American prestige abroad. If a larger appropriation was sought—and Saigon was defeated anyway—no one could accuse the United States of having brought on the disaster through ill-timed parsimony.

The President and the others at the White House session were well acquainted with these arguments. Kissinger had used them before to try to justify raising the price tag on the Administration's aid requests. Yet in the end the group agreed to hold off any final decision until Weyand had completed his mission. If what he found on the battlefront proved the need for a massive new infusion of aid, then it would be that much easier to float such a proposal through Congress.

By the time the conference came to an end the Administration's course was set, at least for the time being. But the air of decisiveness that characterized the proceedings was in effect just that, pure air. For the essence of the Administration's strategy was still the stall-off, a postponement of all crucial decisions until Weyand could find a firm rationale for them. Time was running out for the South Vietnamese, but the policy-makers were still gambling on eons.*

When Erich Von Marbod learned of the Weyand mission to Saigon, and his role in it, he suggested to the general that they create a "team" to go along with them, so that if Saigon should fall, they would not have to take all the blame for whatever final mistakes were made on the American side. Weyand agreed, and from that point on, his prospective fact-finding trip became one of the hottest items in Washington. Anybody on the bureaucratic battlements who pretended to expertise on Vietnam wanted to be cut in. Kissinger suggested that George Carver, the CIA's veteran Saigon-watcher, be included in the group. This did not, however, please others in the CIA who considered themselves equally qualified. Ted Shackley, head of the agency's East Asia Division, was particularly put out, since he and Carver had long been rivals, and he contacted his old acquaintance Von Marbod to see if he could wrangle something for himself. Von Marbod was more than willing to accommodate him, securing him a seat on Weyand's plane.

Meanwhile, Ambassador Martin, in a final meeting with Kissinger, proposed a last-ditch solution to Saigon's ills. If all else failed, he said, the United States should be ready to make détente pay off for the South Vietnamese; Moscow should be forced to realize that the Vietnam peace was still a linchpin in American-Soviet relations.

His suggestion was hardly a passing inspiration. Martin had long believed (as he later told me) that the Soviets would never tolerate a Peking- or Hanoi-dominated Indochina and would, if necessary, intervene to head off such an eventuality. Although Kissinger apparently did not share this view, Martin clung to it until the last days of the war, and it would give him one more incentive to postpone the evacuation indefinitely, for he would remain convinced, in the face of each new disaster, that the Soviets could finally be induced to bail Saigon out.

The day after the White House meeting, Kissinger went before the press to put his own strategic views in perspective. Opening with a few remarks about another perennial trouble spot, the Middle East, he declared that the United States was now willing to consider a new, comprehensive solution to the crisis there, since his step-by-step approach had failed. He then plunged headlong into more philosophical waters. "We understand that peace is indivisible," he emphasized. "The United States cannot pursue a policy of selective reliability. We cannot abandon friends in one part of the world [read: Indo-

---

*As a token of Kissinger's own appreciation of the crisis—or lack of it—he went before newsmen shortly after the White House session to say that the Administration was again thinking of putting before Congress a proposal for a long-term grant-in-aid to Saigon, one sufficient to cover its needs for the next three years. Even at this late date he apparently remained convinced that Saigon's "decent interval" had considerable life left to it.

china] without jeopardizing the security of friends everywhere."

None of the reporters bothered to ask Kissinger what he was driving at; nobody had to. Clearly, in his eyes, American steadfastness in Vietnam had become a measure of American steadfastness everywhere, all the more so since he now had no other card to play in his effort to maneuver Israel and the Arabs toward accommodation.

But Kissinger did not stop there. "The problem we face in Indochina," he said, "is an elementary question of what kind of people we are. For fifteen years we have been involved in encouraging the people of Vietnam to defend themselves against what we conceive as external danger." To abandon them now, therefore, would be tantamount to betraying a sacred trust.*

Many of them came without shoes or weapons and arrogantly planted themselves in the middle of the streets as traffic careened and eddied around them. Others prowled the sidewalks in small groups, demanding handouts. The people of Danang warily eyed these demoralized stragglers from Truong's army, and wondered where the greater danger lay—with the enemy or with them.

Hundreds of ARVN officers thrust their way into the consulate on the twenty-sixth to seek succor and refuge for their families. Many of the Americans responded generously, squeezing the soldiers' wives and children in among the consulate's own employees destined for Cam Ranh or Saigon. Francis himself played savior for a purpose, agreeing to evacuate the dependents of several high-ranking air force officers if they would guarantee the security of Danang's two airfields.

At first the airlift ran smoothly, all things considered. The World Airways 727s and the choppers and C-47 transports from Air America shuttled in and out throughout the day, and each time the ramps went down, hundreds of Vietnamese surged forward across the tarmac, clutching the precious tickets in one hand, their lifelong belongings, their dogs, pigs and children, in the other. If the children stumbled or the old gray-haired mama-sans shuffled along too slowly, the younger ones scooped them up or elbowed them toward the aircraft.

Just before noon Colonel Garvin McCurdy flew up from Saigon to help Francis organize his airlift. But scarcely had he touched down than he was airborne again, heading back to Saigon at Francis' request to see if he could pry some helicopters loose from the U.S. Air Force.

When he arrived at the Embassy late in the day he placed a call to the

---

*Elsewhere in the news conference Kissinger decried the latest aid cutbacks, claiming that Saigon was now suffering grievously from a shortage of spare parts for its military equipment. In a sly effort to undercut him, however, someone in the Pentagon leaked statistics to the press a day or two later showing that much of the latest annual military aid appropriation for Saigon—$700 million—had yet to be spent and that there was no real shortage of spare parts, despite what had been lost in MR 1 and 2. Since Schlesinger himself was known to oppose a massive supplemental aid appropriation, he was held responsible for the leak by Kissinger associates.

U.S. Special Advisory Group headquarters in northern Thailand, asking that two helicopters be put at his disposal for use in the Danang evacuation. But USSAG's chief of staff told him he was asking the impossible. His entire helicopter fleet, he said, was already committed to the prospective evacuation of Phnom Penh—"Eagle Pull." Not one chopper could be diverted elsewhere without Washington's approval, and that would take time.

McCurdy could hardly believe his ears. American lives were in grave jeopardy in Danang, but the Air Force could do nothing to help!

As the evacuation of Danang ground forward, government holdings in MR 2 dwindled toward the vanishing point. On the morning of the twenty-sixth a small town in northern Binh Dinh Province on the central coast was abandoned after a seven-hour battle. The NVA 3rd Division then thrust south toward Qui Nhon, the third largest city in South Vietnam, while other Communist units continued to batter away at the remnants of the 22nd ARVN Division, strung out west of the town. At the same time thousands of residents of Qui Nhon and Tuy Hoa City to the south abandoned their homes and fled down the coast toward Nha Trang, some by foot via Highway 1, others battling the dangerous surf in small fishing boats.

The dozen or more State Department, USAID and CIA men who made up the consular establishment in Tuy Hoa were quick to follow suit. Early on the twenty-sixth they received warning from a CIA source that Communist commandos were preparing to strike at their compound. Within the next few hours they packed up and flew to Nha Trang. Now all that remained of the once-expansive American presence in MR 2 was the Consulate General itself and small outposts in the cities of Phan Thiet and Dalat to the south.

With the entire northern part of the country fast slipping under enemy control, Thieu hardly needed anything else to worry about. But for him, as for his generals, misfortune seemed to come in legions. At noon on the twenty-sixth his arch-rival and former Vice-President, Nguyen Cao Ky, hosted a luncheon for several of his cronies and sympathizers at Tan Son Nhut, and after a long harangue and several bottles of champagne, persuaded them to join him in calling for a new "interim regime capable of rallying the army and negotiating from strength."

Within an hour of the meeting, Thieu's own agents apprised him of what had taken place, and from that moment forward he would spend almost as much time devising counterplots as he devoted to rallying the army.

Meanwhile, the flow of consulate personnel from MR 1 was beginning to swell the ranks and test the nerves of the American community in Saigon. Despite the ordeal many of the new arrivals had suffered, few seemed inclined to drift away to their hotel rooms to sleep off the tensions. Instead, day after day, night after night, they wandered among us, in our exclusive bars and restaurants, spreading their horror stories and their sense of impending doom.

Polgar and other senior Embassy officials, fearing contagion, moved quickly to avert it. They advised their office chiefs and seconds-in-command to soft-pedal the awful truth of what was happening to the north of us in conversations with their own wives, secretaries and subordinates. In addition, Lehmann, still operating as Chief of Mission in Martin's absence, carefully muffled all potential sources of "bad news," including "American Radio," the English-language FM outlet operated and financed by DAO. Every hour one of his subordinates would review the taped news "feeds" from the United States, editing out anything that might alarm Embassy wives listening at their portables alongside the swimming pool. The CIA-controlled *Saigon Post,* the capital's only English-language daily, likewise began playing down recent government setbacks.

As of noon on the twenty-seventh uncertainty and tension had become so much a fact of life in Danang, part of the population seemed to be growing inured to it. Several of the city's largest shops and food markets had reopened after a day's hiatus, and food prices continued to hold steady. One CIA man, caught up in the miasma, took part of the morning off to evacuate his two pet dogs, sending them out on the lap of a disgruntled ARVN officer.

At the CIA logistics compound not far from the consulate, the mass of Vietnamese gathered for evacuation alternately shrank and expanded during the morning like some self-renewing organism. Over 300 people were trucked to the deepwater pier or to the main airfield to await a ship or plane to safety, but during the same interval an equal number slipped through the front gate with their few belongings, and their hopes for an American miracle. Ron Howard, the CIA logistics officer, watched the ebb and flow from the window of his office at the far end of the compound, and tried to bring his own hopes and apprehensions under control. There must be over 3,000 of them out there now, 3,000 Vietnamese who worked for the consulate or for Americans "up country" or who knew someone who did. And they continued to pour in hour after hour, one arrival for each departure, their anxieties weighing as heavily on him as his own.

As a small convoy of jeeps and cars pulled through the front gate, Howard pushed his way into the courtyard to see if he could help with the loading. He was not happy with the way the selection of passengers had been handled so far. The CIA man in charge was himself a recent evacuee from one of the outlying provinces, and he tended, in assigning seat space, to give preference to Vietnamese friends and co-workers who had escaped with him to Danang. Howard's own employees were being largely ignored. Twice during the morning he had radioed the CIA "watch officer" at the consulate—"Cannonball to Papa Lima"—to ask for a more equitable spread, but each time he was told simply, "We're doing the best we can."

Once the convoy had been loaded and sent rumbling off through the front gate, Howard trudged back to the isolation and claustrophobia of his office. Some of the Vietnamese around him had already broken into a warehouse nearby and were pilfering it openly, almost defiantly, as if challenging him to a showdown.

But he had learned long ago not to take note of such provocations or to dwell on the danger, for it was only too apparent to him anyway. As the only American on the spot, with several long blocks between him and the consulate, he was certain his life would be forfeit if the unrest in the streets outside ever boiled over into the compound.

By midafternoon the city was awash with fresh rumors of an impending NVA attack and the population was again teetering on the threshold of wholesale panic. At the large airfield on the western edge of the city hundreds of frightened civilians swept out onto the tarmac, pushing and trampling each other, at the sight of each incoming plane. Jammed in among them, officials of the French, Taiwanese and other foreign consulates tried desperately to keep their balance.

Shortly after two o'clock Al Francis arrived by jeep at the terminal. He was weary and nerve-taut, having slept little in the past few days, and he watched with growing impatience as two CIA officers tried to herd a crowd of Vietnamese toward the departure gate. Finally the nerves gave way and he stalked over to take charge himself. But within minutes, as yet another plane taxied in, the crowd surged past him, and Francis, normally the most disciplined of men, did something no one would ever have dreamed he was capable of—he began flailing away at the Vietnamese nearest him with a hand-held walkie-talkie, stumbling, screaming at them. A CIA man ran over and steadied him, pushing the crowd away. "Get me the mayor," Francis gasped. "Get me the mayor."

The mayor of Danang, standing back in the crowd, seemed little inclined to help. But one of the CIA officers grabbed him and dragged him over. "Goddamnit," Francis snapped, summoning up what must have been his last ounce of strength. "Give us a hand here! These are your people, after all." With that, the Consul General slipped to the ground in a dead faint.

With each passing hour the panic continued to build, much faster now than anyone had foreseen, and as crowds of refugees washed time and again across the airfield, Air America choppers began ferrying passengers over to the smaller airstrip near Marble Mountain east of the city to pick up outbound flights there. "Don Williamson," one of Custer's trusted subordinates, worked at Marble throughout the afternoon, mustering out local Vietnamese marine units to secure the perimeters.

In the meantime, a clutch of Vietnamese waiting at the small ICCS helicopter pad across the street from Francis' own residence in downtown Danang was becoming increasingly unruly. Early in the afternoon the USAID official in charge of loading there had abruptly climbed onto a waiting chopper with his Vietnamese girl friend and left. Now, as twilight set in and nervous Vietnamese passengers pressed onto the pad itself, the remaining CIA controller put in a frantic radio call to the consulate for help. Once again it was Don

Williamson who came to the rescue. Wheeling and dealing with his Vietnamese marine friends, he managed to get a few troopers detached to him on "security detail" and immediately sent them down to the ICCS pad—just in time to prevent a blow-up.

Later, at 8 P.M., Francis called a temporary halt to all Air America flights out of the main airfield out of concern for the growing turbulence and confusion there. Some of the Americans assembled at the terminal when the order came through were choppered directly to Marble Mountain; others were shuttled back downtown to an apartment complex known (aptly now) as the "Alamo."

Over thirty consulate officials were still holed up in the city as night settled in, together with thousands of their Vietnamese employees—many of whom were now waiting apprehensively at the CIA logistics compound.

The radio message from Saigon crackled in over the emergency radio console just down the hall from Custer's office. John Pittman, Polgar's deputy, came up on the other end, and despite the static of the transmission, Custer could discern the strain in his voice. Pittman was anxious for him and the remaining CIA officers to leave Danang at once; Polgar didn't want anybody risking his life in unnecessary heroics.

Custer tried to calm him, assuring him that he, too, was aware of the dangers and was taking every precaution. By the time he signed off, he was confident he had Pittman, and Saigon, out of his hair.

At approximately 10 P.M. the small crowd of Americans at the Alamo received their orders. One of Francis' deputies slipped in from the outside and quietly advised them to pick up their belongings and move at once to Francis' own home around the corner. "But Americans only," he emphasized. "Don't alert your Vietnamese staffers."

"Cannonball to Papa Lima, Cannonball to Papa Lima." Ron Howard tried again and again to raise Custer by radio. The Vietnamese in the compound outside were now jeering at him through the window, ranting about American betrayal, and it was apparent to him that he would need help, lots of it, right away if he was to forestall the onslaught he had feared all day. But the radio remained silent.

Early that same evening President Thieu went on national television with a curt five-minute speech, urging his countrymen to "stop the enemy advance short." His reemergence in the public spotlight was almost as significant as the message itself, for over the past two weeks he had kept himself nearly invisible, making only two brief television speeches, thus giving rise to rumors around the city that he had been killed or deposed.

Shortly after the broadcast Thieu left the Palace in his bulletproof limousine and scurried off to a private hideaway near the Majestic Hotel on the waterfront. He sat up late into the evening talking with senior aides. Even more than the terrible news from the battlefront, the coup rumors and Ky's maneuverings seemed to haunt and trouble him. Earlier in the day Ky had audaciously issued another public appeal, again calling on Thieu to step down. But the President had been ready for this one. Within an hour or so, hand-picked officers of the National Police had arrested several of Ky's confederates, three journalists and four fringe politicians on charges of "plotting to overthrow the government." None of the principals in Ky's entourage had been touched, at least not yet, but the arrests clearly were meant as a final warning to them.

Just before midnight Special Assistant George Jacobson put in a call to Colonel McCurdy at his quarters and asked him to get those helicopters over from USSAG on the double. McCurdy slipped into his uniform and hurried to the Embassy. When he finally reached the commander of the 7th Air Force in Thailand on a secure phone, he was treated to a replay of the message of the day before: no aircraft available, higher approval required, all assets tied up with "Eagle Pull" in Cambodia.

McCurdy rushed to Jacobson's office and found the grizzled old veteran huddled behind his desk, talking into an open line to Francis in Danang. Suddenly McCurdy had an inspiration. He dialed the 7th Air Force again, asking the operator to patch his call into Jacobson's hot line so Francis could talk directly to the commander in Thailand. Hopefully, Francis and Jacobson together could persuade him to release some choppers for the Danang airlift. But somewhere in the conversation Francis inadvertently punctured his own best argument by promising to make one last try the next day to move his people out by fixed-wing aircraft.

As the night wore on, the battlefields around Danang turned suddenly calm. Only the occasional thud of government howitzers served to remind the populace that the war was still out there, in the darkness of this final night. But the quiet was illusory. The 35,000 NVA forces now on the outskirts of Danang were deliberately holding back, letting the worm of fear and anticipation do its worst. They would repeat the same tactic later on, around Saigon, as they moved in for the final blow.

At approximately 1:30 A.M., 28 March, Ron Howard finally made radio contact with Custer. He could hardly keep his voice steady as he explained the dangers he faced: the Vietnamese around him in the logistics compound were already breaking into cars and warehouses, looting at will. Custer's voice came snapping back at him like a whip: "Keep calm. Leave the compound, move to the waterfront and put the boats in the water. We're all going out." The logistics man was weeping now, and tried to make it clear he could not move, he was trapped. Custer repeated his orders and signed off.

Howard sat at his desk, his head reeling. There were five consulate motorboats down at the waterfront; they were his way out. But in between were 3,000 Vietnamese employees and untold numbers of the city's own residents who viewed him quite rightly as their hostage to safety. They would never let him leave, not unless he arranged something for them, or pretended to.

He wandered around his small office, trying to pull his thoughts together, nervously dolloping up deviled ham from a tin he had liberated from abandoned commissary stocks earlier in the day. A ruse, he thought. Figure out some way to make them believe they are to be rescued—and you save yourself.

Out at his headquarters on the road to the beachfront, General Truong was meeting with his staff one last time. It would take at least forty-five days to bring the army and the population to heel, he explained grimly, and to evacuate all the civilians in the city who wanted to go. "But I doubt," he added, "we have any more than a day or two left."

Ides of March

Long before daybreak on the twenty-eighth the deepwater pier outside Danang had become a promontory of terrified, brawling humanity. Its old gray plank boards creaked and groaned under the weight of a thousand pattering sandals as mobs of Vietnamese pressed out toward the end to await their last voyage out. Soon barges and tugboats were clustered around each pylon, three and four deep, and as the press of the crowds at the gangways grew more intense by the hour, the consular officers who were to supervise the loading began throwing their passengers aboard like sacks of potatoes.

Meanwhile, on the western side of town, within range of North Vietnamese snipers, other desperate evacuees seized the control tower of the main air terminal, forcing temporary suspension of all outbound flights. Not long afterward, at 4 A.M., Francis stumbled back to his villa after a brief but exhausting tour of the city and announced to the thirty or more assorted Americans, Vietnamese and other foreigners assembled there that conditions had so deteriorated, he was ordering an immediate and total evacuation of all those for whom he was responsible.

Part of the group beaded their way through the crowds out front to the small ICCS chopper pad across the street as the first Air America Hueys fluttered in. Others jogged down to the pier across from the consulate itself, where a motor-driven barge had just arrived from the deepwater port. But no sooner had the loading began than hundreds of Vietnamese rushed for the gangplank, grappling for space, and in less than twenty minutes over 4,400 people, twice the normal passenger load, had hurled themselves aboard. Custer, looking on helplessly from the dock, knew then that his last hope for evacuating his own charges was dead.

In the midst of all the pushing and shoving, Francis grabbed a DAO officer and two CIA men and told them to follow him. "Here, you may need this," he yelled, tossing an M-16 rifle to one of them. "Don't hesitate to use it." He then dashed across the street to the consulate as several startled Honda riders dipped and weaved around him.

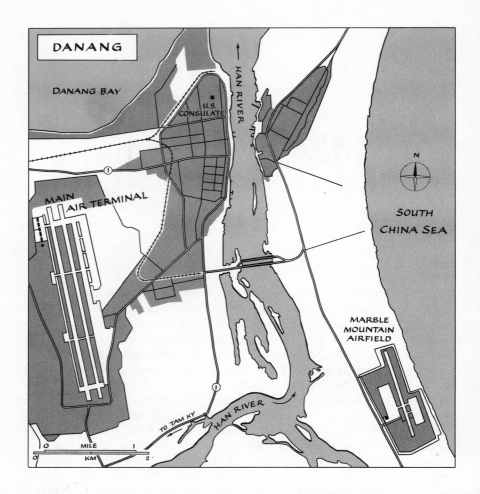

After making a quick sweep of the building, Francis and his three companions gathered up the remaining top-secret CIA radio equipment, loaded it onto vans and drove to the pier. For the next ten minutes they heaved it along a human daisy chain, cramming it into the barge alongside squirming refugees.

In the meantime, at an abandoned CIA residential compound on Gia Dinh and Le Loi Streets the Chinese "Nung" guards were making a last sweep of their own. Realizing they were about to be abandoned by their American employers, they began looting and burning the building for spite, and when two CIA men crept over a back wall to pick up some personal belongings, the Nungs turned their carbines on them, sending them scrambling out the front gate amid a fusillade of stray rounds.

It was not a very clever trick—nor a noble one—but it was the best he could think of. Pulling aside several of his Vietnamese employees, Ron Howard quickly rattled off instructions: they were to gas up the trucks at the far side of the logistics compound and begin loading passengers as fast as they could. All 3,000 of the refugees in the compound, he said, were to be hauled to a point in the middle of town. There American helicopters would soon pick them up.

His minions followed these directions to the letter, Howard himself helping to lift many of the women and children aboard the trucks. Then, one by one, the big deuce-and-a-halfs rumbled off through the front gate in the direction of the bogus staging point.

But as Howard had suspected, the trick was not a very clever one. The loading dragged on for more than an hour, and just as the last of the trucks was pulling out of the compound the first ones came wheeling back in, and the Vietnamese aboard were killing-mad. They had waited and watched for the promised choppers, but none, of course, had materialized.

By the time Howard managed to shut and bolt the front gate, hundreds of the disgruntled "evacuees" had gathered in the streets outside and were pounding on the high chain-link fence rimming the compound. Suddenly Custer's voice broke in over his pocket radio, urging him again to get to the waterfront: *they were all leaving.* Sick with fear, Howard hardly bothered to acknowledge the call. He looked at his watch in the half-light: 5:30 A.M. It was then he started bargaining for his life.

He played it straight this time. There was no other choice. He collared one of the Vietnamese, a mechanic and an old friend, and promised on the strength of everything he was worth to assure him and his family a place on an airplane or barge if he would help him escape. The Vietnamese was dubious, but he, too, had run out of alternatives. So he agreed, and while a dozen or more refugees who had slipped back into the compound were busy setting fire to the fuel pumps and pilfering to their heart's content, the two of them, and the mechanic's family, crept behind a building and climbed into an abandoned truck. The Vietnamese took the wheel, and as Howard hunkered down beside him, he rammed the truck headlong through a small back gate, scattering startled bystanders like chaff in the wind. Minutes later they were at the waterfront.

The airlift out of the main terminal resumed just after dawn. As the first World Airways 727 glided in, a convoy of military trucks packed with South Vietnamese army dependents pulled out onto the tarmac and began unloading. Instantaneously 5,000 other Vietnamese who had been waiting patiently at the entrance gate bolted toward the plane, trampling the women and children in their midst. American security guards showered a few of them with Mace, but to no avail. The pilot immediately throttled his engines and began pulling off, the hatch jammed half-open by countless arms and groping fingers. Scores of Vietnamese were still clinging to the wheel wells as the plane left the runway.

Ten feet into the fog Ron Howard was steering blind, but out in the dimness, over the lash of the waves, he could hear Vietnamese voices screaming for help.

He had found Custer and sixteen other Americans waiting for him at the waterfront, the outboards already churning. They had shoved off without so much as a backward glance, Howard taking the wheel in the lead boat, Custer beside him, Brunson McKinley, three other Americans and Howard's Vietnamese rescuers jammed in the stern. Off to the starboard the consulate's two other motorboats coughed and spluttered through the heavy swells.

Howard had no idea where they were headed, but he didn't much care. It seemed enough to be out of Danang and safe—for the first time in days. Checking his pocket compass, the young logistics officer set course for a small fisherman's island to the southeast.

Custer, dog-tired and drawn, slumped at his elbow. Only several minutes later did he muster the strength to speak. "We've got a 240 LZ waiting to pick us up," he shouted over the whine of the motors. Soon, as if on cue, a red, white and blue smokestack and the dark shape of an American cargo vessel loomed up out of the fog. The nameplate read: *Pioneer Contender*.

When Francis learned of the riot at the main terminal he shifted all Air America flights to Marble Mountain, this time permanently. Although the airstrip there was too small to accommodate the World Airways 727s, Air America transports and helicopters could negotiate it with ease—provided the Vietnamese marines did not interfere.

Over 10,000 Vietnamese were jammed inside the terminal at the time of the shutdown. Some were consulate employees and their families, and Francis immediately called in two Air America Hueys to ferry these "legitimate passengers" to Marble. But hardly had the two choppers bounced to a landing than the crowds again lapsed into an orgy of rioting and bloodshed.

When the small outboards pulled alongside the *Pioneer Contender* several of Ron Howard's companions let out whoops of joy and slapped each other on the back. One of the Vietnamese pressed a small crucifix to his lips. Howard stood up and reached for the scaling ladder draped over the side of the ship. He then turned to Custer and offered to help him up. But the Base Chief brushed his hand aside and shook his head. He was not going aboard, he said. He still had responsibilities. He would have to go back into Danang to search for stranded Vietnamese employees. Anybody willing to help?

Howard could hardly believe he had heard correctly. He looked around at the others in the boat. No one moved. Finally Brunson McKinley nodded. Yes, he would go back in, he said. But he was the only one.

"Good luck and take care of yourself," Custer called out as he waved the rest up the ladder. Then the motorboat pulled off and disappeared into the fog. Howard caught a last glimpse of it over his shoulder as he clambered up toward the main deck. "Thank God, I have no taste for heroics," he shouted to his Vietnamese friend a few rungs above him.

But Howard's relief was premature. For the scene that greeted him as he swung up over the railing of the *Contender* was every bit as nightmarish as anything he might have found in Danang. Over 1,500 South Vietnamese troops were sprawled, lounging, fighting among themselves on the main decks and the bridge, and *practicing their aim* at the hapless Vietnamese civilians in their midst. Less than thirty yards away an ARVN trooper was in the process of raping a Vietnamese woman while another soldier held her male companion at gunpoint. The thirty-five or more American evacuees already on board were cringing by the gangway.

"They want to sail to the Philippines," one of them bellowed at Howard, pointing at a group of armed Vietnamese troopers on the deck just above. "They've locked the captain on the bridge."

Howard scarcely paused to think what he was doing. He motioned to several of the U.S. Marine guards who had come out of Danang with him and quickly outlined a plan. After checking their weapons they began the climb to the bridge. The four Vietnamese troopers at the forward rail were too busy talking among themselves to notice, and before they could do so much as lock and load, Howard and the marines rushed them and pinned them to the deck. Moments later one of the marines broke the lock on the hatchway, and a flustered captain and several crew members emerged from the recesses of the cabin. "You know," the captain grumbled as he tried to compose himself, "they told me in Saigon we were coming here to pick up surplus American vehicles. I had no idea we'd be facing this."

In Saigon none of us had the slightest idea what any of our MR 1 colleagues were facing. On the morning of the twenty-eighth the information from Danang was a mixed but limited bag, mainly journalists' accounts, pilot reports and some overhead photography. And to make matters worse, Custer's reluctance to hasten to Saigon as Polgar wanted had left us all with a false confidence. The Base Chief had things in hand, we assured ourselves, and then went about our business.

Our "business," as it happened, was anything but routine, for the twenty-eighth was the day Martin and the Weyand entourage touched down in Saigon. Even as Ron Howard and the rest of the MR 1 consulate were struggling for their lives, Pat, Joe and I were busily preparing briefings and studies to help bring the great men abreast of events we ourselves hardly understood.

McKinley sat at Custer's elbow, the salt spray pelting his glasses as the motorboat sliced inland. Off in the mist they glimpsed a tugboat, the *Oseola* (a good American name, McKinley mused), and steered toward it. Maybe there were some empty barges strung out behind, Custer shouted. They would need someplace to unload their evacuees.

In fact, none of the barges was empty—it was standing room only on them —but the two men agreed to make the *Oseola* their base of operations anyway, and threw McKinley's briefcase aboard before veering off toward shore.

Out at the deepwater pier they spotted Al Francis. He was glassy-eyed and stumbling-tired, but he refused to be evacuated. He had to stay in the city awhile longer, he said, if only to stiffen the backbone of the Vietnamese. "Stay in touch," McKinley joked grimly as he and Custer shoved off again. It was the last time they would see Francis in Danang.

McKinley left Custer at the small pier across from the consulate and trotted up the street toward Francis' villa, scanning the crowds for familiar faces. Looters had already broken into houses and apartments abandoned only hours before, and throngs of Vietnamese, with booty-filled tarpaulins over their shoulders, rushed past him as the ping of stray rounds echoed down the side streets.

Howard and his American companions gazed nervously out over the thousands of Vietnamese troops who shared the decks of the *Pioneer Contender* with them. They had been on board over an hour now; they had managed to free the ship's captain and calm the more distraught members of the crew, but the chaos and mayhem that raged around them showed no signs of slackening. Gunfire reverberated up from the fantail of the ship as ARVN troops summarily executed "Viet Cong suspects." Soldiers and civilians were battling each other murderously on the lower decks, and rumors were circulating that Communist underwater sappers would soon try to sink them. One of the marines had a proposal: Maybe they should try to clear all Vietnamese off the bridge and upper deck and cordon themselves off. Then, at least, they would be able to defend themselves if the masses amidship turned against them.

Clearing the deck obviously would not be easy. There were nearly 1,000 ARVN troops on the upper portion of the ship, most of them armed, and any effort to force them into the confines of the hole or the fantail might itself spark a confrontation. But what other choice was there? Howard and several others consulted the captain. He agreed. Then they went to work.

Laying down his weapon, Howard waded into the group of Vietnamese nearest him. He pulled the officers aside, cajoled and reassured them, explaining that it would be impossible to sail so long as there was anarchy on deck. Again and again throughout the morning and early afternoon he repeated the same arguments, even as he collected weapons and nudged bewildered and sometimes hostile troopers toward the stern. His American companions did likewise.

Only once did the enterprise threaten to degenerate into outright confrontation. Shortly before noon a small Vietnamese patrol boat pulled alongside the *Contender* with its machine guns leveled at the deck. The Vietnamese skipper, shouting over a bullhorn, demanded that the ship be surrendered to him. Those were the last words he uttered. One of the Americans immediately opened fire, putting several rounds through the pilot's cabin. The small boat quickly backed off without returning a shot.

When McKinley elbowed his way back to the dock at the consulate he had several Vietnamese friends in tow, and he and Custer hurriedly pushed them onto the motorboat. The return run to the *Oseola* took forty-five minutes, the unloading maybe five. Custer then swung the outboard around and was off again toward the city.

The *Oseola,* meanwhile, began dragging its barges toward a groaning foghorn in the mist. According to a recent radio message, the *Pioneer Contender* was somewhere out there, taking on passengers.

Throughout the morning two Air America helicopters ferried evacuees continuously from the small ICCS pad near Francis' villa to the Marble Mountain airstrip. By midday both were running low on fuel and the pilots advised Francis they would have to fly out to an island seventy miles off the coast to pick up emergency rations. Determined to make every minute count, Francis called General Truong's headquarters and asked for an additional chopper to keep the shuttle going. Truong obliged, volunteering his own chopper and pilot.

With this extra lift, Francis was able to clear the ICCS pad by three in the afternoon. As the last of the passengers were boarding he leaned into the cockpit and instructed the pilot to make this final trip without him. He was determined to go back to the consulate to look for more stranded Vietnamese employees.

Ten minutes later Truong's pilot set his chopper down at the east end of the Marble Mountain airfield and unloaded his passengers there. But totally unbeknownst to him, Air America controllers had just shifted pickup operations to another section of the landing strip. Thus, when the scheduled transport came in, these latest arrivals were overlooked.

Later in the afternoon Francis choppered over to Marble for a final spot check. He found the abandoned evacuees huddled together in a frightened little clutch, and immediately radioed for another Air America flight. In the meantime, ARVN troops had begun setting up an artillery battery just off the tarmac, with the tubes pointing down the runway, and Francis strode over to confer with them. Only by promising to take out some of the officers and men was he able to persuade them to hold their fire long enough for the scheduled transport to land. Of the ninety-three people who scrambled aboard that last outbound C-47, over half were Vietnamese troopers.

But even this concession proved insufficient. As the plane began taxiing down the runway hundreds of other soldiers charged after it, grabbing at its wings and fuselage as if determined out of sheer spite to keep it from taking off. Francis sprinted alongside, screaming warnings and insults, beating some of the troopers with his fists. His provocations were not in vain. Several of them soon turned on him and pummeled him to the ground, delivering blow after blow to his neck and face as the plane itself groped skyward. Francis might have been killed then and there, in the midst of those he was trying to help, had he not had the presence of mind to go limp like a dead man. That shocked his assailants and caused them to back off. Eventually they lost interest in him altogether, and wandered back down to the runway toward their guns. As the last of them disappeared into the smoke and mist, a German and two British charity workers who had been watching from a distance ran over and pulled the battered Consul General to his feet. Though shaken and dizzy he seemed no worse for wear, except for the neck bruises. They would trouble him two years after the collapse of Saigon.

By early afternoon on the twenty-eighth the ARVN 3rd Division on the southwestern flank of Danang had disintegrated under the stress of the "family syndrome" and the battering of Communist artillery fire, and the few marines north of the city were falling back toward the beaches in the face of massively superior Communist forces. As news of these reverses filtered into his head-quarters General Truong called President Thieu in Saigon and asked for "flexibility" in waging his final defense of the city. Thieu did not bother to ask for clarification. He knew what "flexibility" meant—immediate and total evac-uation by sea.

To some of their worried colleagues already on shipboard it seemed that Francis and his CIA Base Chief were now vying for the distinction of being the last American in Danang. Immediately following the near-miss at Marble Mountain the Consul General and his British friends choppered off to Truong's headquarters on the edge of town to offer their assistance there. Custer for his part spent the rest of the afternoon shuttling between the *Oseola* and the piers along the Han River. Just before dusk his motorboat ran out of gas not far from the consulate, and he and his pilot were obliged to hitch a ride on a passing barge for their last trip out to the tugboat.

By late afternoon the fog had lifted, and as far as the eye could see, the ocean was littered with the refuse of a city bent on saving itself—sampans, small fishing boats, flat-bottom barges, all packed to the gunwales and wallow-ing in the swells. In the past few hours Ron Howard and his companions had succeeded in sweeping most of the Vietnamese off the bridge and upper deck of the *Pioneer Contender,* but amidships the press of humanity was now so great, it was obvious to the Americans they could no longer reserve part of the ship for themselves.

Throughout the afternoon the loading of the *Contender* had continued unabated. As the smaller vessels pulled alongside, gangplanks or ladders were dropped down to them, and the passengers would begin their perilous climb to the main deck. Many of them, often the youngest and oldest, lost their footing and fell overboard, to be crushed to death as their own vessels slammed into the side of the ship in the pitch of the waves. By dusk Ron Howard had stopped counting the casualties. He had already seen nearly 1,000 people go over the side.

When Francis and his two British friends arrived at Truong's headquar-ters the general was destroying the last of his files and battle maps. Most of his staff had already deserted him. The westerners helped him burn the documents, then climbed aboard his private helicopter and flew with him out to the Vietnamese naval headquarters on a small peninsula near the deepwater pier. Darkness had settled in by the time they landed, but in the dim lights of the compound they could see several barges, all of them packed with soldiers, hovering alongside nearby docks. Dozens of troopers were clinging to the sides of each vessel, their fingers locked in the chain-link fence surrounding the gunwales, their feet skimming the waves. Francis asked one Vietnamese officer if he could "borrow" a barge to go back upriver to the consulate. The soldier hardly bothered to shake his head.

Ron Howard squinted at his watch in the darkness: 10 P.M. In the past eight hours the *Pioneer Contender* had taken on nearly 7,000 evacuees, and the crackle of gunfire continued to echo up from the lower decks as Vietnamese soldiers murdered more and more civilians to make room for themselves. Some of the Americans wanted to intervene, but the rest were unwilling to risk a showdown with the troopers. The best they could do, they all agreed, was to force an end to the loading.

Even at that moment three large barges were moving alongside the *Contender,* each with some 3,000 aboard, far more than could be accommodated. If there was to be a quarantine, it might as well start now. Several of the Americans moved to the railing on the bridge. They waited till the first of the barges had disgorged its load, but once the gangplank had been extended to the second, they fired a volley of warning shots just off its prow. A tugboat to the rear immediately began backing off. Its nameplate glinted briefly in the sweep of a spotlight: the *Oseola,* an American vessel.

Planes from Danang streamed into Saigon's Tan Son Nhut air base long after dark. Bleary-eyed Vietnamese and Americans stumbled down the ramps onto the tarmac with all that remained of their worldly possessions cradled in their arms. Several officers from USAID and the Embassy's administrative office set up a reception center to sort out the arrivals. Americans were quickly bundled off to hotels or to official Embassy residences, but the Vietnamese, many of whom had never been out of Danang before, had no place to go. The government was still working frantically to prepare emergency relocation camps, at Cam Ranh Bay and in the delta.

I remember walking among the Vietnamese evacuees at the terminal that night. Many sat motionless and silent on the hard cement floor, elbows propped on suitcases, their eyes staring wide and unblinking in amazed shock. A few Embassy secretaries and State Department personnel moved among them, handing out tea and small sandwiches.

Some of the CIA officers who had flown in from Danang during the day tried to tough it out, strutting into the Duc Hotel bar to tell of their adventures. But after a while many of them excused themselves and returned to their rooms. One old paramilitary officer broke down and cried in front of his wife. They had left so many Vietnamese behind, he said, so many of their employees.

And he recalled, despite himself, how he had spent the afternoon moving his Vietnamese friends and associates through a series of wire cages that had been set up at Marble Mountain to control the crowds. It would be his most vivid memory of his last days in Vietnam, those cages with the panic-strained faces behind them, the eyes bright with fear and uncertainty as the children wept.

By eleven o'clock Custer, safe aboard the *Oseola* with several of his CIA colleagues, had given up trying to rescue Danang single-handedly. He was now sprawled on the deck, letting the adrenaline drain away. The cacophony of gunfire and the cries of the dying, stabbing in out of the darkness, made it impossible to sleep. In the pilothouse the skipper could see the lights of the *Pioneer Contender* off in the distance. But he was determined now to stay well clear of it, particularly after that little shooting incident an hour before. Evidently someone on the *Contender* was against taking on any more passengers. He would, therefore, have to find some other way to relieve himself of the thousands of evacuees packed in the barges drifting out behind. One of the CIA men on the *Oseola* had already beamed a "Mayday" call to all shipping in the South China Sea.

Shortly after midnight the first round came in, impacting just behind the headquarters building. The second one struck in front, and the third smashed dead center into the Quonset-like structure. A fourth hit one of the barges, killing hundreds of people. The navy compound on the small peninsula just outside Danang, Truong's last stronghold, was now under direct and intense Communist artillery fire.

When the shelling commenced, Al Francis was wandering around the docks, still trying to borrow a barge to go upriver. In his bleariness he thought the first rounds were 122-mm rockets, and he felt strangely relieved, for he knew the 122-mm was notoriously inaccurate; the Communists would be lucky to hit anything. But as the bracket tightened, he realized there must be a forward observer working and that the incoming were not rockets at all but artillery rounds, probably from captured 105-mm howitzers. In a stumbling imitation of broken field running, he and his British friends dashed down to the beach and out into the surf. A small river patrol boat was idling its motors just beyond the breakers. They splashed toward it and clambered aboard.

The South Vietnamese navy picked up Francis and his companions nearly a mile from shore. They were transferred to the "HQ 5," an old coast-guard cutter. The troops aboard, Francis noted thankfully, were still well disciplined, for their commanding officer had stayed with them throughout the evacuation. The skipper informed Francis that he would have to remain on the vessel until the evacuation was complete. He was their surety of American assistance.

The radio on the "HQ 5" was not equipped to communicate on the channels being used by the civilian shipping in the area, and Francis had to send a message to South Vietnamese naval headquarters in Saigon and have it relayed back to the cargo ships now collecting around him in the South China Sea to let Custer and the rest of his comrades know he was safe.

All through the night the Americans on the *Oseola* took turns standing watch, now and again firing warning shots to ward off the overpacked fishing boats and sampans that drifted too close. Embassy communicators in Saigon periodically fed them instructions and encouragement over the emergency transceiver. But one message was anything but encouraging. According to an Air America spotter plane, a Vietnamese tugboat off their stern had just been commandeered by rampaging ARVN troops. The Saigon radio operator cautioned the *Oseola*'s crew and passengers to stay alert for boarding attempts, as if such advice were necessary.

Custer repeatedly queried Saigon for some news of Francis, but the South Vietnamese navy had yet to relay the message from the "HQ 5." The CIA man vowed to stay in the harbor until he was sure his friend, the Consul General, was safe.

Several hours after midnight the passengers of the *Oseola* saw the lights of the *Pioneer Contender* drift away in the distance as the ship set its course for Cam Ranh.

The voyage of the *Contender* lasted over fifteen hours. There was enough food in the galley for the crew, the forty or so Americans and the hundred other westerners aboard, but far too little for the masses on the main deck. Ron Howard and his companions tried to dole out water to the Vietnamese passengers through a fire hose, but each time they reeled it out, Vietnamese soldiers managed to cut it behind them.

The only doctor on board, an old Russian émigré, set up a makeshift hospital in the galley. At one point Howard helped him deliver a healthy Vietnamese baby. Soon afterward the young CIA officer himself became a patient, passing out from heat prostration on a metal butcher's table.

It was raining at daybreak on the twenty-ninth and uncommonly cool, and the ocean seemed no less capricious than the day before. As first light broke over the horizon, one of the CIA men on the *Oseola* climbed up the watchtower and gazed out over the barges nearby. From his vantage point he could peer directly down into some of them. Clearly visible among the thousands of passengers were hosts of standing dead, corpses so tightly wedged in among the living, it would have been impossible for anyone to pitch them overboard.

A few abandoned barges were drifting close by, their passengers having been pulled aboard the *Pioneer Contender* the night before. Refuse cluttered the decks, and as the mist lifted, the CIA man realized that what he had first thought were sticks poking up from the mounds of clothing, suitcases and steaming waste . . . were human limbs.

●　　　　　●　　　　　●

Sometime during the morning of 29 March, General Ngo Quang Truong, reputedly the best commander in the South Vietnamese army, entered the treacherous surf off Danang. He was a poor swimmer and an aide had to assist him as he paddled to a waiting Vietnamese patrol boat.

For the next two days he remained on shipboard, watching the remnants of his once-proud army burn and loot the second largest city in South Vietnam. Some of his military colleagues would later criticize him, accusing him of cowardice for not having stayed ashore to die with his command.

Of the 2,000,000 refugees still in Danang, probably 100,000 were soldiers, stragglers from the 1st, 2nd and 3rd Divisions, and the famous Marine Division, all trapped like rats in a cage. And now they were willing to do anything —betray, steal or kill each other—to secure a means of escape for themselves and their families.

In Saigon, Polgar read the "progress" reports from MR 1 with increasing alarm. Just before the Danang consulate had closed the previous day, he had again instructed Custer to fly to Saigon at once. But the Base Chief, determined to play the hero's role out to the end, had ignored the order as he had the others before it. And now he was sitting in Danang harbor, refusing to pull anchor. He would later insist he had stayed on to help evacuate more people, to collect intelligence and to ensure Francis' safety. But Polgar thought Custer was taking unnecessary risks and told him so in no uncertain terms when he was finally able to put a radio call through to the *Oseola*.

As President Ford prepared to leave Washington on the twenty-ninth for an Easter vacation in Palm Springs, California, he notified Congressional leaders that four U.S. naval transports and several charter vessels had been sent to the waters off South Vietnam to assist in the evacuation of the embattled seaports. Daniel Parker, the director of the Agency for International Development, was named to coordinate the refugee resettlement operations, with supporting funds to be drawn from USAID's own budget. The Navy Department was to bankroll the sealift itself.

Ford described the undertaking as "strictly humanitarian" and emphasized that the ships would stay well clear of combat areas. Coincidentally, the Embassy in Saigon announced the start of an emergency airlift of medical and military supplies from the United States.

Shortly afterward the North Vietnamese publicly denounced Ford's actions as a "grave violation of the Paris agreement" and promptly intensified their shelling attacks against Danang.

Throughout the morning of the twenty-ninth the Saigon radio controller assured the weary little band on the *Oseola* that South Vietnamese naval craft were close at hand and other ships were streaming to their assistance. But the only vessels visible through the curtain of rain were those that made up their own motley armada from Danang.

Finally Mel Chatman surrendered to his impatience. "I'm going back in to see if I can find some of my people," he said. His companions tried to dissuade him, but Chatman, a black USAID employee, insisted. He climbed into an outboard, cranked the motor and bore off toward the shoreline. Several hours later he returned, discouraged and empty-handed. The city was in such chaos he had not even been able to put ashore.

Chatman was not the only American to attempt a last rescue mission into Danang that morning. So did the irrepressible president of World Airways, Edward Daly. Embassy representatives in Saigon had argued with him through the night, trying to persuade him not to go. But he did so anyway, at his own expense and on his own authority, insisting that his planes were now the only hope for the thousands still trapped in the city. Shortly after daybreak two of his 727s took off from Tan Son Nhut and flew north toward Danang. Daly himself was in the lead aircraft.

When the first plane touched down at the city's main airstrip thousands of armed soldiers and civilians were swarming at the edge of the tarmac. As the boarding ramp descended, the stronger and swifter of them charged the aircraft. Daly tried to slow them down by firing several warning shots in the air, but to no effect, and a British television crew that had just disembarked to take pictures was literally overrun. Later an Air America chopper had to be sent in to rescue the cameramen.

In less than ten minutes over 270 people—all soldiers except for two women and a child—jammed themselves inside Daly's plane. As the big jet lumbered down the runway, one trooper who had not been able to get aboard ran alongside and threw a hand grenade at the wing. The explosion ripped the landing flaps into open position as North Vietnamese rockets began dropping in at the far end of the runway. The second 727 did not come in.

An American reporter who was among the passengers called it a "flight out of hell." Scores of people clung to the wings and the landing gear as the plane took off, and many were crushed under the wheels. Others fell off after it was airborne, and several bodies were later found mashed in the wheel wells themselves. The center aisle in the cabin glistened with blood. It was the last American plane out of Danang.

Later in the morning ten small South Vietnamese helicopters took off from the city's main airfield. Each had twenty troopers aboard, double the maximum capacity. Since the airstrip at Marble Mountain was mobbed, they were unable to put in for a fuel stop. One pilot, unaware that Chu Lai had already fallen, flew his chopper to the airfield there and was promptly captured. Four other helicopters were brought down by ground fire. Another limped out to an island southeast of Danang. The rest disappeared without a trace.

Surveying the cordon of barges and fishing boats drawn up around the *Oseola,* Brunson McKinley estimated their total human cargo to be somewhere near 10,000—10,000 Vietnamese of every age, description and state of health. Yet as the day wore on, the population of those vessels began to shrink, more and more of the old and infirm succumbing to deprivation and exposure as the chill rain continued without respite. During the morning the Americans put in a call to Saigon, requesting an airdrop of fresh-water containers. Earlier they had parceled some of their own stocks out to the nearest barges by way of a fire hose; now they needed more.

The Embassy in Saigon was suffering its usual emergency cramps. Ambassador Martin, freshly ensconced in his office, asked USAID officers to assemble provisions, particularly water, for the evacuation fleet. The local USAID chief said he could have everything ready in four or five days. That wasn't good enough, Martin snorted, and turned to Polgar. Within hours Air America aircraft on CIA charter were winging north from Nha Trang with huge containers of water and other supplies.

By dusk the rain had let up slightly. Suspecting this would be his last day off Danang, McKinley went up to the bridge of the *Oseola* for a final glimpse of the battered city. He could hear the sporadic crunch of rocket and artillery, and from time to time muzzle flashes, or lightning, pulsed off the low clouds rolling in over the mountains behind the city.

Suddenly, as he was about to turn away from the railing, a crash swept across the water like a rifle shot. A short distance away two small boats had just rammed each other and were pulling apart again. One of them was already listing badly, and McKinley knew immediately what the South Vietnamese troopers crammed aboard had in mind. Clearly, they were aiming to seize the other boat for themselves. But there were troopers on that vessel too, and no room for additional passengers, and now they were firing point-blank at their attackers to drive them off. As the boats drifted away from each other, tracers darted between them in the dim light, and for a moment McKinley had a sense of being ringside at an ancient gladiatorial contest, the champions stalking each other for the kill. But there was nothing he could do to stop it, and as the rest of the passengers on the *Oseola* crouched behind the starboard rail to watch, someone on the sinking vessel fired a grenade launcher at the other, and in a hail of gunfire both boats began going down.

In less than five minutes all the troopers were in the water, some already dead, others flopping about in their final agonies. The Americans on the tugboat looked on in horror, knowing they could not help.

General Le Trong Tan's NVA divisions were now within two miles of Danang. The city itself was under heavy shelling, a rocket or artillery round occasionally landing in the midst of the refugees on the beaches. Several hours before, North Vietnamese troops also had rolled into the city of Hoi An, fifteen miles down the coast, capital of the province in which Danang was located.

It was the thirteenth province seat to fall to the Communists since the beginning of their winter-spring offensive.

That evening the *Pioneer Contender* put in at Cam Ranh. An Air America transport was on hand to carry Ron Howard and his fellow CIA officers to Saigon. When they landed at Tan Son Nhut an hour later, CIA security men insisted on disarming them. Howard later confided he was thankful they had. Otherwise, he said, he might well have gone gunning for the Embassy officials whose stupidity and misjudgments had set them up for their ordeal—if he could only have figured out who they were.

The Air America transport came in low in the darkness. A CIA communicator on the *Oseola* talked it down, guiding the pilot in for the drop. The first water container, a fifty-pounder, burst on impact just off the prow and the CIA man called the plane around again for another try. Custer and his fellow passengers could hear the motors almost on top of them as the second container fell away.

It came down like a rock, smashing dead center into the conning tower, shards of plastic pummeling one of the Vietnamese passengers and slicing the radio mast to ribbons. The Vietnamese, miraculously, survived with only two black eyes, but the CIA communicator had to spend the next three hours rigging up another antenna. In the meantime, Custer and the rest floated the surviving containers over to the boats and barges lying astern.

Later that night the radio message from Francis, announcing his own rescue, was relayed to them from Saigon. McKinley and his companions were hugely relieved, both for themselves and for Francis, for they could now bring their own vigil to an end.

The following day was Easter Sunday, 30 March. At a morning news conference in Saigon, Phan Quang Dan, South Vietnam's Deputy Premier, made it official: "It is lost. The Communists have taken Danang." Later a Viet Cong spokesman at Tan Son Nhut claimed that the flag of the Provisional Revolutionary Government had been raised in Danang the previous afternoon. In Palm Springs, California, Presidential Secretary Ron Nessen quoted President Ford as saying the loss of the city was an "immense human tragedy."

At midday on the thirtieth the big ships began arriving off the coast of MR I—Japanese, Vietnamese and American freighters and still more tugboats, nearly twenty vessels by final count—and within hours they were taking on passengers from the barges and other evacuation craft. There were three U.S. cargo vessels among them, the *Pioneer Commander,* the *Transcolorado* and the USS *Miller,* an old victory ship, all of them under contract to the Military Sealift Command.

Throughout the afternoon small South Vietnamese patrol boats darted in and out of a sheath of Communist artillery fire to pull still more evacuees off the beaches. Aside from the shelling, the North Vietnamese made no effort to stem the outflow, for they knew it would free them of the necessity of purging the entire society once they took over.

In the meantime, the passengers of the *Oseola* parted company. McKinley transferred to the *Pioneer Contender,* which had just arrived back from Cam Ranh. Custer and most of the CIA men ended up on the *Pioneer Commander.* This time the *Contender* turned out to be a model of tranquillity, for its crew now included Vietnamese security troops. But when Custer and his CIA colleagues climbed over the side of its sister ship, they found ARVN stragglers in control of the main deck and battling among themselves. Over twenty-five people died violently amidship before the *Commander* put in at Cam Ranh the following day.

Three of the U.S. cargo vessels left Danang harbor later in the afternoon. By midnight the other ships, barges and tugboats that made up the evacuation fleet had taken on over 50,000 refugees, far more than capacity, and were also obliged to suspend loading.

Twelve hours later the only vessels that had yet to depart for Cam Ranh were those of the South Vietnamese navy. In the confusion Admiral Cang in Saigon had forgotten to order them to withdraw. Finally Francis himself, on board the "HQ 5," radioed General Smith in Saigon, asking him to suggest to Cang that the time had come to pull anchor.

There was little food or water on any of the vessels in the rescue flotilla, and almost no sanitary or medical facilities, and all passengers, American as well as Vietnamese, had to improvise on the voyage south. A busy Vietnamese doctor on the USS *Miller* delivered four babies in a deckside tent between Danang and Cam Ranh. The newborn automatically became American citizens by virtue of their having entered the world on board a U.S. vessel in international waters.

As the lead ships steamed into Cam Ranh throughout the thirtieth and thirty-first, refugees stumbled off the decks and fell on their knees, gratefully pawing the dry land. Many were desperately seasick, having spent more than four days at sea with almost no provisions. At Cam Ranh itself the heat was overpowering, a hundred degrees or more, and USAID employees and Vietnamese and American charity workers from Saigon and Nha Trang moved among the sweltering masses, handing out water and salt and what little food there was. Meanwhile, hundreds of armed stragglers prowled through the outlying hamlets, drinking beer and stealing food from terrorized peasants.

On the afternoon of the thirty-first six South Vietnamese and American ships sailed back toward Danang to pick up other refugees still adrift in the open sea. A day later authorities in Saigon appealed to the United Nations to intercede with the North Vietnamese to assure food and assistance to refugees in Communist-controlled areas. In fact, the U.N. was already flying relief supplies to Hanoi for shipment south to newly captured areas.

Radio Hanoi announced on 2 April that a coalition government now ruled

Danang. Actually, General Tan was in charge and in the process of restoring order. Several of the city's top police and civilian administrators, who had been left behind, were rounded up and shot. On the same day President Thieu, in one of the more comic epilogues to the entire tragedy, ordered the exhausted General Truong to try to establish a beachhead on an island off the coast of MR 1 as a prelude to a counteroffensive to retake the entire region. Truong nearly laughed in the President's face.

The debacle in Military Region 1 cost the government dearly. Of the 3,000,000 people who had been under its control there at the outset of the offensive, less than 70,000 escaped, the vast majority by sea. Some 16,000 troops were among the final evacuees, but four divisions, including the Marine Division—Truong's best—had been obliterated as fighting units.

The consulate had not fared much better. Francis conceded some months later he had no idea how many of its 500 Vietnamese employees had made it out. Custer admitted that less than half of the 500 on the CIA's roster had escaped, either by his efforts or their own.

Although the Ford Administration would blame Congressional aid cutbacks for the disaster, the root cause was shoddy leadership, particularly in Saigon. Having promised Truong not to withdraw the Airborne Division precipitously, Thieu had reversed himself overnight, without giving his MR 1 commander adequate time to adjust his defenses, and he had changed his mind at least twice about the defense of Hué. To add to the chaos, he had refused to keep his own commanders—or his allies—informed of his plans.

But Thieu was not alone in mishandling the crisis. Even after the loss of Hué the Embassy in Saigon had failed to provide adequate warning or guidance to personnel in the field, and Francis had been equally slow in attempting to fill the gap.

Part of the reason for his delay was his misplaced belief that the U.S. military would come to his aid with helicopters, as promised. But the more basic inhibition was his obvious attachment to all those myths about ARVN strength and Thieu's survivability, which Ambassador Martin had so carefully nurtured in his own effort to prop up Kissinger's Vietnam policies—and American credibility elsewhere in the world.

Piece of My Tongue

The fall of Danang was decisive, strengthening Hanoi's resolution for total victory the way nothing before had. But it also came as a surprise and a shock to the North Vietnamese leadership. As Premier Pham Van Dong confided to a western newsman, he and his colleagues had never dreamed the South Vietnamese army would collapse so quickly.

On 31 March the Politburo held another of its "historic" policy reviews. Judging the South Vietnamese to be "strategically stymied" and the United States "completely impotent," it decided that the war "had entered a period of gigantic development" and called on Dung (in his own words) "to stage a general offensive at the earliest possible date—specifically, no later than April."

A "strategic plan" to this effect was drawn up and dispatched to the NVA commander in the field. It formalized the Politburo's commitment to total victory and tightened the deadline by which Dung was to accomplish it. The previous Politburo directive, issued six days before, had instructed him "to defeat Saigon before the rainy season—in May." Now he was under explicit orders to do it all in the next four weeks.

While setting out firm guidelines for the offensive, the Politburo also sought to sow confusion and political unrest in Saigon. Within hours of the Politburo meeting on the thirty-first, Liberation Radio announced that the PRG was ready to engage in talks with the Saigon government—minus Thieu —"to settle affairs." This formula, conciliatory as it seemed, actually had only one insidious purpose: to bring political opposition to Thieu to the flashpoint.

Throughout all this, the manpower and military hardware needed for the final NVA drive were being marshaled and rammed into the infiltration corridors leading south. Three of the divisions that made up the NVA Ist Corps, based in North Vietnam, were ordered to prepare to join in the fighting. Several units of the NVA IInd Corps, which had captured Danang, were pulled out of the city and sent rumbling down the coastal highways toward MR 3, and General Dung himself activated a IIIrd Corps headquarters to coordinate the operations of his own forces once they, too, pushed on to Saigon.

In order to ensure adherence to its directives, the Politburo sent one of its own number to the battlefront to look over Dung's shoulder. The chosen emissary was none other than Le Duc Tho, who—with Le Duan—had been one of the primary advocates of the offensive from the start. Despite Tho's perennial hawkishness, there was something almost ironic about his new assignment, for it was he, after all, who had co-authored the peace treaty in 1973 which he was now to put to the torch.*

On the day of Tho's departure, North Vietnam's rickety figurehead President, Tong Duc Ton, advised him: "You must win. Otherwise you should not return." The admonition undoubtedly was delivered in dead earnestness. The leadership was now committed to a high-stakes gamble it could not afford to lose.

During the hectic few days leading up to the Politburo decisions of the thirty-first, General Dung became embroiled in a controversy with his colleagues over his own best course of action. The Politburo wanted him to shift the three divisions under his direct control to the Saigon area immediately to prepare for the drive on the capital. But Dung had something more conservative in mind. Ever the methodical field commander, he proposed to complete his blitzkrieg across MR 2 to the coast, destroying all government forces there, before turning south for the final offensive. The Politburo, after some debate, bowed to his arguments and gave him authority to continue pushing east toward Tuy Hoa, Cam Ranh and Nha Trang. Thus the fate of MR 2 was sealed.

By the time Dung forced his wishes on the Politburo, a few lead elements of General Phu's evacuation column from the highlands were trickling into the coastal city of Tuy Hoa, but the majority of the seven regimental-size units that had scrambled out of Kontum and Pleiku two weeks before had simply disappeared. Strung out along Route 7B, they had been systematically worn down and annihilated by half as many North Vietnamese units. Now Phu was without reserves to defend what was left of his holdings on the coast. His only remaining division, the ARVN 22nd, had already lost two of its regiments and was now pinned down in the coastal province of Binh Dinh. Aside from a few companies of militia, the only other unit available to him to fend off the five opposing NVA divisions was the 3rd Airborne Brigade, now deployed to defend Nha Trang.†

During the last days of March the North Vietnamese pressed their advantage with incredible speed, thrusting eastward out of the highlands to attack and destroy Phu's battered units wherever they could find them. Three NVA

*Tho in fact was perfectly suited to his new task. He knew the war in the Saigon area intimately, having served as chief political commissar there in the mid-1950s, as successor to Le Duan himself. More recently he had traveled to the COSVN command zone on at least three different occasions —in 1967, 1971 and 1972—each time to make sure field commanders understood Hanoi's wishes at a moment of a crucial policy shift.
†The 316th, 320th and the 10th NVA divisions of Dung's command, plus the 968th Division in Kontum and Pleiku, were in control of the highlands, while the 3rd NVA Division was operating in Binh Dinh Province.

regiments pushed deep into Binh Dinh to strike at the tattered remnants of the 22nd Division as they fell back toward Qui Nhon, the third largest city in the country. Others pursued the stragglers on Route 7B to the very outskirts of Tuy Hoa and bore in on Nha Trang itself, site of Phu's new headquarters and the American consulate in MR 2. By the twenty-seventh, the 3rd Airborne Brigade was pulling back to positions northwest of the city, leaving its western suburbs utterly exposed to attack.

The following day Communist forces opened a new front in the southern part of the region, marching unopposed into the capital of Lam Dong Province, within three hours' drive of Saigon. At that moment Thieu and his generals were again weighing the feasibility of establishing a forward defense line just north of the capital, running from Tay Ninh in the west to Nha Trang. Shortly before nightfall Polgar called the Palace to inform them that their plan had been pre-empted. Lam Dong Province, which was to be the centerpiece of the line, was now in enemy hands.

Throughout the chaotic last week of March the Consul General in Nha Trang, Moncrieff Spear, attempted to project an image of coolness and confidence. Part of it was pure pretense, for he wanted to do nothing that might undercut the morale of the Vietnamese around him. But part of it was also a blind faith in Phu's army. Despite the collapse of the retreating units along Route 7B, he refused to believe that the withdrawal from the highlands had been a failure or that Nha Trang itself was now in grave peril.

Because of his optimism, and his concern for Vietnamese sensitivities, he did little to prepare rationally or comprehensively for a possible evacuation of the city or his consulate. Unlike Francis in MR 1, he never bothered to update his standing evacuation plan, and although he had recently initiated a draw-down of his staff—each time another province outpost was abandoned he would order the resident American personnel to Saigon—the rate of departures had been far slower than the disintegration of government defenses, mainly because of his own indecisiveness. Many State Department and USAID officers who had been stationed in the highlands or the central provinces of MR 2 were now walking the halls of the consulate with nothing to do. Significantly, Spear's own wife would remain in Nha Trang until the day before the final American pullout.

Spear had hoped to keep his personnel cutbacks discreet and low-key so as not to excite the local populace, but the size and the talkativeness of the American community (roughly 200 strong) made this impossible. By the middle of the last week in March news of the drawdown was already circulating through the city and hundreds of anxious residents were showing up at the consulate gate each morning to beg for a seat on an Air America flight.

To give Spear his due, not all the crimps in his evacuation planning were self-inflicted. As the drawdown in MR 1 accelerated, large numbers of Francis' staffers stopped off in Nha Trang to catch their breath and await orders from Saigon, thus adding dozens of surplus bodies to those for whom Spear was responsible. And with the designation of Cam Ranh Bay just to the south as a refugee resettlement center, his bureaucratic headaches were aggravated even further, for many of his own staffers were now obliged to put in long hours there, assisting in the care and feeding of evacuees from MR 1 and from the highlands.

Finally, there was the problem of aircraft. Once the evacuation of Danang was set in full motion, most of the planes operated by Air America, World Airways and Bird Air, another charter company, were diverted to MR 1, and Spear found it impossible to line up enough flights to speed his own cutbacks.

Some of Spear's staffers were deeply troubled by his sanguine views of the military situation and by his inability to provide for the consulate's evacuation needs. Phil Cook, his lanky, sun-tanned deputy, had made up his mind as early as the eighteenth—the day the American contingent in Phu Bon Province was evacuated—that the withdrawal from the highlands, and perhaps Nha Trang itself, were doomed. And some who had seen the panic and chaos of the highlands pullout firsthand were already pushing for the evacuation of Vietnamese friends and employees in Nha Trang in hopes of averting a replay here. Earl Thieme, the heroic organizer of the airlift out of Pleiku, spent his own last days in Nha Trang frantically trying to arrange seat space on cargo planes and freighters for the Vietnamese and montagnards he had brought with him out of the highlands. The equally resourceful Walt Martindale from Quang Duc Province did likewise. Working together, he and Thieme finally managed to smuggle out to Saigon at least 250 local friends and employees before the Americans themselves abandoned their last citadel in MR 2.

One other member of Spear's staff also was in favor of instant action, though the focus of his concerns turned out to be somewhat different from Martindale and Thieme's. Howard Archer, the CIA Base Chief in Nha Trang, had concluded a week before that Phu's strategic withdrawal was bound to fail, and he had begun pressing at that moment for a dismantling of the American presence in the path of the advancing North Vietnamese army.

But unlike the other advocates of early evacuation, Archer was preoccupied with only one side of the problem: the salvation of the Americans in his care. As he had told his subordinates in Pleiku two weeks before, when he had ordered their precipitous pullout, he considered CIA men intelligence operatives, not consular officials, and he saw no reason for them to risk their lives to help with the airlift of large numbers of Vietnamese. His indifference (or skewed sense of priorities, to put it more delicately) extended even to the Vietnamese on his own payroll. He had made little effort in the past week and a half to prepare for their possible evacuation, and had even become a little annoyed when some of them, sensing his attitude, had abruptly abandoned their posts to try to save themselves.

"It really frosts me," Archer remarked to a friend after the loss of South Vietnam, "to hear some of these refugees complain that the U.S. abandoned them. At Nha Trang they betrayed and abandoned us. Their generals didn't bother to tell us about their plans, and when the pullout came almost everybody in town insisted on lugging out all his household belongings, as well as every aunt, uncle and grandmother. Just how did they try to accommodate us?"

Archer's complaints about the Vietnamese were not wholly unjustified, although he could not know at the time to what extent he was right about them. Unbeknownst to him, General Phu met with his airborne commander on Friday, the twenty-eighth, and told him unequivocally to prepare to give up Nha Trang—without telling the Americans. In the event of a full-scale NVA assault, Phu declared, it would be necessary to hold the defense line west of the city only long enough for him and his staff to escape. After that, he couldn't care less what happened.

The following day General Frederick Weyand, in one of his first official acts since his arrival in Vietnam, dropped in on Phu's headquarters for a firsthand look at the crisis. Phu assured his visitor (disingenuously) that he would attempt to establish a new defense line north of the city. Weyand in turn tried to put on a brave face for his host and the accompanying newsmen, insisting that the South Vietnamese were "not demoralized in any sense of the word."

Throughout the remainder of the afternoon the airborne brigade on the fringes of Nha Trang continued to give ground, and as the chatter of gunfire drew nearer, the city's 500,000 citizens turned volatile and skittish. Refugees from Tuy Hoa and other points further north, meanwhile, staggered in by the thousands, some camping out on the beach, others roaming the streets in search of food or an American friend, and by Sunday morning hundreds of nervous, bedraggled Vietnamese had stationed themselves just outside the consulate gate.

Spear, gauging the mood, debated with himself and his staff what should be done. Phil Cook favored speeding up the evacuation of non-essential staffers, and urged that the palm trees in the consulate's parking lot be pulled down so that, if necessary, choppers could be landed there in a hurry. But Spear, still fearful of sparking a Vietnamese backlash through overhasty action, decided to postpone any such "drastic moves" for a little while longer.

Further north, panic was spreading from hamlet to village like some virulent plague as NVA forces pushed on toward the coast. Air Vietnam canceled flights into and out of Qui Nhon City just before nightfall on the thirtieth, when hysterical refugees stumbled onto the airfield, and General Phu's second-in-command, who had arrived only hours before to pick up a cache of greenbacks he had left with the local province chief, was cornered by ARVN deserters and forced to surrender his personal helicopter to them. (He was later captured by NVA forces when they entered the city.) During the next few hours air force officers at nearby Phu Cat air base abandoned their posts in droves, leaving huge quantities of equipment and aircraft fully intact for the onrushing North Vietnamese army.

On the morning of the thirty-first a new and expanded "non-essentials" list was circulated through the consulate, and Spear announced that all those whose names appeared on it were to depart at once, whether or not they had packed up their personal belongings (most of them hadn't). Even taking these cutbacks into account, the number of Americans and other foreigners on Spear's "potential evacuee" roster still hovered close to a hundred. The number of Vietnamese in the same category seemed to stretch toward infinity.

Since the consulate's Vietnamese employees were normally paid on the first day of every month, many of those who gathered in the courtyard on the thirtieth and the thirty-first had money on their minds, as well as the imperatives of saving themselves. But sometime during these turbulent two days the Vietnamese woman responsible for arranging contracts for the consulate's guards and doorkeepers evacuated herself and the payroll, and on the evening of the thirty-first Spear discovered he had nothing with which to cover the salaries of his local employees. In desperation he put in a call to Saigon, asking for an immediate emergency allocation, hoping against hope there would still be time to get it delivered and counted out before close of business the following day.

But Spear might as well have saved himself the trouble, for time had finally run out for him. Tuesday, April Fools' Day, would be his last one in Nha Trang.

By the morning of 1 April the last survivors of the 22nd ARVN Division were scrambling back through Qui Nhon toward the beaches, lead elements of the 320th NVA Division were pushing headlong into the western suburbs of Tuy Hoa, and the 10th NVA Division had finally outflanked the 3rd Airborne Brigade just northwest of Nha Trang.

Phil Cook awoke shortly after daybreak, dismissed his house servants and drove across the city to Phu's headquarters for the standard morning briefing. Phu, looking more disheveled than usual, remained mum as the briefer ticked off the latest reports from the battlefront. Afterward Cook hurried to the consulate to pass on what he had heard to Spear. By the time he got there, crowds of Vietnamese were already gathered outside the front gate, many of them consulate employees come to collect their paychecks.

In the meantime, the local province chief, a perennially ebullient man who favored an ascot, called Phu from his own headquarters across town to inform him that the municipal bureaucracy, including the police, had literally disintegrated overnight. Although he did not admit as much to Phu, it was the province chief himself who had precipitated the breakdown. During the past two days, as panicky officials stumbled in from Lam Dong and Tuyen Duc Provinces to the southwest, his own nerve and self-confidence had evaporated, and the night before, without consulting Phu or anyone else, he had abruptly closed up his office and dismissed his staff. Other province and municipal officials had quickly followed his example, leaving no one to maintain law and order in the city.

Phu, already in the throes of an emotional breakdown, was in no condition to absorb this latest piece of bad news, and even before the province chief had finished his sad tale the harassed MR 2 commander slammed down the phone and leaped up from his desk in a frenzy. "Get out!" he screamed at the top of his voice to the secretaries and orderlies around him as he dashed out of his office, down the steps of the headquarters building and out into the courtyard, where his own private helicopter was idling. "Get out!" he yelled to the pilot, who promptly began revving the motors. Moments later the commandant of the Academy for Noncommissioned Officers in Nha Trang came pounding across the parking lot and jumped in beside him. The chopper then lifted off and headed for Phan Thiet, where Phu (as he later informed superiors in Saigon) intended to establish a new field headquarters. In fact, the MR 2 command was no more.

A half-hour later Cook tried unsuccessfully to raise the MR 2 headquarters by phone, and then drove over to see why no one was answering. He found the headquarters building nearly deserted, and quickly drew the inevitable conclusion. Reaching Spear by radio, he urged the immediate evacuation of all consulate personnel and "third country nationals" in the city.

The first Air America Huey set down in the consulate's parking lot shortly before noon. But the short-sightedness that had characterized Spear's contingency planning up to now continued to make itself felt. In all the confusion of the morning no one in the consulate had remembered to lock and bar the front gate. Thus, when that first small chopper hovered in over the treetops, some 150 Vietnamese rushed past the Marine guards and into the main courtyard. Cook, who had just returned from Phu's headquarters, hurled himself into the mob and finally, with the help of Walt Martindale and several others, managed to get the gates closed. He then herded the Vietnamese already inside into a small fenced-in area at the edge of the parking lot and began counting off manageable chopper loads.

Soon Air America Hueys were arriving every five minutes, taking on up to twenty passengers at a time and ferrying them out to the main airfield on the edge of town, where they were transferred to transports bound for Saigon. Once the original group of 150 had been loaded and flown out, another fifty or sixty Vietnamese were squeezed through the front gate and assembled for boarding. Walt Martindale took it on himself to police the gate and to point out who should be let in and who shouldn't. Within an hour or so, he was sweating so profusely under the exertions of the job, his blue denim jumpsuit was beginning to fade white.

As word of the American pullout flashed through the city, the masses outside the consulate's front gate quickly swelled into the thousands. At first the Marine guards handled them gently, carefully and politely sorting out those to whom the Americans (by Martindale's reckoning) had a special responsibility. But eventually, as the more energetic members of the crowd began hauling themselves up the big cyclone fence that surrounded the consulate, the marines pulled out their truncheons and went to work with terrible efficiency. As heads were bashed and would-be intruders fell off the fence like crippled flies, the mobs in the streets outside turned murderous.

Several miles away, the airfield itself also was slipping rapidly into the morass of panic and confusion as more and more of the city's residents showed up to grapple for seat space. Sometime around midday the Vietnamese colonel in charge of security there shut down the front gates in an effort to stem the flow, and soon honking cars, jeeps and Hondas were packed twenty and thirty deep around the main entrance.

Up to this point consular officials had been hoping to move some of their Vietnamese evacuees to the Air America terminal, inside the airfield, by car or bus convoy. But now, with the main gate barred, this obviously was impossible. Early in the afternoon Phil Cook drove to the airfield, slipped in through a little-known back entrance and tried to persuade the base commander to allow American vehicles past his checkpoints. But to no avail. The convoy plan thus had to be scrapped, and the chopper shuttle out of the consulate became the only means of conveying passengers to the Air America loading zones. The Vietnamese employees who had been directed to assemble at the convoy pickup points out on the beachfront were simply abandoned.

Around one o'clock Howard Archer wandered into the vaulted CIA office complex on the fourth floor of the consulate to check safes and desk drawers for forgotten classified material. By his own recollection, he felt penned in by the chaos outside and was convinced it would now be impossible to locate, much less rescue, any of his key Vietnamese contacts and employees around the city. Nor did he feel any more inclined than he had a few days earlier to risk life and limb for them, particularly after so many had deserted him.

As he walked from safe to safe, spinning the dials, he remembered a cache of classified documents at a "safe house" not far from the consulate. Several days before, he had deliberately passed up an opportunity to dispose of it, lest his Vietnamese clerks and secretaries become alarmed about a possible American pullout. Now, as he thought over what was in the files, he debated making one last attempt to reach the safe house and destroy them. But finally he decided against it. He was convinced, as he explained later, that the files contained nothing of real intelligence value to the Communists.*

After checking the tumblers on his own empty safe, Archer tucked a .38-caliber revolver in his belt, picked up his briefcase and walked upstairs to talk with Spear. He told the Consul General that although he would be glad to stay and handle radio traffic if necessary—a reasonable enough offer, since the CIA was responsible for maintaining the consulate's communications center—he would prefer to leave. Spear nodded agreeably. Telephone lines to Saigon were still open, he pointed out, and he could use them in lieu of the radios. Besides, it was imperative to begin clearing the consulate of Americans.

Archer and his four remaining CIA staffers spent the next few minutes demolishing the CIA's radio gear. Then they trooped downstairs to the parking lot. At approximately two o'clock an Air America chopper disgorged them at the Nha Trang airfield.

One of the CIA men, however, was suffering qualms of conscience as he

---

*Other CIA officers who served in Nha Trang disagree with this assessment. By their account, the documents included extensive biographical information on potential agents and sources of information—the kind of data which the Communists could have used to identify people close to the Americans and hostile to their own cause.

climbed out onto the tarmac. "Lew James," a young paramilitary officer, had been bothered all morning by the prospect of leaving so many of the agency's Vietnamese employees behind, and now as Archer and the rest strode toward a waiting C-47 transport, he made up his mind to do what he thought was right. He asked Archer if he could stay a little longer to help with the evacuation, then broke out of the crowd and headed for a chopper. He was back at the consulate within ten minutes, even as Archer's own plane flew south toward Saigon.

By three in the afternoon George Jacobson, Martin's special assistant, was bombarding Spear with telephone calls from Saigon, pleading with him to terminate the airlift as soon as possible. Spear in turn was becoming tense and irascible. "I can't have this last-man syndrome," he kept telling his staffers as one after another insisted on staying until all of the Vietnamese in the courtyard had been evacuated. Finally Spear stopped asking for cooperation and demanded it, ordering Cook and the rest of the consulate staff to get to the airfield at once. But even then Cook stood his ground, arguing that it would be impossible to bring the airlift to a successful conclusion if all the Americans responsible for organizing and managing it were withdrawn from the consulate too quickly.

Spear's concern for his staffers was not without basis, for as the afternoon progressed, some of the bolder ones began slipping out of the consulate to search for Vietnamese employees in the confusion of the city itself. One of those who spent much of the day on the streets was Nelson Kief, the young DAO officer from Pleiku who had assisted Earl Thieme during the evacuation of the highlands two weeks before. Having discovered a small hole in the consulate fence, he ventured out through it time and again to track down employees who had been abandoned or forgotten. During one such foray, he stumbled across a group of Archer's Vietnamese employees huddled at the gate of the CIA residential billet not far from the consulate. Among them were several highly skilled English-language translators, who had been responsible for processing captured documents and whose lives would certainly have been forfeit if they had fallen into Communist hands. They told Kief they were waiting, "as instructed," to be picked up by their American employers.

Without wasting time on an explanation, Kief lined them up and led them through the crush of the street crowds to the back of the consulate. CIA officer Lew James helped him funnel them one by one through the hole in the fence.

Around 5:30 P.M. Spear's mentors in Saigon finally reached the end of their tether. Jacobson instructed the Consul General by telephone, "Get the hell out of the city now, you and the rest of the Americans." Spear was already so confused and distracted he could think only of doing exactly as Jacobson told him. Hanging up the phone, he dashed downstairs and boarded a chopper bound for the airfield. A few minutes later Phil Cook wandered into the Consul General's abandoned office and was surprised to discover that Spear was gone.

He picked up the phone and called Jacobson in Saigon for an explanation. "For chrissake, he's been ordered out!" Jacobson boomed at him over the line. "And you'd better get out too. That's an order!"

Realizing he had no other choice, Cook quickly gathered together the nineteen other Americans still in the compound and led them out to the landing zone in the parking lot, where about thirty Vietnamese were waiting to board. Minutes later the first of two Hueys shuddered to a landing and Cook and several others pulled themselves through the hatch as the Marine guards with them fired warning shots over the heads of the Vietnamese to keep them away. The second Huey came in soon afterward, and among those who rushed for it was a thoroughly exhausted Walt Martindale. As the pilot throttled the motors and prepared to pull off, an old Vietnamese man with a baby in his arms hobbled out of the crowd at the edge of the pad and lifted the child up toward the cabin, beseeching the Americans to take it aboard. One of Martindale's American companions moved to the edge of the open hatch and smashed the old man full in the face with the heel of his boot. The baby dropped to the ground, and almost at the same instant the chopper, the last one out of the consulate, soared skyward.*

During the final half-hour of the airlift Consul General Spear paced nervously around the Air America terminal at the Nha Trang airfield. His gray short-sleeved shirt was splotched with sweat and a huge 9-mm automatic bounced and rattled ominously in a black shoulder holster as he picked his way from one group of passengers to another, urging them to be ready to board up as soon as the next transport came in. At one point he literally stumbled over DAO officer Nelson Kief and his CIA companion Lew James, who were sitting on the floor of the terminal building waiting for their names to be called. Kief had been trying to keep out of Spear's way ever since he and James had choppered in with Cook's group a few minutes before, for he knew the Consul General was unhappy about the way he and the CIA man had conducted themselves during the afternoon, with their repeated forays through the city. But now, as Spear untangled his feet from his two prone subordinates, Kief saw he was in for a reckoning. "Goddamnit, Kief!" Spear spluttered at him as his own tensions bubbled over. "If you don't get out of here at once, you're going to catch a piece of my tongue."

The young DAO officer looked up at the Consul General and almost burst out laughing. Here was the very image of mildness—Moncrieff Spear—with that ludicrous cannon strapped on his shoulder, finally warming to the role of assertive commander in chief he had eschewed for so many weeks.

Soon afterward, at around six o'clock, Spear, Cook, Martindale and the

---

*In addition to the thirty Vietnamese assembled in the courtyard and the thousands more outside the gate, the Americans left at the consulate several boxes of classified documents which had been stacked in the foyer for burning earlier in the day, but which had been subsequently forgotten. The files, prepared by State Department and USAID representatives, contained information obtained from friends and collaborators of the consular outposts in the provinces.

few remaining Americans at the terminal climbed into an Air America chopper, flew to a remote section of the airfield, far from the surging masses of Vietnamese, and there they transferred to a twin-engine Air America Volpar. Minutes later, amid the stutter of distant gunfire, the plane roared off down the runway and lurched abruptly up into the night sky.

Almost at the moment the last Americans departed Nha Trang, the Politburo in Hanoi sent new instructions to General Dung, urging him (once again) to pull his troops out of the battlelines in MR 2 and send them immediately to the more important target area, Saigon. This time Dung did as he was told, and the following day, 2 April, he diverted both his 316th Division (from Ban Me Thuot) and his 320th Division (from Tuy Hoa) south toward MR 3. Only one of his principal units, the 10th Division, remained on the central coast to complete mopping-up operations, bearing in on Cam Ranh Bay itself.

Because of the reshuffling of Dung's forces, Nha Trang was not actually occupied by Communist units for nearly a week. This led to considerable confusion among Vietnamese and Embassy analysts in Saigon—was the city a casualty, or not?—and our bewilderment was only compounded by an almost comic episode that occurred shortly before the Communists moved in to fill the vacuum. On 4 April, three days after the consulate had closed down, a wayward South Vietnamese artillery officer wandered into Nha Trang across the beaches in search of his wife and children. He did not find them, or any North Vietnamese troops for that matter, but he did run across an old radio transmitter still in working order. He cranked it up and called Saigon, boasting he had recaptured the city. There was a surge of euphoria throughout the government, and the Joint General Staff quickly dispatched a small team to Nha Trang to help consolidate the "victory." The joy was short-lived, however, for we soon realized Communist forces had simply by-passed Nha Trang and were pressing on toward more vital targets further south.

As General Dung shifted his units out of MR 2, the entire Communist war-making apparatus was regeared to support the coming offensive against Saigon. North Vietnamese sea lanes were quickly extended to newly captured ports in MR 1 and 2. South Vietnamese prisoners of war were pressed into service as auxiliary drivers and guides for the hundreds of truck convoys that were now rolling south day and night, and an air shuttle was set up between North Vietnam and captured airfields at Danang and in Kontum Province. At the same time a third and then a fourth reserve division departed North Vietnam for the front, a new NVA headquarters was established (and almost instantly detected by American intelligence) east of Saigon, and the movement of forces from the Danang area to MR 3 was accelerated. General Le Trong Tan, the NVA commander at Danang, was told to have at least three of his divisions assembled east of the capital no later than 11 April.

There was also a sudden and dramatic upgrading of Communist antiaircraft capabilities in MR 3. Within the first few days of April truck convoys, bearing cigar-shaped SA-2 surface-to-air missiles, wound their way south through the western highlands toward Phuoc Long Province. Never before had such weapons been sighted outside North Vietnam and the borderlands of MR 1, and their appearance so close to the capital was an awesome development, for it was the SA-2, after all, that had taken such a heavy toll on U.S. B-52s over North Vietnam in the mid-1960s.

In tandem with the feverish military build-up, Communist policy-makers continued to hold out false olive branches in an effort to keep their enemies in Saigon confused and off guard. The day after the Nha Trang evacuation, Madame Nguyen Thi Binh, the PRG's Foreign Minister, told newsmen in Algeria, "We understand General Duong Van Minh [Thieu's chief rival] is ready to negotiate for peace and we are ready to talk with him." Optimists in both Saigon and Washington took the remarks as a sign the Communists might be willing to bargain, but in fact the only thing Hanoi was angling for was the removal of Thieu himself, the one man who seemed capable of holding the South Vietnamese army together during the trials and tribulations ahead. Within a few days, moreover, the true shape of Hanoi's intentions became somewhat more apparent. Radio Hanoi and Liberation Radio began dropping references to negotiations and substituting something far more ominous: an appeal for a "general uprising" in Saigon and other major cities throughout MR 3 and the delta. It was the kind of euphemistic declaration of total war that had been repeated over and over prior to the massive Communist offensive of 1968.

Meanwhile, the man who was to lead the final Communist thrust against Saigon had just arrived in MR 3. On the afternoon of 3 April, General Dung's battered field car pulled into the township of Loc Ninh, about sixty miles due north of Saigon. Weary and dust-covered after his day-long drive from Ban Me Thuot, the general immediately went to look for the local Communist commanders, for Loc Ninh had long been one of the principal headquarters of COSVN, the Communist command for the Saigon area and the delta. In a ramshackle old bamboo shack on the edge of town he found one of those he was seeking, COSVN's august chairman, Pham Hung. Later that evening Hung's deputy, General Tran Van Tra, arrived from the newly established field headquarters in eastern MR 3.*

*Pham Hung, a short, burly man in his mid-fifties, was fourth in line in the Hanoi Politburo, outranking even Dung himself. Since his appointment to COSVN in 1967, his name had gone unmentioned in the North Vietnamese press—Hanoi's way of camouflaging the fact that one of its major leaders was running the war in the southern half of South Vietnam. Dung's military deputy, General Tra, was already well known to Americans in Saigon as the original chief of the PRG's delegation to the Joint Military Commission—a post he had vacated at the end of March 1973. An unassuming, taciturn officer, Tra had been the primary architect of the 1968 offensive against Saigon and apparently had never quite recovered politically from its failure, for although he was a secret member of the Party Central Committee in North Vietnam, he had yet to be admitted to the select company of the Politburo.

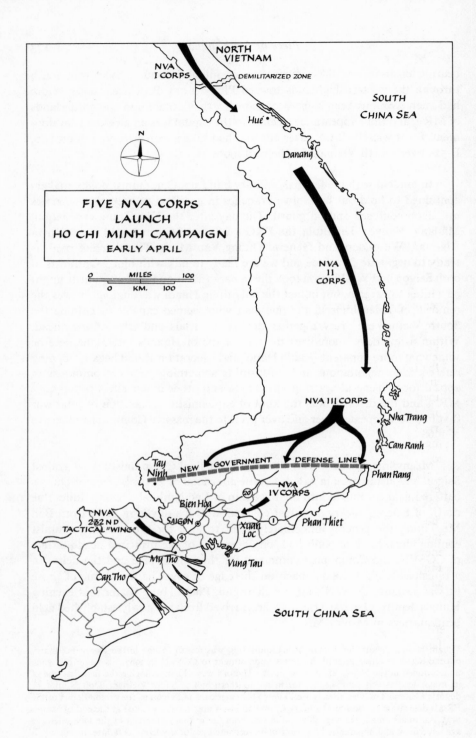

FIVE NVA CORPS
LAUNCH
HO CHI MINH CAMPAIGN
EARLY APRIL

MILES 0 — 100
KM. 0 — 100

NORTH VIETNAM
NVA I CORPS
DEMILITARIZED ZONE
SOUTH CHINA SEA
Hué
Danang
NVA II CORPS
NVA III CORPS
Nha Trang
Cam Ranh
Tay Ninh
NEW GOVERNMENT DEFENSE LINE
Phan Rang
Bien Hoa
NVA IV CORPS
SAIGON
Xuan Loc
Phan Thiet
NVA 232ND TACTICAL "WING"
My Tho
Vung Tau
Can Tho
SOUTH CHINA SEA

During the next few days Dung and the two COSVN officers consulted endlessly over tactics and strategy, finally agreeing to mount a three-front assault against Saigon, with a main thrust to come in the east against the village of Xuan Loc. It was here, at Xuan Loc, that the main highways leading to Saigon and to the coast intersected, and Dung knew that whoever controlled this crossroads town would have a direct line of march to Saigon's eastern suburbs and the outlying city of Bien Hoa, where well over sixty percent of the government's remaining war matériel was stockpiled. The conquest of Xuan Loc was to be the key to his strategy.

While Dung and his colleagues planned and debated, NVA forces in southern MR 2 continued to chip away at remaining government real estate. On 4 April the citizens of Dalat, shorn of their own defenses, invited NVA units to enter the city and help them restore order in the face of rampaging ARVN stragglers. Two days later the 10th NVA Division overran the refugee center at Cam Ranh Bay itself. The loss of this strategic facility left only a small sliver of MR 2 in government hands—Phan Rang air base and Phan Thiet City just to the south.

By the end of the first week in April, General Dung and his commanders at Loc Ninh had finished their planning exercise, and on the seventh the entire COSVN central committee was called together to consider (and rubber-stamp) their handiwork. Just as the meeting was called to order, a roar and a backfire echoed through the assembly hall, and "a motorbike came to a stop in the courtyard," Dung recalled. "The rider was a tall comrade wearing a light-blue shirt, khaki trousers and a stiff troops' hat. He had a big black leather sack slung over his shoulder. We immediately recognized him as comrade Le Duc Tho."

The following day Tho briefed Dung and his colleagues on the Politburo's latest decisions, including a plan for a special new command, superseding COSVN itself, to coordinate the offensive against Saigon. General Dung was to be the supreme commander; Pham Hung, the chief political officer; and Generals Tran Van Tra and Le Duc An, their deputies. A few days later General Le Trong Tan, conqueror of Danang, was named Dung's second in command, with responsibility for orchestrating the crucial campaign against Xuan Loc.

Within a week of the Nha Trang evacuation, the North Vietnamese thus were embarked on the path to "total victory in the shortest possible time." The balance of forces, moreover, had shifted so dramatically in their favor they were within easy reach of their goal.

In less than a month 150,000 South Vietnamese troops and militia in the northern half of South Vietnam had been dispersed, abandoned or annihilated. Sixteen thousand troops had been pulled off the beaches of MR 1, but only one unit had remained intact, a marine brigade. Out of the two ARVN divisions in MR 2, only two regiments, plus the airborne brigade west of Nha Trang, were still even remotely combat worthy. During the same brief period fifteen provinces had been lost to the Communists; $1 billion worth of equipment had been destroyed or left behind; nearly half of the government's four hundred planes and helicopters, including at least twelve sophisticated F-5 jet fighters, had been abandoned (many of them intact); and the government's entire intelligence apparatus in MR 1 and 2 had been obliterated. Had it not been for continuing American intelligence operations, our South Vietnamese allies would have met their fate in the next few weeks without the slightest inkling of how or why.

Six infantry divisions, an airborne and an armored brigade, and a few newly created ranger groups were all that remained of Thieu's once-proud army. It was these meager forces (roughly 90,000 men), plus whatever units could be salvaged from the debris of MR 1 and 2, that would now be responsible for the defense of Saigon and the delta.

On the other side of the ledger, the North Vietnamese had over 300,000 men, already in the south or preparing to move, to throw against the government. By early April at least eighteen NVA divisions were engaged in the fighting; five more were standing by in North Vietnam to assist, and all but two of these would be thrown into the fray before the war was done. Altogether, a record 30,000 NVA regulars would be sent south in April alone.

An intelligence appraisal which I prepared for Washington shortly after the fall of Nha Trang summarized the arithmetic and its grim implications: "Counting regular forces alone, the current balance of forces is roughly three or even four to one in the Communists' favor . . . The South Vietnamese in fact face a 'new enemy' which can offset through infiltration or modest troop deployments any steps that might be taken to rebuild government strength in MR 3 and 4. Hanoi may not fully appreciate its advantage, and that may delay military defeat for the government for a short while longer, but in the absence of decisive U.S. action [and here Polgar penciled in "not necessarily military," for he did not want anyone to think we were advocating the reintroduction of combat forces] it is about the only thing that can."*

---

*Polgar and I were not alone in our pessimism. For one brief moment the intelligence pundits in Washington also seemed tó have a clear view of the realities, unblinkered by the hopes for a political settlement that would later confound their vision. On 2 April, CIA Director Colby told WSAG: "The balance of forces in South Vietnam has now shifted decisively in the Communists' favor . . . The process of demoralization and defeatism already under way could prove irreversible and lead quickly to the collapse of the GVN and its will to resist." The following day an interagency intelligence memorandum declared: "We believe that in a matter of months, if not weeks, Saigon will collapse militarily or a government will be installed that will agree to a settlement on Communist terms."

Nguyen Van Tai, one of the highest-ranking North Vietnamese ever to fall into government hands, became the focus of secret exchanges that might have brought the release of some American prisoners even prior to the Paris agreement.

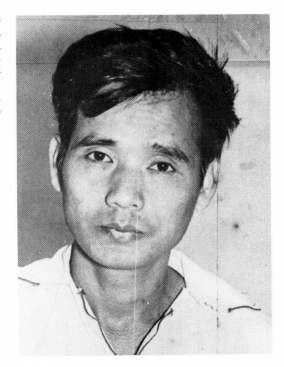

State Department officer Douglas Ramsey (center, with Frank Scotton on right), shown here on the day of his release, spent an extra year and a half in a Communist prison because Washington refused to trade Tai for him.

The author, on board the bridge of the USS Denver, *three days after he and the last CIA contingent in Saigon were helo-lifted out of the Embassy.*

Bill Johnson, veteran CIA counterintelligence officer, rescued Hungarian and Polish ICCS members from Communist shelling attacks on the last morning of the war.

Pat Johnson, CIA analyst, wrote a prophetic estimate in late 1974 pinpointing South Vietnamese morale problems, but was unable to persuade the Station Chief to send it to Washington.

Colonel Bill Legro, DAO's chronically pessimistic intelligence chief, helped to lay the groundwork for the evacuation long before the Ambassador authorized it.

General Homer Smith, last U.S. Defense Attaché in Saigon, had frequent "inspirations" that ultimately saved the evacuation from total disaster.

Tom Polgar, the CIA's bespectacled Station Chief, realized the hopelessness of the military situation early on, but was misled by the French and by social contacts in the Hungarian ICCS delegation into believing a negotiated solution was possible.

General Murray (center), Smith's gloomy predecessor as Defense Attaché, enjoys a lighter moment with his wife and Ken Moorefield, Martin's aide, whose heroics in the final days contributed to the evacuation of over 20,000 Vietnamese.

General Charles Timmes, the CIA's principal liaison to the South Vietnamese command, parlayed tennis games into political clout with "Big" Minh.

When President Thieu met with General Frederick Weyand and his fact-finding team in early April 1975 he was still hopeful of massive American military aid— and B-52s. (Seated at table, starting far left clockwise): CIA officers Ted Shackley and George Carver, General Smith, Deputy Assistant Defense Secretary Von Marbod, Weyand, Martin; Thieu (at head), Vice-President Huong, Prime Minister Khiem, General Vien.

MR 2 Consul General Spear (with hat) left his consulate in Nha Trang before the last of his staff, while MR 1 Consul General Al Francis stayed in Danang until the NVA were on the edge of the city.

Lacy Wright, a State Department officer inured to conservative dress and understatement, organized the evacuation of hundreds of Vietnamese relatives of American officials.

Alan Carter, USIA chief in Saigon and Martin's nemesis, found himself constantly ignored in Saigon's final days, and ended up leaving most of his Vietnamese employees.

Embassy officer Walt Martindale spirited montagnard and Vietnamese friends out of the highlands and Nha Trang, and helped organize the final airlift out of Saigon.

General Ngo Quang Truong, MR 1 commander, gave up Hué and Danang without a fight because of conflicting and changing orders from Saigon.

General Pham Van Phu, MR 2 commander, abandoned his army in the highlands and Nha Trang—and precipitated the unraveling of government defenses throughout the country (shown here with General Smith).

General Nguyen Van Toan was appointed MR 3 commander in Saigon's final days, despite a reputation for corruption, and managed to slow the Communist advance.

Hoang Duc Nha, Thieu's cousin (on left), battled furiously with Prime Minister Khiem (with glasses)—and lost, leaving the government in the hands of a slavishly pro-American faction.

Nguyen Van Thieu geared his policies to pleasing the Americans, and was misled by the Ford and Nixon Administrations into believing they would always be behind him.

During follow-up negotiations in Paris in June 1973, Kissinger and Le Duc Tho seem in good spirits, but a year and a half later Tho would have the last laugh as he joined General Dung and Pham Hung to lead the offensive against Saigon.

Party First Secretary Le Duan: the moving force behind Ho Chi Minh's vision of a unified Vietnam and mastermind of the final offensive.

Last American plane out of Danang after landing in Saigon: 400 government troops mobbed the plane in Danang; some crept into the wheel wells—only to be crushed to death on takeoff.

The Pioneer Commander, *one of several cargo ships committed to the evacuation of Danang, had become a floating charnel house by the time it reached Cam Ranh Bay.*

USDAO COMPOUND SAIGON 30 APR 75

A unique high-altitude photograph of DAO headquarters the day after Communist forces moved into Saigon; U.S. demolition charges had left the building a ribbon of crumpled metal.

Thieu's last memory of the Americans in Vietnam—the sign he saw when the author drove him to Tan Son Nhut four days before the final evacuation.

THE NOBLE SACRIFICE OF ALLIED SOLDIERS WILL NEVER BE FORGOTTEN

The next best thing to a B-52: Ambassador Graham Martin in a rare moment of relaxation and good humor.

An exhausted Martin disembarks from the chopper that brought him out of Saigon—flanked by Admiral Whitmire (on his right) and John Hogan, his press spokesman.

Though reporters wanted a statement, Martin, ill and exhausted on board the USS **Blueridge** *after the evacuation, is ordered into silence by Kissinger.*

Weyand and Martin debate who shall be first to disembark from the plane as they arrive from Washington in early April to face Saigon's final reckoning.

The aging Hamlet of Saigon politics —"Big" Minh—was embraced by the Americans and the French in the final days, but scorned by the Communists.

CIA man—identified by alias "T.D. Latz"—helps evacuees up ladder to make-shift chopper pad on last day of the war.

General Cao Van Vien, commander of government forces, proposed the withdrawal from the highlands without studying the escape route beforehand, and thus set the stage for the destruction of the army.

General Van Tien Dung and Pham Hung, as they appeared at victory celebrations in Saigon, directed the final offensive from their command post thirty miles north of the city.

Part 3

Collapse

Polgar

Martin

Van Tien Dung

Thieu

Primary Responsibility

As parts of South Vietnam dropped off the body of the country like pieces of a disintegrating ice floe, the Republic of Cambodia dissolved into nothingness.

On the day Danang was lost, the Embassy in Phnom Penh announced that Premier Lon Nol would soon be heading off on a "good-will tour" of Indonesia and the United States. Four days later, the decrepit, partially paralyzed Cambodian leader climbed aboard an American transport and flew to Thailand to begin his journey. He would never return. Almost within the hour Communist artillerymen lifted their sights on the center of Phnom Penh, as if to give the Americans and other foreigners on Embassy Row an opportunity to leave as well. By nightfall the last government outpost on the Mekong River southeast of the capital had been overrun, and 10,000 Khmer Communist troops were wheeling north to join 30,000 of their brethren already drawn up around Phnom Penh, defended by half as many government forces.

The departure of Lon Nol signaled an end to Henry Kissinger's four-year experiment in Cambodia, for the U.S. government had been instrumental in nudging him off center stage, and was now embarked on a new policy aimed merely at easing the country's death agonies. At long last, after stonewalling for over a year, Kissinger had decided to pursue the political compromise long advocated by Martin, Ambassador Dean and the French. The United States would support the restoration of deposed Cambodian leader Norodom Sihanouk as a way of bridging the gulf between the nationalist factions in Phnom Penh and the KC leadership in the bush.

In the meantime, a no less decisive drama was being played out in Saigon itself, for it was during this same momentous period, from late March to early April, that General Weyand and Graham Martin put their intellects, and their illusions, together to try to save what was left of South Vietnam. It was sadly ironic that they should have arrived in Saigon in the very midst of the final dissolution of the army in MR 1 and 2, for having so much to comprehend, and so little time to do it, they would never fully appreciate how close we were to the final reckoning.

By the time they showed up in the Embassy on 28 March, two lines of analysis had emerged among those of us who had been watching the crisis develop at close range. The CIA Station and the Defense Attaché's Office, in agreement for perhaps the first time on a strategic issue, were now convinced Saigon's military position was "untenable." In his initial briefing for Weyand, Colonel Legro, DAO's intelligence chief, stated flatly that nothing short of B-52 strikes against Hanoi had a chance of stopping the North Vietnamese—and even that was questionable. In his view, the only constraint the Communists faced was logistics. The problem of feeding and reequipping their fast-moving army, he surmised, might keep them from consummating their inevitable victory before June.

In our own assessments for the Weyand team Polgar and I hammered away at the same points, with one significant emendation: we argued that logistics would not be a serious handicap and that only U.S. intervention, or a negotiated surrender, could avert a total Communist military victory in the next few weeks.

On the other side of the debate, Chargé Lehmann and several other senior State Department officials vehemently objected to such "defeatism," as they described it. With a little more ammunition, they maintained, the South Vietnamese would "pull through," at least to the extent of being able to defend the southern half of the country and strike an "equitable" bargain with the other side. It was a precise echo of Martin's own desperate theories.

Just before his departure from Washington, Weyand had conceded privately that Vietnam was in deep trouble. But the very nature of his mission did not allow for such pessimism. He had been sent to Saigon to develop solutions, or options, not to rule them all impractical from the outset. He had been told, moreover, not to be deterred or diverted by political obstacles in the United States, Congressional or otherwise. If B-52s could do the job, he should acknowledge it. If additional U.S. aid was the panacea, he should say so. In effect, he had been given carte blanche to come up with anything but a realistic assessment of Saigon's staying power.

Nor was Weyand the kind of observer who could have approached the subject with total objectivity. As the last of the commanders at MACV, he had helped to usher Saigon into the era of Vietnamization and of the cease-fire, and he felt a deep personal responsibility for what had transpired—and what had not. As he once told a friend, he believed (with Kissinger) that the United States had a moral obligation to stand by the South Vietnamese till the end, particularly if they wanted to go down fighting.

The other members of Weyand's entourage were equally burdened with the myopia of past commitments. Erich Von Marbod had helped to formulate many of the Pentagon's fiscal policies toward Vietnam since the cease-fire and was determined to see them succeed. George Carver, Kissinger's hand-picked observer from the CIA, had framed his perspectives on the war during two decades as the agency's principal Vietnam specialist and was scarcely prepared to admit that all of our "nation building" programs, rural pacification and the like, had come to naught. His CIA colleague Ted Shackley likewise had a personal stake in the fortunes of the Thieu regime, for as Station Chief in Saigon in the late 1960s and early '70s, and more recently as head of the agency's East Asia Division, he had done much to make it what it was.

To have convinced such committed "experts" that Saigon was finished would have taken months, perhaps even years, of persuasion. In the few days available, those of us in the Embassy who glimpsed the worst had no chance at all.

Equally impervious to our gloom was Martin himself. He had been away for several weeks, was hopelessly behind on his facts, and would hardly have been predisposed, under any circumstances, toward the grim assessments the Station and DAO favored. He had lost a son in Vietnam and had put his own prestige on the line in the past year and a half for the sake of the Thieu regime, and his emotions and his ego were now fully engaged. To have admitted that all he had worked for and had believed in had been dashed in a mere three weeks would have required an act of self-effacement of which he was simply not capable.

To some extent, moreover, he was spurred on in his optimism by the presence of Weyand himself. Kissinger's decision to send the general on his fact-finding tour was, after all, a challenge to Martin's own competence and authority, and now the Ambassador had to prove he had been right about Saigon's staying power, if only to keep the general from upstaging him on his own turf.

The game of one-upmanship began the moment Weyand's plane set down at Tan Son Nhut. As the general and his entourage lined up to disembark, Martin insisted on being the first down the gangplank so that there would be no doubt among the Vietnamese officials waiting below that he was still the "President's representative on the scene."

On Martin's first morning in the Embassy, Polgar sent me down to his third-floor suite to brief him on the crises in MR 1 and 2. When I walked in with my charts and battle maps, David Kennerly, President Ford's personal photographer, who was traveling with the Weyand team, was leaning on the edge of his desk. "Hey," Kennerly said to me, "can you tell me how I can hitch a ride to Danang or Nha Trang? I'd like to get some pictures of the refugees."

I replied (as patiently as I could) that Danang was under attack and that we were having troubles enough simply getting Americans out of the place. It simply wouldn't be possible to spare a seat for him on a plane. Kennerly shrugged and walked out. I then turned to Martin. "Sir, Polgar wants me to give you some data on the situation," I said. He nodded and beckoned to George Carver, who was standing in the anteroom, to join us.

At best, Martin was a briefer's nemesis, always ready to interrupt, correct and even to humiliate when it might serve his purposes. Now, with Carver at his elbow, he was determined to discredit the grim picture I conjured up for him. What was the date of that report? Who was the source? he asked again and again. How can you be sure that this or that commander is not out rallying his men?

At the end of the hour I felt broken and utterly defeated. Carver later assured me I had "turned Martin around," but he could not have been more wrong. Up until mid-April, Martin would continue to tout the virtues and viability of an enclave Saigon, making it so difficult for the Station to clear "field appraisals" with him, again questioning every detail, that for the first time ever we began sending our assessments to Washington without the usual tag line "the Ambassador has read this appraisal and offers no objection to its dissemination."

Polgar and I were not the only ones who found Martin immune to the facts. Only a few hours after disembarking from the HQ-5, Al Francis, his face pinched and haggard behind the coal-black beard, arrived at the Embassy to give the Ambassador the full tragic details of the Danang evacuation. "Sir," he said wearily as he sat down on the sofa in a corner of Martin's suite. "Danang is lost. General Truong's army is no more."

Martin smiled benignly and shook his head. He had just been informed of Thieu's plan to try to retake MR 1 and was not prepared to count Danang out just yet. "No," he purred in a barely audible whisper, "MR 1 is not lost. I have information to the contrary."

That assurance, delivered so soothingly and condescendingly, cut through Francis' usual reserve. "But, sir," he burst out, "I've been on shipboard for days with the remains of Truong's army. MR 1 has fallen, I tell you. If you don't believe me, get a helicopter and go up and take a look for yourself."

Martin stared for a moment, then changed the subject, inquired of Francis' health, and at last showed him out of the office.

From this point on, Francis, the supreme insider, would be an outsider like the rest of us. By disagreeing with his old mentor at this critical juncture he forfeited his collateral with him, and for the next week or so would be consigned to a minor office down the hall, with no special access to the Ambassador's suite. Lehmann later tried to explain Francis' ostracism to me by impugning his emotional stability: "Francis was a little high-strung and overwrought, you know, particularly after all those awful things that had happened to him during Danang's final days."*

---

*Not even the growing proximity of the war seemed to diminish Martin's optimism. From the very moment he arrived back in Saigon it was apparent that the southern reaches of MR 2 would soon be in grave danger, but Martin refused to accept this. His reluctance nearly resulted in the loss of a small nuclear reactor in the city of Dalat which the United States had established there in the mid-1960s (as part of an electrical generating plant) under its Atoms for Peace Program.

• • •

Because the Weyand team was top-heavy with "ranking" officials, much of the drudgery of their mission was left to middle-level officials like myself. I soon learned, however, that involvement did not necessarily equate with influence, particularly where vital policy considerations, and reputations, hung in the balance. George Carver brought this truth home to me with stunning clarity when he called me to his quarters on Sunday, 31 March, to help prepare the initial draft of his own "situation assessment."

"Weyand is going to put together his own analysis," he explained to me as I plunked myself on the edge of his bed, "but I'd like to do something on my own for Bill Colby. Here's my initial draft." He handed me a sheaf of papers littered with typos. The gist was that while things were awfully bad around the country, there was still a chance that a victory or two, plus additional American aid, could galvanize the army. I told him I thought it was overly optimistic.

"Hmmm, well, what I really want from you," he sniffed as he paced back and forth, "is statistics. Could you dredge up some order-of-battle figures, you know, comparative-strength stuff to flesh out the text. I'd like to have it by this afternoon."

Pat and Joe came to the office to lend a hand and we spent the rest of the day drawing up a study for Carver. Our arithmetic said all there was to say about the hopelessness of Saigon's military prospects. Given the balance of forces, the outcome of the war seemed to us self-evident.

Our statistics so impressed Carver, he made certain they were later incorporated into Weyand's final report. Unfortunately, however, he did not see fit to include our conclusions as well, for like the rest of the Weyand crowd, he continued to believe for another week or more that a miracle was still possible.

During the confused eight days of the Weyand tour, a number of other experts from Washington trekked through the Embassy to double-check the general's findings. Among these independent canvassers were two staff investigators from the Senate Foreign Relations Committee, Dick Moose and Chuck Miessner, who happened to be old friends of mine. I had first met Miessner back in 1970, during my first assignment in Vietnam, when he was MACV's resident expert on Cambodia, and I had worked closely with Moose during his many previous trips to Vietnam on behalf of the committee. I respected them both for their knowledge and integrity and was determined to do all I could to help them. If anyone could shake the Ambassador and Weyand out of their contrived optimism, I decided, it was Congress.

I got a chance to brief the two staffers shortly after their arrival. My

---

Shortly before the evacuation of Nha Trang the U.S. Atomic Energy Commission sent a special plane to Vietnam to haul out the radioactive rods that comprised the heart of the reactor, but Martin refused to permit the extraction until literally within hours of the Communists' entry into Dalat on 4 April.

opening two-liner was specially calculated to rivet their attention. "The military situation is irreversible," I said. "The South Vietnamese will be defeated decisively in the next few weeks unless the United States intervenes." The rest of my briefing was pretty much in the same vein, and at several points Lehmann, who was sitting in on the session, tried to interrupt to temper my judgments. But each time he did Moose or Miessner would cut him off, challenging him to address specific points I had raised. Lehmann apparently was unwilling to become embroiled in a factual debate, for he eventually subsided.

Afterward Miessner thanked me for my candor and told me to expect to hear from them again before they departed for Washington. It was the beginning of a collaboration between us that ultimately, a week and a half later, would have an important impact on Congressional attitudes toward the Vietnam crisis and the conclusions of the Weyand team.*

From the moment he set foot in Saigon, Weyand focused his energies on a very few basic objectives. Aside from the rather straightforward business of fact-finding, he concentrated heavily on developing a new strategy of survival for the South Vietnamese. The essence of his plan was a variation of Thieu's own "Light at the Top, Heavy at the Bottom." Initially, under this concept, Thieu had hoped to establish a forward defense perimeter for Saigon extending from Tay Ninh in the west to Nha Trang on the coast. But now, with the deep Communist penetrations into southern MR 2, some modifications obviously were required. Weyand suggested, as one alternative, that the new defense perimeter be anchored at the coastal city of Phan Rang, with Xuan Loc as its centerpiece and Tay Ninh as its western hinge. Since Thieu had few other options, he accepted the proposal outright. He made only one demand on the Americans. At a session with Weyand, Martin and several others on 3 April, he asked if B-52s might be brought into play to help with Saigon's defense. Von Marbod, startled and dismayed that Thieu might still be counting on American bombing, explained that this was impossible. But he promised, as a kind of consolation prize, to make available to the South Vietnamese an array of sophisticated weapons, including monstrous "Daisy

---

*Moose and Miessner were not the only Washington luminaries who passed through Saigon during the period of the Weyand tour. One evening, at the Duc Hotel, I ran into an old acquaintance, Bill Christison, who had risen to become the CIA's National Intelligence Officer for South and Southeast Asia, largely through Carver's patronage. He explained to me that he was not part of the Weyand team, but had come out to Saigon to do some fact-finding on his own. "And boy, am I going to stay out of their hair," he continued as we joked about the exertions of Carver and the rest. "No profit in it. In fact, I'm flying to Can Tho tomorrow to play some tennis with our boys down there."

And so he did, the CIA's principal operations officer for Vietnam and Cambodia. He went off to the delta and played tennis for two days while Weyand and his team dug a political hole for themselves. Of all of Washington's leading "experts" on Indochina, Christison would be the only one who could honestly claim when the whole tragedy had run its course that he had had nothing to do with the Weyand mission and its misjudgments. He had been too busy on the courts.

Cutter" and CBU bombs, that would enable them to maximize the effectiveness of their own air force.*

As a first step toward realizing the new defense plan, Thieu placed Phan Rang under the control of General Toan, his MR 3 commander, and Toan in turn directed his old friend General Nguyen Vinh Nghi, the former MR 4 commander (fired the previous fall for corruption), to establish a forward headquarters there with part of the Airborne Division. He also deployed an armored brigade and several ranger units to eastern MR 3 to reinforce the 18th ARVN Division at the crucial town of Xuan Loc.

In addition, Thieu and his commanders agreed to do everything they could to rebuild some of the units that had been evacuated, mostly in shambles, from MR 1 and 2. From the beginning, however, they seemed determined to complicate their task through abysmally poor planning. Only at the prompting of General Smith, the Defense Attaché, did they bother to put together a blueprint to guide them, and even then, to no real purpose. When Smith and his staff looked it over during the first few days of April they found it to be wholly impractical, and immediately set to work on a substitute. But no sooner had they completed their prospectus than the South Vietnamese produced a new one of their own. Under its provisions, 4,000 marines and other stragglers from MR 1 and 2 were to be regrouped at the coastal city of Vung Tau, southeast of Saigon, and at other nearby training camps, and to be formed into new units, hopefully before the end of April. Although the plan was somewhat more realistic than the original one, it suffered from a defect which Smith considered fatal. Whereas he wanted all rebuilt units incorporated into existing ones to minimize problems of command and control, the Vietnamese insisted on deploying each one independently, as soon as it was whipped back into fighting shape. Despite Smith's protests, it was this procedure they followed up until the last day of the war, and as a result, the four infantry regiments and four artillery battalions that finally emerged from the reconstitution process were sent into the field piecemeal, to be chewed up in equally piecemeal fashion on Saigon's shrinking battlefronts.

Because Saigon's high command was now in total disarray, Smith and his staffers shouldered other basic tasks that ordinarily would have been left to it. They became deeply involved, for example, in locating and distributing Saigon's remaining supply stocks and parceling out equipment newly deliv-

---

*The "Daisy Cutter," originally designed for clearing helicopter pads in the jungle, explodes just above the target area, scouring the earth for a hundred yards around. The CBU (cluster bomb unit) is an even more awesome weapon. Essentially an airborne aerosol can, it detonates at a preset altitude, producing a cloud of kerosene-like fuel fifty feet in diameter and eight feet thick. Once ignited, the cloud itself generates a down-pressure of about three hundred pounds per square inch, sufficient to crush anything in its field. Anyone who survives the initial blast quickly suffocates in the post-explosion vacuum. By any measure, the CBU is one of the most lethal non-nuclear weapons in America's arsenal.

ered from the United States. So efficiently did they perform this task that they soon had supplies flowing to the field faster than the South Vietnamese could rebuild their units.

There was, of course, one unfortunate side effect to all this activity. For the first time since the cease-fire the North Vietnamese were completely justified in their claims that a large number of Americans in Saigon were serving as "military advisors" to Thieu's army.*

As a corollary to refurbishing Saigon's war machine, Weyand and his colleagues decided early on that some changes in the government also were in order. What they had in mind was not the elimination of Thieu himself (as the Communists demanded), but the broadening of his cabinet to include moderates and even a few token members of the non-Communist opposition, so if some sort of negotiations with the Communists became necessary, a large segment of the political spectrum would be lined up behind the government.

On their second or third day in Saigon, Shackley and Carver visited the Palace to test this concept on Prime Minister Khiem, who had always showed himself highly receptive to American advice. Once again he behaved true to form, nodding and agreeing wholeheartedly with the Americans. Afterward he tried to plant the seed in Thieu's ear. Maybe the time had come to broaden the government, he told the President; maybe a peace offering ought to be made to the other side, while the army was still strong enough to serve as a bargaining counter. Khiem also resolved (as he told a CIA contact) to try to force the issue by threatening to resign.

Meanwhile, domestic opposition to Thieu continued to mount. On the day after the Nha Trang evacuation the South Vietnamese Senate, normally a rubber-stamp body, unanimously approved a resolution calling for new governmental leadership, and Nguyen Cao Ky, convinced that such public appeals were useless, began pressing actively for a coup d'état. Since his own "air force" clique was not strong enough to bring it off alone, he sought the support of various old friends in the army's chain of command, including General Le Minh Dao, commander of the crucially placed 18th ARVN Division at Xuan Loc. But Dao refused to commit himself without the backing of the Joint General Staff itself. This in turn led Ky to seek the assistance of the one man whose participation could tip the scales overnight, JGS chairman, General Cao Van Vien.

Meeting with Vien around midday on the second, Ky set forth his arguments and asked for support. Vien, cautious to a fault, hemmed and hawed and finally promised to get back to him in a day or so with an answer. That afternoon Vien informed Khiem of what had taken place and suggested that they check with the Americans, before alerting Thieu himself, to determine if

---

*DAO's logistics activity also was of questionable legality in view of Congressional proscriptions against American involvement in the war.

Washington was behind Ky's plotting. Within an hour or so, Khiem queried Polgar and was told unequivocally that the Americans would not support a coup by Ky or his cronies, since none was considered sufficiently "moderate" or "centrist" to deal with the Communists.

Thieu, in the meantime, had just gotten wind of Ky's scheme. Through a contact in the Thu Duc Military Academy near Saigon, his cousin, Hoang Duc Nha, learned of Ky's contacts with General Dao and immediately alerted the President. This, more than any of the advice the Americans had given him or his cronies, cinched Thieu's decision to make some changes in the government. He was particularly put out with Khiem, for he suspected the Prime Minister knew far more about the conspiracy than he had let on. Consequently, when Khiem finally got around to offering his resignation on the afternoon of the third, Thieu promptly accepted it.

The following day Thieu went on national television to announce a governmental housecleaning. Assembly Speaker Nguyen Ba Can was to head up a new government of "war and national union," he said, and outgoing deputy Prime Minister Tran Van Don was to become concurrently deputy Prime Minister and Defense Minister. The cabinet of Tran Thien Khiem, who had held the Defense Minister's portfolio as well as the Prime Ministership, was to stay on for a few more days to ensure an orderly transfer of power.

Within Saigon's political community the reaction to these changes was a collective shrug of indifference, since Thieu still retained the reins of power. Perhaps the only satisfied onlooker was the Embassy itself. Martin was particularly encouraged, for he believed (mistakenly) that the new line-up would be seen by the domestic opposition as a real change and would enable Thieu to rally the army and the country. Polgar, though hardly so optimistic, could console himself with a somewhat more parochial consideration. One of the highest-ranking members of the cabinet-to-be had long been a fully recruited, well-paid and responsive CIA agent.

With the renovation of Thieu's entourage, many of my colleagues were strengthened in their belief that politics might eventually save the day for the South Vietnamese, that the right combination of strength and moderation in the government might set the stage for "equitable" negotiations. Indeed, by the time Weyand and his team left Saigon on the morning of 4 April, this notion had become a central ingredient in their plan for salvaging the lower half of the country.

Yet whether any of the underlying assumptions were valid or not remained open to question. The persistence of the Communist offensive, coupled with Hanoi's continuing appeals for a general uprising, seemed to imply a distinct aversion to any kind of deal with the Thieu government.

On 1 April, I decided to try out the negotiations thesis on a highly reliable informant, who had just come in out of the field. Meeting with him at a safe house not far from the Embassy, I questioned him throughout the morning about various aspects of Communist planning. My efforts were well repaid, for the source had some startling things to say about the mood and thinking of the "enemy." As he explained it, the Hanoi leadership was now on a "blood scent" and would stop at nothing short of total victory. Even a negotiated surrender, with all the uncertainties that implied, might be unacceptable to them, he said.

Around midday Shackley, Polgar and his deputy, John Pittman, joined us for a quick lunch. Over salad and hamburgers I reviewed what the source had told me. Shackley was intrigued (if somewhat negatively) and directed me to draft a memorandum at once on the conversation so he could fully brief Weyand. Polgar was more skeptical, however. He could not believe that the Communists would blast their way to victory as the source suggested, when they could achieve it bloodlessly through negotiations.

Polgar's views on this issue would have a profound impact on the course of American policy in the next few weeks. But the irony was that he drew his inspiration not from any exaggerated hopes of saving South Vietnam, but from precisely the opposite. By the time Nha Trang was given up, he had persuaded himself that there was no chance of stabilizing the military situation and that efforts should be made at once to reach an accommodation with the Communists on whatever terms possible. So firm was his belief in the wisdom and urgency of this course of action, he could not conceive that it, too, might be impractical.

Apart from the continuing advance of the North Vietnamese army, one other factor helped to shore up his conviction that negotiations were the only way. This was the almost palpable danger of a popular backlash against the American community in Saigon. The evacuation of Danang and Nha Trang proved beyond doubt that under the turbulent conditions of defeat, the Americans could not count on the tolerance of their allies. Now, with the North Vietnamese army pressing toward MR 3, the prospect of a direct attack on the capital itself had to be reckoned with. And if that happened, and an American evacuation became necessary, how would the army and the population react toward us?

On 2 April, Polgar received an unsettling answer to that question. During the morning a contact in the Vietnamese Ministry of Defense reported that certain army officers had agreed to make the Americans in Saigon hostage to their own safety if the Communists moved on the city. In particular, Major General Nguyen Ngoc Loan, a "special assistant" to General Vien and one of Ky's closest allies, wanted it "known" at the Embassy that if the Americans did nothing to help their Vietnamese friends in the event of an evacuation, the army would turn on them.*

---

*Loan himself was a ruthless and uncompromising man, having achieved a certain notoriety during the Communist offensive of 1968, when as Saigon's police chief he had put a bullet through the head of a Viet Cong prisoner in full view of American television cameras. If anyone was capable of leading a march on the Embassy, Polgar concluded, it was this audacious one-legged general.

The report sent Polgar into a quiet frenzy, and reinforced his conviction that something must be done straightaway to promote negotiations. Unlike Weyand and the Ambassador, he doubted that any variation of the Thieu regime would ever be able to strike a bargain with the Communists. He therefore made up his mind that the removal of Thieu and his replacement by someone acceptable to Hanoi were imperative.

Since it was obvious the Ambassador would never sanction such a move, Polgar resolved to go over his head. Around four o'clock on the afternoon of the second, he called me to his office and explained what he intended to do. Together we were to draft a cable to Washington, pointing out Thieu's liabilities and the prospects (such as they were) for an accommodation with the Communists. Hopefully, Washington would draw the appropriate conclusions.

The document we prepared in the next two hours was unlike anything that had come out of the Mission since the cease-fire—and perhaps ever. We argued that Thieu's days were numbered, that he had lost the support of a large segment of the military establishment, and that a coup against him was likely, perhaps even imminent. Although we did not ask explicitly for authority to replace him with someone amenable to surrender, we made it clear that factions favoring negotiations were mobilizing against him: "While moderate politicians, including some of the opposition, would like him to stay on as a titular president for the sake of constitutional continuity, there is nearly unanimous demand that Thieu surrender the substance of his powers." Nor did Polgar hesitate to spell out what he felt would be the consequences of a rejection of our views in Washington: "Should Washington perform as most of us expect, then we have to conclude that neither Thieu nor an independent South Vietnam has any prospects of surviving more than a few months."

Next came an analysis of Hanoi's military intentions which I had specially prepared to strengthen our argument for Thieu's removal. "We believe," I wrote, "that the North Vietnamese will move to the very brink of a military victory, isolating Saigon and destroying its military potential, and then call for negotiations"—on terms designed "to ensure the quickest possible transition to the kind of Communist-dominated coalition Hanoi has long envisioned as a way station to reunification."

In essence, Polgar and I were suggesting that Hanoi was still interested in a negotiated victory, rather than a strictly military one. It was a purely speculative point and at odds with the intelligence I had gleaned from my informant the day before. But Polgar was determined to make it anyway, for he was convinced that if Administration officials could be persuaded that Hanoi was still willing to negotiate, they might be prepared to authorize the removal of Thieu, the opening of talks with the Communists, and other "radical" measures to defuse the threat to Saigon itself.

As Polgar and I sat down at the end of the day to review our draft, I voiced some reservations about our treatment of the political option and its practicality, reminding him of what the informant had told us—Hanoi was on a "blood scent." But Polgar was unconcerned. In his view there were several compelling reasons to suppose Hanoi would prefer to seize power by way of the conference table rather than by direct assault. For one thing, he said, a negotiated victory would be far easier for them to rationalize to friends and allies abroad, particularly since the prospect of Soviet T-54 tanks rattling down the streets of Saigon could hardly go over well with the "détente-minded" Russians. Secondly, as he saw it, the North Vietnamese simply did not have enough political cadres to administer all the territory they would have to absorb if they were to seize power outright. By going through the motions of a political settlement, with a mock coalition, elections and so on, they could buy time to build up their control before unification.

As Polgar warmed to his subject he harkened back to the pattern of Communist takeover in his own native Hungary, where the Soviet-controlled party apparatus had managed to seize power in the mid-1940s, first by working through proven patriots and then by subverting and eliminating them. This was how the Vietnamese Communists, he believed, would consolidate their own victory.

When he had finished his little spiel he asked me again what I thought. I told him I was leery of locking the Station so firmly into an analytical position when there was so much conflicting information. But I conceded, to my everlasting regret, that our estimate seemed consistent with Hanoi's long-standing plan for victory, with its emphasis on the utility of negotiations and coalition politics as bridges to a final takeover.

Polgar looked at me for a moment, then penciled in an additional paragraph on the final page: "The finer points of a possible interim political solution should not distract us from what would seem to be the primary responsibility of the U.S. government. This we define as the orderly evacuation of United States nationals and the many thousands of Vietnamese who have laid their lives on the line, trusting in our promises and in our commitment to the Paris agreement . . ." He then signed his name to the cable and sent it off to the communications room for transmittal to Washington.

The message, for all its novelty, struck a responsive chord at home, and part of its thesis was immediately embraced by a segment of the intelligence community. On 4 April the CIA, State and Defense Departments declared confidently in a joint memorandum: "While a quick, decisive military stroke may be in the works, we believe that Hanoi will opt for a less costly and politically more expedient alternative, calculating that a South Vietnamese collapse is near at hand."*

The larger concept Polgar had been hoping to get across to his colleagues, however, fell on deaf ears. Two days after we filed our cable, CIA Director Colby sent back a top-secret reply which made it clear that the Station should

---

*The memorandum also endorsed DAO's thesis that an NVA victory would not be likely before June, although it emphasized that "the only question over the defeat of the Republic of Vietnam is timing."

do nothing to promote Thieu's downfall. His objections centered not on the desirability or undesirability of a coup—Colby made no comment on this—but rather on the adverse political fallout that could be expected at home and abroad if it ever became known the CIA was again in the business of over-throwing governments. It would be "an institutional and a national disaster," he wrote, "if there was any remote connection between us and such an event." He went on to say that the agency should present itself to Saigon's political community as a guardian of life and the status quo. "If things get complicated at all," he concluded, "advise, and I will recommend the strongest effort to facilitate Thieu and family safe passage and haven."*

Colby's directive plunged Polgar into deep despair, for it meant that if there was to be a governmental change at all in Saigon, it would have to be accomplished through protracted legal means, consistent with the South Vietnamese constitution. And by then, Polgar feared, a negotiated settlement, and even an evacuation, might be impossible.

---

*Colby's aversion to coups d'état traced back to 1960, when as Station Chief in Saigon he and Ambassador Eldridge Durbrow frustrated an initial attempt by South Vietnamese dissidents to overthrow President Diem. In opposing a coup attempt against Thieu, Colby also was reflecting Kissinger's thesis that we should do everything we could to foster America's image abroad as a steadfast ally.

Limp Little Rags

The message Polgar and I drafted and sent to Washington on 2 April highlighted a problem which Weyand and his team seemed all too determined to ignore. By reminding Washington of our responsibility to help those Vietnamese who had helped us, we threw into focus the monumental implications of a total American withdrawal from Vietnam.

As the war drew into its final month the Embassy's only evacuation plan was the standard blueprint provided to all U.S. Missions around the world—plus the special annexes drawn up by DAO in February. For all its size and complexity, the two-inch document was largely a waste of paper. Not only did it impose an arbitrary and totally unrealistic ceiling of 8,000 on the number of potential evacuees, American and Vietnamese, but it also presupposed the cooperation of the populace, a prospect that could scarcely be counted on in view of recent experiences in MR 1 and 2.

During the past two weeks several Embassy staffers had tried to modify the plan to bring it into line with the lessons of Pleiku and, finally, Danang and Nha Trang. Shortly after Phu's withdrawal from the highlands Marv Garrett, the Embassy's security officer and the man technically responsible for the safety of everyone in the Mission, had drafted several new paragraphs and tried to insert them in the text. But when his immediate superior, administrative counselor Henry Boudreau, discovered what he intended, he promptly put a stop to it. As a Martin appointee and thoroughgoing loyalist, Boudreau was not about to let his subordinates delve into such a sensitive topic as evacuation until the "front office" gave the word. Indeed, he quickly adopted the studiously unruffled air which Lehmann and ultimately the Ambassador himself displayed toward each new crisis. Refusing to discuss the fall of Danang with his staff, Boudreau told Garrett and several others privately that the collapse of MR 1 was not a "matter of concern."*

---

*Garrett, for his part, was too ill-acquainted with military realities to realize how far he was being misled. At a dinner party in late March he and I nearly came to blows over the seriousness of

Not all senior Embassy staffers were as sanguine as Boudreau. General Smith, for one, had both the experience and the common sense to recognize a poor military show when he saw one, and sufficient resources at his disposal to pursue his own evacuation planning in his own way.

"I used to lie awake at night," he later remarked, "and contemplate ways of getting my people out of the country. That's when I got my inspiration, during those long, sleepless hours."

Initially, however, it was not so much inspiration as the exigencies of pulling manpower and supplies out of MR 1 and 2 that forced his hand. On the eve of Danang's collapse Smith had created an evacuation control center to coordinate the evolving sea- and air-lift out of the city and also had set up a special planning group to review his "evacuation options." At the same time his intelligence chief, Colonel Legro, had attempted to persuade Lehmann and his political counselor, Joe Bennett, to draw up lists of "sensitive" Vietnamese whose lives might be endangered by a Communist takeover. Neither of them had been willing to consider such a politically controversial step, but Legro had pushed ahead anyway, and during the last weekend in March he and his staff put together a preliminary list of "non-essential" American personnel at DAO and a roster of Vietnamese employees who ought to be helped in an emergency.

Among the Embassy's other senior officials, only Polgar was in a position to match DAO's efforts in the evacuation field. Not only did he have the requisite strategic intelligence at hand, but he was also supported by a vast bureaucracy, stretching from Saigon to Washington, capable of providing aircraft and other needed resources.

In late March, when it became apparent to him that Danang was finished, and Nha Trang doomed, Polgar requested authority from CIA headquarters to accelerate the removal of CIA wives, dependents and household effects from Saigon, and to grant "early departure" to officers nearing the end of their tours.* Agency officials in Langley gave their approval at once. But, as an integral part of the Mission, the Station was unable to follow through without the cooperation of the Embassy's administrative section, and here, predictably, it encountered a roadblock in the person of Henry Boudreau. True to the official line that the Americans were in Saigon to stay, he refused to provide assistance in shipping out CIA officers' personal effects. Finally, Polgar was obliged to dip into his own contingency funds to cover the costs of packing

---

the threat to Saigon. Throughout the evening he had been arguing for the elimination of hazardous duty "bonuses" for Embassy personnel, on the grounds they were unwarranted. I pointed out to him rather emphatically that even then the equivalents of six North Vietnamese divisions were arrayed within a sixty-mile radius of the capital—a justification for hazardous duty pay if there ever was one.

*There were, then, roughly 370 CIA employees in South Vietnam and 160 "company" wives and dependents, plus 43 officers from the code-breaking National Security Agency, who were dependent on the Station for both administrative support and security.

and freight. Such was the inauspicious beginning of the CIA's departure from Vietnam.

Early in his own contingency planning Colonel Legro asked Polgar if he would like to join in preparing for a Vietnamese evacuation as well. Polgar told him he would "get back" to him, but never did.

His unwillingness to be drawn into such a project so early on was, in part, politically motivated. Polgar wanted to go about his own planning in his own way, without becoming entangled in DAO's vast bureaucracy. He also was somewhat more impressed than Legro and his colleagues with the necessity of operating within the framework of Mission policy. Though hardly the Ambassador's flunky, he sat only three floors away from the power center, and the obstacle, and at that distance he found it far more difficult to circumvent official guidelines than did the DAO staffers, comfortably situated as they were five miles away at Tan Son Nhut.

Besides the loss of Danang and Nha Trang, one other factor helped to bring the prospect of an evacuation into focus for all of us: the continuing crisis in Cambodia. By early April, with the KC on his threshold, Ambassador Dean had already updated standing arrangements for the use of helicopters in the final, "Eagle Pull," phase of a complete withdrawal, and CIA and State Department officers were busily compiling lists of Americans and "third country nationals" whom the Embassy would assist in such a contingency. In addition, Admiral Gayler in Honolulu had activated a "marine amphibious brigade" to provide protection during a helo-lift, and had created a naval squadron—Task Force '76—under Admiral Donald Whitmire to facilitate the assembling of U.S. vessels in Indochina waters on an emergency basis. By 4 April some eight warships, including the helicopter carrier *Okinawa,* had already taken up station in the Gulf of Thailand off Cambodia.

In Washington, meanwhile, the planning for a full American withdrawal from Indochina proceeded far less systematically. In late March the Pentagon put together a thirty-man staff to keep the Joint Chiefs of Staff abreast of what Smith, Gayler and the U.S. Special Advisory Group in Thailand were doing to prepare for such an eventuality.*

At the State Department, however, what little planning was done was confined mainly to the administrative section, and focused primarily on Cambodia. The problem of extracting Americans from South Vietnam received only passing attention, particularly after the Weyand team began rummaging around Saigon. There was, in fact, a tendency among top-level State Depart-

---

*From the outset, one substantive consideration haunted and stymied the JCS planners. No matter how they tallied the available "assets," they kept coming up with the depressing conclusion that there were simply not enough ships and aircraft in the Pacific area to handle emergency evacuations under hostile conditions in Saigon and Phnom Penh simultaneously. If the Americans in both cities were to be safely extracted, one group would have to be removed far in advance of the other.

ment officials to assume that Weyand and the Ambassador would tidy up most of the loose ends on their own. One high-ranking official who worked closely with Assistant Secretary of State Habib and Undersecretary Ingersoll through-out the last weeks of the war confided to me a year later that neither he nor any of his colleagues had ever really appreciated the evolving crisis in Vietnam or the need for decisive action on the Washington end. No one, he said, realized until very late how little Martin was doing to prepare for an evacua-tion, or wanted to try to second-guess him, given his special relationship with Kissinger. And since Dean in Cambodia seemed wholly capable of making responsible decisions without Washington's interference, the consensus was that Martin could do likewise. "Dean's demonstrated competence," my con-tact explained, "left us with the feeling we should let the man on the spot handle the show."

Despite such complacency at the top, however, there was a group of young men down in the bowels of the foreign policy establishment who saw early on what was coming in Vietnam and the need to plan for it. Most of the principals were middle-grade movers in the State Department and the USIA who had begun their careers in Vietnam as executors of American policy in the countryside and who therefore knew the country from the rice roots up, far better than any of their superiors. The acknowledged organizer and spokes-man for the group was Lionel Rosenblatt, a thirty-one-year-old State Depart-ment officer and the very quintessence of the young Vietnam-veteran-on-the-rise. A district advisor in Vietnam in the mid-1960s, he had been appointed aide to Undersecretary Ingersoll on his return to Washington and had watched the crumbling of Vietnam in recent weeks from the unique vantage point of one who had all the top government appraisals and policy papers at his fingertips. Up to now Rosenblatt had been careful to play the bureaucratic game by the rules, keeping his complaints and objections to himself and operating through "channels," but with the loss of Ban Me Thuot and then the highlands and Hué, he had become increasingly restive, and finally, on the eve of Weyand's visit to Vietnam, which he considered a time-waster, his experience and sensi-tivity got the best of him.

The "conspiracy" he masterminded began as a strictly informal affair. One night just before the fall of Danang he and some friends, all Vietnam veterans and bureaucratic comers, were sitting around his apartment, sipping cognac and mulling over the latest bad news from the front. Each of them was convinced the loss of Ban Me Thuot and the highlands spelled the end of South Vietnam and that the Administration was not moving fast enough to provide for the safety of the Americans there and their Vietnamese employees. Accord-ingly, Rosenblatt suggested they take matters in their own hands and try to force their bosses toward some hard, realistic decisions.

During the next several days the group began meeting over lunch in the State Department's antiseptic cafeteria. In addition to Rosenblatt, the regulars included Al Adams, special assistant to Kissinger; Jim Bullington, the State Department's Vietnam deskman; Frank Wisner from the Department's Public

Affairs office; Ev Bumgardner, an experienced USIA officer; Craig Johnstone from Kissinger's Secretariat; Ken Quinn of the National Security Council staff; and Frank Scotton, the USIA man who had engineered my contacts with the Congressional visitors in February.

At first the group concentrated on developing a practical evacuation schedule. Assuming the fall of South Vietnam was only two months away at most, they agreed that the withdrawal of Americans would have to begin immediately so seat space on the final flights could be given over entirely to Vietnamese. Bullington produced a thumbnail estimate of the number of "potential" Vietnamese evacuees. Counting the 17,000 local employees of the various agencies in the Embassy, and their dependents (ten per household), plus some 93,000 others who had worked for the United States sometime in the past, he figured the total came to well over a million. No one needed to be reminded of the mammoth task these statistics implied. At the end of the first Indochina war in 1954 it had taken over three months to move less than 800,000 refugees from North to South Vietnam—and that under relatively stable conditions.

Rosenblatt and company also pinpointed what they saw as holes in the existing contingency planning. All felt the standing Embassy document, with its blasé assumptions about a quiescent populace, was totally unrealistic. Therefore, as one of their immediate priorities, they agreed to try to persuade their bosses to form a real task force to address the evacuation problem systematically.

When the Weyand team flew off to Saigon at the end of March, Ken Quinn, one of the luncheon-group regulars, managed to get himself assigned to it as a "staff aide." Apart from his inevitable curiosity, he had a deep personal motive for wanting to visit Saigon at this time. His wife was Vietnamese and many of her relatives were now streaming into the capital, looking for help and refuge in the face of the advancing North Vietnamese army.

A day or so after his arrival, Quinn quietly contacted his in-laws and put them in touch with various Embassy officers. If there was an evacuation, he told them, these Americans would help. He then rounded up a bunch of friends in the Embassy to discuss the status of the Ambassador's evacuation program. Lacy Wright, an accomplished young State Department officer who had served briefly as chief of the consulate in the delta in late 1973, was one of his contacts. So was I. The three of us agreed to keep each other informed of the progress of the Embassy's planning, and of the North Vietnamese army. I was to provide the intelligence input, while Wright would have responsibility for ensuring that certain of our Vietnamese friends (or relatives) were included in any prospective evacuation. Eventually I became so preoccupied with my work for Polgar that I was unable to lend assistance, but Wright, backed by Quinn, Rosenblatt and their mafia in Washington, managed to save hundreds of Vietnamese who otherwise might have been left behind.

•   •   •

During the eight days of the Weyand visit, the Embassy's own evacuation planning fell prey to the aims and illusions which the general and the Ambassador were so avidly pursuing. Admitting no imminent military threat, Martin himself saw no need to rush to the helicopters or even to prepare to do so. Nor was he willing to add to Thieu's already considerable burdens by confronting him with the prospect of an American bailout. A pretense of steadfastness became a key element in his own formula for saving the Saigon regime.

Essentially, this policy meant gambling the lives of the 6,000 Americans in Vietnam on the promise of a last-minute miracle, and because of the hazards it implied, Martin knew he would need a powerful rationale for it. He did not, in fact, have to look very far for one. The recent reports indicating that the army might turn against us in the event of an American evacuation served nicely, providing him with a perfect excuse for doing almost nothing at all in the evacuation sphere. Drawing on this intelligence, he could argue convincingly that any overhasty planning would bring on the threatened backlash, and that this in turn would make an orderly withdrawal impossible.

Although the intelligence certainly gave cause for concern, some of us doubted that Martin was ever as committed to this apocalyptic vision as he professed. I, for one, remained convinced that he was deliberately exaggerating the danger of "chaos in the streets" to ward off decisions that might undercut American support for Thieu. My suspicions were heightened by his approach to another problem. Within a day or two of his return to Saigon, for example, he ordered political counselor Bennett to build a noisy press campaign around recent reports that the Communists were torturing and mutilating recalcitrant civilians in newly captured areas of MR 1 and 2. Obviously he was hoping that this would generate sympathy for the South Vietnamese abroad. But what he seemed to overlook in the bargain was the effect such disclosures might have on the South Vietnamese population itself. If there was one easy way to spark the panic and chaos he claimed to fear, it was by invoking the specter of wholesale slaughter and mayhem at Communist hands.

Not all of the Ambassador's alarms, of course, were overdrawn. There was, to be sure, a very real danger the South Vietnamese would turn on us if Saigon came under attack. But the lesson of both Pleiku and Danang was that the riskiest course of all lay in the direction Martin now seemed determined to follow. If the local populace was led to believe, rightly or wrongly, that we underestimated the military crisis, or the need for evacuation planning, they were almost certain to succumb to panic and murderous hostility when the moment of truth arrived.*

*In testimony to Congress following Saigon's collapse, Martin attempted to minimize how far he had gone to frustrate evacuation planning, insisting that he had ordered Lehmann and special assistant George Jacobson to assume "watching briefs" over the Embassy's program in late March. In fact, this overstated the case. Jacobson did not receive a formal mandate to this effect until mid-April, and as Martin himself later admitted to me, Lehmann never even bothered to read the Embassy's standing evacuation plan. During the same hearings Martin cited the restrictive character of American immigration law as the main reason for his failure to plan adequately and in advance for a Vietnamese evacuation. The only way an alien can resettle in the United States or

•   •   •

On 1 April, only hours after the Nha Trang evacuation began, Colonel Legro drove to the Embassy to try to coax Martin off dead center. The family syndrome, he explained, was already taking a terrible toll on Saigon's high command as more and more officers cast aside their military duties to look to the safety of their families. As an antidote, he proposed that the dependents of some ARVN generals and colonels be moved at once to the Philippines or other points of safety outside Vietnam.

Martin nodded indulgently, but rejected the idea. The exodus of a privileged few, he insisted, no matter how discreetly carried out, would wreak havoc with morale in the army's lower ranks and could lead to the unraveling of what remained of Saigon's defenses. He did agree, however, to provide an immigration visa to the family of one of Legro's Vietnamese army friends as a personal favor to him. The beneficiaries of this select act of generosity were the first Vietnamese to be evacuated under Embassy auspices.

Martin's refusal to be any more forthcoming did not discourage Legro's superior, General Smith. Later the same day he hit on a scheme that would enable him to begin trimming his own American staff, despite the Ambassador's objections. In the past twenty-four hours the airlift of emergency supplies to Saigon had been cranked into gear, and Smith knew that large numbers of cargo planes would soon be shuttling between Clark air base in the Philippines and Tan Son Nhut. Since the return flights to Clark were to be made with the cargo bays empty, the airlift provided a unique opportunity to begin flying Americans out of Saigon in large numbers. The problem was to find a way to make this palatable to Martin and the South Vietnamese.

For a solution, Smith turned to Martin's old adversary, Admiral Gayler in Honolulu. In a personal message to Gayler around midday he proposed accelerating a series of routine DAO personnel cuts that had been slated for the following June. This would give him an excuse to begin moving out some of his own staffers. Gayler approved the scheme without hesitation—and in an effort to give it urgency, pointed out in his return cable that the Communists could attack Saigon within five days if they wanted to.

Armed with Gayler's message, Smith called on Martin to try to win his approval. He knew the Ambassador would not be happy with the plan, but he attempted to cast it in terms Martin could accept. The removal of DAO's non-essentials, he said, could be presented to Thieu as an economy measure, designed to release funds for Saigon's war effort. Happily, Martin was im-

---

its territories is on a visa as an American dependent or some other special-category *immigré,* or under a "parole" granted by the Attorney General, and as Martin correctly pointed out to Congress, he did not have benefit of the broader, more inclusive parole until the end of April. What he failed to mention, however, was that he had been instrumental in obscuring the need for a flexing of the immigration rules. If he had seen fit to alert Washington earlier to the desperateness of the military situation, officials in the State Department and the White House would have had a better case to put before the Attorney General and the Immigration and Naturalization Service.

pressed with this logic and by the end of the meeting had agreed to let Smith proceed as he wanted.

Later that afternoon, Smith's deputy, Air Force Brigadier General Richard Baughn, summoned the service attachés to his office, read them Gayler's cable and ordered them to set the planned staff reductions in motion. At the same time two high-ranking naval officers were dispatched from Gayler's headquarters to assist the DAO planners in their work. Rear Admiral Owen Oberg was sent in to serve as liaison with the 7th Fleet, backstop for Task Force '76, and Rear Admiral Hugh Benton arrived to supervise sealift operations out of the northern half of the country.

During the next few days Smith and his colleagues eagerly exploited the momentum they had injected into the Embassy's evacuation planning. Food and bedding sufficient to support 1,500 people for five days on a self-sustaining basis were moved into DAO's fledgling evacuee processing center, and Smith asked Gayler for two Marine companies to reinforce DAO's already jittery Vietnamese guards.

In addition, on 2 and 3 April, Colonel Charles Wahle met with other Embassy officials to try to prod them into following DAO's example. Lehmann, who presided over the meetings, found himself rapidly backed into a corner, and out of desperation, finally agreed to several of the more modest steps Wahle suggested. He would not object, he said, if the 7th Air Force in Thailand upgraded its alert status, or if DAO insisted on keeping four or five cargo ships close at hand on the Saigon River, or even if each Mission component drew up lists of Vietnamese to whom it felt obligated. Nor would he or the Ambassador oppose the departure of non-essentials or some Embassy dependents, as long as it was done discreetly.

When Wahle asked him, however, to *order* all surplus personnel out of the country, Lehmann put his foot down. All departures, he said, must remain strictly voluntary. Otherwise the South Vietnamese might suspect we were preparing to abandon them.

This stipulation, reasonable as it seemed, would have a disastrous effect on the pace of departures during the next few weeks, for as long as Lehmann and the Ambassador refused to order any American out of Saigon, each non-essential staffer remained free to choose the date and time of his leaving. And since the Ambassador continued to minimize the military crisis, few of the foot-draggers realized the risks they were running.

On the afternoon of the third Smith and his staff attempted to push the Embassy's planning one step further. Summoning representatives of other agencies to DAO, they set out to identify and locate all 6,000 Americans in the city. They finished the job in three days, using a variety of ingenious tracking techniques, including an exhaustive examination of liquor-ration files at the commissary and the membership list of the downtown sports club, Le Cercle Sportif. The resulting "density plot" served as the basis for all subsequent evacuation planning.

•   •   •

As Smith and his staff pressed ahead, others in the Embassy inevitably became caught up in their enthusiasm. Alan Carter of USIA and officials at USAID began contemplating personnel cutbacks of their own, and Polgar asked for, and received, permission from CIA headquarters to expand his own drawdown lists to include "excess" personnel in Saigon as well as "non-essentials" from Danang, Nha Trang and the other cities lost in the past few weeks. In addition, Ted Shackley began snatching an hour or two each day from the schedule of the Weyand team to try to help the Station adjust to the mounting crisis.

One of the questions he and Polgar had to address at once was whether to begin laying in the plumbing for "stay-behind" espionage operations to provide intelligence in the event of an NVA victory. In all the years of American involvement in the war the CIA had never developed such a cadre of deep-cover agents who could indeed "stay behind" to operate in a Communist-controlled Vietnam. Now, with the enemy at the gates, older Station hands who had seen Eastern Europe fall to the European Communists in the mid- and late-forties were agitating for some fast backing and filling.

Among the most outspoken was Pat Johnson's husband, Bill, a veteran counterintelligence officer and Chief of the "Saigon base" which handled the Station's intelligence operations in the capital. From the moment the Weyand team appeared on the scene, Johnson had been begging for permission to recruit some "stay-behinds" and to establish a Vietnamese émigré organization in Bangkok as a springboard for long-range agent penetration networks into Vietnam. As a concept, it was simple enough. The CIA had done the same thing with émigré groups in Eastern Europe years before.

But Shackley remained opposed. He could not believe, he said, that Congress would react to a defeat in Vietnam—if indeed one was in the offing —as it had to the falling dominoes in Eastern Europe in the 1940s. "No one will want to spend the money on such frivolities here," he insisted.

Despite such objections, Johnson eventually was allowed to undertake a few limited initiatives, but the broad strategy he proposed never got past Shackley's reservations. As a result, when South Vietnam did collapse, the CIA had no significant intelligence networks in place to keep it informed of the policies and eccentricities of the new Communist regime.

While stay-behind operations and evacuation planning continued to oc-cupy part of the Embassy staff, another problem began to weigh heavily on the calculations of all of us. Within a day or so of the loss of Nha Trang, thousands upon thousands of refugees were flooding into MR 3 from points further north, and 70,000 of them were already gathered at Vung Tau, the beach resort forty-five miles to the southeast. To ease the pressure and danger posed by the refugee flow, Admiral Benton, Gayler's man at DAO, quickly set up a plan-ning group of his own and began marshaling American resources behind the ongoing sealift out of MR 1 and 2. On 3 April the amphibious cargo ship

Durham took on 1,400 refugees at sea off Phan Rang, and the Navy's landing dock *Dubuque* picked up eighty more. They were the first American warships actually to participate in the sealift (although American freighters under charter from the Pentagon had of course been involved from the very beginning). In Washington the Administration immediately sent a letter to Congress, detailing the operation and drawing attention to the provisions of the War Powers Act that required the President to notify the lawmakers whenever American forces entered a war zone. Clearly, Ford was seeking to test the elasticity of the act. For the moment Congress did not object.

Under Benton's basic operating plan, a large number of the refugees were to be shipped south to Phu Quoc Island off the tip of the delta and resettled there. It was hoped that their isolation would prevent their fear and panic from spreading to the rest of the population. But the very feature that made the scheme so appealing to the Embassy—the remoteness of Phu Quoc—made it unacceptable to the refugees themselves. The last thing they could tolerate after the terrible ordeal of their passage south was the prospect of being separated from friends, relatives and governmental protection on the mainland. Consequently, no sooner had the first shiploads been disembarked on the island than rioting and fighting broke out, and the government was obliged to send security forces to restore order.

In addition to isolating the refugees, Embassy officials resorted to one other trick to keep their panic from seeping into Saigon itself. Hours after the collapse of Nha Trang, Ted Shackley paid a call on the chief of Saigon's municipal police force to ask him to cordon the city off against both refugees and army stragglers. Reluctantly, the Vietnamese official agreed, and on 3 April the city was officially closed to all but legitimate, fully documented residents. It was a crucial decision, for it fenced the city off from the fires of panic and chaos smoldering in the countryside, permitting all of us to ride out the final days of the war in a vacuum of relative tranquillity.

For Graham Martin the plight of the refugees was particularly painful, for he had once served as a State Department coordinator for a U.N. refugee program and knew the misery of the world's uprooted firsthand. But Martin also saw in the vast human tragedy now sweeping across South Vietnam an opportunity for political maneuver and gain. The idea first came to him as the result of the exertions of Ed Daly, the imaginative owner of World Airways, the charter airline that had been so instrumental in the evacuation of Danang. For days Daly had been trying to organize an airlift of Vietnamese orphans to the United States as another personal contribution toward easing the suffering he saw around him. When Martin heard of the scheme he promptly urged the White House to organize a similar airlift of its own. As he explained in a letter to Saigon's Minister for Refugee Affairs, he hoped that the spectacle of hundreds of Vietnamese babies being taken under the American wing would generate sympathy for the South Vietnamese cause around the world. The White House apparently shared this sentiment, for on 2 April, AID officials in Washington announced "Operation Baby-lift," an emergency program whereby over two thousand Vietnamese orphans were to be flown to foster homes in the United States under a new immigration "parole."

In a sense "Operation Baby-lift" was a fraud from the start, for few of the children who were to benefit from it were refugees. Most of them, in fact, had been languishing for years in Saigon's orphanages and were in no immediate danger from the Communist offensive. But the majority of us in the Embassy chose to overlook this minor detail, and applauded the enterprise as a worthy first step in the right direction.

General Smith was especially enthusiastic, for he quickly realized that the baby-lift could be made to serve his own purposes. What better way to smuggle out large numbers of DAO's female employees, he reasoned, than by slipping them onto the orphan flights as nurses and bottle-washers? Within hours of Washington's announcement he and his staff were already alerting DAO wives and secretaries to prepare to depart.

In the meantime, the war continued to sweep in toward Saigon like an onrushing tide. During the first few days of April three NVA divisions pushed deep into southern Tay Ninh Province to try to interdict the road running south to the capital, and on the third the 341st NVA Division dislodged the defenders of Chon Thanh forty-five miles due north of Saigon, the only remaining government outpost in the area.

As news of these setbacks swirled through the capital, the western community was seized with a fit of wanderlust. The demand for seats on the twice-weekly Pan Am international flight doubled almost overnight, China Airlines found itself booked solid through the ninth, and a large proportion of the 600 Iranian, Hungarian and Polish ICCS members began packing their bags.

Ambassador Martin tried to damp down the nervousness with a show of unconcern. "There's no danger to Saigon," he declared confidently to a newsman on the third. But his blitheness was beginning to wear badly, both on the Saigonese and on some of his American colleagues. Intelligence analysts at Gayler's headquarters sent a cable to the Pentagon on the same day, disparaging the Ambassador's contention that Saigon or the surrounding area could be defended as an enclave—"the chaos resulting from the influx of refugees," they wrote, "would cause the collapse of the GVN"—and in Washington, Secretary of Defense Schlesinger began voicing his own reservations more forcefully. The next thirty days, he told reporters, would tell whether South Vietnam in any form lived or died.

At the State Department, meanwhile, Lionel Rosenblatt and his luncheon conspirators continued to agitate for an expanded evacuation program, sufficient to assure the rescue of 200,000 Vietnamese or more. Despite considerable resistance among their superiors, none of whom wanted to commit themselves until Weyand's return, they won an important preliminary concession. On the basis of their recommendations, Assistant Secretary Habib agreed two days after the collapse of Nha Trang to convert an informal working group in his own office into a task force to coordinate the Department's evacuation planning.

For the past several days, ever since Weyand's departure for Saigon, the White House itself had been refraining from direct comment on the Indochina crisis. But with the upsurge in fighting around Saigon on the third, President Ford finally broke his silence. In a statement to newsmen at his vacation retreat in Palm Springs he openly criticized Thieu for his overhasty decision to withdraw from the highlands and admitted that the evacuation of the 6,000 American citizens in Vietnam was indeed under consideration. Touching on one of the most sensitive issues of all, he also made it clear that by his interpretation of the War Powers Act he was entitled to use forces to assist in evacuating American citizens from any war zone in the world.*

His remarks on this point were hardly fortuitous, for in addition to the mounting pressure in the immediate Saigon area, the Administration was now facing imminent catastrophe in Cambodia. In fact, Phnom Penh's military situation had grown so perilous in the past day or so, the White House had finally decided to move ahead with the withdrawal of the entire American community there.

On the morning of the fourth Ambassador Dean called his staff together to announce the decision. The evacuation of all Americans in Cambodia, he said, was to be undertaken in two days' time. For Dean himself this dramatic turn was something of a personal triumph, for he had been pleading with Washington for days not to risk the lives of Americans as the angling for a political settlement went on.

But, as it happened, he was not to gain satisfaction just yet, for within the next few hours he received another top-secret advisory from Washington, this one postponing the final evacuation for a little while longer. At the last minute Kissinger had decided that the American presence in Phnom Penh was still needed as a "stabilizing influence" while he continued to try to work out a deal with Sihanouk and his Chinese patrons.

By midday on the fourth the Defense Attaché's compound in Saigon was bustling with activity. Carpenters and technicians were hard at work, tearing down fences, uprooting lampposts and installing facilities for a functioning evacuation center.

---

*During the past few days White House lawyers had prepared a brief for Ford on the legislative debate surrounding the War Powers Act. Among other things, they pointed out that when the bill was being discussed in committee and on the floor of Congress, even its proponents had allowed for the use of forces to rescue American citizens abroad in an emergency. For lack of any better authority, Ford was now determined to use this loophole to justify the commitment of the marines who were standing by on shipboard off the Indochina coast.

During the morning an Air Force C-5A Galaxy jet, the largest air transport in the world, touched down with a huge shipment of new war matériel for Saigon's army. As the plane was unloaded, DAO staffers assembled the 243 orphans and the forty-four DAO employees and other Americans who were to be flown out to the Philippines on the same plane that afternoon. It was be the first evacuation flight under General Smith's "thinning-out" program and "Operation Baby-lift."

What happened in the next several hours doubtless would remain forever imprinted on the memories of those who lived through it. Thirty minutes out of Saigon, as that big C-5A winged its way toward the coast, the pilot noticed a blinking red light on his instrument panel, signaling trouble with one of the hatches. He radioed the control tower at Tan Son Nhut to say he was turning back, and then swung the transport around and began nosing it down. But just as he was beginning his final approach to the airfield, an explosion rocked the plane, the bottom ramp was blown away, leading to immediate decompression in the lower cabin, and many of the fifty adults and children strapped in their seats there died instantly from lack of oxygen. Others were sucked out through the gaping hatchway.

The plane skidded for almost half a mile in a rice paddy just south of Tan Son Nhut, as debris and twisted metal churned into the lower deck. Once the plane shuddered to a stop, water rushed in, drowning many of those who had survived the pressure loss and the crash itself.

Air America choppers were on the scene almost at once, and for the next several hours ferried the survivors and the dying to ambulances waiting on the tarmac. A CIA secretary who had gone out to Tan Son Nhut to see the orphan flight off later described what she witnessed. "As the children were carried off the choppers and piled into the ambulances, you couldn't tell if they were alive or dead. Nearly every one of them was covered from head to toe with mud, and only after the ambulance began unloading at 'Third Field' [the former U.S. Army hospital near Tan Son Nhut] were we able to sort out the casualties. The nurses would simply pass the children under the shower, saying, 'This one's alive, this one's dead.'

"After a while several other Americans and I began stuffing the uninjured children into jeeps and cars to take them back to the orphanages. Some were still so frightened they couldn't even cry. They were just like limp little rags in our arms.

"None of the babies had name tags, simply wristbands saying 'New York,' 'New Jersey,' and so on, the addresses of their new foster homes. So one of the big problems we faced was simply figuring out who the survivors were. I ended up spending the rest of the afternoon checking wristbands against name lists—and drawing up death notices to send to foster parents in the States."

The downing of the C-5A struck all of us like a blow to the heart. Those of us who remained in the CIA situation room throughout that terrible afternoon and evening listened in stunned silence as our contacts at Tan Son Nhut read off the names of the American casualties, letter by letter, over the CIA's "Diamond" radio network. By final tally, the crash was the second worst in aviation history: over 200 children and all but one of the DAO employees on board had been killed.

Nor were the broader implications of the accident—the result of a faulty latch on the cargo doors—lost on us. If one hastily organized flight could end so disastrously, how much more dangerous a massive airlift under full wartime conditions might be!

General Smith was particularly anguished by the tragedy, for it was he, after all, who had insisted on packing so many Americans onto the baby-flight. But he refused to allow what had happened to divert him from the task he had set for himself. The following day, as DAO teams picked through the wreckage for bodies, hundreds of additional orphans and DAO non-essentials were hustled aboard newly arrived air transports for their own flight out.

Ambassador Martin, meanwhile, did his best to contain the shock and trauma in the Embassy. Among the first of those he ministered to was Alan Carter, the USIA chief. On the morning after the crash Carter drafted a cable to Washington warning of "growing unrest in Saigon bordering on panic." When Martin received a copy, he exploded. "There's no panic here," he thundered at Carter, "and we all have to be careful not to promote panic in Washington." Then he added, "And if Washington had checked with me before using that C-5A, I wouldn't have given authorization. Those kids would still be alive."

Carter staggered out of Martin's office, his head reeling. Not only did the Ambassador seem cynically preoccupied with assessing blame for the accident; he also appeared convinced that a sense of urgency, such as Carter's own, had led to it. The USIA man resolved, from this point on, to communicate his own private worries to Washington by long-distance telephone, without clearing with the Ambassador at all.

The Bombing

The day after the C-5A crash General Weyand and his team flew into Palm Springs, California, to present their findings on the Indochina crisis to the President and Henry Kissinger. The report they brought with them contained snippets of the military assessment I had prepared for Carver several days before, including references to the almost ludicrous imbalance of forces and even to the possibility of military defeat for the government. "The odds are," it declared, "that in pure capability terms the North Vietnamese can move existing units in South Vietnam faster than the GVN can form new ones."

Beyond this bold beginning, however, the authors slipped rapidly into platitudes and vague generalities. While acknowledging that recent defeats had weakened "the social and political structure of the country," they argued that it was impossible to tell to what extent. Nor were they willing to be any more precise in projecting Communist intentions. Two options, they said, were now open to the North Vietnamese: a direct military takeover or, alternately, consolidation of recent gains followed by a lopsided negotiated settlement. But they refused to try to guess which Hanoi preferred, arguing that the Politburo itself had probably not had time "to digest the developments of the past few weeks, even days."

Having thus begged all the vital questions, Weyand and his colleagues felt free to champion the policy the Administration clearly preferred. As they were all well aware by now, Kissinger himself favored a massive new aid allocation for South Vietnam, so if Saigon was lost, the United States could not be held responsible. Accordingly, Weyand and his group recommended a stunning $722 million in emergency military assistance for Saigon.

Initially they attempted to justify such generosity in Kissinger's own geopolitical terms. "The governments of the world know the past," they wrote, "but they will surely see any present failure to support the Vietnamese in their current crisis as a failure of U.S. will and resolve . . . Continued U.S. credibility, worldwide, hinges on whether we make an effort, rather than on an actual success or failure. If we make no effort, our credibility as an ally is destroyed, perhaps for generations. Failure now will only encourage aggression later, possibly at an immense cost in human lives, instead of only American treasure."

Once such cosmic considerations were dispensed with, Weyand and his team got down to cases. Arguing that the money was needed as a palliative for South Vietnamese morale, they insisted it would also have a restorative effect on the capabilities of the army. In attempting to demonstrate this last point, however, they encountered difficulties. Von Marbod and General Smith had arrived at the $722 million projection on the basis of what they figured was needed to refurbish four ARVN divisions and to cover the cost of equipping the army for up to "sixty days of intensive combat"—through the end of the dry season. But because the South Vietnamese themselves already had so arbitrarily revised their force reconstitution plans, there was no way of knowing if the money could now be effectively applied toward its intended purpose. Weyand and his team could not acknowledge this, of course, without overturning their argument for some massive display of support. So they avoided making any precise or grandiose claims for the $722 million, saying only, "This money is urgently needed for basic military necessity, to provide an even chance for the survival of the Republic of Vietnam."

Elsewhere in their report Weyand and his colleagues raised the ticklish subject of an evacuation. "A major multi-divisional operation by U.S. forces supported by tactical aircraft," they noted, would be necessary to ensure the safe extraction of the "6,000 Americans and the tens of thousands of Vietnamese and third country nationals to whom we have incurred an obligation." They did not go so far as to suggest, however, that evacuation planning be accelerated or that cutbacks in the American presence in Saigon be pursued in tandem with the drive for additional aid. Instead they presented the evacuation option as an alternative, to be acted upon only if and when Congress failed to provide the proposed $722 million: "If rapid tangible U.S. support is not forthcoming, we must begin now to plan a massive evacuation."

The Administration would follow their cue, postponing a final pullout until the aid debate had been resolved. American lives in Vietnam thus became hostage to that $722 million—money which by Weyand's own admission offered only an "even" chance for Saigon's survival.

Weyand's initial meeting with Ford lasted ninety minutes. By the time he, Shackley, Carver and Von Marbod sat down with the President, Kissinger had already read their report, for he had specifically directed that he be given a copy before the President received his.

Because Weyand's views so closely paralleled his own, Kissinger had no trouble endorsing them. He agreed with the general's assessment that the military situation was retrievable, if just barely, and (naturally) shared his conviction that some show of support was needed as a surety for American prestige abroad. "There is also a moral question for the United States," Kissinger told reporters after the meeting, "a question of whether when an ally with whom it has been associated for ten years wishes to defend itself, it is the United States that should make the decision for it by withholding supplies."

Throughout the discussions the one man in the Administration who might have effectively challenged Kissinger's platitudes or Weyand's recommendations was cooling his heels and his ego in Washington. Once again Defense Secretary Schlesinger had been barred from the President's inner councils. Kissinger, in fact, had explicitly ordered Weyand not to alert Schlesinger to the contents of his report until the session with the President had been concluded.

One reason Kissinger insisted on keeping Schlesinger at bay was the latter's continued negativism. Not only was the Defense Secretary still deeply skeptical of the kind of guarded optimism Weyand was peddling; he was also strongly opposed to any large new aid appropriation for Saigon. American credibility requirements, and Saigon's needs, he felt, could be adequately met with the $322 million supplemental-aid proposal that had been tabled two months before. Anything beyond that seemed to him wasteful and pointless, particularly since the South Vietnamese in his judgment were as good as defeated already.

Kissinger vehemently disagreed. He was particularly annoyed by Schlesinger's opposition to the concept of a maximum aid donation, for he felt there could be no cut-rate approach to Saigon's survival or to the preservation of American credibility in the world. He was also convinced that nothing short of the $722 million could adequately ensure Vietnamese acquiescence in an American evacuation if that should become necessary. "Our objective," he later explained to Congress, "is to bring about a military stabilization, but if that should fail and the worst should come to pass, then this request [for the $722 million] will also be the most effective way to bring about the evacuation of Americans and those Vietnamese to whom we have a moral responsibility." In short, it was Kissinger's view that if a ransom was to be paid for American lives in Saigon, only a kingly sum would do.

Kissinger never managed to persuade Schlesinger of this, and the debate over the precise amount to be requested of Congress continued for the next several days. In the meantime, the acrimony between the two men intensified, Kissinger doing his best to keep the Defense Secretary as far away from the President as possible.*

Both Weyand and Von Marbod suffered considerable anguish at this spectacle. Although they agreed with Kissinger that a maximum aid allocation was necessary, they had an abiding respect for Schlesinger and were distressed to see him so ill-treated. Several days later, as a kind of penance for being a party to it all, both offered him their resignations. Schlesinger, however, turned

---

*Ultimately President Ford ordered Schlesinger to speak out in favor of the aid proposal despite his opposition to it. Thus the one top Administration official who seemed to perceive the extent of the crisis in Vietnam, and the need for stepped-up evacuation planning, was effectively neutralized.

them down, and in an act of magnanimity that left them both moved, publicly commended them for their work and awarded them special service medals.

For those of us on the firing line, Saigon's death watch was fast becoming an around-the-clock vigil. Pat Johnson, Joe Kingsley and I were now on call day and night, seven days a week. Each of us was showing up earlier and earlier each morning to try to get a jump on the mass of cable traffic that always broke on us just after daybreak; and in the evenings, whenever a top-priority intelligence report clattered in over the teletypes, it was always one of us who was called in by the "watch officer" to look it over and determine if the Station Chief or the Ambassador ought to be disturbed.

In the past three weeks, since the abandonment of Pleiku, over 600 intelligence reports had flowed in to be processed, reviewed and absorbed, and the pressure for instant judgments on the most complex issues showed no signs of slackening. By now I was turning out a field appraisal every two days, a record for the station, and providing impromptu briefings at about the same rate.

The ten-man analytical staff at DAO and many of our State Department colleagues were straining under a similar schedule, and leisure time throughout the Mission had become a thing of memory. Our official lunch break already had been cut back from the usual two hours to a quick half-hour, if that, and the swimming pool behind the chancery was going almost wholly unused. Some of the Embassy wives later told me that they had known the end was near when a sign was posted indicating that Mike, the lifeguard, had been relieved for want of bathers.

And as if we were not facing problems enough, many of us were suddenly discovering we had many more Vietnamese "friends" than we realized. They were beginning to show up at all hours, often camping out on the doorstep overnight, so if the helicopters came in unexpectedly, they would not miss out on a seat.

Among my particular burdens was a short-stemmed twenty-one-year-old reformed "hostess" from Mimi's named Tu Ha who was desperately afraid that her long association with Americans would make her number one on the Communists' blood list. Absurd, you may say, but none of us could be sure in those days what was absurd and what wasn't. So I let her stay around, to do odd jobs and to fix dinner when the maid left early. And here was one more straw for the camel's back.

"We're all suffering from a lack of sleep now," I wrote in my pocket notebook on the seventh in the melancholy spirit of the times. "You suddenly come alive at three in the morning to the thud of not so distant artillery and listen for the rattle of tank treads in the streets signaling the move on the Palace, the coup. Sometimes you almost wish it would happen, to relieve the agony of waiting.

"Pat Johnson insinuated into a conversation yesterday, 'Well, we might not survive this ordeal,' and for the first time I fully sensed what the Vietnamese must be living with. Pat and her husband Bill have already made a death pact between themselves. If the North Vietnamese overrun the city and they can't get out, he puts a .38 slug through the back of her head, then finishes himself off.

"The lines outside the consulate building are getting longer by the day, as the homesteaders show up in droves to try to buy their Vietnamese girl friends out for one last and most important time. But Embassy management continues to pretend it's business-as-usual on all fronts, as if the rumble of artillery on the outskirts were no more than spring thunder.

"The pool in the recreation compound is mostly empty now, but the Vietnamese construction teams who've been hammering away on the upper stories of the bathhouse for weeks are still hard at it. Apparently Boudreau and his administrative staff are reluctant to call off the work lest the locals come to suspect the Americans might not be around much longer.

"But the question, of course, is not if, but when, the North Vietnamese will strike. Polgar wondered out loud yesterday if we were overestimating their strength. I told him that was the least of our worries: we've overestimated the strength of our allies.

"Company tradition notwithstanding, there're plenty of raw nerves in the Station, among both sexes. In fact, the secretaries seem, if anything, just a little calmer than their male colleagues. They don't dwell on the danger. They simply admit it to themselves and go on with their business. But the men, inevitably, are determined to prove themselves. So they strut about, exchanging weapons and war stories and slapping each other nervously on the back, even as they pop Valium tablets and advance cocktail hour toward noontime.

"Some of my associates insist on treating our occasional contingency preparations like a game, to ease the tensions. When Polgar ordered us the other day to begin destroying classified files, the secretaries in Security brought in pitchers of Bloody Marys and everyone had a great, somewhat drunk old time venting aggression and fears on the shredding machines.

"Station regs forbid any of us packing side arms except with express approval, but Polgar himself has begun toting a Browning automatic under his suit jacket and the Hawaiian-style shirts he favors on weekends, and the Station's logistics officers are handing out weapons as freely as the medics used to dispense Tetracycline and faulty diagnoses. Through some old Special Forces contacts, my office colleague [Joe Kingsley] has unearthed a vast array of exotic killing machinery—from hand grenades to Thompson submachine guns and AK-47s—as well as an ample supply of helmets and flak jackets. I've already taken one of each."

By the end of the first week in April some of my friends and colleagues were complaining there were two realities, the one they actually perceived, and the one the Ambassador and his senior staff were trying to foist on them with their eternally glad tidings. During the past few days, despite the crash of the C-5A, the latter variety had been given new currency by no less an optimist than Lehmann. In a speech before a group of local American businessmen earlier in the week he had proclaimed exuberantly that there was no danger to Saigon. The city was as secure as the American dollar, he told them. So reinvest!

Even Polgar was helping to promote this myth, though for reasons somewhat different from Lehmann's. Shortly after the C-5A accident he reminded senior Station officers for perhaps the second time in as many days not to discuss the mounting military threat with wives, children or secretaries. He also ordered Pat and Joe to begin preparing a daily "situation report" that was systematically to downplay the Communist threat and to overdramatize government strengths. This rather novel item was to be cabled to U.S. Embassies around the world, for use in generating positive comment in the international press, and in Congress, about Saigon's chances for survival. In addition, senior Station personnel were to display copies of it prominently on their own reading boards so their own staffers could "benefit" from its benign pronouncements.

Such efforts at obfuscation did not work very well, however, particularly in the Station, where the accumulation of disheartening data was simply too much for Polgar to conceal. The rumor mill and the inevitable cocktail-hour conversation provided perhaps the most telling insights into the tragedy unfolding around us, for it was here, through the personalized revelations of those who had lived through Danang and Nha Trang, that we learned what it was actually like to be caught on some remote airfield, without a chopper, in the midst of thousands of panicked Vietnamese. Then, too, as scores of nonessential staffers from Cambodia began streaming through Saigon en route home, the rumors and horror stories they brought with them gave a new edge to our worst imaginings, for it was through them that we first savored the ugly sights and smells of a lost cause on the verge of extinction.

But rumor was not the only telltale sign that the confidence in the front office was a sham. Despite his continued efforts to project a brave face, Polgar managed to cast doubt on the sincerity of this image quite early on. On 7 or 8 April, in reaction to a breakthrough in the Station's shipping arrangements, he decided to pack up his household belongings (and his wife) and move them out of the country. Needless to say, others in the Station took notice and quickly concluded that the situation must be far worse than he was saying.

Martin was especially upset over the rather hasty removal of Polgar's personal effects, and later, after the fall of South Vietnam, complained bitterly to one and all that the Station Chief had thereby helped to undermine morale within the Embassy and among the South Vietnamese.

As the days passed, Pat, Joe and I contributed in our fashion to the growing awareness of friends and associates. Periodically, one of us would slip off to a vacant office to brief an ill-informed colleague about military developments or to hand him a copy of one of my latest field appraisals, which were rapidly gaining wide if not always authorized circulation within the Embassy, like a kind of *samizdat.* At the same time I began feeding substantial information to my old friend Ken Moorefield, Martin's former aide, who after a series of assignments was now one of the Embassy's liaison officers to the ICCS. Moorefield in turn passed the gist of my most alarming intelligence to the two "friendly" ICCS delegations, the Iranians and the Indonesians, who because of Martin's moratorium on bad news had no other way of gauging the dangers around them.

While the majority of us thus groped for perspective, General Smith continued to try to nurture his fledgling evacuation program to full potential. By 7 April the number of American cargo planes shuttling into and out of Tan Son Nhut had risen dramatically, nearly a dozen mammoth C-141 transports flying in and out each day, with a smaller number of the more compact C-130s arriving nightly to pick up freight, and Smith had put his staff on notice to begin moving out at least a hundred DAO non-essentials each day.

But, alas, his directives went unfulfilled. One of the main obstacles to a speed-up was the reluctance of the several thousand American contract personnel and Army retirees who lived in Saigon and who drew a salary from DAO to leave without their Vietnamese friends. Many of them were married to local girls or had common-law Vietnamese wives and children, but without a special dispensation from immigration authorities in Washington—in the form of special paroles or some other legal document—they had no right to move these "dependents" to American soil. And, since few of the dependents themselves had passports and exit visas from the Saigon government (it normally took up to six months, and hundreds of dollars in bribes, to obtain them), even those Americans who might have considered moving their Vietnamese families to Hong Kong or Bangkok for a "brief vacation" were hamstrung.

With departures threatening to grind to a standstill, someone in the office of Smith's deputy, General Baughn, finally decided to ignore the red tape and to begin flying Vietnamese dependents and friends of DAO personnel to Clark air base in the Philippines without any documentation whatsoever. This "underground" airlift effectively solved one problem but also gave rise to a far more formidable one, for it flagrantly violated the laws of the Vietnamese, Philippine and American governments.

From its inception, the air shuttle to Clark was reserved mainly for DAO personnel and their families. Other Embassy non-essentials were expected to make their way out of the country on commercial aircraft. To speed up this process, State Department officials (at the prompting of Lionel Rosenblatt and his group) contacted Pan Am on the seventh and asked for additional flights into Saigon. The airline's executives were unwilling to bend that far, since additional flights would mean a further increase in already skyrocketing insurance rates for the Indochina circuit, but they did agree to expand the seating capacity of one of the 747s already scheduled for the Saigon run.

The Embassy, in the meantime, made a first feeble effort to deal with the "local nationals" problem. A small Mission-wide task force, inspired by DAO, met on the fifth to establish guidelines for identifying Vietnamese employees and others whose past or present contacts with Americans might invite Communist retribution. Each agency was asked to draw up "key Vietnamese personnel lists," and Shep Lowman, a State Department officer, was given responsibility for boiling them down into a master roster.

At the same time Polgar was prodded by CIA headquarters into accelerating the withdrawal of non-essential Station personnel and dependents. Our first non-essentials list was completed and circulated on the eighth, and the thirty-seven employees whose names appeared on it were ordered to be out of the country on the earliest possible commercial flight. Sadly enough, few of them complied. Some were suffering from the same inhibitions that beset their DAO counterparts and were unwilling to leave without Vietnamese families or friends. Others simply succumbed to pangs of guilt. "I remember little Lan over in our ticket office," one of them told me. "There she was, making out airline tickets for all of us, while knowing there was no way for her own family to escape. When I went by to pick up my own tickets, she was crying. She said to me, 'My country is dying.' I felt so ashamed I canceled my flight on the spot."

Perhaps unavoidably, the selection of non-essentials also became a source of tension and confusion in the Station. Polgar himself was partly to blame, for he often put the premium on rank or friendship in determining who should go or stay.

The jealousies and acrimony sparked by such practices ultimately helped to frustrate their purpose. Operatives with injured egos often postponed their departures for days as they pleaded with Polgar to reconsider their cases. Others merely ducked their check-out dates without telling anyone and retreated to the bar of the Duc Hotel to drink and complain among themselves about the inequities of the "system."

The injustice and occasional illogic of the cutbacks also proved disastrous for many of the Vietnamese on the CIA's payroll, for thanks to a bureaucratic fluke, many of the earliest non-essentials were officers responsible for running intelligence operations in the immediate Saigon area itself. As one after another of them was pulled off the streets and sent home, their "cases" were passed on to other Station officers, who often had only scant knowledge of the agents they were inheriting, no personal attachment to them and no particular interest in assuring their safety in the event of a total evacuation. It was partly for this reason that so many of our Vietnamese employees would finally be left behind.

Even as he initiated our first staff cutbacks, Polgar also reshuffled the Station's top command in an effort to bring officers to the fore whom he felt he could count on in an emergency. Bill Johnson, who apparently was not numbered among these select few, was shifted out of his position as head of the Saigon base and put in charge of organizing some kind of "stay-behind" spy network—a job which because of Shackley's objections was considered relatively unimportant. To replace him as Base Chief, Polgar chose Custer from MR 1, and also named Archer from MR 2 to head the Station's reporting and analytical staff, of which I was part.

Whatever the logic behind these changes, and some claimed it was no more than cronyism, the result was pure chaos. Neither Custer nor Archer had even a rudimentary knowledge of the military or political dynamics of the Saigon area or of the principal Vietnamese players. Their subordinates realized this at once and largely ignored them, deferring to recognized experts like Johnson for direction. The Vietnamese around Saigon did likewise (the chief of the city's municipal police force refused even to meet with Custer without checking with Johnson beforehand), and as a result, lines of command in the Station soon became hopelessly snarled, posing one more obstacle to effective contingency planning.

The elevation of Custer and Archer had yet another unfortunate consequence, for it seemed to signify official approval of their performance during the pullout from MR 1 and 2 and of their attitudes toward the entire evacuation question. One of the awful lessons their experience taught was that you could indeed survive bureaucratically even if you did not manage to save your Vietnamese employees. Management would reward you regardless.

By the second week in April both men were spreading this gospel by explicit word and deed. During a visit to Bien Hoa, fifteen miles to the east, they spelled out their views to the consulate staff with appalling candor, emphasizing the need to move out Americans early and expeditiously in the event of an evacuation. They also freely acknowledged that they had done little to provide in advance for the safety of local employees in Danang and Nha Trang.

The CIA Base Chief in Bien Hoa, "Bill Taggart," and the Consul General himself, Dick Peters, took their advice to heart and henceforth focused their own evacuation planning primarily on the salvation of their American subordinates. Some of the young CIA and State Department officers on their staffs, however, were repelled by what Custer and Archer told them. One of those who found it particularly troubling was John Stockwell, Chief of the small CIA outpost in Tay Ninh City. In his twelve months "in country" Stockwell had developed a strong personal attachment to the locals under his care, both his agents and his translators, and he was now determined to do all he could to assure their safety, whatever the oracles from Saigon said.

But Stockwell faced a practical obstacle quite apart from the attitude of his superiors. The road from Tay Ninh to Saigon was now being shadowed by Communist forces, and though helicopters could still get in and out, many Air America pilots were already reluctant to make the run because of the high concentration of Communist antiaircraft artillery in the area.

To add to Stockwell's problems, Taggart himself was becoming increasingly edgy about Tay Ninh. He had tried to chopper in a few days before, only to be driven off by Communist ground fire, and now he wanted Stockwell to withdraw his two-man American staff at once, even if it meant abandoning his twenty Vietnamese employees.

But Stockwell would not consider the proposal. He would hold his staff in place, he said, until helicopters were made available for his local employees. Finally, after several days of bickering, Taggart caved in. All of Stockwell's employees and translators were flown to Bien Hoa, just as he had demanded.

During the predawn hours of 8 April the war around Saigon suddenly heated up. Communist forces shelled a district town just south of Bien Hoa, commandos struck the Thu Duc military academy five miles east of the capital, and for the third straight day elements of three NVA divisions in the northern delta mounted harassing attacks against National Highway 4, interdicting it briefly at a point fifteen miles south of us.

I arrived at the Embassy at my customary six A.M., looked over the initial after-action data, and wondered gloomily if the city itself would remain immune for long.

Approximately two hours later I called a friend at USAID several blocks away to exchange some gossip on the evacuation planning. Hardly had I got out a full sentence than the question I posed to myself only a short while earlier was definitively and somewhat abruptly resolved. The first warning came with a burst of gunfire in the streets. Then suddenly the whine of a jet engine swept through the Embassy like a shock wave, followed by a massive explosion that set my plastic windows trembling in their frames like delicate timpani.

"What the hell was that!" my friend bellowed on the other end of the line. Without bothering to answer I dropped the phone and ducked behind my desk, fumbling in my briefcase for my .45 automatic. Almost at that instant several secretaries from the office next door rushed past me to the windows to try to peer out. I grabbed one of them and pulled her to the floor. "Get away from that window!" I screamed at the rest. "Get away and stay down!" Moments later, after forcing them all behind chairs and desks, I dashed down the hall to Polgar's office. But he, too, seemed oblivious of the danger and was standing blithely by his own window, trying to catch a glimpse of what was going on outside through the portholes in the cement artillery shield.

"Looks like someone's bombed the Palace," he said at length, his voice strained and thin. "Go up to the roof and see if you can spot the damage."

The Presidential Palace was at the end of Thong Nhut Boulevard, within easy eyesight of the Embassy, but frankly, the last place I wanted to be at the moment was up on our roof, trying to assess the impact of an air-strike-in-progress. But orders were orders, and dutiful subordinate that I was, I immediately headed for the interior stairwell to do as Polgar commanded.

As I stepped out onto the roof I could see a curl of smoke rising from an injured corner of the Palace less than a mile away. I also discovered that I was not to be alone in my vigil, for secretaries and other Embassy personnel were already hurrying up to the roof to watch the show. "An A-37 jet," someone yelled at me. "Three passes. Hit the Palace on the last one." But by now I was hardly listening. My attention, my every sense, was riveted on the brightness of the morning sky to the east where the plane had first appeared. I stared into the sun, scanning its face for an incoming black speck, straining for the whine of an engine that would signal yet another pass. Next time the pilot might aim for the Embassy itself, and if he did, the twenty or thirty of us now crowded up there on the parapets would literally be blown away like clay pigeons.

But luckily the speck had vanished, and the stillness that had settled over the street below in the wake of the plane's final dive gradually gave way to raucous voices and a frantic honking of horns as Vietnamese pedestrians pulled themselves out of the gutters and from under cars where they had sought momentary shelter.

When I finally went back downstairs, a secretary was holding a telephone call for me. It was Tu Ha, calling from her apartment. She was sobbing hysterically and I could hardly make out what she was saying.

"Are they here?" she stammered. "Are the VC in Saigon?"

"No, certainly not, Tu. Are you all right?"

"Okay," she said, "but scared. When that big bang went off I was . . ."

"Yes?" I coaxed, trying to sound calm and unconcerned.

"I was taking a shower."

"Well, you were lucky," I said, unable to keep from laughing. "The bathroom's a safe place. Well away from the windows."

"No, it was terrible," she insisted. "I don't want to die with no clothes on."

I laughed again and reassured her all was well. But as I hung up the phone I couldn't help wondering at how curious her reaction was. Tu Ha, after all, had spent much of her childhood dodging shrapnel in the streets of her native village in the delta, and a good many of her teenage years working the bars on Tu Do. And now, as if she were still an innocent in the world, she was worrying about dying in the buff!

When I hurried into Polgar's office he was already at his typewriter, banging out an after-action report for Washington. He paused long enough to take a call from an informant at the Palace: Only one minor official had been injured. Thieu was safe.

Moments later a secretary ran in with an agent dispatch that had been lying in someone's in-box since the night before. According to the report, the chief of the 23rd Tactical Air Wing at Tan Son Nhut had approached two officers the previous afternoon and proposed a bombing run on the Palace, implying he was speaking for Air Marshal Nguyen Cao Ky.

General Timmes was immediately sent out to Ky's house at Tan Son Nhut to try to check on the story. The Air Marshal vigorously denied he had had any hand in the bombing.

Later the Communists' clandestine "Liberation Radio" proclaimed that a South Vietnamese air force officer, Nguyen Thanh Trung, had been responsible. In the words of the broadcast, Trung had long been a Communist agent and had been preparing for the attack for months. CIA informants, however, soon provided another slant, claiming that Trung was merely a befuddled pilot trying to do Ky a favor without his knowledge or approval.

Whatever the truth, the incident provided some significant object lessons for us all. Most important, like nothing else in recent years, it underscored Saigon's vulnerability. For all of the sophisticated weaponry and warning systems the Americans had installed around the city, the government had been unable to prevent one determined pilot from going in for the jugular.

The Embassy had been chastened as well, for it was now painfully clear that few of us knew how to conduct ourselves in the face of direct hostile fire.

Alan Carter, the USIA chief, found the episode particularly poignant. Immediately after the plane's first pass he had phoned Boudreau's administrative office in the Embassy and asked what to do. Since the USIA headquarters was quite near the Palace, he had good reason to be concerned. One of Boudreau's subordinates took the call, but could think of nothing better to tell Carter than "use your judgment."

"Well, should we all try to move to the Embassy?" Carter asked.

"Use your judgment," the administrator repeated.

"How the hell can I use my judgment," Carter spluttered, losing what was left of his patience and temper, "if I don't know what's going on! We need guidance over here."

The following day Carter dipped into his contingency funds and bought three hundred and fifty dollars' worth of C-rations and medical supplies for the USIA compound. Boudreau's staffers installed a special radio so Carter could communicate with the Embassy in an emergency. But that was the extent of their response to his pleadings, and on the final day of the war Carter and his staff would again find themselves stranded and forgotten.

As Saigon rolled with its first body blow, our colleagues an hour away by air in Phnom Penh were facing the *coup de grâce.* By 8 April there were no more than fifty-eight U.S. officials still in the Cambodian capital, plus thirty-five other foreign diplomats, most of them now busily packing out. Ambassador Dean had offered the day before to evacuate all 300 of the Embassy's Cambodian employees, but few of them had shown any interest. If there is one thing a Theravada Buddhist (the dominant variety in Cambodia) fears more than death, it is dying outside his own native land.

The Khmer Communists, meanwhile, pushed ever closer to the city, seizing a government outpost four miles away from the airfield on the afternoon of the eighth. Shelling of the airport continued without cease, though the center of Phnom Penh remained untouched. Soon Khmer police began stopping Embassy cars on the way to the airport, ostensibly to search for illegal Cambodian evacuees. Dean and his staff reacted with alarm, since several renegade army officers had already threatened to make the Americans hostage to their own safety.

A friend of mine who had been in Cambodia for many years wrote in his own pocket journal: "Now we're expendable, for the Cambodian government as well as for Kissinger."

Spotlighting

The bombing of the Palace on Tuesday morning, 8 April, forced cancellation of my weekly military-situation briefing to the Mission Council, Martin's senior staff. I would never do another one, partly because of Polgar's increasing reluctance to risk frightening his senior colleagues with the facts and partly because both he and Martin were now convinced that negotiations, not warfare, were the key to Saigon's future.

The two of them had arrived at this conclusion from totally divergent viewpoints. It was pessimism over the military situation that led Polgar to look to the political option as the only way of saving Saigon from the torch, whereas Martin was ready to pursue negotiations because he believed that the government was still able to lead from strength. Polgar, moreover, was quite prepared to cast Thieu and his cronies aside to get negotiations started, while Martin, convinced that the government was still viable, felt it must be preserved and strengthened for the political haggling ahead. Such differences would ultimately cause considerable friction between them as they pursued their common goal, but at least initially they were reaching out in the same general direction.

From beginning to end, the evidence on which they based their hopes for a political deal was distressingly thin. On the positive side, there were the remarks by the PRG's Foreign Minister on 2 April to the effect that her government might be willing to parley with Saigon if only Thieu would step down beforehand. Since then, PRG spokesmen in Stockholm and other listening posts in Europe had reiterated this line.

The import of such straws-in-the-wind, however, had to be seriously questioned. For one thing, the North Vietnamese had often held out the promise of negotiations simply as a way of undermining support for Thieu. Also, the credibility of the PRG sources themselves remained very much in doubt. Over the years Hanoi had frequently used the PRG as a vehicle for obscuring, rather than clarifying, its intentions; indeed, the PRG spokesmen in Europe who were now declaiming about the negotiating prospects had never been regarded by the CIA or anyone else in the U.S. government as a reliable window on Hanoi's thinking.

It therefore required an almost monumental leap of faith to believe that negotiations were still possible. But Polgar and Martin accomplished this intellectual gymnastic with very little difficulty at all.

Undoubtedly one of the reasons they did so was desperation itself. How difficult it was for any of us in the Embassy in those days to ignore the few glimmers of hope on the horizon! But there was also a more concrete influence weighing in on them that constantly strengthened their illusions. For countless different reasons many Vietnamese politicians and other foreign observers in Saigon likewise had grown confident by early April that a political settlement, or at least a peaceable surrender under the guise of negotiations, had a chance. In the pressure-cooker atmosphere of the final weeks these "optimists" encouraged each other in their own vain hopes, and reinforced Polgar and Martin in theirs.

Predictably, the most desperate of those who looked to the conference table for a solution were those who believed with Polgar that the South Vietnamese had already lost the war. By the second week in April sentiment to this effect extended deep into Thieu's own entourage, and pressure for his resignation, as a first step toward accommodating the Communists, was growing even among those who had once been his staunchest supporters. Outgoing Prime Minister Khiem was perhaps the most adamant of these loyalists-turned-agitators, and it was he who drove the first wedge between Thieu and his new cabinet. Meeting with Defense Minister–designate Tran Van Don on the seventh, he persuaded him that Thieu must be removed for the good of the country.

Don actually needed little persuading. An opportunist by inclination and a plotter by habit, he had already become caught up in the anti-Thieu maneuvering through the intervention of a totally unexpected outside party. On 1 April, during a stopover in Paris after a vacation abroad, Don was contacted by representatives of French Prime Minister Jacques Chirac and asked to come to the Elysée Palace for an interview. During the meeting (as Don recounted it) Chirac told him that South Vietnam was done for, that the "three great powers" were in agreement—*"ils sont d'accord"*—that Saigon should be handed over to Hanoi, and that the North Vietnamese were ready to accept such a solution, provided it could be consummated within eight days through French mediation.

Before leaving Paris, Don opened private contacts with the PRG mission there and with exiled Emperor Bao Dai, who some dreamers believed might serve as a bridge between the two sides. A day or so later, when he returned to Saigon, he asked a long-time friend to establish a secret channel for him to the local Communist underground. Finally, after all this was done, he called on Thieu to apprise him of what Chirac had told him.

Thieu, needless to say, was unmoved, and insisted the French were lying.

Later, on the afternoon of the fifth, Don received a long-distance call from Chirac's office in Paris, reminding him that only three days remained of the deadline the Communists had set for a deal. Unable to budge Thieu, Don could offer no hope that it would be met.

It was against this backdrop that Don's meeting with Khiem took place on the seventh. Since Don saw no other way of bringing peace to the country, he readily seconded the Prime Minister's contention that Thieu would have to go.

The man whom Don and Khiem agreed to support as Thieu's replacement was none other than their old comrade-in-arms General Duong Van Minh. In 1963 they had joined with Minh to form the triumvirate that overthrew President Diem. Now they were convinced that their old alliance could be resurrected to rid the country of yet another authoritarian who had outlived his usefulness.*

For years Minh had been widely regarded both at home and abroad as the aging Hamlet of Vietnamese politics, indecisive to the point of paralysis. After the coup in '63 he had been abruptly swept aside by young generals grown impatient with him, and the Americans likewise had looked elsewhere for a spokesman and front man for their own cause in Vietnam. Only General Timmes of the CIA had bothered to stay in touch with him, often meeting him for a game of tennis at the Cercle Sportif.

The collapse of MR 1 and 2, however, had recently put a new burnish on Minh's image. Almost overnight he had become the last prayer of those who yearned for a negotiated settlement—in part because he was the only non-committed political figure in Saigon who seemed to attract any attention on the Communist side.

Minh for his part considered himself well suited to the role so many now wished on him. A self-styled neutralist, he had long believed that there were many others out there in the limbo of Saigon politics who could be rallied to the government if some way could be found to broaden its appeal. As he told Timmes in early April, he was certain he would be able to reach them. Minh also was convinced that the PRG itself and its principal figures were more southern than Communist, and that given a choice between a Hanoi-

---

*Minh, Don and Khiem jointly launched the plot that resulted in the assassination of Diem and his notorious brother Ngo Dinh Ngu in early November 1963. Several weeks before, with the knowledge and acquiescence of the American Embassy (and Washington, for a cable had recently arrived from Assistant Secretary of State Roger Hilsman indicating the Embassy should not attempt to frustrate any plotting), the three Vietnamese conspirators, as well as several other army officers, had met at the JGS compound to devise a plan. General Nguyen Ngoc Le was the first to propose killing Diem, but the job was actually left to Minh's personal bodyguard, Captain Nhung. On the night of the coup Nhung bundled Diem and Ngu into an armored personnel carrier and then shot both of them through the head as the vehicle stopped at a railroad crossing in a Saigon suburb. Nhung himself was later found dangling from a rope in his own sleeping quarters. Allegedly he had committed suicide out of remorse.

dominated unified Vietnam and a coalition with other Saigon "neutrals," they would choose the latter.*

In late March, shortly after the loss of Hué, Minh had begun playing his political hand in earnest, getting in touch with the head of the National Liberation Front and the president of the PRG. Since his own brother was a high-ranking PRG official, he could pursue these contacts quite informally, without making any commitments in advance. At the same time, upon learning of Don's exchanges with Chirac, he attempted to draw the French openly into his corner, declaring publicly that they had an important "role" to play in the quest for a settlement. The French quickly rose to the bait, and on the very day Khiem and Tran Van Don agreed to join forces against Thieu, the French Ambassador in Saigon asked for and got a secret interview with Minh.

Two days later Minh invited Khiem to his villa for a chat. Admitting he had been communicating secretly with the PRG, he declared that the French considered him a viable alternative to Thieu and capable of working out an accommodation with the Communists. By the end of the conversation Khiem had offered to support him to the hilt.

Throughout all this maneuvering CIA agents kept the Embassy informed of each new twist and development, and as the intelligence accumulated, Polgar and the Ambassador were strengthened in their assumption that negotiations were a viable alternative.

It was not Minh or Khiem, however, who nourished these hopes to full bloom, but rather, the French themselves. From the moment Chirac contacted Tran Van Don, they remained a primary force behind the search for a last-minute political deal—and unwittingly helped to bring Saigon to the very brink of self-destruction.

Why they became so deeply and cynically involved in the "peace" gambit can only be guessed at. Part of their motive may have been a simple impulse toward vengeance. Old Gaullists in the French Foreign Ministry had never forgotten, or forgiven, Washington's refusal in the mid-1960s to let them try to mediate an end to the war. The breakdown of the cease-fire was thus seen by many of them as an apt comeuppance for the Americans—and as a political windfall for them, providing an unparalleled opportunity to recoup some of France's lost influence in Indochina.†

Perhaps, too, they were spurred on by a basic misunderstanding of the Vietnamese Communists themselves. The Foreign Ministry's Indochina spe-

---

*Minh's views on the southern front organizations traced back to the mid-1950s when he had been friends with Nguyen Huu Tho, a Saigon doctor who was later coopted by the Communists to head the National Liberation Front. Minh remained convinced up until the last day of the war that individuals like Tho owed their loyalties first to the south, and then to Hanoi, and therefore could be maneuvered into supporting a neutralist coalition in Saigon.

†The French also continued to have a fair economic investment—estimated at $275 million—tied up in South Vietnam, and this no doubt contributed to their abiding political interest in the country.

cialists had long believed the "revolutionary movement" in Vietnam was far
more fragmented than the Americans claimed. Like Minh, they saw the southern half of the Communist apparatus, capped by the PRG, not as a tool of
Hanoi but as a force unto itself, capable of independent action. On the basis
of historical experience they also felt that Hanoi would never attempt to seize
power outright, but would attempt to disguise its intent by working initially
through a coalition arrangement.*

In late March and early April the flurry of ambiguous statements from
the PRG and Hanoi about the prospects for peace strengthened the French
in their conspiracy theories, and led them to believe that long-standing rivalries
between northern and southern revolutionaries were finally breaking into the
open. If French diplomacy was quick to move into the breach, they reasoned,
there was a possibility the war could be brought to a conclusion beneficial to
French interests.

The goal they set for themselves was in effect a return to history, a revival
(with some variation) of the three Vietnams that had existed throughout much
of the French colonial period. Alongside historic *Tonkin* (now the Communist-dominated north), a coalition regime was to be coaxed into existence in
central Vietnam (MR 1 and 2), where the French had once ruled through the
Emperor Bao Dai. To the south, in old *Cochin China* (MR 3 and 4), the Thieu
regime was to give way to a more broadly based government capable of dealing
with Hanoi and the new authorities to the north.

To bring this Balkanized Vietnam into being, the French devised a four-
pronged strategy. Hanoi had to be persuaded its interests lay in negotiations.
Thieu must be convinced his lay in resignation. General Minh was to be
groomed as his successor, and the Americans were to be made to believe that
their only workable option was the one French policy charted for them.

By the time Danang was lost, the French were already embarked on an
ambitious effort to realize these objectives. Secret exchanges had been opened
with the North Vietnamese at the "presidential level," and with PRG representatives in Paris, and a number of retired French army officers who had once
served in Indochina were on their way to Saigon to try to persuade old
Vietnamese comrades-in-arms that negotiations along Paris' preferred lines
were essential.

The French overtures to Tran Van Don on 1 April were part of this skein,

---

*The "coalition government" syndrome was a legacy of the 1940s' transition period in Indochina,
and many of us in Saigon still suffered from it. In August 1945 Ho Chi Minh had moved into the
political vacuum left by the defeated Japanese and the discredited Vichy French and had set up
an ostensible coalition government in Hanoi to rule over a unified Vietnam. Ho had scarcely more
claim on popularity in those days than many of the other nationalist factions in the country, and
knowing this, opted for the coalition mechanism as a way of lining up support for himself. The
experiment was short-lived. As result of decisions taken at the Potsdam conference, British forces,
landing in Saigon, soon paved the way for reassertion of French colonial rule over Vietnam, and
the country was plunged back into war. In light of the brief experience of 1945, however, the
French and others continued to believe that coalition politics was an integral part of Vietnamese
Communist strategy.

and undoubtedly were undertaken in good faith. In recent conversations with North Vietnamese and PRG representatives at various levels the French *had* been assured there was a chance for a negotiated transfer of power in Saigon, if accomplished within eight days through French offices. Yet the reliability of these assurances should almost immediately have been questioned in the Quai d'Orsay, for within a day or two of the Chirac–Tran Van Don exchange French diplomats in Hanoi sent an urgent message to Paris warning that the prospects for a negotiated settlement were being overestimated and that the North Vietnamese seemed committed to immediate and total victory. Almost coincidentally, as if to confirm this prognosis, the North Vietnamese Mission in Paris advised French officials that the precondition for anything and everything was the removal of Thieu and the severing of all ties between Saigon and the Americans—a formula that clearly left no room for bargaining. On 5 April the French duly passed these demands on to Washington, perhaps in the belief that the Americans would swallow their pride and agree to them.

Kissinger was not so obliging. In his judgment the three-Vietnams proposal put forward by the French was merely a self-serving attempt at political gerrymandering, one that would leave them a dominant influence in Indochina. And insofar as it implied an "extralegal" solution to Saigon's problems —General Minh would probably have to overleap Saigon's constitution to assume power—he feared that the result would be chaos, endangering American lives. He therefore advised Paris on the seventh that Hanoi's demands were unacceptable.

Whereupon the scene of the action again shifted to Saigon.

Jean-Marie Mérillon, the wiry and diminutive French Ambassador to South Vietnam, had two overriding passions, his job and game-shooting. Since his arrival a little less than a year before, he had shown himself adept in both. I had once seen a photograph of him taken during a hunt at Ban Me Thuot. He was shown standing over a deer he had bagged during a night excursion. First, it seemed, he had blinded the animal with a spotlight, then shot it down as it stood dazed. "Spotlighting" was the Ambassador's specialty, both in diplomacy and in the bush. He would apply the same technique in Saigon during the last weeks of the war, dazzling his political contacts with the bright light of exaggerated hopes and promises and thus rendering them vulnerable to his—and, inadvertently, Hanoi's—final ministrations.

During the first week in April he tried the tactic on Thieu's cousin, Hoang Duc Nha. Touting the viability of a tripartite Vietnam, he urged Nha to support its realization. With no trace of irony he cited the example of the French army in 1940, reminding Nha that timely accommodation with the Nazis had saved France from destruction. Nha's response was blunt and to the point. "You're crazy," he told Mérillon. "The plan is ridiculous."

The French Ambassador was not discouraged, however. In the next few days he focused his spotlight on a far more formidable prey, Graham Martin.

Mérillon's private residence and his Embassy were just next door to the

American Mission, and he could therefore drop in on Martin easily and unobtrusively at any hour of the day, to share ideas with him over a cup of coffee. Each time he did, he regaled the Ambassador with the virtues of a negotiated settlement. No, he assured him, there was no guarantee the North Vietnamese would agree to terms. But was there any harm in trying?

Martin's initial reaction was negative. He was convinced (with Kissinger) that if there was to be any change in leadership in Saigon it would have to be accomplished "constitutionally" so as to preserve some measure of stability and to maximize the chance for equitable negotiations between Thieu's successors and the Communists. Nor could he quite bring himself to accept Mérillon's contention that Saigon was now so weak, it had to sue for peace.

Still, Martin was not prepared to reject the French ideas out of hand. He was a chess player, not a wild-eyed gambler, and rather than risk everything on his own assumptions and preferences, he decided to keep his lines open to Mérillon if only to preserve his options. He ordered a door cut in the wall between the French and the American Embassies and had a private bug-proof phone line strung between them so he could confer with Mérillon discreetly, without drawing the attention of the Vietnamese or his own staff.

For privacy's sake Mérillon's own extension was installed in the bathroom just off his office, and as the days wore on, secretaries and clerks in the French Embassy grew greatly concerned for his health, for he seemed constantly to be excusing himself to go to the WC.

Even as Mérillon sought out American support for his schemes, he also drew a bead on another crucial objective. For months the French Embassy had been pursuing a discreet dialogue with General Minh through its intelligence chief, Pierre Brochand, and in early April, when Minh publicly expressed an interest in Paris' peacemaking role, Brochand seized on the remarks as a pretext for introducing Mérillon himself into the exchange.

At their first meeting on the seventh, Mérillon outlined his government's contacts with the North Vietnamese and emphasized his own conviction that Minh himself now had an important contribution to make. He did not say so precisely, though it was implicit, that Minh was Paris' first choice as Thieu's successor.

Several days later French President Valéry Giscard d'Estaing publicly called on Thieu himself to show a greater disposition toward "reconciliation." Thieu's reaction, however, was not what Paris had wanted or expected. Far from cringing before these admonitions, the Vietnamese leader promptly ordered all contacts with the French Embassy suspended until Giscard had "withdrawn" them. Mérillon thus found himself locked out of the Palace at the very moment he was supposed to be closeted with Thieu, persuading him to resign for the sake of a non-Communist Cochin China.

In an effort to regain the initiative, Mérillon resorted to a new and desperate tactic. Through Vietnamese friends and contacts he spread a rumor around town to the effect that the Communists, impatient with Thieu's delays, had decided to attack Saigon forthwith. As this chilling forecast gained currency, it sent the high command and the U.S. Embassy into a panic and diverted all of us momentarily from Hanoi's actual planning. Mérillon finally admitted to a CIA contact that he had been fibbing. Even so, the ruse continued to have perverse effects. Thereafter, whenever a report indicating Communist attacks fell into our hands, many of the stalwart optimists in the Embassy would simply shake their heads and insist, "That's only the French trying to frighten Thieu into resigning."

The French, of course, were not the only poachers who ventured into Saigon's political wilderness during the final weeks of the war to blind and befuddle the government and the Embassy. Indeed, much of the maneuvering and self-deception that beset us during those hectic days was inspired by an even more dangerous interloper, Hanoi's principal ally, the Soviet Union.

At the outset the Soviets attempted merely to capitalize on the myths the French were disseminating. On 5 April the party newspaper *Pravda* published a commentary by Yuri Zhukov that seemed to reinforce Paris' vision of Vietnam's future. Venturing beyond the latest North Vietnamese and PRG statements, which promised only "peace" in exchange for Thieu's removal, Zhukov held out the possibility of actual negotiations as a quid pro quo. "The new situation taking shape," he noted cryptically, "opens up a clear prospect for the establishment of peace."

Kissinger reacted to this smoke signal as he had to the French feelers— with indifference. Since Thieu's removal was the basic prerequisite for "peace," he saw little in it to suggest flexibility.

His reservations did not keep the Soviets from plying their objectives elsewhere. If Kissinger was not receptive, there were always those in Saigon who might be. To reach them, Moscow turned to its natural surrogates on the scene, the Polish and Hungarian delegations to the ICCS.

The Poles pursued Moscow's strategy largely through a surrogate of their own. For over a year a leading member of the PRG delegation at Tan Son Nhut had been an agent and collaborator of Polish intelligence. He also had become a frequent contact of Ambassador Mérillon. In late March, at the direction of his Polish friends, this admirably connected agent began skillfully shaping Mérillon's views to suit the purposes of Moscow and Hanoi. It was he who confirmed the French Ambassador in his conviction that Thieu's removal could lead to a political breakthrough.

The Hungarian ICCS team, meanwhile, exploited to similar effect an inside channel to the American Embassy. After months of cocktail parties and friendly socializing, the Hungarian political counselor, Anton Tolgyes, and his Military Attaché, Colonel Toth, enjoyed an easy and comfortable relationship with Tom Polgar. In early March, Polgar had tried to justify this camaraderie to CIA headquarters, explaining that the Hungarians had promised to provide him with advance warning if the North Vietnamese should decide to launch a major new offensive. His superiors in Washington had remained dubious, and as it turned out, justifiably so. The North Vietnamese had launched their attacks on Ban Me Thuot and then Hué and Danang without so much as an apologetic peep from the Hungarians.

Polgar, however, had not let that discourage him. He continued his contacts with Tolgyes and Toth and duly reported what they told him to Washington. By early April the two of them were telling him precisely what Moscow and Hanoi wanted him to hear, dropping hints that the war need not end in disaster and humiliation for the Americans. Polgar was too devoted an anti-Communist, and too experienced an intelligence officer, to accept everything they said at face value. But since he now so much wanted to believe that Saigon could be saved from the holocaust, his well-developed skepticism began to fail him.

Polgar's growing fascination with the prospect of a negotiated settlement also affected his judgment on other matters. In his determination to convince the Ambassador and the rest of us, for instance, that he was right about the chances for a truce, he soon began ignoring the countervailing intelligence. I reacted by doubling my efforts—writing more field appraisals, expanding my briefings—to underscore what our agents actually were telling us, which increasingly seemed to boil down to this: no negotiated settlement, a disguised surrender or otherwise, was remotely feasible.

As spokesman for this line, I was, admittedly, on somewhat weak footing. It was I, after all, who had helped Polgar write his cable of 2 April setting out his basic arguments for a settlement. During the past few days, however, Communist troop movements and the tone of our agent reports had convinced me I had made a terrible mistake. The North Vietnamese were indeed on a "blood scent," as the agent had warned me on April Fools' Day.

A few hours after the bombing of the Palace on the eighth I made another attempt to swing Polgar over to this viewpoint. Pat Johnson and I drew up a cable for CIA headquarters, citing "tentative indications" of impending Communist attacks "closer to the capital," including a report from "an untested agent source" who claimed that Hanoi had decided to assault Saigon itself. Since our cable did not directly address the issue of a negotiated solution, Polgar found it incontestable—and unpersuasive. He cleared it without debate, almost indifferently.

That night the Station's best agent supplied us with a crucial update of the intelligence already in hand. The Communist high command, he reported, had just issued a new "resolution" calling for the "liberation" of all territory north of Saigon during April and a move against the capital at an as yet unspecified date, with *no allowance whatsoever for a negotiated settlement*. All the "talk" of negotiations and a possible coalition government, he emphasized, was merely a ruse to confuse the South Vietnamese and to sow suspicion between them and the Americans.

When I was called into the office during the night to read over the report, I felt a strange sense of relief, despite its terrible implications. Here, from our most reliable agent, was proof of the cynicism of Hanoi's political demands and of the falseness of the French hopes for a settlement.

After scanning the document I phoned Polgar. A half-hour later he showed up to review it himself. Unshaven and rumpled, he kept shaking his head as he picked through each line for some glimmer of the impossible dream.

By the time the Embassy opened for business the following morning several corroborative reports had been filed by other sources. One forecast attacks against Saigon no later than 15 April, with the main thrust to come through the suburb of Gia Dinh on the city's southwestern flank. Another proclaimed that a new Communist field headquarters (actually General Dung's command, about which we still knew nothing) had just been set up to coordinate a three-pronged offensive against the capital.

We also received intelligence pointing to increased pressure east of Saigon, against the town of Xuan Loc. During the past few hours the Communists in fact had launched their first attacks against this all-important target and had thereby set in motion the final offensive of the war.*

I immediately sat down and wrote a field appraisal for Washington based on the new information. "The indications are," I concluded, "that the North Vietnamese have altered their plans and timetable to include attacks against Saigon possibly as early as mid-April," with "no provision for negotiations or a tripartite government."

Neither Polgar nor the Ambassador was pleased with my analysis—it was "too alarmist" for them—but since it was drawn almost exclusively from available intelligence, with little conjecture, there were no grounds for scuttling it.

Polgar did make one critical change in my draft, however. Where I had predicted "attacks *against* Saigon" he amended the text to read "attacks in and around the Saigon area." He was still trying to make room for his own wishful thinking.

The importance of the intelligence reports of 8 and 9 April cannot be overemphasized. Together with my field appraisal, they provided Martin, Polgar and Washington with an absolutely accurate picture of what lay ahead, including the lines of attack the Communists would pursue. And if someone could have brought himself to make the decision, there was still time enough

---

*It is worth noting that the opening wave of attacks against Xuan Loc corresponded precisely with the lapsing of the eight-day deadline French officials had mentioned to Tran Van Don as the grace period for a negotiated surrender. As pointed out in a previous chapter, however, preparations for the final NVA campaign had continued feverishly up through the seventh, whereupon Le Duc Tho arrived at COSVN to brief the entire command staff on Hanoi's plans for victory and to establish the coordinating committee, with Dung at its head, which was to guide it. It thus seems likely that the eight-day "grace" was merely the lead time required to lay the groundwork for the offensive and was not really related to any political motive on Hanoi's part.

(prior to the predicted offensive on the fifteenth) for an orderly evacuation, or at least a coordinated effort to plan for one.

Yet most policy-makers in Washington and Saigon now stood dazed and transfixed in the multiple spotlights of Kissinger's priorities, the Weyand report, the French initiatives and Soviet deception.*

---

*On April 9 CIA Director Colby briefed the National Security Council on our latest intelligence, but inexplicably neglected to mention the most crucial detail, the recent disclosure that all the talk of a negotiated settlement was a sham. Later in the day, however, my more perspicacious colleagues in the CIA's analytical division made up for Colby's oversight. Quoting almost verbatim from my latest field appraisal, they wrote in their daily intelligence wrap-up: "New instructions to Communist cadre in South Vietnam call for a continuation of the present offensive until 'total victory' is achieved this year. The instruction said that talk of negotiations . . . will be used merely as stratagems." It was noted that the instructions left little room for political solutions and that the Communists might now be moving into position for final attacks. "They currently have eight divisions in Military Regions 3 and 4," the CIA analysts reported; "at least four of them are positioned in an arc north of Saigon and the others are threatening population and supply routes in the area."

Eagle Pull

The Ambassador made no attempt to block my miasmic field appraisal of the ninth. But he was less indulgent with my colleagues at DAO. When a draft of their Monthly Intelligence Update reached his desk on the same afternoon he told Legro he wanted to delay its distribution for a day or so until he could make some changes.

The DAO analysts had concluded the war would be over by June, with the Communists victorious. Martin found the forecast objectionable. When Legro asked him why, the Ambassador replied simply, "Political factors. They haven't been given enough weight." Mérillon's spotlighting was already having its effect.

In addition to tinkering with the intelligence, Martin found other ways of making his optimism felt in Washington. Soon after my own intelligence appraisal was filed, he cabled off to the White House a study prepared by his economic counselor, Dan Ellerman, which purported to show that whatever the Cassandras said, the southern half of the country could be made to stand on its own. Later, in a television interview, he reiterated its conclusions. "With the exception of the coastal plain around Danang and Hué," he declared, "the lost territory [of MR 1 and 2] constituted a drain on the revenues of Saigon. What is left is the old Cochin China, the great heartland of the country. It is economically viable." It was as if he was suggesting that the war itself, and the terrible toll it had already taken, did not really matter at all.

Martin also attempted to rein in some of the more vocal naysayers on his senior staff, including Alan Carter, the USIA chief. Carter's "hysterical" reaction to the crash of the C-5A had already convinced Martin that he was a dangerous source of "negativism," but now Carter was posing another problem, demanding that the Ambassador make the USIA bureau the focal point for all Embassy contacts with the press. Martin was not about to stand for this, for he knew it would enable Carter to spread his own gloom to the already nervous media. He called the USIA man to his office on the ninth to deliver his verdict.

"All of the assets of the Embassy are mine," he said, "and I'll decide how to use them."

"I just thought we might better coordinate our dealings with the press," Carter replied.

"Please write me a memorandum on the subject."

"Oh, come on, Mr. Ambassador, we're up against the wall. We don't have time for bureaucratic niceties."

At this, Martin shifted tack. "You know, Alan," he said, "my colleagues view you as a loner. You don't join the team."

Carter asked him to name his accusers, but Martin merely shrugged. "*I'm* not saying you're a loner," he continued. "I'm simply repeating what some of my colleagues say." He then instructed the USIA chief to draw up a plan for the reorganization of the entire Vietnamese Information Ministry.

"My God!" Carter cried. "That's unrealistic. There's no time for that."

"Well, I guess my colleagues are right," Martin sighed. "When I ask you to do something really important, you turn out to be a loner . . ."

Martin would have the last word in more ways than one. Shortly after their meeting he directed Carter to go on Vietnamese television as an Embassy "spokesman" to announce that there was no real danger of a Communist takeover and that the Americans intended to stay. Reluctantly Carter did as he was ordered. His sermonette was videotaped, with Vietnamese voice-over, and within a few days it began to run on the government-sponsored television station, Carter's image materializing again and again before Vietnamese viewers, advising them all was well even as North Vietnamese forces moved to within a mile of the city.

In Washington, meanwhile, the Administration was wallowing in the backwash from the Weyand mission. Beginning on the eighth WSAG and the National Security Council launched into two days of secret sessions to consider the general's conclusions and recommendations. The debate over the efficacy of his proposed $722 million aid package continued unabated, Kissinger arguing for it, Schlesinger against. At the same time several Administration officials began pressing for a little more activism on the evacuation issue. CIA Director Colby, increasingly dubious of Saigon's survival prospects, urged a step-up in the withdrawal of Americans and "high-risk" Vietnamese, and challenged Martin's view that such a move might provoke reprisals against the American community. Schlesinger and the chairman of the Joint Chiefs of Staff, General George Brown, also were in favor of accelerated cutbacks, but unlike Colby, they were concerned primarily with the removal of Americans and high-cost military equipment, not the rescue of Vietnamese. Schlesinger insisted that the cold, hard realities of U.S. interest demanded the first, but not necessarily the second.

Kissinger was unwilling to embrace either extreme. Citing Martin's own expressions of confidence, he maintained that an immediate evacuation was not necessary, and would only weaken Thieu's hand at the very moment additional American aid might save him. He also hammered away at his old argument, so neatly limned in the Weyand report, that nothing must be done (including an evacuation) to signal to the world a lessening of support for our Saigon ally.

Ultimately Kissinger's views prevailed. The decisions reached during the two-day session represented merely another stall-off to win time for the aid debate. While preparations for a total withdrawal were to be expanded, the final "hard pull" itself was to be postponed. Under Kissinger's scenario, Gayler and Martin were to complete their evacuation planning by 19 April—by which point (it was hoped) Congress would have reached some determination on both the aid proposal and the legalities of introducing combat forces to protect an evacuation. In the meantime, Martin was to step up the "thinning-out" process already under way, cutting the American community down to 1,100 in the next two weeks so that if a full evacuation became necessary after the nineteenth a small fleet of choppers would be sufficient to handle it.

The Administration also was to seek a relaxation of U.S. immigration rules so Vietnamese dependents could accompany their American relatives to the United States. Unlike Schlesinger, Kissinger considered it vital to provide for the rescue of as many Vietnamese as possible—for the sake of America's global honor and prestige.

To the dismay of some of his colleagues (and the French), Kissinger continued to reject any direct political overtures to the North Vietnamese, since in his view they were holding all the bargaining chips. But he did agree to certain indirect initiatives, including a demarche to the Common Market nations, calling on them to issue a cease-fire appeal to Hanoi and a diplomatic note to the Soviets and the Chinese inviting them to reconvene the Geneva conference on Indochina provided for in the Paris agreement. He also endorsed continued efforts to promote peace in Cambodia through French mediation and the restoration of Sihanouk, but was still unwilling to order a total American evacuation from Phnom Penh.

To some of those who participated in the WSAG and NSC sessions Kissinger in fact had never seemed so inflexible on so many issues—or so intolerant of debate. He did not attempt to maintain even a façade of amicability toward his two severest critics, Colby and Schlesinger, and time and again subjected them to incredibly abusive language, accusing them of trying to "cover your asses" with their warnings and their pleas for early evacuation. His impatience no doubt stemmed from his own awareness of just how great his gamble was. "I can recall no set of discussions between the President and his senior advisors," he later told a Congressional committee, "that were more prayerfully conducted than these."

While the Administration's top officials dickered over grand strategy their aides and subordinates attempted to keep the main priority in view. Throughout the marathon discussions in WSAG and the NSC, Ken Quinn of the National Security Council staff saw to it that the latest and most alarming intelligence reports were inserted in the front of the President's briefing book each morning so they would not be overlooked. Parker Borg, Habib's assistant and one of the most active members of Rosenblatt's informal planning group, persuaded the Pentagon to press for an updating of the Embassy's own evacuation plans, and Rosenblatt himself succeeded in mobilizing his State Department superiors behind an effort to avert a cutback in Pan Am commercial service out of Saigon.

One young State Department officer even went so far as to leak to reporter friends the gist of my latest appraisal of the military situation so Kissinger would have no excuse to ignore it.

As the Administration continued its policy deliberations the Embassy quickly became caught up in the swirl. Within hours of the first WSAG meeting we were deing deluged with requests and proposals, particularly with respect to the evacuation issue, and almost in spite of ourselves we were forced to address it more closely ourselves.

At Kissinger's insistence, one of the first things we attempted was a sorting out of our own evacuation plans. Al Francis suggested that General Smith be put in charge of the undertaking, since he and his DAO staff already seemed to have a good idea of what it might entail. Given the pressures of the moment, Martin agreed, and on the ninth directed Smith to assume control of all the Embassy's contingency preparations.

Smith moved promptly to test his prerogatives. In an effort to hasten "voluntary" departures he canceled PX privileges for the retired Army personnel living in Saigon and ordered a revised estimate of the number of his own 1,000 contract and staff employees he could release without putting DAO out of business. In addition, his Army Attaché, Colonel Wahle, was directed to begin translating four prospective evacuation schemes into practical options.

The first two options Wahle "gamed out" provided for the step-by-step evacuation of 3,000 to 5,000 Americans and select Vietnamese on charter and commercial planes; the second two envisioned a combined sea- and air-lift involving many more people, possibly culminating in an extraction by chopper out of DAO or some other staging area. Since commercial as well as military aircraft were still flying into and out of Saigon in large numbers, part of Wahle's task was simply organizational, the fitting of all these assets into complementary operating schedules. But one of the options, the last one, demanded much more. Since the crux of it was a helo-lift out of the DAO compound itself, special flight routes, landing zones and numerous other technical arrangements were required. "Option IV," as it was code-named, also posed a special security problem. As the final stage of an American withdrawal, it was bound to bring to a head any smoldering resentments among the population.

By the evening of the ninth, the Navy Attaché, Captain Carmody, had completed plans for a riverborne evacuation—to complement any final airlift —involving three or four freighters operating from the Newport docks just outside the city. In the meantime, a group of Marine officers had arrived from

Gayler's headquarters to help Wahle prepare for Option IV itself. Under the blueprint they devised, bus convoys and small Air America choppers were to collect passengers at designated assembly points around town on "E-day" and shuttle them to Newport or to waiting planes and helicopters at Tan Son Nhut. Since this pickup and delivery phase was one of the most delicate aspects of the entire operation, several DAO technicians set to work on it at once, charting bus routes and collection points around the city. Ultimately twenty-eight Embassy buildings were designated as official bus stops. Of these, thirteen were found to have roofs sturdy enough to support a small UH-1 helicopter, and soon DAO construction teams attacked the buildings like marauding huns, tearing out chimneys and television antennae, uprooting elevator cupboards and anything else that might inhibit the incoming Hueys. They also asked the Embassy for permission to paint large H's to the exact dimension of helicopter skids on each of the pads to facilitate landings. At first Martin turned them down flat, claiming the H's would excite maids and washerwomen as they went up each day to hang out their laundry. But finally, as a compromise, he agreed to allow the skid lines to be marked out in dots.

No one was fooled. Vietnamese could read the meaning of a dotted line as well as the rest of us. And each day, as the DAO workmen on the roof of my own apartment complex at 6 Chien Si Circle sent loads of cement and rooftop refuse scuttling down long vertical chutes to the street, the maids and valets would gather out front and lay bets on when the big birds were coming in.

As the DAO planners plunged ahead with their myriad schemes, others in the Embassy pitched in to help. The Air America operations chief briefed the thirty-four pilots on his staff on the rooftop evacuation plan and offered to release any of them who thought it too risky. Only three of them did, and the rest stayed on to perform heroically on E-day. Al Francis, meanwhile, gathered together some of his former staffers from Danang and put them to work locating Vietnamese from MR 1 and 2 who ought to be included in any airlift out of Saigon.

Throughout all this initial planning Martin remained fervently opposed to one aspect of it everybody else thought was essential—the introduction of American combat forces to provide assistance and protection. Such a move, he argued, could precipitate the Vietnamese backlash he was so desperately trying to avoid.

The U.S. military, however, was unmoved by his arguments, and on the ninth, Admiral Gayler sent Washington his estimate of what a full American evacuation out of Saigon would require in terms of armed security. In the event of a withdrawal over the beaches through Vung Tau, he said, an entire Army division plus 3,000 marines would be needed to secure the road from Saigon to the port city. A full-scale airlift out of Tan Son Nhut would demand two divisions, and a helo-lift out from the airfield or from other pads around the city, 3,000 to 5,000 marines with an Army division standing by in reserve.

Gayler's projections actually overdrew the requirement—less than a thousand marines would prove sufficient for the final airlift—but it helped to clinch Washington's thinking on the need for some kind of security force on E-day.

It also drove Martin into a fury.

Around midday on the tenth General Baughn, Smith's deputy, chaired the first Mission-wide evacuation-planners' meeting. It was not a very productive session, since the Ambassador had refused to authorize discussion of anything more than the drawdown of non-essentials. But a few hours later Baughn himself ventured somewhat further. Responding to a Pentagon query, he drafted a message to Washington—similar to Gayler's the day before—outlining various evacuation "options" and calling for the commitment of troops for protection. He then submitted the cable to the Ambassador's representative at DAO for clearance. The officer on duty apparently did not realize how controversial its topic was, for he "signed off " on it without checking with Martin at all.

Meanwhile another project with which Baughn's name had become associated was running into trouble. During the past several days the airlift of undocumented Vietnamese to Clark air base in the Philippines had continued unchecked, and Ambassador William Sullivan in Manila was now under intense pressure from the Philippine government to stop the influx. He had already sent several cables to Washington and Saigon, demanding a halt and proposing that all the illegals be sent back to Vietnam.

His messages caused considerable unease at the State Department, since no one wanted to backtrack as he suggested. Finally Rosenblatt and his luncheon group devised a compromise and got it approved: while no more "illegals" were to be admitted to Clark, those already there were to be "detained" and "processed" until a special immigration parole could be worked up for them. Appropriate instructions were immediately dispatched to both Manila and Saigon.

When Martin received the directive on the afternoon of the tenth he tore it up and neglected to inform either Smith or Baughn about it. He resented Sullivan's imperious tone and Washington's interference. But an hour or two later, as he was going through some other cable traffic, he came across something that prompted him to look again at DAO's activities. It was a copy of the message Baughn had sent to Washington earlier in the day on the combat-troop requirement for Tan Son Nhut. Reading over the cable, Martin was infuriated, both by its content and by the fact that Baughn had presumed to send such a message home without clearing it directly with him. Without batting an eye, he picked up a secure line, put in a direct call to the Pentagon and demanded that Baughn be removed immediately, on grounds of insubordination. In particular, he tried to implicate Baughn in the unauthorized airlift to Clark.

The following day the Pentagon did as Martin demanded, yanking

Baughn out of Saigon—and thus divesting the Embassy of one of its most energetic evacuation planners.

How quickly the bureaucracy attacks its own! Let a man fall from grace and even those he considered friends are likely to turn on him. So it was with Baughn. After the collapse of Vietnam, General Smith insisted that the Air Force general had been little more than a "fighter jockey," and other members of the Embassy staff tried to blame him for a variety of Saigon's own problems, including the weakness of the South Vietnamese air force.

But the truth is that Richard Baughn, through someone else's bureaucratic error, had become a symbol for the Ambassador of all the dangers he sensed around him: the pressures for an accelerated evacuation and the threat of insubordination among a restive staff. And Martin had reacted characteristically, with massive preemptive action.*

As the Embassy struggled with Martin's inhibitions, three NVA divisions continued to hammer away at Xuan Loc, thirty-eight miles northeast of Saigon. During the first two days of battle, 9 and 10 April, over 1,000 rounds of rocket and artillery fire rained in on the city's 100,000 hapless residents, and a single NVA regiment briefly penetrated the city's limits. The following night government forces, now numbering 25,000 troops (nearly a third of the remaining South Vietnamese army), counterattacked and drove the invaders out. But the shelling continued without cease and the South Vietnamese air force added to the carnage by hurling its bombs in from the now-customary 10,000 feet.

Against this backdrop Polgar decided to make another pitch to Washington for some remedial political action. On the morning of the tenth his deputy, John Pittman, called me to his office and outlined the plan. I was to prepare a new field appraisal, he said, this one examining all the possible ways of carrying out an evacuation. In conclusion I was to show that *none of them would work.* "That's right," he emphasized as I gasped in surprise. "Polgar wants to convince Washington there's no alternative to political intervention."

As I walked back to my office I felt numb, and totally disheartened. The upsurge in military activity obviously had had the "wrong" effect on Polgar. Instead of focusing his attention on the need for an accelerated evacuation, it had merely quickened his resolve to force a settlement. And now I was to contribute to this ill-considered scheme by showing there was no other way.

---

*In testimony before Congress a year after the fall of South Vietnam, the Ambassador denied he had fired Baughn—which was technically true: he had had the Pentagon and Smith do it for him. In another Machiavellian twist he also tried to associate himself with the very issue he had used as a pretext for getting rid of the Air Force general: "My only point was that it was alleged General Baughn—I don't know whether this was true or not and I certainly would have great sympathy for him were it true—noticing the reverse empty lift going back to Clark, began to put . . . the Air Force Vietnamese employees on these planes going back. As I say, I had great sympathy with that."

It took little imagination, however, to make a credible argument for Polgar's basic thesis. If we attempted, for example, to move large numbers of Vietnamese overland to Vung Tau for evacuation over the beaches, as some Embassy planners suggested, the army or the Communists themselves might well interfere. Alternately, any attempt to airlift masses of Americans and Vietnamese out of Tan Son Nhut would very likely lead to wholesale rioting. Conclusion: a large-scale evacuation, involving 100,000 people or more, was impossible, or nearly so.

My study was sent off to Washington "back-channel" in a highly classified format and was not circulated within the Embassy at all. Only Martin got a chance to review it before release. He told me he did not entirely agree with its conclusions. Although he was willing to concede the difficulties of an evacuation—particularly one involving large numbers of Vietnamese—he was not ready to write it off as impossible.*

By the time my study had been flashed off to CIA headquarters I was close to despair. Having glimpsed the full scope of the evacuation problem, I was distressed by the inadequacy of our preparations and determined to alert colleagues at home to it. The problem was: how to accomplish this without incurring Polgar's wrath. Luckily I did not have to search very far for a solution. Just before the end of the day on the tenth I received a call from my two friends Moose and Miessner, who were still snooping around Saigon on behalf of the Senate Foreign Relations Committee. They wanted me to provide some additional background information for their final report to Congress. I realized at once that here was the opportunity I had been looking for.

That night the three of us met at the café of the old Majestic Hotel down by the waterfront. After a tranquilizing Scotch-on-the-rocks I began spinning out the particulars of our crisis: the North Vietnamese were now advancing against Xuan Loc; the most recent intelligence foreshadowed an attack on Saigon perhaps as early as mid-April; and the Embassy's evacuation planning, apart from DAO's contribution, remained haphazard.

Moose nervously fingered his mustache as he listened, and twice Miessner nearly choked on his water-buffalo steak. The two of them had been in Phnom Penh for the past day or so. They had no idea the Vietnam situation had worsened so dramatically.

After our conversation they drove to the Embassy and sent a cable to their superiors in the Senate, advising them they were returning home immediately with bad news. They also drew up a preliminary report on what I (and others)

*In Washington my dismal thesis was more readily accepted. The National Security Council, in a study of its own, likewise concluded that the chances for a large-scale evacuation (100,000 people or more) were minimal. Similarly, in his cable to the Pentagon on the ninth, Gayler argued that without the tacit acquiescence of the Saigon government and the populace, not even the commitment of substantial numbers of U.S. security forces could assure success.

had told them, and were about to cable it out through the Embassy's communications room when Moose had grim second thoughts. They had better file it through the Embassy in Manila the following day, he suggested, so Martin would have no chance to censor it.

Within hours of my conversation with the two Senate staffers, President Ford went before a joint session of Congress to announce several of the decisions recently hammered out by WSAG. Promising a prompt cutback in the number of American civilians in Saigon, he asked Congress to reaffirm his authority to use military forces in any full-scale evacuation. He also called for $722 million in military aid for South Vietnam, and $250 million in emergency economic assistance, saying that the money was needed to give Saigon "a chance to save itself "—and to buy time for a "political settlement." Moreover, "if the worst were to happen," he declared, such generosity "would at least allow the orderly evacuation of Americans and endangered Vietnamese," whose numbers, he said, ran into the "tens of thousands."

Nowhere did Ford mention the Administration's peace plan for Cambodia. In discussing the situation there, he said only that additional U.S. aid might be "too late."

Congressional reaction to the speech was swift and almost uniformly negative. Within hours, even Senators and Congressmen who were normally sympathetic toward South Vietnam were decrying the uselessness of throwing more good money after bad.

The President's remarks concerning the use of combat forces also drew heavy fire. Some Congressmen were opposed to the idea on general principles. Others, while favoring the commitment of troops to protect American lives, were against their being used to help evacuate Vietnamese. Much of the controversy sprang from the vagueness of the Administration's own pronouncements on the issue. In draft legislation sent up to Capitol Hill, Ford asked merely that none of the existing Congressional strictures on military activity in Indochina be interpreted as "limiting the use of armed forces" to assist "in a humanitarian evacuation." Many legislators read a sinister meaning into this loose language. It was, after all, just such a vaguely worded document—the Gulf of Tonkin Resolution of 1964—that had originally deprived it of its prerogatives in the war-making sphere. And hadn't the Johnson Administration committed forces to the fighting in Santo Domingo in 1965 on the pretext of evacuating Americans?

In an attempt to find a middle ground, several Senators suggested an alternative to the President's request, one that would have granted the authority he sought under rigidly defined conditions, while establishing Congress' right to approve or disapprove the use of American forces in any evacuation. But the White House quickly signaled its opposition, claiming that any such measure would represent an intolerable intrusion on the President's own Constitutional powers.

For all practical purposes the debate was very nearly beside the point even as the White House and Congress squared off. Several days before, Ford had unilaterally committed warships to the sealift operations off MR 1 and 2, and had thus established a precedent for taking such action without express Congressional approval. Moreover, within twenty-four hours of his speech the pressures for an even more ambitious initiative along these lines—this time, in Cambodia—would make all Congressional objections irrelevant.

By the morning of the eleventh Khmer Communist forces had entered three villages just north of Phnom Penh and had stepped up their shelling attacks against the airfield. Shortly after daybreak a chartered American DC-3 was struck by shrapnel as it taxied down the runway, and four of its crew members, including the free-lance American pilot, were killed. Soon afterward Dean cabled Kissinger, once again asking permission to evacuate his remaining staff. For the moment Kissinger held him off, arguing that an evacuation still might not be necessary. An American representative in Peking, he said, was to open discussions with an official of Sihanouk's government-in-exile that very afternoon.

The meeting in question took place at 5 P.M., Peking time. The American spokesman, State Department officer John Holdridge, informed Sihanouk's chief aide that the United States was now fully prepared to support the exiled leader in his efforts to work out a settlement and would keep an American presence in Phnom Penh to help him do so. The Cambodian official indicated that Sihanouk would fly to Phnom Penh immediately.

Within the next few hours, however, Communist shelling effectively closed the Phnom Penh airfield, and Ambassador Dean again pleaded with Kissinger to authorize a full evacuation. This time the Secretary felt he had no choice but to agree. Consequently, just before dawn on the twelfth, Holdridge passed word to Sihanouk that the military situation around Phnom Penh had so deteriorated, the Embassy would have to close. In Washington the Administration promptly informed Congressional leaders that the President had authorized the use of helicopters, air support and Marine security forces to remove the remaining Americans in Phnom Penh under his prerogatives as Commander in Chief. The final "Eagle Pull" phase of the Cambodian evacuation was now a reality.

The Embassy's consular office in Phnom Penh had deliberately over-booked, projecting a passenger turnout of over 300, so that if any Americans or "third country nationals" who had not been contacted in the past few days showed up at the chopper pad two blocks from the Chancery, there would be plenty of seat space.

The first of the Phantom jets that were to fly protective cover entered Cambodian airspace at 8:34 A.M. An hour and a half later the big CH-53 helicopters began swooping in low over the edge of the city, arriving in waves of three, the first of them ferrying in members of the 350-man Marine security force.

About a hundred Cambodians soon gathered outside the Embassy's front gate and at the nearby chopper pad. There was no panic among them, no chaos in the streets. Many assumed that the choppers were bringing American troops in to save the city and offered to help Khmer police control traffic and crowds near the landing zones.

During the next hour thirty-six American choppers landed and took off without incident. Eighty-two Americans, thirty-five "third country nationals" and 159 Cambodians, including a number of Embassy employees, were evacuated.

Just before noon Ambassador Dean tucked the Embassy's American flag under his arm and climbed aboard one of the last of the choppers. Lieutenant General Saukham Khoy, the acting Cambodian President, was at his elbow, but several other Cambodian leaders had refused his offer of assistance. Sirak Matak, a former Prime Minister under Lon Nol, had sent Dean a note explaining his own reticence: "Dear Excellency and Friend: I thank you sincerely for your letter and your offer to transport me to freedom. I cannot, alas, leave in such a cowardly fashion. As for you, and in particular your great country, I never believed for a moment that you would have the sentiment of abandoning people who have chosen liberty. You have refused us protection and we can do nothing about it. You leave and it is my wish that you and your country will find happiness under the sky . . . I have only committed the mistake of believing in the Americans."

As the Ambassador's chopper lifted off, the marines began tightening their perimeter around the pad. Almost immediately KC artillerymen on the edge of the city opened up on Embassy Row, pummeling it with rocket and mortar fire as they had not done in two weeks. The marines scrambled for their own choppers as the crowd scattered.

For the next few days American cargo planes dropped load after load of food and other supplies into the besieged capital. Finally, on the seventeenth, as hordes of ragtag Communist troops who had been fighting along the Mekong River poured into the city's southern suburbs, the "Generals' Committee" that had been set up to wage the final battle asked for a cease-fire. The request was rejected. "We enter Phnom Penh as conquerors," the clandestine KC radio announced. "We order the surrender of all officers and officials of the Phnom Penh puppet regime under a white flag."

The following day thousands of civilians in Phnom Penh and other cities were ordered to leave at once and find new homes in the countryside. This forced migration, carried out in accordance with long-standing KC plans, left American espionage networks throughout the country broken and useless, for despite extensive intelligence pointing to such a "pastoralization" of the society under Communist rule, the last CIA planners in Phnom Penh had chosen to focus their stay-behind operations on the cities, establishing all of their

secret radio terminals and clandestine spy cells there. When the cities themselves were cleared, the networks collapsed, leaving us with almost no way of
gathering intelligence in postwar Cambodia.*

Following the Communist takeover, the few remaining foreigners and
newsmen in Phnom Penh, including members of the Soviet Mission, took
refuge in the French Embassy and holed up there for the next several weeks,
fighting among themselves for the scant food rations while keeping the gates
barred against Cambodians. When Sirak Matak and former Premier Long
Boret showed up to seek asylum among them, they were summarily turned
away. Both were later executed by the Communists.

In May the motley denizens of the French Embassy finally left by overland convoy to Thailand. The twelve journalists among them brought out
stories of widespread slaughter and starvation, and American intelligence
channels buzzed with rumors that at least two Americans, old homesteaders
who had elected to stay behind in Phnom Penh, had been killed by vengeful
KC. During the next several months evidence of such KC excesses continued
to accumulate as more and more terrified Cambodians fled across the border
to Thailand. But incredible as it might seem, there was never any international
outcry, no liberal voices calling for a Red Cross inquiry. All those concerned
humanitarians around the world who had once so righteously protested the
barbarity of the American bombing of Cambodia remained uncharacteristi-
cally silent.†

His picture was on the front page of *Pacific Stars and Stripes* a few days
later: Ambassador John Gunther Dean, stern-faced, with the furled flag under
his arm, preparing to board that chopper of his out of Phnom Penh. I stared
at the photograph a long time, and wondered if the humiliation, the rage and
the inevitable relief wore well together. But the face told nothing, and except
for the flak-jacketed marine in the background, the image might well have been
that of a wealthy American banker or industrialist, dark-suited, distinguished,
climbing into his private helicopter to head off to a businessmen's convention.

There was no drama to it, no seeming danger. If the parting could be so
benign, I thought, then we in Saigon had nothing to worry about.

*This unfortunate development was a direct result of a failure to heed our own intelligence, for
we had known for years that KC leader Khieu Samphan intended to raze the cities and turn the
society into a great rural estate if his movement was ever blessed with victory. This was one of
the main tenets of a dissertation he had written as a student. Moreover, in the last months of the
war the Communists had systematically depopulated every major town they had captured, thus
providing further proof of their overall aim.

†Rough estimates show that perhaps 300,000 Cambodians perished, either from deprivation or
execution, during the exodus from the cities which extended over the first six months of KC rule.
Within the next two years the number of victims may have quadrupled. Khieu Samphan himself
has provided perhaps the most reliable estimate of the casualties. During a conference of non-
aligned countries in Colombo in August 1976 he admitted to an Italian journalist that the population of Cambodia had dropped by a million since the end of the war. When asked what had
happened to all these people, he replied, "It's incredible how concerned you westerners are about
war criminals."

But such comparisons were inapplicable. Only 1,200 Cambodians had left their country during the three-week drawdown prior to Eagle Pull, while in Saigon "key" Vietnamese evacuee lists already were running into Ford's "tens of thousands."

The Saigon government tried to squeeze some benefit from Phnom Penh's tragedy by giving extensive air time to rumors of KC atrocities. If the object was to galvanize anti-Communist sentiment among the populace, however, the trick succeeded all too well. Many Saigonese were more terrified than steeled by what they heard, and with the Asian's sense of fatalism, concluded the tide was now running decisively in favor of the Communists on both sides of the border.

The North Vietnamese apparently reached a similar judgment. Writing later about the collapse of Cambodia, General Dung claimed that he and his comrades had viewed it as further proof that the United States was now prepared to abandon the "puppet" regimes in Indochina. The road to Saigon was open.*

*Following the collapse of Saigon, information surfaced which indicated that one NVA division may in fact have been diverted to Cambodia in mid-April to provide a backstop for KC forces targeted against Phnom Penh.

Discarded Luxury

The day after the evacuation of Phnom Penh several NVA commando units swung north around Xuan Loc and bore in on the highway running west toward Bien Hoa and Saigon itself, and Communist forces in the lower delta briefly penetrated government defenses north and northwest of the city of Can Tho, seat of the American consulate in MR 4. As if to capitalize on their battlefield successes, the Communists also struck a new hard line politically. A PRG spokesman at Tan Son Nhut warned of a massive uprising in Saigon unless Thieu resigned and the "military advisors disguised as civilians" left at once.

When I learned of these remarks I suggested to Polgar that Hanoi might be handing the Embassy itself an ultimatum. Since the Communists had long portrayed all of us as "military advisors," it seemed they were telling us in no uncertain terms: get out or else. Polgar was not so sure.

Several hours later Hanoi provided a clarification of sorts. In a public communiqué the North Vietnamese Foreign Ministry announced that an American evacuation could easily be carried out without the use of marines and helicopters if it were done "immediately." Evidently the Politburo was becoming increasingly concerned about the expanding U.S. naval fleet off-shore and was anxious for us to get on with our evacuation as quickly as possible.

As the saber-rattling continued, General Dung and his senior staff began grappling with some crucial policy decisions. On Monday, the fourteenth, a four-day policy conference was convened at their command post at Loc Ninh to consider a series of new directives from Hanoi. The most important dealt with the dramatic change in the timetable for victory.

Shortly after the initial attacks on Xuan Loc several days before, Dung had contacted the Politburo and asked for additional time to prepare for the offensive against Saigon itself. The reasons for his request—according to his memoirs—were strictly tactical. For one thing, the 18th ARVN Division at

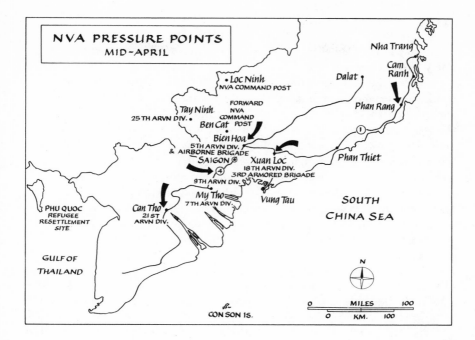

Nha Trang

Cam Ranh

Loc Ninh
NVA COMMAND POST

Dalat

FORWARD
NVA
COMMAND
POST

Tay Ninh

25TH ARVN DIV.

Ben Cat

Phan Rang

Bien Hoa

5TH ARVN DIV.
& AIRBORNE BRIGADE

SAIGON

Xuan Loc
18TH ARVN DIV.
3RD ARMORED BRIGADE

9TH ARVN DIV.

Phan Thiet

My Tho
7TH ARVN DIV.

Vung Tau

SOUTH
CHINA SEA

PHU QUOC
REFUGEE
RESETTLEMENT
SITE

Can Tho
21ST
ARVN DIV.

GULF OF
THAILAND

N

CON SON IS.

0   MILES   100

0   KM.   100

Xuan Loc was putting up a far stiffer defense than expected. For another, there had been difficulties in shifting units south out of MR 2, in part because of the dogged resistance of General Nghi's makeshift blocking force at Phan Rang. In addition, Hanoi's own planners had been unable to move men and supplies fast enough to meet Dung's needs in the Saigon area, and had just informed him that the last units of the NVA 1st Corps from North Vietnam would not be in place in MR 3 until the twenty-fifth, over one week away.

Given these problems—and perhaps, too, out of concern for the U.S. naval armada—the Politburo acceded to Dung's proposal, authorizing him to push back the date for the final offensive (which according to our latest intelligence had been scheduled to begin between the fifteenth and the nineteenth) for several days more.

Apparently there was never any serious question, however, that the campaign would be brought to a climax as quickly as possible. "The rainy season is now approaching," Le Duc Tho reminded his colleagues at the opening session on the fourteenth. "We must act quickly to fulfill our mission before it arrives." A day or so later Pham Hung proposed a new deadline for victory: "We must manage to be in Saigon to celebrate Ho Chi Minh's birthday" (19 May).

To expedite the progress of North Vietnamese arms, Dung decided during the conference not to waste any more time on Xuan Loc but to by-pass it altogether. He also proposed to his comrades in Hanoi that the offensive against Saigon itself be given a designation appropriate to its historic purpose. The Politburo quickly sent back a reply: "Agree that the campaign for Saigon be called the Ho Chi Minh Campaign." The message was signed "Le Duan, Party First Secretary."*

Under the new guidelines set out at the policy session, the offensive quickly gained momentum. On the morning of the fifteenth NVA artillerymen shelled the airfield at Bien Hoa with long-range field guns for the first time in the war, and further to the east, a fourth NVA division, the 325th from Hué, arrived in position on the Xuan Loc front even as other NVA units began quietly outflanking government defenses north and south of the town, as Dung had ordered. Xuan Loc itself was now under unremitting shellfire—over 2,000 rounds had fallen in the past twenty-four hours—and the remnants of General Dao's 18th Division were being plucked from the eastern suburbs by helicopter, as women and children battled with the wounded over body space on the skids.

Northeast of Xuan Loc, three other NVA divisions bore in on the government's only remaining real estate along the central coast, a seventy-five-mile stretch of lowland extending from Phan Rang (President Thieu's hometown) to Phan Thiet City. General Nghi's patchwork army, which had momentarily slowed the advance, was now beginning to break up under the pressure.

As the Ho Chi Minh campaign lurched forward, those in Saigon who favored a political settlement redoubled their efforts. Twenty-six of Saigon's most conservative politicians circulated a manifesto on the thirteenth, urging the government to cede territory to achieve peace, and the new Defense Minister, Tran Van Don, met secretly with his colleagues in the incoming Can cabinet and persuaded them a cease-fire had to be arranged under any circumstances.

In the meantime, the French decided to put out new feelers to the Americans in an effort to enlist them in their own stalled peace efforts. This time Mérillon chose to make Polgar, rather than Martin, the object of his blandishments, for he knew the Station Chief was already strongly committed to the idea of some kind of negotiated deal.

The French made their approach poolside at the Cercle Sportif, on the afternoon of the thirteenth. Polgar, decked out in his fading blue swimsuit, was surveying bikinied bathers over the edge of his *Saigon Post* when Pierre Brochand, the French intelligence chief, sidled over. Seating himself on a footstool at Polgar's elbow, the Frenchman proceeded to outline his government's position carefully and persuasively. While the French did not expect Saigon's defenses to collapse in the next few weeks, he said, they considered the military situation beyond recall. Therefore, something had to be done at

---

*During the next several days Dung parceled out assignments to his field commanders. General Le Duc An, commander of the four divisions that made up the 232nd Tactical Group, was to drive up Route 4 toward Saigon from the delta. General Vu Lang, IIIrd Corps commander, was to hurl his three divisions against the capital from the direction of Tay Ninh. General Nguyen Hoa's Ist Corps was to attack from the northeast, and the six divisions of the combined IInd and IVth Corps, under Dung's protégé, General Le Trong Tan, were to concentrate on the Xuan Loc–Bien Hoa front.

once to assure the survival of an independent Cochin China, at least "for a while." As he explained it, the French had reason to believe that the North Vietnamese "were not in a hurry" and would agree to the establishment of an ostensibly neutralist peace government in Saigon as a kind of bridge to Communist rule. "Big" Minh would probably be most acceptable to them as a chief of state, he said, though Khiem, Tran Van Don, former Foreign Minister Tran Van Do and Senate Chairman Tran Van Lam were all considered possible alternatives.*

Brochand's remarks, speculative as they were, pumped new hope into Polgar's flagging illusions, and by the end of the conversation he had offered to do what he could to realize the French objectives. As both he and Brochand knew, this meant persuading Martin that Thieu was now a major obstacle to peace and that a change in government must occur immediately.

An hour after the poolside tête-à-tête Polgar returned to the Embassy, summoned me to his office and directed me to prepare a new field appraisal. This one was to demonstrate that Thieu had become an intolerable liability.

The estimate turned out to be Thieu's political epitaph. "The catastrophic and costly military pullbacks in Military Regions 1 and 2," I wrote, "have convinced most Vietnamese, both civilian and military, that the President of the Republic has lost the mandate of heaven . . . Thus, many senior military officers and government officials feel he must relinquish power if a total and final military defeat is to be averted. Most would prefer a constitutional transfer of power, but some are willing to pursue any means to this end.

"Given the precarious military situation, the pressures for a violent coup d'état are likely to increase in the next few days, particularly if the army should suffer a major defeat at Xuan Loc. In the event of a coup, the successor government's ability to command the army and to maintain law and order would be nil."

The following morning, 14 March, Tran Van Don provided further encouragement for the optimists among us. During a private visit to the Embassy he advised Martin that he had just been contacted by a PRG intermediary and had been assured there was still a chance for a negotiated settlement. In particular, he said, the PRG representative had told him three things: (1) he, Don himself, was acceptable as a replacement for Thieu; (2) there would be no Communist attempt to interfere with the evacuation of select Vietnamese; and (3) the United States could maintain a small Embassy presence in Saigon, provided all other "official Americans" were withdrawn.

I was highly skeptical of Don's remarks. They seemed too pat and self-serving and a little too reminiscent of what the French wanted us to believe. I suspected that Mérillon, not the Communists, had inspired them.

Polgar did not agree. Neither, as it turned out, did Martin. Indeed, the information Don provided, together with Brochand's disclosures and the obvi-

---

*Brochand also promised that the French Embassy would ensure the evacuation of 50,000 Vietnamese if necessary—a pledge that was not kept.

ous problems I had cited in my field appraisal, finally altered the Ambassador's views on the sanctity of the status quo. By the end of the day on the fourteenth he had decided to propose to Washington what had been unthinkable up to now: the removal of Nguyen Van Thieu as the first step toward promoting a cease-fire.

When Martin sat down the following morning to draft a cable to the White House, setting out this startling idea, his mood was none too rosy. Not only was he galled at the prospect of having to admit the expendability of the Thieu regime, especially after he had so loudly proclaimed its virtues over the past two years, but also, to make matters worse, he was now facing an inordinate amount of criticism on his flanks. A number of Congressmen and editorialists at home were calling for his removal; his old rival, Assistant Secretary Habib, was trying to dictate to him on the evacuation issue; and even Kissinger seemed to be increasingly impatient, with his constant admonitions to him to speed up the Embassy's contingency planning.

In the opening paragraphs of his message the Ambassador thus sounded very much like a man on the defensive. "The relatively few people about whose opinions I really care," he wrote, "will not change their opinion of me. Even the sly anonymous insertion of the perfumed ice pick into the kidneys in the form of quotes from my colleagues in the Department is only a peculiar form of acupuncture indigenous to Foggy Bottom, against which I was immunized long ago. There are only two important considerations I keep in mind, the safety of the people under my charge and the integrity of U.S. policy. Both of these objectives, especially the first, seem to me to demand that we not be diverted by any kind of pressure, press or Congressional, from coolly pursuing a course best designed to achieve them." Martin went on to portray himself as the very model of coolness, an observer trying to view the situation as dispassionately as from "a seat on the moon."

Having thus vented his frustrations, he then turned to the matter at hand. Quoting liberally from my field appraisal, he underscored Thieu's weakness and warned that a cabal might be mounted against him, and "quickly," if additional aid was not forthcoming. Although he did not call specifically for Thieu's removal—that would come later—he left no doubt that the man had outlived his usefulness to U.S. policy.*

Elsewhere in the cable Martin attempted to ease concern in Washington over the status of his evacuation planning, insisting that he was already prepared to move out 200,000 people by sea, land and air if necessary. He also tried to diminish the precariousness of Saigon's overall position. Citing once again the economic potential of MR 3 and 4, he ruled out a total collapse of the army—even in the event of a negative vote on the aid measure—although he conceded that the Americans, under such circumstances, might be in for

---

*All of these points had been spelled out in my appraisal, and because Martin embraced them so completely, my draft was never sent to Washington.

a bad time "for a while." In perhaps his most extraordinary flourish, he also suggested that the Administration begin looking for ways of arranging a five-year loan for South Vietnam—as if the country had that long to live.

The cable, for all of its quirks, represented a remarkable about-face for Martin and a turning point in American perspectives on Vietnam. But it did not produce the immediate effect in Washington that he and Polgar and Martin desired. Because the proposed $722 million aid bill was still being debated by Congress, the Administration chose to delay any decision on Thieu's fate for another day or so.

By the time Martin fired off his message, the Embassy was busily trying to make good on one other objective we had set for ourselves—the refinement of our evacuation plans. Two days before, shortly after Baughn's dismissal, Martin had given Admiral Benton responsibility for completing a revised evacuation scenario in time for Kissinger's deadline of 19 April, and Smith's own planners had launched into the final phase of "Project Alamo," the establishment of a fully operational evacuee processing center in the DAO compound itself.

For all this commotion, however, one important aspect of our evacuation program continued to drag badly. By the afternoon of the fifteenth only 1,500 Americans had left for Clark air base in the Philippines on the military shuttle since the beginning of the month, and even fewer had departed by commercial aircraft.

The primary brake on the outflow was still red tape, in particular the restrictions against the movement of large numbers of Vietnamese friends and dependents to American soil. As long as the old homesteaders could not legally transplant their common-law wives, girl friends and illegitimate children, they were not about to budge themselves.

The Administration itself already had attempted to provide one solution. On the afternoon of the fourteenth the Embassy had received word that under a new "parole," U.S. immigration restrictions were to be waived for all Vietnamese with an American relative actually resident in Vietnam. Within hours of this happy news Al Francis, working unobtrusively on his own, managed to persuade Saigon's Ministry of the Interior to ease up on its *emigration* rules. Henceforth, in place of the standard exit visa or passport, a special document known as a *"laissez-passer"* was to be issued to any Vietnamese who could demonstrate that he or she was an American dependent.

When General Smith learned of these dual breakthroughs he called his non-essentials and contract employees together and urged them to take advantage of them at once. Other Embassy personnel set out to test the elasticity of the new regulations. Some (including the wife of one of Martin's senior counselors) bought or manufactured bogus marriage and child-support certificates so they could claim large numbers of Vietnamese as dependents.

Unhappily, however, the new rules achieved only part of their purpose. While greatly facilitating the departure of Vietnamese, they did little to speed up the American drawdown. Many of Smith's employees looked upon the flexing of the regulations as a portent of things to come and decided to stay on until all the obstacles to a large-scale Vietnamese evacuation had been swept aside. Worse still, since the new U.S. parole made it impossible for an American to sponsor a Vietnamese at long distance, its immediate effect was to promote an influx of good Samaritans from abroad. Almost overnight hundreds of U.S. citizens who had been living in Hong Kong, Bangkok or Singapore began crowding into the city to marry or otherwise "legitimize" as dependents girl friends or Vietnamese children. (A number of cynical entrepreneurs showed up as well, offering dependent's status for gold and hard cash.) In addition, a large number of Army deserters who for years had been living illegally in Vietnam suddenly emerged from the rice paddies to register themselves and their dependents with the Embassy, so they, too, could take advantage of the new travel regulations. As a result, within a day or two the list of potential American evacuees had expanded by over a thousand names.

Hoping to reverse the trend, General Smith asked Martin on the fifteenth to call on the Thieu government to declare all Americans not engaged in the war effort *personae non gratae.* Martin turned the proposal down, on grounds it might be misunderstood by Congress, but he did agree to set up a consular desk in the DAO gymnasium so Smith and his staff could assist in processing the massive backlog of parole applications as they accumulated at the Embassy.

Shortly before Eagle Pull in Cambodia, Martin had told a reporter he would never allow himself to be evacuated until all of the Embassy's Vietnamese employees had been taken care of. So far, however, his planning for the withdrawal of the Mission's locals and other Vietnamese charges had remained haphazard at best. Part of the problem was Martin's own concept of how such a rescue operation ought to be handled. Because of the massive number of Vietnamese for whom the Embassy was responsible, he was convinced an airlift out of Tan Son Nhut would never be able to do the job. As an alternative, he was toying with the idea of sending the majority of our Vietnamese evacuees overland to the coastal city of Vung Tau on E-day, to be picked up on the beaches by American ships and helicopters. But this option, too, was fraught with hazard and difficulty. For as I had pointed out in my recent study of our evacuation prospects, there was always a chance the Communists or the army would interdict the Saigon–Vung Tau highway in a crisis.

During the past few days Martin had sent a CIA man to Vung Tau to survey the landing areas and had asked General Smith to explore the feasibility of the plan with Saigon's high command. Smith did as he was told, but remained skeptical. In his opinion the Vung Tau option could never be made workable. Consequently, he and his staff were already quietly looking into ways of removing at least high-risk Vietnamese from Saigon by air. By the afternoon of the fifteenth Air Force Attaché Colonel McCurdy had drawn up a schedule for ultra-secret "black flights" and had struck a bargain with Vietnamese security personnel at Tan Son Nhut to assure their acquiescence if and when it became necessary to smuggle large numbers of Vietnamese onto the airstrip. His quid pro quo was guaranteed seat space for the families of the security officers themselves.

In the meantime, two Embassy staffers, Bob Lanigan and Mel Chatman, who had served in Nha Trang and Danang, began pulling together a small flotilla of ramshackle barges at the Newport docks outside Saigon, in case other means of transport proved inadequate on E-day. Both Smith and Captain Carmody scoffed at them, claiming that barges and tugboats would never be able to negotiate the river under the chaotic conditions of an evacuation.

Lanigan and Chatman were not the only Embassy staffers who were now attempting to improve on existing contingency plans. Marv Garrett, the Mission's security officer, also seemed determined to do so. In the past day or two he had called together some of his own colleagues and put them to work on a problem the military had all but ignored: the modification of the Embassy compound itself to accommodate large numbers of evacuees on E-day. Under their direction a metal gate was soon constructed at the passageway between the Embassy and the adjacent recreation compound so that access between the two could be shut off in an emergency, and barbed-wire hedges were strung along the top of the back wall of the recreation compound.

In yet another burst of initiative Garrett and his colleagues also took it upon themselves to revise a large section of the standing evacuation plan, without bothering to confer with DAO at all. But unfortunately, in this instance, their handiwork proved less than satisfactory. On the morning of the fifteenth, as I was on my way back to my office from the Embassy coffee shop, I spied several mimeographed copies of their blueprint on a table in the lobby of the chancery building. I picked one up, scanned it, and suddenly felt very ill. In his attempt to refine the original plan, Garrett had significantly (and ineptly) altered a number of important elements, including the procedures for the pickup and delivery of evacuees on E-day. If there had been an evacuation at that point, hundreds of Americans under his scenario might well have been left behind.

I raced upstairs to the Ambassador's suite and flung a copy at Brunson McKinley, the young State Department officer from MR 1 who was now serving as Martin's personal aide. "Who authorized distribution of this?" I gasped. McKinley, white-faced, said he didn't know. I told him about the batch of them in the lobby and suggested he tell Martin immediately, before they could be circulated.

Soon afterward Garrett was summoned to Martin's office. What the Ambassador said to him never became common knowledge, but within an hour the rooftop incinerators were gobbling up hundreds of his diagrams. For all the right reasons Garrett had come perilously close to putting part of the Embassy's contingency planning back to square one.

Throughout all of this hurly-burly, one man in the Embassy, my own boss, Polgar, remained strangely aloof. Now increasingly preoccupied with the promise of a political solution, he let the Station's own evacuation planning idle. Although he was fully aware that many of us were slipping Vietnamese out illegally on forged papers, he offered little encouragement or guidance. Nor did he heed Washington's pleas for a step-up in the Station's personnel cutbacks. Non-essentials continued to set their own pace.

His attitude quickly became infectious. Officers in charge of drawing up the Station's non-essentials lists went about their task almost casually, without troubling to coordinate with others involved in evacuation planning, and those responsible for identifying potential Vietnamese evacuees soon succumbed to a kind of fatalistic unconcern. When I asked one of them if I could slip a name or two onto his roster, he replied with a shrug, "Why not? None of this is going to work anyway. If you want to waste your time, be my guest."

In Bien Hoa, meanwhile, CIA Base Chief Taggart remained equally skeptical of the prospects for a large-scale Vietnamese evacuation and refused even to go through the "charade" of preparing an appropriate evacuee list. Some of his subordinates were chagrined. "When are we going to start trying to help our locals!" John Stockwell, the young operative from Tay Ninh, screamed at him during one particularly contentious staff meeting. And from then on, the two men were at loggerheads, Stockwell pushing for more contingency planning, Taggart dragging his feet all the way.

On the morning of the fifteenth Polgar flew down to the delta city of Can Tho to confer with CIA officers there. To the dismay of the local Base Chief, "Larry Downs," he seemed determined to put a bright face on the overall situation. Touting the prospects for a negotiated settlement, he predicted that the Embassy would probably be able to maintain a small presence in the country, even after a change in government, and insisted that a full evacuation would therefore be unnecessary.

Throughout the discussions, Downs and his staff grumbled and protested, reminding Polgar that six NVA regiments were poised just north of Can Tho. Finally, in an effort to meet their concerns halfway, Polgar agreed to let them accelerate their contingency preparations, to the extent of moving some of their Vietnamese personnel to Phu Quoc Island.

Downs and his staff, in fact, were already several steps ahead of Polgar. During the past weekend, after a heavy shelling attack on the Can Tho airfield, the dozen or so CIA personnel spread through the provinces of MR 4 had been withdrawn to the consulate. Some of them had been bundled off to Saigon (together with the wives of several CIA officers) and a formal non-essentials list had been drawn up by Downs' deputy, "Tom Franklin." Now there were no more than a dozen CIA officers in Can Tho and only a few remaining dependents.

Despite the obvious need for such precautions, Downs had faced stiff opposition throughout from Terry MacNamara, the mid-fortyish, somewhat modish State Department officer who served as Consul General in the delta. MacNamara took his role as chief of the local U.S. Mission quite seriously and was determined not to be overridden or stampeded by his CIA colleagues. He was also somewhat more impressed with the need to adhere to directives from Saigon than Downs was. And one directive he was resolved to follow to the letter: avoid a precipitous drawdown of Americans or Vietnamese, Martin had told him; do nothing to panic the local population.

As the Americans throughout what remained of the Republic wrestled with the evacuation problem, the threads binding Vietnamese hopes and illusions continued to fray. The new Can cabinet, installed on the fourteenth, quickly became the butt of caustic metaphor. "Old wine in a new bottle," some of its critics sneered. Others were put off simply by its inappropriateness. Only two military men were to be found among its ranks—Defense Minister Tran Van Don and Brigadier General Phan Hoa Hiep, the new Information Minister—and neither of them was a model field officer. Worse still, Thieu himself seemed increasingly out of touch with reality. His only decisive act in recent days, since the start of the Communist drive against Xuan Loc, had been to close all bars and brothels in Saigon—temporarily—"to save money for ammunition."

The malaise at the top levels of government was matched by a growing sense of defeatism throughout the society. Tri Quang, the famed Buddhist activist, declared sadly to an American friend on the fifteenth, "The war is lost. Everything, including religion itself, is doomed to perish in a Communist takeover." Later in the day Senate Chairman Tran Van Lam bitterly complained to reporters about America's failure "to react immediately and vigorously" to the NVA offensive, as Nixon had pledged to do at the time of the cease-fire.

"A little busy," I wrote in my notebook on the evening of the fifteenth. "Nerves working overtime. Small stimulus sufficient to set them all firing at once. Long hours. Weight dropping. I go to the office each morning at six to shuffle through the nightmares reported in soft copy.

"Strange, the effect such pressure has on you. Suddenly I've discovered I'm a latent gun-hound. I now set aside a few minutes every night to hand-load magazines, oil down the stocks, arrange and rearrange piles of grenades and bullet pouches around the apartment. Addicted, too, to rock music, from Joe Cocker to Neil Diamond, particularly the melancholy sound track from the movie *Jonathan Livingston Seagull.* Come day's end, the volume goes up to the last decibel to shatter what remains of the tensions.

"No use, though. Wherever you turn now, the end seems foreshadowed in countless small ways. I was walking past the Embassy pool yesterday and found proof there too, flakes of charred classified waste from the rooftop incinerators floating mid-depth, intimations of our own sinking fortunes.

"The city continues to enjoy a false immunity from the chaos of the countryside behind its cordon of police checkpoints. But all of us have paid a price for this, for our lives have been compressed into intolerably small spaces, and brief fourteen-hour intervals delimited by the curfew.

"Last night at nine I wandered out on my balcony to watch the city close down as the curfew took hold. A few loudspeaker trucks were cruising lazily around the traffic circle, their rooftop megaphones blaring out last-minute warnings to dawdlers: 'Get inside! Get inside!' And within minutes the streets around my apartment building were swept clean of all form of humanity— except for a lone white-shirted policeman in the lamplight on the other side of the traffic circle. It was then, in the stillness, I could hear the distant thud of artillery at Bien Hoa.

"Colleagues who saw Danang or Phnom Penh in its final hour claim to recognize here the first symptoms of the siege mentality they know only too well. Beggers are out en masse now, and increasingly aggressive, tearing at your pockets or your car windows as you scuttle through the city to an agent meeting or to fast pre-curfew cocktails with friends. And much of the population seems to be on a mad selling spree, as one journalist friend put it the other day. The thieves' market along Nguyen Hue and Le Loi Boulevards has become a cornucopia of discarded and cut-rate luxury. Iceboxes, stereos, air conditioners, anything too large to fit in a suitcase, can be had for a third or a fourth of the usual bargaining price, and over on the tree-lined, wealth-studded boulevards like Pasteur or Tu Xuong, one after another of the beautiful old French villas are being boarded up and abandoned as their owners depart precipitously, often without making a sale.

"For Vietnamese without American friends or sponsors the price of a way out is astronomical, and still rising. The cost of a passport and exit visa in under-the-table gratuities has jumped from the equivalent of $500 to $3,000 in the past two weeks. The price of a modest seagoing junk has tripled and is now $10,000 or more. Gold prices are up too, now $725 an ounce, but few of the Chinese merchants in the suburb of Cholon are anxious to sell. Most of them are hoarding their gold on the theory that it will be legal tender even in a Communist society. No one is so sure about the acceptability of the U.S. dollar, but for the moment it seems preferable to the piaster itself. In only five days the black market exchange rate for American currency has surged from 1,200 to 2,000 piasters for every dollar.

"With the evening curfew now so drastically cut back, Vietnamese friends and associates are showing up at first light, and breakfast has become the time for exchanging courtesies and doing business outside the framework of the normal working day. Establishing a common ground for understanding remains excruciatingly difficult, for you don't want to confront your maid, girl friend or contact in this or that government ministry with the stark, disheartening truth. So you talk around it, alluding euphemistically to the prospect of harder times ahead, to the 'usefulness' of staying in touch with American friends and colleagues so that if 'something does happen, well . . .'

"The Vietnamese remain equally circumspect. No one asks bluntly for help in fleeing the country, at least not yet. Their appeals are always more subtle. 'Would you mind,' they ask tentatively, 'exchanging these few piasters for me? Prices are rising and the banks are freezing deposits and how nice it would be to have some green in one's pocket if worse comes to worse.' And before you know it, you are brokering illegal dollar-piaster transactions for this or that friend, providing him with the capital that may save his life, allowing yourself to become his last hope of deliverance.

"Nor are the legal barriers the only ones breaking down. Vietnamese who've always remained aloof are now opening up, telling you of their worries, families, mistresses or boyfriends, and of their buried views on politics. They don't hate the Communists, they say. They fear them. They've lived so long with the French and the Americans and with Thieu's loose autocracy, they can't imagine any other way. Change may be all right for the peasants in the countryside. But what will happen to them?

"Cynical or steeled as you might be, it is impossible not to sympathize, for the face of the victor is fast becoming discernible through the mesh of rumor and government propaganda. Some of the images are intimidating simply for what they say of the enemy's efficiency, his seeming ability to dominate whatever he chooses. Refugees still struggling south out of MR 1 and 2 claim the North Vietnamese have already imposed 'military management committees' on captured towns and cities, elbowing aside the front organizations and home-grown Viet Cong apparatus which till now were their camouflage. 'They've even restored water and electrical service in many of the villages!' an old Vietnamese friend exclaimed to me recently. 'How can we hope to defeat such people?'

"Atrocity stories abound too, now imaginatively embroidered by Saigon radio, the local press and the Embassy. At the Ambassador's orders, Joe Bennett [the political counselor] is still zealously churning out his share of them, playing on thirdhand reports relayed out of Ban Me Thuot by a Buddhist monk. 'They're tearing out women's fingernails up there and chopping up the town council,' one of Bennett's younger staffers advised me gleefully this afternoon. 'That should turn some heads in Congress.'

"Normally, as one of the Embassy's 'experts' on Communist policy, I would be asked to review such reports and to check their veracity. But not now. The Ambassador and Polgar apparently consider the latest crop too useful to risk putting them to any such test.

"Many Vietnamese friends and contacts take the tales at face value, particularly now that Cambodia has been abandoned, with all that that implies. 'Do the Communists really torture women who've been with Americans?' Tu Ha asked me one night. I told her no and tried to change the subject.

But later as I watched her at my window, staring apprehensively at the muzzle flashes out toward Bien Hoa, I could not deny my own doubts. No one, except perhaps the misguided young officers in Bennett's office, expects a massive purge on the heels of a Communist takeover. But there was Hué in 1968—some 2,000 people died there at Communist hands—and the North Vietnamese land-reform program of the mid-1950s in which some 30,000 to 50,000 intransigent peasants and landowners were killed or imprisoned. South Vietnam's peasant population is hardly any more malleable than those victims must have been. Probably far less so, since Thieu's land-to-the-tiller program has eliminated the absentee landlord and made each small farmer master of his own domain. If the Communists try to communalize the south, resistance, or at best reluctance, must be expected. And what then? If a bloodbath is unlikely, there is still the ghastly possibility of a slow internal hemorrhaging.

"The Communists, predictably, claim otherwise. Since early April, Liberation Radio has been promising leniency to anyone who will repent his 'anti-PRG' activity. Yet amid all this sweetness and light, there lingers one dark shadow. The commentaries also warn that anyone found 'resisting' the revolution will be 'severely punished.'

"I wouldn't want to gamble my own life on such ambiguity. Do I have the right to gamble anyone else's?

"Friends and neighbors in my apartment building already are arming for a bloody last stand. [Joe Kingsley] and I agreed several days ago to become security wards for the building, responsible for protecting the rooftop helo-pad on E-day, and now, each night before turning in, we trek up to the roof to adjust the sights of our M-16 rifles and arrange sniper cover. Since the building has just been selected as one of DAO's assembly points, hundreds of irate Vietnamese will undoubtedly congregate at our front gates on E-day, and there's bound to be need for crowd control and possibly even protective fire. Under the plan Joe and I've worked out, he'll police the lobby entrance downstairs and I'll cover him from the roof as our neighbors board the choppers. Personally I don't think there's much chance the plan will work. Fourteen Americans and forty assorted Vietnamese are permanent residents of the building, and other Vietnamese 'visitors' already are vying for sleeping space in the lobby and hallways. The rooftop pad, however, can accommodate only one Huey at a time, and that means any extraction operation will be a long, drawn-out affair. Considering the fact that only one malcontent in the streets with a rifle could bring the entire helo-lift to a halt, I just can't see how we can all expect to get out . . .

"Among friends and colleagues in the Embassy, meanwhile, the prevailing mood would do justice to a wake. The alcoholics among us are hitting the bottle at first light and tranquilizers are going like peanuts. I've eased back on the booze myself and am staying away from tranquilizers altogether. I have no desire to be any more fuzzy-headed than I am.

"Joe and I are trying (vainly) to keep up a brave front for our colleague Pat, whose pessimism seems to know no bounds. Whenever Joe shows up with another armload of weapons and war gear, she says something half mocking, like 'Clank, clank, clank. Here he is again, our warrior.' Usually Joe simply smiles at this and offers her a helmet or hand grenade or whatever else he's peddling. But already the joke's wearing thin. 'No,' she said this morning when he laid a Thompson on her desk. 'I've made my peace. Since the airfield can be shut down anytime, your guns will do no good.'

"Pat drove to Tan Son Nhut around noon today and put her two pet Siamese cats on an outgoing cargo plane. She's agonized over the decision for days, ashamed to devote such attention to two animals when so many of our Vietnamese friends are living on the edge of hope. But balance and perspective are scarce in the Embassy these days, and if it's possible to save something of value, be it no more than a favorite pet, who can be faulted for doing so?

"Pat's also been suffering pangs of guilt over the shipment of her household effects. The Station's logistics staff now have packers on call around-the-clock (Polgar's major concession to the crisis) and if they're too busy to crate up something at once, they'll give you the packing material so you can do it yourself. But Pat has been unwilling to make the effort. So have I. It just doesn't seem right to worry over the detritus of two or three years in a war zone when at last the war is making an appearance. Even so, Pat struck a compromise of sorts yesterday, mainly at the pleadings of her husband. Her records and stereo were sent out, but most of her clothes stayed on the racks. This morning the children of her Vietnamese maid were gleefully frolicking about in her discarded dresses and shoes, oblivious of the implications of their good fortune."

Even as I was finishing up these entries on the evening of the fifteenth, the military crisis continued to deepen. Shortly after nightfall heavy fighting erupted around a district town on Route 4 some twenty-four miles southwest of Saigon, and to the east, as choppers continued to pull government defenders out of the shell crater that had been Xuan Loc, an armored brigade, which had been guarding the northern approaches of the capital, was shifted in to meet rising pressure on the highway linking Xuan Loc to Bien Hoa and Saigon. The shelling of Bien Hoa airfield, meanwhile, had all but immobilized what remained of the South Vietnamese air force.

By the following morning NVA forces were lining up another devastating blow against us. The units General Dung had sent barreling down the central coast after the capture of Nha Trang and Cam Ranh were now closing around General Nghi's headquarters at Phan Rang in southern MR 2.

The mounting threat in this area had special poignancy for us in the Station. Several days before, one of our colleagues had been sent to Phan Rang to serve as liaison with Nghi's staff. Now he was directly in the path of 25,000 advancing North Vietnamese.

The hapless point man was Lew James, the same young operative who had refused two weeks before to leave Nha Trang until he had done all he could to rescue the CIA's local Vietnamese employees. In the past several days

Polgar had decided to make further use of his grit and personal courage by stationing him at Nghi's imperiled headquarters.

When my own office colleague, Joe Kingsley, had first learned of the assignment, he had objected vehemently. Communist forces were moving so fast, he had told Polgar, they might be able to overrun Phan Rang without any warning at all. But Polgar had refused to reconsider, and had merely advised Taggart in Bien Hoa, who was "control officer" for the mission, not to keep James on location overnight if an attack against Phan Rang seemed imminent.

Incredibly, however, Taggart and Pittman, the backup man in Saigon, had failed to take even this precaution and had left James in Phan Rang night after night despite the mounting Communist pressure. Taggart later tried to justify this to me by insisting the Station had not kept him adequately informed of the developing threat at Phan Rang. He may have had a point, particularly in view of Polgar's reluctance to share alarming intelligence with his subordinates. James himself may also have contributed to the confusion, for as a former Special Forces officer, he enjoyed a good fight and had neglected to keep Taggart or the Station as fully apprised of the evolving crisis as he might have.

In any case, the end came, on the morning of the sixteenth, faster than any of us had anticipated. I had just finished reading the morning intelligence file when a radio message from James flooded in over the "Diamond" radio transceiver in the communications room next to my office. Joe Kingsley and I were at the console immediately. Through a hash of static James explained that he, Nghi and Brigadier General Pham Ngoc Sang, commander of the 6th Air Division, were in a bunker together. They were all right, he said, but North Vietnamese tanks were even then probing the perimeter. Joe told him we would send a chopper to pull him out at once. No, James replied, that wasn't necessary, not yet anyway. ARVN forces were still holding. Besides, Nghi had his own chopper.

At that moment Howard Archer, the former Nha Trang Base Chief, walked in on us. Seizing the microphone, he asked James to describe his predicament. He then made a decision, one that left Kingsley and me astounded. James was to stay in place for the time being, he said, but was to call in every half-hour to assure us he was okay. So ended our last radio contact with Lew James.

When Communist forces moved into the city hours later, they put James, Nghi and Sang under arrest. Liberation Radio soon disclosed the capture of the two Vietnamese, but failed to mention the American. In Saigon we took the omission as a sign the CIA man had escaped—or had been killed. Actually, the North Vietnamese were keeping silent about him until they determined who he was.

Unraveling his identity turned out to be fairly easy. Like so many of us, James had been sent to Vietnam under "light cover," his official "I.D." card describing him as an "employee of the U.S. Embassy" and a "Foreign Service Reserve Officer." These titles were transparent. Journalists, Vietnamese officials and almost anyone else with an interest in ferreting out the Embassy's CIA contingent had long ago seen through them.*

In James' case, the cover problem had been compounded by bureaucratic stupidity. Within hours of his disappearance Station administrators discovered that no one could be quite sure what his cover was, whether he had been given an "Embassy employee" designation or something more elaborate.

Officials at CIA headquarters immediately began building a new cover for him, labeling him a "U.S. consular officer" so that if the press discovered he was missing, his agency affiliation could be concealed. This could hardly benefit James himself, of course. On the contrary, it could only do him harm, for having no idea what new label the CIA had given him, he could scarcely defend it—or himself—credibly to his North Vietnamese interrogators.

The day after his capture NVA officers began grilling James on the spot. At first they threatened to beat him, then made good on their threat. Despite the harsh treatment, he initially held firm, relying on the technique, so favored by Soviet agents, of feigning ignorance of anything but a fragment of the "big picture."

After a week or so his captors, frustrated but determined to break him, trucked him and the two South Vietnamese generals to Hanoi. There they penned them up in Son Tay Prison, where countless American fliers had waited out their capture years before, and began putting James through intensive interrogation, eventually confronting him with a large dossier that had been compiled from "sources" in Laos, where he had once served. The file identified him unequivocally as a CIA officer, largely on the basis of testimony from a Laotian who had known him well. From that point on, it was utterly futile for him to try to deny knowledge of the CIA, its operations or its agents.

The breaking of Lew James was, in large measure, a reflection on the ineptitude of those for whom he worked. The young CIA officer had been sent on a useless and dangerous assignment with little guidance or protection from the Station. If he betrayed certain "secrets," CIA management, not James, should answer first.

Over a half year after the fall of South Vietnam, James was freed by Hanoi (along with the handful of westerners captured at Ban Me Thuot) under a "professional arrangement" worked out by the CIA through another western intelligence organization. He was indeed the last CIA operative in Vietnam.

---

*The flimsiness of such "cover" apparently had never troubled CIA headquarters, at least not enough to prompt a change. With the departure of the U.S. military in the wake of the cease-fire, the CIA had lost most of its military cover "slots" in Vietnam. (Many of us had been masquerading as civilian employees of the Army.) Since then, the personnel office in Langley had been unable to dream up a credible alternative. As a result, many CIA officers ended up with almost no cover at all and constantly faced exposure by Vietnamese, Hungarian or Polish intelligence operatives.

Worst Case

When news of James' disappearance filtered through the Station, some of his friends rushed mindlessly for planes and helicopters and spent the next two days scouring the shoreline between Vung Tau and Phan Rang for him. The search turned out to be both futile and dangerous. North Vietnamese forces, now traveling the coastal highways at all hours, did not particularly relish being buzzed by Air America aircraft, and at one point, when a two-engine Volpar swooped in too low over a troop column on a road north of Phan Thiet, several AK-47 rounds ripped through the wing, and the pilot was forced to make an emergency landing on a beach several miles away. An Air America Huey went in and pulled out the crew and the CIA officer on board. "No casualties," a voice crackled in over the "Diamond" radio net. But after that Polgar was unwilling to take any more chances. The search was called off.

In Washington, meanwhile, the Administration was reeling from new shocks of its own. Kissinger's indirect peace feelers had come to nothing. The Soviets and the Chinese seemed unwilling to convene a new international peace conference on Indochina, and the nine Common Market nations had just informed Washington they would not approach Hanoi, as the Administration had requested, to ask for a cease-fire, lest they be accused of partisanship in the Vietnam conflict.

At the same time a mood of pessimism, even defeatism, was settling over the Administration itself. Kissinger's own top advisors, Habib and Ingersoll, were now deeply disturbed over Martin's performance, or lack of it. Bill Hyland, the State Department's intelligence chief, had recently told a WSAG session that the South Vietnamese could last only a few more days, and analysts at the Defense Intelligence Agency were privately confiding to reporters that the Saigon high command probably would not be able to rally stragglers from MR 1 and 2 in time to avert a Communist victory.

Particularly disturbing to CIA and defense analysts was the recent appearance of SA-2 missiles in MR 3. Once these highly sophisticated weapons were emplaced—the latest sightings showed them still in transit in the north-eastern part of the region—the North Vietnamese would be in a position to block any air evacuation out of Saigon.*

Outside the "official community" glimmerings of panic and confusion also were increasingly apparent. In the past few days the television networks and various newspapers and magazines had begun badgering the White House for help in evacuating their own Vietnamese employees in Saigon, claiming that Martin would never be able to accomplish it on his own. Congress, too, was becoming restive. Senate Majority Leader Mike Mansfield had recently accused the White House of dragging its heels on the evacuation issue, and more and more legislators seemed convinced that the Administration was deliberately holding the American community in place in Saigon to force a positive vote on the aid bill and to justify introduction of American forces.

As it happened, a principal catalyst for such Congressional attitudes was the field report prepared by my friends Dick Moose and Chuck Miessner, the staff investigators for the Senate Foreign Relations Committee. On Monday, the fourteenth, only hours after returning to Washington, they briefed the Committee on their findings. On the basis of what they had learned from me and others in Saigon, they predicted the Communists would try to consolidate their control around the capital by the first of May.

Warning of increased opposition to Thieu and growing hostility toward the American community, they reported a "consensus" in the Embassy urgently favoring evacuation. But they also pointed out that there was opposition in the highest quarters. "This sense of urgency is not shared, and indeed is being actively resisted, by Ambassador Martin and a few of his senior officers," they noted. "The Ambassador does not regard the military or security situation as critical and therefore he does not perceive or acknowledge the risks seen by others. He deplores what he regards as 'panic' on the part of others. Instead, he stresses the need to avoid taking action which would convey to the Vietnamese government signs of American uneasiness." As a result: "Serious Embassy planning for full-scale evacuation of Americans and Vietnamese began only last week. By week's end it had not progressed beyond the preliminary stage. Coordination between the various elements of the Mission has been minimal and primarily because discussion of the problem seems to have been discouraged."

To compensate for all this, Moose and Miessner proposed that Congress

---

*The malaise that gripped at least part of the intelligence community was reflected in the daily bulletin prepared by CIA analysts for the White House. Witness the following entries: April 14: "The Communists are moving additional forces into position for an assault in the western approach to Saigon . . . [They] now have almost three full divisions—the 3rd, 5th and 9th—along Saigon's western defense perimeter." April 15: "Recent reports continue to refer to Communist plans to carry out [sabotage] attacks from inside Saigon in the near future." April 16: "The recent shellings of Bien Hoa air base suggest the Communists also now may be planning to shell the outskirts of Saigon and the Tan Son Nhut air base with their heavy field guns. An offensive by newly arrived divisions north of Saigon, coupled with sapper attacks and shellings of the city itself, might lead to a rapid crumbling of the government's position."

call on the Administration to waive all immigration restrictions and to accelerate the evacuation of both Americans and Vietnamese even before the aid vote
—which was, of course, at odds with Kissinger's strategy. They also suggested
delaying debate on the use of military forces until most Americans were out
of Saigon, since "already nervous and irritated elements of the Vietnamese
public may take considerable offense" at it. As for the aid proposal itself: "No
one including the Vietnamese military believes that more aid could reverse the
flow of events."

The two staffers were no more optimistic than I about the prospects for
negotiations—"at worst they would amount to surrender talks and at best a
deck stacked heavily against the present government"—but they felt there was
no harm in trying. The difference between their view and the Ambassador's
was that they were not willing to defer evacuation planning for the sake of the
peace gambit.

Following their briefing, Senator Clifford Case called the White House
and asked the President to meet with the committee at once. Later in the day
the entire membership showed up at the Oval Office. During the interview the
Senators offered to support a small sum in humanitarian aid and to authorize
use of forces to evacuate Americans, provided the White House agreed to
withdraw the American community promptly. Ford equivocated, refusing to
commit himself to a specific deadline. He also objected to the idea of making
additional aid and the use of forces contingent on a full American pullout, and
denied he needed Congressional authority to protect American lives. In addition, he was adamant about "our obligation" to help endangered Vietnamese,
claiming that the numbers ran as high as 174,000.

The meeting ended inconclusively. Senator Robert C. Byrd, the Assistant
Majority Leader, was so disturbed over what had taken place, he decided to
introduce immediately a resolution restricting the use of American forces to
an Americans-only evacuation.

Facing such resistance, Kissinger and his Administration colleagues were
now eager, even desperate, for alternatives. But because they still were hopeful
of rallying Congress behind the proposed $722 million, they could not yet
bring themselves to embrace the option Martin suggested: the abandonment
of Thieu.

On the morning of the fifteenth, only hours after Martin had first
broached this prospect to the White House, Kissinger and several other Administration officials launched a last, concerted assault on the various Congressional groups that held the key to the aid vote. Kissinger himself spent most
of the day with the increasingly skeptical Senate Appropriations Committee.
He reiterated most of his now-familiar arguments and elaborated on one other,
claiming that "the sum we have requested would enable the government of
South Vietnam . . . to negotiate under conditions that are more consistent with
self-determination." When asked precisely what this meant, he explained, "I
suppose they [the South Vietnamese] could hope to achieve an implementation

of articles of the [Paris] agreement that called for a National Council of National Reconciliation and Concord." The remark was telling. No one, not even the French, had suggested that the Communists might now be willing to join in such a tripartite coalition. The source of our first definitive report on Hanoi's plans, the one on 8 April, had expressly ruled it out. Evidently Kissinger was indulging his own wishful thinking at the expense of the intelligence.

General Weyand, appearing before the same committee, claimed that Saigon would collapse in one month without additional assistance, and Secretary Schlesinger, in testimony of his own, offered an even grimmer prognosis, warning that over 200,000 Vietnamese (conveniently the number the President wanted to evacuate) would face death if the Communists seized power. The following morning, copies of the *Pacific Stars and Stripes,* with his claims emblazoned in bold headlines, circulated around Saigon, strengthening hundreds of Vietnamese in their own worst nightmares.

Congress itself remained unmoved, however. In addition to all the old doubts about the utility of additional aid, there was considerable skepticism about the Administration's veracity, particularly its statistics. Schlesinger assured one group of legislators on the afternoon of the fifteenth that the number of Americans in Saigon had been reduced by one-third, to less than 4,000, in the past two weeks. But within hours the Pentagon was forced to acknowledge that perhaps as many as 5,000 Americans were still in the South Vietnamese capital, including some who had just shown up on the books. The Senate Foreign Relations Committee, suspecting duplicity, postponed its vote on the aid proposal pending a clarification.

In Hanoi the party leadership moved deftly to exploit the mounting confusion and controversy in Washington. As if to goad Congress into a quick decision on the evacuation issue, the North Vietnamese Foreign Ministry announced on the sixteenth that "liberation forces" had always been ready to guarantee the immediate safe withdrawal of "U.S. military advisors." Meanwhile, a PRG spokesman in Paris told a *New York Times* reporter that his side would pose "no obstacle" if the Americans wished to withdraw all "25,000" of their military advisors in Saigon (four times the actual size of the American community).

Ambassador Martin viewed these pronouncements, and the furor in Congress, with deep alarm. Certain that Saigon's house of cards would collapse around us if the Administration was stampeded into an evacuation, he felt he had no choice but to continue playing for time, holding off a too-hasty drawdown until Congress had made up its mind on the aid bill. Whatever its decision, Kissinger might then agree to the political solution that now seemed the only safeguard for American lives.

Since the aid vote was so critical, Martin considered it incumbent on him to help lobby for it from Saigon, and soon he began placing hourly long-distance phone calls to friends and allies in Congress, offering to evacuate this or that Vietnamese (or American) of their choice while soliciting their support of the aid measure. He also attempted to keep his Administration colleagues at bay by disparaging the prospect of an easy or rapid drawdown of American personnel. In a press interview on the sixteenth he stated flatly that he would not be able to reduce the American community to 1,100 as fast as the White House wanted, and warned that the effects of even the latest cutbacks would not be felt for "two or three days."

He also hit upon a scheme for damping down one other major source of pressure, the American press corps. Although he certainly had no love for this venerable institution, he realized that the only sure way of keeping the journalists quiet was by making some special effort to meet their concerns. On the afternoon of the sixteenth he therefore directed his own press "spokesman," John Hogan, to arrange a special "black airlift" for the Vietnamese employees of the American news organizations in Saigon.

The press "shuttle" turned out to be one of the Embassy's most successful evacuation operations. During the next several days Hogan and the local CBS bureau chief in Saigon, the primary contact on the media side, secretly evacuated some 600 Vietnamese through the auspices of Air America. Not a word of this was leaked to the public. Nor was it widely discussed in the Embassy. Martin later told Congress that this was precisely how the newsmen had wanted it. By his account the CBS chief had been particularly insistent that Alan Carter not be informed because of his supposed "unreliability."

When Carter learned of this after the collapse of South Vietnam, he was not at all amused. Neither were a good many CIA men. While no one begrudged the Ambassador his generosity, his willingness to extend special assistance to outsiders while the Embassy's own local employees floundered seemed less than reasonable. Who was in the greater danger, after all—CBS office workers or Vietnamese attached to the CIA or other Embassy components? Obviously, the Ambassador had opted first for public relations.*

In the meantime, Martin continued to try to limit the outflow of Vietnamese for whom he had no special use. Even as the press shuttle got under way he made it clear to all of us in the Embassy that we were not to put active-duty military officers, government functionaries or Vietnamese males of draft age on any outgoing flight. The Embassy, he said, would not be a party to desertion or dereliction of duty. He also attempted to bring the Embassy's own evacuation machinery under even tighter control to ensure adherence to his dictates. On the afternoon of the seventeenth his "special assistant," George Jacobson, announced to a group of colleagues that he had just been appointed the new "evacuation coordinator" and that Jim Devine, head of the political-military section, was to serve as his deputy. Some of us were a little

*In authorizing the press shuttle Martin clearly was bending U.S. immigration rules to facilitate an evacuation he considered politically expedient. At the time he set this black airlift in motion it was legal to move to the United States only Vietnamese "dependents" with American relatives actually resident in Vietnam. Few of the Vietnamese slated for the press shuttle fit this definition.

surprised at these choices. The coordinator's job up to this point had been held
by military men, first Smith and Baughn and then Admiral Benton. Since
DAO already had the organization, the aircraft and the cargo ships, the switch
to civilian management seemed pointless. But Martin evidently thought otherwise. Now that a real evacuation was in the offing, he was determined to have
his own men up front. Jacobson and Devine, both of whom owed him their
careers, could be counted upon to follow his directives to the letter.

To one member of the Ambassador's staff the shake-up had all the appeal
of a slap in the face. Al Francis had been urging Martin for days to retain Smith
as coordinator, and when he learned Jacobson had been chosen instead, he felt
rebuffed. He informed Martin of his feelings and said he was leaving Saigon
right away. Thus the Ambassador's one-time protégé, the hero of Danang,
severed his remaining ties to the man whose support had made him one of the
fastest-rising stars in the Foreign Service. Within a day or so Francis was gone.

By close-of-business on the seventeenth, Martin's desk was piled high
with cables from Washington admonishing him to speed up the evacuation and
to take stock of the deteriorating military situation. One of them, from Kissinger, requested an assessment of Thieu's plans for the defense of Saigon, as
well as an analysis of the threat posed by the SA-2s. Martin read them over
with ill-concealed impatience. The State Department and the White House still
did not seem to grasp the importance of approaching such problems coolly and
dispassionately. He sat down at his desk and scratched out a reply in longhand,
his secretary, Eva Kim, typing each paragraph as he wrote.

The one thing that could spark a backlash against the Americans in
Saigon, he warned, was a sudden effort to evacuate them. Another would be
for "some goddamn fool" in Washington to send the marines to the rescue.
Such a move, in his view, would trigger "a hell of a mess."

On a more soothing note, he promised to try to meet the President's
schedule for personnel cutbacks. All Embassy wives would be flown out the
following weekend, he asserted, and an effort would be made to squeeze the
American community down to 2,000 in one week's time. He also assured the
President and Kissinger that as far as he could determine, there would be no
direct Communist assault on the city (hence, no need for an assessment of
Thieu's defense plans). Nor did his own "advisors," he said, expect morale to
crumble, or popular sentiment to turn against the American community for
one week or more, even if Congress voted down the aid proposal.

He then turned to the subject he had raised in his cable two days before.
Thieu would be effectively "finished," he insisted, if Congress were to vote no
on aid. Therefore, said the Ambassador, he proposed to go to the South
Vietnamese President in the next day or so and suggest that he step down
before his generals forced him to.

Martin also reminded Kissinger of what he had told him during their
meetings in Washington in late March. There should be a price for détente,
he said. The Soviets and the Chinese should be made to realize that their own

interests would be served by exercising constraint on Hanoi.

Even by Martin's now well-established standards the cable was somewhat extreme. The only "goddamn fool" in Washington who could ultimately dispatch troops to Vietnam, after all, was the President himself. Then, too, for the first time Martin was here urging a change in the Saigon government and a real peace initiative (through Hanoi's allies) even prior to the Congressional decision on the aid proposal. The very suggestion was a measure of Mérillon's persuasiveness.

For the Administration the message was the last straw. Its shrillness was galling enough, but to add to its unpleasantness, it reached Washington at the very moment Congress was demolishing last hopes for the $722 million aid proposal. That same afternoon the Senate Armed Services Committee voted not to support additional military aid at any price. Although several other committees were still to be heard from, Kissinger, dejected, conceded defeat. "The Vietnam debate is over," he told a group of legislators. "The Administration will accept the Congress' verdict without recrimination or vindictiveness."

An hour or so later the State Department, acting on directives from WSAG, began pulling together an interagency task force to take charge of the evacuation in Martin's stead. Dean Brown, a fifty-eight-year-old former Foreign Service officer, was called out of retirement to head it up. Brown, who had left the Department only a month before, had served in various overseas posts, and as Deputy Undersecretary of Management, had impressed Kissinger with his administrative skills.*

To alert the Ambassador to this change of plan, Kissinger sent him a back-channel message just before midnight, Saigon time. Opening in a conciliatory vein, he assured Martin that he and the President were now seriously considering his proposal for Thieu's removal. (In fact, the State Department had just been ordered to begin canvassing various "friendly" countries in Southeast Asia in search of a point of refuge for the South Vietnamese leader.) In the meantime, Kissinger went on, the situation in Congress had gotten out

---

*The Administration's decision to seize the initiative was also prompted by continuing pessimism among intelligence analysts over the military picture. CIA Director Colby lavished his own gloom on Kissinger during a meeting of WSAG on the seventeenth: "We believe that the Communists will have overpowering forces deployed into positions for an assault on Saigon within a matter of days . . . A Communist military victory is likely within one to three weeks. The Viet Cong's Provisional Revolutionary Government has maintained that the best protection the U.S. can afford its personnel is to withdraw them immediately, and that such withdrawals would 'not encounter any difficulties or obstacles.' . . . As for the evacuation of South Vietnamese, the Communists are maintaining a hostile public attitude, but we have tenuous indications of possible flexibility in this position." Here Colby cited the recent report from Tran Van Don. Although he went on to describe Don as an "opportunist" and said "we are skeptical about his veracity," he added, "nonetheless the Communists do appear to be peddling the line that if Thieu were replaced, a less bloody outcome would be possible. This theme surfaced in a recent report of a conversation between Buddhist leader Thich Tri Quang and an individual whom he believed was a PRG representative. North Vietnamese and PRG representatives in Paris have made similar statements in the past week or so." Colby thus managed to underscore the prospects, such as they were, for a disguised surrender even as he wrote Saigon off militarily.

of hand. Furthermore, various agencies were becoming increasingly convinced that the "worst case"—a helo-lift during a full-scale NVA attack on Saigon —was inevitable, and were therefore pressuring the White House to withdraw all surplus Embassy personnel as soon as possible. "Given the political realities," the Secretary continued, "drastic action is required" to ensure a Vietnamese evacuation as well as an American one. Therefore, every effort was to be made to reduce the American community to 1,100 within less than a week. Martin also was to submit a plan at once for evacuating as many as 200,000 Vietnamese.

In the final paragraphs of his message Kissinger asked Martin to comment further on a matter he had raised in his own previous dispatch—the feasibility and wisdom of approaching the Soviets for help in bringing about a cease-fire and a settlement.

Martin wasted no time in responding to that last query. As he later explained to me, he called Washington by secure phone shortly after receiving Kissinger's cable and told the Secretary "by all means go ahead with the overture to Moscow." The bargaining chip was to be the resignation of Nguyen Van Thieu.

He was less enthusiastic, however, about some of the other things mentioned in Kissinger's message. The reference to the growing concern in Washington over the "worst case" particularly troubled him, for he felt it denoted a sense of panic, even unreality, that could upset his own carefully calibrated plans, especially his hopes for arranging some kind of breathing spell through Thieu's removal. In an effort to put a brake on those who would move too hastily, Martin filed a full comment on Kissinger's remarks the following morning.

With the "airlift available," he assured the Secretary, it would be possible to cut the American community to 1,700 people by "close-of-business" on the twenty-third. Yet, "we cannot," he said, "possibly broaden the categories of Vietnamese citizens excluded from the Vietnamese travel ban [active military officers and government officials] without engendering panic we should all be striving to avoid." Consequently, "we do not consider it feasible to try to assume responsibility to lift all the Vietnamese [200,000], to whom the President refers, from Saigon. We will instruct our own local employees to make their way to designated spots on the coast where they can be evacuated." He also assured Kissinger that "press principals" had been informed that "after the fall of South Vietnam we will be able to negotiate for the release and safe exit of Vietnamese nationals who worked for Americans." (In fact, the North Vietnamese had never guaranteed this to anyone.)

With respect to those panic-stricken "agencies" Kissinger had alluded to, Martin suggested coyly that evacuation planning be left to appropriate military officers and warned that "automatic assumption" of the worst case could "automatically bring it about." He also advised against attempts by anyone in Washington to give "instructions" to any separate element of the Embassy itself. (He undoubtedly had Alan Carter and his USIA and CIA contacts in mind.) "We are a close-knit family here and such end runs will not work," he emphasized. "But constant attempts could cause chaos if they continued."

By any standard, it was a classic Martin performance: rhetoric as a straight-edged razor. But if he was hoping to cut the alarmists at home down to size, he failed miserably. Some of those in Washington who saw the message concluded he had become unbalanced. Several members of Habib's staff suggested he be removed for "reasons of health." Kissinger himself was furious. "Unacceptable!" he bellowed when he read over the cable—and he promptly ordered Martin to begin planning for an evacuation of both Americans and Vietnamese along the lines he had prescribed.

What particularly rankled Kissinger, and frightened so many others, was Martin's cavalier treatment of the Vietnamese evacuation issue. Only a few days before, President Ford had explicitly committed the Administration to saving at least 200,000 locals; now Martin was unilaterally rejecting the idea as "not feasible." He was even threatening to make his prognosis self-fulfilling by casting all of his plans in terms of an unprotected withdrawal through Vung Tau, a contingency the Pentagon considered wholly impractical.

Despite the outcry over Martin's evacuation proposals, however, his views on the political option did find an echo. In a speech to a group of newspaper editors on the seventeenth, Kissinger proclaimed solemnly, "We shall not forget who supplied the arms which North Vietnam used to make a mockery of its signature on the Paris accords." With that, he put Moscow publicly on notice, as Martin had suggested, that Vietnam was still part of the fabric of détente.

Aside from the Ambassador, no one in the Embassy was made privy to the Administration's plans for Thieu or for the Soviets, at least not at once. But the futility of the negotiating track now seemed scarcely in doubt to many of us. Neither the Soviets nor the Chinese had shown any willingness to help work out a compromise, and the North Vietnamese were hanging toughest of all. While insisting on the ouster of the entire "Thieu clique," they were now pressing hard for the withdrawal of an extravagant number of American "military advisors," with no clear indication of who qualified and who didn't. Nor were they offering anything concrete in return.

Moreover, within hours of Martin's message to Washington on the seventeenth, one of the Station's best-informed agents provided fresh intelligence that should have cast doubt on all the Ambassador was angling for. As it happened, I was the instrument of his revelations.

Just before noon a senior case officer called me at my office, said the agent was coming in out of the field, and asked if I would like to join him for discussions at a nearby safe house. I told him I would be there within the hour.

As I drove across the city to the rendezvous point, I could scarcely contain my excitement. The agent had long been a wellspring of extraordinarily accurate intelligence. If anyone could give us an insight into Hanoi's plans, he could.

He arrived in full disguise, and though we had met several times before, I hardly recognized him behind the false glasses and other paraphernalia. He greeted me politely, and after a few sips of canned Budweiser (a delicacy behind Communist lines) he began spinning out his story, the gleanings of recent top-level briefings.

The North Vietnamese, he said, would fight on until total victory, whether or not Thieu was overthrown or the United States supplied additional aid. On the basis of decisions made in late March, they felt it was better to sacrifice men in a large military push than to waste time trying to achieve victory through a coalition government. There would be no negotiations and no coalition, he emphasized (he was quite categorical about this).

When I asked him about the projected attacks against Saigon, he indicated there had been slippage. The offensive would not be mounted as scheduled, on 19 April. But the Communist high command, he said, was determined to celebrate Ho Chi Minh's birthday, 19 May, in Saigon (precisely the objective Dung and his comrades had set for themselves only a day or so before). Given the lead time they would need to meet this deadline, he speculated, they would initiate their final drive by the first of May at the latest.

Their primary targets would be air bases, ammunition depots and military installations. Long-range artillery and even air power would be used against the city, and radar had already been set up on Black Virgin Mountain north of Tay Ninh City to help guide the air strikes. The high command, he added, was even now making "arrangements" for the protection of the Communist delegations at Tan Son Nhut.

When I arrived back at the Embassy, Polgar was not in his office, and I went to see Pittman next door. As I was rehashing what I had learned, Polgar walked in, listened impassively a few minutes, then cut me off. "Nothing new in that," he muttered. "We've heard it all before. No need to disseminate it." With that, he walked out.

For a moment I stood dazed. No dissemination? Surely there must be some mistake. Ignoring Pittman, I grabbed up my notes and rushed after Polgar into his office. As he settled in behind his desk, I was already trying to change his mind. Yes, we had received such gloomy information before, I conceded. But this source had brought it all together and added crucial detail —the absolute veto on negotiations, the air strikes and the targets of the campaign, and above all: the slippage and the rescheduling of the launch date. No other recent report had provided us with so much data on Hanoi's latest plans.

Polgar rubbed his nose nervously and appeared not to hear. I pleaded with him to let me send my notes home through "operational channels" at least, so analysts at CIA headquarters could crank them into their own analyses. At last he agreed—but "ops channels only," he emphasized.

And so the report was transmitted, clattering out over our high-speed transmitters as an in-house "ops cable" for headquarters background use only. No one else in Washington was to receive a copy. Seldom had such high-level intelligence been relegated to such low-level treatment.

Thankfully, the reception in Washington was more enthusiastic. CIA headquarters immediately broke the report out of the "ops channel" format, turned it into a priority intelligence dispatch and flashed it to all key consumers, including Kissinger's staff, Gayler's headquarters in Honolulu and the Saigon Embassy itself. Gayler was so impressed that he called the Station directly over his hot line to check into several details, particularly those concerning the planned radar-guided air strikes.

That night corroborating information poured in through other channels. Highly sensitive sources revealed that North Vietnamese pilots were training with captured aircraft at Danang airfield, and a reliable agent confirmed that the offensive against Saigon had been delayed for a short while, though was still in the offing.

"We did have information from a long-range penetration in the so-called COSVN," Martin later explained to Congress, "which indicated that regardless of all the other by-play, the North Vietnamese were now determined to press a strict military solution. At that time the report was not given that much credibility by the CIA Station Chief. It was not until he was pressed by the officer who was in direct contact with his penetration that this man was allowed to send it back through operational channels."

The problem, of course, was that Polgar, for the most humane reasons, had become so emotionally committed to the idea of a negotiated "way out" that he could no longer judge contradictory intelligence objectively. Although some of the information the source had provided me had been reported elsewhere, many of the specifics were new. So was the mesh. For the first time we had a complete blueprint of Hanoi's own "end game."*

Notwithstanding his later remarks to Congress, Martin initially was no more receptive to the report than Polgar was. To accept its veracity and its implications was to concede disaster, for if the North Vietnamese were indeed bent on moving against Saigon by the first of May, there was little chance for an orderly evacuation of Americans or Vietnamese, or for the change in government Martin now considered essential. Thus, rather than acknowledge these hopeless realities, he chose simply to shrug off what the agent had told me and to proceed as if nothing had changed. His only concession to the

---

*After the collapse of South Vietnam, Polgar persisted in arguing that my report of the seventeenth had added nothing new to what we already had known about Communist intentions, thanks to earlier disclosures by the same source and others. To support his judgment he noted that the intelligence evaluators in Shackley's East Asia Division had given it a rather modest "value rating" when it was first filed. In my view this "defense" merely underscores the fact that Polgar was not the only man in the CIA who was misled by Hanoi's peace propaganda in the last days of the war. But more to the point: even if my report had not been so revealing and useful, it would have been wrong under any circumstances to block its dissemination as Polgar tried to do. For given the confusion and conflicting signals that assailed us in those final days, intelligence analysts and policy-makers in Washington needed every scrap of information available to try to clarify Hanoi's intentions. Apart from its content, the report was doubly crucial, for the agent who generated it was someone generally recognized throughout the U.S. government as our best source on Communist intentions.

intelligence was purely tactical. A few hours after I had filed the report, he canceled the Joint Military Team's liaison flight to Hanoi so that the last ranking North Vietnamese delegate at Tan Son Nhut would be unable to depart, as he was evidently planning to do. Martin thus thwarted the "arrangements" the Communists were making for the safety of their representatives at the air base.

My imbroglio with Polgar left me bitter and frightened. As long as he and Martin refused to accept the inevitability of a Communist assault, it seemed likely they would continue to subordinate the evacuation effort to their peace gambit. In my anxiety I resolved to try to signal to Washington once again (as I had earlier through Moose and Miessner) how far off-track I thought they were.

Alan Carter, the maverick USIA chief, was giving a dinner party that evening for several American journalists. The dinner was another of his rebellious little acts, since Martin had outlawed all contacts with the press except those he personally approved.

I called Carter and asked if I could wangle an invitation. "No problem," he said. "But I got to warn you most of the guests probably know your agency affiliations. They'll be asking leading questions." I said that was exactly what I wanted.

The group was a perfect cross section. The electronic media had its spokesmen in Garrick Utley of NBC and Bob Simon of CBS. Keyes Beech of the *Chicago Daily News* and George McArthur of the *Los Angeles Times* were our token old-timers, both veteran war correspondents who had made a life and career of Vietnam. Fox Butterfield, patrician gadfly of the *New York Times,* who prided himself on his contacts with Polgar and the Ambassador, showed up stylishly late. So did the Embassy's most unlikely *bête noire,* Phil McComb, former speech writer for New York's conservative Senator William Buckley, who had managed to offend Martin several months before by writing a series on corruption and morale problems in the South Vietnamese army for the *Washington Post.*

Most of the guests had heard me brief before and knew me to be well informed. So they listened with more than casual interest to what I told them over dinner. After briefly detailing the balance of forces, I turned to my main topic. Without identifying my source, I emphasized that there was good evidence the Communists had decided in favor of a military solution and were determined to celebrate Ho Chi Minh's birthday in Saigon. Their planning apparently did not allow for a negotiated settlement, or even a disguised surrender. I said I was telling them all this in hopes they would get the message to Washington.

McArthur and Butterfield protested. Both had recently interviewed top Embassy officials, and they accurately played back to me what they had been told: (1) the Communists had neither the manpower nor political "assets" to absorb the country in one sweep; and (2) with some satisfactory changes in the

Saigon government, they might be willing to work through the existing political structure for a while, if only to maximize their chances of attracting non-Communist aid and investment.

I acknowledged that all this made good sense in purely speculative terms, but stressed that what I had told them was not speculation but fact, a precise reflection of Hanoi's most recent guidelines.

None of the reporters filed stories on what I said. Several months later Beech apologized to me for his failure to do so. The Ambassador, he explained, had done such a "snow job" on the press corps—denying interviews, then parceling them out with exquisite timing—that no one could quite accept what other officials (aside from Polgar) were leaking to them.

Still, my performance was not an utter waste. Several of the reporters who had been at the dinner began calling me regularly to fish for additional information and to pass on observations from their own forays to the battlefront. As days passed and the Station's own agents disappeared, the intelligence they provided became an invaluable window on what was taking place only a few miles away.

Controlled Conditions

Friday morning, the eighteenth, the substance of my agent report was nervously discussed at a pre-WSAG priming session at the State Department. "Who was the originator?" one of the more skeptical State Department officers demanded. A CIA representative identified me by name and said my work was generally considered "trustworthy." The State man nodded and suggested Kissinger ought to be informed "soonest."

The suggestion withered on the bureaucratic vine. Because of the circuitous dissemination process occasioned by Polgar's objections—ops channels first, then regular distribution channels—the report did not reach Kissinger's desk until much later in the day. By then he had already launched the negotiating initiative that now seemed so much in question.

As he had advised Martin in their phone conversation the night before, his approach was directed not at Hanoi itself, but at its principal ally, the Soviet Union. Meeting with Soviet Ambassador Anatoly Dobrynin around midday in Washington, Kissinger handed him a note from Ford to Brezhnev. "Our overriding concern," said the message, was to achieve "controlled conditions" for the evacuation of Americans and select Vietnamese. To this purpose, the United States was prepared to discuss a cease-fire and "political problems." An immediate reply was requested.

During the conversation Kissinger elaborated on these points. Should a cease-fire be arranged, he told Dobrynin, the United States would immediately stop supplying Saigon. Moreover, pending a response to its queries, the Administration would expect the North Vietnamese to refrain from launching attacks against Saigon, Tan Son Nhut or evacuation aircraft. Any attack on an American plane, he emphasized (and here he obviously was thinking of the SA-2s), would create a "most dangerous situation" for Hanoi.

He also assured the Soviet Ambassador that there had been no direct overture to Hanoi or China. The United States, he said, was intent on dealing exclusively with the Soviet Union on this matter, in the interest of preserving their "special relationship."

Kissinger's remarks were both a plea and an ultimatum, a request for Soviet assistance and, implicitly, a warning that détente could be imperiled, and Hanoi threatened, if such help was not forthcoming. His comments also gave new meaning to trends on the battlefield, for all of us would now be looking closely for any signs of constraint on Hanoi's part, a lull in the fighting.

As the meeting broke up, Dobrynin promised Kissinger that Moscow would supply an answer to his questions as soon as possible. In fact, the answer was already at hand. The definitive agent report on Hanoi's plans filed on 8 April had warned that the "talk of a coalition and negotiations" was merely a ruse to keep us, and the South Vietnamese, off balance. My more recent debriefing of our primary agent had corroborated this and revealed that the delay in the Communist drive on Saigon was tactical, not political: the Ho Chi Minh campaign would enter its climactic phase in precisely two weeks.

Within a few hours of the Dobrynin-Kissinger discussion, the *New York Times* reported from Moscow that "Soviet diplomats" had recently informed "well-placed sources" there that they did not expect the Communists to attempt to seize Saigon or to win the war in the "current campaign." The story undoubtedly reflected the essence of Dobrynin's most private assurances to Kissinger, or at least what Moscow wanted us to believe. According to the newspaper account, this analysis of North Vietnamese intentions was based on dispatches from the Soviet Embassy in Hanoi on the thirteenth and fourteenth. The North Vietnamese, said the *Times*, had informed Soviet diplomats on these dates that their resources were stretched too thin to permit an early victory.

As General Dung acknowledges in his own memoirs, the fourteenth did indeed have special significance. It was then that he and his field commanders met at Loc Ninh to chart out their next move and to reaffirm their intent to achieve victory "before the beginning of the rainy season," despite logistically imposed delays. It would appear, then, that the Soviets were deliberately misleading the *Times'* "well-placed sources" in suggesting there would be no attempt to seize Saigon in the "current campaign," or were being misled themselves by the North Vietnamese. Since Moscow had its own spy-in-the-sky satellites and its agents inside the North Vietnamese command, it is in fact inconceivable that the Soviet leadership did not know the outlines of Dung's true plans at the time Dobrynin conferred with Kissinger on Friday morning.

Dean Brown, head of the new interagency evacuation task force, was one of the few officials in Washington to be fully briefed on the Kissinger-Dobrynin meeting. He told several of his subordinates that there was a chance for negotiations, that political issues were being discussed at various levels, but he emphasized that none of this would affect their work. They were to plan for an evacuation as if they were racing the clock and the North Vietnamese army.

Brown began laying the groundwork only hours after receiving his marching orders from Kissinger. Shuffling bodies and desks in the State Department's situation room, he quickly pulled together the semblance of a staff. Since he already knew of the exploits of Rosenblatt and his luncheon group, he immediately made them charter members. Eventually, representatives from thirteen separate government agencies were dealt in as well. It was a large group, almost too large for effective crisis management, but unlike Habib's informal task force before it, it did not have to concern itself with such diverse and essentially extraneous matters as trying to sell the Administration's aid bill to Congress. Its only task was to stage-manage an evacuation.

From the outset Brown accepted as a "given" that large numbers of Vietnamese would have to be included in any evacuation program. The main questions were how many and under what kind of immigration authority.

There was also the subsidiary problem of where to put all the beneficiaries. Initially, Pentagon officials and the military proposed merely a localized shift, a mass relocation of endangered Vietnamese to Can Tho or to Con Son or Phu Quoc Islands off the coast of the delta. But this was quickly dismissed as pointless. If the Communists scored a decisive victory, it was decided, they undoubtedly would bring such outlying areas under control. Another proposal focused on Thailand, but the State Department turned this one down on the sensible grounds that the new center-left civilian coalition in Bangkok would never tolerate a massive influx of Vietnamese refugees.

One foreign government did offer substantial assistance, however. The regime on Taiwan privately informed the State Department on the eighteenth that it would accept large numbers of South Vietnamese military personnel if they would bring their arms, aircraft and equipment with them. Kissinger ruminated on the proposal, but ultimately rejected it, lest the Communist Chinese be offended.

With so few practical alternatives available, it quickly became apparent that the United States itself would have to absorb the vast majority of the evacuees. But who was to take charge of this potentially mammoth enterprise? After some debate at the White House and the State Department, the decision was made to give the job to the Army, Navy and Air Force, for of all the agencies of government, they seemed best qualified to handle a national disaster, as the evacuation was already being described in some quarters of Congress. Each branch of the Armed Forces was promptly invited to "volunteer" an installation as a temporary resettlement center.

Even before the task force became fully operational, a search was undertaken for a series of way stations across the Pacific to support the expanded airlift. Since the Marcos government in the Philippines was already complaining bitterly about the influx of refugees, it was questionable whether Clark air base could be used as a transit point much longer. One logical alternative was the old U.S. B-52 base on the American protectorate of Guam. At the prompting of the State Department, the governor of the island soon offered to accept 25,000 Vietnamese as permanent residents and announced that the island could be used as a rest station for others if necessary.

One of the most awesome hurdles facing the task force was the Immigration and Naturalization Service itself. With the American economy in recession and unemployment hovering close to eight percent, the INS and its Congressional watchdogs were in no mood to open the door to a flood of Asian refugees.

Only at the direct intervention of Lawrence Eagleburger, Kissinger's special assistant, were the agency's inhibitions finally overcome. Throughout the day on the eighteenth, Eagleburger pleaded with Kissinger to go to the President and demand a broadening of the latest immigration parole. At last Kissinger was persuaded, and through him, so was Ford. Within the next several hours the Attorney General, at the President's direction, drew up a new parole that would enable thousands of Americans and Vietnamese in the United States and elsewhere outside Vietnam to arrange for the evacuation of relatives in Saigon simply by filing a visa petition with the INS. In short, it became possible to sponsor Vietnamese evacuees long-distance, so long as you could demonstrate some family tie.

As the State Department marshaled its resources, the Pentagon did likewise. During the next several days Whitmire's fleet was expanded to include five carriers, a dozen destroyers, nearly as many amphibious naval craft, eight cargo ships and 4,000 marines. Additional American jet fighters were shifted to Thailand to provide air cover if necessary.

At the same time Administration officials redoubled their efforts to win Congressional approval for a militarily supported evacuation. In a series of committee hearings on the seventeenth and eighteenth Kissinger battered away at the obstacles. While pleading with the legislators not to tie the President's hands, he attempted to restore confidence in Martin's own responsiveness and capabilities. "An accomplished diplomat," he said of the Ambassador. "A man performing with great skill the difficult job of protecting American lives and upholding South Vietnamese morale."

He also began leveling with Congress on a number of key issues. Discussing the prospect of negotiations, he acknowledged that Hanoi was showing no flexibility and was still demanding Thieu's resignation. "I don't believe any one personality is going to be the key to a settlement," he added, as if to shoot down the French notion that "Big" Minh might be. He also spoke frankly of the real utility of additional aid, *any* aid. Merely a "bargaining chip," he conceded, "to achieve negotiations, a humane transition of power and controlled conditions" for a safe evacuation.

In a final concession to Congress, Kissinger provided the Senate Foreign Relations Committee with a copy of his plan for reducing the American community in Saigon to less than 2,000 in one week's time. With this prospectus in hand, the committee's attitude softened, and on Friday afternoon, the eighteenth, it voted to recommend $200 million for relief and evacuation as well as the use of troops (on a limited basis) for the evacuation of both Americans and "endangered" Vietnamese. The only thing that remained was for the full Congress itself to give its approval.

• · • •

With the Administration now bent on a speedier drawdown, there was more room than ever for improvisation in Washington, and Rosenblatt and his colleagues were quick to take advantage of it. One of their number, Ken Quinn, showed himself particularly adept at this. On Friday afternoon he dropped by the White House and persuaded the President's staff to send a cable to Saigon calling for a special evacuation program for the friends and relatives of Foreign Service officers, such as Quinn's own Vietnamese in-laws. As an added precaution, he called his State Department friend, Lacy Wright, in Saigon and asked him to put his wife's family on an outgoing flight if the Ambassador failed to do so.

When Martin received the message Quinn had inspired, he called Wright to his office. Although he knew nothing of the private communications between the two young officers, he considered Wright the logical man to organize the operation the White House prescribed, since he had been agitating for weeks for the evacuation of Vietnamese friends and employees.

During their conversation Martin emphasized the need for secrecy, pointing out that some of the potential evacuees had no Vietnamese exit papers and would have to be spirited out without the knowledge of Saigon's emigration authorities. Wright frowned and nervously fingered his pin-stripe vest. Secrecy might be difficult, he allowed, particularly since State Department contacts had already sent him the names of over 200 so-called Vietnamese "dependents."

During the next several hours Wright frantically organized, assembling a small task force to help him. His plan of action was something reminiscent of James Bond. Each morning a certain number of seats were to be blocked out on military flights to the Philippines or Guam. Then a corresponding number of evacuees were to be assembled at one of four safe houses (high walls, away from the street) around town, and from there smuggled directly to the loading ramp at Tan Son Nhut without any stop-off at the consular checkpoints in the DAO gymnasium.

At first Wright and his team tried to hold to Martin's guidelines, excluding draft-age males and active-duty troopers. But eventually their passenger lists were expanded to accommodate just about anybody, including a great many "low-risk" individuals—chauffeurs, cooks and gardeners. Such charity was not without cost. Each time one of Wright's marginal cases was secreted aboard a C-141, another Vietnamese, perhaps equally deserving but with no special ties to an American Foreign Service officer, was forced to step back one place in DAO's waiting lines.

Wright, of course, was only one of many who flaunted the rules for magnanimous purposes. Fred Gulden, an architect for USAID, had refused several days before to leave when his name had appeared on a non-essentials list, and had taken it upon himself to arrange for the evacuation of some of his own Vietnamese employees. Similarly, Walt Martindale, the young Embassy officer who had played such a pivotal role in the evacuation of Nha

Trang, was now shuttling secretly between Saigon and Phu Quoc Island, trying to identify refugees from MR 2 so he could assure them a seat on the airlift out of Tan Son Nhut.

General Smith, meanwhile, was pressing the Ambassador to authorize a secret airlift for Vietnamese who for one reason or another could not obtain exit papers, or whose departure, if known, might affect the morale of the population at large. On Thursday afternoon two of his trusted subordinates, Legro and Colonel McCurdy, visited Chief Consul Walter Burke at the Embassy to inquire into the "legalities" of such an airlift. Burke conceded that Smith could order up "black" flights on his own, provided they were kept within modest bounds and the evacuees had legal American immigration papers.

The next morning two C-141 transports were loaded with variously documented Vietnamese and sent out of the country under totally "black" conditions. Neither the Thieu government nor the Ambassador, for that matter, was informed. A few hours later Kissinger's deputy, Brent Scowcroft, sent Martin a curt message directing him to launch a "black" airlift himself.

Within an hour or so of these first "black" flights George Jacobson ordered up a secret Air America run to Thailand to haul out the families of the CIA-trained technicians who worked for the Vietnamese Ministry of Defense. The 143 passengers, mostly women and children, were the first Vietnamese to benefit from a CIA "black" flight. Unfortunately, there would not be many more. Although individual CIA men continued to smuggle friends and co-workers onto DAO "black" flights and the regular military shuttle, the Station itself did not mount any sizable "black" airlift on its own. Polgar's continuing hopes and illusions were partly to blame, but there were other obstacles as well, bureaucratic ones. As long as Martin refused "officially" to open the gates to draft-age males and government officials, Polgar could not authorize the departure of any agents or Vietnamese employees of the Station who fell into these categories. And since a great many of them did, we remained stymied in our efforts to move out large numbers of Vietnamese, secretly or otherwise.*

As the Embassy stumbled into the first phase of its accelerated drawdown, the consulate in Bien Hoa, fifteen miles away, was in the process of closing up altogether. By the morning of the eighteenth the local CIA base had been cut to eight officers and the State Department contingent to five, and a cloud of incinerator dust hung over the parking lot like some baleful talisman of defeat as the Marine guards burned the last of the classified files.

*Nor did CIA headquarters do much to help. At one point Polgar asked Colby by cable to dip into the agency's contingency funds to cover the costs of evacuating a group of "sensitive" Vietnamese. Colby refused. Since he was under orders from Kissinger to do nothing to upset the political chemistry in Saigon, he felt it would be impossible to justify an airlift that in effect overstepped the country's laws.

Shortly before noon Taggart, the local CIA Base Chief, hustled his young subordinate, John Stockwell, onto a chopper bound for Saigon. For the past three days the friction between the two men had steadily worsened as Stockwell had continued to press for the evacuation of large numbers of their Vietnamese employees. The final blowup had come when Stockwell, totally disregarding Taggart's orders, had tried to organize a small flotilla to take his own Vietnamese friends and co-workers downriver to the sea. Taggart had learned of the scheme before it could be carried very far and was now determined to be rid of his zealous subordinate before he did something that might panic the city's population.

When he and Stockwell got in to see Polgar later in the day, Taggart accused the young officer of insubordination and asked the Station Chief to veto once and for all the riverborne evacuation plan. Although Polgar had always respected Stockwell, he decided to act on Taggart's recommendation, particularly since Stockwell seemed insistent on taking all sorts of personal risks (to the point of accompanying the boats downriver) to ensure the success of the operation. Having just lost Lew James to the Communists, Polgar was not about to let another CIA man put himself in jeopardy.

After the meeting Taggart returned to Bien Hoa alone and promptly handed the boats Stockwell had assembled over to the local province chief. He then completed plans for evacuating the Americans on his staff.

Although some of Taggart's Vietnamese employees ultimately got to Saigon on their own, few of them were included in the airlift out of the capital itself. Both Taggart and Dick Peters, the Consul General from Bien Hoa, departed the country several days before Saigon's collapse and merely left it to colleagues in the Embassy to provide for the Vietnamese who had served them so well.

As Martin had feared, the step-up in the evacuation had an immediate and adverse effect on the mood of the population, giving rise to fresh apprehension and bitterness. On the evening of the seventeenth, during a dinner party at the home of former Prime Minister Khiem, Charlie Timmes discovered how deep these emotions ran. Throughout the five-course repast Madame Khiem, a plump, bejeweled lady, wept openly and loudly, pleading to be allowed to leave the country now that the Americans were making their own exit. Khiem himself seemed equally despondent, though for reasons of his own. There was little chance that Thieu would step down voluntarily, he confided to Timmes. Ky was again threatening a coup and there was no clear evidence that the Communists would be willing to deal with "Big" Minh. Therefore, he hoped Timmes would remember his Vietnamese "friends" when the time came.

From the ramparts of his own cloistered existence Thieu himself was also beginning to glimpse the inevitable. He could hardly avoid it. Shortly before dawn on the eighteenth a Communist commando squad struck at the Phu Lam radar installation in Saigon's western suburb, thus bringing the war to the city's doorstep. An hour or so later General Toan, the MR 3 commander, flew in from his headquarters in Bien Hoa to advise Thieu that the war in fact was already lost. The army was in disarray and hopelessly outnumbered, he said, and could not be expected to hold for more than another two or three days. He also confirmed the fall of Phan Rang and the capture of General Nghi, and advised Thieu that the President's own ancestral gravesite outside Phan Rang had been bulldozed by ARVN stragglers just before the Communists moved in.

As if this were not enough to ruin Thieu's morning, a group of distinguished moderates and opposition figures got in touch with him just before noon to warn him time also had run out on the political front. They would call for his resignation in six days, they promised, if he refused to step down.

In a vain effort to placate his critics, Thieu promptly ordered the arrest of several military officers who, he claimed, were far more responsible than he for the debacles of the past few weeks. Among those tossed in jail was the pathetic General Phu, who for days had languished in a near-comatose state at a tuberculosis sanitarium outside Saigon. His accomplice in disaster, General Truong of MR I, was not included in the roll-up, however, for he was still considered too essential a field commander to be cashiered so abruptly.*

Later in the day the Embassy came to Thieu's assistance in deflecting yet another threat. In light of what Timmes had learned at the Khiem dinner the night before, Martin had decided something must be done to rein in that constant troublemaker Nguyen Cao Ky. Therefore, around midafternoon he and Timmes paid a call on the Air Marshal at his home at Tan Son Nhut.

In the course of the two-hour conversation they repeatedly assured Ky that he and his followers "had a role to play" in bringing about a settlement. In fact, Martin believed quite the opposite. If Ky were to insinuate himself into any future government, there could be no hope for negotiations. But the Ambassador also realized that the only way to keep the road clear for a smooth, fully constitutional transfer of power was to give Ky and his hotheads the impression that their interests would be served in the bargain. As Ky himself later admitted, Martin succeeded magnificently in this. By the end of the exchange the Air Marshal had agreed to "allow" Thieu to remain in office, even as effective power was handed over to someone else. (He supposed himself.)

Sadly for historians, the Martin-Ky dialogue was never fully documented. When Timmes sat down that evening to draft a memo on it, he discovered that the tape recorder he had hidden in his briefcase during the meeting had jammed. He had to stay up all night dredging the details out of memory and never quite got them straight, as the Ambassador later emphatically observed.

•   •   •

*Not that Truong was suffering his disgrace gladly. Several days before, Timmes had visited him at a field hospital, where he was recovering from a case of jangled nerves. Truong, in tears, had lambasted Thieu for changing his marching orders so often and capriciously during the final days of MR I.

Apart from conspirators and the North Vietnamese, Thieu also was facing another compelling problem at the moment—money. Earlier in the month, on 2 and 3 April, he had shipped most of his own personal fortune and household effects to Taiwan and Canada. But the nation's fortune—the sixteen tons of gold, worth $220 million, that made up a large part of Saigon's treasury—had yet to be "expatriated."*

Initially, Thieu had hoped to ship the entire cache surreptitiously to the Bank of International Settlements in Basel, Switzerland, where $5 million in South Vietnamese gold was already on deposit, and to use it—so he claimed to subordinates—as collateral for loans to buy equipment for the army. But several days before the transaction was to be completed, the Embassy had learned of it through one of the CIA's intelligence sources, and someone on Martin's own staff, who apparently mistrusted Thieu's motives, had in turn leaked word of it to the press. The resulting publicity had aborted Thieu's plan, for the charter airlines with which he had been negotiating for shipment contracts quickly backed off for fear of drawing public criticism themselves.

In the meantime, Martin had intervened to try to limit the damage Thieu seemed determined to do to himself and his image. In hopes of dispelling the aura of suspicion surrounding the entire affair, the Ambassador had suggested to him that instead of shipping the gold to Switzerland, he deposit it in the Federal Reserve Bank of New York, where many other countries maintain quite legitimate gold reserves.

Thieu, anxious to clear himself, had readily agreed, and on the sixteenth the Embassy had cabled Washington to ask for a special military flight, complete with insurance coverage, to ferry the gold to New York. But here again obstacles loomed. The Air Force and the Federal Reserve Bank both were leery of insuring such a large amount, particularly since the pickup was to be made in a war zone. Much foot-dragging ensued, and now, two days later, as nearly eighteen NVA divisions converged on Saigon, the gold, a king's ransom, was still gathering dust in the national bank.

---

*Thieu was not the only Vietnamese notable who had seen to his personal effects by mid-April. On the sixteenth Khiem likewise shipped his household belongings—and his fortune—out of the country. Somewhat earlier, at the time of Danang's collapse, Saigon's Ambassador to Washington had directed his wife to begin looking for a new and permanent residence for them in Maryland.

Panic Button

How far do you trust your intelligence reports? You can never be sure. Saturday, the nineteenth, came and went. There was no direct assault on Saigon; the communist timetable had slipped. Apparently, that much of what our agents were telling us could be believed. But there was no slackening of the NVA offensive, either. For the first time Communist artillerymen shelled Phu Quoc Island, now home of over 50,000 refugees; two NVA divisions began their assault on Phan Thiet, ninety miles northeast of Saigon, and most ominous of all, trucks hauling SA-2 batteries continued to wind their way toward Saigon from the northeast.

Politically the signals were equally intimidating. At his regular Saturday-morning press conference the PRG's chief delegate at Tan Son Nhut, Colonel Vo Dong Giang, upped the ante, still without offering anything in return. Demanding (as usual) the withdrawal of all "American military advisors disguised as civilians," he added a new twist, insisting that Martin leave as well. "He's cloaked as an American diplomat," said Giang, "but actively directs all military, political and economic policies and is responsible for all criminal acts of the Thieu regime." Did this mean Hanoi was ruling out even a residual American presence in Saigon in the event of a Communist victory? Giang was excruciatingly vague: "There's no problem about a thousand American civilians staying, but the presence of even one American advisor would be a major violation of the Paris peace agreement."

Polgar thought he had deciphered Giang's meaning. Yes, there was a "bitter-end option," he insisted to me, a chance we could keep a residual presence in Saigon, whatever happened, just as Tran Van Don had assured us several days before. Perhaps, too, there was still room for some real political bargaining.

I wrote a memorandum in rebuttal, emphasizing Giang's vagueness, his failure to mention any form of reciprocity. Polgar read it, pigeonholed it, never sent it out—or to the Ambassador.

My skepticism turned out to be a minority position. Malcolm Browne, the

New York Times bureau chief, wrote that Giang's remarks "implied there was still time to meet" Communist conditions. It was a precise echo of Polgar's own views. This convergence of opinion, in fact, was no accident. During the past several days Polgar had been feeding the newsman opinions and classified information. The two had become confidants.

Polgar had always liked playing pundit, so his affinity for Browne, his willingness to leak data to him was understandable. Browne, moreover, was a natural ally, for some of his own "sources" were saying precisely what Polgar wanted to hear. One of them, a PRG delegate at Tan Son Nhut, had been hinting for days that a negotiated ending might be possible. Like any responsible journalist, Browne had cross-checked the story with a man in the Embassy, Polgar, who was in a position to render judgment on it. Polgar's observations apparently strengthened him in his own belief in the source's veracity, and since Browne had no way of separating Polgar's speculation from fact, he was misled into overplaying the prospects for a settlement in his own news dispatches. Hanoi could not have put together a more effective team of disinformation specialists if it had tried.

Soon after Giang's press conference, one of Polgar's own "sources" provided a further "clarification" of the North Vietnamese position. Colonel Toth, the Hungarian Military Attaché, called Polgar around midmorning and asked for a meeting. When the two got together an hour or so later, he offered the Station Chief a tantalizing new peace formula. There might be grounds for a "deal," he asserted, provided Thieu resigned "expeditiously," the Americans ended all military "intervention," and a regime "dedicated to peace, independence and neutrality" was installed at once. As Polgar later recounted the conversation to me, Toth also indicated that Minh might be an acceptable replacement for Thieu.

In addition, he assured Polgar that the Communists had no desire to "humiliate" the United States and would permit the Americans to retain an Embassy in Saigon. He emphasized that the PRG, not Hanoi, was the author of all he said.

At a compact two hundred pounds Polgar was not one to orbit easily. Yet when he bounded back into the Embassy after the meeting his feet were hardly touching ground. He felt he had been handed the key to salvation. Till now, Hanoi had been offering merely "peace" in exchange for Thieu's removal. Toth had promised much more—an actual political solution that would enable the United States to get out without humiliation or bloodshed.

Polgar immediately cabled a gist of the conversation to Washington. He then went to brief the Ambassador.

Martin was less enthusiastic. Implicit in Toth's scenario was a complete dismantling of Saigon's constitutional structure, something Martin was certain would bring on a final confrontation between the Americans and the population. Still, there was enough in what the Hungarian had said to tempt him. He therefore urged Polgar to continue the contact and to solicit more information, and advised him of Kissinger's own overtures to Dobrynin, including the demand for a hold-down in the fighting pending a reply from Hanoi.

Polgar left the Ambassador's office with his hopes and illusions intact. From this point forward, the contradictions and ambiguities in the intelligence disappeared for him. Everything he read or saw seemed to corroborate his vision of the future. The failure of the Communists to hit Saigon as expected, on the nineteenth, suddenly became in his eyes a signal, an indication that the fix was in and that Hanoi had reined in its forces as Kissinger had demanded. He advised Malcolm Browne of this theory. Soon journalists and diplomats around town were earnestly opining on the "lull," the last chance for negotiations.

Following his discussion with the Ambassador, Polgar bustled into my office to levy a new assignment. I was to write another field appraisal on the military situation. "Make it as bleak as you can," he said, "The Ambassador is going to use it to convince Thieu it's time for him to go." I was so numb with fatigue and so discouraged with Polgar, it took a few moments for the significance of the remark to register.

I needed no prompting, however, to write the appraisal as he wanted. Its bleakness was a simple reflection of the facts. "With the collapse of government defenses around Xuan Loc and the continuing NVA build-up in MR 3, the balance of forces in the greater Saigon area has shifted irreversibly in favor of the North Vietnamese and the Viet Cong," I concluded. "Although the government might be able to reinforce one of the major target areas now in imminent danger of attack—Bien Hoa/Long Binh to the east of Saigon; Long An and Hau Nghia Provinces to the west; or Binh Duong Province to the north—it does not have the strength to defend them all equally. The NVA/VC, on the other hand, will have the capacity within three or four days to launch concerted, multi-divisional assaults on all of these objectives . . . The government thus faces a situation in which Saigon itself could become isolated and cut off from the outside in a matter of two weeks or it could fall to NVA/VC forces in three or four weeks." (I wanted to suggest sooner; Polgar did not.)

My appraisal eventually became a document of some historical note, and not only for the reasons I had expected. When Thieu finally did step down he left his files intact in the Palace. No one bothered to destroy them, and among the papers the Communists captured when they seized the place was a copy of the appraisal. General Dung apparently was impressed with it, for he included near-verbatim extracts in his own postwar memoirs.

As I was busy at my typewriter, Polgar closeted himself with other Station officers to discuss ways of assuring a rapid transfer of power. Once Thieu was out, Vice-President Tran Van Huong must be prepared to give place immediately to "Big" Minh, and the National Assembly must be ready to approve the move, so it all could be done "constitutionally" (Martin's emphasis) and "expeditiously" (the Hungarians').

Next door in the French Embassy, Mérillon and his staff spent much of the morning plotting along similar lines. Martin informed them at once of the Hungarian overture, and Mérillon scheduled a meeting with Thieu for the following day.

Thieu and his entourage were not unaware of the developing cabal. On the same morning President Lee Kuan Yew of Singapore called Hoang Duc Nha and invited him to fly down at once. "Something critical to discuss," he said. When Nha arrived in Singapore hours later, Lee advised him that American officials had already queried his government and others around Southeast Asia about possible asylum for Thieu. Nha immediately called Saigon long distance. "Yes," Thieu replied after hearing Nha out. "I had expected as much."

In Washington only a handful of top-level policy-makers were briefed on Polgar's conversation with Toth. Consequently, few of the desk officers in the State Department or the CIA, who worked with the intelligence each day and who knew the situation most intimately, had a chance to weigh Polgar's (or Kissinger's) projections against the facts.

One expert who did was Douglas Pike, the Indochina specialist on the State Department's Policy Planning Staff. But Pike had already convinced himself that the Communists would rather take Saigon by subterfuge than by force, and he therefore considered the Hungarian-Soviet gambit "credible." He assured Ev Bumgardner, the USIA official on Brown's task force, that Hanoi would surely opt for a kind of Vichy regime in Saigon, and a bloodless take-over, for the sake of world opinion. Bumgardner disagreed. He could not believe the North Vietnamese would gamble on the threshold of victory. But his reservations went unheeded. He had no direct access to Kissinger. Pike did.

Several other Indochina experts, however, turned their back on optimism once and for all on Saturday the nineteenth. Within hours of Giang's press conference staffers attached to the CIA's analytical division in Washington were called in to dissect the meaning of the PRG official's remarks. Undiverted by knowledge of the Hungarian-Soviet ploy, they quickly concluded that Giang's ambiguous statements signaled a final shutting-off of the negotiating option. Like me, they were particularly struck by his failure to offer any kind of reciprocity, his omission of any reference to a possible coalition. In light of what he had said, they were prompted to review once again the latest intelligence reports from Saigon, including the one I had filed two days before. After sifting through this data, they hammered out a new intelligence estimate in time for an upcoming WSAG session. For the first time they committed themselves unequivocally to the view that Saigon was doomed; there was little chance for a negotiated settlement or even a disguised surrender.

Their conclusion did not please those in the State Department or the

upper echelons of the CIA who saw a glimmer of hope in the latest message
from the Hungarians. Shackley, who as Polgar's immediate superior felt bound
to defend his conclusions, protested the gloom. He advised Director Colby that
some allowance ought to be made for a political breakthrough, particularly in
light of Toth's remarks to Polgar.*

Meanwhile, planning and preparation for the evacuation the White House
now seemed determined to have continued to inch along. Even as Polgar was
meeting with Toth, the Embassy was notified of the new parole lifting immigration restrictions for Vietnamese dependents of Americans living outside Vietnam. Martin read over the explanatory cable with a twinge of discomfort. He
was still smarting from Kissinger's latest admonitions to him to step up the
evacuation.

A short while later a final insult was added to the injuries he had recently
suffered at the hands of his Administration colleagues. During one of my
late-morning trips to the coffee shop behind the Embassy, I realized a storm
was brewing when four or five black limousines with stars on the bumpers
pulled up just outside the back entrance. One of them I recognized as General
Smith's. According to an awed Marine guard, the largest and the shinest
belonged to "the biggest brass of them all"—Admiral Noel Gayler, commander in chief in the Pacific.

Gayler, hardly one of Martin's favorite people, had been dispatched to
Saigon this hectic Saturday morning to see to it that his old adversary understood the latest directives from Washington. He had brought a cheering section
with him, including Lieutenant General John J. Burns, commander of the U.S.
Advisory Group in Thailand. Perhaps Gayler was hoping to dazzle Martin
with all these stars and stripes of high military rank. If so, he was sadly
mistaken.

The atmosphere of the meeting would have chilled an interrogator's
sweatbox. As if to ensure the Ambassador's irritation, Polgar led off by insisting that the military situation was hopeless. Gayler agreed, and attempted to
put the "worst case" in a time frame. Reflecting on the latest intelligence, he
predicted that the Communists were on the verge of moving against the city.

---

*On the nineteenth Colby himself told WSAG, "South Vietnam faces total defeat—and soon"—
perhaps "in a few days." He repeated this estimate in a WSAG meeting the following day, and
on the twenty-first emphasized, "at this point the best a new government [in Saigon] can probably
obtain would be negotiated surrender under the guise of a political solution." He also pointed out
that "the Communists have assumed an even tougher line on negotiations," to the extent of
insisting that "final victory is at hand and that there will be no negotiations or any form of
tripartite government." He did not, however, go on to offer an opinion of his own on the chances
for such a solution. Lower-ranking CIA officials were somewhat less cautious. "The Communists
appear to be ruling out any consideration of a genuine negotiation of the conflict," they wrote in
their daily intelligence bulletin for the President on 21 April. "At a press conference in Saigon
Saturday the Viet Cong spokesman carefully avoided mentioning negotiations with the present
government or even a reconstituted one such as they had been demanding . . . An equally tough
line emerged from a secret briefing of senior Communist officials in COSVN." Here the analysts
cited my report of a few days before.

The offensive could come within ten days, he said, or within three weeks at the outside. Therefore, he wanted to "pull the cord" on the evacuation. Martin should attempt to cut the American community to a manageable 1,100 at once. At the same time all Vietnamese who were to be evacuated should be put aboard the freighters currently standing by in the Saigon River and sent out through Vung Tau. Although such a riverborne evacuation was hardly the best or safest way to rescue Vietnamese, there now seemed to be no other choice, particularly since the White House was intent on clearing the decks for a helo-lift of Americans as soon as possible.

Martin listened, nodded, but would not commit himself. And as had often been his tactic in the past when his preferences were challenged, he waged his counterattack on points of detail. How many evacuees could be accommodated in the final daylong helo-lift? he asked. Burns conceded 1,900, plus an 800-man Marine security force. If that was so, Martin rejoined, then it was unnecessary to cut to 1,100 immediately, as the White House demanded. Up to 2,000 Americans could be left in Saigon till the last minute without prejudicing the chances for a successful helo-lift.

But what about the Vietnamese? Gayler posed. The freighters were ready to sail. No, Martin replied softly, they could not be used, either now or in the next day or so. If Vietnamese with no exit papers were to be put aboard them, the city would be plunged into chaos.

Throughout the exchange General Smith sat quietly, offering no opinion for or against the Ambassador's views. Yet when Martin had finally (it seemed) demolished the case for an immediate evacuation by river, he felt obliged to inject an observation. If the freighters could not be used, he said, then some other means must be found to move out Vietnamese who could not qualify as American dependents under the latest immigration parole. As one solution, he suggested a dramatic broadening of the definition of "dependent." Perhaps a simple "affidavit of support" would suffice, he said. It need only be a scrap of paper with the Embassy's consular seal on it, the name of a Vietnamese beneficiary and the signature of an American sponsor. By signing the document, any American in Saigon could legally declare himself financial guardian to any Vietnamese he chose and thus make him eligible as a "dependent" for entry into the United States.

Martin did not like the idea at all. It could lead to a sudden mass exodus of Vietnamese and thus imperil the entire evacuation. Yet of all the possible alternatives, it perhaps carried the least risk. It was obvious, moreover, that some provision would have to be made for common-law wives and bastard Vietnamese children who could not meet the legal dependents' criteria. Otherwise the old American homesteaders in Saigon would never leave. Reluctantly Martin agreed to give Smith's proposal a trial run.

Few other problems were so neatly resolved. Martin told Gayler that he would take his suggestions under consideration and cable his own recommendations to the White House. As the President's personal representative on the scene, he reserved that right for himself.

•   •   •

As the meeting broke up, General Smith acted promptly to realize the small concession he had wrung from the Ambassador. He stopped off at Eva Kim's desk in the anteroom outside Martin's office and scribbled out a model for the "affidavit of support." Eva immediately typed it on stencil and thousands of copies were mimeographed and distributed that afternoon.

With the issuance of this document, the whole complexion of the Vietnamese evacuation program changed. Previously, only the legal dependents of American citizens had been eligible for resettlement in the United States. Now any Vietnamese who could find an American willing to assume financial responsibility for him could be slipped in under the new Attorney General's parole. General Smith immediately gave blanket authority to his own senior staffers to sign affidavits of support for whomever they wanted.

The only remaining obstacle to the evacuation of Vietnamese (apart from Martin's age and rank restrictions) was the still formidable problem of obtaining exit papers, the *laissez-passer,* from the Saigon government. To speed up the process, the Embassy invited the Vietnamese Ministry of the Interior to set up a consular office inside DAO's evacuation center at Tan Son Nhut.

Gayler's visit left Martin in a dour mood, and several hours after the admiral's departure he set out his complaints in another of his finely wrought back-channel cables to Kissinger. He would try, he wrote, to cut the American community to the lowest possible number by Tuesday, the twenty-third, and to be ready for a full evacuation in ten days. Yet none of this, he emphasized, would be easy. "Our biggest bottleneck," he explained, were the Americans with Vietnamese dependents. As long as they stood their ground, the only way to pull the American community down to 1,100, as the White House wanted, was by stripping the Embassy of its own personnel. But that, the Ambassador pointed out, would leave no one to manage the evacuation program. Reiterating his objections to an immediate evacuation of Vietnamese, he urged that Gayler be directed to withdraw the freighters now standing by on the Saigon River.

Elsewhere in the message, he repeated his plans for Thieu, stressed the significance of the Hungarian overture, and attempted to diminish the military threat, insisting (quite erroneously) that the SA-2 missiles in northeastern MR 3 had been around for months. Their likely purpose, he said, was to protect the Communist headquarters, not to strike at aircraft over Saigon.

In his final paragraphs he indulged his well-known penchant for the vernacular. Everyone in Washington, he asserted, seemed to be "trying to cover his ass." The intelligence community was veering toward "worst case" predictions; Gayler and the military had presented their own direst estimates; and "you, Mr. Secretary, have given me a directive [the prescribed drawdown to 1,100 Americans in one week's time] that won't work." The only "ass which isn't covered is mine," Martin complained. But, he added, he was used to that.

When the message arrived in Washington, it won Martin no new friends, and several members of Brown's task force prepared a formal memo calling on Kissinger to fire the Ambassador at once or to send someone out to hold his hand. Kissinger read it, but declined to act on either recommendation. Given the delicate status of the new political initiatives, it was simply impossible to withdraw Martin at this time.

Kissinger did not hesitate, however, to give the Ambassador a piece of his own mind by return cable. Reemphasizing his determination to see the American community reduced as quickly as possible, he rejected Martin's self-pitying remarks. "When this thing is finally over," he told the Ambassador, "I'll be hanging several yards higher than you."

Martin informed almost no one in the Embassy of the Kissinger message or of Gayler's advice to him. For most of us, his plans and objectives remained shrouded in a fog of rumor and contrived optimism. At a staff meeting on Saturday afternoon Alan Carter, still unaware of the Ambassador's private arrangements with the American press corps, asked if Marv Garrett's security office could brief reporters on evacuation planning. Administrative counselor Boudreau said Garrett and his staff were providing no briefings whatsoever. "Not so," Carter replied. "They briefed the business community only a few days ago." At that, Joe Bennett, the political counselor, perked up. "Really?" he injected. "Well, if that's so, maybe Garrett could brief the rest of us on what's going on."

Carter remembered that remark. It was the first time Bennett, the Martin loyalist and spinner of atrocity tales, had expressed any dissatisfaction with the way the Ambassador was handling business. Carter, of course, was deeply dissatisfied himself. He wondered, How the hell can any of us know what's happening if every disclosure is accidental?

Carter and Bennett were not the only confused denizens of the Embassy. When "Jerry Locksley" moved his overnight kit into the duty officer's cubicle on the second floor later in the day, he had no inkling of the trials and tribulations facing him. By the luck of the draw, Locksley, a CIA officer under full State Department cover, was to be the Embassy's chief duty officer during the last week of the war, responsible for keeping the Ambassador and other top officials informed after hours as each new crisis developed. Although he had some knowledge of the Hungarian ploy, he knew nothing of the evacuation planning. As soon as he had settled in at his new office, he asked for a briefing from Jacobson.

Locksley and Shep Lowman, the State Department officer in charge of compiling lists of "sensitive Vietnamese," got in to see Jacobson an hour later. The session was revealing, though not in the way Locksley had expected. Lowman knew far more about the military's ongoing airlift than Jacobson did. DAO personnel, he said, were already moving out hundreds of Vietnamese who were neither high risk nor legally eligible. Some Americans had already signed for eighty or more "dependents." Jacobson seemed to pale.

●   ●   ●

In the meantime, another young Embassy officer was suffering revelations of his own. That same afternoon my good friend Ken Moorefield, formerly Martin's aide, who had also served in Nha Trang and in the ICCS liaison office in the Embassy, was shifted again, this time to DAO, to help with evacuee processing. Like much else about the evacuation effort, his assignment was makeshift. He had no consular experience whatsoever and no idea of the scope of DAO's planning.

Four or five officials from the Vietnamese Ministry of the Interior were setting up a desk in the DAO movie theater when he arrived. The DAO auditor general's office was directly in charge of the processing, and its two principal representatives, Bill Guy and Jack Brown, treated him as an interloper.

"The place was in pandemonium, inside and out," Moorefield recalled. "Guy and Brown were accommodating too many Vietnamese applicants, and the Vietnamese themselves were on the brink of riot."

As a West Point graduate and former infantry commander, Moorefield was not one to tolerate such disorder for long. He immediately set up a desk for himself, laid down guidelines (no more than 300 to 400 Vietnamese were to be admitted to the theater at any one time), and soon had the applicants formed up in neat lines, waiting their turn, which was no mean trick in itself.

"If you didn't have an exit visa," he later explained to me, "you had to get a *laissez-passer* from the Ministry of Interior officials on the spot, and for that you needed my consular stamp and an 'affidavit of support' certifying that you were an immediate relative of a U.S. citizen.

"Technically we were authorized to clear only those Vietnamese who were legal American dependents. But it was obvious from the beginning that there were many who couldn't meet any of our criteria or who had lost their paperwork. The first hour or so, I sent each of these unfortunates back into the city to clear up their problems with the proper Vietnamese authorities. But I soon realized my nit-picking was only serving to benefit the black marketeers. Given the laws of supply and demand, the price for a quickie marriage in town or for adoption papers had risen from the equivalent of seventy dollars to over a thousand dollars.

"So by nightfall I was beginning to improvise. I had the Vietnamese secretaries working with me type up different forms, which I handed out to anybody who needed them. One of them said simply, 'I've lost my paperwork, but I'm an American dependent.' Another, 'This is my legally adopted child.' At first the Vietnamese consular officials wouldn't have anything to do with these phony papers, but after we promised to evacuate their families they became more cooperative and began issuing exit papers on the basis of them."

Given the crush at his desk, Moorefield tried to dispense with each case in less than three minutes. "Sometimes I was facing families of fifty or sixty members," he said, "all of them supposedly the 'immediate relatives' of an American sponsor. At first I tried to restrict each group to ten or fifteen on the theory I had to make space for others. But how do you explain to a Vietnamese that he is going to have to leave a half dozen of his loved ones behind? Many of them wanted me to make the selection for them, since they couldn't face up to it themselves. I tried to do it the best I could, with all the compassion I could muster. But God, it was impossible! Imagine: hundreds of people sliding before you every few minutes, tears running down their faces, beseeching you to recognize their particular problem.

"Sometimes the Vietnamese themselves made decisions I couldn't abide by. No one, for instance, wanted to leave a breadwinner behind. Usually it was the old, the very infirm or the very young who were to be discarded—none of whom of course could look after themselves. I tried to make it clear that a breadwinner would have to be included among those left. But then, in trying to persuade them to show compassion toward their own, toward the old people and the young, I often talked myself into what I had been trying to avoid all along, and gave them all clearance."

During his first few hours on the job Moorefield approved the departure of over 200 Vietnamese. Word of his flexibility and generosity quickly spread through the Embassy. I alerted several of my CIA colleagues, and many began mustering Vietnamese friends and co-workers in hopes of slipping them out through Moorefield's sieve the following day.

As Moorefield labored at the processing center, Lacy Wright launched the "black" airlift Martin had authorized the day before. Just after dusk on the nineteenth he drove the first of his passengers, all of them Vietnamese relatives of fellow Foreign Service officers, to Tan Son Nhut in a battered white van. One or two of the old mama-sans had second thoughts just as the front gates of the air base loomed into view and pleaded to be let off. But Wright, relying on his fluent Vietnamese, managed to calm them, and everyone was finally packed off without further complaint or incident.

Shortly after curfew that same night Jerry Locksley, the Embassy duty officer, was plunged into his first crisis. He was sitting in his second-floor cubicle in the Embassy, reading a war novel, when the secure phone rang. To his horror, the operator informed him that it was the White House calling.

The man on the other end was Frank Wisner, a State Department officer on Brown's task force. He said he was speaking for the President of the United States. He wanted to know how many Americans had been evacuated from Saigon during the day.

"The situation is this, sir," Locksley stammered. "It's very difficult to get information. Perhaps tomorrow . . ."

Wisner (hot under the collar): "The President wants to know now!"

Locksley: "Look, the curfew is already down. I can't move without hazard. I can hear C-130s taking off in the distance, though, so the outflow must be continuing."

Wisner (very hot now): "I'm Frank Wisner. I'm calling for the White House. Get me an answer *now!*"

Earlier in the day one of Locksley's friends had been to Tan Son Nhut to see his Vietnamese girl friend off. He had later mentioned that five to six Vietnamese seemed to be getting out for every American. For lack of any other figure, Locksley cited that one to Wisner. "Not good enough," the State Department official snapped. Locksley promised to get back to him in an hour or so with a better one.

He called for a car and armed escort from the Mission Wardens' office and drove over to Boudreau's villa. The administrative counselor had no idea how many Americans had left that day. In desperation Locksley decided to ask Wolfgang Lehmann, but the Deputy Chief of Mission was no more helpful. "Go back to the Embassy," Lehmann told him "and get the statistical break-down from yesterday. We'll use that to keep the White House satisfied."

By the time Locksley arrived back at Lehmann's villa with the statistics in hand, the DCM was not in good humor. Looking quickly over the tally, he sat down at the secure telephone in his study and put in a direct call to Washington.

When Wisner came on, Lehmann let him have it between the eyes. The verbal abuse to which he treated the White House staffer turned Locksley cold. "What do you think you're doing (you so-and-so), asking my subordinates those questions!" Lehmann screamed. Then, shifting key, mockingly: "You must be under terrific pressure."

After several more choice volleys, Lehmann reeled off the figures: 612 Americans had left on the military airlift the day before, bringing the total since the beginning of the month to 2,237, plus 2,776 Vietnamese and other alien nationals. He reminded Wisner those figures applied only to departures through DAO and did not take account of those Americans who had left by commercial aircraft for whom the Embassy had no tally. As a matter of fact, he added, the Embassy had no way of knowing how many more Americans there were in Saigon.

Before Wisner could respond, Lehmann offered a final, somewhat extreme observation (particularly extreme, since he was, after all, addressing a White House representative): "And keep your fucking finger off the panic button!" With that, he hung up.

If there were any Soviet spy-in-the-sky satellites tapping in on that conversation, the code breakers must have been up for days trying to figure out the secret meaning behind it all.

As Locksley climbed into his car and headed back to the Embassy, he felt a distinct queasiness. If this was an example of how Saigon and Washington were communicating on key issues, were any of us safe?

Ambassador Martin himself did not spend the evening at home. Without bothering to inform his immediate staff, he paid a call on the Polish Ambassador to the ICCS, Ryzard Fialkowski. The two of them had not seen each other for some time. Several weeks before, Martin had managed to insult and offend Fialkowski by accusing his government of providing arms to the North Vietnamese to carry on the offensive. The confrontation had been carefully staged for maximum impact. After inviting Fialkowski to his office, Martin had flung a Polish-made machine pistol down in front of him. "That," Martin had exclaimed, "was found at the site of a Communist ambush in the delta." Fialkowski had stalked out in protest.

But now Martin wanted to smooth over the relationship, at least to the extent of enlisting Fialkowski in his last-minute search for peace. He opened the conversation with a rather straightforward warning. If those SA-2s were used against evacuation aircraft, he emphasized, the American Air Force would have a "perfect excuse" to bomb Hanoi. He then turned to the subject of negotiations. What the two men discussed in this regard Martin never disclosed to me, but several days later a newspaper story, based on an Embassy leak, noted that both the Poles and the Hungarians were now involved in the American peace initiatives. According to the story, a message delivered to the Embassy during the weekend had set out "stringent terms for Communist acceptance of a tripartite government" and had demanded Thieu's resignation by Wednesday, the twenty-fourth.

A Bargain Whose Day
Has Passed

"What role did you play, if any, in persuading President Thieu to resign?" the Congressional inquisitor asked Martin a year after the loss of South Vietnam. "None," replied the Ambassador. "I did attempt to lay before him as candidly and as accurately and objectively as I could the situation as we perceived it."

"Did he at any point ask whether you thought he should resign?"

"Yes, he did . . . I told him that that was a decision that he would have to make, only he, in light of his own concern for the people of Saigon, for Vietnam as a whole, for everything that he had worked for, and in light of Vietnamese sensibilities and Vietnamese culture."

Martin drove up to the Palace to see Thieu on the morning of the twentieth, shortly after Mérillon had been in for an interview—same theme, same purpose. "I had obtained from the Defense Attaché and the CIA Station," the Ambassador later told a Congressional committee, "the latest information available to us on both the realities of the military situation and the feelings of the senior Vietnamese civilian and military leaders . . . The conclusion was inescapable that should Hanoi rapidly move in for the kill, it would be difficult for Saigon to last more than a month, even with the most skillful and determined defense, and probably not more than three weeks. I said that while it was my opinion that Hanoi wanted Saigon whole, not a pile of rubble, one could not escape the possibility they might elect the latter, if there was no move toward negotiations.

"President Thieu asked about the prospects for additional military aid. I said that even if by some miracle it were now approved, it might preserve the opportunity for a better negotiating position, but it could not arrive in time to change the balance sheet he had just read. As of now, the balance arrayed against him was overwhelming . . .

"I said I was speaking to him only as an individual, not for the President or the Secretary of State, or even as the American Ambassador. I said I was speaking only as one who for a very long time had watched events in Southeast

Asia and who for the past two years had worked very hard at understanding the interweaving of the fabric of Vietnamese affairs. I said the older I got, the more I knew that I did not know it all, and a reasonable doubt was always present. But it was a difficult time, and perhaps my perceptions were as accurate as those of any other westerner.

"A few things were very clear to me. The military situation was very bad, and the Vietnamese people held him responsible for it. The political class, both his supporters and his enemies, did not believe he could lead the country out of its present crisis. I said it was my conclusion that almost all of his generals, although they would continue to fight, believed defense was hopeless unless a respite could be gained through the beginning of the negotiating process. And they did not believe such a process could begin unless the President left or took steps to see that the process began immediately. I said it was my feeling that if he did not move soon, his generals would ask him to go.

"President Thieu asked whether his leaving would affect the vote in Congress. I said it might have changed some votes some months ago, but it could not now change enough to affect the outcome. In other words, if his thought was to offer to resign if Congress assured a level [of aid] sufficient for South Vietnamese survival, that was a bargain whose day had passed, if indeed it had ever existed . . . The important thing was perhaps the effect his leaving would have on the other side. I said I did not know the answer, but it seemed that most South Vietnamese now seemed to think it would facilitate negotiations. I personally thought it would make little difference. Hanoi would be opposed to any strong leader. They would insist on a much weaker man, if indeed they were really interested in negotiating. But his colleagues felt it might buy time, which was now the essential commodity for Vietnam. Some felt if the destruction of Saigon could be avoided, if an independent Vietnam could continue to exist, one might hope, even if reason recognizes the dimness of the hope, that things might improve. The conversation went on for about an hour and a half . . . On [my] leaving, President Thieu said he would do what he thought was best for the country."

In a brief follow-up cable to Kissinger, Martin speculated that Thieu would bow out in a short time, perhaps two or three days. He also betrayed his own repugnance at what he had done that morning. After the interview, said Martin, he had returned home, climbed into the shower and scrubbed himself down with strong soap. Then he had taken a long nap.

While Martin rested after his ordeal, Kissinger experienced a change in heart, in part as a result of a telephone call from Soviet Ambassador Dobrynin. The request for a cease-fire, Dobrynin told him, was now "in train." In view of this fact, it suddenly occurred to Kissinger that Thieu's immediate departure might not be such a good idea, after all. Instead, as he pointed out to Martin in a message later in the day, it might be useful to keep Thieu around a bit longer, so the "promise" of his resignation could be used as a bargaining card in further discussions with the Soviets.

When Martin read over the cable he could hardly contain his anger. Kissinger seemed to be making policy by the seat of his pants, starting, then stopping, with no real sense of direction.

Shortly after daybreak on the twenty-first the government's last defenses at Xuan Loc finally collapsed. The last of four surviving battalions of the 18th ARVN Division, plus the commander himself, General Dao, were pulled from the rubble of the city by chopper. Some 600 ARVN troopers under Colonel Le Xuan Hien volunteered to stay behind to cover the withdrawal. In a few hours they were literally inundated by the advance elements of the 40,000 NVA troops directly committed against them.

An hour or so later, Defense Minister Tran Van Don, in frantic meetings with the remaining power brokers in Saigon, forged an informal coalition against Thieu. His most important recruit was General Vien, who conceded under prodding that the army could no longer fight and could not hope to win. Well then, Don posed, the only alternative was to sue for peace. That meant Thieu's removal and his replacement by someone, preferably Minh, who could negotiate with the other side. Would Vien be willing to go along? The general agreed, and the rest was academic. With Vien behind him, Don was able to bring the other principal members of the Can cabinet around: the Prime Minister himself, and Economics Minister Nguyen Van Hao. The four of them then made a pact. The next day they would call on Thieu to resign. If he refused, they would force him out.

Thieu, in fact, was already several chess moves ahead of them. Overnight he had decided not to give his tormentors the pleasure of picking over his corpse. He would step down at once and let them tear each other to pieces. "Yes, my timing was just right," he told a friend on Taiwan several months later. "I waited until the patient was on his deathbed. No one could save him. Then I left. I wanted no one to be able to surpass what I had done for my country."

Just before noon on the twenty-first Thieu summoned former Prime Minister Khiem and Vice-President Huong to his office. He was resigning, he told them. He would make the announcement that very evening. Recalling his conversations with Mérillon and Martin the day before, he emphasized that neither had advised him to bow out. Yet because of the military situation, which he described as "hopeless" (Khiem and Huong agreed), his continued presence, he said, was purposeless and would only prevent a solution. He had only one wish: the transfer of power must be achieved "constitutionally" to avoid chaos. Whether he was hoping thereby to forestall the installation of his old rival, "Big" Minh, was unclear; he mentioned no potential successor, apart from the inevitable one, the Vice-President himself.

As Thieu spelled out his decision to his two old comrades, the CIA's electronic listening devices in his office picked up every word. Soon afterward, around 1 P.M., Polgar rushed into my office. "We've scooped everybody on the biggest news since the cease-fire," he shouted at me. "No need to worry about

the military situation any more. You'll just have to switch to coalition politics."

Polgar wasted no time in preparing for this contingency himself. He
informed both the French and the Hungarians of Thieu's impending departure, and then, around midafternoon, sent General Timmes to see Minh.
Timmes was blunt: Would Minh be willing to take over and negotiate a peace
as soon as a way could be found to move Huong aside? Minh nodded, expressed confidence he could placate the other side, said he wanted to send a
representative to Paris to open discussions at once. Timmes reached into his
briefcase and pulled out a handful of crisp green dollar bills: one thousand
dollars, to cover travel expenses. (Minh would never use the money, nor return
it.)*

Meanwhile, another Station officer conferred with one of Minh's aides
about tactics. It might be useful, said the CIA man, for Minh to accept the
Prime Ministership from Huong. That might ease the transition. The aide
shook his head. No, he said, Minh would never join the Huong government.
He must assume power on his own terms. His remarks provided a first ominous
sign that the change in government might not go according to the Embassy's
plans.

Thieu's nationwide address began at 7:30 P.M., Saigon time, lasted approximately two hours, and eventually produced considerable shuffling and
many not so stifled yawns among the 200 or more ranking South Vietnamese
officials in attendance at Presidential Palace. As might have been expected, it
was a plea for the vindication of history. He had resisted signing the Paris
agreement, Thieu declared, because there was no provision for the withdrawal
of North Vietnamese forces from the south. He had relented only when the
United States threatened to cut off all aid and only after President Nixon had
promised to use military force to halt any Communist offensive. But domestic
difficulties, including Watergate, had destroyed America's resolve, he said.
And the North Vietnamese had reacted by building up their forces in the south
and by leeching territory. South Vietnam, in his view, was now like a planta-
tion owner at the mercy of a thief who stole pieces of fruit every day.

American aid had always been critical, Thieu went on. It had tipped the
balance against the North Vietnamese in 1968 and 1972 and had helped to deter
them immediately after the cease-fire, and when the first deep cuts had been
made in the aid allocations in early '74, Vietnamization still had a long way
to go.

*Martin was never informed of this overture to Minh. When I told him about it following Saigon's
collapse, he reacted with a certain display of partisanship, claiming that Polgar had meddled where
he shouldn't have. Indeed, he insisted that in giving Minh money the CIA had destroyed his credit
with the Communists and thereby prejudiced the chances for a negotiated settlement. As General
Dung points out in his memoirs, the Communists did become aware at some point that money
was a factor in Minh's last-minute bid for power: "And, as we already knew," he writes, "the
political marionettes of the U.S. puppets . . . would suggest one thing or another, use their dollars
for bribery or offer to act as mediators . . ."

After an hour and a half of such sermonizing Thieu moved on to his only real news, tearfully announcing his decision to resign and to turn over the government to Vice-President Huong. Now that half the country was lost, he said, he was willing to sacrifice himself for the people.

Following the address, General Vien briefly went on national radio to announce his troops would continue fighting to "defend the homeland against foreign aggressors." At his swearing-in ceremony the new President, Tran Van Huong, seventy-one, arthritic, nearly blind, pledged to stand fast until "the troops are dead or the country is lost."

Sages in the American Embassy shrugged off these hard-line remarks. "Merely pap for Ky and the right wing to keep them from stepping in," they insisted. "Actually, Huong wants to negotiate." And as if to prove the point, the new government did call promptly for a cease-fire and creation of a tripartite "National Council" with Communist participation.

But to some of us the bombast had an ominous ring: To placate Ky and the rightist elements the new government already seemed to be staking out a position that could only offend the Communists.

"Thieu resigns, Saigon remains quiet," I wrote in my notebook the evening of the twenty-first. "A new curfew, from 8 P.M. to 6 A.M., is on to discourage demonstrations, though I suspect the people are really too traumatized to want to dance in the streets.

"Some colleagues rejoiced at the news. I didn't. Merely felt sad, not so much over Thieu's going—that was inevitable—as over the spectacle itself. We'd all known it was somehow wrong, our grafting had never taken. But you always hoped it would never come to this, or at least you wouldn't be around to see it."

As news of Thieu's resignation flashed through Washington, Kissinger sent Martin a melancholy message. Expressing his continued "respect" for the South Vietnamese leader, he offered to assist him in leaving the country, and emphasized that the Administration had not been involved in any of the French maneuvering to unseat him. And as of now, he added, there had been no reply from the Soviets.

Within Saigon's own political community, the reaction to Thieu's departure was as diverse as the motives that had led to it. Some principals applauded the ex-President's parting shots at the Americans. Others, many of the younger military officers, were simply embarrassed by them, feeling that Thieu should have shouldered more blame himself. No one seemed happy with Huong. "Too old, out of touch" was the consensus, but there was no agreement on what should be done next. And when those in favor of a cease-fire speculated on the possibilities, they did so in fairly confidant terms, as if they expected to be able to approach the Communists as equals. Abject surrender was still far from their minds.

"Big" Minh was as guilty as the rest. In conversations with associates on Tuesday, the twenty-second, he spoke hopefully of "striking a bargain" with the other side, and in Paris a spokesman for him called publicly for a cease-fire, a resumption of the Paris peace talks, and the establishment of a genuinely "representative" government. In a similar vein, former Prime Minister Khiem told a CIA friend he wanted to establish a new cabinet—he and General Vien as the prime movers, Minh as a figurehead President—to stall off the Communist offensive and gain time to build the army's morale.

Whether any of them actually believed such options were practical can only be guessed at. Pretense had always been a prime ingredient of Saigon politics, and as far as the moderates were now concerned, bravado was the very key to survival, theirs and the Republic's, for it was the only way they could hope to keep Ky and his cronies tranquilized as the peace gambit was pursued.

Martin and Polgar, of course, were only too well aware of the dangers Ky posed and were equally determined to blunt them. Tuesday afternoon Polgar dispatched Timmes to talk with the Air Marshal and to sound out his views. The meeting turned out to be oil on the fire. As Ky later acknowledged, he thought the CIA man had come to tap him as Huong's successor, but when Timmes absently questioned him about the possibility of a coup "against 'Big' Minh," he realized that Minh, not he, was the American candidate. Complaining bitterly to Timmes about Minh's "inappropriateness," he resolved privately to carve out a new niche for himself. Timmes' slip of the tongue thus cost the moderates what little maneuverability they had left to them. The right was now on full alert.

The French in the meantime continued to meddle. Pierre Brochand, Mérillon's intelligence chief, was now spending every waking minute with Minh, coaching and encouraging him, and warding off all potential challengers. On the morning of the twenty-second, when he learned that Tran Van Don had some vague designs on the presidency, he promptly contacted the Vietnamese general and warned him that only Minh would be acceptable to the Communists.

Later in the day Don paid a call on the American Embassy to pass the same message on to Martin. The visit actually had been inspired by the French for a special purpose. Martin, still desperately intent on preserving a constitutional façade in Saigon, did not yet seem to grasp the urgency of moving Minh to the fore at once. Instead, he wanted to maintain Huong in place for a while, or failing that, to replace him with Senate Chairman Tran Van Lam, who by law was next in line for the presidency. The French considered such adherence to legal form suicidal and were determined to get this point across to the Ambassador.

The Communists' own initial response to the changing of the guard at the Palace was far less ambiguous than the public's. A PRG spokesman at Tan Son Nhut promptly advised newsmen that Thieu's departure changed nothing, and rejected Huong's call for a cease-fire. Radio Hanoi denounced Huong as a "reactionary and traitor" and demanded that the United States "abandon the Nguyen Van Thieu clique, not just the person of Nguyen Van Thieu" and "end its interference in Vietnam, including military aid." These were ultimata ("the only way out" for the United States, according to Radio Hanoi), hardly negotiating points, and there seemed little doubt about the threat behind them. "If the U.S. does not really respond to the legitimate demands and seeks to undertake maneuvers to deceive public opinion," proclaimed Liberation Radio, "nothing can be settled and it must assume full responsibility." In other words, surrender now, or else.

Hanoi's commentaries also seemed to offer little hope for an orderly evacuation. There was no suggestion that Thieu's departure might buy additional time for a drawdown, and within hours of Thieu's speech, Liberation Radio explicitly tightened the deadline for removal of all American "advisors" —to "two or three days or even twenty-four hours."

Despite all this, however, Martin and Polgar and Kissinger in Washington continued to believe there was room for maneuver. The day after Thieu's resignation Polgar once again tested his own hopes on the Hungarians. Now that Thieu was out of the way, he asked Colonel Toth, what could we expect? Toth was painfully obscure. The PRG, he said, was now interested in an American declaration of "non-interference." But what does that mean? Polgar inquired. Toth, in effect, offered no reply. As Polgar later noted, the Hungarian had said simply, "If you play gin rummy, you know that when you put down a card, your opponent picks it up to determine whether to keep or discard it. We have picked up your card." That was all.

The analogy to gin rummy later appeared in one of Malcolm Browne's articles in the *New York Times,* a story dealing with "signals" certain "intermediaries" were receiving from the Communist side. Polgar again was leaking to Browne for a purpose: to give Washington a sense that he had latched on to something truly important. Yet all he managed to do was to nurture the dangerous impression in Washington that there was more to the negotiating gambit than there was. Browne's articles became "false confirmation" for what Martin himself was saying to the White House in his own back-channel cables.

The Hungarians were not the only source of Polgar's enduring optimism. Some of his Vietnamese friends also had a hand in it. On Tuesday afternoon General Binh of the National Police assured Polgar exuberantly that the period since Thieu's resignation had been the quietest since the cease-fire. The Communists, he said, must have accepted the change in government as a "signal." Polgar, obviously in agreement, repeated this conclusion to Malcolm Browne. The *New York Times* carried a story the following day alleging a cutback in the fighting.

The claim was absurd. During the three days bracketing Thieu's resignation, the Communists had made spectacular gains. Phan Thiet, the last town in MR 2, had been lost. Ham Tan, a district town twenty-nine miles to the south, where government stragglers were trying to regroup, was already under intense attack. Xuan Loc had finally been abandoned, and Communist forces were now pushing beyond it, along highways leading east toward Bien Hoa and south toward Vung Tau. To fend off the five NVA divisions now committed in the area, the South Vietnamese had only the pitiful remnants of the 18th ARVN Division and two marine brigades in a blocking position east of Bien Hoa, and an airborne brigade and two battered infantry regiments poised between Xuan Loc and Vung Tau. Bien Hoa itself was still under heavy shelling, and a few hours after Thieu's resignation, General Toan, the MR 3 commander, had begun shifting his own headquarters from there to Saigon.

If this was a lull, a respite from the fighting, then a full-scale offensive would have swept us off the map.

I wrote two memoranda for Polgar late Tuesday afternoon, setting out my views on the subject. First, I argued there was no lull at all; the Communists were quite systematically eliminating the targets left to them. Secondly, I stressed the continued inflexibility of their political line, in particular the absence of any guarantee of reciprocity should we meet their demands. Polgar refused to pass either memo to Washington or to Martin. Even Howard Archer, now my nominal superior as chief of the analytical section, was surprised at this, though not enough to try to change Polgar's mind. At the end of the day, at Polgar's direction, he dutifully drafted a brief and bland cable to CIA headquarters, skating over all the points I had raised.

Thus, for the second time in a week, Polgar was attempting to squelch information that did not conform to his own view of things. But this time the consequences were far more serious than when he had tried to block my agent report of the seventeenth. My office was now the only real clearing house in the Embassy for intelligence and analyses on the military situation. The Defense Attaché's Office had virtually ceased performing this function, in its concentration on the evacuation problem. If my own colleagues and I failed to provide timely information to Washington, the likelihood was that it would simply not get there.

Kissinger himself seemed to realize something was dropping out of the intelligence picture, and asked Martin by cable on Tuesday to comment on the suggestion of "some sources" that there would be no negotiated settlement. Martin replied that "we have many sources who are saying this" and emphasized that the CIA had changed its estimates so often before, they could hardly be considered credible.

On the very evening Thieu delivered his farewell address, General Van Tien Dung, Le Duc Tho and Pham Hung were reviewing the final blueprint for the Ho Chi Minh campaign at their Loc Ninh headquarters. In concept, the "unified plan" of attack, drawn up by Dung's deputy, General Le Ngoc Hien, somewhat resembled the peeling of an onion: North Vietnamese forces were first to strip away Saigon's outer defenses, destroying government units on the outskirts; then they were to penetrate the city itself with mechanized units, concentrating on five targets, all military in nature—the Presidential Palace, the General Staff headquarters just outside Tan Son Nhut, the headquarters for the Saigon City Military Command, the General Police Director-ate and Tan Son Nhut airfield. There were two projected springboard dates: 27 April for the attacks on the city's perimeters; 29 April for the final drive. By Tuesday, the twenty-second, Dung makes clear in his memoirs, these dates had been decided on.

The campaign was to have a single focal point: Saigon. The primary objective of Communist forces in Tay Ninh to the northwest and in the delta to the south was merely to tie down ARVN units and prevent them from redeploying to help defend the capital.

By Dung's own account, one aspect of the "unified plan" required partic-ularly "great effort"—the positioning of "antiaircraft missiles" (read: SA-2s) around Saigon. Equally difficult and time-consuming was the task of preparing for the artillery attacks on Tan Son Nhut, predicted by my source on the seventeenth. The prerequisite was the capture of Nhon Trach, a marshland on Saigon's southeastern rim, for it was here that the rocket launchers and batter-ies of 130-mm field guns were to be emplaced. By Tuesday afternoon General Le Trong Tan, commander on the eastern front, had arrived at his command post just north of Bien Hoa to coordinate the operation. Dung sent him an urgent message sometime during the day: "Nhon Trach must be occupied on 27 or 28 April at the latest."

Although the North Vietnamese wanted no war with the remaining Americans in Saigon, lest Washington retaliate militarily, their plans did provide for the elimination of some of us, if only to give the rest an incentive to leave. Shortly after Thieu's speech the South Vietnamese police, acting on an informant's tip, warned a senior CIA officer that NVA commandos were to strike his home in the center of the city that very night. Exhausted from the day's work, the CIA man spent the next few hours hand-loading M-16 magazines and barricading his doors. Around midnight the police contacted him again: the attackers had been apprehended at the city's limits. He was safe—for the time being.

To judge from Dung's memoirs, he and his field commanders were well aware of all the political and diplomatic maneuvering surrounding Thieu's resignation. The details were spelled out for them in a flash message from Nguyen Duy Trinh, Hanoi's Foreign Minister. Trinh left no doubt of his own attitude toward the American and French peace gambits, describing them simply as "perfidious tricks," an epithet that surfaced almost simultaneously in Communist press play. Dung apparently was equally unimpressed. As he tells it, Trinh's disclosures merely strengthened him in his conviction that "total victory" must be won as soon as possible. Another message, from Le Duan himself, no doubt reinforced his sense of urgency. Military and political conditions were ripe for a "general offensive," Duan told him. "Timely action is the firmest guarantee of victory."

Dung's contempt for the diplomatic by-play fairly oozes from the pages of his postwar account (although predictably there is no mention of the Soviet or the Hungarian role). "What a gang of silly ignorant people!" he writes of those in Saigon who would have altered the government simply to "check our troops' advance and to avert total defeat."

Special encomium is reserved for Polgar: "The U.S. CIA clique in Saigon crept around like a venomous snake to spy and conduct many insidious plots," Dung declares. "It spread a report Huong would be an interim President and that the U.S. was ready to reach an agreement and was waiting for a reply [precisely the message Polgar delivered to the Hungarians]." Dung also has some sneering words for General François Vanuxem, an old French army officer who had known Thieu in the early fifties and who had arrived in Saigon several weeks before to "advise" him in his final hour. Despite Thieu's resignation, Vanuxem stayed on to urge a strategy of counterattack on the South Vietnamese command, something Dung describes as "pettifoggery."

None of this can be taken to mean the North Vietnamese were dead set on a bloodletting. Undoubtedly they would have accepted an unconditional surrender if it had been offered to them clearly and "expeditiously." Indeed, there are hints in Dung's memoirs that he and his field commanders were not inattentive to this possibility. At one point he complains that the "Minh solution" came too late. Had it come earlier, would the North Vietnamese have accepted it? Dung provides no clue.

In any case, shortly after Thieu's resignation, his and Hanoi's patience gave out. Sometime on the twenty-second Dung and Pham Hung signed the actual "resolution for attack," and the command staff itself was broken down into two elements. Dung and his chief deputy, Tran Van Tra, were to go to a forward headquarters at Ben Cat in Binh Duong Province, northeast of Saigon, while the old gray-hairs, Le Duc Tho and Pham Hung, were to stay behind at Loc Ninh for the time being to coordinate "political, diplomatic and military activities," and possibly to keep an eye cocked for the unconditional surrender that would make the final offensive unnecessary.

Secret Caller

Sunday, the twentieth, the day before President Thieu's resignation, the Big Push began. Whether Martin discussed the accelerated airlift with Thieu during their conversation at the Palace that morning is not a matter of record. In any event, it wasn't necessary. You could hear the roar of jet engines as the C-141s lumbered off the tarmac at Tan Son Nhut five miles away.

The new parole document and Smith's affidavit of support were partly responsible for the step-up. DAO and a few overworked Embassy officers did the rest. Ken Moorefield, Lacy Wright and General Smith's staff were now ramming bodies onto aircraft as fast as their ingenuity allowed.

Since that first disastrous baby-lift of 4 April, two to four military transports had been shuttling between Saigon and Clark air base each day. Now, suddenly, the Joint Chiefs of Staff in Washington flooded Tan Son Nhut with many more C-141s than the DAO flight controllers could efficiently handle. Colonel McCurdy, the Air Attaché, asked the JCS to throttle back and let his staff determine the rhythm. The Pentagon gruffly agreed.

During the morning, as the crowds outside the DAO movie theater grew into a seething mob, Smith ordered all processing moved next door, to the DAO annex, to minimize the risk of infiltration or sabotage of the headquarters building itself. Moorefield and the Vietnamese consular officials immediately began the laborious shift, closing out operations in the theater, setting up again in the Quonset huts and gymnasium a half mile away. The complex of fragile wood and tin-framed buildings that was to serve as their new headquarters had once provided a home away from home for the American army, and many of the Vietnamese who now pushed and shoved their way through its portals still remembered its old nickname: "Dodge City."

Soon after the shift was announced, DAO staffer Ms. Sally Vinyard and a group of volunteers assaulted the place with mops and brooms. The mess hall and cafeteria were outfitted with new propane and electric grills; the bowling alley was packed wall to wall with canned food; and two field kitchens were rolled into the parking lot in front of the PX to assist in dishing out the fare, which included such non-Vietnamese delicacies as beans and franks, cheese sandwiches and a variety of unidentifiable soups. Smith also ordered the beer and liquor concession closed out, and asked for ten additional Marine guards from the Embassy to help maintain order and discipline among the rapidly expanding masses.

DAO's personnel division assumed responsibility for preparing the passenger manifests and an Air Force and a Navy officer shared the onerous task of checking luggage for firearms or hard drugs. Under the evolving operating procedures evacuees were first cleared by Moorefield at the gymnasium's front door. Vietnamese without exit visas or *laissez-passer* documents were sent to the government's consular desk tucked away in a corner of the building, while the rest were shunted into the long lines of passengers awaiting manifesting and baggage checks just under the basketball nets. Then it was a short walk (or bus ride, if you were lucky) to the marshaling area at the nearby DAO swimming pool, where Hungarian and Polish ICCS members had once frolicked in the sun courtesy of the American taxpayer. From there, buses and vans hauled the passengers to the flight line across the highway inside Tan Son Nhut air base itself.

Around midday on the twentieth, five top-ranking Marine officers choppered to Tan Son Nhut from the evacuation fleet to help Smith put his house in order and to try to strengthen cooperation between DAO and the Embassy. That last job was to prove the far more difficult. "The major problem," they concluded in their after-action report, "was coordination with the Embassy in ascertaining numbers of Americans and Vietnamese to be evacuated. The estimated number of Americans varied widely (1,500 to 5,000) and Vietnamese figures were consistently less precise." The report did not attempt to place blame, but since Jacobson was technically in charge of Mission planning, there was no question where it belonged.

The same afternoon Colonel Legro called Shep Lowman, the State Department officer who was to compile lists of potential Vietnamese evacuees, and asked him for some names. But Lowman had nothing but excuses. So many names had been turned in to him, he explained, there had been no time to tabulate them.

Legro, impatient and discouraged, didn't bother arguing with him. He decided simply to force the issue himself. During the next several hours he and his top assistants divided up the seat space on the outgoing flights among the Embassy's various agencies. Hopefully, with such quotas in hand, the bureaucrats downtown would be moved to action.

The expansion of the regular airlift did not obviate the need or demand for "black" flights. From the twentieth onward, one or two were flown each day, although most of those who benefited from them were not "politically sensitive" Vietnamese but, rather, friends and relatives of DAO officers who were simply impatient to get out of the country.

From the outset, one of the most difficult aspects of the "black" airlift was the fundamental first step, the smuggling of paperless persons past the police checkpoints at Tan Son Nhut. Colonel McCurdy continued to promise the police and security personnel at the front gates assistance in evacuating their families if they would be "flexible," but time and again convoys of evacuees were turned back as they tried to enter. Finally the Embassy and DAO resorted to another ploy, an old and honored one in Saigon: the greasing of palms. Eventually over $50,000 in bribes were paid to police and military personnel at the airfield to assure their cooperation in the evacuation of their own countrymen.

Money, of course, was not an answer to all problems, and from time to time the Vietnamese exacted a price that threatened to bring the entire airlift to a halt. An incident Sunday evening was only too typical. Around 10 P.M., DAO's evacuation control center got a call from the flight line: Vietnamese air force officers were holding up the departure of one "unmanifested" C-141. Marine Major R. J. Delligatti hurried out to the runway, where, to his infinite discomfort, he found a large group of high-ranking, heavily armed Vietnamese police and military officers drawn up in a cordon around the aircraft. Among them was Brigadier General Phan Phung Tien, commander of the Vietnamese 5th Air Force Division. When Delligatti climbed out of his jeep, Tien saun-tered over to him, his hand playing ominously over the .45 on his hip. There were Vietnamese "illegals" aboard that plane, he sneered, and he and his men were going in to pull them out. Delligatti stiffened. "Sir," he said, "there're also armed American security guards inside, and if anyone tries to force his way in, they'll open fire." As Tien gawked and fumbled with his holster Delligatti reached for the radio telephone in his jeep and called General Smith. "Stand by," Smith told him. "I'll do what's necessary." Minutes later the Defense Attaché called back and told him to inform Tien and the rest that General Binh had ordered the plane cleared for takeoff. Tien glowered at Delligatti, but motioned to his men to give way.

The accelerated airlift was not limited merely to warm bodies. Sunday afternoon DAO also began ferrying operational and intelligence files to USSAG in Thailand. Martin had authorized the transfer on the theory that further military aid to Saigon was unlikely and that DAO, in its current manifestation, would not be staying on.

He was not so flexible with other agencies. He refused, for instance, to authorize the removal of USAID's economic records, in the belief (as he later explained to Congress) that the Administration would continue economic aid even after a "change" in the Saigon government. Many of the agency's files would thus ultimately be lost, creating countless problems for USAID officials in Washington as they tried in the wake of Saigon's collapse to sort out financial obligations to the companies that had served them in Vietnam.

The CIA Station itself had begun destroying its fourteen tons of classified trash—dossiers, biographical files and intelligence reports—earlier in the month. But so far only a dent had been made in the backlog, principally because the Ambassador had been unwilling to permit burning and shredding during the day. As he had explained to Station security personnel, he did not want incinerator dust wafting across the parking lot and besmudging Embassy limousines.

Now that the evacuation was on the upswing, however, Martin's attitude changed, and many Station officers began toiling before the incinerators eight hours a day, sweat and flecks of charred paper clinging to their faces and arms like the symptoms of some ancient plague. The two incinerators on the roof just above my office soon were working constantly, their earsplitting whine setting my nerves sputtering.

When Martin advised senior Embassy officers on Sunday of Kissinger's demand for a speedier drawdown, General Smith ordered his own staff to prepare a new non-essentials list for DAO. Anyone whose name appeared on it, he warned, had better be airborne by the end of the day, or else reconcile himself to abrupt and early retirement. That afternoon I called DAO's think tank and asked to speak to a particular analyst. I was told there was no think tank any longer. The only analyst still around was busy tearing out wall maps.

With the curtailment of DAO's intelligence activities, my own office became all the more important to the Embassy. We were not immune to personnel cuts, however. During the past few days my colleague Pat Johnson had found her own name on the Station's latest "non-essentials" list. Her nomination, Polgar emphasized, in no way reflected on her competence. Her husband, Bill Johnson, had insisted on it, for he was desperate to get her out of the country so he could concentrate his energies and emotions on piecing together his stay-behind spy network.

Pat spent her last two days in town making her farewells. It was a strange time, she later told me: an air of unreality. Some Vietnamese friends seemed oblivious of the dangers closing in. She found one of them out in his garden on Saturday morning, quietly tending flowers. Later she went by her tailor's shop and bought a memento, an *ao dai,* the traditional Vietnamese tunic. When she walked into her hairdresser's salon just before noon, the manager seemed surprised. "Oh, you're still here!" the woman exclaimed. "But you're the only one. The American customers are all gone." An hour later, hair done, fingernails manicured, Pat prepared to leave. The manager asked anxiously, the normally soft voice going shrill, "You'll come back, won't you? You're the last one."

Pat had particular trouble telling her maid goodbye—the old *chi ba,* husband dead, five children, several cousins all living together in Pat's household. She went out to the kitchen just before her departure on Sunday, embraced the old woman and gave her one last handful of dollars. There were tears all around. Pat had debated taking the old lady and her family out and resettling them in the States, but had decided against it. They wouldn't fit, she concluded. Besides, they were part of the masses. They had a chance to survive. The Communists couldn't kill everybody.

Pat left on a special flight to Bangkok that evening. There were few other passengers. The management of Air Vietnam had scheduled the run for a special purpose, to ship the liquid assets of the airline, $20 million in gold, out of the country. Pat took a seat amid innocuous gray canvas bags stuffed with the treasure. After the fall of the country the gold dropped out of sight, undoubtedly into some expatriate's private coffer.

She danced in Bangkok that evening, partied till dawn with old friends. It was a strange and false gaiety, born of nerves. She heard the following evening: President Thieu had resigned.*

He had never been known for patience or an easy manner, but according to associates, Secretary of Defense Schlesinger was now angrier than they had ever seen him. During the past several days he and Kissinger had been arguing violently over the pace and scope of the evacuation. In his pique, Schlesinger had leaked his objections to the press. The accelerated evacuation had begun so late, he told one reporter, that plans for removing Americans by civilian and military aircraft had been "overtaken by events." Helicopters and Marine security forces would have to be used.

Kissinger rose to the provocation. During a WSAG session on Monday morning he heaped abuse on Schlesinger, insisting that the Defense Secretary was simply trying to protect his reputation with his jeremiads to the press. Furthermore, he insisted, the immediate evacuation of the Americans still in Saigon would bring on the panic Martin predicted.

Later in the day, he sent a directive to Martin urging him to move out the majority of DAO's employees as soon as possible, before a helo-lift became necessary. That at least would steal some of Schlesinger's thunder.

The tremors in the upper echelons of the Administration rattled some of those below. Lionel Rosenblatt, now firmly entrenched in Dean Brown's task force, found them particularly troubling, for they seemed to betoken continuing indecision and confusion at the top that could only produce tragedy for his Vietnamese friends. Sunday morning he and a young State Department colleague, Craig Johnstone, therefore reached a crucial decision. Convinced they could no longer count on the bureaucracy to meet their obligations for them, they signed out of the State Department on "annual leave," bought airline tickets to Saigon and a few hours later were off. When Assistant Secretary Habib found out, he cabled the Embassy and ordered Martin to send

---

*On the very day Pat left for Bangkok, Hoang Duc Nha flew into the Thai capital from Singapore. Whether he was involved in disposing of the treasure on Pat's Air Vietnam flight—Thieu's family had often used the national airline as a screen for personal transactions—was never determined. Nha did, however, make good use of his brief stopover in Bangkok. On the evening of the twentieth he called Saigon's Ambassador to Washington and asked him to plead with the CIA for assistance in evacuating his own family from Saigon. Ambassador Phuong obliged him, promptly contacting Shackley at CIA headquarters. Shackley promised to do what he could.

them back. Several young State Department officers made sure the message never got to the Ambassador.

For the next several days Rosenblatt and Johnstone, operating out of the Caravelle Hotel, labored around-the-clock, secretly funneling Vietnamese into DAO's processing center. By the time they packed themselves off on the twenty-fifth they were exhausted and several pounds lighter, but they had managed to smuggle out twenty key locals and their families, over 200 people, none of whom had exit papers. Unlike many other "illegals," theirs were truly "high risk," the majority of them former "provincial reconnaissance" cadres who had been responsible for mounting terrorist operations against the Communists.

Monday, the twenty-first, the day of Thieu's swan song, Admiral Gayler expanded the airlift into a twenty-four-hour affair, C-141s flying in and out during the day, C-130s at night, to accommodate the crush of applicants at DAO. Initially each passenger load was held to a hundred, but DAO officers quickly discovered that by limiting each passenger to one suitcase, they could nearly double the capacity.

Over 1,500 American and Vietnamese evacuees, three times the number on Sunday, were flown into Clark air base in the Philippines during the next twelve hours, raising the resident refugee population there to 3,-000 or more. New arrivals were herded into a makeshift tent city in the base's central courtyard, a grass-covered quadrangle known as "Happening on the Green."

Sometime during the day the resourceful entrepreneur Ed Daly of World Airways flew into Saigon to try to help take up the slack. Over 250 crippled Vietnamese orphans, few of them with any documentation at all, were bundled aboard one of his 727 jets and whisked off to California, where they were all taken under the wing of a fundamentalist church near San Jose.

With the evacuation rapidly assuming a life of its own, Martin felt obliged to begin preparing for the release of some of the Embassy's Vietnamese employees. At his direction, DAO sent a priority cable to the Pentagon on Monday morning, asking that $12.5 million be dispatched to Saigon to cover severance pay, and Don Hays of the administrative office was instructed to draw some $4.2 million from DAO's existing caches to provide an initial funding pool. Since Martin wanted none of the locals to know about the rift in advance, the administrative office was obliged to count out the pay envelopes by hand, without Vietnamese clerical assistance—$1.5 million for over 3,000 employees of State and USIA alone. Eleven Mission officers did nothing but this for two days.

"There were piles of piasters and dollar bills in our vaults," Hays recalled. "I remember walking among them, feeling nervous as hell, knowing that if even one greenback was lost or misplaced, I'd be held responsible. It was a sobering thought, what with thousands of NVA troops within a day's drive of Saigon."

Because of the limited number of "black" flights, Colonel Legro and several other DAO officers agreed on Monday to begin slipping some of their own "illegals" onto the regular military airlift. The decision profited no one but the immediate beneficiaries themselves, for the flood of additional passengers quickly destroyed Legro's recently established quotas, and within hours the evacuation degenerated into a case of every man for himself. Several CIA officers "penetrated" Moorefield's consular operation and other critical points along the processing route to assure space for their own friends and co-workers, DAO retaliated in kind, and other agencies in the Embassy began vying frantically for the leftovers.

As confusion spread through the evacuation program like a paralysis, the Station's own drawdown continued to falter, partially for reasons beyond our control. Under a long-standing arrangement with the Pentagon, several air transports scattered throughout the western Pacific were supposed to be available for CIA use at all times. But now, as the military airlift geared forward, we discovered that none of the transports could be released to us. As an alternative, John Pittman asked CIA headquarters to authorize a shift of all Air America's transports to Taiwan, Thailand and Singapore, his aim being to turn the outgoing flights into a passenger lift. But CIA headquarters said no. Neither Thailand nor Singapore, Shackley argued, would agree to a massive influx of CIA-sponsored Vietnamese.

Many of us were shocked by the decision, and one of my colleagues began putting in nightly telephone calls to USIA officer Frank Scotton in Washington to try to prompt reconsideration at that end. This "secret caller," a high-ranking and experienced field operative, told Scotton that we were shaving it too close, that a helo-lift was in order. Martin was incompetent, and Polgar diverted, he said, and he begged Scotton to persuade officials there to intervene. Scotton and his USIA colleague Ev Bumgardner, already convinced something was terribly wrong in Saigon, went to Brown's deputy on the interagency task force, Clay McManaway, and repeated what the "secret caller" had told them. McManaway contacted Colby and advised him. But Colby, for all of his own concern about the evacuation, was under strict orders from Kissinger to let the White House run the show in its own way. So he stalled, asking for the identity of the "secret caller" so he could "assess" the value of his information. Reluctantly McManaway provided it. This gave Colby his pretext: he turned down the plea for immediate action on the grounds the "secret caller" was not in a position to know the "big picture."

Actually, the "secret caller" had his facts down perfectly. I had been briefing him for the past week and a half on the military situation. With his rank and my information, I felt certain Washington would be forced to react. But as usual, I was wrong.

•　　　　•　　　　•

The "secret caller" and I were hardly the only Station officers trying to force a decision at the center. Larry Downs, the CIA Base Chief in Can Tho, was now bombarding Saigon with cables requesting assistance, principally in the form of helicopters, to help haul out local employees. USAID officials had already "reserved" all the space on the daily Air America flights to Saigon, and Consul General MacNamara, intent on evacuating his own employees down the Bassac River by whaleboat if need be, had refused to order up any additional aircraft. In spite of Downs' repeated queries, however, no one in Saigon saw fit to respond.

Station officer Bill Johnson, meanwhile, was facing a bureaucratic stonewall of similar proportions, but he made up his mind not to be daunted by it. The evening of the twenty-first he and several colleagues, working secretly and totally on their own, launched what was to become the Station's most successful evacuation effort—the removal of the entire staff of an ultra-secret CIA-run radio station known popularly among company hands as "House 7."

The "House 7" operation traced back to the first days of the cease-fire. Soon after wrapping up the Paris agreement, Kissinger had directed the CIA to set up a clutch of "gray" propaganda radio stations to harass the North Vietnamese and the Viet Cong. The designation "gray" meant they were to represent themselves to the world as non-Communist radio voices with no government affiliation. The CIA base in Saigon, under Johnson's direction, had been given the job of putting them on the air. Studios were built in a ramshackle old building at No. 7 Hong Tap Tu Street—hence the nickname "House 7"—and eventually no less than five stations, each operating on a separate frequency, were nurtured into being. Two of them, broadcasting in Cambodian, beamed their subliminally anti-Communist programs across the border. The three others—the "Voice of the Southern Nam Bo," the "Voice of the Sacred Sword" (ostensibly the vehicle of an "independent" revolutionary group) and "Mother Vietnam"—were all directed at indigenous audiences in the north and south.

"Mother Vietnam" was the most effective. Featuring a seductive female voice, nostalgic music and plenty of soft news, it was meant to remind the North Vietnamese trooper out in the paddies what he had left behind. The political message lay buried deep in the sentimentality—an appeal to the Vietnamese people's sense of oneness, the feeling of family, less Tokyo Rose than Radio Berlin: Himmler attempting to woo the British in the late 1930s with visions of ethnic solidarity.

The seductress herself was not one person but two, a pair of Vietnamese girls whose voices were all but identical. The older was a sophisticated beauty named Mai Lon who had studied broadcasting in the United States and whose father was a ranking official in the Thieu government. Thoroughly westernized, she lulled her audiences each night with homilies to a homeland she only vaguely knew.

Mai Lon was an instant hit with the boys on the front line—and with her American sponsors as well. Johnson was particularly intrigued with her and always included her among his guests whenever he threw a party for visiting CIA bigwigs. Her English was flawless, her manners impeccable. She was a Vietnamese to whom westerners could "relate."

At the beginning of April, Johnson had promised the "House 7" crew he would do his best to ensure their safety. Accordingly, he had tried to persuade Polgar and CIA headquarters to let him relocate the entire radio complex to a point outside Vietnam, preferably Thailand. But Shackley vetoed the idea. He did not think the Thais would accept, or Congress would fund, such an "expatriate activity." Polgar had refused on other grounds, claiming such a move would antagonize the North Vietnamese at the very moment he and Martin were trying to nudge them toward an accommodation.

Johnson, undiscouraged, had kept pushing, finally persuading Pittman to authorize the shift of "House 7's" entire staff to Phu Quoc Island off the delta. Ostensibly he was to set up a transmitter there so "Mother Vietnam" could resume broadcasting. His real purpose was simply to put Mai Lon and her associates out of harm's way.

Just after nightfall on the twenty-first the airlift began, Air America C-46s and C-47s shuttling loads of fifty and a hundred down to Phu Quoc. Three CIA men stayed with the broadcasters and their families throughout, moving them clandestinely to Tan Son Nhut, flying with them to Phu Quoc, helping them set up a small kibbutz on the island.

When the "House 7" airlift was completed four days later, all 144 Vietnamese employees of the station and their families, a total of 1,000 people, had been safely relocated. Yet because of bureaucratic error, the ship carrying their radio gear, valued at $4 million, sailed off to the Philippines and was not seen for months.

During the last several days of April rioting broke out among the other 100,000 refugees on Phu Quoc and one of the broadcasters was killed in a gunfight. The rest were picked up by the *Pioneer Challenger* and ferried to Guam.

Apart from that single casualty, Johnson thus kept his promise to his Vietnamese employees. He was one of the few Station officers who did. But the ultimate credit for the salvation of "House 7" belonged to Mai Lon herself: vivacious, Americanized, she had won the affection of her CIA patrons, and was thereby able to ensure that she and her co-workers would not be forgotten.

"Began the melancholy business of packing out today under threat of losing everything," I recorded in my pocket notebook on the twenty-second. "In deference to the special services I'm performing for Polgar, the logistics people said the only thing I had to do was to put my stuff in the middle of the living room. The packers would take care of the rest. The Embassy itself has become an empty shell; hallways strewn with litter, scuff marks along the floor from the packing crates. Hundreds of Vietnamese camped in folding chairs outside the consulate building, waiting anxiously for visas or affidavits of support.

"Even the blessed of the society, the wealthy westernized elites, are scrambling for the refugee flights. Many who'd never sold themselves to us before are willing now, simply for a way out. An ad in the *Saigon Post* today: 'Fairly pretty high school girl, eighteen, holder of baccalaureate degree, piano player, from well-to-do family, seeks adoption by or marriage with a foreigner of either American, French, British, German or other nationality who could take her abroad legally, to enable her to continue her college studies outside Vietnam, at her own expense . . .'."

Within twenty-four hours of Thieu's farewell speech, the departure rate doubled. Over 3,000 evacuees left Saigon via DAO on Tuesday, the twenty-second, bringing the total number since the beginning of the month to over 10,000. American transports were now arriving and departing Tan Son Nhut on an average of two per hour.

Washington helped to accelerate the pace by once again flexing the immigration rules. On Kissinger's urgent recommendation, the Senate Judiciary Committee unanimously approved, and the Justice Department made public on the twenty-second, a plan for waiving entry restrictions for over 130,000 "aliens from Indochina," including 50,000 Vietnamese in the "high risk" category. It was a monumental concession from Congress and from the Immigration and Naturalization Service. Normally, only 20,000 entry visas can be issued to citizens of any one country each year, and no more than 130,000 to residents of the "eastern hemisphere." The last time such an exception had been made was back in the early 1960s, when over 600,000 Cuban exiles were admitted to the United States after the Bay of Pigs fiasco.

Since the new parole provided explicitly for the immigration of "high risk" evacuees as well as American dependents, the last bit of American red tape in effect was eliminated. It was no longer necessary to pair each evacuee with an American relative. Those with no affidavit of support or petition from a next-of-kin in the United States could simply be declared "high risk" and packed off under the 50,000-man quota. And, as Martin later wryly conceded to Congress, "using the John Marshall broad construction approach, we stretched the authority to cover the problem."

Soon after learning of the new regulations, Martin ordered General Smith to begin moving out the families of ranking Vietnamese military personnel. Although officially the new quotas were not to go into effect for another day or so, the Ambassador saw no reason not to take advantage of them at once.

At the DAO processing center itself the easing of the immigration strictures had little practical impact, since rules and regulations had already given way to expediency. The only change in procedure that really affected the routine there was the lowering of Saigon's curfew to eight o'clock in the wake of Thieu's resignation. Since Moorefield and his colleagues could not possibly finish their work before the new curfew took hold each evening, they decided to begin keeping evacuees in the DAO annex overnight and to turn the processing into a continuous business. Apart from the availability of aircraft, and their own endurance, only one consideration threatened to limit their efficiency. Smith insisted on having the annex cleared by dawn each morning, so that if Option IV were suddenly ordered up, there would be no milling crowds near the helo-pads.

Under the new operating schedule the gymnasium soon took on the disheveled quality of a carnival at closing time. "It was hot as a son-of-a-bitch," Moorefield later remarked, "and once the people began camping in overnight, we had a tremendous problem controlling bodies. Discarded luggage was everywhere, the snack bar had been cleaned out in the first few hours, the toilets were backed up and overflowing, and many of the Vietnamese were sick with fear. We had three or four cattle chutes set up to funnel the folks along, and two other Embassy officers [Joe McBride and Bill Mosher] were now working at my elbow, but still the load was too much to handle."

Part of the chaos was deliberate. With the start of the twenty-four-hour airlift Moorefield and his associates agreed to backlog as many people as possible so no plane would leave the country half empty. But part of it was a product of Moorefield's own generosity. "Look," he explained, "you had to find a way to take care of the people who'd fallen through the slats. USAID was supposed to be ushering out the employees of the volunteer agencies, but something went wrong. Locals from World Vision, and other charity groups, were left stranded at DAO, with nobody but a Vietnamese honcho to speak for them. So were the employees of many American companies. They'd step up to my desk, show me some kind of documentation, and say they'd been promised assistance. And of course they had, and deserved it. I had no choice but to try to help them.

"And then there were those goddamn quotas, people blocking out seats in advance. We never knew how many would be available after DAO and various Embassy types had finished slipping their own 'special cases' past us.

"I was on the phone to the Embassy every twenty minutes fishing for guidance. But it soon became apparent no one was in control. So I began applying my own remedies. When Rosenblatt or someone from the agency [the CIA] came in with a Vietnamese they said was 'high risk,' I stamped the papers and sent them through. No further questions."

The Vietnamese bureaucrats on the scene also posed obstacles. "By Day Two or Three," Moorefield recalled, "it was obvious the fellows from the Ministry of the Interior were slowing the pace. They were sending all *laissez-passer* applications downtown for approval—and that normally took about a day. So what we did was organize around them. We set up several different lines in the gym, winding this way and that, making it impossible for them to keep track of who'd been processed and who hadn't.

"Every once in a while I'd look up from my desk and see that one or two of the officials had packed up and left. I later found out that several had decamped with whole satchels full of blank *laissez-passer* forms and were selling them down on the black market at extravagant prices."

By Tuesday afternoon the refugee population at Clark air base in the Philippines was spilling out of the reception area like a potful of exploding popcorn. The task force in Washington hurriedly notified the Guamian government to prepare to absorb the excess—5,000 evacuees daily, to be bedded and boarded for up to ninety days. Within a few hours the first of them arrived at Guam's Andersen Air Force Base, and were put up in a complex of metal barracks known as "Tin City," home of American B-52 pilots when the island was a jumping-off point for bombing missions against North Vietnam. The ovenlike structures offered little in the way of creature comforts—their air-conditioning units had gone with their last American tenants—but with each passing day, more and more refugees tried to crowd in, for the only alternative was a tent in the relentless tropic sun.

At first immigration officials on Guam and at Clark tried to cleave to the letter of the law. Each refugee's paperwork was carefully checked for errors or forgery. Criminals, prostitutes and drug addicts were duly identified and isolated. After a day or so, however, it became obvious the traffic would not bear such scrutiny. There were bar girls aplenty in the tidal wave of arrivals, and not a few wore a tattoo of needle pricks. Moreover, in attempting to review each case in full, the immigration men were causing traffic jams at Guam's arrival center that threatened to bring the entire airlift to a halt. So, like Moorefield and so many others on the Saigon end, they began using their discretion.

Polarized Thinking

Despite the quickening pace of the evacuation, Congress remained dissatisfied. There was still widespread suspicion on Capitol Hill that the Administration was deliberately delaying an American pullout to assure time for a Vietnamese one. "We don't want any more Americans in Saigon than can be removed in one swoop of a helicopter," one ranking Senator told newsmen.

The White House tried to deflect such concerns by promising once again to cut the American community down to 1,500 in the next day or so. In addition, the Pentagon acknowledged that the evacuation fleet was being further expanded, so that a large-scale helo-lift could be mounted on a moment's notice if necessary. If this was meant to ease nerves in Congress, however, it did not succeed. Several legislators clamored that the Administration was stumbling into a new war. The North Vietnamese seemed equally discomfited. "This adventurous course," Radio Hanoi warned, "could lead to dangerous consequences."

Ford tried to lay such fears to rest in a speech on Wednesday evening at Tulane University. Declaring the war in Indochina "finished" as far as America was concerned, he called on the country to "stop refighting the battles and recriminations" of the past. "Some seem to feel," he said, "that if we do not succeed in everything everywhere, then we have succeeded in nothing anywhere. I reject such polarized thinking. We can and should help others to help themselves. But the fate of responsible men and women everywhere in the final decision rests in their own hands."

A presidential spokesman tried to explain to reporters what it all meant. "Not a shift in policy," he commented, but an appeal to the American people to "shift their attention."

In Saigon, halfway round the world, you could feel their presence now, those eighteen North Vietnamese divisions, backed by countless armor and artillery units, closing inexorably in around us like the coming monsoons. They revealed themselves by pinpricks as the week wore on: a bus ambushed on the road from Tay Ninh, a flare-up on Route 4 seventeen miles southwest of Saigon, heavy pressure on the road between Xuan Loc and Bien Hoa. The Phu Lam radar installation, five miles from the heart of the capital, was struck again by commandos. This time the defenders did not make even a pretense of holding. They fled at the first shot.

Rumor had it the Communists, once victorious, would round up all unmarried girls and force them to wed their disabled veterans. So in the past few days there had been a rash of weddings as the city's fairer citizens sought to put themselves out of the running. Others, the plainer sort, bought bottles of sleeping pills or straight-edged razors.

The airfield at Bien Hoa was now effectively closed; the consulate as well. John Stockwell made a final trip to the city on Wednesday, the twenty-third, to look for Vietnamese employees who might have been left behind. Only a few Chinese "Nung" guards were still at the compound. Dick Peters, the Consul General, waited until the end of the day—the last minute—to depart, not so much out of a sea captain's sense of duty, as for the sake of simple prudence. He would not drive to Saigon, he advised the Embassy, until he had been provided with a chopper escort. His caution was well advised. Disgruntled Vietnamese troopers fired burst after burst over the roof of his car on the way in.

As General Dung tightened his grip on Saigon, Kissinger tried to make the most of the time left to us. There were two possible options, he observed in a cable to Martin early on the twenty-third. We could try to keep the Huong government afloat for the time being, or as the French (and Hungarians) were advocating, we could attempt to put together a new regime acceptable to the Communists. In his view, the first option assured us far more leverage in dealing with the Soviets. He therefore urged Martin to do what he could to bolster old Huong, pending a reply to our cease-fire request from Moscow.

Martin followed Kissinger's mandate to the letter, and made sure his staff did too. When Polgar asked permission to buy and bribe members of Saigon's National Assembly to hasten Minh's elevation, Martin would not hear of it. The South Vietnamese, he insisted, must work out their own destiny in their own way, without American interference.

The South Vietnamese seemed determined to do just that, though often with little regard for what might best assure their survival. Rather than unite in the face of their common enemy, they continued to give rein to countless rivalries and jealousies. On the extreme right, there was Ky. Haranguing his followers at a banquet on Wednesday, he urged the army to fight on so that a new "peace cabinet" could negotiate with the Communists from strength. In the meantime, the more pragmatic General Vien and Tran Van Don, fearing a coup from Ky and his faction, agreed tentatively to mount one of their own.

Minh for his part continued to favor an extraconstitutional change as the only way to preserve his credit, such as it was, with the Communists. He would never accept a cabinet appointment from Huong, he advised Vien and his growing entourage. Nothing less than the presidency itself, offered by an informal "coalition of neutralists," would satisfy him.

As for Huong himself, the ancient and embattled caretaker, he remained intent on playing the head of state he thought he was. "Thieu has fled destiny," he told Ambassador Mérillon. "Destiny has come to me." As if to prove his authority, he ordered the removal of all anti-Communist banners and posters around the city and dispatched an aide to Tan Son Nhut to attempt to open "negotiations" with the North Vietnamese delegation to the Joint Military Team.

The following morning, Thursday the twenty-fourth, Huong also attempted to make a virtue of defeat. At his direction General Vien formally and with great flourish ordered the army to assume a "defensive posture," to "reassure" the Communists of Saigon's sincere interest in peace.

Reasonable as the gesture was, several of Vien's generals objected to it. Though under no illusions about the army's staying power, they wanted to give the Communists one last taste of cold steel, if only to prove that negotiations were still a two-way street. Two days before, only hours after Thieu's resignation, General Toan, the MR 3 commander, had suggested asking the Americans for one last B-52 raid. Vien had dismissed that idea for obvious reasons; he finally understood, as Toan evidently did not, that there would be no B-52s. The proposal did give rise, however, to a kind of pale imitation of the great bombing runs of yesteryear. With the help of DAO technicians, South Vietnamese pilots rigged up a special bomb rack for the piece of ordnance Von Marbod and Weyand had offered them earlier in the month: the terrifying killing device known as the CBU-55.

The effectiveness of this awesome weapon was proven beyond any shadow of a doubt Tuesday afternoon. A C-130 transport with a CBU on board took off from Tan Son Nhut, circled once over Xuan Loc to the east, and dropped its load virtually on top of the command post of the 341st NVA Division just outside the newly captured town. The casualties were enormous. Over 250 NVA troops were incinerated or died from suffocation in the post-explosion vacuum, and for a moment General Dung's forces staggered in midstep.

Radio Hanoi immediately cried foul, accusing the Americans and the South Vietnamese of resorting to "illegal" biological warfare. The Communist Chinese protested with equal vehemence, describing the bomb-wrought havoc as "mass murder" and charging the United States with directing the attack. It was the harshest criticism Peking had leveled at us in over two years.

As the protests continued, other punishment was visited on the enemy. Scores of Daisy Cutters, those monstrous 15,000-pound bombs developed for clearing chopper pads in the jungle, and pallets of 500-pound bombs were rained down on Communist units around Xuan Loc, and at one point a special air strike was flown against a convoy of mobile SA-2 launchers in northeastern MR 3. The ordnance was a sophisticated homing missile known as the Wild Weasel and the attack planes were American. Neither Polgar nor any of us on his staff was informed of the mission. The White House did not want it known that American aircraft were again engaging in the hostilities.

The Communist response to these torments was instant and effective. Within hours of the CBU strike, the shelling of Bien Hoa airfield intensified to such a point that the runways were no longer fully serviceable. The few F-5A jets there were quickly pulled back to Saigon and the remaining A-37 light bombers were shifted to Can Tho.

Even as Saigon flexed its muscles for the last time, the political breakthrough Kissinger had been yearning for loomed into view. By Wednesday evening Ambassador Dobrynin had passed to the White House the eagerly awaited note from Brezhnev. Kissinger immediately cabled the text, together with his own comments, to Martin. Seldom before, he remarked in his preface, had he ever made an Ambassador in the field privy to such high-level communications with the Soviets. As one who appreciated flattery himself, he evidently felt it would not be lost on the envoy in Saigon.

The Soviet message touched on several crucial points. Not only had the "Vietnamese side" assured Moscow it had "no intention" of posing obstacles to an American evacuation; it also had indicated that it had no desire to "humiliate the United States," and was willing—with respect to political questions—to "proceed from the Paris accords." In a postcript, Brezhnev expressed hope that "no action by the United States" would exacerbate the situation in Indochina.

Aside from the references to the evacuation, the message was a masterpiece of ambiguity. It skirted almost as many questions as it answered, and gave no clear sign of Hanoi's willingness to negotiate. In his covering note to Martin, however, Kissinger attempted to read his own hopes into it. In his opinion, he said, the message could be interpreted to mean: (1) that the withdrawal of both Americans and select Vietnamese could continue; (2) that we could retain a bantam-sized, 800-man Embassy in Saigon; and (3) that the "PRG" was prepared to "negotiate within the framework of the tripartite commission" envisioned in the Paris agreement. In addition, he speculated, the note seemed consistent with his own estimates concerning the amount of time available for an evacuation. As Martin later explained, Kissinger had originally proposed two weeks to the Soviets. Having received no specific comment on this point, the Secretary was now ready to assume two weeks were acceptable to Hanoi.

Kissinger's gloss on the message was nothing if not generous. But according to State Department officers who had watched him negotiate in the past, such overreaching was characteristic of him. During the latter stages of the Paris talks in 1972, he had put words into Le Duc Tho's mouth (particularly on the Cambodian issue) in an effort to create a basis for understanding. He was now doing the same with Brezhnev.

On Kissinger's orders, Martin advised few of his colleagues of the Soviet communiqué. He briefed neither Smith nor Legro on it, and though he did show Kissinger's cable to Polgar, he warned him, graphically, that if he told anybody about it, he would "cut off his balls and stuff 'em in his ears." Polgar, unintimidated, hinted to me soon afterward that something was in the wind: the Soviets might let us out of Saigon with our hides.

Since the Soviet message followed so hard on the Hungarian approach to Polgar, it was natural to assume they were part of the same cloth. As one high-ranking State Department officer later remarked, the Hungarians and the Poles had provided the "nest," and the Brezhnev message seemed to be "the egg that fit."

The combination inevitably buoyed Martin and Polgar in their hopes for some kind of political deal. Even so, the two remained at odds on one essential point: what to do next. Polgar, now deeply impatient with Martin's concern for legal proprieties, again insisted on pushing Huong aside by whatever means necessary. Martin, by contrast, was strengthened in his belief that a constitutional turnover was the sensible way. Indeed, now that Hanoi had agreed not to interfere, the only real danger to the Americans, in his view, was the chaos of uncontrolled change, a coup.

Within hours of the Brezhnev note, one of Kissinger's key assumptions was tentatively confirmed. In a private conversation with an American visitor, Pham Van Ba, head of the PRG mission in Paris, remarked that "his side" would not object to the evacuation of Americans or select Vietnamese—the same assurance a PRG contact had given Tran Van Don in Saigon a week before.

Beyond this, however, there was little else in diplomatic channels to provide encouragement. In a comment of its own on the Brezhnev message, the American Embassy in Moscow cast doubt on the most critical assumption of all—the projected time frame for an evacuation. By the Embassy's account, working-level contacts at the Kremlin were intimating that the North Vietnamese actually would pull their punches only through the weekend—not beyond Tuesday, 29 April.

That projection, of course, would prove dead accurate. The twenty-ninth was the day Dung meant to unleash his final offensive against Saigon.

When Douglas Pike, the State Department's Indochina expert, saw the Embassy cable he cast off his own last hopes. That evening he went home thinking, This is it. Saigon really has only five days left.

Soon afterward the *New York Times* quoted a senior Republican on the House International Affairs Committee as saying he had learned of a "tacit understanding" whereby Hanoi had accepted not to attack Saigon until Monday to permit evacuation of Americans. Someone on Kissinger's staff apparently had leaked part of the Moscow advisory to the Congressman, who in turn had leaked it to the press.

Amid the flurry of speculation on Hanoi's plans, the principals themselves offered a new, if discouraging, clue. Liberation Radio, in a political commentary on Thursday, the twenty-fourth, explicitly rejected Martin's "constitutional solution" and insisted on the creation of a "new administration" in Saigon composed of "sober-minded individuals" who had not "taken sides." It also demanded an end to all American aid and the withdrawal of "U.S. warships" and "intelligence personnel," as well as "military advisors disguised as civilians."

The broadcast confirmed my own worst suspicions. Hanoi's demands clearly were expanding balloonlike with each passing hour. The references to "warships" and "intelligence personnel" had not seen before.

My views were not shared in the front office. Against the backdrop of the Hungarian feelers and the Brezhnev note, Polgar saw the new political statement as "a blueprint for political accommodation"—inferentially an endorsement of the "Minh solution," since it specifically ruled out all others.

I was almost too weary to argue the point. What was lacking, I emphasized to him, was what had been lacking in Hanoi's pronouncements since early April—any hint of reciprocity. Once again, it seemed to me, we were simply being offered an impossible ultimatum on a take-it-or-leave-it basis. Nor could I believe that Minh would ever be acceptable to the Communists, even as a transition figure, not with the concessions he would have to make to the rightists merely to survive his first day in office.

Polgar shrugged, and asked for a brief analysis of the broadcast. Within an hour I sent my draft to his office. By the time I got it back, it had been "Polarized," emended into oblivion. "As presented, the new PRG statement," Polgar had written in a concluding paragraph, "leaves open the possibility of negotiations with such figures as General Minh, who is not a member of the Thieu government."

Polgar circulated the study among members of the National Assembly that afternoon. Although Martin had ordered him not to tamper with the constitutional machinery, Polgar felt there was no harm in suggesting to a few legislators that negotiations might be possible if Minh was quickly installed. He also broached this idea to Malcolm Browne. The *New York Times* promptly reported that the PRG statement of the twenty-fourth "hinted" that Minh might be acceptable as a chief of state.

Polgar's views, as amplified by the *Times,* had immediate impact in Washington. In a briefing to WSAG, on the twenty-fourth, Colby proclaimed that while a "negotiated surrender" was probably the best that could be obtained from Hanoi, "we may be near the formation of a government [in Saigon] with some chance of dealing with the Communists on this basis."*

At the very moment Polgar and Colby were pushing their latest peace theories, General Dung was finalizing his plan of attack. On Thursday after-

---

*Unfortunately, Colby was not the only one at CIA headquarters now afflicted with "peace fever." On the twenty-third Theodore Shackley, evidently reflecting the latest disclosures from the Soviets, told Saigon's Ambassador to Washington that there was now hope the evacuation could continue for two weeks.

noon his commander on the Xuan Loc–Bien Hoa front, General Le Trong Tan, asked him for authority to launch his own initial thrust ahead of schedule —on Saturday, the twenty-sixth—so that he would have plenty of time to position his guns at Nhon Trach in preparation for the final assault and the shelling of Tan Son Nhut three days later. Dung let the request simmer for the next twelve hours.

Tank leader Quang Tan, meanwhile, was frantically poring over his maps of downtown Saigon. He had been informed earlier in the day that his unit, NVA Armored Brigade 203, was to spearhead the final assault on the South Vietnamese capital and was to have the supreme honor of capturing the Presidential Palace. He was thrilled at being entrusted with such a historic mission, but deeply worried as well. By the afternoon of the twenty-fourth his brigade had yet to form up for the attack. Two units were still on the road to the northeast. Nor did he have any real "feel" for his objective. He had never seen Saigon and knew nothing of its street patterns or of the surrounding countryside. He could only hope that the cartographers in Hanoi, who had hastily prepared the map he was now trying to commit to memory, were better informed than he.

As Dung's troops girded for battle, they became increasingly careless, flooding the airwaves with often only thinly coded messages about their tactical plans. Many of the transmissions our monitors plucked out of the air pointed unmistakably to an impending drive on Saigon. But Polgar could not bring himself to believe them. There was a good possibility, he remarked to me on Thursday, that the Communists were merely "spoofing"—that is, churning out bogus messages to mislead and frighten us. In an effort to prove his point, he sent a message to Washington, requesting a review of the entire intercept package. He would reserve judgment, he said, until Washington had rendered its own.

With that, he turned his back on the radio leaks, and thus blinded himself to our last source of credible information on Hanoi's planning. By now most of our agents in the field had vanished, or had lost touch with us, and aside from a few gratuitous handouts from journalists, there was little other data available, even on tactical developments.

While Polgar and Martin tried to draw solace from the latest political signals, Mérillon and his staff at the French Embassy continued to exude an air of confidence. By the afternoon of the twenty-fourth they had alerted all 10,000 French citizens in the city to plan to stay on, since a cease-fire was "imminent." As a result, many Frenchmen who had been preparing to help Vietnamese friends and associates escape decided not to make the effort.

Other elements of the foreign community were not so gullible. On Thursday morning no less than four Embassies shut their doors for good. None of them quitted the field with honor. The British and Canadian Missions simply abandoned their Vietnamese staffs, the Canadian chargé explaining irritably to newsmen that he was not in the business of providing succor to refugees without proper documentation. The Taiwanese Embassy went further, abandoning not only its Vietnamese employees but also the 1,000 nationalist Chinese citizens in the city, many of whom were part-time intelligence agents.

Taking their cue from Embassy Row, several oil companies and foreign airlines suspended business on the same day. Even the redoubtable Pan Am was forced to discontinue its twice-weekly service, on orders from the Federal Aviation Administration, which now considered the airspace over Cambodia and Vietnam unsafe for commercial flight.

Unlike the diplomatic establishment, the business community went to some lengths to provide for the Vietnamese in its care. Representatives of Chase Manhattan, First National City Bank and Bank of America had already filtered back into Saigon (after their own hasty departure earlier in the month) to arrange for the evacuation of local employees, and several smaller firms were discussing pooling their resources to charter a special airlift to Bangkok.

In an effort to be helpful, Martin's economic counselor, Dan Ellerman, approached IBM and the three western oil companies in the city and offered to organize an airlift for those on their payrolls. He made it clear, however, that timing was critical. Over the years foreign firms had plugged western technology into myriad aspects of Vietnamese life, and if the Vietnamese technicians manning the various "systems" were now yanked out prematurely, much of the society and the governmental structure would simply disintegrate. Since Martin was determined to avoid that at all costs, Ellerman urged IBM and the oil companies to delay the departure of their locals till the last possible minute.

The continuing shrinkage of the foreign community considerably aggravated tensions in the Embassy. Why aren't we moving faster? The question echoed up and down the corridors of the chancery, and since no answer was forthcoming from the third-floor suite, bitterness and frustration built to the boiling point.

Ironically, Smith and his staff drew much of the fire. With their superior organization and their proximity to the flight line, they were moving out far more Vietnamese than anyone else in the Mission, and some of us were beginning to feel slighted. On Thursday afternoon Jim Devine finally attempted to establish some kind of equity. He drew up a new set of quotas to replace those Legro had tried to enforce two days before and established an "auxiliary" evacuation control center at the Embassy to promote cooperation between DAO's flight controllers and the rest of us.

But as with so many other recent innovations, these came too late to make much difference. DAO continued to overfulfill its quotas, other agencies responded by leeching yet more space from Lacy Wright or from Moorefield, and chaos and improvisation reigned on supreme.

•   •   •

Meanwhile, the Embassy's administrative officers were trying to come to grips with the bureaucratic implications of our leaving. Not the least of their concerns was purely fiscal. Late Thursday morning the $12 million that had been requested from Washington to cover severance pay for local employees and other expenses was delivered to DAO by a flying safe-deposit box, and Don Hays and other administrative staffers immediately began dispensing pay envelopes to Vietnamese staffers. But in order to avert widespread panic and resentment, many of those "separated" were promptly "rehired" and kept on till the last day of the war. Few of them ever realized therefore that the end was near—or felt any need to prepare for it.

Since most of the foreign and domestic banks in the city were already closed, Hays and his companions also were obliged to handle currency conversions for hundreds of departing Americans. Initially they put an arbitrary limit on such transactions, refusing to change any more than $2,000 worth of piasters per person. But after the first day or so, in the face of mounting pressure, they began converting any "acceptable" amount, provided the customer could produce a note from his employer showing that he was to leave the country the same day. The deadline was meant to prevent departing Americans from cycling their money repeatedly through the Embassy and the black market for huge profits. Apparently it worked. Hays could later recall no instance in which an American had showed up with more than a few hundred dollars in piasters to exchange.

To add to their burdens, Hays and fellow administrative officer Jim Gagnon also were nominated Thursday afternoon to help evacuate some of the Embassy's locals. Gagnon drove out to DAO shortly after lunch to survey the assembly areas. "Pure chaos," he told Hays by phone. Sanitary facilities were taxed to the limit and food supplies were nonexistent. Hays contacted the manager of the Embassy canteen and asked for help. In the next few hours the fourteen Vietnamese waitresses on duty there whipped up 2,000 sandwiches, trucked them out to DAO, and set up shop in the bowling alley just off the main courtyard. Soon they were handing out their wares free of charge.

That night Hays and several colleagues assembled a convoy of army buses and picked up their first passengers. When the caravan arrived at the marshaling area inside "Dodge City," however, no one from the Embassy was on hand to guide the frightened and confused evacuees through the system. Hays and Gagnon had no choice but to shoulder the job themselves.

By the time the Embassy began moving out its own locals in earnest, Martin was under pressure to evacuate another item of value: military hardware. On Thursday afternoon Assistant Defense Secretary Erich Von Marbod arrived in Saigon to coordinate the operation. He had been sent out from the Pentagon on orders from Schlesinger himself. Convinced that the end was now only a few days away, Schlesinger was determined to prevent additional U.S.-made military equipment from falling into Communist hands, and since Von Marbod was a proven logistics specialist, he seemed just the man to handle the job. Von Marbod, in fact, had already laid the groundwork by the time he showed up at the Embassy. The day before, during a stopover in Bangkok, he had managed to persuade the Thai military to let him use several local bases as parking places for the planes and equipment he was hoping to spirit out.

When Martin learned what Von Marbod was up to, he was furious. The withdrawal of any military equipment, he protested, would sabotage Vietnamese morale and destroy whatever slim chance existed for an orderly, fully constitutional change in government. But Von Marbod ignored his plaints and plunged into his task with fervor. ("Went off like some goddamned unguided missile," Martin later complained of him.) A few hours after his arrival he contacted old friends in the Vietnamese navy and made them a proposition. If the worst came to pass, he said, they should be ready to put their families and select navy personnel on every available vessel on the Saigon River and sail them out to sea. As Schlesinger's personal representative, he could guarantee that the American military would welcome them—and their ships—with open arms.

Von Marbod was not the only "unguided missile" now threatening the Ambassador's carefully framed universe. For the past several days Captain Carmody, Smith's Navy Attaché, had been trying to trace an orbit of his own, clamoring for authority to put Vietnamese aboard the freighters standing by at the Newport docks just outside the city limits. Like Gayler, he felt conditions for a riverborne evacuation would never be better than they were now.

But Martin remained unpersuaded. "Had we attempted to load those ships," he later told Congress, "there was universal agreement from those who understood Saigon that we would have had an immediate panic situation." He therefore ordered Carmody to stand easy.

In the meantime, an issue of equal delicacy was teetering on the point of decision. Earlier in the week the State Department had finally arranged insurance coverage for the military flight which was to ferry the $220 million in gold that made up Saigon's treasury to the Federal Reserve Bank in New York. Officials of the Economics Ministry were already packing up the bonanza. The plane was slated to arrive for the pickup Friday morning, the twenty-fifth.

But now, at the last minute, a snag developed; the plan became a hostage to politics. Thursday morning Economics Minister Hao informed Dan Ellerman that Huong had ordered the shipment delayed indefinitely, until a new government was formed. Martin promptly scheduled an appointment at the Palace to discuss the matter with the new President. The meeting failed to break the logjam. Whether with Huong's agreement, or without, Martin decided then and there to leave the gold in place for the time being, if only to lend an aura of stability and permanence to the government, and to add to the collateral it might bring to bear in negotiations with the Communists. He told Ellerman: "Keep the plane here until midnight, the twenty-seventh."

Martin had failed to reckon, however, on one other player at the gaming table: Economics Minister Hao. After the fall of Saigon several reliable sources advised me that Hao had been a pawn of the Communists all along. As they explained it, he had received word from North Vietnamese agents in early April that he would be treated leniently by the "new regime" if he succeeded in thwarting the shipment of gold out of the country. Though Hao was no agent himself, he was young, excitable and somewhat idealistic (fatal alchemy), and he evidently took his Communist contacts at their word. Not only did he ultimately refuse to be evacuated himself; he also managed through polite run-arounds to prevent Ellerman from smuggling the gold out. The entire $220 million in bullion would thus still be lying undisturbed in a cargo room at Tan Son Nhut when Dung's forces rolled triumphantly into the city.

As I nosed my Ford Pinto through the rush-hour traffic on Thursday evening, I toyed with the idea of asking Polgar to ship me out. Obviously, nobody in the Embassy was really interested in intelligence appraisals any longer. Polgar and the Ambassador were intent on reading the signals as they chose.

But no sooner had I made up my mind than I changed it again. Five years I had given to Vietnam—five years and my own best illusions. To have packed up and pulled out at this point would have been tantamount to casting off a long-running love affair, and about as easy. No, there was really no choice open to me: I knew I would have to stay on till the end, if only to be able to satisfy myself that I had put the last of my illusions to rest.

When I walked into my apartment Tu Ha was clattering about in the kitchen, deliberately banging pots and pans to muffle the pounding at Bien Hoa. She did not even bother to say hello. She had become so transfixed by her own fears and uncertainties during the past week, she might as well have been on a permanent drug high. As I stood in the hallway listening to her, I made my only sensible decision of the day. If I was going to be so foolish as to indulge in last-minute heroics, I had no right to expect the same of her.

By any logical standard, Tu and her family had nothing to hide or to fear from the Communists. They had never actively supported the government or lionized the Americans. Tu's parents would have been appalled to discover she was even on speaking terms with a "round-eye." In all the years she had toiled in the dives at Vung Tau and on Tu Do Street, they had never known.

And yet, what if the Communists misinterpreted her past, her American associations? That infinitesimal possibility far outweighed all other considerations, rational and otherwise.

As we sat down to dinner, I asked her what she wanted to do. Tears welled up in the almond eyes. "I'm too scared to go to America," she sobbed, "but too scared to stay here."

"There are ways of getting you out," I mumbled, struggling with my chopsticks and my reserve. "Ways of finding papers and an escort."

She sat for a moment, saying nothing. Then inevitably she asked me the central question, for which I had no answer: "Will the VC kill me?" I said I didn't know, and at that moment I realized further discussion was pointless. I told her to be ready to leave in twelve hours. She looked at me beseechingly. "There's one more thing," she whispered, as if afraid to broach it. "Can I take my family with me?" Not realizing how far the restrictions had broken down, I told her that was impossible.

The next morning Joe Kingsley and I agreed on a division of labor. He would see to the evacuation of our mutual Vietnamese friends, wheeling and dealing them through the system. I would handle the office. "Helluva good idea!" he exclaimed. "Getting tired of this analytical crap anyway. No profit in it." I knew what he meant.

Within the next several hours Kingsley rounded up forged documentation and persuaded an old office chum to sign on as Tu's sponsor and escort. A call to Moorefield at Tan Son Nhut assured them seat space.

In the meantime, Tu and her father tried to close out her bank account, a little over $1,000 in piasters. But they found it had been frozen, along with all others.

Her father, a merchant, must have guessed Tu's plans, though she told him nothing, only that she might be away from the city for a while. When she returned home to pack, her mother was away at the market.

Shortly after lunch she arrived at my apartment with one suitcase. She asked my maid to deliver a note to her parents, explaining everything. Two hours later Kingsley came by to pick her up. Before he left her at the processing center, he handed her an envelope with $1,000 in it from me.

At eight o'clock the following morning Tu, her American companion and his Vietnamese mistress clambered aboard a U.S. Air Force C–141. The flight, icebox-cold, took nearly nine hours. Some of the passengers became desperately ill; the toilets spilled over; there was no food or drink. But later, Tu's most vivid memory of the ordeal was the silence behind the roar of the engines. None of her fellow Vietnamese passengers seemed capable of talking. They merely wept in silence.

When the plane touched down in Guam it was four in the afternoon. Navy personnel handed out cookies and cups of soup to the passengers as they filed out. That first night Tu and eleven other people slept on the floor of an old wooden shack, thirty by thirty feet. At dawn they all went together, men and women, to the shower rooms, but none of the fixtures worked.

Tu remained stranded on Guam for over a month and a half, passing her days in that broken-down building. Immigration authorities quickly discovered her forged papers and refused to let her go on to the United States with her "sponsor." In the weeks in the sun, she turned "brown as a soul sister," she later told me. Some of the girls she got to know went off to sleep with Navy men or immigration authorities to assure themselves an early exit.

The price of Tu's own liberation was merely hard cash. One of her Vietnamese friends had lined up a plethora of "sponsors" in California and offered to sell her one for $100. What she received in return was a signed petition and an address and a quick clearance from the immigration officials.

The couple that greeted her on the West Coast seemed reassuringly conventional, even familiar—a retired U.S. military officer and his wife. But after a week or so, the man began making overtures, and the wife, sensing the competition, became broodingly jealous, refusing even to acknowledge Tu's presence.

There were neighborhood friends, to be sure—fresh young Californians of Tu's age who found her exotic and attractive, all the more so for the size of her wallet. They took her out to dinner and to the movies, inviting her in good-natured fun to pay the fare. Before long they had run through her $1,000 as if it were some kind of public philanthropy. Then they dropped her.

At last, in desperation, Tu wrote to a Vietnamese friend and her husband in New Orleans and asked them to sponsor her. They agreed, and there she resettled. By the time I tracked her down, months after the collapse of Saigon, she had taken a job as a seamstress and an apartment by herself, and was beginning to weave the latest Americanese into her own broken accent.

High-Class Chauffeur

"Le Duan murders his chief political rival in Hanoi! Chinese troops pour across the border into North Vietnam to avenge the death!" These dazzling headlines were flung across the airwaves by Saigon Radio on the morning of the twenty-fifth. And you almost wanted to believe them. But of course they were nothing more than a hoax, a piece of psychological warfare conjured up by the Saigon authorities to confuse and demoralize the North Vietnamese troops on our doorstep.

Most Saigonese found the story so preposterous they did not even bother to tune in for further details later in the day. The North Vietnamese presumably were no more impressed. The only listeners who seemed to have been taken in were American journalists. All morning I was deluged with calls from reporter friends seeking confirmation. I told them it was merely Saigon's idea of a bad joke.

"The city is a short, sizzling fuse," I wrote in my notebook the same day. "The latest John Wayne flick plays downtown to an empty house. No one needs vicarious thrills in this town. The reality is here.

"Money as usual is a barometer of the mood. It takes five thousand piasters now to earn a dollar on the black market, up from three thousand only a day or so ago. Lesser omens abound as well. According to a reporter friend, the last of the lovelies at Mimi's bar were seen packing their bags into an old Chevrolet this morning. Undoubtedly, some ingenious American has found a way to sneak them all aboard the great 'Freedom Bird.'

"In the Embassy, a false camaraderie—call it the 'Alamo syndrome'—has sprung up among those of us who're still considered 'essential.' Colleagues who've never spoken to each other before are suddenly fast friends, lunching together (quickly), exchanging stories about the Ambassador's parentage, his behavior, and about Communist planning. In a way, the new bonhomie is the outcropping of mutual need. The continuing exodus of maids, cooks and shoeshine boys has denied us our usual props; only by pulling together can we compensate. A State Department wife (one of the few left) has begun playing part-time cook in the restaurant behind the Embassy, and the manager of my apartment building has persuaded a neighbor with culinary skills to form a task force to feed the rest of us.

"Now that Tu Ha is on her way, I'm holding up pretty well, though one of the secretaries claims to see traces of strain. 'It's your wardrobe,' she told me yesterday. 'Those tailor-made contour shirts are beginning to bag like tents in the wind.'

"I continue to try to keep my friends and colleagues on top of the news, on the theory that knowledge is more consoling than imagination run rampant. But apparently not everyone agrees. Eva Kim told me the other day she nearly has heart failure whenever I walk into the third-floor suite with an intelligence report in hand.

"I seem to be beating a hundred paths now, dashing from the Ambassador's office to Polgar's and back to mine, churning out instant analyses, picking through the ever-diminishing intelligence for some thread of hope. Polgar's confident the opposition will soon be signaling its 'flexible' intent by way of Radio Hanoi 'or Liberation Radio, so every hour or so I trek across the lawn to the monitoring offices of the [CIA's] Foreign Broadcast Information Service to scan the latest translations.

"So far the reams of copy have been anything but uplifting. The real drama is in the monitoring office itself. The manager, an old Far Eastern hand, has been in agony for days over the fate of the Vietnamese translators on his staff. He wants to move them to Bangkok so they won't be caught in the crush of a final evacuation. But Martin and Polgar are opposed, since most of those in question are males of draft age. I told the manager yesterday to ship them out anyway; Moorefield would give them clearance. But he's a dedicated CIA bureaucrat who can't conceive of breaking the rules. So his Vietnamese staffers are stuck here, with his scruples—and the entire North Vietnamese army less than thirty miles away."

Early Friday morning the new immigration quotas became official. The Attorney General in Washington formally approved the 130,000-man ceiling to which we had been alerted two days before.

A few hours later several Vietnamese paratroopers tried to cut their way through the barbed-wire fence surrounding the DAO processing center. A platoon of marines was rushed in from the fleet to help reinforce the compound. "After that we didn't have any trouble maintaining control," Smith recalled. "There's something about a United States marine that demands respect from the Vietnamese people."

Among the leathernecks who choppered in was Brigadier General Richard Carey, commander of the special Marine force that was to provide security under Option IV. He and General Smith conferred for several hours over crucial details. In line with Gayler's wishes, they decided that if and when a final helo-lift was mounted, the central staging area would be the DAO compound. Air America choppers would be used only to ferry passengers from rooftop pads downtown to the flight line.

Smith's staff suggested at one point that the Embassy grounds be turned into an alternate springboard for the "Sea Knights" and other giant helicopters that were to form the backbone of the helo-lift. But Gayler himself ruled that out, arguing that the Embassy could never be properly secured. Martin (for once) agreed with him. In his opinion, there need be no more than 200 people at the Embassy on E-day; indeed, a larger number, he felt, could set off panic in downtown Saigon. "And in the worst possible case," he told a subordinate, "I can always take refuge with Mérillon next door."

This decision would very nearly be the undoing of us all. Focusing their plans exclusively on DAO, Smith and Gayler would never prepare adequately for massive chopper landings at the Embassy or for the sealing-off of the compound. Under their working scenario, the Embassy was merely to be one of several assembly points on the bus routes to DAO.

Since there were now too few DAO personnel in town to man and monitor the twenty-eight designated bus stops, Carey and Smith decided to cut the number in half. They also devised a new emergency warning system in the interest of security. In case of Option IV, DAO's American radio would alert its listeners with the code phrase "Mother wants you to call home," followed by a recording of Bing Crosby's "I'm Dreaming of a White Christmas."

Although the White House remained opposed to the idea of marching Vietnamese to Vung Tau for evacuation, Martin continued to hold out hope for it. On Friday morning he sent George Jacobson to Polgar's office to be briefed on the military situation around the coastal city. I pointed out during the give-and-take that the North Vietnamese had just created a new field headquarters in the Vung Tau sector—a sure sign they were planning offensive activity there.

Martin did not let this little inconvenience sway him. Later in the day he dispatched Captain Carmody to Vung Tau to discuss security arrangements with the marine commandant, Bui The Lan, whose troops, all stragglers from MR 1, were the main garrison force there. Carmody was to promise Lan assistance in evacuating "select" marine dependents, if the marines in turn would guarantee safe passage for evacuees and free access to the beaches.

Lan was dubious. He wanted American marines put ashore to fend off the North Vietnamese. His own troops, he said, should be left to control the crowds and the wharfs, since—"unlike the Americans"—they would have no qualms about shooting down "unruly" Vietnamese civilians.

But Carmody told him firmly there would be no American ground forces, and after some haggling, Lan agreed to do as Carmody proposed.

That night the Embassy fulfilled its side of the bargain. Despite Gayler's strenuous objections, two C-130s were flown to the airfield at Vung Tau to haul out several hundred Vietnamese families, all marine dependents. Lan, for his part, was never called upon to follow through on his part of the deal. The country would collapse before he got a chance.

For Washington, Vietnam had once again become a numbers game, and as in the days when the Pentagon and the White House batted body counts back and forth like race-track odds, no one was sure how far to trust the figures. Assistant Secretary Habib told reporters on Friday that the American community in Saigon had dropped to 1,357 officials and private citizens. Within hours, Martin's own press spokesman at the Embassy issued a correction— "more like 1,500 to 1,800."

The confusion was not merely a token of bureaucratic incompetence (although that may have played a part). As one official in Washington pointed out, Americans never before counted on anybody's rolls were still "crawling out of the woodwork."

The changing and conflicting tallies tipped the scales in Congress. After an explosive fourteen-hour debate, House-Senate conferees voted Friday morning to impose strict limits on the President's maneuverability. While agreeing to support over $300 million for relief work and for the evacuation, they insisted, as a proviso, that the White House reduce the number of Americans in Saigon to a "minimum" without delay. They also stipulated that American troops could be engaged "only in numbers, areas and for the length of time" required to complete the withdrawal of Americans. No separate evacuation could be mounted for Vietnamese. As Kissinger had feared, Congress had projected itself into the very bull's-eye of policy.

Several hours later the Senate approved legislation incorporating these points, but the House remained suspicious and hesitant. Many of its members insisted on further proof of the Administration's good intent, and consequently, the leadership decided to postpone the final vote on the aid measure for a few more days, to 29 or 30 April.

Hamstrung and hemmed in by Congress, Administration officials suddenly developed a sympathetic affinity for their embattled colleagues on the front lines. During an afternoon meeting at the State Department, Habib, apparently discouraged by the Congressional action, refused to countenance any further criticism of his old foe Graham Martin. Actually, he conceded, the Ambassador had done his best to meet the directives from Washington.

Out in Langley, Virginia, CIA Director Colby also experienced a twinge of generosity toward Polgar. In a personal message to the Station Chief, he commended him for his efforts and announced that he was recommending him for the CIA's highest award.

To the White House, the stiffening of Congressional attitudes raised the specter of a severe crisis of command, one that could jeopardize the successful completion of the evacuation. Martin, however, was more sanguine. In his view, the Soviets had already assured us a way out.

Around noon on Friday he wandered into the canteen behind the Embassy for soup and a sandwich. He sat down with Station officer Bill Johnson, and chatted idly with him for half an hour. At one point Johnson mentioned that he was already laying the foundation for a stay-behind spy network. Martin smiled. "I hope that won't be necessary," he said in that soft southern drawl of his, "the stay-behind network, I mean. I hope we'll all be staying on."

His optimism had received another boost that very morning. Hungarian ICCS representative Toth had again contacted Polgar to pass on some new advice and hopeful hints to the Embassy. Not everything he said was encouraging, to be sure. Reminding Polgar of the need for "expeditious" action, he demanded a "clear break" with the South Vietnamese constitution and insisted that the United States pledge unequivocally not to intervene militarily. But in a far more conciliatory vein he also advised the Station Chief that the PRG delegation at Tan Son Nhut now wanted him, Polgar, to serve as its liaison in discussing political problems, and was willing to meet with him on Sunday, two days away.

Polgar rushed back to the Embassy to spread the good news. "You see," he exclaimed as he dashed through my office. "I was right. There is a chance for some kind of deal. They want me as intermediary."

I tried, politely, to inject a cautionary note, reminding him of the Liberation Radio broadcast the day before: in particular, the demand for withdrawal of all American "intelligence personnel" in Vietnam. I could not see how that could be reconciled with the PRG's "request" that he operate as a go-between. Polgar frowned, and suggested that maybe Liberation Radio was not plugged into Hanoi's overall game plan.

Martin evidently agreed with him. Although he could not be comforted by Toth's rejection of Saigon's constitution, he saw the remarks about Polgar as a positive sign. By midday he had cabled the gist of the latest Hungarian overture off to Washington.

In light of what Toth had told him, Polgar again pleaded with the Ambassador to let him push Huong aside at once. But Martin stood firm. It was imperative, he argued, to engineer the next change in government in a way consistent with law and order. Months after the collapse of South Vietnam, Polgar would remain convinced that Martin's refusal to authorize a "clear break" with the constitution had caused the breakdown of the negotiating gambit.

The Hungarian overture was not the only beguiling smoke signal of the day. Late the same morning Colonel Harry Summers, deputy chief of the American delegation to the Joint Military Team at Tan Son Nhut, made his last liaison flight to Hanoi. During the trip one of his North Vietnamese counterparts sidled over to him for a few private words. As Summers later reported, his contact "made three significant comments": (1) the four-party Joint Military Team, and implicitly the fifteen-man American delegation, must stay in South Vietnam, whatever happened; (2) the Defense Attaché's Office must go in its entirety; and (3) the American Embassy must work out its future with the "new government."

The remarks were cryptic to a fault. Were the North Vietnamese holding out an olive branch to the Americans—or merely trying to ensure DAO's removal? Martin chose to read the emphasis in a way that squared with his own hopes. The "significant comments" that most interested him were those pertaining to the Embassy and the Joint Military Team. As he saw it, the North Vietnamese were reaffirming their willingness to agree to a residual American presence in Vietnam.

He therefore immediately instructed Summers and the rest of the American delegation to prepare to stay on. As a token of "good faith," he also directed them to pass to their North Vietnamese counterparts a tally showing the exact number of DAO personnel still in Saigon (327), together with assurances that the entire bunch, Smith and everybody else, would be out of Saigon by 30 April.

By the end of the day Martin was in high spirits. Toth's revelations and those of the North Vietnamese seemed to support Kissinger's broad and optimistic interpretation of the Brezhnev message. Not only was there still time for an American evacuation and perhaps for a political solution; it appeared Hanoi, indeed, had no desire to humiliate the United States.

That afternoon Polish ICCS Ambassador Fialkowski was giving a cocktail party in honor of one of his departing comrades. Although Martin generally avoided ICCS functions like the plague, he decided to put in an appearance, if only to shore up the deal that now seemed so much within grasp.

When he strode into Fialkowski's villa there was a stir among the guests. "So Graham Martin really exists!" one startled diplomat exclaimed. Martin nodded slightly to the crowd and then began his rounds, exuding charm and self-assurance as only an actor of his consummate skill could do. Finally he drew his host aside. It was time, he told Fialkowski, for everyone to work together to bring an end to the bloodshed. The Polish diplomat fidgeted. If peace was what the Americans desired, he posed, then why were they assembling a naval armada offshore? "Well," Martin replied, "if the North Vietnamese try to interfere with our evacuation, you'll find out what those ships are for." Fialkowski paled. The threat obviously was not lost on him. "And by the way," Martin continued, "perhaps you could explain the purpose of the continuing build-up of SA-2s around Saigon." Fialkowski turned almost apologetic. "They're only for defensive purposes, I assure you, Mr. Ambassador. Only for defensive purposes."

Martin left the cocktail party convinced he had played his hand just right. While the North Vietnamese obviously were confident of ultimate victory, they must now reckon anew with the threat of American retaliation. Perhaps that would keep them from attempting to seize the prize before the evacuation had run its course.

●   ●   ●

According to Van Tien Dung, he and his comrades already knew by Friday afternoon precisely how and when they *would* seize the prize. Indeed, as he explains in his memoirs, the twenty-fifth was the day they locked the final details in place. General Tan, commander on the eastern front, was given permission definitively to launch his initial attacks against Bien Hoa the following afternoon. In the meantime, Dung met with the deputy commander of the North Vietnamese air force, who had just arrived from Hanoi, to wrap up plans for the projected air strike against Tan Son Nhut. Dung cautioned the airman that he would have only one chance, on the twenty-eighth, to bring his planes into play, since the second and final phase of the offensive would be mounted the day after.

Late Friday afternoon Dung's deputy, General Tran Van Tra, left for the command's forward headquarters at Ben Cat, north of Saigon, to begin gearing the rest of the army up for attack.

While the NVA planned and rehearsed for the final act, old President Huong attempted to do the same. In secret exchanges with the North Vietnamese delegation at Tan Son Nhut during the day he offered to send an intermediary to Hanoi to discuss the cease-fire. The proposal was rejected out of hand. Next he offered to open up the jails and free all "political prisoners," including the eighteen journalists imprisoned in February, as a sign of his good intent. The North Vietnamese did not even bother to comment.

Huong also met secretly with "Big" Minh in a last desperate effort to persuade him to join the cabinet as Prime Minister. Minh was no more accommodating than the Communists.

As Huong faltered, other political figures closed ranks against him. Tran Quoc Buu, the noted labor leader who had long been a CIA collaborator, called on followers to push Huong out of office. Tri Quang, agitator for the An Quang Pagoda, pleaded with the old man to give place to Minh. At a rally on the outskirts of the city Air Marshal Ky whipped 5,000 right-wing Catholics into a frenzy of anti-Communist, anti-government sentiment. "The so-called Communist victory," he bellowed, "resulted from our generals and officers choosing to run even before they were asked!"

Soon afterward one of Ky's old defenders, Robert Shaplen, reporter for *The New Yorker*, dropped by Polgar's office to try to generate CIA support for the Air Marshal's cause. Polgar could hardly conceal his impatience.

Surveying the wreckage of his own hopes and ambitions, Huong quickly concluded that he was blameless. It was Thieu's shadow, falling across his regime like a stigma, that had destroyed his credit with the Communists, he decided. To rid himself of it, he could think of only one solution: Thieu himself would have to be cast out of Saigon.

Ever since his resignation on the twenty-first, Thieu had been playing Goneril to Huong's King Lear. Pacing the halls of his empty villa on the waterfront, he had given himself over entirely to visions of revenge and restored grandeur. His wife, frightened beyond tolerance, had left for Bangkok by commercial jet on Thursday morning, and his brother, Saigon's Ambassador to Taiwan, had flown in to try to persuade him to leave as well. But Thieu would not hear of it. He was convinced he still had a role to play. "And if I go, I must go with honor, with a staff," he told his cousin Hoang Duc Nha.

Nha had not seen Thieu since his own return from Singapore the previous weekend, and when he visited the fallen leader at his villa Thursday afternoon he found him altered, lost in his own dream world. And as so often before, Nha tried to cast himself as a spokesman for reality. "No, my President," he told Thieu, "there is no longer any time for honors or revenge. You must leave now."

Thieu, normally aloof, reserved, seemed touched by the concern. "You are the only one who has stood beside me, Nha," he exclaimed, "and after all the harm I did you—the firing and the disgrace."

Nha, dipping into his fertile imagination for a last consoling word, found one, appropriately, in the history of the country that had first framed Thieu's perspectives. "Simply think of me as Cambronne," he said, "the general who stood by Napoleon on Elba."*

Huong could not conceive of forcing Thieu's exile himself, lest some of the ex-President's die-hard supporters wreak a terrible revenge on him. He therefore asked Martin to arrange a solution for him.

Martin was hardly enthusiastic at that prospect. So far he had managed to sustain the fiction that the Embassy had had no direct hand in Thieu's political demise. He wanted to do nothing to alter that impression.

Yet there was now another overriding consideration. "Big" Minh had become convinced that Thieu's continued presence in Saigon was an obstacle to his own maneuvering. He asked the CIA's Timmes to see to it that Thieu was sent into exile. That clinched Martin's own thinking.

Around 5 P.M. on the twenty-fifth Polgar called me, Joe Kingsley, General Timmes and one other Station officer to his office. "Can you fellows find your way around Saigon at night?" he asked coyly. We all nodded, though actually I was not too sure about myself, what with the city's countless side streets and French traffic circles. "Good," he continued, "because I want you to help me get Thieu and Prime Minister Khiem off to Taiwan tonight. It's a piece of cake from me to you, partial payment for the commendable job you've all been doing."

Polgar himself had been cut in on the caper only in the past several hours. Initially Martin had intended keeping it a strictly military affair, and had relied exclusively on DAO to make all the necessary arrangements, including a

*Tran Van Don was also instrumental in spurring Thieu's departure. Meeting with the former President on the afternoon of the twenty-fifth, he told him that Ky and the air force wanted him to stay—so they could kill him.

special "deep black" flight out of the Air America terminal at Tan Son Nhut. But at the last minute, perhaps out of appreciation for Polgar's efforts with the Hungarians, he decided to give the Station a role.

Martin later confided to me he regretted doing so. "He couldn't get anything right," he complained of Polgar. "I'd asked him to have Thieu's parole documents typed up and to bring them with him when you fellows came out to Tan Son Nhut. But he couldn't even manage that. He forgot the papers. He said he hadn't been able to find a typewriter." As a result, Thieu left his own country on an American plane without either Vietnamese or American clearance.

Timmes, the two other officers and I collected three limousines from Station garages at around 8:30 P.M. and drove to the South Vietnamese military headquarters just outside Tan Son Nhut, where Khiem had his private residence. Joe and I had stashed sidearms under our seats; we had managed to spook ourselves by speculating generously on the odds for a replay of the Diem assassination. We could both conjure up the vision in vivid detail: young Vietnamese military officers halt us at a roadblock, order us all out of the cars and cut us down. At least we wanted to be able to take a few of them with us, melodramatic as it may sound.

Shortly after 9 P.M. Polgar arrived at the Khiem residence with his own car and driver. While he had a restorative drink with Khiem and Timmes inside, the rest of us cooled our heels in the courtyard. Kingsley and I tried to divert ourselves by chatting with the Vietnamese guards on the perimeters. Some were playing cards. Most seemed indifferent to the comings and goings of all the "great men" around them. There was a crackle of gunfire on the rim of the air base a short distance away. Suddenly a radio came alive with a cross-channel message between the Embassy duty officer and a Mission Warden patrol car. A fire fight had just erupted near the Vietnamese cemetery behind the Embassy. Two edgy South Vietnamese soldiers had opened up on each other. "But apparently no casualties," one caller reported. "Now everything seems quiet."

As the radio chatter died away, a gray Mercedes pulled into the driveway. A man of medium height, silver hair slicked back, face oiled, gray suit immaculately pressed, clambered out. In the dimness Nguyen Van Thieu looked more like a model for a Far Eastern edition of *Gentleman's Quarterly* than a former head of state. He did not deign to look at us as he hurried up the steps to the front door.

Moments later several burly aides scrambled out of a patch of woods at the edge of the compound, each hefting a mammoth suitcase. They demanded we open our car trunks for them and insisted on stacking the luggage themselves. The clink of metal on metal broke through the stillness like muffled wind chimes as they heaved the bags into place.

Not long afterward Thieu, Khiem, Polgar, Timmes and several senior South Vietnamese staffers emerged from a side porch and quickly dispersed to the limousines. Thieu got into the back seat of mine, sandwiching himself between Timmes and a Vietnamese aide. "Stay down, Mr. President," Timmes advised him, "for your own sake." I wondered if there was any way I could do the same and still drive the car.

The trip lasted ten minutes, though it seemed like hours. Timmes engaged Thieu in extraordinary small talk, largely about the past. They had first met over a campfire in MR 1 sometime in 1961, and Timmes had occasionally briefed him in succeeding years on the progress of pacification ("one of your great achievements, Mr. President"). At one point Timmes introduced me as "an outstanding Embassy analyst—therefore, a high-class chauffeur." There was forced laughter and Thieu murmured in his French-accented English that all the drivers in Saigon were "high-class," but "maybe the worst around, even by comparison with the maniacs in Bangkok."

"How are your wife and daughter?" Timmes asked. "They've gone to London to buy antiques," Thieu replied disingenuously. I could see the ex-President's face in the rear mirror, eyes glistening as the streetlights flashed by. The odor of Scotch hung in the air-conditioned vacuum like a pall.

As we approached Tan Son Nhut's front gate my headlights played briefly over the Vietnamese monument to American war dead, with its inscription "The Noble Sacrifice of the Allied Soldiers Will Never Be Forgotten." Thieu sighed audibly and looked away.

Again Timmes warned him to stay down. Normally the Vietnamese security police on the front gate would not bother to look twice at an American car with diplomatic license plates, but it was already past 9:30 P.M., an hour after curfew. They might be skittish. Thankfully, this time they weren't.

As the caravan swept out onto the tarmac beyond the Air America ticket offices, the driver of the car just ahead of me extinguished his headlights. I did the same, and for a few horrible moments I could see nothing at all, the big Chevrolet plunging on in the blackness as if by a will of its own. Suddenly, as my eyes adjusted, I caught a glimpse of Polgar bounding across the tarmac a few yards ahead. Flooring the brake to avoid hitting him, I pulled to a screeching, swerving stop, Thieu and all my other passengers bouncing against the front seat. The cars behind me careened and slid around each other like paddy wagons in a Keystone Cops' chase scene. Polgar, his arms pumping, ran up and opened the door for Thieu.

An American Air Force four-motor C-118 was dimly visible a short distance away. Several plain-clothes American Marine guards, Ambassador Martin's private escort, stood off to one side. The Ambassador himself was waiting at the foot of the boarding ramp.

As the back door clicked open, Thieu leaned over the seat and tapped me on the shoulder. "Thank you," he said hoarsely, offering his hand. He held my grasp for a few moments, blinking away tears, then slid out and trotted up the ramp. Khiem and the claque of aides, packages underarm, cameras and shoulder bags banging lapels, rushed after him.

"I just told him goodbye," Martin later recalled of their final conversation. "Nothing historic. Just goodbye."

To Joe Kingsley and me that last conversation seemed interminable. Outside on the tarmac, we stood nervously by ourselves, scanning the perimeters of the airfield and joking (lamely) about the sputter of gunfire beyond. At last Polgar and then Martin ducked out of the hatchway and the plane's motors began revving. As the Ambassador stepped off the bottom rung of the ramp, he turned and grasped the handrail and began dragging the whole structure away at a dead run, as if he were trying in some symbolic way to snatch the present from the past. "Mr. Ambassador!" I yelled, puffing along beside him. "Can I do that for you?" He stopped and stood staring through me, his chest heaving. He was wearing his usual oval-shaped glasses with their flesh-colored frames, and he looked more like a well-tailored don than a man who had just bidden farewell to the last vestige of three decades of bad policy.

Our Turn

The exodus from Bien Hoa was in full flood by the following morning. Many of those caught up in it moved by taxi and car with the regalia of wealth strapped on behind, for Bien Hoa had always been an appendage of Saigon's own affluence, an extension of its consumer's market. The four-lane highway running west toward the capital, pride of American engineers, seemed to come alive with the bumper-to-bumper flow, rippling and undulating under a canopy of exhaust fumes like some giant serpent. Security forces tried to establish checkpoints every few miles to filter out Communist infiltrators, but soon were swept aside.

General Vien, Tran Van Don and others spent the morning at the Presidential Palace pleading with Huong to resign. Finally, around noontime, the old man agreed, but out of spite, or legalistic reflex, or in deference to Martin, he demanded a final price for the constitution. Under no circumstances, he said, would he simply hand power over to Minh. The National Assembly would have to "legalize" such a change by formally electing Minh itself. In a message to the Assembly he explained his position, adding: "If you cannot decide to replace me with General Minh, and if we cannot successfully and happily negotiate, then Saigon must be turned into an ocean of blood and we will still have to fight for our national honor."

As Huong thus threw up one more obstacle to an easy surrender, new and perplexing signals concerning Communist political intentions seemed to assail us from every quarter. Around midday, Tran Van Don was contacted by another of his "PRG intermediaries" and given a "firm" assurance that a cease-fire would be possible if Minh assumed power at once and the Americans made no attempt to evacuate large numbers of Vietnamese or to extract war matériel from the country (as Von Marbod was trying to do). Soon afterward Madame Binh, the PRG's Foreign Minister, passed word to French contacts that the Viet Cong would indeed consider negotiating with Minh, provided his new government included no one sympathetic to Thieu. A similar pledge was obtained by French diplomats from the PRG's chief delegate in Paris, Pham Van Ba. In an excited message to Washington on the twenty-sixth the French government reported that Ba had just advised them that a "political formula" which left Minh in charge of a regime "inspired by a spirit of national reconciliation" would be agreeable.

This sudden blossoming of olive branches naturally caused quite a stir in both Washington and Saigon. But were they to be taken seriously? The similarity of the various overtures gave rise to speculation that they were simply part of a concerted campaign of deception. Moreover, for each conciliatory statement, a tough, hard-line one could be found in the Communist media or in diplomatic channels. Within hours of Ba's comments, for example, Radio Hanoi demanded total abolition of the Saigon government and its army and called on all "third force" figures to join the people in a "general uprising." There was no reference to the possible formation of a new "administration" in Saigon (as there had been in a similar broadcast two days before), and since Minh had often referred to himself as a "third force neutralist," the statement seemed to imply rejection of any kind of dealings with him.

There were also discouraging bleats from the PRG spokesmen at Tan Son Nhut. At a press conference around midday Colonel Vo Dong Giang, when asked about the prospects for negotiations, would say only, "Our troops continue to advance."

Giang knew whereof he spoke. He and his fellow PRG delegates had been informed in a secret message from Dung's headquarters the day before that the attack on Saigon was imminent, and he and his colleagues were even now digging bunkers under their compound as shelter against the artillery bombardment they now knew was less than three days away.

None of us who picked through the ambiguity of his statements, however, could know what truth they concealed. The best anyone could do was guess, and depending on the hopes and assumptions you labored under in the first place, there was ample evidence to support almost any case.

In Washington the tendency was to read some measure of hope into the confusion. Shortly after learning of Madame Binh's comments, Colby advised WSAG: "We now believe that Hanoi has been deliberately holding back militarily in order to allow time for the evacuation process and for a government of surrender to be established in Saigon . . . In sum, the action for the moment has shifted to the political arena." In the meantime, Kissinger sent the Embassy a summary of the French message concerning Ba's recent disclosures in Paris. He also appended a stern admonition. Because of the increasing delicacy of the negotiating process, he asserted, he was now thrusting himself to the fore. Any further political initiatives were to be undertaken in Paris—by him—not in Saigon. The Embassy was to restrict its own exchanges with the PRG to strictly tactical military questions.

Polgar needed no prompting to realize these chidings were directed at him. Although the PRG might want him as mediator, Washington evidently did not. The trouble, Martin remarked to me, was Polgar's zeal. If he were to have his way, Huong and Saigon's constitutional system would quickly be discarded for the sake of an easy peace. There would be no give-and-take with the Communists, no effort to turn Huong's potential resignation into a bargaining chip. And in view of the recent message from Brezhnev, Kissinger believed that bargaining was still a possibility.

Despite Kissinger's remonstrances, Polgar continued to agitate for the "easy peace" he felt was essential, and throughout the afternoon of the twenty-sixth he pressed Martin to authorize an approach to the Communists, or at least some symbolic gesture, to reassure them we were trying to meet their demands. Martin, however, remained unreceptive, and rejected all of Polgar's proposals, except one: he did agree to let the Station mount a modest telephone canvass to help Tran Van Don and others convince the National Assembly that an immediate cease-fire was imperative.

"Goddamn! The Old Man is sick, irascible," Polgar exclaimed to me as he trudged through my office after one of his bouts with the Ambassador. "He hasn't been sleeping at all, and he's taking his frustrations out on the rest of us."

Ironically, the first real negative comment on the latest Communist statements, at least in Saigon, came from Mérillon's Embassy. In a conversation with Polgar around midday Brochand confided that he was fast losing faith in the peace prospects and was afraid that even the chances for a negotiated surrender had already been lost to the haggling of Saigon's politicians.

Nor was Brochand the only member of the local peace lobby whose confidence was waning. On the same afternoon the Station learned from a reliable source that the Polish ICCS delegation had decided, three days before, to evacuate Saigon. A Polish IL-18, due to arrive within hours, was to move all 280 Polish delegates to Warsaw via Bangkok the following morning, 27 April.

While observers in Saigon and Washington debated Hanoi's intentions, General Dung was dodging potholes in a dirt road in northern MR 3. Shortly after daybreak on the twenty-sixth he and his senior aides set out by car from their rear headquarters at Loc Ninh and headed south toward the abandoned government ranger camp at Ben Cat, thirty miles north of Saigon, which was to serve as their forward base. It was here, from a thatched-roof hut, that Dung would coordinate the final phase of the Ho Chi Minh campaign.

When he arrived at the command post shortly before noon, he found his deputy, General Tran Van Tra, sketching out lines of attack on terrain maps. At another field headquarters further to the east, General Le Trong Tan, commander of the Bien Hoa front, was supervising feverish last-minute preparations for his own initial thrust, which was to come that very afternoon.

Only two members of the Communist command team had yet to assume their place on the ramparts. Politburo members Pham Hung and Le Duc Tho were still at the rear base at Loc Ninh, undoubtedly taking final measure of the political winds.

Aside from Brochand and the Polish ICCS team, plenty of others in Saigon now seemed to sense the hopelessness of the political maneuvering. In the past twenty-four hours the number of Americans and Vietnamese lining up for seat space at the DAO evacuation center had outstripped the "system," and on the morning of the twenty-sixth McCurdy was forced to close the gates temporarily to give his men time to dispose of the backlog.

For the three consular officers now working with Moorefield in the processing area itself, the pressures had become all but intolerable. None of them was getting any more than three or four hours of sleep each night, and the exigencies of the job were demanding far more than most were used to. "Every few minutes," Moorefield recalled, "we were having to make life-and-death decisions, dismembering families, turning away people who we knew would face reprisals at the hands of the VC if left behind. As a former combat officer, I had some experience with this sort of responsibility, but the State Department fellows didn't."

One of Moorefield's colleagues, a consular officer, literally broke under the strain. Sometime around midday he suddenly jumped up from his desk and smashed a Coke bottle against the wall, screaming insults at the hundreds of distraught Vietnamese pushing and shoving to reach him and his precious consular stamp. Moorefield called the Embassy at once and had the man relieved.

Others reacted to the pressure more coolly—and calculatingly. "I remember this one American," Moorefield declared, "who showed up at my doorstep at six-thirty one of those last mornings. He had a Chinese friend, he said, who was prepared to make us both very wealthy young men if only I would stamp his papers. I told this guy I couldn't do it. I was surprised he even asked. He was a friend of mine, a person of integrity. But I guess the strain had got to him too."

By the afternoon of the twenty-sixth Jim Devine, deputy Mission coordinator, had planted a small group of overseers at the DAO center to ensure adherence to his newly established quotas, and Don Hays and Jim Gagnon—now involved full-time in moving out the State Department locals—had begun handing out improvised identity tags, a different color for each stage of the processing game, in an effort to keep track of their charges.* At the Embassy, meanwhile, Shep Lowman and the other staffers responsible for keeping book on key Vietnamese personalities were falling further and further behind. Countless names had been collected from the various Mission agencies. Iden-

---

*Devine's overseers rapidly succumbed to the same "generous" tendencies that beset Moorefield. Although they had been assigned to DAO to enforce Embassy quotas and ensure the evacuation of Vietnamese to whom we had a special obligation, they spent much of their time simply smuggling Vietnamese friends onto aircraft.

tity cards stood row upon row on tables and desks. But Lowman and his cohorts still had not found time to draw up a master roster. The problem was simply volume, Lowman later explained, too many names to handle.

Early in the afternoon Walt Martindale paid a call on Nay Luette, a former government minister and the self-styled spokesman for the montagnard tribesmen whom the young Embassy officer had gotten to know so well during his own tour of duty in the highlands of MR 2. Luette grasped Martindale's hand and pleaded with him to guarantee the evacuation of at least a hundred montagnard children "so the seed of our people will be preserved." Martindale knew that the statement was no mere melodramatic flourish. In view of the traditional Vietnamese animosity toward the montagnards, he had no doubt that Hanoi's victorious army would exact a terrible price from Luette's fellow tribesmen.

Immediately after the session Martindale drove to the Embassy to seek the assistance Luette had requested. Jacobson listened to his pleadings and was obviously moved. But he did not offer much in the way of encouragement. "I'm afraid, Walt," he said at length, "that we're the only people in this Embassy who give a damn for the montagnards."

Nor did Jacobson seem convinced of the need for immediate action. He assured Martindale that a "settlement" was in the offing, and urged him to begin making plans for his own departure.

Martindale was stunned and begged Jacobson to let him stay on to help. Jacobson finally relented and gave him permission to make another trip to Phu Quoc Island to collect more of his Vietnamese friends from MR 2 so they could be included in the airlift out of Saigon. Within an hour Martindale was on his way.

With more and more evacuees crowding onto the outbound C-141s, the pressures on the receiving end of the airlift were beginning to approximate those at the point of origin itself. Finally, late in the afternoon on the twenty-sixth, officials in Washington ordered some of the evacuation flights diverted from Guam to Wake Island, 1,300 miles to the northeast, so the Guamian reception team could catch its breath.

From his headquarters east of Saigon, General Le Trong Tan tried to keep track of the American airlift as the day drew to a close, through radio reports from Communist commandos on the rim of Tan Son Nhut. One question remained uppermost in his mind: Were American warplanes among the aircraft now flying into and out of Saigon? So far his spotters had detected none.

At 5 P.M. the NVA commander glanced at his watch, then nodded to his radio operator. Within seconds a coded message heralding the start of the Communist push on Nhon Trach and Saigon's eastern suburbs was flashed to the commanders of the six divisions under Tan's direct control. The "Ho Chi Minh campaign for the liberation of Saigon" was now truly under way.

•   •   •

As the offensive kicked into motion, the politicians in Saigon remained locked in dispute. By the end of the day the various factions in the National Assembly were still at loggerheads over whether, and by what means, to alter the government to the Communists' specifications. Some of the legislators, those once firmly allied to Thieu, opposed Minh's candidacy for fear of reprisals at his hands. Others, the rightists, favored Ky in Huong's place. At last, hopelessly deadlocked, the two houses of the Assembly agreed to hand the problem back to Huong himself, and unanimously approved a joint resolution authorizing the old President to do whatever he felt necessary to deal with the crisis. It was not exactly the clear-cut mandate for change Huong had been pressing for.

Just before curfew I drove over to the Duc Hotel. First reports on the fighting around Bien Hoa were already trickling into the Station, but there were still few details, and I decided I might as well get a solid meal and a good night's sleep to arm myself against the inevitable pressures of the following day.

The scene that night at the Duc bar might have been lifted from a Brechtian tragedy. Hordes of colleagues had shown for a fortifying nightcap, but there was none of the conviviality that usually characterized the after-hours crowd. It was general knowledge by now that the so-called "lull" had ended, if it had ever begun, and some officers stood in morose silence at the plastic windows watching the flashes off along the skyline. Others talked quietly among themselves, exchanging grisly tales about the processing at DAO and the lack of Station planning.

I pulled up a stool beside an old friend, a veteran Latin-American hand who at some distant point in his career had been reassigned to Vietnam. His face was chalk-white, glistening sweat, and his hand trembled as he lifted the double Scotch. I asked if he was all right (I knew he had a record of heart trouble). Yes, he assured me, it was simply the strain. He had been at DAO all day trying to help some of his Vietnamese friends find a place in the chutes. What an ordeal! All day in the sun, a little beer to drink. That was all. You would think . . .

I interrupted him, not really wanting to hear the nightmarish details. What about his Vietnamese wife and family? I asked. Had they been evacuated? He nodded. Yes, several days before. Then he smiled, adding that they'd been none too happy, though, with the DAO flight controllers. You see, the family had been raising a styful of pigs in the backyard and had wanted to take at least one or two along to the States. His wife wouldn't be dissuaded and had bundled two of the larger ones off with them to the DAO processing center. McCurdy and his people, needless to say, had drawn the line.

I laughed, and we joked about the Vietnamese's innate practicality and I bought him another Scotch. He stared at it a few moments, his face going tense again. I told him goodnight. He was crying.

• • •

I was about four hours into my "good night's sleep" when the phone on my night table rang. It was the CIA duty officer at the Embassy. Radio Hanoi had just broadcast another "authoritative" political statement: a warning to Saigon authorities to meet PRG demands at once. I told him not to bother Polgar with it. He already knew, and had dismissed Hanoi's deadlines.

An hour or so later this particular deadline came due. The first ear-splitting explosion sent me tumbling out of bed. As the second one buffeted the air, I was already groping around the floor in the dark for my flak jacket and M-16. Then, with the percussion drumming the windows, I crawled over to my night table, grabbed the telephone and dialed the Embassy. "Unknown number of rockets," the duty officer stammered. "All in the center of town." I told him I would be in as soon as I could throw some clothes on.

I slipped into a shirt and some jeans and was about to buckle up my flak jacket again when a frantic hammering rattled the front door. I opened it cautiously, flicking off the safety on my M-16. My neighbor and colleague, Joe Kingsley, was standing there in the half-light in his flak jacket, helmet and undershorts. "Looks like war," he declared, grinning broadly. "You going in?" I told him I was and suggested he stay put, so if an evacuation was ordered up, there would be somebody around to help with the helo-lift off the roof as we had planned.

The 122-mm rocket, a seven-foot tubelike projectile of Soviet or Chinese manufacture, has one major drawback: inaccuracy. But the North Vietnamese had managed to compensate over the years by using it principally against "soft" targets, such as civilian population. Not since December 1971 had Saigon itself felt its lethal effect.

When I got to the Embassy details were pouring in from police sources: five rockets in all, two in the center of town, the rest in the Chinese suburb of Cholon; six civilians dead, twenty-two wounded. One of the rockets had smashed into the luxury penthouse at the Majestic Hotel down by the river, leaving the night watchman a bloody spot on the floor. Another had spun into a slum neighborhood near the central police station, igniting a fire storm among 500 or more tinderbox hovels.

Polgar walked into the CIA situation room around seven, looked at me and shook his head, mumbling something about a "shot across the bow." I knew he wanted to believe that's what it was, merely a warning, not a harbinger of things to come, for the very thought of a massive rocket or shelling attack on the center of the city was enough to chill the bone. The neighborhood now in flames was typical of many others: rows upon rows of wooden shanties, closely packed. Two or three random shots would be enough to turn them all into a raging inferno.

As the morning dragged on, Polgar sent several CIA officers out around the city to gauge the mood and to pick through the embers for signs of panic. But the Vietnamese were reacting like Vietnamese, philosophically, almost fatalistically. One old woman whose shanty had disappeared in the morning's holocaust remarked laconically to a journalist, "In the past week we saw refugees sleeping under tents. We could not stand the sight. Today it is our turn."

With General Tan's preliminary thrust in the east now several hours old, the rest of the North Vietnamese army began falling into stride. Shortly after daybreak on the twenty-seventh the NVA 232nd "Tactical Wing" under General Le Duc An pushed past a town on Route 4 twelve miles southwest of Saigon. To the northwest, elements of the NVA Ist Corps severed the Tay Ninh–Saigon highway, bottling up part of the ARVN 25th Division at the village of Cu Chi. Several hours later another NVA unit cut the road between Saigon and Vung Tau, thereby making Martin's planned evacuation over the beaches impossible.

As Dung had envisaged, the outer layers of Saigon's defenses were being systematically and effectively peeled away like the skin of an onion. Yet Dung himself was not quite satisfied. He sent an urgent message to General Tan. All "difficulties," he reminded him, had to be overcome at once if the army was to be in position for the final drive into the capital on the twenty-ninth.

By midmorning Communist forces were on the edge of Bien Hoa and moving fast. Two French journalists, who had dragged their heels in hopes of a good story, were captured by vanguard units. West of the city a small group of Communist commandos struck at a vital bridge on the highway to Saigon. Government troopers hastily planted explosives at other crucial river crossings beyond.

Stragglers from the 18th ARVN Division and the airborne units that were supposed to be defending Bien Hoa fell back on the city and began looting and burning. Erich Von Marbod dispatched a C-130 transport to the airfield to pull out remaining military equipment, and then choppered in himself to supervise. But just as he put down, several shells came crashing in only yards away. He ordered the C-130 out, and dashed for his own Huey.

Meanwhile, Liberation Radio leveled a new set of demands at Washington. In addition to withdrawing all "warships, intelligence personnel and military advisors," the Americans were now to "abstain" from any further "interference in Vietnamese affairs." Some of us took this to mean the Embassy itself was to be out of business.

The White House soon registered its displeasure with the one party whose help it had been counting on. An Administration spokesman announced that President Ford and Soviet Party Leader Brezhnev had "agreed" to postpone until the fall a summit meeting that had been scheduled for the following summer.

In the midst of all this, old President Huong suffered another attack of juridical vapors. He informed Senate Chairman Tran Van Lam just before noon that while he was ready to designate Minh his successor, he was deter-

mined to submit the decision to the entire Assembly for approval so he would
not have to bear sole responsibility for it.

Lam immediately rounded up the 134 legislators who were still in town
and called them into extraordinary session. To ensure that they appreciated
the need for prompt action, he invited Vien, Tran Van Don and Economics
Minister Hao to brief them. Political and parochial jealousies, however, continued to play havoc with resolve, and the debate raged throughout the afternoon. At several intervals Lam took leave of his colleagues to confer with
Minh. If the Assembly could not arrive at a consensus quickly, they agreed,
Huong would have to be ousted by force.

Finally, after hours of bickering, the Assembly managed to reach a decision of sorts. With one-third of the legislators abstaining, the two Houses voted
unanimously to grant full powers to Minh in accordance with Huong's recommendation. The swearing-in was scheduled for the next day. Huong insisted
that the ceremony be postponed till the afternoon so he could boast to his
family and friends that he had been President of the Republic for at least one
week.

Minh immediately began interviewing candidates for his own cabinet. It
was a complicated task, since most of the available politicians were in some
way heirs to the "Thieu clique." Only one choice was apparent. Minh announced outright that his old political protégé Vu Van Mau would become
Prime Minister. Air Marshal Ky, realizing there was no possible role for him,
gave his endorsement to Minh and ordered his followers to do likewise.

Shortly before the assembly vote Ambassador Mérillon, in a last desperate
bid for peace, made a secret trip to Camp Davis at Tan Son Nhut to confer
personally with the Communist delegations there. But to his dismay, NVA and
PRG officials merely repeated the latest hard line from Radio Hanoi. While
offering "peace" in exchange for a total U.S. military withdrawal, they refused
to commit themselves to negotiations with Minh.

Even as Mérillon's final hopes were dashed, Polgar got in touch with
Colonel Toth and the Hungarian ICCS team to sound them out on his own.
This was the day, after all, they had invited him to meet as "intermediary"
with the PRG delegation at Tan Son Nhut. But now, as everything Polgar had
been working for seemed finally to be falling into place, the Hungarians had
some bad news. The clock, they said, had run out; an accommodation with the
other side was impossible.

Polgar's reaction was one of shock and disbelief. How could the fix be off
just at the moment Minh was to assume power? Had he not done his utmost
to ensure that Communist demands were met? Surely Hanoi would take that
into account.

His incredulity and unflagging optimism were reflected in a cable he sent
back to Washington just after the Assembly vote. "The big question remains,"
he wrote, "whether the changes [in government] come in time and whether the
Communists will view them as decisive enough to divert them from the mili-

tary solution of which they remain fully capable" (as if that were ever possible). In another message he attempted to read a political meaning into the latest NVA military initiatives: "The Communists are clearly bringing significant pressure to bear . . . to manifest their displeasure at the slow pace of preparations on Saigon's part for negotiations to end the conflict." It apparently did not occur to him—and he was now well beyond asking my opinion on the subject—that the Communists might be exerting military pressure for purely military reasons.

In Washington, at least a few observers remained as doggedly optimistic as he. Despite Schlesinger's own skepticism, senior analysts in the Defense Intelligence Agency commented in their Daily Intelligence Summary on the twenty-seventh: "These [morning] rocket attacks . . . are probably designed to prod the South Vietnamese to move ahead with negotiations at this time. It appears the Communists will probably delay an all-out attack against Saigon as they weigh political developments." At that very moment Van Tien Dung's divisions were already in the first stages of an all-out attack.

Although the intelligence community still did not seem to grasp the significance of events on the battlefield, analysts and policy-makers in Washington did agree on one point. In a cable to Martin on the afternoon of the twenty-seventh Kissinger remarked that there was now no great "sentiment" among the "principals" of WSAG for the evacuation of large numbers of Vietnamese. The opportunity had been lost; such an undertaking was now considered both impractical and dangerous. The Navy was convinced that the deteriorating military situation east and south of Saigon ruled out the use of Vung Tau as an exit point, even for a riverborne evacuation from the capital. Therefore, the cargo ships docked at Newport were to be pulled out immediately, before the entire Saigon River corridor fell prey to North Vietnamese artillery.

Shortly after the message was filed, the White House instructed Admiral Gayler to stand by to initiate a vastly accelerated airlift. At the same time Kissinger reminded anxious colleagues that it was still up to Martin to determine when the "plug" should be pulled.

When Martin received the Secretary's cable he promptly directed Captain Carmody to release the cargo ships at Newport, as the Pentagon wanted, and send them downriver to safety—without passengers. He then drafted a reply to Kissinger, assuring him that the American community in Saigon was already close to the nub, no more than 1,000 strong (a projection that would prove grossly inaccurate). He also urged against a further acceleration of the airlift, or Option IV, arguing that the time was not yet ripe for either. "I believed I could get a maximum number of Vietnamese and Americans out by the thirtieth, without resorting to extraordinary measures," Martin said later. "The thirtieth was my outside estimate of how soon the North Vietnamese could make their smash into Saigon."

Actually, the Ambassador's motives for this final stall were rooted in political as well as military considerations. As he explained to me, he did not want to pose an additional handicap for the new Minh government—as he was sure an accelerated airlift would be—at the very moment it was maneuvering for a settlement. Nor did he believe that a final dismantling of the American presence was necessary, despite the latest bombast from Radio Hanoi and Liberation Radio. Like Polgar, he remained convinced that an accommodation was still within grasp. He assured General Smith on the twenty-seventh, "We'll be here till July or August. I'm not at liberty to tell you how I know that." Smith was only vaguely aware of the Hungarian initiatives, and could not judge for himself. He therefore accepted the Ambassador's assurances at face value. He cabled his own wife in Bangkok and urged her to return to Saigon; it appeared there might be a settlement. That afternoon she arrived by military aircraft.

Martin's confidence in the negotiating option finally set him at odds with the very man who seemed to hold Saigon's political future in his hands. On the evening of the twenty-seventh General Minh asked for, and was granted, a meeting with the Ambassador through the Embassy's political counselor, Joe Bennett. When Martin showed up at his villa, the old neutralist told him flatly that in the interest of appeasing the Communists, he wanted all Americans attached to DAO to be out of Saigon by the time he took office the following day. Martin objected, explaining that he had already made it clear to Hanoi through Colonel Summers and the Joint Military Team that DAO would be closed by the thirtieth. The North Vietnamese, he said, seemed to be reconciled to that; therefore it was unnecessary to shut down DAO any earlier. Minh finally bowed to these arguments and agreed to give DAO another twenty-four hours—up until the thirtieth—to complete its withdrawal.

With that, Minh committed himself to what may have been the gravest political error of his life. If there was one demand the Communists now seemed determined to have fulfilled at once, it was the removal of all "U.S. military advisors" in Saigon. Any prolongation of DAO's existence was thus an invitation to disaster.

While Minh, and Kissinger, continued to defer to the Ambassador on the evacuation, CIA headquarters suddenly became far less indulgent with Polgar. Throughout the day on the twenty-seventh it pummeled him with cables, urging him to step up the withdrawal of non-essentials and key Vietnamese. To provide an additional incentive, agency officials prevailed on the Pentagon to release an aircraft for the Station's exclusive use.

Shortly after nightfall, at headquarters' direction, Polgar and several other Station officers collected various Vietnamese VIPs and herded them aboard a special "black" flight bound for the Philippines. Among the privileged passengers were Nguyen Khac Binh, Hoang Duc Nha and Nguyen Ba Can. For the past week Can had been pleading with the station to save him, but Martin had refused until now to let Polgar do anything for him. None of the country's visible leaders, the Ambassador had argued, could be spared until Minh was assured the presidency.

By the time I stumbled out of my office at eight o'clock that evening, I had no doubt the end was upon us. The road between Saigon and Vung Tau was cut at several points, the 700 remaining troops of the 18th ARVN Division east of Bien Hoa had been out of contact for several hours, and Route 4 out of the delta was a tatters of NVA roadblocks. Saigon had become an island unto itself, with only one bridge to the outside—the airlift.

I did not have the heart for my usual after-hours trek to the Duc bar and restaurant. Instead I dropped by Joe Kingsley's apartment, a few doors away from my own, for a martini and commiseration. Joe was in a particularly jovial mood, despite the day's events. I soon discovered why. We were just finishing our second martini and umpteenth war story when the doorbell rang. "Her name is Tue," he said, smirking, as he undid the latch and ushered in a lovely nineteen-year-old Vietnamese girl with a large smile and pneumatic breastline. "A refugee from Mimi's bar. She didn't want to leave town with the rest of the girls and was looking for business, so I decided to do her a favor—and you too. She's yours for the night, compliments of the house."

Hedonism and weariness never mix well—not with me, anyway—and I was sorry Joe had been so thoughtful. I tried to decline his "gift" but he wouldn't hear of it. And since it was now well past curfew, there was no question of simply turning little Tue into the night.

All other options exhausted, I therefore took her hand and led her to my apartment. She gasped when we walked in. The place had been scavenged by the packers during the day; crates and packing materials were strewn everywhere. I fixed her a drink and we sat down to talk, and after a while I began to feel, well, maybe this was not such a bad idea after all. Then the phone rang: the duty officer as usual. Radio Hanoi had treated us to still more fluff; he wanted me to come in for a look.

I told Tue to make herself at home and drove to the Embassy. The streets were deserted except for a few barbed-wire barriers and scatterings of teenage militiamen snoozing on the curb.

The broadcast was predictably tough, describing the impending governmental overhaul, Huong's departure and Minh's accession, as a "very pernicious and dangerous scheme aimed at replacing Thieu and Huong and reassigning their henchmen to save the Saigon administration." If Polgar needed any more evidence that negotiations were out and Minh unacceptable, this would suffice. I called him at home and read him the statement over the line. He merely grunted and hung up.

When I arrived back at my apartment I found my houseguest fast asleep in the middle of my bed. I did not try to wake her—not even when another round of rockets shattered the predawn calm. The next morning, after she had gone, I discovered she had pocketed some cuff links and other petty jewelry the packers had overlooked the previous day. They were to be among my last contributions to postwar reconstruction in South Vietnam.

They're in the Halls

It was a cool morning with mist, unusual for Saigon. Shortly after daybreak NVA commandos attacked and burned a USAID warehouse on the other side of the Saigon River and seized two government outposts on the far end of the Newport bridge only a few miles from the center of town. Then they set up a machine-gun nest in the middle of the span and began blasting away at anything that moved. Helicopter gunships were called in to provide counterfire, and Joe and I went up to the Embassy roof with our first cups of coffee of the morning to watch them swoop and turn over their prey. Not since 1968 had the war stabbed so close to Saigon.

The attack on the bridge effectively closed the Saigon–Bien Hoa highway. Bien Hoa itself was now under continuous shelling, and stragglers already were raging through the abandoned headquarters of the MR 3 command.

To the south, NVA units were pressing en masse up Route 4 out of the delta and fanning out toward Saigon's southern suburbs. Tay Ninh City, to the northwest, was reeling in the aftershock of a massive predawn shelling attack, and the 25th ARVN division was still struggling vainly to break through an NVA roadblock on the highway to Saigon.

The severing of the main arteries into the capital was the final blow, sapping the army's morale, destroying its last lines of supply and retreat. But it was not without some benefit for the rest of us. As one government unit after another became bottled up in the hinterlands, Saigon itself was granted a stay of execution. The North Vietnamese would feel no need to put the city to the torch. Nor would we be faced with the resentments and depredations of a defeated army in its death agonies. By peeling away the outer layers of the onion cleanly and systematically, General Dung in effect saved our lives.

At Dung's forward headquarters, thirty miles to the north, Le Duc Tho and Pham Hung had just arrived to take their place at the helm. They quickly outlined the latest political news, advising the NVA commander there was no alternative to a military solution. Dung nodded, turned back to his battle maps.

•   •   •

The capital itself was tense as a drumhead. The rattle of gunfire at Newport echoed through the center of town. Street traffic quickly became hopelessly snarled as thousands of infantrymen and civilians walked, rode and
pedaled in from the countryside. Along the more isolated thoroughfares, police
and army officers cast off their uniforms and changed into civilian clothes to
avoid detection, and retribution, at the hands of the victors.

Over 6,000 terrified Vietnamese squeezed themselves aboard the airlift out
of DAO before the last plane late that afternoon. American departures continued to lag—only 123 during the day—as non-essentials and others put off
leaving to help Vietnamese friends.

Martin was not happy with his subordinates' charity. He would have
preferred that all non-essentials pack out now, without delay, particularly
those at DAO. He was determined to meet his promise to the North Vietnamese—the liquidation of DAO by the thirtieth.

On Guam and Wake Islands the masses of refugees at the reception
centers continued to swell. Only 1,200 of the 20,000 logged in since the beginning of April had so far been shuttled on to Travis Air Force Base in California. The rest were entangled in paperwork. The Immigration and Naturalization Service was partly to blame. No more than ninety officials had been sent
out to Guam to handle processing.

Soon after the attack on Newport, four of five cargo ships at the nearby
docks sailed for Vung Tau, all of them empty. A remaining freighter, three tugs
and four barges prepared to move to the more secure navy yards closer to the
center of town.

DAO still considered the barges impractical as a means of escape, but
several Embassy officials were now beginning to take them quite seriously,
particularly as it became apparent that the airlift itself could not accommodate
all the potential evacuees on their lists. Pittman asked Jacobson at a morning
staff meeting if the Station could use one or two of the vessels to move out the
families of police contacts. Jacobson agreed. Since he had never attached much
importance to the barges himself, he saw no harm in letting the CIA do with
them what it wanted. Pittman promptly got in touch with top police officials
and promised them passage out if they would help to secure the waterfront.

The two men who had turned the barges into a viable option were not
consulted on any of this. And as the Station and others in the Mission began
haggling over the passenger space they had husbanded so carefully, Mel Chatman and Bob Lanigan of USAID alerted their own Vietnamese charges to
prepare for boarding.

During the morning a large, unruly crowd blossomed in the recreation
compound behind the Embassy as more and more Vietnamese, most of them
employees of various Mission agencies, showed up by instinct or instruction

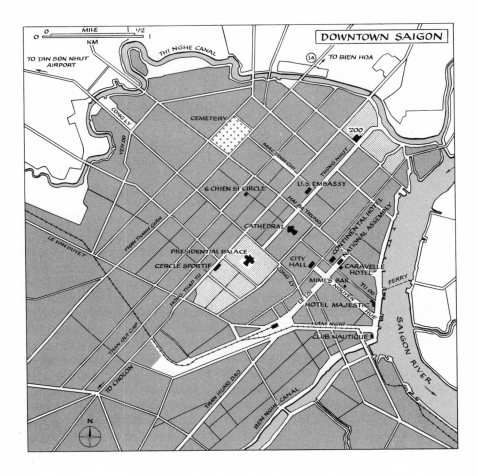

to angle for a ride to the airport. The water in the pool, unused and unattended for several days, had turned the bright gold of urine, but some of the new arrivals began wading or washing clothes in it to kill time. The canteen itself had been shut the day before and the last of the waitresses spirited away to Guam. An American associated with the Embassy's administrative section had taken advantage of the last-minute crush to peddle affidavits of support for a profit.

Around midmorning a Chinese girl, an old acquaintance, called to ask my help. Her American husband had abandoned her and her children, she explained tearfully; she had no one else to call on but me. I told her wearily I could do nothing at the moment. I was chained to my desk. "But contact me again in an hour," I said. "I'll see what I can do." There was a brief silence on the other end of the line. Then her voice drifted in, cool and distant. "If you won't help me," she said, "I'm a dead woman. I'll kill myself and my children. I've already bought the pills." I glanced at the papers piled high in front of me. Polgar wanted something written, another useless analysis, as soon as possible. No, I could not break away. "Look," I said, "just phone in an hour. I'll help you then."

Precisely on schedule, an hour later, she called again. As it happened, I was away from my desk. She left a message with the duty officer: "I would have expected better of you. Goodbye." That was the last I heard from her.

Many of my colleagues were now sweating and straining before the incinerators, destroying mounds of classified files. In a few hours the normally sparkling limousines in the parking lot were dulled with ash.

USAID officials, reluctant to do away with their own precious records, once again asked the Ambassador for permission to fly them to Thailand or the Philippines. Once again the Ambassador refused. There would be ample time, he assured them, to consolidate and remove records after a cease-fire.

While the incinerators ground on, gobbling up a fortune's worth of dossiers, intelligence reports and other official papers, some staffers busily thumbed through mountains of cold cash. The Administrative office drew another $3 million from DAO strongboxes during the morning to cover severance pay for the last of the Embassy's locals. By noon only twenty of the State Department's 900 Vietnamese employees had yet to receive their due.*

In the meantime, government staff cars began beading their way in through the Embassy's back gate. A Vietnamese general or colonel or ranking politician would slide out and nod sheepishly at the Marine guards and then scurry into a waiting elevator. None of us needed to be told they were on their way out. Since first light, Air America choppers had been landing and taking off intermittently from the rooftop pad, hauling Saigon's elite to Tan Son Nhut and a rendezvous with outbound American aircraft.

One of our most celebrated transients that morning was General Cao Van Vien, chairman of the JGS. As he strode into the Embassy foyer he saluted the Marine guards and shook hands with the State Department escort who was holding an elevator for him. Then he stepped in, the doors closed behind him, and he was off on his own final journey out of Vietnam. "He was one happy fellow," General Smith later remarked of him. "When he got to DAO, you would have thought we had a little kid on our hands. He was practically beside himself as he changed from his uniform into civvies." Shortly afterward Vien was helo-lifted out of the DAO tennis courts and ferried to the task force offshore. Meanwhile, President Huong, as one of his own final acts, designated General Lam Son as Vien's replacement. Pending the change of regime later

---

*This was not true of employees of other Embassy agencies. On the morning of the twenty-eighth two representatives of the Mission Wardens' office informed the Vietnamese guards who stood watch over Embassy residences around the city (the Embassy used Vietnamese for this purpose, while the CIA relied on Chinese "Nungs") that they could pick up their pay envelopes the following day. Because of the confusion of the final airlift, however, the pay envelopes were never distributed, and Vietnamese security personnel and other employees were deprived of over $800,000 in back salaries.

in the day, General Khuyen, chief of staff at JGS, doubled as the acting chairman. In effect, the army was leaderless.

Not all of Saigon's great and near-great, to be sure, had yet taken their leave. General Quang, CIA confidant and Thieu's former security advisor, stalked around the JGS headquarters all morning, bellowing out invectives against Thieu and the Americans. He was furious that neither had seen fit to guarantee him a free ride out. Nguyen Cao Ky, also feeling a little helpless and unwanted, considered having Quang arrested on general principles, simply to stop the noise. But when several air force officers arrived at the JGS compound to perform the deed, the ever-resourceful Quang ducked out a side door and eluded them.

Over breakfast, Bill Johnson jotted a quick letter to his wife Pat, still in Bangkok. "We're going to have a negotiated settlement," he assured her. "No need to worry." He then drove across town to see several top officers in the Vietnamese Special Police Branch and the Central Intelligence Organization. Already aware that the Station would control one "black" flight that day, he wanted them all to be on it. Should a coalition government be formed, he felt they would be of greater use elsewhere. "I wasn't really interested in helping these fellows for humanitarian reasons," he recalled. "I did so because they could help set up intelligence networks into Saigon from the outside."

In his conversations with the officers Johnson did not broach the possibility of evacuating their subordinates, the 800 or more high-risk Vietnamese employed at the CIO and Special Branch headquarters. Neither did they. "Our concerns were purely professional, not humanitarian," he explained.

Technically, Johnson was acting out of turn, anyway. Phil Custer, his replacement as Chief of the Saigon base, was officially responsible for looking after the local police and intelligence operatives in the city. But Custer was playing his Danang scene all over again, holding off any decisive action till the last possible minute. After the fall of South Vietnam he insisted he had had no other choice. If the 400 Special Branch officers had been evacuated, he maintained, Saigon would have been plunged into chaos.

His argument had some validity, but only some. While the officers of the Special Branch may have been essential custodians of law and order in the city, their 400 colleagues in the CIO were not. Since they operated in a closed little world of espionage and intrigue, their departure would hardly have been noticed. Yet Custer made no more effort to evacuate them than he did the police.

Nor did he tend to basic incidentals. Over the past several years the Station had helped the police and the CIO put together massive files identifying defectors, collaborators, prisoners, anyone who had helped us or seemed likely to. A North Vietnamese prisoner once told me that the lot of them would serve as an ideal blood list if the Communists ever took over. Any far-sighted intelligence officer should have arranged to have them destroyed days, even weeks, before the Communist victory; indeed, the task should have been relatively easy, since we "controlled" most of the Vietnamese officials who controlled the files.

But Custer so far had failed to take action on the matter, partly because of unfamiliarity with Saigon's "operational climate" and partly because Polgar refused to sanction any move that might signal despair to our allies. Consequently, the files, many of them computerized for easy retrieval, would be captured fully intact by Dung's forces.*

Just before noon Johnson dropped by the Special Police compound to bid goodbye to the officer who was now in charge. "He was in tears," Johnson recalled. "He was the top man now, but he knew it meant his life. I shook his hand, patted him on the shoulder, and said, 'Keep your chin up if you can.' "

Two days later the same officer would put the muzzle of a Browning automatic under his chin and blow his head off.†

Polgar chose to view the morning's pandemonium philosophically. At a brief staff meeting he joked about the proximity of NVA forces—"even the Hungarians are uneasy"—and when Joe Kingsley alluded nervously to the machine-gun nest on the Newport bridge, Polgar suggested he drive over for a firsthand look, as if he were consigning him to routine surveillance. "Well, give me a gunfighter to back me up," Joe stammered, his face going white. Polgar told him to pick someone from Custer's office, then waved him off.

"We got to within a few hundred yards of that goddamned bridge," Joe remembered. "I had a cigarette with one of the police fellows and we cheered the friendlies on as the gunships pummeled the VC with mini-rockets. About five or ten minutes after I got there, some fool ARVN jumped over the sandbags and dashed out on the bridge, shouting something about 'mother and country.' I think our own fire cut him down."

Soon after Joe set off on his mission, Polgar called me to his office and

---

*The failures and omissions of CIA men like Custer paled in comparison with those committed by senior Vietnamese officials themselves. One may ask, for instance, why General Binh, chief of the National Police, had not bothered to have the computer files destroyed before his own departure on a CIA "black" flight the day before. They were his direct responsibility, after all. The fact is that many senior police and intelligence officials were simply too busy with their own affairs to worry about such technical problems. It is known, for example, that two top men in the police force spent their last days in the city making the rounds of the gold shops, forcing the proprietors to make large contributions in bullion "to Saigon's final defense." The booty, needless to say, was spirited out of the country in the policemen's own suitcases. And all the while the intelligence files for which they were responsible went unattended and ignored.

†In addition to meeting with his police friends on the morning of the twenty-eighth, Johnson completed plans for several "dirty tricks" that were meant to confuse the Communists if and when they seized Saigon. He ordered subordinates to prepare a batch of bogus "secret documents" and plant them in empty safes around the Embassy so if the Communists ever got into the building, they would be led to believe they had stumbled on a CIA treasure trove. Two or three of the documents erroneously identified top-ranking Communist officials as CIA agents, their purpose being to cause the Communists to turn on their own. Unfortunately, the end came so fast, none of the documents were ever distributed. By contrast, when American and French intelligence officers fled Hanoi in 1954, they went to great lengths to make life difficult for the Communist victors, even to the extent of putting sugar in the petroleum stocks left behind.

gave me a "very special assignment." I was to deliver a message to his "old friend" Malcolm Browne at the *New York Times* bureau downtown. It was a query for Browne's PRG "source" at Tan Son Nhut, as supplicatory as all those that had gone before. Would the Communists accept Minh as a new chief of state? Would they agree to a continued American presence in Saigon? Speed was essential, Polgar emphasized to me. "Don't bother taking your own car. Use mine. My driver, Ut, can negotiate traffic a lot faster than you can."

He was right. Ut rammed through the jungle of Peugeots and Hondas on Tu Do Street in less than five minutes.

Browne was out when I got to the disheveled *Times* office. Two journalists, who I assumed were *Times* staffers, were sitting in his anteroom. I gave them Polgar's message and asked them to pass it on to Browne. They seemed puzzled, but thanked me profusely. I later learned they were reporters from the *Washington Post.* I had given Polgar's top-secret communication to the competition! No wonder the two were so grateful. In any case, the message soon reached Browne and he in turn conveyed it to the PRG delegation at Tan Son Nhut.

There was no immediate reply. Hanoi did telegraph a message to us subliminally, however. During a routine news broadcast Hanoi's domestic radio service assured the home audience the Defense Attaché's Office would be out of Saigon by the thirtieth. Apparently even the news editors at Radio Hanoi had been informed of DAO's impending pullout.

Although Polgar was still desperately hopeful of a last-minute fix, he was beginning to weigh the alternatives as well. All morning he and Martin argued strenuously about several of them, and the prerequisites. Much of their haggling revolved on a seeming inconsequential: the fate of a gnarled tamarind tree in the center of the Embassy parking lot. Polgar wanted it cut down so if a full-scale helo-lift had to be staged out of the Embassy itself, there would be landing space.

Martin said no. The felling of the tree, he said, would be seen as the felling of U.S. resolve—a signal to everyone the Americans were leaving. Besides, the Embassy was to be no more than a bus stop on E-day: only 200 potential passengers there at the maximum. The tree would stand.

Several blocks away, in his private villa at Number 3 Tran Quy Cap Street, General Minh, the incoming President, was wrestling with alternatives of his own. His press spokesman was urging him to declare an unconditional surrender and be done with it. But Minh was unwilling to bend that far. He felt the army could still serve as political collateral.

In one gesture of conciliation, however, he directed his newly designated Vice-President, former Assembly Speaker Nguyen Van Huyen, to announce the decision worked out with Martin the night before. Around midday Huyen declared publicly that the new Minh government would have "no objection" if American military advisors were out of the country in twenty-four hours.

Throughout the morning Minh also continued to scratch about in the debris of Saigon's once teeming political arena for cabinet appointees. One after another the candidates dropped by his villa to plead their case. Minh greeted each one with a handshake and a noncommittal nod, then ushered him into his private garden, where he conducted the interview politely and nonchalantly, even as he himself dawdled over his cherished pet orchids. None of those he talked with, however, quite suited him—some were too hawkish, some too dovish—and in the end he decided to postpone his choices until after he had been sworn in. He was to assume office only with Vice-President Huyen and Prime Minister Vu Van Mau at his side.

At one point during the morning General François Vanuxem, the old French army officer, called on Minh and urged him to fight on. Minh tried to humor him over a cup of tea. General Timmes showed up as well—three times, in fact, before midafternoon. He asked Minh about his cabinet appointments, assured him DAO would be leaving, and arranged to set up a hotline between his new office in the Palace and the Embassy.

When Timmes questioned Minh about his view of the future, the old general smiled. There was still a chance for negotiations, he said, since Saigon, Tay Ninh and the delta were still "viable."

"But what if they're not?" Timmes replied. "What will you do? The Embassy will gladly provide asylum if you want." Again Minh smiled, shook his head. "The Vietnamese are my people," he said. "I cannot leave." He did ask Timmes, however, to arrange for the evacuation of his grandchildren and his daughter, who was married to a Vietnamese army colonel.

Shortly before lunch Erich Von Marbod pushed through the crowd in the Embassy's third-floor suite for a brief chat with the Ambassador. He was startled by Martin's appearance. Gray, haggard, Martin was suffering from a worsening case of pneumonia, his voice barely audible for the hoarseness. Von Marbod thus broached his subject as soothingly as he could. He wanted permission to pull all remaining surplus war matériel out of Saigon.

Martin leaned across his desk and leafed through a stack of cables. Finally he found what he wanted: the message from Kissinger on the Brezhnev demarche. He handed it to Von Marbod. "I repeated the request I had previously made to Mr. Von Marbod," Martin later said of the conversation, "that we do nothing that would degrade the capacity of the South Vietnamese armed forces to resist as long as they had the will and the capacity to do so. Obviously, no capability, actual or potential, remained on April 28th to defeat the North Vietnamese forces. However, the South Vietnamese armed forces did provide a significant bargaining chip in any negotiations the Minh government might be able to undertake." He went on to outline for the astonished Pentagon official his ideas on a settlement. There would be a cease-fire-in-place within three days, Martin said. After that we would have thirty days to form a new government, a coalition. One of the terms of agreement with the Communists would be the demilitarization of South Vietnam and the removal of all equipment of war. Von Marbod would therefore have "all the time in the world" to salvage American matériel.

Von Marbod glanced hurriedly through the cable traffic. He could find nothing in it that seemed to justify such optimism. Martin, evidently sensing his doubts, indicated that his views were based on assurances from the French and various Vietnamese contacts.

After the session Von Marbod drove with the Ambassador to his villa for a quick lunch. He was appalled to discover that Martin had shipped out none of his household effects—except for a prized stuffed ocelot—and that Mrs. Martin herself was still in town. "For Christ's sake, Graham," Von Marbod exclaimed, "put Dottie on a plane now!" But Martin refused. His wife's continued presence, he said, was a "stabilizing influence" for the Vietnamese.

An hour later Von Marbod moved quickly to circumvent the constraints the Ambassador had placed on him. Although Martin had ordered him not to remove the military stockpiles in Saigon, he had said nothing about the remaining ones at Bien Hoa. Seizing on this omission, Von Marbod immediately sent his aide, Rich Armitage, to Bien Hoa by chopper to see to the task.

In the meantime, he himself paid a call on General Khuyen at JGS headquarters. He informed Khuyen of his plan to withdraw the equipment at Bien Hoa and suggested that the air force prepare to fly some of its surplus aircraft at Tan Son Nhut to Can Tho or to Phu Quoc Island. He also asked Khuyen to schedule air strikes against the Bien Hoa airfield later in the day to destroy whatever matériel Armitage could not haul out. Khuyen agreed to do what he could.

Just as Von Marbod was preparing to leave, the general received a call from Minh. "I want you to hold the army together a bit longer," Minh told him. "We'll soon have a cease-fire-in-place."

"There were fifty Vietnamese maintenance types at the airfield when I got to Bien Hoa," Armitage recounted. "I promised to take them to Saigon if they'd help me with loading, and told them to shoot anyone who tried to come in over the fence and interfere. During the next half-hour or so a few stragglers did try to climb over the wire. We held them off, though, and in the meantime, packed up fifteen pallets.

"We were about to tackle a few more when Von Marbod called me on the radio. 'Get out!' he shouted. 'I can't tell you why on the air.' I later learned somebody at DAO had picked up an NVA radio message which said: 'We have the enemy surrounded at Bien Hoa. Don't let him escape!'

"I told Erich I couldn't leave without my fifty Vietnamese. He said, 'Okay, load them on the chopper. But get the hell out now!' We did." So ended Von Marbod's salvage operations at Bien Hoa.

Within the next hour Von Marbod offered to turn over to General Smith and to Polgar several of the transports he had earmarked for the Bien Hoa supply lift. Smith eagerly took him up on this, immediately using the planes to fly out equipment and files. Polgar responded less decisively. "I'll get back to you on that," he assured Von Marbod. He never did, thus forfeiting an opportunity to bring several more planes to bear in his last-minute efforts to evacuate Vietnamese friends and employees of the Station.

When Armitage, harried but in one piece, choppered back to Tan Son Nhut from Bien Hoa, Von Marbod was waiting for him on the tarmac. "One more stop," he told him. "Get in." Armitage slipped into the jeep beside Von Marbod and the two drove downtown to Vietnamese naval headquarters.

Admiral Chung Tan Cang, the chief of naval operations, was an old friend of Von Marbod's and quickly ushered him and Armitage into his office. No one wasted time on courtesies. Saigon might not have much time left, Von Marbod explained. The navy should be ready to set sail with everything that would float. The rendezvous point for all vessels would be Con Son Island off the eastern coast of the delta. Once they put in there, Admiral Whitmire's task force would guide them to safety.

"Do we leave now?" Cang inquired. Von Marbod said no, not yet. Perhaps tomorrow or the next day, though. Stand ready.

Around midday I climbed into my Ford Pinto and inched my way through four blocks of murderous traffic to Le Cercle Sportif, where I had spent so many leisurely afternoons in the past. Out of a conspirator's sense of curiosity I wanted to see if there were any monied Vietnamese still in town who felt secure enough for a relaxed lunch break of their own. Only a fool or a Communist agent would be capable of such indulgence.

To my disappointment, the sun deck and the poolside café were deserted except for a small clutch of Frenchmen. They eyed me hostilely from a corner table as if offended that an American dared to intrude on their now truly exclusive little world.

As I plodded through a few minutes of free style, I felt exposed and vulnerable, like a fly on glass. How terrifying it must have been for early-morning swimmers three weeks before when those disgruntled pilots strafed and bombed the Palace next door! My musings, it turned out, were something of a premonition. In three hours Saigon would suffer a second air strike, this time by the North Vietnamese.

An hour's flight away, at Can Tho City in the delta, Consul General Terry MacNamara was having second thoughts. It was not, however, the feasibility of his planned downriver evacuation that inspired them (he was confident it would work), but rather, his irascible Base Chief. The day before, he and Larry Downs had had a stormy confrontation over a private CIA evacuation effort. For want of any help or guidance from Saigon, Downs had begun flying some of his own Vietnamese employees to Phu Quoc Island in Air America choppers. MacNamara, discovering the plot, had lost his temper and had "fired" the CIA man on the spot, accusing him of insubordination. But now MacNamara was beginning to suffer misgivings. Downs, after all, had merely been doing his duty as he saw it in arranging those unauthorized flights. Moreover, with the military situation deteriorating by the hour, it would hardly be prudent to deprive the consulate of its CIA Base Chief.

MacNamara called Downs to his office just before noon, apologized, and gave him permission to push ahead with the helo-lift to Phu Quoc. Downs nodded, shook hands, made conciliatory noises. But he was not mollified. His feud with MacNamara had cost him a valuable day.

By midafternoon Saigon was facing its first monsoon storm of the season. The sky had turned bleak and forbidding and occasional bursts of thunder overrode the rumbling of artillery at Bien Hoa. Around 4 P.M. various notables began gathering in the reception room at the Presidential Palace. There were over 200 of them by final count—legislators, retired and active generals and a large number of opposition figures, many of whom had not set foot in these august surroundings for years. All had come to welcome the new chief of state, President Duong Van Minh.

Outgoing President Huong opened the ceremonies with a rambling, self-congratulatory speech. When he had finished, two army officers promptly strode forward, unhitched the official presidential seal and replaced it with Minh's own personal coat of arms: a stylized version of the Confucian symbol of reconciliation, the yin and the yang, complementary opposites. A murmur of approval rippled through the audience.

Minh's inaugural address was notable for its brevity and for its lack of realism. Pitching his remarks explicitly to the "PRG"—the first time any Saigon leader had officially acknowledged its existence—he called for an immediate cease-fire and peace talks within the framework of the Paris agreement, and promised to establish a broadly based government composed of individuals "with a clear-cut stand for reconciliation." One of its first acts, he said, would be to release "those who have been detained for political reasons and to end the coercive system imposed on the press." The pledge clearly was aimed at meeting a recent PRG demand for a "dismantling of all the government's coercive machinery," but even as a sop, it must have caused Ambassador Martin some anguish as he listened to a simultaneous translation in his office. How many times had he assured Congress and others there were no political prisoners in South Vietnam and that Saigon's press was one of the freest in the world? Apparently the new President disagreed.

Minh also had a few special words for the South Vietnamese army. "You have a new duty," he said. "This is to defend the territory that is left . . . Keep your spirits high, your ranks intact and your position firm to accomplish that duty. When the cease-fire order is given, your mission will be rigorously to execute that order in accordance with the clauses of the Paris agreement and to maintain order and security in your areas." Such firmness was not exactly what one would have expected from a man on the verge of surrender. But Minh, of course, still felt surrender was avoidable.

After introducing his Vice-President and Prime Minister, Minh nodded to the audience. A flash of lightning ricocheted through the Assembly hall amid nervous applause. It was exactly five-fifty in the afternoon.

Within the next ten minutes the Communist wing leader nosed his plane in for the attack.

Contrary to what some observers said later, the air strike that afternoon was not a response to Minh's speech. As my agent-source had reported to me on 17 April, it had been planned weeks before. That it coincided with Minh's swearing-in was merely one final irony.

The DAO's official after-action account was crisp and to the point: "28 April, eighteen hundred hours: a flight of five A-37 [captured South Vietnamese jet] aircraft equipped with MK 81 ordnance attacked a flight line area of Tan Son Nhut. A total of six bombs hit the Vietnamese air force parking area destroying numerous aircraft [at least three AC-119s and several C-47s]. The last two bombs hit between the base operations center and the control tower. No U.S. Air Force aircraft was damaged. The A-37s were equipped with both [wing] tip and four undersling wing tanks. Dive-bomb tactics were used with an estimated roll in altitude of 5,000 feet and a release altitude of 2,500 feet. Pullout was estimated to be below 2,000 feet."

In his own memoirs General Dung described the strike as a "splendidly coordinated attack, the most perfect joint operation ever by our armed forces and branches." Part of the credit for its success, he acknowledged, belonged to the lead pilot, Nguyen Thanh Trung. A recent defector from the government side, Trung knew Saigon and Tan Son Nhut well. It was he, after all, who had flown the bombing mission against the Presidential Palace only three weeks before.

I was at my desk on the top floor of the Embassy when the first of the planes came in. It was heralded by the ping of a few stray rounds. Then suddenly the world seemed to explode in a cacophony of cannon and machine-gun fire. I tried to stand, my knees gave way. I tried again and ran in a crouch into the interior hallway, keeping my head and shoulders below the plastic-paned windows. Colleagues next door were scrambling into the hallway pell-mell. Some fell to the floor, clawing at it as if trying to burrow in. I caught my breath, ducked back into my office, and kneeling beside the secure telephone behind my desk, dialed DAO, flipping off the overhead light with my free hand. I could hardly hear the voice on the other end for the din of the bombing and automatic-weapons fire. "We're under direct attack," my DAO contact screamed. "Several A-37s diving in on the runways. One or two F-5s may have scrambled but most are still on the ground. Very bad. Don't know if the refugee center was hit. How bad are you?"

"Can't tell yet," I said. "Aircraft seem to be on top of us. Everybody in the street is firing wildly."

I hung up and ran to Polgar's office down the hall. His two secretaries were sitting frozen at their desks in the reception area only a few feet away from the windows. "Under your desks!" I yelled as I dashed past them.

Polgar was standing at his own window, trying to catch a glimpse of the aircraft. I stammered out what I had learned from DAO, then waited for a reply. He just stood for a moment, staring at the cement screen beyond his window. "Sir," I said, "maybe you'd better get away from there. A stray round . . ." Abruptly he came to. He turned and followed me into the anteroom. Pittman was trying to calm the secretaries. All at once a voice echoed up the stairwell in the outside hallway: "They're in the halls! They're in the halls!" Apparently I was not the only one shocked into visions of 1968, when NVA commandos had tried to penetrate the Embassy. Up and down the corridor there was an orchestrated rasp of metal on metal as one officer after another chambered a round. I reached for the snub-nosed .38-caliber pistol on my back hip. Someone darted out of a side office with an M-16 in his hand. There was a clatter of footsteps on the stairwell. Two flak-jacketed Marine guards dashed out and ran past us to the little stairway leading up to the roof. One tossed off an aside: "False alarm. The Embassy's secure."

At that moment Bill Johnson and Jerry Locksley, the Embassy duty officer, were scurrying for cover in the Norodom complex next to the main chancery. They had first mistaken the gunfire for thunder, but as the second and third explosion reverberated through the building, they recognized it for what it was. Johnson yanked a Chinese AK-47 rifle off the wall as they scrambled under a stairwell. Maybe the airborne troops up the street at the zoo were simply practicing? Locksley guessed. "Christ, no!" Johnson growled, trying to force a round down the chamber. "It's a ground attack. Even the marines on the roof are blasting away." As if on cue, there was a burst of machine-gun fire from the rooftop pillboxes on the chancery itself. They switched on Locksley's portable radio. "Hello, Tiger, hello, hello!" Locksley bellowed into the mouthpiece. "What the hell is going on?" A voice stuttered in over the Mission Warden net: "Ground assault negative. It's an air strike at Tan Son Nhut."

On the top floor of the Embassy, Polgar was trying to restore order. "All right," he said, holding up his hand. "Put the weapons away. We're intelligence officers, not an assault force. We're not going to try to hold off the North Vietnamese army."

As each of us reluctantly holstered our arms, Pittman pulled out a cigar, lit it and took several thoughtful puffs. Maybe we'd better set up a temporary operations center on the floor below, he suggested; less danger from aircraft down there. Polgar mumbled agreement, then motioned to me. "I'm going downstairs to write this up," he said. "Keep funneling data to me and try to get hold of some of our people at DAO." Since all of our secure lines and the radios were in the sixth-floor situation room next to my own office, I realized, to my discomfort, I had just been nominated to stay topside.

Don Hays had not slept for three days, and when the first bombs went away he felt his nerves slip a notch or two. He was on the rooftop patio of the recreation compound behind the Embassy, amid crowds of Vietnamese. As the chatter of gunfire intensified, he shooed them all downstairs to the restaurant and hustled the children into the interior bathroom. He than ordered the rest to begin turning over tables as cover, in case the plate-glass windows were blown out. A short while later Wolfgang Lehmann, Boudreau and Jazynka strode in. Hays would always remember the expression on Boudreau's face. He was chuckling to himself as if in another world. "What the hell are you doing?" Lehmann snapped as he caught sight of the young administrative officer sitting on the floor with his back against an overturned table. "No need to rearrange the furniture." At that moment the percussion from some distant explosion rattled the front door on its hinges. Lehmann almost dove into Hays' lap.

As I darted around my office, pulling together notes, taking telephone calls, I suddenly remembered Joe Kingsley. If ever I needed his help, and his warrior's instincts, it was now.

But Joe was currently "indisposed." An hour or so earlier he had driven downtown to pick up a ring for his wife and to drop by some bars. Now he was in the thick of it.

"I was driving along Tu Do when the planes struck," he later told me. "Right away I knew what was happening. I jumped out of my car and ran around to the trunk. I had an arsenal in there—Thompsons, M-16s and hand grenades—and I pulled out an armful. Just then two Marine guards from the Embassy came stumbling out of a corner bar. They were in civvies and drunk as loons. 'Give us a ride!' they yelled, and I said okay, tossing them a .45 automatic or two to keep them happy. Then we hopped in; I floored the thing and barreled off toward the Embassy, banging cars out of the way as I went, like they teach you to do in obstacle-course driving. Every once in a while my passengers would take a pot shot at somebody along the way. I hope to hell they didn't kill anybody.

"When we got to the Embassy the gates were bolted. One of the guys with me took out his .45 and poked it at the Vietnamese gatekeeper. 'No keys! No keys!' the little fellow screamed in Vietnamese. My man didn't understand, and was about to shoot him through the head. I grabbed the .45 and told him to cool it. Then, suddenly, some idiot off down the street, over near the British Embassy, started pinging away at us. We ducked behind a tree while the Marine guards inside looked for a key. At last they found one and sprang the gate. As it swung open we dashed across the street into the compound, with stray rounds zipping about our ears. I don't believe I'd seen so much action since Quang Ngai in '68."

In the eye of the storm, at Tan Son Nhut, at least some of those under fire were taking satisfaction in it. Just before the bombing run, the North Vietnamese and PRG delegations at Camp Davis had filed quietly into the underground bunkers they had been building for the past week. They remained there throughout, fielding telephone calls from contacts downtown and congratulating one another on the skill of their pilots.

About a mile away, at DAO headquarters, a far less contented Colonel Legro was trapped in the command mess with a handful of Vietnamese waitresses. One of them was weeping uncontrollably. "You're okay," he assured her, patting her on the back. "The North Vietnamese aren't here."

"That's not why I'm crying," she sobbed. "I know now you'll all be leaving tomorrow."

Members of the American delegation to the Joint Military Team, who only three days before had been invited by the Communists to stay on, were now darting from building to building in the main DAO compound, pulling panic-stricken Vietnamese inside, pushing them into corners and under tables, trying to restore calm. Several hundred yards away, in the processing center itself, another reluctant good Samaritan was simply trying to do his job. "We were working like crazy as usual," Moorefield later commented, recalling the moment the first plane swooped in. "All of a sudden there were these tremendous explosions and the lights fell out of the ceiling. One of them crashed right on Joe McBride's desk, on his shoulders. But he just kept right on working.

"But then there were more explosions, and the Vietnamese with us— maybe a hundred in total—started screaming and running around like decapitated chickens. I jumped up and grabbed my revolver, and McBride and I began herding them out of our building and into a sturdier one across the street.

"As we made the dash I saw several planes coming in for a second run. There were three or four of them and smoke and airbursts were splattered all over the sky. Since the target zone itself was only a quarter of a mile away, the concussion was tremendous.

"I guess we stayed hunkered down for an hour or two, though the strikes themselves lasted no more than fifteen or twenty minutes. One thing was particularly discouraging to me: the long delay between that first sortie and the time South Vietnamese interceptors got off the ground to give chase. The Assistant Air Attaché later told me the strike had effectively knocked out the air operations center, so the planes that did go up were flying blind.

"I remember thinking throughout it all how ironic this was. How many times in my two years as a combat officer in the delta had I called in air strikes against the VC! Now I knew what it felt like to be on the receiving end, and totally defenseless."

During the first hour or so the leg muscles got a workout. I must have stumbled up and down the interior stairwell in the Embassy twenty or more times, delivering radio and telephone reports to Polgar in his fifth-floor refuge, carrying messages from him to others around the building.

A North Vietnamese prisoner had once tried to convey to me the feeling you get in an air strike: the sense of helplessness and claustrophobia. I knew now what he meant. And as I rushed around the Embassy, doing Polgar's bidding, I couldn't help shuddering at the odds: even if an evacuation got under way in the next hour, North Vietnamese aircraft would quickly be able to block access into and out of Tan Son Nhut, shutting us in for good.

In the situation room next to my own cubbyhole, three other CIA officers soon took over at the radios. All of them were obliged to work dangerously close to the windows, since the consoles were fixed in place, immovable. The primary operator, a secretary normally assigned to another office, performed valiantly, sitting calmly before the microphone hour after hour, passing messages to panic-stricken Station personnel on the outside as stray rounds sang past the windows at her elbow.

At first Polgar was convinced that the air attack was the opening shot in a coup attempt. Dozens of A-37s were still available to the South Vietnamese air force, and Nguyen Cao Ky no doubt still had designs on the presidency. Within minutes of the first bombing run, Ky's old friend Robert Shaplen, of *The New Yorker,* called from the Continental Hotel downtown to assure me the Air Marshal was not involved. "But tell Polgar," he screamed over the line, his gravelly voice barely discernible over the weapons chatter, "I'll check with Ky right away to make sure." He soon called back to say that the flamboyant airman had categorically denied any role in the attack.

Not long afterward a colleague handed me an intelligence report that proved North Vietnamese complicity beyond doubt. The planes, it revealed, had been launched from the captured air base at Phan Rang on the coast. I took the report and Shaplen's message down to Polgar on the floor below. He was sitting at a secretary's desk in a borrowed office, pounding out a cable to headquarters on a rickety old typewriter. He had just run up the steps from the Ambassador's third-floor suite; beads of sweat stood out on his bald head and he was panting for breath. He incorporated my notes and the intelligence into his cable and told me to get in touch with Malcolm Browne at the *New York Times* to see if he had had any reaction from the PRG delegation at Tan Son Nhut.

"Any word from Toth?" he shouted to another officer, who was trying to reach the Hungarian ICCS Military Attaché by phone. "No, sir," the officer replied, slamming down the receiver. "The Hungarians apparently aren't answering."

Before I could dial the *Times* office, Browne put in a call to us. As I picked up the phone, he sounded excited and distraught. His staff had spotted a MIG-19 over the cathedral only three blocks from the Embassy, he spluttered, and several A-37s had made strafing passes over the Palace. But the worst news he had was from the PRG. A spokesman for its team at Tan Son Nhut had just advised him by phone that "Big" Minh was totally unacceptable to their side. "The United States must meet articles I, IV, and IX of the Paris agreement and respect the will and fundamental rights of the Vietnamese people," the spokesman had explained, recalling the provisions of the agreement that provided for a total U.S. withdrawal, a cease-fire and elections. "Secondly, the United States must annul the Saigon administration, which is an administration of war and repression. The declarations of General Minh do not meet these demands."

Polgar blanched when I passed this message to him. It was final proof that all of his maneuvering had been for naught. As the intelligence of early April had indicated, the Communists were bent on total victory, without even a semblance of political accommodation.

Predictably enough, the air strikes had brought the airlift to a full stop. Only minutes after the first pass, General Smith put two inbound C-130s into a holding pattern southeast of Tan Son Nhut. He also directed his staff to move all available buses to the prearranged staging areas. Since he was under orders to dismantle his entire shop within the next twenty-four hours, he wanted to be able to send convoys into the city on a moment's notice to pick up remaining employees once the shooting stopped.

At approximately seven-fifteen Ambassador Martin called Smith from the Embassy for an initial damage assessment. Had the refugee center been hit? No, said the general. No casualties at all he knew of. Well, what about the runways? Were they in good enough shape to permit a continuation of the C-130 flights? The general hesitated; he had not been able to conduct a firsthand inspection yet. But based on preliminary reports and what he could see from his office, there was still room enough for the big birds to maneuver. He assured Martin as much.

The Ambassador breathed a sigh of relief. Some of his senior staffers, Polgar included, were already agitating for an immediate helo-lift, Option IV. But with the runways still serviceable, he could argue them down. A helo-lift would panic the Vietnamese, destroy all hope for a negotiated settlement. Better to proceed with a fixed-wing airlift as planned; less risk involved.

In Washington, a half-day behind Saigon, it was early morning. Kissinger briefed President Ford on the bombing and said Martin was convinced the fixed-wing airlift was still feasible.

The President was not satisfied. As he later revealed to aides, he did not understand what had brought the South Vietnamese to this horrible pass anyway. Nor was he sure of the wisdom of leaving so many crucial decisions to Martin alone. This business of negotiations was particularly puzzling. Schlesinger saw no real chance for it. Even Kissinger was increasingly skeptical. Only Martin still believed the chestnut could be pulled from the fire.*

---

*Colby's attitude remained a compromise between Schlesinger's and Martin's. On the twenty-eighth he told WSAG: "Bien Hoa and its air base should fall in a few hours if the North Vietnamese press the attack. Resistance at Long Binh [a military base near Bien Hoa] will probably soon come to an end. Tay Ninh and Tan An will fall soon to the Communists. In sum, the North Vietnamese have resumed military pressure on Saigon. Minh's dilemma is whether he can arrange a capitulation in which non-Communists have some role in a new government before the North Vietnamese bring about a total collapse of the Saigon government. There appears to be little time left to reach such a denouement—probably one to three days."

Finally, after airing his concerns with Kissinger, Ford decided on a compromise. While it would be left to Martin to determine if and when all Americans should leave, a massive fixed-wing airlift, to reduce the backlog, was to be set in motion in the next twenty-four hours. Kissinger would also query the Soviets again, to see if they could ensure Hanoi's cooperation.

At approximately 8 P.M., Saigon time, General Smith gave landing clearance to the two C-130s still orbiting above Tan Son Nhut. Some 360 passengers were quickly pushed aboard and the two planes took off without incident. Meanwhile, Admiral Gayler contacted Smith from Honolulu to advise him of Washington's latest decisions. All C-141 flights, he said, were to be discontinued immediately to make way for some sixty C-130 "sorties" in the next twenty-four hours. Ten thousand people, including all DAO personnel, were to be moved out on them.

Other senior Mission officers were quickly informed of the plan. Acting on Martin's instructions, Jim Devine directed all agency chiefs to begin notifying and assembling those they intended to send out. It was the Ambassador's assumption, he said, that we would have at least two days, up through the thirtieth, to complete the evacuation of key Vietnamese personnel.

Several agency heads protested. Saigon police had just imposed a twenty-four-hour curfew. So how could they assemble evacuees? Devine suggested the majority be brought to the Embassy and to nearby agency compounds to minimize travel time. In the morning they could be bused to Tan Son Nhut itself.

In the next few hours some 1,000 Vietnamese were marshaled at the Embassy and another 200 at the USIA compound on Le Quy Don Street. Don Hays and other officers counted heads and prayed the convoy system would hold up the following day. As they were all now well aware, the standing evacuation plan provided for only 200 potential passengers at the Embassy on E-day. A substantially larger number would necessitate a massive helo-lift out of the chancery grounds, something nobody had planned for.

In fact, the Embassy's role under Option IV was already being rethought and revised. In the wake of the air strikes Gayler suddenly became convinced that the Embassy might have to be used as a major helicopter pickup point, after all, and he quickly alerted General Smith to this possibility. Smith in turn advised the Marine guards downtown to clear all cars out of the Embassy during the night so the parking lot could quickly be converted into a landing pad if necessary. When Marv Garrett, the Embassy security officer learned of this, he knew he could no longer delay the inevitable. The great tamarind tree, which spread like a sheltering umbrella over Martin's own limousine, would have to come down.

A half-hour later several of Garrett's subordinates crept across the parking lot with a chain saw. They unsheathed it, lined it up on the tree trunk and flipped the switch. To their chagrin, nothing happened; the saw was jammed. One of the Embassy's Marine guards brought out an armful of fire axes and they all went to work with these, the crunch of each blow resounding loudly through the parking lot. Minutes later Lehmann, his tie askew, raced out of the building, shaking his fist at them. "What do you think you're doing!" he stammered, nearly incoherent with rage. "Nobody told you to cut that tree down." Garrett and his boys laid down their axes. The tree had gained a reprieve—for the time being.

As the last of the gunfire died away, Erich Von Marbod left General Smith's office, where he had sought refuge during the air strike, and drove over to JGS headquarters. He was anxious to determine if the South Vietnamese air force had managed, in the confusion, to carry out the preemptive bombing run on Bien Hoa he had requested earlier in the day.

When Von Marbod walked into the chaotic situation room, Air Marshal Ky, impressively chic in his tailor-made flying suit, was picking through piles of documents strewn across a desk top. The wall maps, once testimony to the myths of pacification and the glory of South Vietnamese arms, were now Kandinsky abstracts of red and pink chalk marks showing the latest Communist advances. Scribbled in the corner of one of them were the numerals "308," punctuated with a large question mark. The 308th Division, the best in the North Vietnamese army, had not been heard from for weeks; in fact, it was the only combat-ready NVA unit that had yet to be thrown into the offensive. As intelligence sources would later reveal, it was still being held in reserve in North Vietnam, as a hedge against unforeseen contingencies.*

Von Marbod shook hands with Ky and and quickly got down to cases. He wondered if the Air Marshal could "use his influence" to assure the air strikes at Bien Hoa. He also asked him to try to persuade the air force command to fly all surplus planes—all except the F-5s—to Takli air base in Thailand.

Ky agreed to help. But why leave the F-5s behind? he posed. Von Marbod explained that Martin wanted him to do nothing to "denigrate" the air force's fighting capability. The F-5s would have to stay until the last minute.

In subsequent testimony before Congress, Martin accused Von Marbod of violating that understanding. "I later learned that after the bombing run on the air base," the Ambassador said, "he went to see Air Marshal Ky and persuaded him to influence the commander of the Vietnamese air force to fly out a considerable portion of serviceable planes that afternoon. The net result seems to have been a breakdown of discipline at the air base. The severe rocketing of the air base the next morning [on the twenty-ninth] to forestall any further removals was also a consequence." What Martin was implying was that his unguided missile, Von Marbod, had driven the North Vietnamese over the brink and precipitated their final attack on Saigon by arranging for the removal of South Vietnamese planes. This was patently untrue. No South

---

*In addition to the 308th, a training division in North Vietnam was being readied for combat and probably would have been committed to the offensive had not Saigon collapsed so quickly.

Vietnamese aircraft landed at Takli until midmorning the following day, well after the North Vietnamese had mounted their final attack.

Ky, for his part, also played false with Von Marbod. Not only did he fail to arrange for the departure of vital South Vietnamese aircraft; he also neglected to set up the bombing of Bien Hoa, as he had promised. Consequently, a large proportion of the air force's equipment and planes were left for the victorious North Vietnamese.

As Ky later explained, he had been preoccupied with something else that evening. Shortly after his conversation with the Pentagon official, he drove to a nearby hangar and helped outfit several F-5 fighters for a retaliatory raid against Phan Rang, where the A-37 attack force had originated.

Meanwhile, General Van Tien Dung and his aides were nailing down their final objectives. "On the evening of 28 April," he reports in his memoirs, "the campaign command, analyzing the overall situation, noted that the enemy was very perplexed, his command had become disorderly . . . In the first two days of the campaign, our columns had operated according to plan. Therefore, we ordered that the general offensive be launched on all fronts on the morning of 29 April and the advance into Saigon be made." Messages reflecting this decision were duly dispatched to Hanoi and to all field headquarters.

A short while later Tank Brigade 203, which was to spearhead the drive into the capital, was rattling toward its jump-off point at Bien Hoa, picking its way along Route 1, east of the city, with headlights extinguished as South Vietnamese aircraft droned purposelessly overhead.

By 10 P.M. we were beginning to pull ourselves together. Convoys of cars and limousines already were threading their way through the police roadblocks around the city, some delivering exhausted Embassy personnel to their residences, others picking up the first of the Vietnamese employees who were to go out on the C-130s the next day. With the twenty-four-hour curfew now battened down, the streets were deserted and bleakly ominous with their hedgerows of barbed wire.

Alan Carter dropped by the USIA compound on Le Quy Don Street to help subordinates bed down the Vietnamese already assembled. As he walked through the crowds, he recognized only a few of his own locals. The majority were USAID employees and other unfamiliars who had simply slipped past the front gate. He tried to think of some way to seal off the compound. No use: the Embassy's public-affairs office had not been built as a fortress.

At the recreation compound behind the Embassy, Don Hays and two of his colleagues were packing boxes of frozen food into the back of a battered old station wagon. Hays was desperately tired, almost ill, but knew he could not succumb now. He had been summoned to the DAO processing center to relieve two colleagues who had been on duty throughout this nerve-racking day, and there were still over 700 State Department evacuees to be fed and processed before the start of the C-130 airlift in a few hours.

Just as he was climbing into the vehicle, Boudreau and Jazynka sauntered through the parking lot, laughing and talking. Why in such a hurry? they called to him. No need to overdo things. Why, they were even going to a late-evening cocktail party. Come on and join them.

Hays merely stared, too weary to react.

Within the next few hours three more C-130s put in at Tan Son Nhut, each carrying "hot cargo," more Daisy Cutters for the nonexistent South Vietnamese air force. Given the time required for unloading, none of the planes could immediately take on passengers. The milling crowds in the processing center quickly swelled to over 2,800.

With more and more people filtering into the annex, Ken Moorefield cast about for pacifiers. All it would take to stall all the "systems" governing the evacuation was wholesale rioting there, in the compound, and he and everybody else were desperate to avoid that at all costs. Since many of the evacuees were now hours away from their last meal and showing the strain, he decided, as Hays had, that food was the answer. Around ten-thirty he and several other consular officers raided the canned stocks in the bowling alley and lugged them over to the kitchen in one of the larger buildings. They then put a team of American and Vietnamese cooks to work preparing a meal of rice and beans for the multitude.

While the concoction simmered, Moorefield made a last inspection tour of the annex and its perimeters. Slightly after eleven he walked out to the checkpoint just beyond the front gate. He found thirty or forty Vietnamese huddled there, and he guided them down the road into the compound so in the event of another air strike they wouldn't be caught in the open. He also talked briefly with the two young Marine guards on duty. Both were nervous and jumpy, as might be expected. Lance Corporal Darwin Judge had been in Vietnam only a month; his companion, Corporal Charles McMahon, only slightly longer. Moorefield tried to bolster their spirits, assuring them everything was under control. He was the last man to see them alive.

Downtown at the Embassy, evacuation coordinator George Jacobson had spent the past half-hour phoning all agency chiefs, alerting them to an urgent conference at midnight. Each was to send a special representative to help draw up plans for the airlift the next day.

As soon as Dan Ellerman, the economic counselor, received word of the meeting, he began rummaging about in the debris on his desk for his lists of business community employees. Over the past few days representatives of various American concerns had managed to fly out over 300 Vietnamese, most of them bank staffers. Still to go: those who worked for Esso, Shell and IBM.

A short time later Ellerman was summoned to the Ambassador's office to take a long-distance phone call from a senior IBM representative in Bangkok. The man was furious. He had been due to fly into Saigon during the day to arrange for the evacuation of the company's locals, but his landing clearance had been revoked because of the congestion at Tan Son Nhut and the air strikes. Now he wanted to know what the Embassy was going to do to help him. There were nearly 300 Vietnamese employees of IBM plus their families to be taken care of.

Ellerman tried to calm him down. He would do what he could, he promised, but right now, with a twenty-four-hour curfew in effect, his hands were tied. The IBM representative asked if he could fly in at once. Ellerman said no; there were too many Americans in Saigon already. "Well, if you don't get our people out," the IBM man retorted, "I'm going to call the White House." Ellerman sighed: "Go ahead."

In Washington, IBM executives did just that, contacting the White House and demanding assistance. None was forthcoming, and all IBM locals were ultimately left to fend for themselves. Company representatives complained "unofficially" after the fall of Saigon that their Vietnamese employees had been made hostage to the Ambassador's pipe dreams. In the interests of promoting a political settlement, they said, he had deliberately left the highly trained IBM technicians in place, as a gesture of conciliation toward the Communists. The Ambassador flatly denied this.

Since the majority of my colleagues were now absorbed in contingency planning, there was little more I could do. I debated going out to DAO to lend Moorefield a hand, but Polgar ordered me to "stay on call" so if there were any dramatic military developments during the night, I could handle coverage for headquarters. I told the CIA duty officer I could be reached at my apartment if needed, and then drove over to 6 Chien Si Circle with an escort from the Mission Wardens' office.

Before turning in I went next door for a nightcap and a chat with Joe Kingsley. The portable radio on my belt was giving off a monotonous little purr, but otherwise remained silent. When Joe opened the door he was already on his third martini. "Just trying to forget the close call today," he mumbled. At that moment one of his old Green Beret chums staggered up behind me. He was a good five sheets to the wind, and the only complete sentence he could utter was "I'm going to stay in Saigon, goddamnit, to go down with the ship." Joe fixed him a chaser and we all sat down to review our rooftop evacuation plan one last time, each of us agreeing to make sure the other two were up and moving if there should be any emergency during the night.

When I returned to my apartment a short time later, I spent a few minutes arranging my helmet, flak jacket and M-16 rifle on the floor by the night table so I could find them easily in the dark.

Morning

The meeting was called to order in the Embassy conference room just before midnight. They were a weary and ragged bunch, all twenty of them, and as George Jacobson slid into the Ambassador's chair on the far side of the table to preside in Martin's stead, one of the State Department men gave up a silent prayer that his colleagues might be less long-winded than usual.

He was not to be surprised. The session dragged on for over an hour, as each of the Embassy's would-be evacuation experts took his turn.

Jacobson had the first word. The Ambassador was confident, he said, the North Vietnamese would hold off for another forty-eight hours before making a final decision on whether or not to attack. The Embassy thus had some time to evacuate its chosen 10,000.

But there was a problem: quality. Too much seat space had already been given over to the cooks and bottle-washers. The Ambassador was determined that the next 10,000 evacuees be truly "high risk." Jacobson looked over at Shep Lowman, the Embassy's master list maker. "See if you can dredge up the names of 2,000 Vietnamese who 'really' deserve help," he told him. Lowman was amazed. It was the first time he had ever been given a specific quota for VIPs.

The discussion then turned to bus routes, pickup points and a hundred other technicalities. Finally Lacy Wright raised his hand. "Has anyone got plans for getting us out?" he inquired. "If so, what are they?" Jacobson smiled, mumbled something no one could hear.

As the meeting broke up, Lowman buttonholed Alan Carter, the USIA man, and asked him to provide a new list of his own "priority contacts."

"For God sakes!" Carter exclaimed. "I turned one in days ago."

"I know," Lowman replied. "But our tabulations have broken down. We'll have to start again."

Before any of his own subordinates could escape for the night, Lowman called several of them together and formed a small staff of "volunteers" to help with pickups and deliveries the next morning. He and colleague Don Brewster then began phoning the first of the Vietnamese nominees.

In Washington, meanwhile, Soviet Ambassador Anatoly Dobrynin was mulling over a new query from Kissinger. The Secretary of State had just advised him of the expanded airlift, and asked again if Hanoi would negotiate with Minh, permit a residual American presence in Saigon and assure the evacuees a free exit—in particular, an open-air corridor over the Saigon–Vung Tau highway. For the moment the Soviet diplomat had no reply.

Hanoi's own spokesmen were not so tongue-tied. Liberation Radio declared an hour or so later: the "most important and correct action now is for our people to rely totally on their political and armed forces to rush forward valiantly . . . and liberate the whole of the Fatherland's southern territory." Another broadcast dismissed the Minh government as "a dishonest administration and powerful war machine" of which "members of the third force [read: Minh himself] are victims."

Hanoi also had some discouraging words for the Americans. "The mere proposal [by Washington] that the United States maintain only an embassy [in Saigon], with the normal number of personnel, cannot be regarded as a suspension of American involvement," said Liberation Radio. "The question is what such an embassy has the right to do and why the Americans are not immediately and urgently withdrawn. [No distinction here between military advisors and the rest] . . . The question is whether the U.S. imperialists agree to compensate for and heal the deep and extensive wounds they have caused the Vietnamese people." In short, if the Americans wanted to keep any kind of official presence in Vietnam, they would have to pay cash on the line and agree to tie their hands in advance. These demands clearly ruled out any normal diplomatic mission. The "bitter-end option," the retention of a small American embassy, was now out of the question, although the White House would take several more hours to realize it.

Besides the propaganda, policy-makers and analysts in Washington had something even more ominous to ponder as their working day drew to a close. Intelligence specialists had just finished the review of Communist communications Polgar had requested several days before, and had confirmed the original findings. The messages were not spoofs, as Polgar suspected, but a valid reflection of Communist plans and troop moves. There was no longer any doubt that the entire North Vietnamese army was pressing in on Saigon from all directions and preparing to shell various key targets, including Tan Son Nhut itself.

By 2:30 A.M., Saigon time, 29 April, the 2,000 or more Vietnamese in the DAO annex were munching away contentedly on the rice and beans Moorefield's culinary experts had whipped up. The airlift had been shut down, since the bombing and DAO technicians were still unloading the three C-130s that had arrived several hours before.

Moorefield himself was staggering-tired, and after a final tour of the grounds he climbed into his battered staff car and drove back into town to his apartment. "I had this homing instinct," he said later. "I had to get back one last time, if only to pick up my getaway bag and rifle."

In the next hour and a half, two of the C-130s finally were cleared for boarding. Don Hays, working the chutes in the processing center, was so numb with fatigue he could hardly count off the prescribed passenger loads. At last one, then another of the planes rumbled off the runway. The third began taxiing over to the loading ramp. Hays glanced at his watch: 4 A.M. A few seconds later the first rocket came screaming in.

The explosion rocked my apartment. I rolled out of bed, groping around the floor in the darkness for my helmet and flak jacket. As I crawled to the window I tried to gauge the distance of the series of lesser explosions that followed: a few miles away, probably Tan Son Nhut. Over the treetops I could see huge fireballs careening into the night sky, the horizon pulsing with artillery flashes. The radio transceiver on my desk burped and came alive with an ear-piercing *bleeep!* A voice clawed through the static: "Tan Son Nhut taking rockets and 130-mm!" Then a brief silence followed as another message cut into the channel. I scrambled to my feet, kicked on some trousers and shoes, and dashed out onto my front porch. In the streets below, Vietnamese police were peering timidly out from under parked cars and from behind sandbags. I ran in a crouch across a small catwalk spanning the face of the building and hammered on Joe Kingsley's door to make sure he was awake. He was—just barely. "Looks like this is it," he said groggily as he pulled on his flak jacket. "And wouldn't you know it. I've got one helluva hangover." We then scrambled up the outside stairwell to the roof.

One of the first rockets dropped in only a few feet away from the taxiing C-130, crumpling part of the fuselage as easily as a piece of tin foil. A third, then a fourth slammed into the guard post Moorefield had visited only a few hours earlier. Corporal McMahon and Lance Corporal Judge were killed instantly.

Another rocket spun over the processing center and careened into the DAO squash court. Fifteen hundred Vietnamese caught in the open near the swimming pool swept this way and that, like wheat stalks in a strong wind. Hays tried to grab those closest to him and force them to the ground, but was nearly trampled as hundreds surged past him. Seconds later another rocket crashed into the corner of the gymnasium, slicing off a piece of roofing and sending it boomeranging toward a Vietnamese woman in the courtyard below. Three or four hundred evacuees trapped inside the building ripped and clawed at the metal walls, trying to get out. A few hundred yards away the earth erupted in a geyser of flame as another rocket burrowed in. General Smith and Erich Von Marbod in the nearby DAO command billet were thrown to the floor. Upstairs an air conditioner spun out of the wall and landed at the foot of another officer's bunk. The shaken occupant grabbed his M-16, dashed out of the building and flung himself into a ditch. Only moments later did he realize he had forgotten to put his pants on.

On the roof of my apartment building, three miles away, you could tick off nearly five seconds between each muzzle flash and the shock of impact. "Definitely 130-mm artillery," Joe commented almost reverentially. "No rocket could do that kind of damage." One of the fuel depots at the edge of Tan Son Nhut took a direct hit and burst instantly into an incandescent cloud, showering fiery petroleum in a hundred different directions. Seconds later another rocket streaked out of the darkness into the holocaust.

"Must be taking incoming there too!" Joe shouted, pointing off toward the Chinese section of the city. Sure enough, the night sky over Cho Lon was flickering with an eerie pink glow, a fire storm gathering wind.

The first explosion tore Moorefield out of a deep sleep and flung him out of bed. For a few moments he lay on the floor, on his back, more dazed than frightened, not quite sure if he was dreaming. As reverberations from the third or fourth blast pummeled the air, Lacy Wright, at his own villa several blocks away, was already struggling into an old suit. The buzzing of his telephone cut through the din. "Get in right away!" Shep Lowman shouted over the line. "The C-130 lift may be in jeopardy."

Bill Johnson meanwhile was eagerly gathering up the assorted weapons he had stashed around his bedroom. His own villa just off Cong Ly Street lay on the route Viet Cong forces had followed from Tan Son Nhut in 1968. He was sure he would see some action today; in fact, was itching for it.

Within the next few minutes Ambassador Martin himself was dialing the Marine duty officer at the Embassy. "What the hell is going on?" he asked, his voice stony calm, almost frighteningly so. "We're not sure, sir," the marine stammered back. "Looks like rockets at Tan Son Nhut." Martin clicked him off in midsentence and put in a call to Eva Kim at her residence nearby. All senior Mission Council members, he told her, were to be summoned to the Embassy at once.

Unhappily, Jerry Locksley, the Embassy duty officer, was not at his post this unpropitious Tuesday morning. He had decided not to spend the night at the Embassy. With all the other contingency planners around, it hadn't seemed necessary. But by 4:25 A.M. he was cursing himself for being so short-sighted. Not only was he now hopelessly out of touch with what was going on; he couldn't seem to reach anyone who knew better. Finally, after countless frantic calls on his radio, he managed to raise one of Marv Garrett's Mission Warden officers at Tan Son Nhut. He learned little more than he could have guessed: the rocketing was continuing; a few Vietnamese wounded. He immediately called Polgar to pass on this scanty news. "Keep me apprised," the Station Chief murmured sleepily.

In the next half-hour General Smith and his staff began pulling themselves out from under the rubble to take stock of it. Colonel Bill Michler, the Assistant Air Attaché, was among the first to scuttle out to the flight line. After a quick once-over he hurried back to the control center to radio a damage report to the 7th Air Force "battle staff" in Thailand and the evacuation fleet itself.

Smith, still a bit shaken, called Michler from his quarters and asked for an estimate of the rate of fire and incidentals. He was advised soon afterward —nearly a round per minute; estimated firing position: Nhon Trach, southeast of the city.

Jerry Locksley rang up Polgar again at 4:45 A.M.: no word on the state of the runways. Rockets still falling. "Could have figured out most of that myself," Polgar grumbled. He sounded peevish, annoyed. Evidently he disliked getting information this way—indirectly, through Locksley. But Marv Garrett's Mission Warden officers had forgotten to give Polgar a radio that could tap in on their net. So Locksley was his only recourse. He told the young officer to pack up and prepare to head to the Embassy at once. He and his driver, Ut, would be around to pick him up in a few minutes.

Most of the thirteen Americans who shared my apartment building were soon huddling around Kingsley and me on the roof. The three women in the group had outfitted themselves in helmets and flak jackets and were as calm as any of the rest of us. Our pocket-size two-way radios crackled with the flow of messages between the Embassy and Tan Son Nhut, but against the thunder of the bombardment it was all but impossible to tell what was being said. Joe's old Green Beret friend, his drinking companion of only a few hours before, kept shaking his head, mumbling, "Going to go down with this goddamn ship."

After the first twenty minutes or so, Joe leaned over and shouted in my ear, "I think we'd better get to the Embassy. All of us. If the NVA turn those things on the city, we'll be stewed in our juices." His imagery seemed only too apropos against the backdrop of the roiling fire clouds over Tan Son Nhut. I told him I'd go in immediately to start processing the intelligence; he agreed to stay behind to make sure everybody in the building got the word.

From the instant the first rocket was sent hurtling toward the enemy, General Van Tien Dung followed the progress of the bombardment through a stream of reports from NVA commando teams just north of Tan Son Nhut. At approximately 5 A.M. he was called to the telephone.

"As our troop columns were simultaneously opening offensive fire," he recounted in his memoirs, "we at the command post received a message from the Politburo, including an appeal and the following directives: all cadres, combatants and party and union members are now called on to display their highest determination, to launch a quick and direct attack on the enemy's last stronghold and to use the powerful force of an invincible army to smash all enemy resistance, to liberate the Saigon–Gia Dinh municipality completely and to win a total victory for the historic campaign bearing great Uncle Ho's name."

After reading the message back to others in the command post, Dung and his senior colleagues drew up a final "mobilization order." Pham Hung, as the senior Politburo member on the spot, had the honor of signing his name to it, the directive that sealed Saigon's fate.

In a series of follow-up messages the leadership in Hanoi advised Dung of Kissinger's latest exchanges with the Soviets. A large number of Americans and Vietnamese, he was told, were to be flown out of Saigon in the next few hours, including the last of the American "military advisors." Although the army was to continue to tighten its noose around the city, it should not attempt to target the airlift itself.

Dung was hardly enthusiastic about this restriction. He had long been suspicious of the evacuation, seeing it as merely a ruse to deny him final victory and perhaps to justify last-minute American intervention. And was it any coincidence the Americans were again asking for a reprieve at the moment the offensive was entering its decisive stage?

The general made his reservations clear to the Politburo, but Le Duan and the rest overruled him. Unlike Dung, they reasoned that completion of the airlift would minimize the risk of American intervention, not increase it.

On this note the long-distance debate was broken off, and Dung turned back to his battle maps. Like any good field commander, however, he resolved to be prepared for the worst. He sat down at a wicker table and jotted out a message to General Tan, commander of the eastern front: If the evacuation were deliberately prolonged—or if the Americans should turn it into a pretext for intervention—Tan should be ready to shell the heart of Saigon itself.

While Dung composed this death warrant, Colonel John Madison, chief of the American delegation to the Joint Military Team, sent a radio message to his North Vietnamese and PRG counterparts at nearby Camp Davis. "The U.S. delegation," he declared, "strongly protests the threats to our safety by your wanton shelling, and calls upon you to immediately guarantee our safety as required by the agreements on privileges and immunities." The Communist delegates, who had once again retired to their bunkers, must have had a good laugh at this one, but in their return message they feigned innocence. "Even we don't know the reason for all this," they told Madison. "We're in the same boat."

Not far away, at the ICCS compound, several others who were "in the same boat" were far less jubilant about it. The remaining members of the

Polish and Hungarian teams had spent most of the previous evening drinking and partying and toasting their Communist brothers on the front. But as the first rockets sailed in just before dawn, the festivities had come to an abrupt halt; now the Hungarian and Polish delegates, the same men who had so expertly duped Polgar and Martin, were running around like frightened sheep, ducking for cover wherever they could find it. Their comrades-at-the-front apparently had not seen fit to inform them in advance of the little surprise they had planned for Tan Son Nhut this morning.

Shortly after 5 A.M. General Smith, in combat fatigues with a .45 on his hip, jogged across the tennis court to the DAO headquarters building. He was still huffing when one of his aides called him to the phone to speak with Martin at the Embassy. "Yes, we're still taking rockets," he told the Ambassador, "and a C-130 is burning." Then he remembered the grimmest detail: two casualties—marines, killed at the gate. There was a pause on the other end of the line. Not sure Martin had heard, Smith started to repeat himself. "Yes, understood," the Ambassador interrupted, the voice choked by laryngitis. He then reminded Smith of the main priority: all DAO personnel must be out of Saigon within the next twelve hours, shelling or no. The C-130 airlift would have to begin at once. What was holding it up? "The runways," Smith said quietly. "We're not sure they're usable."

Back in my apartment I showered and shaved as calmly as I could, slipped into some old pants, a shirt and sports coat, plunked the steel pot back on my head, and stuffed two .38 revolvers into my belt and shoulder holsters. After squeezing back into my flak jacket, I took a last rueful look around my apartment, the few remaining clothes, the radios, the accouterments of an American colonialist in his final hour. I then headed for the elevator.

The Vietnamese and Chinese "Nung" guards at the downstairs entrance saluted as they unlocked the gate for me and ushered me out into the bleak morning. Nungs had long been employed as security personnel at official CIA residences and were considered "reliably" anti-Communist, since many were refugees from North Vietnam or Laos. All of those who greeted me this morning had been promised a seat on an evacuation flight, and expected it. One of them, the husband of my Vietnamese maid, helped me load my battle gear into the back of my Ford Pinto. He saluted again as he opened the door for me. "Remember us," he stuttered in one of his few English phrases. That was the last I saw of him. He and all the rest would be left behind.

My apartment was only a three-minute drive from the Embassy, but as I careened through the empty streets I felt as though I would never cover the distance. When at last I pulled up behind the recreation compound, a Marine guard in battle dress pointed me to a parking place on the street. I shouldered as much of my gear as I could, locked the car, and stumbled up to a back gate. A marine cracked it just enough to let me through. As I hurried past the barred and shuttered canteen building in the recreation area I noticed a lone figure out front—George McArthur, one of those reporters at the Carter dinner two weeks before who'd refused to accept my version of Hanoi's intentions. "Good day, brother!" he drawled, his southern accent drifting like smoke through the dank morning air. "Looks like you're a little burdened down." A few minutes earlier McArthur had learned of the expanded airlift from his old friend Eva Kim; obviously, he was determined not to be left behind. I nodded and hurried on.

Polgar was not yet in his office when I trudged into the operations room on the sixth floor. The duty officer handed me a score of cables and radio messages, including Hanoi's latest propaganda statements, and a copy of Washington's communications review. I sat down at my desk and scribbled out two commentaries for Washington. The intercepts, I concluded, left little doubt of Hanoi's intentions to seize Saigon; the propaganda seemed to close the door definitively on any kind of accommodation. They were the last full-fledged analyses, political, military or otherwise, anyone filed from the American Embassy in Saigon.

Weary of playing spectator, Ken Moorefield left the roof of his apartment building around 5:45 A.M. and clambered downstairs to his apartment to call the motor pool for a car. "I wanted to get to the Embassy and talk to the security people," he said later. "But I might as well have saved myself the trouble. Garrett and his Mission Warden staff were as ignorant of what was going on—the status of the airlift—as I was. So I said, 'What the hell! I'll go where the action is,' and asked Garrett to provide me an escort to Tan Son Nhut.

"The drive out was easy enough. Not many people were too anxious to be out on the streets just now. But when we got to the front gate of the airfield we ran into a problem—my first of the day: the guards wouldn't let us in. Maybe they thought we were journalists, or were just too nervous to be thinking straight at all. Can't blame them for that, though. Rockets were streaming in all over the place. Vietnamese aircraft were taking off in droves, and everybody on the ground, airmen and security police, seemed to be blasting away at will.

"Frankly, I thought we'd never get in. But just when we were preparing to turn back toward town, two rockets spun in only several hundred yards away and all of us dove for a drainage ditch. By the time we pulled ourselves out, the guards were so shaken they didn't give a damn what we did."

By 6 A.M. senior Mission officials were drifting into the Embassy. Polgar had arrived a few minutes earlier and was already in the Ambassador's office, filling him in on the latest news from Tan Son Nhut. Maybe it was time to consider a helo-lift, he suggested—"At the least, cut down that tree in the courtyard." The Ambassador did not even bother to argue with him. The C-130 airlift was still practical, he insisted. That was all. Polgar, exasperated, pulled George Jacobson aside. "Let's cut that tree down anyway," he mumbled, "just to be on the safe side."

At that moment President Ford was holding a late-afternoon conference with his primary energy advisors at the White House. Just as one of the experts began opining drearily on the prospects for another Arab oil embargo, General Brent Scowcroft, Kissinger's principal deputy, tiptoed in and handed the President a note. Tan Son Nhut under shelling attack, it read. Two marines dead. Evacuation temporarily suspended. Ford cleared his throat, thought a moment, then told Scowcroft to summon all members of the National Security Council to an emergency meeting in one hour.

At his headquarters in Honolulu, Admiral Noel Gayler was pacing the floor. He wanted desperately to go to Option IV, but Martin, it seemed, was still stalling. He had tried to put in a direct call to the Embassy a few minutes before, but had been told the Ambassador was "unavailable."

At 6:30 A.M. General Smith issued new instructions to his staff: all remaining DAO personnel were to be ready to leave the minute the C-130 airlift resumed. Colonel Wahle, the Army Attaché, quickly drew up an alert message to be telephoned or radioed to the assembly points downtown, and directed Marine Captain Tony Woods to begin pulling together bus convoys. "Officially" only DAO personnel were to be picked up, but if any other Americans wanted to come aboard, Wahle emphasized, they could.

Shortly before seven a Marine officer dashed in off the runways to give Smith an updated status report. Things were bad out there, he said. Very bad. Vietnamese aircraft were weaving all over the tarmac like crippled birds. Jettisoned fuel tanks, live bombs and other equipment were strewn everywhere, and one F-5 jet, its engine still running, had been abandoned on the taxiway just in front of the loading ramp. Smith kept shaking his head as he listened. How the C-130s were going to land in this chaos, he couldn't imagine. After hearing the officer out, he called Gayler in Honolulu. The next inbound transports, he told the admiral, had better have a fighter escort.

Several hundred yards from Smith's headquarters, Moorefield had just pulled into the DAO processing center. "The place was a madhouse," he recalled, "wall-to-wall chaos. No security, no control, no nothing. There was this Marine captain—Woods was his name—over at the operations center who was supposed to be helping with the evacuation. I decided to go over and ask him for some extra marines to police up the annex. But when I found him I saw he was in no position to offer any kind of assist. Christ, he needed help himself! He had just been ordered to throw together some convoys. But he didn't even know where the assembly points were around town. I did, of course. So I volunteered to give him a hand."

At approximately 7:23 in the evening, Washington time, the National Security Council was convened in emergency session at the White House. They were all there, all the principals of the defense and intelligence establishment:

Ford at the end of the table; Kissinger on his right; then, counterclockwise, Deputy Secretary of State Ingersoll; CIA Director Colby; Schlesinger and his principal deputy, James Clements; General George Brown, chairman of the Joint Chiefs of Staff; and finally, a few other lesser lights. Kissinger opened with a plea for caution. No sense in going to a helo-lift right away, he argued (echoing Martin). The runways at Tan Son Nhut might still be usable. Schlesinger and Brown disagreed, asserting that Option IV was already overdue.

Finally, in an attempt at compromise, Brown suggested a test run: seven C-130s would be ordered to Saigon from the Philippines and Thailand. If they could land, the fixed-wing airlift was on. If not, it had to be Option IV. He also urged dispatching a fighter escort to accompany the planes in, as Smith had recommended to Gayler. But Kissinger was opposed. Any show of force, he insisted, would be misinterpreted by Hanoi.

That much settled, the next topic on the agenda was the status of the Embassy itself. Hanoi's latest statements seemed to make any residual American presence unthinkable, but Martin was still unpersuaded. Perhaps Martin was wrong and the North Vietnamese were right, someone quipped. Kissinger frowned; Ford started to smile, but didn't. At last a decision was reached—again a compromise: the Embassy would be reduced to 150 "hard core" officials. The rest would be moved out during the day with their DAO counterparts.

After the session Kissinger retired to the White House operations center to place a call to Martin. The President, apparently satisfied that his crisis managers had things in hand, joined his wife for a pre-dinner martini in their second-floor living quarters.

By the time Alan Carter arrived at the Embassy around 7:30 A.M., most of his colleagues were already crowded into the Ambassador's suite. "May I join you?" he asked as he walked in. The Ambassador gestured to a sofa. Polgar had just finished highlighting for the group my analysis of Hanoi's latest propaganda statements. He added, as an afterthought, "My people out at Tan Son Nhut say the runways are unserviceable. Perhaps we should consider Option IV." His deputy, Pittman, shifted uneasily in his chair; he and everybody else could see what was coming. Martin's face suddenly had gone taut as old parchment. "How do you know the runways are out?" the Ambassador rasped. "You're going to take the word of a subordinate over the phone?" Polgar tried to answer, but the Ambassador ignored him, sliding neatly into a digression. "Anyway," he said, "I still think Hanoi intends to negotiate."

At this point a hand shot up in the back of the room. "Where do you find evidence of that?" asked Joe Bennett, the political counselor, trying to sound authoritative. Two or three of his colleagues looked at each other in surprise. Joe Bennett, Martin loyalist, anti-Communist to the core, was hardly one to question the Ambassador's judgments. But there he was, letting his doubts show.

Martin did not deign a direct reply. "I can tell you this," he said, "before I make any decision I'm going out to Tan Son Nhut to have a look for myself." Carter felt his mouth drop open despite himself. There were murmured protests, but before anyone could pose a coherent objection, Martin was summoned to the phone to take another call from Kissinger.

When he returned a few minutes later his face had lost some of its toughness. "The President agrees to go with the fixed-wing airlift for now," he murmured. Then he paused, and added with a resigned sigh, "But he wants us to pare this Embassy down to a hundred and fifty people, a small hard core."

Everybody was suddenly talking at once. Polgar started to say something, but apparently thought better of it. Instead, he merely sat back, shaking his head. So this was Washington's idea of crisis management. A small hard core! That meant he and everybody else would have to spend the next few hours drawing up new manning tables. Fiddling while Rome burned. That's what it amounted to.

As the group scattered, Jim Devine, motioned to Shep Lowman. How was he doing with those Vietnamese VIPs? he asked. Lowman assured him most of the principals had been contacted. Nonetheless, he was worried: What if the C-130s couldn't land? What then? No chopper lift could take out all the nominees. Devine thought a moment. There were always the barges, he suggested. Better start building a plan around them.

Ten minutes later Lacy Wright and the rest who made up Lowman's vest-pocket task force were on the phone, contacting the hundreds of Vietnamese they had called hours before. An airlift might not be practical, they warned. But there was an alternative, much riskier. (The barges were not mentioned explicitly.) Who would be willing to try it? Those who agreed were told to ignore the twenty-four-hour curfew and to make their way as quickly as possible to one of several designated villas around town. An Embassy officer would soon be around to provide instructions.

As Wright dialed his twentieth or thirtieth Vietnamese, he was suffering severe misgivings. "We're calling too many," he told a colleague. "We'll be inundated." Sadly, he was right.

On his way back from the Ambassador's office Polgar stopped by my own to tell me I was to be part of the Station's own fifty-man "hard core." We might take casualties, he remarked almost nonchalantly. Was I willing to risk it? I nodded. By now I was so weary—and so inured to the nightmares being played out around me—I felt almost bulletproof.

George Jacobson, meanwhile, was frantically searching for a chopper to fly Martin to DAO. He called the Air America terminal at Tan Son Nhut, but the harried and exhausted flight controller on the other end said he couldn't put any of his fleet in the air just yet. At the time the shelling began, only two Air America pilots had been on duty at the terminal; the rest were still being rounded up and briefed. Several choppers, moreover, were even now tied up in Can Tho, on assignment to the CIA base.

When Martin was advised of this, he angrily pulled on his suit jacket and stalked out to the elevator. "Goddamnit," he muttered, "I'll drive."

At 7:30 A.M. the Assistant Air Attaché, Colonel Michler, and several other officers made another jogging tour of the loading area across the highway from the DAO compound. "In their opinion," General Smith later remarked, "the resumption of a fixed-wing evacuation was not possible at that time." The general considered this judgment final and ordered all DAO personnel to prepare for a helo-lift out of the tennis courts. He called the Embassy to alert Martin. But the Ambassador was "not available," Eva Kim explained. He was already on his way to Tan Son Nhut to survey the runways himself. Smith literally had to steady himself on the edge of a desk as he absorbed this piece of bad news.

The general suffered another jarring surprise a few minutes later. Without any warning at all, five or six top officers in the Vietnamese air force marched into DAO headquarters and demanded asylum and help in leaving the country. Smith greeted them coolly, had them disarmed, and then shoved them into an empty office. Ready to give up the fight, were they? Well, not quite yet. They could still perform one useful function. Smith ordered his staff to keep the airmen under lock and key until DAO had completed its own pullout, just to ensure the cooperation of the rest of the Vietnamese military.

Moorefield had never driven a bus in his life. But when he and Captain Woods slid like base-stealers into the DAO motor pool, he knew at once that inexperience was going to be the least of his worries this morning. Despite Smith's alert the night before, none of the dozen or so buses slated for the downtown pickups even had a full gas tank. The gas pumps themselves were locked shut and the Vietnamese drivers and attendants had run off. Worst of all, he and Woods seemed to be in the center of the cross hairs. "Rockets began slamming in all around us," Moorefield recalled, "one of them no more than forty meters away. The VC obviously had us bracketed, and I remember thinking as I ran for the tall grass, Ain't gonna be any evacuation today. They'll blow us away. There was a Vietnamese trembling in the dirt beside me. I grabbed him and asked him if he knew how to drive. He was so scared he couldn't think of anything to say but 'Yes.' I dragged him up, flung him into one of the buses, and said, 'Okay, prove it!' Woods found some others and did the same. The two of us then jumped into a jeep and a staff car and took off for Saigon, four or five buses trailing behind."

The time was 8:15 A.M. To all intents and purposes, the first phase of the final evacuation of Vietnam was under way.

In the DAO processing center, Don Hays had a wailing Vietnamese baby under one arm, two suitcases under the other, and was scanning the crowd desperately for the proprietors. Through the smoke and haze over the airfield he saw a small plane take a direct hit and spin out of the sky like a burned-out meteor. Moments later an American Air Force colonel pushed toward him through the crowd. "We got orders," he yelled to Hays. "All Americans gotta clear this compound now and regroup over at the pads in the main headquarters area."

"Can't do that," Hays exclaimed, dropping the suitcases. "There're maybe three thousand Vietnamese in here. You can't just abandon them." The colonel pushed his face toward him. "I don't take orders from the ranks!" he snarled. "Move!"

Hays, having once been a infantryman himself, knew there was no point arguing with a colonel. He handed the baby to the officer and ran off to look for a telephone. He finally managed to reach Jazynka at the Embassy. "No need to worry," Jazynka told him. "The Ambassador is coming out there for a personal assessment. He'll know what to do." Hays hung up and walked back to the colonel. "Okay, I'll cooperate," he sighed, "provided you keep me informed." The colonel nodded, surrendered the baby, and sauntered off. Hays began quietly passing word to the fifty or so Americans scattered through the crowds to move toward the gymnasium. A CIA man was waiting to usher them out through a back door.

Downtown at the Presidential Palace, General Timmes climbed out of his Embassy limousine and followed a shriveled old functionary up the steps to Minh's office. To his surprise, there was not one army officer or security guard to be seen.

The new President of the Republic, in a simple tunic, greeted him warmly. Timmes apologized for troubling him; he had come only to see if there was anything more the Americans could do. Minh frowned thoughtfully, then shook his head. The initiative had passed to the French, he said. Mérillon was due to arrive for an interview in a few minutes. He felt there was still a slight chance for a settlement.

Timmes leaned forward, scribbling notes. What led the French to believe this? he inquired. First of all, replied Minh, they reckoned the Chinese were still opposed to North Vietnamese hegemony across Vietnam and would use their influence to stall off a total Communist victory. Secondly, Hanoi did not have an administrative apparatus sufficient to govern the entire country and might therefore be receptive to a transitional regime. Most important, the PRG itself was against North Vietnamese domination. Timmes sighed. All of these were the same tired arguments the French had been peddling for the past month, to no avail. But there was no use debating them now. Timmes assured Minh he would convey this information to Martin.

Three blocks away at the Embassy, Polgar was taking an utterly different line—at last. He told his morning staff meeting the bombardment of Tan Son Nhut was "an important signal."

"Like a bullet through the brain," someone whispered in the back of the room. There was a titter of laughter. Pittman chewed his cigar, adjusted his glasses. "Anybody with Vietnamese to take care of should send them to

Newport or the navy yards," he said. "We've got barges there to take them out." Several officers gasped in surprise. Few of us had ever heard of the barges before.

Around 8:30 P.M., Washington time, Nancy Kissinger arrived at the White House in evening clothes. She and the Secretary had tickets for *Present Laughter,* a Noël Coward revival, and had planned a night on the town. But Kissinger told her the evening's entertainment was out. Vietnam was in its final hour.

A few minutes later, as President and Mrs. Ford sat down to dinner, Kissinger and General Scowcroft, walked across the White House lawn to the Executive Office Building next door. "Any news?" a reporter called out to them. Kissinger smiled benignly, but said nothing.

Across the Potomac, Secretary Schlesinger and General Brown had just wolfed down hamburgers from the Pentagon's mess and were heading for the operations center on the second floor. When they walked in, the loudspeakers on the wall were barking and screeching with long-distance radio pickups from Task Force '76, USSAG in Thailand, and DAO in Saigon.

At approximately 8:47 P.M. a call was patched in from Gayler. How about a fighter escort for those C-130s due into Saigon? he suggested. Brown picked up the microphone and gave him the bad news: the President was against any undue saber-rattling. The few moments of silence on the other end of the circuit spoke volumes.

Under the best of circumstances the drive from Tan Son Nhut air base was a fifteen-minute warm-up for the "Indy 500." But this morning, as Moorefield and Captain Woods guided their bus convoy into the heart of the city, the fifteen minutes stretched out to an hour; the entire population seemed to have shrugged off the twenty-four-hour curfew and taken to the streets in a frenetic last effort to save itself. "Cars and trucks were hurtling everywhere," Moorefield noted. "Blind old mama-sans and panicked army officers were behind every wheel. And the police at the checkpoints had no qualms about putting a few bursts in the air just to keep you awake.

"Halfway into town we got a radio message from the DAO ops center: 'Proceed to the Ambassador's Residence at once.' Woods nearly drove into a tree when he heard that. He hadn't been briefed on any pickup at the Ambassador's—didn't even know where the place was. I did, of course, and told him we could swing by with no difficulty. We soon discovered the reason for the detour: it was to pick up the Ambassador's household staff and their families.

"Woods really got pissed off at that. Both of us felt we were wasting valuable time. But in fact the trip turned out to be a sort of a plus. When we got to the Residence an Embassy maintenance guy was on hand with a fuel truck, so we were able to gas up the buses we had brought from DAO half empty.

"The Ambassador wasn't there. Mrs. Martin may have been in the house somewhere, but we didn't see her. One of the two security guards on duty said we were to take the housekeepers and maids down to the docks.

" 'The docks!' I yelled. 'I don't know what you're talking about.' 'You know, the barges,' he said. Well, that set me on edge a little. Woods too. We didn't have the faintest idea what, or where, these 'barges' were. The only thing we knew was we were being told to make another detour and again delay our pickups.

"I decided to call the Embassy to straighten things out. Jim Devine came to the phone. 'Look, the captain and I are in the dark,' I said. 'What's going on?' Devine seemed very uptight. 'You have an order, direct from the Ambassador,' he replied. 'Don't question it.' He wouldn't even tell me where the barges were! Luckily, the security guards had some details.

"I went back outside to discuss tactics with Woods. We agreed to squeeze all the Vietnamese into two buses and send them down to the docks with one of the security guys. We would take the other two and continue on our way.

"Once that was worked out, I walked back into the Residence to see who was left. I found Martin's number-one houseboy, Mr. Chinh, and his cook, Mr. Canh, sitting quietly in the kitchen. 'Mr. Chinh, aren't you leaving?' I asked. He shrugged. 'Maybe I go tomorrow,' he said. 'There isn't going to be any tomorrow,' I told him. But I saw he really didn't understand. So I shook his hand and wished him good luck. Then I was off and running."

While Moorefield and Woods were biding their time at the Ambassador's, other DAO and Embassy personnel put the rest of the buses on the streets. By 9 A.M. one convoy had already made its first passenger run and was rumbling back to Tan Son Nhut to unload. Soon Embassy officers downtown began bombarding the DAO operations center with orders and requests, demanding pickups at this or that address. Lehmann insisted that four buses be diverted to the Embassy and placed at his disposal. DAO dutifully complied, but after an hour or so Lehmann lost track of the vehicles, and the lot of them remained parked, unused, behind the Embassy throughout most of the day, even as DAO frantically shuffled and reshuffled the remaining convoys to ensure coverage of all the designated assembly points.

Under DAO's standing "surface extraction" plan, Air America choppers were to operate in tandem with the bus convoys to move evacuees from the downtown area to the flight line at Tan Son Nhut. But because of the difficulties of alerting and assembling pilots at the Air America terminal, only a few of the choppers were airborne as the first of the convoys fanned out around the city. Within the next half-hour the Air America landing strip itself was struck by several rockets, and in the panic and confusion a group of armed Vietnamese paratroopers hijacked four of the company's choppers, leaving only eighteen for the rooftop roundelay.

General Smith immediately directed Air America to shift its flight control center to the more secure confines of the DAO compound itself. But this, too, created problems. Several weeks before, the airline's management had refused

Smith's invitation to set up auxiliary fuel pumps inside the DAO grounds. Drums of emergency stock had been stashed at several of the thirteen rooftop pads around town, but none was outfitted with the pumps and gauges necessary for fast fueling. Consequently, as one after another of the choppers ran low on gas, they had to peel off and fly out to the fleet offshore to pick up more. Initially this seemed a drawback, threatening to complicate and infinitely prolong the entire surface extraction plan. But soon General Smith and his flight controllers realized they could turn a profit from it. Instead of dumping their passengers at the Embassy or DAO before heading out to the fleet, each of the choppers began making the forty-minute run with a full load. Air America thus began hauling Americans and Vietnamese out of the city long before the military itself got into the act.

Shortly after 9 A.M. the Ambassador's bulletproof black Chevrolet limousine wheeled into the DAO compound. General Smith quickly ushered Martin into the downstairs operations bunker where several Vietnamese and American officers were gathered to brief him. Colonel Luong, intelligence chief for the JGS, wasted few words. The military situation was hopeless, he said, the army was collapsing and NVA commandos had already penetrated the northern perimeters of the air base. Legro and McCurdy outlined the sad state of the runways.

"Are there any troops to defend Tan Son Nhut?" Martin asked. No, Legro replied. Luong was right. The army was falling apart. The Ambassador nodded, then motioned to Smith to follow him into a side office. He was determined, he told the general, to evacuate as many Vietnamese as possible. A helo-lift would never be sufficient for that. The C-130's would have to land.

As Smith tried to object, Martin turned his back, picked up a secure phone, and put in a direct call to Washington. Scowcroft came on the line. The Ambassador repeated his views to him: a resumption of the fixed-wing airlift was mandatory. Scowcroft tried to sound sympathetic. The National Security Council, he assured the Ambassador, was fully in favor of that option at the moment. The C-130 airlift would continue as long as possible. Before hanging up, Martin scribbled down those last words and read them back out loud for Smith's benefit. He then slammed down the receiver and strode back into the main operations room.

Erich Von Marbod was sitting on a desk in a far corner, sipping coffee. Decked out in a khaki flight suit, with a Swedish K machine gun slung over his shoulder, he looked more like a pint-sized guerrilla fighter than an Assistant Secretary of Defense. The immaculately tailored Martin gave him a deprecatory stare and started to brush past. But just as he reached the door he turned and walked back to Von Marbod, his face suddenly going soft. "Well, Erich, how are you this morning," he said, smiling, as he put an arm around Von Marbod's shoulder. "I wonder if you could do me a favor. It's about my wife, Dottie. How about arranging a flight for her out of the country? You've got a lot of friends over at 7th Air Force headquarters in Thailand. Think you could get them to send a special plane over for her?"

Von Marbod stared at him. "Goddamnit, Graham!" he sputtered. "Don't you realize what's happening? We're catching a ration of shit out there on the airfield. There's no time for a fixed-wing operation. Any plane that survives the first ten minutes on those runways will be mobbed by Vietnamese in the next ten. Only way I can get Dottie or anybody else out is by chopper."

The tired eyes turned dead-cold. "I've just told the President we'll go fixed-wing," Martin said archly, and started to walk off.

Von Marbod grabbed him by the sleeve. "Why not come out to the flight line with me and see for yourself?" Martin shook his head and tried to pull away. At that instant a tremendous explosion pulsated through the building. Von Marbod felt a shudder run through the Ambassador's arm. "Still want to go with fixed-wing?" he asked.

Martin simply looked at him, his mouth moving wordlessly. Then he turned and without saying anything walked to the door. Von Marbod later told a subordinate he was convinced at that moment the Ambassador had changed his mind.

Smith was not so sure, and as soon as he had packed Martin off in his Chevrolet, this time with a full armed escort, he placed a call to Gayler in Honolulu. Back in Washington, at the White House and the Pentagon, other officials listened in on the conversation as it was played back over their long-distance monitors.

When Smith had finished explaining the Ambassador's views, Gayler cleared his throat, said it looked as though everything hinged on those C-130s now heading for Saigon. If they could land, the Ambassador would have his airlift.

Smith put down the phone and summoned Colonel John Madison of the the Joint Military Team. Madison and his deputy, Colonel Harry Summers, were to take their boys downtown to the Embassy, he said. Since the North Vietnamese had already indicated they wanted the American delegation to stay on even after the DAO's departure, maybe it would be wise for them to set up shop closer to the nerve center—and to the Ambassador.

A few minutes later a Marine officer, in helmet and flak jacket, rushed up to Smith. Just no way those C-130s could set down, he told the general. There was debris all over the runways. Worse, Vietnamese troopers had just attacked and overrun one of the main loading areas.

"Good God!" Smith gasped. "Pull everybody out of there at once—passengers, marines, everybody!" He then grabbed a microphone and ordered the incoming C-130s to swing into a holding pattern.

In Washington, Schlesinger was already on the phone to the White House. "For Christ's sake, let's go to the helos," he yelled at Scowcroft. For the first time Kissinger's aide seemed ready to agree.

Smith placed another direct call to Gayler at 10:25 A.M., Saigon time. "It's got to be Option IV," he insisted. The admiral breathed a loud sigh that could be heard over the line in Saigon. He would immediately relay the proposal to the Pentagon, he promised.

Smith then called Martin, who by now had arrived back at the Embassy. The C-130 airlift was a washout, he stammered. It was Option IV or nothing. Well, the Ambassador replied, his voice struggling against the laryngitis, he would take Smith's views under consideration. He would go with the helicopters if necessary.

Kissinger, meanwhile, had just called Ford from his office in the Executive Office Building to say Option IV was imperative. But Ford was puzzled; the signals were now changing so quickly he couldn't be sure which ones to believe. Before making a final decision, he said, he would ask Martin's advice one last time.

At 10:43 P.M., as the Washington Special Action Group went into emergency session, Kissinger got hold of Martin on a secure line. He explained his own views and waited for him to take the cue. After a long pause the Ambassador said simply, "Let's go with Option IV." Kissinger murmured agreement and promised only one hour's lead time before the first choppers came in.*

With Martin committed, Kissinger contacted Ford to apprise him. The President immediately directed Schlesinger to set the operation in motion. At 10:51 P.M., Washington time, the execute order for Option IV, "Frequent Wind," flashed out over command channels.

At the operations center in the State Department somebody walked out of the communications room and said to the assembled officers, "Looks like it's Code 3—total evacuation by helicopter. Agence France-Presse has just picked it up off the airwaves." At first no one could quite believe it, but a few minutes later a cable from Gayler in Honolulu provided confirmation. Frank Scotton, the USIA officer who had spent much of his career in Vietnam, felt anything but elation. He wondered: Would there be time?

Within the next half-hour American Service Radio in Saigon spun an old familiar ballad—"I'm Dreaming of a White Christmas." After letting the piece run through several times, station staffers put on a long-playing tape of Sousa marches and left for Tan Son Nhut.

Word of the impending helo-lift circulated only informally within the Embassy. Few of us were alerted in any systematic way, and some remained unaware until the big choppers were actually overhead. Shep Lowman, whose role in the evacuation of Vietnamese was so crucial, did not learn of Option IV till midafternoon. All he knew as he called the last of his Vietnamese VIPs was that two helicopters, presumably from the Air America fleet, would be

---

*The verdict rendered by intelligence officers at the morning's WSAG session only strengthened the case for Option IV. Said CIA Director Colby, "Communist forces are now on the outskirts of Saigon and clearly in position to occupy it. The Minh government has been overtaken by events, and a complete North Vietnamese military takeover in Saigon appears inevitable today or tomorrow."

available for a few pickups later in the day. His own contacts would have to rely mainly on the barges.

When Lowman had finished briefing the last candidate on his list, he hung up the phone, ripped it out of the wall, and slipped into a light tweed jacket. He had chosen his wardrobe carefully this morning. If he was dressed like a diplomat, he assured himself, the Vietnamese would treat him like one. He then went downstairs and into the Embassy courtyard, squeezed through the side gate, and climbed into his battered car as hundreds of Vietnamese bystanders pressed around him. Inching forward, with his horn blaring, he drove to a villa a short distance away where he had told a group of the VIPs to gather.

At about the same time one of his colleagues embarked on a similar mission of his own. After alerting the Vietnamese on his list, Lacy Wright borrowed Eva Kim's Toyota and picked his way through the traffic to a villa he had been using as an assembly point for friends and relatives of Foreign Service officers. There he collected his remaining name lists and the Vietnamese who'd been helping him. He then drove with them back to the Embassy. There was a huge crush outside the front gate when he pulled up, and Wright and his companions were obliged to slip in through the recreation compound to the rear.

As they elbowed their way through the crowds alongside the swimming pool, three Mission Warden officers and several marines struggled past them with large canvas bags over their shoulders. Wright later learned that the sacks contained over $2 million in Embassy contingency funds. The Ambassador had just ordered the money destroyed.

The marines dumped the cash into metal drums at the far end of the compound, sprinkled on some gasoline, and struck a match.

But just as flames swirled through the first container, Boudreau came running through the crowds. "Stop! Stop!" he shouted. The Ambassador had changed his mind. He wanted to keep the money around a bit longer, in case he could work out a last-minute settlement. The marines clamped the lid on the flaming mass, trying to snuff it out.

Some of the money was salvaged, much of it stained and charred. Later in the day, as the first of the helicopters came in, the downdraft ripped open several of the bags that had been left at the edge of the parking lot, scattering much of the remaining cash to the four winds. In the meantime, one Embassy officer managed to palm at least $80,000 of it. His Vietnamese girl friend tucked the bonanza under her dress and smuggled it onto one of the choppers. Once aboard the evacuation fleet, he was searched for contraband but she was not. Hundreds of slightly damaged $20 bills later turned up at the refugee resettlement points on Guam and Wake Islands.

Among the first of the evacuees General Smith sent out to Admiral Whitmire's fleet as the Air America shuttle gathered speed during the morning were his own wife and the two top-ranking naval officers, Admirals Hugh Benton and Owen Oberg, who had been part of the DAO planning staff since the beginning of April. Simple prudence dictated Mrs. Smith's departure. Admiral Gayler, on the other hand, had insisted that Benton and Oberg be withdrawn. As he had explained to Smith he wanted no U.S. "flag officers" in Saigon as the situation deteriorated.

Erich Von Marbod also was included in this early group of evacuees— by his own choice. Since daybreak he had been desperate to get out to the fleet so that he could arrange for the removal from Saigon of what remained of the South Vietnamese air force.

Von Marbod's Air America chopper had no sooner set its wheels on the deck of the USS *Blueridge,* Whitmire's command ship, than he was off and running at full speed. He headed straight for the radio room and sent a flash message to Secretary Schlesinger in Washington. Explaining that he had just come out of Saigon with one of the first chopper loads, he asked for immediate assistance in completing the salvage operation for which Schlesinger had made him responsible a week before. What he wanted most of all, he said, was use of one of Whitmire's aircraft carriers.

A reply "eyes only" from the Secretary soon came sizzling back over the ship's radio circuits. Whitmire immediately called Von Marbod to the captain's deck. He was not exactly happy with Schlesinger's message. Not only had the Defense Secretary reaffirmed Von Marbod's mission; he had also given him direct command of the USS *Dubuque,* one of Whitmire's "landing dock transports," a helicopter carrier. What was going on, anyway? Whitmire spluttered at Von Marbod as the two read over the message. Putting a civilian in command of a U.S. Navy warship! Why, it just couldn't be done!

But it was done, for the cable from the Pentagon was signed by Schlesinger himself.

Von Marbod thanked Whitmire for his understanding and then choppered over to the USS *Dubuque.* The ship soon set sail for An Thoi Island, near Phu Quoc off the delta, where Von Marbod planned to set up a communications net to help guide wayward Vietnamese aircraft to Thailand.

In the meantime, his assistant, Rich Armitage, boarded another of Whitmire's ships and directed it to Con Son Island, off the eastern coast of the delta, for a rendezvous with the Vietnamese naval vessels that were to leave Saigon within the next few hours.

Around midmorning Moorefield's bus convoy finally arrived back at DAO to unload the first of its passengers. "As we pulled up to the post office building, the rockets started raining in on us like the Fourth of July," he recounted. "The NVA obviously had a forward observer staked out to call in the shots whenever a convoy rolled in. As you might expect, our passengers went berserk over the shelling. All of them suddenly were screaming, ducking under the seats, crying to get the hell out of those buses. Another American and I pulled them off as fast as we could and shoved them into the post office. There were some who couldn't walk—babies and old women—so we carried them, all the while kicking excess luggage out of the way. And those goddamn newspaper photographers with us—they were getting all tangled up in their equipment. 'Leave it!' I yelled to them. 'For chrissakes, leave it!' But not a one of them would part with his precious tripods or tote bag—or raise a hand to help with the Vietnamese.

"By the time we rammed everybody into the building, my Vietnamese driver had run off and I had to bargain with another poor son-of-a-bitch to take his place. Only by promising to evacuate him and his family could I persuade him to cooperate. Unfortunately, he later got lost along the way and I was never able to make good on that promise. Anyway, for better or worse, we were off again."

Even on his best days Joe Kingsley was hardly a couturier's delight. But when he limped into the office sometime after ten o'clock he looked like a man who had been caught in the back blast of an F-5 jet fighter. The black hair was sweat-plastered, the shirt torn and grease-smudged, and the eyes looked like red springs, and as he flung the armload of hand grenades and machine guns down on the desk he might as well have been casting off the burdens of the world. He had spent the past three hours helping Americans and Vietnamese at our apartment building claw their way to the Embassy. "Maybe still some people in the building, for all I know," he grunted. "Every time I sent somebody out, somebody else sneaked in. The Viets all thought a 747 was going to land on the roof and haul them out. I tried to tell them otherwise, but . . ."

The buzz of the intercom interrupted him: Pittman—front office. "I'll handle him," Joe said, and wavered off down the hall. Pittman had a new task for him, as impossible as his last. "Go down to see Jacobson," Pittman told him. "Try to arrange to get some of our Vietnamese out to the barges at Newport."

"Newport!" Joe exclaimed. "Jesus, that place has been out of bounds since yesterday. VC all over the place. No way we're gonna get people there."

But Pittman persisted, and Joe, good soldier that he was, did as he was told. He went down to Jacobson's office on the third floor to seek guidance. And Jacobson confirmed his suspicions: even on this side of the bridge the roads to Newport were impassable. Carmody, the Naval Attaché, had already directed that the few remaining vessels there be shifted to the Khanh Hoi docks downtown, where Mel Chatman and Bob Lanigan had their own flat-bottoms lashed up.

While Joe tried to promote an understanding between the third and sixth floors of the Embassy, I continued to spend my energies far less usefully. For the past few hours I had been riffling papers and trying to make sense of what little intelligence there was. Whenever a cable or radio message was slipped into my In box, I scanned it quickly, memorized what was meaningful, and then tossed it into a "burn bag" destined for the incinerators. Each piece of intelligence pointed to the conclusion I had reached weeks before: the Communists intended to capture this city in the shortest possible time.

I also began destroying the last of my situation maps and classified files.

Though I was to be part of the Station's hard core, I had no desire to face a victorious North Vietnamese army with even one drawerful of sensitive data. Most of the maps were mounted on heavy "briefing boards" and there was only one way to break them apart—with bayonets. I felt almost elated as I hacked and slashed through the accumulated wisdom of the past two years. By late morning my office was a garbage heap, shreds of cardboard everywhere. Only one item was left untouched—a huge poster-size photograph of a Japanese calendar girl with her T-shirt hitched up to her shoulders. Joe and I had often joked there were two ways of looking at that poster. On good days there was no question the tanned, smiling model was taking her shirt off. But on bad days you had to allow she might be putting it back on. Now I saw only the cover-up.

Elsewhere in the Embassy other staffers were frantically shredding their way through their own remaining files. One secretary gleefully threw a $500 typewriter down the stairwell. The shimmering grind of the two rooftop incinerators continued to muffle the explosions at Tan Son Nhut.

Outside, in the Embassy compound, Marine guards were now pacing nervously along the walls. Countless hands groped at the latticework of the front gate as hundreds of Vietnamese begged to be let in, many shaking white slips of paper, undoubtedly some sort of claim to passage. Inside, several of their more fortunate countrymen, most of them cooks and chauffeurs who had shown up with their Embassy employers at sunrise, stood patiently to one side of the parking lot waiting for a bus ride to Tan Son Nhut. In the recreation area nearly a thousand more Vietnamese were wandering about in no particular order. A few of them had quite openly and calmly broken into the small grocery store and were now pilfering the stocks. Several of my CIA colleagues decided to join them, and soon turned up in Polgar's office with armloads of wines and cheeses they'd managed to "liberate" from the masses.

Just before eleven I took an elevator down to the ground floor. The lobby, overflowing with Vietnamese and American families, looked like the economy deck on a third-rate freighter. TV cameramen with huge backpacks trudged back and forth in the parking lot outside, and CIA officers bobbed and weaved to avoid the indifferent glass eye as they circulated in and out of the building. Two correspondents from the *New York Times,* perched on a packing crate in a corner, started to jump up when they spotted me. But I turned my back on them. In their trembling eagerness they reminded me a little too much of jackals on a death scent. I simply had no stomach for a journalist's curiosity any more.

In the meantime, Polgar, my energetic if not always detatched commander in chief, was beginning to show the strain. It was not the fear or tension that now broke down his reserve, at least not that alone, but a last obsessive concern as compelling as the passion for a settlement that had dominated him during the past few weeks.

Among the senior Mission Council members, Polgar was one of the few who had actually become "Vietnam-imprinted" during his tour, developing close personal ties to Vietnamese high and low that went beyond the demands of the profession. Now, as the morning wasted away and the old order collapsed around him, his sympathies and attachments began tearing at him like a guilty memory. Hour after hour I watched the disintegration take place, the tough little man I knew so well dissolving into someone I hardly recognized at all. I was moved to the depths of my feelings; I wanted to help, but knew it was pointless to try. As Polgar himself later told me, he was sinking rapidly into an "emotional coma."

One group of Vietnamese in particular riveted his attention—thirty old friends and associates he'd promised to help days before. It was a strange and mixed group: politicians, policemen and simply a few old social contacts, including a woman employed by the Vietnamese Ministry of the Interior for whom he had great admiration.

He had called them all the night before and instructed them to assemble at his residence at eleven o'clock the following morning. But now, as the appointed hour approached and he prepared to go out to pick them up, he suddenly found himself locked in.

The barriers at the side gate came down just as Polgar's chauffeur was bringing his limousine up to the back door of the Embassy. It had all happened so fast: someone in the street had triggered a hand grenade, and then, without a moment's hesitation, the marines at the gate had thrown on the padlocks and halted all traffic in and out. When Polgar saw what was going on, he ran up to a Marine corporal and pleaded to be allowed to drive out. But the corporal said no—"and I don't give a damn who you are!" So there Polgar was, trapped in the Embassy at the very moment his favored Vietnamese were gathering at his villa ten blocks away.

As he stood by the gate, staring helplessly into the sea of faces, he heard a familiar voice floating toward him out of the crowd. It was a high, uneven voice, a slight lilt to it. Moments later General Dang Van Quang, Thieu's former security advisor, thrust himself up to the gate. He was wearing a long trench coat and dark glasses and was carrying two leaden briefcases. "Let that man through!" Polgar snapped at the corporal. A heated argument ensued, but finally the marine did as he was ordered, cracking the gate just enough to let fat old Quang wriggle through.

For the next few hours Quang roamed around Polgar's sixth-floor suite, looking very much like a plump kumquat on stilts, in his tailored navy-blue suit and his diamonds. He spent a good deal of time on the phone, for in his haste to slip into the Embassy he had left his son and his nephew outside. Now he was trying to reach friends to ask them to help.

Most of us tried to ignore Quang as we rushed in and out of the front office, for he was nobody's favorite Vietnamese now. The CIA had paid and pampered him over the years and ensured his position with Thieu, and yet in the end he had betrayed us, failing to inform us of Thieu's decision to withdraw from the highlands. So Quang in his final hours in Saigon labored and agonized alone, and when he was choppered off the roof later in the day—without his son—some of us thought, Good riddance.

•   •   •

When Polgar left the courtyard and came back to his office, he looked decades older. "What can I do?" he said over and over again as he paced around the anteroom. "I promised those Vietnamese I'd pick them up at my house. I can't just leave them there." Pittman grabbed him by the arm and began reeling off alternatives. "Maybe we could send a chopper over to pull them out?" he suggested. "Won't work," I interjected. "The Mission Wardens' office reports indiscriminate sniping in the neighborhood. No chopper or bus can get in right now."

I then remembered 6 Chien Si Circle, my own residence, which was not too far from Polgar's, and proposed a pickup there. The roof had been outfitted for choppers; it seemed as reasonable an alternative as any. Polgar nodded. "Good, good, I'll send Ut to guide them over there. A chopper can go in and pull them out. Good, good."

A short while later Ut, Polgar's five-foot five-inch Vietnamese chauffeur, slipped out of the Embassy gate with a portable radio in his back pocket. From that point on, Polgar's overriding preoccupation was the odyssey of those thirty Vietnamese as they tried to make their way to safety.

"T. D. Latz" did not look the part of a hero. A former U-2 pilot with an Arkansas twang, he walked with a limp, was blind in one eye, and his gray scruff of a beard had all the dash of a soiled Brillo pad. But as the ranking Air America officer at the Embassy, he knew the limits and capabilities of the available Air America helicopters as none of the rest of us did, and given the hour and the circumstances, he was the man Polgar now needed most.

Shortly after sending Ut on his way, Polgar gave Latz a call on a two-way radio. The old airman at that moment was high above the city in an Air America Huey, guiding the pilot to a clutch of frightened Americans on a rooftop landing pad. Within the next twenty minutes his chopper clattered to a landing on the Embassy's own roof and Latz ambled into Polgar's anteroom, muttering something about fuel gauges and lost air time. Polgar took him by the arm. "Look," he said. "I want you to go over to 6 Chien Si Circle and pick up thirty of my people." Latz gazed warily over at me. Several days before, we had discussed the evacuation drill at Chien Si and had concluded the chances of a safe follow-through were depressingly slim, particularly in view of the size of the pad and the possibility of ground fire.

"He'd better take some marines along," I interposed as Latz thought through the idea. "There're still some Vietnamese in that building. They'll be looking for a ride too."

Polgar did not hear, or chose not to. "Okay?" he said, clutching the big man's hand.

"Okay, Mr. Polgar," Latz replied, "but I'll have to take me a sidearm for security."

Twenty minutes later T. D. Latz climbed back into his helicopter and was off to 6 Chien Si Circle, to await Ut and his little band.

•   •   •

Soon afterward Polgar was confronted with another equally "delicate" problem. I was on one of my myriad trips to his office when I all but stumbled over it. As I walked into the reception room I noticed an unlikely visitor slumped on one of the sofas. I had seen him at cocktail parties and other Embassy functions, but now, in his sweat-stained gray shirt and brown trousers, Colonel Toth looked like anything but the high-ranking Hungarian military officer he was.

"What the hell is he doing here!" I whispered to one of the secretaries as Toth got up and sauntered into Polgar's office. It was undoubtedly the first time a Communist of his rank and position had been admitted to this innermost of all of Polgar's inner sanctums. "He's trying to persuade the Old Man to rescue the Hungarian and Polish team members at Tan Son Nhut," the secretary said dryly. "They've been under shelling since daybreak."

Over at the CIA's auxiliary offices in the Norodom complex next to the main chancery, Jerry Locksley, erstwhile duty officer, was busy at the incinerators. He and several colleagues had been toiling there for hours, shredding and burning the Station's personnel files, which for some reason had been left to the last minute. There was also something else, equally sensitive, yet to be destroyed—thousands upon thousands of the laminated name cards the Station had had printed up to serve as seat tickets for high-risk Vietnamese on E-day. None had ever been distributed, and as Locksley tossed one after another into the incinerators he felt as though he were consigning the intended recipients themselves to oblivion. He knew they would now be left behind, each of them a long-time agent or collaborator.

As the young officer and his companions heaved another bagful into the flames, Bill Johnson, white fishing hat pulled down on his ears, his face pinched as a dried apple, slouched past the incinerator bin and disappeared into the Norodom office. When Locksley saw who was with him he had to blink twice: it was none other than Colonel Toth, Polgar's visitor. Locksley later learned that Polgar had assigned Johnson to organize the rescue mission Toth had requested, the run to and from Tan Son Nhut to "save" the Hungarians and the Poles.

While Johnson rummaged around his office for volunteer chauffeurs and extra car keys, Toth flung himself into an armchair and began nibbling on dirty fingernails. Other CIA officers rushed in and out, carelessly barking out agents' names and addresses, cryptonyms and case titles, none of them realizing the plump, sweating civilian in the corner was a Communist operative.

On the long drive out to Tan Son Nhut, Toth apologized to Johnson. "I'm sorry," he said, lapsing from German to English and back again. "It just didn't work out. It just didn't work out at all." What he was referring to, Johnson was never quite sure, for if Toth's mission had been to mislead the Americans into believing a negotiated settlement was possible, he had succeeded to perfection.

Once the convoy pulled into the ICCS trailer park at Tan Son Nhut, Johnson had some difficulty rounding up his "evacuees." A rocket had recently demolished two of the makeshift barracks; several of the Poles were in shell shock, and most of the rest were hiding. The Hungarians, meanwhile, were nervously guzzling bottles of barack. By the time Johnson got them stuffed inside his twenty cars and jeeps, a few of them were feeling no pain.

In defiance of the crowds and the traffic, Johnson floored his Ford Maverick and roared back toward town, his entourage straggling along behind. A young Vietnamese policeman who had long been on the Station payroll and had often risked his life for his employers "talked" the convoy through the series of army checkpoints along the way, explaining to the nervous troopers that the ICCS members were bound for the Palace "to arrange a cease-fire." Once or twice the lie didn't work, and thereupon Johnson simply drew his automatic and held the troopers at gunpoint until the motorcade was past.

Finally, a few blocks from the waterfront in the city, the CIA man broke away from the convoy and drove back to the Embassy. The Poles and Hungarians continued on to the Majestic Hotel, there to eat, drink and make merry until NVA forces entered the city the next day.

Months later the Hungarian government awarded a special hero's citation to Johnson for his efforts on behalf of the ICCS team members that final morning. It was surely the first time Budapest had lauded a CIA operative for saving party faithful from a Communist artillery attack.

Johnson was neither amused by the irony nor flattered by the honor. In the course of his extraordinary rescue mission on the morning of the twenty-ninth, he had become separated from the brave Vietnamese policeman who had guided the convoy safely in. The officer would be left behind.

To many of those around him, Graham Martin now looked like a walking dead man. The pneumonia and the doctor's stiff antibiotics were taking their toll. Pasty-faced, drawn, he was even having difficulty standing erect. And now that Washington had ordered Option IV, some of the old spark, the fight, seemed to have gone out of him. For all practical purposes the military and Gayler were now in control. Only one prerogative was left to Martin himself —to ensure at this late date that as many Vietnamese as possible were evacuated.

Even that, however, would have to wait an hour or so, until the first wave of choppers arrived from the fleet. For now, Martin was in effect a free man, with no responsibilities whatsoever, perhaps for the first time since his posting to Saigon. He decided to take advantage of the respite to tend to a personal matter. He would return to his villa to pick up his wife.

His plain-clothes Marine bodyguards objected vehemently when he announced his intention. They would retrieve Mrs. Martin for him, they said. There was no need for him to expose himself again to the chaos outside. But Martin said no. He was the Ambassador; he would not be locked in.

As his limousine wheeled through the parking lot the hordes of Vietnamese in the streets outside went wild, many of them flinging themselves against the gate. "Never mind," said Martin when he was informed. He would make the trip on foot. Before his security chief could recover his composure, Martin beckoned to three of his largest Marine bodyguards and headed for the elevator. With his escort hedging him in on all sides, he slipped out of the Embassy through the recreation compound and walked the four blocks to his home. His houseboy, Mr. Chinh, greeted him at the door. Mrs. Martin, a short, matronly woman, was packed up and ready. Martin directed the valet to make up an overnight bag for him.

He then took one last look around the old French villa that had housed the three Ambassadors before him. Rumor had it the place was haunted—there had even been an exorcism here once—but the phantoms that now flickered through memory were far more of the moment. The autographed picture of President Nixon and his family was still on the piano in the living room. The Ambassador's personal belongings, his furniture and mementos of forty years of government service, were all in their proper places.

As Martin wandered through the house he noticed a favorite antique, a model Chinese pagoda. He picked it up and tucked it in his pocket. He then took his wife on his arm and strode out to the street. The Marine guards closed in around them as Mr. Chinh struggled along behind with the overnight case. They arrived back at the Embassy in less than five minutes.

Before returning to his office Martin ducked through the door in the wall between the French and American compounds and went to look for Mérillon. The French Ambassador was not in his chancery this morning. He had decided to seclude himself in his private villa next door. As he had explained to his staff, he felt his absence from the Embassy itself would discourage miscreants and politicians from seeking asylum there, as had happened at the French Mission in Phnom Penh on the day Cambodia collapsed.

Mérillon greeted Martin in his private study. The two shook hands and briefly exchanged courtesies. Martin then bore in on the essentials. Had Mérillon's interview with "Big" Minh earlier in the morning been productive? Had there been any new peace feelers from the PRG? The Frenchman lit his ubiquitous pipe and took a few puffs, the acrid smell of Algerian tobacco falling like a curtain across the room. No, he said at length, there was nothing very encouraging to report. Minh was continuing to sound out the other side, but the PRG had yet to respond. Martin stared for a moment, then dropped his voice conspiratorially. In that case, he had a suggestion, he said. He would like to meet with the PRG delegation himself. Could Mérillon help to arrange it?

The Frenchman knocked his pipe out on an ashtray. He could try, he said hesitantly, but he could promise nothing. Martin nodded, thanked him, and stood up to go. As he did, he pulled the antique pagoda out of his pocket and set it on Mérillon's desk. He wanted Mérillon to have it as a token of his own appreciation for all that the French Mission had done in the past month to promote the cause of peace.

When Martin walked into his own third-floor suite his wife was talking quietly with the secretaries about a vital concern of her own. She didn't like the way Graham looked at all, she said. Not at all. He was clearly very ill. He needed something substantial for lunch. She wanted to return to the Residence to fix him some beef stew. One of the Ambassador's aides gently dissuaded her: the Residence might soon be overrun by mobs. An hour or so later Mrs. Martin was put aboard an Air America chopper on the Embassy roof and flown out to the USS *Denver,* one of the ships of the evacuation fleet.

Just before 11 A.M. General Timmes made another trip to the Palace, this time with a personal note from Martin. It was a response to a formal request from Minh that all American military officers be out of Saigon within twenty-four hours. Since DAO's departure was already a foregone conclusion, Martin now had no qualms about giving the new President a formal guarantee to this effect. Indeed, he felt it might strengthen Minh's bargaining position with the Communists.

At his headquarters north of Saigon, General Van Tien Dung was becoming increasingly impatient. It had been hours since the Politburo had advised him of the pullout of the American "military advisors." Yet his own forward observers at Tan Son Nhut reported that the Defense Attaché's Office was still bustling with activity.

Dung, cautious and meticulous as he was, decided to take no chances. He dictated another message to his artillery commanders on the eastern front, proposing targets and a specific deadline for the shelling attack on downtown Saigon he had suggested a few hours earlier. If the Americans failed to withdraw by nightfall, he would make them pay dearly for their duplicity.

Even as Dung's message was transmitted to his forward command at Bien Hoa and Nhon Trach, several colleagues and I were slashing through the last of my situation maps and preparing to assault the telephones. Not long afterward, as we were gathering up the scraps and stuffing them into a "burn" bag, a station officer, white-faced and trembling, rushed in and handed me a small piece of teletype. It was the transcript of an intelligence report filed moments before. Unlike most of the others we had received during the past several hours, this one dealt with something more than tactical NVA troop moves. It announced in the garbled syntax of translated Vietnamese that NVA gunners were preparing to lob 200 rounds of 130-mm artillery at the Presidential Palace at exactly 6 P.M., Saigon time—a little over six hours away. I stared at the text, not quite able to believe it. Two hundred rounds of 130-mm fire would not only reduce the Palace to a deep hole in the ground, but would obliterate the American and French Embassies as well. As I reread the report a third time my legs were already pumping. I dashed down the hall, skidded into Polgar's office past the startled secretaries, and thrust the text under Polgar's nose. He gazed at it a moment, his eyes growing wide behind the thick glasses. "To the

Ambassador!" he said hoarsely, pushing it back into my hand. "Now!"

I bounded down the stairwell to the third floor and ran the length of the interior corridor to the Ambassador's suite. Martin was standing at Eva Kim's desk in the reception area. I was still panting hard as he read the document. His expression did not change. He shrugged, handed it back to me without a word.

Back on the sixth floor, I breathlessly told Polgar what had happened. "Get Timmes," he said. "He's to call 'Big' Minh and tell *him* to pass the word to the Communists not to go ahead with that shelling." Minutes later Timmes strode in. He conferred briefly with Polgar, then picked up the phone and began dialing.

Almost coincidentally, Ambassador Martin received an urgent call from Kissinger. The "bitter-end" option was out, he told the Ambassador. All Americans—the 150-man hard core and Martin too—were to leave Saigon by nightfall. Evidently the report on the shelling or some other such sobering intelligence had finally convinced Washington an American presence in Vietnam was no longer tenable.

When Garrett, the Embassy's chief security officer, was notified of the change in plan he decided to buck the bureaucracy. Even if the military was convinced all Americans could be funneled out through DAO, he was not. The Embassy had to be equipped to handle choppers as well. The great tamarind tree in the courtyard must come down.

Around midday Colonel John Madison and the four other members of the American delegation to the Joint Military Team pushed through the gate of the Embassy's recreation compound and waded into the milling crowds. Captain Stuart Herrington, a young blond army careerist with a flair for languages and a distinguished combat record, was appalled by what he saw. Looters had already broken into the canteen's liquor stocks and were guzzling Pinot Chardonnay in the parking lot.

Inside the Embassy compound itself, Marine guards were moving the last of the State Department limousines past crowds at the front gate. Others were flailing away at the great tree in the middle of the parking lot, wood chips sailing around them like shrapnel.

Jim Devine briefed Madison and his men on the latest directives from Washington. A full evacuation was on. Lehmann had overall responsibility for clearing the Embassy; Jay Blowers from the political-military section was to handle operational details. Madison looked Blowers up and down and immediately volunteered to assist him.

A few minutes later, as Herrington wandered back into the courtyard, he reached into his knapsack and pulled out several padlocks. As his own first blow for order and discipline in the Embassy, he was going to secure those liquor cabinets in the recreation compound and throw the bottles over the wall.

•   •   •

With the morning fast drawing to a close, Pittman and I wandered down to the third floor to check on the status of the evacuation. When we walked into Jacobson's office, rows of photographs showing him in various comradely poses with Vietnam's best- and lesser-known luminaries were still clinging to the walls like an indomitable memory. Jacobson himself, dressed as usual in a blue-striped seersucker shirt, was slumped over a secure telephone talking to flight controllers at DAO. Once he hung up, Pittman asked him how long he thought the evacuation had to run. Jacobson shook his head. "I'm only the traffic cop," he said. "Go ask Wolf Lehmann. He should know."

Lehmann, cool and unruffled in his gray-green cotton-knit suit, had no better answer. "Why don't you go up to the fourth floor and ask the people in the evacuation center," he told us.

"But, Mr. Lehmann," I replied, "there's no evacuation center on the fourth floor any more. Everybody is tending to his own."

"Look," Pittman interrupted. "We have to know how much more time we've got. It'll take at least three hours to destroy much of our radio equipment, and if the evacuation is going to wind up any time soon, we've got to start right now."

"I just don't know," Lehmann sputtered. "We've got maybe a thousand, two thousand or even ten thousand more Americans to evacuate, for all I know. Use your judgment." With that, he motioned us out of his office. As we passed through the Ambassador's anteroom, someone in the milling little crowd there raised a glass to us in toast. The favored few who were to share the Ambassador's presence during the next few hours had broken out a bottle of whiskey.

Just as we walked out of Martin's anteroom Alan Carter, the USIA chief, stumbled in past us. He was disheveled and winded, his salt-and-pepper goatee glistening sweat. He had just driven five harrowing blocks from the USIA compound on Le Qui Don Street. He had not wanted to come—there were still hundreds of Vietnamese jammed in that compound and only himself and two other Americans to keep them calm until the buses arrived—but Lehmann had given him no choice. "Get over to the Embassy at once! An emergency!" Lehmann had shouted at him on the phone, and for once Carter had dutifully complied.

"What's going on?" he growled at Martin's aide, Brunson McKinley, as the young Foreign Service officer threw another "burn" bag on the pile in the center of the room. McKinley said he wasn't sure; it looked as though everybody was leaving. He suggested Carter check with Lehmann.

"Oh, didn't you know?" Lehmann stammered when Carter finally cornered him. "We're all evacuating."

"Goddamnit, Wolf!" Carter snapped. "Is that why you called me over here? Don't you know I've still got Vietnamese in my compound and only two staffers to watch over them? You should have let me be."

Lehmann drew himself up. "Two staffers?" he said coolly. "Well, get them over here too. You're all leaving." He made no reference to the Vietnamese.

Carter threw up his hands. "How the hell am I going to get them over here, Wolf?" he exclaimed. "The streets are chaos and the locals in my compound will go crazy if they find out they're being abandoned."

At that moment Lacy Wright walked in and asked in his usual mild-mannered way if there was anything he could do. Carter looked at him and put a hand on his shoulder. "Maybe you can tell me, Lacy, how I can get two of my men over here from Le Qui Don."

"Sure," Wright replied. "I'll drive over and pick them up." Carter offered no objection. Months later, when asked why he, and not Carter, had made the trip, the young Foreign Service officer simply shrugged. "I guess Carter thought it was a lot more dangerous out there than it was. But you gotta remember. Conditions were changing all the time. He may have passed through town at a bad moment and assumed it was like that everywhere. In any case, I'd just been out and knew it wasn't."

Within the next twenty minutes Wright nudged Eva Kim's Toyota through the traffic to the USIA compound on Le Qui Don. John Swenson and Ken Jackson, Carter's two staffers, were waiting for him at the gate. Hundreds of Vietnamese in the courtyard surged after them as they dashed for the car.

In Washington it was now just after midnight. President Ford, weary and nerve-taut after the long day, climbed into bed and reached over to his side table for his usual nightcap: a glass of warm buttermilk.

Downstairs Kissinger was still reading through traffic from the front. According to the latest report from Smith's office, Saigon's army was in collapse and its command nonexistent.

In fact, the headquarters of the Joint General Staff on the outskirts of Tan Son Nhut was now all but deserted. Air Marshal Ky wandered alone through the litter-strewn halls, looking for General Khuyen, the outgoing chief of staff. Ky had sent his own wife and family out of Saigon that morning and now (as he later told it) wanted to take a plane up for a last bombing run against the enemy. But Khuyen had disappeared, and when Ky rang up the office of the air commander he was told everyone had decamped to DAO. As he hung up, General Ngo Quang Truong, former MR 1 commander, now a bitter and broken man, slumped into the operations room. "I don't know what to do any more," he sighed. Ky nodded, put his hand on Truong's shoulder. "Come with me, then," he said. They walked out of the headquarters building, climbed into Ky's private chopper, and flew off to the USS *Midway* in the South China Sea.

At the DAO compound itself, another Vietnamese army notable was paying a last call on General Smith. He stood before the American, in a neatly pressed dress uniform, campaign medals glittering on his chest. Then General Pham Van Phu, the man who had surrendered the highlands without a fight and had abandoned his command to destruction, executed a slow formal salute, turned on his heel, and walked out. He had asked General Smith to evacuate some of his family. He had requested nothing for himself. A short while later Phu put a bullet through his head.

Downtown at the Palace, President Minh gazed sadly at his old comrade-in-arms, Admiral Diep Quang Thuy, navy chief of staff, and shook hands with him for the last time. Thuy had come to plead with him to leave the city with the navy flotilla that was even now taking on passengers at the waterfront. Minh said no, he must stay till the end, but he urged Thuy—ordered him—to save himself and the others in the navy command. If the Americans were willing to receive them, they should set sail at once. Thuy nodded, straightened his tunic, and saluted his last commander in chief.

When John Swenson and Ken Jackson walked into the Ambassador's suite they found their boss, Carter, on the phone. He was talking to Mel Chatman in the Mission Warden's office on the other side of the Embassy parking lot. "We've got hundreds of Vietnamese at the USIA compound," Carter was saying. "How can we move them?"

"Any Americans among them?" Chatman asked.

"Not any more," Carter said, flicking a glance at the new arrivals.

Chatman hesitated. "Well, we'll try to get some buses over there when we can." Carter asked if he should try to go back to the compound himself. Chatman urged against it.

Pittman wandered through a few minutes later and mentioned to someone that the barges were already loading. "The barges!" Carter exclaimed. "What barges?" It was the first time he had ever heard of them. One of the Ambassador's assistants filled him in, adding that the vessels were due to push off no later than 3 P.M.

Carter immediately placed a call to his own compound and asked the Vietnamese employee who answered if the buses had arrived yet. The Vietnamese was crying. "Just now," he said, "but they're mobbed. None of the USIA staffers can get near them."

Carter again contacted the Mission Wardens' office, but was told no more buses were available. He and his deputies then debated alternatives. They could send their employees down to the docks unescorted, but if they did, the group might well be turned back at the gate to the navy yard. Besides, time was too short. The vessels were to leave at three o'clock. The USIA people would never make it in time, not on foot through the city. At last Carter decided to order the group over to his own residence, only a few blocks from the Embassy. A bus convoy might be able to negotiate that distance.

But when Carter called Mel Chatman back and outlined the idea, he was again told, "No buses available."

For the better part of the morning Larry Downs and his CIA colleagues in the delta city of Can Tho had been running a makeshift helo-lift from a rice field on the edge of town. Every few minutes an Air America chopper would shuttle in from the fleet, take on another batch of local employees, and haul them off to the ships or down to Phu Quoc, as Consul General MacNamara had authorized the day before.

Some of the pilots, however, were already grumbling. They could hear the cross-channel chatter from Saigon on their radios and were anxious to join in the fun.

Shortly after Option IV was ordered up, Jacobson called the consulate from Saigon, directed MacNamara to put his riverborne evacuation plan into effect, and insisted that all choppers be diverted immediately to the capital.

MacNamara had hardly put down the receiver than he was snapping out orders. "Assemble the staff! Prepare the boats!" One of his colleagues had a fleeting image of General Patton on the eve of the Bastogne offensive.

When MacNamara strolled into the consulate's briefing room he indeed bore some simularity to old Patton. He was sporting a tailored bush shirt, a .45 automatic on one hip, and a helmet specially made up to his specifications. The helmet was perhaps the most striking part of his costume; glistening black it was, with a leather strap and a single gold star in front as a token of rank. Some of his staffers were embarrassed at the very sight of it.

But MacNamara was unconcerned about such sentiment in the ranks. He was all business now. Slipping easily into the role of field commander, he announced his first order of the day: Downs' helo-lift was to be canceled, and everyone was to assemble at the docks on the Bassac River in one hour. Two motor-driven "mike" boats, each with a capacity for 300 passengers, would be waiting to take them on. Any overflow could put aboard an old rice barge and the CIA's five Boston whalers.

Tom Franklin, Downs' deputy, interrupted with a suggestion: "What about sending some of the Vietnamese women and children out with the last choppers?" MacNamara shook his head. "Everybody goes out on the boats," he insisted. With that, he closed the meeting.

Franklin and Downs immediately alerted their own five remaining staffers. All except their communications officer were to drive at once to the logistics compound. The radio man would join them there once the consulate's communications gear had been spiked.

Everybody seemed clear on the drill. But later the communicator forgot the most important detail: the rendezvous point. After destroying the radio gear he dashed down the street, collected his Vietnamese girl friend and her family, and then, instead of heading for the logistics compound, returned to the consulate. A few minutes later MacNamara's deputy, Hank Cushing, found him sniveling in a corner, distraught at being "abandoned" by his CIA colleagues. Cushing pulled the man to his feet and pointed him in the direction of the docks.

As Tom Franklin maneuvered his jeep through the swarms of buses and cyclos in the center of Can Tho, he switched on his portable radio and placed a call to one of the inbound choppers. "Don't come in," he told the CIA man on board. "We're going out in the predetermined manner. Return to the ship." The officer on the other end acknowledged with a curt "Roger." But a few minutes later Franklin overheard the same officer, in an exchange with a shipboard controller, announcing that the chopper would set down in Can Tho anyway to fuel up. Franklin radioed Downs at the logistics compound and advised him to round up some passengers. At least the secretary and one or two of the older officers could be spared a ride on MacNamara's "African Queen."

By the time the Consul General arrived at the docks, over 200 Vietnamese and most of his eighteen-man consular staff were already on hand. Although none of the CIA contingent had yet appeared, he decided to begin loading anyway. "No time to spare," he growled to a subordinate.

But as the passengers began lining up on the wharf, MacNamara discovered that Downs and his men were not the only notable absentees. The Vietnamese pilots he had hired to take the convoy down the Bassac were nowhere to be found. Some of the Americans began fidgeting with the gas gauges and dials, trying to figure how to put the boats in gear. "We just prayed and pushed the starter button," one of the younger consulate officers recalled. "Luckily, the damn things cranked up."

It was almost noon when the last of the evacuees piled aboard. MacNamara still had not heard from Downs or the other CIA men, but felt he could delay no longer. No doubt he would find them waiting for him downriver with their whaleboats, as his evacuation plan called for. In any case, it was time to shove off. A few minutes later, as the small armada chugged out into mid-channel, Tom Franklin managed to raise MacNamara by radio. He could hardly believe what the Consul General told him: the boats were already under way! "At least he could have waited to find out if we were safe!" Franklin later remarked bitterly.

MacNamara's departure left the CIA men to fend for themselves. Franklin promptly ordered resumption of the helo-lift and called for several more choppers to pull out the last of the base's Vietnamese employees.

In the meantime, the chopper already on its way in to refuel was running into trouble. As it hovered into the Air America terminal several armed stragglers dashed from behind a hangar and waved it away from the fuel pumps at gunpoint. The pilot, remembering an auxiliary pump at a nearby warehouse, made for it. After gassing up there, he swung the bird around, picked up Downs, Franklin and several others at the logistics compound, and headed for the coast.

As the chopper veered up over the river Franklin spotted MacNamara's "mike" boats in midstream. He radioed down to make sure the CIA communicator was on board and to ask if they needed help. MacNamara assured him the radio man was fine, and that everything else was well in hand too. No help required.

But MacNamara clearly had spoken too soon. Within the next several minutes several Vietnamese navy patrol boats swooped down on his rickety armada like birds of prey, their machine guns chopping the water starboard and port. The commander of the first boat, Commodore Thang from Can Tho, ordered MacNamara to heave to and prepared to board. Several hundred feet above, Downs' Air America chopper strained for altitude.

Thang pushed his way through the frightened passengers on Mac-Namara's mike boat and planted himself squarely in front of the Consul General. The MR 4 commander, General Nam, he said, had instructed him to intercept the evacuation flotilla to make sure there were no army deserters on board. MacNamara's heart sank when he heard that, for many of the evacuees around him were indeed army officers in civilian dress.

But just as he was about to offer some lame protest, Thang broke into a broad, totally unexpected grin. "Don't worry, though," he continued, "I can see there're no army personnel here." He then shook MacNamara's hand and clambered back onto his own patrol boat. As the small naval force pulled off, MacNamara straightened his helmet and breathed a loud sigh of relief. Several days before, he had helped evacuate some members of Thang's own family to Saigon. Evidently the navy man had decided to repay the favor by not looking too closely at MacNamara's current crop of evacuees.

Meanwhile, at the urging of the CIA men in the chopper above, the U.S. Navy had scrambled several Phantom jets to come to MacNamara's rescue. But by the time the American warplanes soared in over the Bassac, the Consul General's mike boats were already under way again, churning their way slowly but surely down the silt-clogged river to the sea.

Afternoon

Admiral Donald Whitmire was a mountain of a man. Hulking, muscular, barrel-gut slipping over the Navy ensign on his belt buckle, he looked more like an aging fullback than the commander of a trim naval task force on the edge of a war. Appearances notwithstanding, he had performed his mission till now with all the skill and dedication for which the Navy is renowned. He had rescued Vietnamese at sea, assembled aircraft and ships, and kept the discipline of his men intact under the most trying and delicate circumstances. To his immediate subordinates aboard Task Force '76, he was the very epitome of the effective commander at sea.

On the morning of the twenty-ninth, however, the skill and efficiency he had so far demonstrated to perfection ran afoul of the circumstances. The problem sprang from the confusion surrounding the crisis itself. Up until the past few hours Option IV, "Frequent Wind," had seemed a remote contingency to be undertaken only if all the political maneuvering came to naught. Thus when at 10:51 the President had actually set the helo-lift in motion, Whitmire and his men had not been fully prepared for it. Before even one military chopper could be sent into Saigon, all eighty-one of them on board the fleet had to be cross-checked for takeoff, the marines loaded, and fighter escorts called in from Thailand.

Then, too, there was a question as to when exactly the launch was to take place. Somewhere between Washington and the task force itself messages had become scrambled and directives confused. When Kissinger had told Martin the evacuation would begin at 11:51—one hour after the execute order—was he calculating on the basis of Washington time, Greenwich mean time or Saigon time? No one in Whitmire's command seemed quite sure. Consequently, by twelve noon not one of the military choppers had yet departed for Saigon.

Martin called Gayler direct and demanded an explanation. That apparently jogged the machinery. Fifteen minutes later the marines aboard the task force were ordered to mount up. At approximately 12:30 P.M. the first wave of thirty-six heavy-duty choppers left the deck of the USS *Hancock* with several Cobra helicopter gunships flying escort. One minute later the first Phantom fighter jets from bases in Thailand crossed over into Vietnamese airspace to provide additional cover.

By now, an hour and a half had passed since the President had called for Option IV. The delay might not have been so serious, except for two other complications. Out of concern for Communist sensitivities, the Pentagon had directed Whitmire to keep his ships well beyond South Vietnam's legal twelve-mile limit. The flight time into Saigon had thus been extended to forty minutes or more. In addition, Whitmire compounded his problems at the last minute by insisting on still more time to complete preparations for the helo-lift. Even after the first wave of choppers was airborne, he sent word to his squadron commanders that the first pickups were to be postponed until two o'clock.

Kissinger awakened President Ford slightly before 1:00 A.M., local time, to clear the text of a proposed press announcement on the evacuation. He also advised the Chief Executive of the slippage in the launch-time. Across the White House lawn, in the Executive Office Building, aides and secretaries were busily dialing prominent Senators and Congressmen to give them advance word.

In Saigon few of us at the Embassy were aware that Option IV was even in first gear, much less encountering difficulties. Martin and his senior staff were now so preoccupied with the immediate problems of collecting and moving bodies to appropriate assembly points, they forgot to keep the rest of us informed.

My own attention remained focused almost exclusively on the intelligence reports still trickling into my office. I carefully picked through each one, hoping to find some proof that the foreshadowed artillery attack had been called off. My diligence was wasted. The picture that emerged from the reams of manila ticker was of a methodical stripping away of the city's outer defenses.

Shortly after midday a reliable source confirmed that two NVA divisions had overrun Tay Ninh Province, isolating and entrapping the headquarters of the 25th ARVN Division at Cu Chi. Elsewhere, other government forces were scuttling helplessly from one embattled position to another, like crabs at high tide. Only to the southwest were ARVN units putting up any kind of fight at all. Two regiments of the 22nd Division, obliterated in MR 2 four weeks before and resurrected in the past few days, were still holding a ragged line on Saigon's southern perimeters.

In an office a few doors away from my own, General Timmes was puzzling over a message just broadcast over Saigon Radio, an appeal from the new Prime Minister, Vu Van Mau, calling on *all* Americans to leave Saigon at once. No more than an hour before, President Minh himself, in his last meeting with Timmes, had insisted only on the prompt withdrawal of DAO. Now, apparently, he was angling for maximum political advantage with the Communists by closing the door on us all.

Timmes rushed up to Polgar's office to alert him to the change, but could hardly wangle two minutes' worth of conversation with him. The Station Chief was now totally absorbed in the peregrinations of his thirty favored Vietnamese.

Around twelve-thirty Ut, Polgar's brave little chauffeur, radioed his first progress report from the rendezvous point at my apartment building on Chien Si Circle. Yes, there *was* a chopper on the roof, he assured us. He could see it. But neither he nor any of the thirty Vietnamese with him could get past the front gate. Over 300 other would-be evacuees were milling around outside. If the gate was opened, the building literally would be overrun.

Polgar stared at the radio speaker. He seemed to be blinking away tears. At last he turned and trudged back to his office. There was a bottle of cognac on his desk. He picked it up and drank. Several other officers outside in the anteroom took their cue from him and began breaking out the stocks of Scotch and cognac which the Station kept around to lavish on Palace contacts on better days.

Gazing warily at the 3,000 sweltering Vietnamese around him, Don Hays felt as conspicuous and vulnerable as a point man on a long-range patrol. He, two Australians and an Air Force colonel were now the only westerners left in the heart of the processing center.

The sun was only slightly past its noontime high and the shadeless assembly area was shimmering with rising heat like a Saharan mirage. Hays reached into his back pocket, pulled out a handkerchief. One of the hazards of going prematurely bald, he mused humorlessly as he wrapped it around his head: the last thing he needed at this point was a good second-degree sunburn along the hairline. The Vietnamese pressing in around him were sweating as profusely as he was and grumbling for water. The last of the stocks had been drained off a few minutes before, and a handful of Vietnamese paratroopers had just broken through the fence and were scavenging the remaining food stores in the bowling alley. Where *were* those goddamn choppers?

Suddenly, from the direction of the Quonset huts at the other side of the compound, the staccato cough of an M-16 broke over the murmurings of the crowds. Little tufts of dirt were blossoming in a neat line across the parking lot as Hays dove behind a tin drum. Vietnamese swept around him in a frenzy, their screams deadening the rattle of the gunfire. Out of the corner of his eye, he saw two U.S. Air Force officers dash from behind the gymnasium, firing carbines from the hip. Just as they were leveling their weapons at one of the rooftops across the compound, several stray rounds ricocheted close to Hays' elbow and he buried his face in his arm. When he looked up again, a single ARVN soldier, the sniper, mortally wounded, was pitching headlong off the roof, his M-16 hitting the ground just seconds before he did.

Hays grabbed a megaphone and staggered to his feet. "Stay calm! Stay calm!" he screamed in Vietnamese to the crowd. "It's all over. The Americans won't leave you. I'll not leave you."

●   ●   ●

Not far away, Ken Moorefield's convoy was threading its way through the front gate of Tan Son Nhut en route back to town. "The traffic was thick as Ban Me Thuot coffee," he recalled, "and the security forces along Cach Mang were determined to keep it moving along even if they had to shoot some of us in the process. Captain Woods and I tried to pull over to the curb to take on a group of passengers, but a Vietnamese cop ran up and lowered his carbine at my belt line. 'No can stop! No can stop!' he kept yelling. Woods tried to negotiate with him. I jumped out of my jeep, ran to the front of the convoy, and pushed everybody on. Then I took Woods' staff car and two of the buses and went forward so the whole convoy wouldn't get bogged down. Only minutes later did I remember: I'd left my getaway bag, with seven hundred dollars in it, back in the jeep. Never saw it again.

"I wheeled the motorcade around and headed back toward Tan Son Nhut. But as we were pulling up to the civilian gate, several other buses wedged themselves in ahead of us. The Vietnamese security guards, maybe half a platoon, got very excited, locked and loaded on us and put several rounds in the air. Well, I'd faced loaded weapons before, but not where I was so seriously outnumbered. I had my drivers pull off and we began careening around and around the traffic maze just outside the gate. We were running low on gas, couldn't unload our passengers, and I didn't know what the hell we were gonna do."

Inside Tan Son Nhut, at DAO headquarters, General Smith soon learned of the fracas from a radio dispatcher with one of the other convoys. He grabbed the Vietnamese base commander, who had skulked into the headquarters building a few hours before, and warned him if he didn't find a way to get those buses past the checkpoints, he would feed him to the Viet Cong and call air strikes in on the security forces there. The officer, very nervous and agitated, radioed the front gate, and was told that the police chief from a nearby precinct had ordered the airfield sealed off until the Americans promised to evacuate him and his deputy. Smith, hearing this, immediately agreed.

By the time the gate came up, however, Moorefield's convoy was already rumbling back toward Saigon. "I had two busloads on my hands and no place to stash them," he remarked. "I thought maybe I'd find Woods at a rendezvous point we'd agreed on, so I went there. But he never showed.

"The population was really on edge by now, and every time I'd stop for a light or for traffic, scores of cops or armed troopers would ring my car, pleading for help or a free ride. I locked the doors and tried to wave them off, and all the while I kept thinking how ironic it would be—after all my close shaves as a combat officer in the delta—to be cut down by a group of our own allies in downtown Saigon."

As Moorefield continued his perilous odyssey, two of his Embassy colleagues were preparing to embark on one of their own. Slightly before one o'clock Lacy Wright and a fellow State Department officer, Joe McBride, climbed into two white-paneled minibuses parked on the street alongside the

Embassy and drove to 62 Truong Minh Giang to pick up their first Vietnamese VIPs.

"The place was mobbed when we arrived, maybe three hundred people in all," Wright noted later. "We'd called too many, so we had to start trimming the group right then and there. We separated out the babies and the old ladies, sent them home, cut the largest families down to manageable size." Finally, after much pushing and agonizing, Wright and McBride got the first of their passengers packed in a van and headed down to the docks at Khanh Hoi, near the old French sailing club, Le Club Nautique, there to transfer them to the fabled barges.

By their third or fourth trip, the graying old Vietnamese guards at the gate to the navy yard were beginning to joke among themselves about the two sweating Americans. "Hey, how about bringing us some cognac!" one called out jovially to Wright. "Sure, sure," Wright yelled back, trying to appear friendly, hoping against hope he would not actually have to produce a bottle as the price of entry on his next run.

The first hour or so, the masses at dockside were reasonably well behaved. Several Vietnamese barges were already lashed up and taking on passengers, the going rate for seat space running as high as $5,000 to $10,000 in American green. Mel Chatman's vessels were moored a short distance away, and as soon as Wright and McBride deposited the first of their charges, loading began there as well, all in a very calm and orderly manner.

In the meantime, on the other side of town, one of my colleagues, "Harvey Mitchell," was facing his first real crisis of the day. It was approximately one o'clock when the cigar-smoking CIA man made his fifth or sixth trip out to the gate of the Duc Hotel to reconnoiter the street for a bus convoy or Embassy van. This time he was in for a surprise, a decidedly unpleasant one. No sooner had he stepped out on the sidewalk than government security forces on the other side of Pasteur Street fired off several bursts from their M-16s. In a flash he ducked back in the gate and ordered the Nung guards to lock it up tight.

It had been touch-and-go at the Duc all morning. All but thirteen of the CIA officers quartered there had left for the Embassy at daybreak. But in the past three hours the hotel had begun filling up with Vietnamese, many of them waitresses, clerks, room valets long employed by the establishment. Mitchell, increasingly uneasy, had ordered the gate closed around midmorning to choke off the flow, but from time to time both he and others had succumbed to their own sense of charity and had let a "few more" friends or co-workers in. Now there were over a hundred assorted Vietnamese scattered through the six-story building—and still no buses to haul them to the Embassy or DAO.

An hour before, Vietnamese troopers had set up machine-gun nests in the playground across Pasteur to backstop security forces at the Presidential Palace a block away. Mitchell had advised the Embassy immediately and had volunteered to stay at the hotel to help move out the Vietnamese. Logically, Polgar should have told him no. Weeks before, he had named Mitchell "coordinator" of the Station's overall evacuation program, such as it was. And now, if Mitchell was needed anywhere, it was at the Embassy itself, overseeing the rescue of all the Station's Vietnamese. He was one of the few officers among us who knew the details of DAO's various evacuation plans. But for some reason, in the confusion of this bleak final day, Polgar concluded the Station could do without its coordinator, and agreed to let Mitchell stay at the Duc to orchestrate the side show there.

Once or twice during the morning an Air America Huey had set down momentarily on the improvised pad near the hotel's rooftop swimming pool, but so far no Vietnamese had been flown out. Since the pad could accommodate only one small chopper at a time, Mitchell had decided to reserve the helo-lift for himself and the few other Americans still in the building. The Vietnamese would have to be evacuated by bus.

"Robert Kantor," Polgar's administrative chief, had just taken over at the radio consoles in the CIA situation room when Mitchell called around one-thirty to remind us again of the need for buses. Kantor, an even-tempered southerner with kinky red hair and a beard to match, promised to send a convoy immediately.

Polgar walked in soon afterward. "Anyone heard from Ut?" he asked, his voice husky with fatigue and worry. "No, Tom," Kantor replied. "But there is this problem at the Duc." He then explained what Mitchell had told him. Polgar listened for a few minutes, but seemed distracted. After tossing off a cursory question or two, he shrugged and walked out.

Halfway down the hall one of the Station's supply officers ran up and caught him by the arm. "Sir," he huffed, "it's about my Vietnamese employees —two hundred and fifty of them. They're out at the logistics compound. How can I get them picked up?"

"Shut up!" Polgar snapped, brushing past him. "I haven't got time for that." Like so many others, those 250 would ultimately be left behind.

On the roof of 6 Chien Si Circle, T. D. Latz took another look at his watch. For the past half-hour he and his pilot had been biding their time there, waiting vainly for Ut and Polgar's thirty Vietnamese. Now Latz was deeply worried. Every minute he wasted on that rooftop was one minute less he could devote to rescuing Americans and Vietnamese elsewhere in the city. And God knows, he later told a friend, there were no choppers to spare.

Kantor put down the microphone and leaned back in his chair. A cloud of cigarette smoke hung, motionless, over his head like a speech balloon in a cartoon drawing. He tried to disperse it with a wave of his hand, but to no effect. With the continued vibration of the rooftop incinerators, the Embassy's always eccentric ventilation system was beginning to break down, leaving everybody's last nervous puff in midair.

As Kantor again hunched over the microphone in front of him, one of his senior colleagues burst into the situation room. "Helluva problem downstairs!" he exclaimed loudly. The Ambassador had waited till the last minute to order his most sensitive cables destroyed. Now a ton or more of the stuff was lying, half shredded, across the commo room on the fourth floor. "It's a God-awful fire hazard!" the officer bellowed.

Kantor raised his hands in a gesture of mock despair. "Well, if there's a fire hazard," he said, "I nominate you to take care of it."

The officer grimaced, started to object, but then reconsidered, and without another word, hurried off to do as Kantor suggested. For the next two hours he and a dozen other Embassy officers crawled around the commo room stuffing classified waste into big plastic bags. Once they had swept the place clean, they carted the sacks downstairs to the courtyard and stacked them neatly against the wall of the Vietnamese snack shop near the Mission Wardens' office. Whereupon they forgot them. A few hours later, when the first choppers came in, the back draft tore into the bags and blew the contents all over the courtyard. Code words and full paragraphs from the Embassy's most sensitive top-secret communications were still clearly legible on many of the scraps as they came to rest on bushes, trees and the elaborate hairdos of some of the wealthier Vietnamese matrons waiting for a ride out.

By 1:45 A.M., Washington time, President Ford had dropped off to sleep. Following his example, several staff aides flung themselves on chairs and couches outside the operations center downstairs to try to catch a few winks before the priorities of the evacuation set them running again.

At 1:50 P.M., Saigon time, the first wave of helicopters from Task Force '76 veered westward from Bien Hoa and bore in toward Tan Son Nhut. They were now just ten minutes away from their scheduled touchdown. In the lead chopper Brigadier General Richard Carey, commander of the Marine security force, was checking his battle gear for the last time.

On board the evacuation fleet Admiral Whitmire, however, was still having second thoughts about his timetable. Preparations for launching the next wave of choppers were lagging badly, and squadron commanders doubted that all forty of those still on the decks could be put into Saigon even within the next hour. "To properly position the ground security force, get the proper number of helos airborne, and assemble the proper waves of aircraft [for protective cover], a two-hour lead time as specified in air operations planning was required," explained an official after-action report.

After weighing all of these factors, Whitmire arrived at a crucial decision. With only a few minutes to go, he ordered the start of the evacuation to be pushed back yet another hour, to three o'clock. By any measure, whatever the justification, it was an extraordinary change in plan. Coming on top of the original delay, it put the helo-lift on a very short fuse, for once the operation did get under way an hour later, pilots would be flying in a dead heat against the clock, the onset of darkness and dwindling North Vietnamese patience. They would also have another handicap to contend with: a heavy storm center had just been detected sweeping in toward Saigon from the sea.

Only minutes after Whitmire imposed the new schedule, General Carey in his command chopper received a radio alert from the fleet: he and his entire sortie were to go into a holding pattern over Tan Son Nhut until the evacuation was formally geared up an hour later. This, too, was a curious change in plan, since Carey's thirty-six helicopters were already over the landing zones and could as easily have gone in as not. And wisely, Carey chose to ignore it. While the rest of the choppers began orbiting south of the airfield, his own Huey swooped in toward the DAO compound.

General Smith watched for a few moments from a window as the helicopter eased in; then he began feverishly revising his own plans to fit Whitmire's new timetable. Under the standing evacuation scenario, each helicopter in the first wave was to disgorge its cargo of marines and then return promptly to the fleet to pick up the remainder of the security force. But with the afternoon now fast slipping away, Smith decided to make every flight count. He told his staff that once Carey's choppers set down, passengers should be boarded immediately and sent out to the fleet on the turnaround.

Carey himself hit upon another shortcut. Because of the recent flare-up at Tan Son Nhut's front gate and the difficulties of assuring continued bus service to DAO, he recommended to Whitmire that some of the choppers be diverted to the Embassy to pull out evacuees there. The admiral and his staff were understandably perturbed, since only 200 people were supposed to be at the Embassy on E-day, and no real security force had been provided for. Before agreeing to the proposal, Whitmire sent Carey a follow-up message, asking exactly how many evacuees were gathered at the chancery and whether the rooftop pad could support the larger military helicopters. General Smith in turn queried Lehmann. To the first question Lehmann responded with now typical imprecision. "Maybe a thousand, maybe two thousand. I just don't know," he said of the hordes of evacuees at the Embassy. To the second question he had no answer at all. A secretary, listening in on the exchange, heard Smith mutter disgustedly on the other end of the line, "You mean you can't even tell me if the Embassy can take big choppers or not!" Obviously, confusion was still the order of the day in the Ambassador's office.

In Washington, Kissinger had just learned of the decision to delay the helo-lift once again. According to aides, he was furious. He had promised Martin at 10:51, Saigon time, the operation would begin in one hour. Now, three hours later, the military was still dithering.

"Where is Ut? Where are those thirty Vietnamese?" Polgar half whispered as he wandered back and forth in the anteroom outside his office. It had been nearly an hour since the abortive pickup attempt at Chien Si Circle, and Ut and his thirty companions were still there, trapped in the street crowds, awaiting fresh orders. Pittman lit yet another cigar and gnawed on it thoughtfully. "There's a small patio on the roof of my own apartment building on Gia Long [Street]," he said finally. "It's not big enough for a two-point landing, but if you could get one chopper skid on the edge of it, you might be able to hover long enough to take on Ut and his group."

Polgar's face brightened. At once he was reeling off instructions: Get Latz! Radio Ut and tell him where to go!

Within minutes Latz's Air America Huey was whirring to a landing on the Embassy roof. When he loped into the anteroom he was dripping sweat, a Swedish K submachine gun dangling from his hand. "No way I could get those thirty Viets out of Chien Si," he apologized to Polgar. "Nung guards locked the front gate, wouldn't open it even when I waved this thing at them [gesturing with his weapon]. Can't blame them. Must've been five hundred Viets in the street outside, banging to get in. We'd have been trampled before we pulled off the roof." He looked at me. "Some boys from the Mission Wardens' office are still in the building, though. Been there since early morning when the rest of you people left. They're waiting word from the Embassy to evacuate. I told them to come with me. Nope, they said, got orders to hold on. Somebody better tell the Ambassador or Jacobson to order those bastards out and send a chopper for 'em."

"Any ground fire?" I asked.

"Strays," Latz said, pulling hard on a cigarette. "But most of the Viets are so damn anxious to get out of this city they're not doing us the damage they could."

Polgar hurriedly explained the new pickup plan, while Kantor contacted Ut by radio and passed instructions to him. Afterward Polgar shuffled back into his office, took a long draught of cognac, and sank down in the chair behind his desk to wait for news.

Back on the roof, Latz climbed into his chopper and spun off toward the rendezvous point atop Pittman's apartment building. Later in the afternoon a news photographer snapped a spectacular photograph of him—a telephoto shot of his backside—as he was helping Vietnamese up a small ladder to that precarious landing pad (or one exactly like it). Replayed in thousands of newspapers around the world, it became one of the immortal images of that last hectic day.*

In the Embassy courtyard, Colonel Madison and the four others from the Joint Military Team had just been advised of the planned helo-lift out of the chancery grounds and were busily preparing for it. No one doubted it was going to be one difficult and complex operation. Not only did it pose immense logistical and technical problems, but it also threatened to complicate established lines of command. Although Madison was now the ranking military officer in the Embassy, the commander of the Marine detachment, Major J. H. Kean, who had arrived a few days earlier, was insisting on his own prerogatives, and only after heated debate was a division of labor agreed upon. The marines would direct the landing of the choppers in the parking lot; Madison

*Among those who made that perilous climb to Latz's chopper was Tran Van Don, Saigon's last peripatetic and imaginative Defense Minister, who with the French had done so much to foster the illusion that the situation would never come to this.

and his group were to supervise the marshaling of passengers.

To complicate matters further, the Embassy's senior staff also continued to aspire to a certain leadership role, as Madison soon discovered. Shortly after learning of the expanded helo-lift, he sent one of his own officers up the Embassy's radio tower to cut down guy wires that might have impeded incoming choppers. When Lehmann found out, he gave him a good dressing down, ranting and raving that no one in the Ambassador's office had authorized such "extreme measures." Madison apologized politely—but had the wires snipped anyway.

By 2:30 P.M. Bob Kantor, still laboring before the radios in the CIA situation room, was beginning to lose his customary cool. It was the crisis at the Duc Hotel that weighed on him now, trying both his patience and his nerve. In the past half-hour the streets around the hotel had become so choked with traffic, not one official bus or vehicle had been able to negotiate the short distance from the Embassy. A few minutes before, Harvey Mitchell had called to say that the Vietnamese troopers across Pasteur Street were again taking pot shots at passers-by. And as he explained it, some of the Americans with him were beginning to panic. Choppers would have to be sent over to pull them out—now!

Kantor had just slammed down the phone when Polgar walked in to inquire again about Ut. Ignoring his questions, Kantor reminded him of the crisis at the Duc and asked what ought to be done. "Well, if the ARVN are shooting over there," Polgar replied, "pull them out."

"The Americans?" Kantor asked.

"Yes, pull them out," Polgar repeated, then shambled off. Having overheard the exchange from the doorway, I suddenly felt terribly ill. In effect, Polgar had just decreed that the hundred or more Vietnamese at the Duc be abandoned. Mitchell and the handful of other Americans there were to save themselves.

Kantor hesitated for a moment, as if he, too, was having trouble accepting that verdict. At last he picked up the phone and relayed Polgar's instructions to Mitchell. He then pressed the broadcast switch and repeated himself over the air to make sure the other Americans at the Duc understood.

Earlier in the day many of the hotel's American tenants had neglected to turn off their two-way radios as they frantically decamped to the Embassy, and now, as Kantor's message crackled out over the circuits, the Vietnamese who had replaced them in the rooms and hallways heard it and realized what their CIA patrons had in store for them. Mitchell hurried from floor to floor, trying to calm them. "No problem," he assured them as he gathered up the scores of weapons that also had been left lying around. "More buses and choppers will be here soon." At the same time he quietly advised his American colleagues to make their way to the rooftop pad at once.

Many of the Vietnamese who looked on helplessly as the Americans began disappearing into the stairwells were long-time CIA employees. Some of them were bona-fide agents or relatives of those who were. Others were hotel waitresses who had turned down earlier opportunities to leave, on the understanding they would be taken care of if they helped to keep the hotel running to the last minute. Several had even prostituted themselves to this or that CIA officer during the past few days to reinforce their chances of getting out. Their bedmates now studiously ignored them as they slipped up to the roof to await the incoming Hueys.

Somewhere on the central stairwell Mitchell found himself cornered by a Vietnamese army major and lieutenant. As he later told the story, one of them reached under his tunic and pulled out a small pistol. "Either you take us with you," they were supposed to have told him, "or you don't leave." Other CIA staffers later denied there were any weapons. They claimed that Mitchell in fact had invited the two Vietnamese to come along. In any case, these were the only locals out of all those in the hotel who saw an evacuation flight that day.

As Mitchell and his companions reached the fifth floor they slid the metal security doors shut, switched off the elevators, then leaped up the remaining few steps to the roof and were dragged aboard a waiting Air America UH 1. Seconds later they were airborne, heading off toward the fleet.

Throughout the rest of the afternoon the Vietnamese at the Duc put in call after call to the Embassy on the discarded two-way radios. "Save me! Tell me where to go!" "I'm Mr. Hai, the cook." "I'm Mr. Anh, the chauffeur; my family is here." Kantor and a CIA secretary, who was now working at his elbow, tried to calm them and to cajole them into clearing the circuits, since their calls were overriding more "urgent" transmissions. "Return to your homes," Kantor told them again and again over the air. "Buses and helicopters will come by to pick you up." Finally, a distraught voice cut into the channel: "Vietnamese soldiers have broken into the bottom floors. They're burning and looting." Soon radio contact with the hotel was lost.

The following morning, as NVA troops entered Saigon, some of the Vietnamese who had remained in the Duc overnight began sniping at them. The North Vietnamese immediately brought up heavy machine guns and B-40 rockets and blasted away at the façade, killing or wounding many of those inside.

In the various post-mortems on the Duc, no one was ever able to agree on what had gone wrong. Mitchell claimed that some of his CIA companions had panicked at the sound of gunfire, making an immediate pullout imperative. Other CIA officers who had been at the hotel with him insisted Mitchell himself had panicked, and in his calls to Kantor had exaggerated the danger posed by the government troops across the street. Whatever the truth, if any of us in Polgar's office had had the presence of mind to consider alternatives, something undoubtedly could have been done to help the Vietnamese left behind. Some could have been directed or even escorted on foot to another collection point, such as the Embassy itself four blocks away; a large number might even have been helo-lifted out despite the size of the hotel's rooftop pad. As it was, we did nothing but save the gentlemen in the white skin. It was as ignominious and callous an act of betrayal as any of us were guilty of that day.

At the very moment the last Americans were plucked off the Duc Hotel roof, Lacy Wright and Joe McBride were on their fifth trip to the docks; T. D. Latz was ramming passengers into his chopper as it hovered on the edge of Pittman's rooftop patio; and Moorefield's bus convoy was still meandering through the city. At one point the convoy pulled up to a tree-shrouded villa not far from the Embassy, where Shep Lowman was waiting with the 1,000 VIPs he had called that morning. Lowman pleaded with Moorefield to let some of the Vietnamese on board. "I called for buses hours ago," he stammered. "We need help bad." But Moorefield shook his head. "Can't take on any more passengers," he shouted from the window of his staff car. "There'd be a stampede." With that, he drove on.

In the meantime, many of the American and foreign journalists who made up Saigon's motley press corps were converging on a designated assembly point in the center of town. Robert Shaplen, veteran of over twenty years of Indochina reporting, was alternately laughing and crying. Distressed at having to leave his beloved Saigon, he nonetheless found himself in a ludicrous predicament. In his rush to pack out of the Continental Hotel earlier in the day, he had broken the zipper on his pants and now couldn't quite keep them up. Since he had always cultivated a stylishly rakish image, some of his younger colleagues thought it only too appropriate that he should be tripping over his trousers at the exit.

Malcolm Browne, Polgar's erstwhile contact, was particularly conspicuous among his journalistic colleagues in his flak jacket and steel helmet. He and his *New York Times* staff, in fact, were the only members of the press corps who seemed dressed for war. Earlier that morning, at the prompting of their superiors in New York, they had decided to leave with the other evacuees, since none wished to end up like so many of their colleagues in Cambodia, helplessly confined to some Embassy compound as Communist forces moved in and took over.

A few of the American reporters in the city, however, had opted to stay on. The Associated Press bureau chief even devised an elaborate charade to fool his competitors at United Press International into thinking he was leaving, so they would do so themselves. After closing his downtown office, he walked to the assembly point with his staff, and then stole back through the crowds to set up shop again. The ruse, as it turned out, was pointless. The UPI staffers waited too long to try to get to the Embassy and were ultimately locked out. Both UPI and AP thus were left in Saigon to cover the Communist takeover.

Among the journalists who gathered at the bus stop this chaotic afternoon was Keyes Beech, dean of the American press corps in Saigon. Like Shaplen, he was hardly enthusiastic about having to turn tail and run, but since his reporting had never been particularly sympathetic to the "revolution," there was little chance he would be welcome as a guest in a Communist-dominated Vietnam.

When a small bus convoy finally swung by to pick up Beech and his colleagues, many of them undoubtedly felt hugely relieved despite all their other emotions. At least they were now on their way. But in fact, their ordeal was only beginning. "Nobody on that bus will ever forget the next few hours," Beech later wrote in a dispatch. "We were a busload of fools piloted by a man who had never driven a bus and had to wire the ignition when it stalled because the Vietnamese driver had run away with the keys the night before. 'I'm doing the best I can,' said Bill Austin of Miami, Oklahoma, the man at the wheel, as we careened through narrow streets, knocking over sidewalk vendors, side-swiping passing vehicles, and sending Vietnamese scattering like leaves in the wind.

"At every stop Vietnamese beat on the doors and windows pleading to be let inside . . . Every time we opened the door we had to beat and kick them back. For no reason except that we were following another bus, we went to the Saigon port area, one of the toughest parts of the city, where the crowds were uglier than elsewhere . . . I got off the bus and went over to John Moore, the Embassy security officer, who was sitting in one of those sedans with the flashing blinker on top. 'Do you know why we are here and what you are going to do with us?' I asked him. Moore shrugged helplessly. 'There are ships,' he said, gesturing toward sandbagged Vietnamese vessels lying alongside the dock. I looked around at the gathering crowd. Small boys were snatching typewriters and bags of film. This, as the Chinese would say, looked like a bad joss. I didn't know how or whether I was going to get out of Saigon, but I damned well knew I wasn't going to stay here. I got on the bus . . . I found myself pushing a middle-aged Vietnamese woman who had been sitting beside me and had asked me to look after her because she worked for the Americans and the Viet Cong would cut her throat. That's what they all said and maybe they are right. But she fought her way back to my side. 'Why did you push me?' she asked. I had no answer."

At approximately 3 A.M., Washington time, Special Assistant Lawrence Eagleburger advised Kissinger that the first choppers had landed in Saigon. General Carey had finally brought his long-delayed sortie in. Option IV, "Frequent Wind," was at last in train.

In the sun-baked courtyard inside the DAO compound, heavily armed marines were soon fanning out toward the perimeters as one after another of the CH-46s and CH-53 Sea Knights fluttered in. There were three landing zones in all—the parking lot inside the DAO annex, a nearby baseball field and the tennis courts alongside the DAO theater in the main compound—and passenger lines quickly formed at each. An Air Force colonel who was organizing the lift at the least hospitable of them, the ball park, was soon covered from head to toe with an oily soot, like a vaudevillian in black face. A few days before, in a vain effort to damp down the dusty surface of the playing field, DAO technicians had sprayed it with oil. Now the downdraft from the incoming choppers whipped up a cloud of grime and grit that clung to everything and everyone it touched.

As a pair of choppers dropped in out of the sun and came to rest in the annex area, Don Hays felt like cheering. For him and the 3,000 evacuees around him, the marines had arrived not a moment too soon. Vietnamese paratroopers had just cut another hole in the security fence and were filtering into the crowds, and would surely have overrun the compound in another fifteen or twenty minutes. But now the marines waded into them, beating them to the ground, disarming them.

"Who're these gooks?" one marine with a foundry worker's build asked Hays, gesturing to the civilians in the compound.

"All legitimate evacuees," Hays shouted over the whir of the rotors. The marine nodded and ordered his men to begin organizing passenger-loads of sixty. He also urged Hays himself to leave. "Not yet," Hays replied grimly. "I made a promise to these Vietnamese. I'm staying till the last one of 'em is on a chopper."

At approximately 3:12 P.M., Saigon time, one of the big CH-53s lifted up out of the DAO compound and headed for the fleet, setting a course parallel to the Saigon–Vung Tau highway. Another chopper, loaded with marines, veered off in the direction of the Embassy. Within minutes it quivered to a landing in the parking lot behind the chancery, as Vietnamese civilians and newsmen fluttered about it like pieces of blown scrap paper. Polgar rushed to a window on the sixth floor and pressed his face against the plastic pane. "Thank God!" he said over and over. "I think we now have a chance."

His optimism in fact was premature. For the next hour and a half the helo-lift out of the Embassy courtyard was held in abeyance as Marine reinforcements, ultimately 130 in all, were flown in from DAO to augment the forty-four-man guard force already in place.

The arrival of the additional troops undoubtedly helped to intimidate and subdue the mobs just outside the gates, but it also added to the command and control problems within the compound itself. Inexplicably, no headquarters unit was inserted with the Marine force, so the commander, Major Kean, was suddenly faced with the responsibility of controlling a large security contingent as well as preparing for the helo-lift. He was unable to devote his attention fully to either task.

Despite the delay in the helo-lift out of the courtyard, Air America choppers were now landing and taking off every few minutes from the Embassy roof, and soon the labyrinthine interior of the building became a throbbing catacomb as hundreds of evacuees crowded into the halls to await an outbound flight. From time to time an acquaintance of Polgar's would break out of the lines and dart into his office to pay final respects. Ted Sarong, the retired Australian brigadier general who had helped to persuade Thieu months before to adopt "Light at the Top, Heavy at the Bottom," dropped by with the girl

friend of a senior Mission Council member on his arm. The South Korean
Ambassador who had abandoned his own Embassy several hours earlier and
had been waiting in Martin's office downstairs also turned up. A distraught
Japanese diplomat drifted in and demanded vainly to be allowed to return to
his own Mission a few blocks away. He had arrived on a diplomatic errand
during the morning and now found himself locked in. We advised him, in view
of the mounting chaos outside, to take his chances with us—which he reluctantly did, departing by chopper for the evacuation fleet a short while later.

Downstairs, on the third floor, Martin wandered forlornly around his
private suite, sifting through the last of his files, stuffing the choicest cables into
manila folders. Earlier, around two-thirty, he had taken a shower in the small
lavatory off his office, and was still in the process of dressing when the first
Marine choppers whirred into the DAO compound. Soon afterward Eva Kim
burst in on him unexpectedly, and prim and proper as she was, nearly collapsed from embarrassment at the sight of America's last Ambassador to the
Republic standing behind his desk in undone trousers and nothing more.
Martin, preoccupied with his papers, never batted an eye.

Several minutes later, suit and tie in place, he walked into the anteroom
and handed the manila folders to one of the secretaries. She was to guard them
with her life, he said, and ensure they were evacuated. They contained his own
most recent communications with Kissinger, "to be preserved for history."

He then turned to his Marine bodyguards and told them politely but
firmly that he intended to return to the Residence once again. Yes, he said,
as he was bombarded with protests, he knew the streets were in turmoil and
that he would again have to make the trip on foot. Even so, he meant to do
it. He had just remembered some important unfinished business at home.

Martin and his nervous Marine escorts strode through the gate of his
rambling villa shortly after 3 P.M. One of the house servants who had chosen
to stay behind was waiting for them at the door. Under his arm he was holding
a wriggling black poodle named Nit Noy ("Small Thing" in Thai), which had
been a fixture of the Martin household for years. Earlier in the day Martin had
decided to leave the dog at the Residence, on the assumption that a political
deal could be arranged and that he himself would be staying on. Nit Noy was
to have been his companion as he stood sentry for American interests in the
wake of a negotiated settlement. But now that the Embassy was to be shut
down altogether, neither the Ambassador nor Nit Noy had any further role
in Saigon. Martin scooped up the dog, turned on his heel, and trudged back
out to the street as his Marine guards scurried after him.

Stamping, screaming Vietnamese were now packed twenty and thirty
deep in front of each of the Embassy's gates, and Martin and his bodyguards
had no choice but to slip into the compound by way of the French Embassy
next door. Martin took advantage of the detour to pay yet another brief call
on Mérillon.

The Frenchman, still cloistered in his private study, had nothing encouraging to tell him. The PRG officials at Tan Son Nhut had rejected Mar-

tin's offer to meet with them. And although President Minh had sent four envoys of his own to their compound around midday to propose a new negotiating formula—a peace conference in Saigon to settle "military questions" and another one in Paris to address "political issues"—the PRG had so far proved unresponsive.

Martin shrugged. Perhaps it was too late after all, he sighed. Perhaps the Communists were bent on total victory. In any case, there was little more he could do. The American presence was to be dismantled. After thanking Mérillon again for "all his help," Martin walked out into the courtyard to the wall between the French and American compounds, knocked three times on the connecting door, and was admitted again to his own shrinking sanctuary.

For once Jean-Marie Mérillon had been right about Communist intentions. The PRG indeed had no interest in Minh's latest proposals. When his four envoys arrived at Tan Son Nhut that afternoon, the PRG delegates brushed aside their overtures and invited them, instead, to sit down and share some bananas with them which they had grown in the garden of their compound. The envoys reluctantly agreed. Finally, after an hour or so of useless banter, they got up to leave, promising to call publicly for the negotiations Minh envisioned. The Communist delegates smiled benignly and kept on chomping their bananas.

Shortly after Martin departed on his final foray outside the Embassy, Lehmann beckoned Alan Carter to his office and told him flatly it was time for him and the remaining USIA staffers to leave. Since the helo-lift was off to such a late start, he said, there wouldn't be time for many flights before nightfall. So it was imperative to begin moving out even senior Embassy officials.

Carter frowned and reminded Lehmann of the group of local USIA employees gathered at his own villa several blocks away. "Don't worry about them," Lehmann assured him. "The Mission Wardens' office will do what it can to take care of them. In the meantime, you would do well just to follow orders. We've got to start clearing this compound now."

A short time later, as Carter wedged himself in among the crowds on the sixth floor, he spotted me in Polgar's anteroom and came in to say goodbye. "I've been told to get out," he grumbled. "Seems there's nothing more I can do." I told him Polgar was in the same predicament—immobilized. Carter nodded, clasped my hand, then walked back into the hall. But just as he was being ushered up to the rooftop pad, his eternal optimism got the best of him. "Damnit, I can't leave now," he muttered as he handed his suitcase to a subordinate. "There must be something I can do for our locals." For the rest of the afternoon he scraped about for a solution, pleading with DAO and Mission Warden officers to send buses to his residence for them. But by the time he placed his third or fourth call to DAO, it was already too late. The convoy system was finally breaking down.

Twice in the past several hours mobs of panic-stricken Vietnamese had

attacked convoys as they wound their way through the center of Saigon, and
the Mission Warden officers serving as escorts were now nervous and trigger-
happy. Finally, around 3:35 P.M., General Smith decided to curtail all bus
service to DAO from the downtown area in deference to the chaos.

At about the same time Captain Carmody ordered the few remaining
American vessels at the Newport docks to depart for Vung Tau or to withdraw
to the more secure Khanh Hoi navy yard near the center of town. Not long
afterward, as the first of three American tugs swung into the Khanh Hoi
loading area, pandemonium erupted on the wharf as hundreds of anxious
Vietnamese pushed and jostled each other to be first in line. The skipper pulled
back into midstream to wait for the turmoil to subside. In the meantime,
another tug arrived with two more barges. As it turned out, the extra passenger
space they provided far exceeded what was needed. During the remainder of
the afternoon only about 6,000 people, well below the combined capacity of
the barges, were taken aboard. In repeated calls to the Embassy, Carmody
urged that additional evacuees be rounded up and sent down to the docks. But
with the streets of downtown Saigon now a bog of humanity, his pleas were
in vain. As Carter, Polgar and so many others in the Embassy searched
desperately for passenger space, the barges sat idle and half empty.

Amid a swirl of visitors and harried Station officers Polgar continued to
prowl his office like a small caged bear. Where was Ut? Why weren't there
more helicopters for the Embassy? Any word from the Palace? He reeled off
questions for which there were no answers as if to divert himself and the rest
of us from the dire implications of each one. At last Howard Archer, the
former MR 2 Base Chief, threw up his hands and told me he was leaving on
the next Air America chopper. He had seen such confusion before, in Nha
Trang, and was not about to stay around for a replay.

Others in the front office also were beginning to succumb to their nerves.
One of Polgar's secretaries had grown so agitated, she was no longer functioning in her usual practical and efficient way. At one point I caught her hammering away at the frame of a wall picture in Polgar's office with the butt of a
cocked .38-mm revolver. "Just taking the pictures down for Mr. P.," she
murmured as I grabbed her hand and thumbed the safety catch. I pushed her
back into the anteroom and suggested that she and the other secretary catch
the next Air America chopper out. There were heated protests from both of
them, but finally, at Polgar's insistence, they did as I recommended. As soon
as they had joined the other evacuees in the hall, I slid behind the reception
desk and began fielding calls and the accumulated cable traffic. From that
moment on, I was a focal point for whatever lines of command and control
still existed within the Station.

Shortly before 4 P.M. Ken Moorefield ended his wanderings through
the limbo of downtown Saigon and guided his small convoy of buses to

the parking lot across the street from the Embassy. As his passengers clambered off he advised them to try to make their way into the compound by the side entrance, or over the wall if necessary. Obviously, it was not going to be easy in either case. By now, thousands of Vietnamese had the Embassy grounds under siege.

Among those who stumbled out into the parking lot and gazed warily across the street at the mobs were Keyes Beech and the Vietnamese woman who had been at his elbow since the beginning of the journey. "I have worked for the U.S. government for ten years," she told him, "but you do not trust me and I do not trust you. Even if we could get to Tan Son Nhut, they won't let me on the plane. I'm going home to poison myself."

As the woman disappeared into the throngs Beech pulled out his notebook and thumbed through it for a telephone number. He knew he was going to need extra muscle to get inside that Embassy. Perhaps the CIA could provide it.

When I picked up the phone at the reception desk in Polgar's office, I immediately recognized the raspy midwestern accent on the other end. "How the hell do I scale the walls!" Beech sputtered at me, explaining that he was across the street with his old friend Bud Merick of *U.S. News & World Report* and several Vietnamese and Japanese newsmen.

I told him to head for the side street paralleling the Embassy's east wing, and to make his way to the small Vietnamese police precinct headquarters located there. The Mission Wardens' office had bribed the precinct chief several days before, and supposedly the police were ready to help any wayward American over the wall and into the Embassy itself.

Beech called back minutes later. The police had turned him away! he screeched. What now? Holding him on the line, I motioned to Phil Custer, who had just walked in. As Saigon Base Chief he should know why the police weren't cooperating. But when I asked him, he simply shrugged. "They've been bribed," he said disinterestedly, and turned his back. I picked up the receiver again. "Go to the Embassy gate," I said to Beech. "Maybe we can pull you over."

"Once we moved into that seething mass we ceased to be correspondents," Beech recorded. "We were only men fighting for our lives, scratching, clawing, pushing ever closer to that wall . . . We were like animals. Now, I thought, I know what it's like to be a Vietnamese. I am one of them. But if I could get over that wall, I would be an American again.

"Somebody grabbed my sleeve and wouldn't let go. I turned my head and looked into the face of a Vietnamese youth. 'You adopt me and take me with you and I'll help you,' he screamed. 'If you don't, you don't go.' I said I'd adopt him. I'd have said anything. Could this be happening to me? Suddenly my arm was free and I edged closer to the wall. There was a pair of marines on the wall. They were trying to help us and kicked the Vietnamese down. One of them looked down at me. 'Help me,' I pleaded. 'Please help me.'

"That marine helped me. He reached down with his long, muscular arm and pulled me up as if I were a helpless child. I lay on a tin roof, gasping for breath like a landed fish."

Beech and Merick stumbled into Polgar's anteroom a few minutes later. Both were sweat-soaked and choked for breath, and Merick looked like a walking cadaver, his face a rubbery white. I got them some soft drinks from the medical refrigerator on the fifth floor and pointed them toward the rooftop chopper pad. Beech turned to me. "Thanks," he said, in reference to nothing in particular. Then he paused and ran his hand nervously over his bald skull. "Goddamnit, though! The marines left our Vietnamese and Japanese friends outside the wall. They couldn't, or wouldn't, pull them over the wall."

At a villa on Tran Cao Van Street, a few blocks from the Embassy, Shep Lowman strode out to the front gate to scan the chaos in the street beyond. After nearly four hours not a single bus—aside from Moorefield's overpacked convoy—had materialized, and the 1,000 Vietnamese VIPs gathered around him were beginning to turn panicky. Nervous and desperate himself, he put in another call to Mel Chatman at the Embassy. Yes, the barges were still at Khanh Hoi, he was told, but as for the buses, well, there just weren't going to be any. Lowman hung up the phone slowly and turned to several of the Vietnamese near him. Believing candor the best policy, he repeated the sad news to them. If any of them wanted to go out by barge, he said, they would have to make their way to Khanh Hoi on foot.

There was a chorus of protests. "Maybe we ought to stay here," one of them argued. "Maybe the buses will come." Lowman shook his head. And then, as the Vietnamese haggled among themselves, he slipped out of the compound and headed off toward the Embassy, pushing and shoving his way through the raucous street crowds.

A block or so away, he passed by his own villa and spotted two old Vietnamese friends, Do Kien Nhieu, former mayor of Saigon, and Senator Nguyen Van Ngai, hovering at the front gate. He hailed them and invited them to come along with him to the Embassy. Both were eager enough, but Nhieu asked if they could wait there at the villa just a few minutes for his wife. He had sent her down to the docks earlier in the day, and now wanted to retrieve her and take her to the Embassy too. Lowman agreed, and they all sat down in his living room while Nhieu's adjutant ran off to the docks to fetch the lady.

Lowman tried to make small talk to ease the tension, but just as he was launching into an idle remark on the weather an explosion rocked the house and a piece of shrapnel sailed in through the window, clattering against the wall behind Senator Ngai's chair. "Do you really think we ought to wait?" Lowman asked anxiously. The two Vietnamese looked at each other, then back at him, and shook their heads. Instantaneously all three bolted toward the door. Fortunately (as they would later learn), Mrs. Nhieu had already set sail.

Because of the crush at the Embassy's front gate, Lowman and his companions went next door to try to gain entry through the French compound.

At first the French guards turned them away, since Mérillon had given them firm instructions not to admit any refugees. But finally, after much pleading, Lowman was able to persuade them to make an exception in his case. Within minutes he and his two Vietnamese friends were squeezing through the connecting door in the wall that led into the American chancery.

Lacy Wright, meanwhile, was wandering down a cul-de-sac on his own last mission of mercy. He had promised one of his Washington colleagues he would do everything he could to rescue his Vietnamese father-in-law. But in all his perambulations of the afternoon, he had yet to run across the man. "Finally I made one last attempt to find him," he recalled. "His house was in an alley—a middle-class neighborhood—across the street from the Ministry of Health. I left my truck outside and walked in to look for him. To my surprise, life back there was going on as if there was no crisis at all. Elsewhere, all over the city, Americans were running for their lives, helicopters were going off roofs, the airport was in flames. But here things were so quiet; the children were even playing in the street."

Wright poked his head into several of the small homes along the alley to ask for his passenger, but no one seemed to know him. At last he gave up and walked back to his van. Nudging it through the street mobs at a snail's pace, he drove over to his own villa near the Embassy. His Vietnamese guards had disappeared by now, and since he had no key of his own to the front gate, he was obliged to heft himself up over the wall. Inside, the neat little world he had created for himself this past year and a half was still intact. The books, clothes, household belongings—almost everything he owned—were all in their proper niches, for during the past two weeks he had never found a moment to ship out any of his personal effects. He had been too busy evacuating Vietnamese.

After tucking a toothbrush and some underwear in his briefcase, he called Eva Kim at the Embassy. He knew that 150 Vietnamese were still waiting to be picked up at a nearby rendezvous point and wondered if he could help. But Eva told him the time for helping was past. Conditions throughout the city were fast deteriorating, she said. Get to the Embassy at once.

It took Wright less than three minutes to jog the short distance from his villa to the back wall of the Embassy. Like Keyes Beech and so many others, he was dragged up over the parapets by U.S. Marine guards as frantic Vietnamese grabbed and clawed at his heels.

Another weary State Department officer who had spent his day on the streets was already inside the Embassy compound, trying to catch his breath. A few minutes before, Moorefield had likewise been pulled in over the wall, and now, after his myriad adventures and close calls of the past twelve hours, his nerves and emotions were demanding a respite. He sat on the back step of the Embassy with his head in his hands, and wondered if he was in any condition to do more. Perhaps he should simply join the passenger lines on the top floor of the Embassy and wait for space on an outbound chopper. But even as the thought came to him he dismissed it. He was a West Point graduate, after all, a former combat officer. Surely his talents and training could be put to some use. He stood up and gazed glassy-eyed at the score of Marine guards pacing along the wall of the compound. Yes, that was it, he thought to himself. At the very least he could do what he knew best: play soldier.

"We had a Marine company inside the compound now," he recalled, "but only a few officers, and none of them was particularly familiar with the layout. With my training and experience I kinda felt it incumbent on me to help them police the place, to try to keep the men in the ranks as relaxed as possible so they wouldn't be tempted to fire into the crowds.

"Some explosive problems had already developed. You'd find one Vietnamese inside the fence, the rest of the family on the other side, and they'd all be weeping and pleading with you to open the gate. But you knew there was no way to let one or two in without having to beat back hundreds more.

"Contrary to what some of the press stories said, it wasn't always so difficult for an American to get inside the compound. Often the Vietnamese would just stand aside and let you haul yourself over the wall. Maybe they thought we had rights above theirs—or were simply afraid no one would get in if the Americans didn't. And of course we were armed.

"They weren't so tolerant of their own, though. Try to get a Vietnamese through the gates or over the wall and it was a free-for-all. The rest probably figured they had entry rights too, and in fact many did. Some of them were waving documentation I myself had stamped the day before.

"By the time I started circulating, Colonel Madison from the Joint Military Team had taken charge of the compound and Marv Garrett's Mission Warden people had been assigned to control the flow of people from the recreation area to the landing zones in the courtyard. George White, Tom Gramatikus and Steve Bray were already lining passengers up so they could feed them to the helo-pad as each chopper landed.

"Dusk seemed to settle in rather early, and we quickly realized there would be a visibility problem for the pilots. The marines moved several cars up to the approach side of the pad and turned the headlights on. Then we brought out a very high ladder and I crawled up to the top and wired a floodlight to the section of the wall between the French Embassy and our own. In the meantime, several of Garrett's fellows got down on their hands and knees and began picking up those goddamn wood chips from the tree that had been cut down earlier in the day. They were all over the courtyard. You can imagine what one of them would have done if it was caught up in the prop blast of a helicopter and hit you in the face or the eye."

Around 5 P.M. General Smith again called the Embassy to check on the size of the evacuee population there. For the first time he got a fairly straightforward answer. One of Jacobson's subordinates had just completed a head count in the courtyard and the recreation compound, and calculated there were some 1,500 to 2,000 to be evacuated.

The mood among this mass of humanity was already turning volatile and dangerous. Only three military choppers had so far arrived to take on passengers, and another forty minutes would pass before the CH-46s and CH-53s were flowing continuously, in an airborne daisy chain, between the Embassy and the fleet. Meanwhile, rumors of abandonment and betrayal whipped through the crowds like random sparks, and time and again, to add to the tension, the sound of gunfire wafted in over the walls as looters and army stragglers rampaged through the abandoned British Embassy across the street.

Up on the sixth floor of our own chancery I tried to shut my mind to the chaos around me as I fumbled through telephone calls and the diminishing cable traffic. But any sort of detachment, I found, was impossible. Like Polgar, I was rapidly falling prey to the terrible emotions of the moment.

I had just hung up on my one hundredth or so distraught Vietnamese when "Harry Linden," a Station colleague, pushed through the crowds in the corridor outside and thrust yet another problem in my lap. As he leaned toward me across the receptionist's desk he was trembling, his thick metal-rimmed glasses flecked with sweat. "Our translators. They've been forgotten," he gasped. "All seventy of them and their families. They're still waiting to be picked up at their compound near the Duc."

Linden, a veteran CIA translator, felt a professional commitment to the Vietnamese who worked with him, for many were specialists in their fields, expert bilinguists who had frequently assisted Station personnel in translating important documents and interviewing prospective agents. Of all of our Vietnamese employees, they were perhaps the best acquainted with CIA operations and personnel. And yet, as Linden now breathlessly explained to me, the CIA officer responsible for assuring their safety had taken a chopper out earlier in the day.

I shoved Linden into Polgar's office and listened as he repeated the details to him. But Polgar quickly became impatient. "Get someone out there to handle the problem," he interrupted, gesturing to the dozen or so CIA officers who were now perched on chairs and sofas in the anteroom, guzzling Scotch and indulging in gallows humor. I took Harry by the arm and pulled him over to a telephone. "Call them," I said. "Tell them to get over to [Pittman's] place. Polgar has sent thirty of his friends there for a rooftop pickup. The translators may have to wait in line, but at least they'll have a chance." Linden nodded, picked up the phone and began dialing.

As he rattled off instructions to someone on the other end, I could hear hammering and muffled explosions echoing up the stairwell from the Embassy's fourth floor. CIA communications officers had begun destroying the radio equipment that linked us to Washington. They had not been officially authorized to do so, but had decided to go ahead anyway, leaving only the most essential gear to the end. Only minutes after they set to work with their axes and grenades, Ambassador Martin stormed up the stairs from his office below. "Cut out the racket!" he rasped through his laryngitis. "I can't hear myself think!" The CIA officers continued to hammer away, though more gently.

I sat there in the reception room, listening to Harry and the hammering, and wondering just how close we were to the end. I reached in my pocket and pulled out a crumpled piece of ticker and read it again. It was the intelligence report proclaiming the Communists' intention to shell the Presidential Palace at 6 P.M. I looked at my watch: less than an hour to go.

General Timmes called the Palace shortly after 5 P.M. to ask Minh about his latest contacts with the PRG. What had his representatives learned at Tan Son Nhut? Were the Communists determined to go through with their artillery attack? Minh was typically himself—vague and uncertain. He had been trying to arrange something, he said, but so far the PRG delegates had refused to deal, claiming that as military men they could not address political issues. But all was not lost, he added. Three professed "neutralists" were even now en route to the PRG compound to try to work out a cease-fire on their own. When Timmes heard the names he could not help feeling a twinge of bitterness. All three—Tran Ngoc Lieng, a lawyer; Professor Chu Tam Luan; and Father Chan Tin, a Redemptorist priest—had long been ardent critics of the U.S. role in Vietnam. That the fate of the remaining Americans in Saigon should now lie in their hands was perhaps the war's final irony.

Timmes knew he would never see his old friend Minh again, but he was determined not to dwell on maudlin farewells. "Goodbye," he said simply, and hung up. The conversation was indeed their last.

According to General Dung's memoirs, Minh's "neutralist" delegates were treated to the same evasions his four envoys had encountered earlier in the afternoon. In a radio message to Dung the PRG team members later gloated over their handling of the visitors. "Comrade Vo Dong Giang [the chief PRG spokesman] received them and confirmed our views outlined in the 26 April statement [calling for total abolition of the Saigon government]. After the talk they asked for permission to leave the camp, but when we told them our artillery was now bombarding Tan Son Nhut airport and it would be better for them to spend the night with us, they agreed to stay."

The neutralists' mission had been Minh's last hope. He had resolved not to take any further political initiatives, or to surrender, until the three returned. Their decision to remain with the PRG delegation left him paralyzed, unable and unwilling to take any action at all.

With the afternoon now all but spent, the last of the American tugs and barges at Khanh Hoi pulled away from the docks and sailed south toward Vung Tau, most of them still only half full. Among those on board was one of the Embassy officers who had made the voyage possible in the first place, Bob Lanigan. Except for a scattering of sniper fire near the mouth of the river, his trip downriver to the sea was as leisurely as a Sunday excursion.

A short while later the last of DAO's bus convoys, with 800 people jammed aboard, careened through the front gate of Tan Son Nhut. For the man in the lead staff car—Captain Tony Woods, Moorefield's former companion—this last trip had been indisputably one of the worst of the day. The troopers at the gate had turned the buses away five times, and only after General Smith had again threatened to call in air strikes had the guards waved them on.

Two miles down the road, in the processing center itself, Don Hays was still loading Vietnamese on choppers as fast as his flagging energies allowed. At approximately 5:30 P.M. General Smith advised the evacuation fleet that there were still some 1,300 potential evacuees in the annex and compound, including the Marine security force, now 840 strong. Analysts at the 7th Air Force headquarters in Thailand estimated it would take at least two more hours to pull all of them out.

Halfway round the world President Ford, still groggy after a fitful four hours' sleep, was even then calling the White House operations center for the latest news from the war zone.

Soon after twilight the weather turned sour, the dead heat of the afternoon giving way to heavy gusts of wind and occasional lightning. Up to now the marines in the Embassy courtyard had been guiding the choppers in by hand signals and body language, but as visibility dropped they switched on their walkie-talkies—only to discover, to their horror, that no one had given them the choppers' radio frequency. After several frantic telephone calls to DAO, Major Kean was finally able to pinpoint the proper channel.

When Lacy Wright wandered into the Ambassador's office sometime after nightfall, he was shocked at what he saw. "There was a lot of confusion up there," he later confided with typical understatement. Fifteen or twenty people were just standing around, wringing their hands or crooking their elbows in the best cocktail-party fashion. Walter Burke, the Consul General, was mixing a drink. Martin himself looked like a man in a sleepwalk as he chatted idly with George McArthur, the *Los Angeles Times* man. Only Eva Kim seemed hard at work, juggling three or four telephone calls at once. Just as she clicked off on one line, the signal light on another began winking frantically. "I'll take it," Wright said, picking up the receiver. The caller could hardly make himself understood for his sobbing. "We've been up here all day and nobody has come to get us," he murmured, identifying himself as a Vietnamese employee of DAO. He and 200 others like him were on a rooftop somewhere in downtown Saigon, still looking for deliverance.

"Too late for cars or choppers," Wright told him wearily. "You'll have to walk down to the docks. Some vessels may still be loading."

There was a brief silence on the line, then: "You mean you're going to leave us here to die?"

"Listen," Wright replied, "you've got only one chance. You'll have to leave the building and go down to the barges."

"So you won't help us. We're all going to die here."

Wright repeated his instructions, trying to reassure the caller, but before he could make certain the man understood, the line went dead.

On the back steps of the Embassy, Ken Moorefield was hurriedly finishing a meal of C-rations and trying to savor a moment's relaxation. But just as he was forking up his last bean and frank, a familiar figure broke away from the masses in the courtyard and dashed over. It was one of the Iranian ICCS members whom Moorefield had met while serving as a liaison officer to the delegation months before, though he was now anything but the cool, detached diplomat Moorefield remembered. A few minutes before, he and his teammates had been admitted to the compound through the secret door from the French Embassy and were now wedged in among the pushing and shoving Vietnamese at the pad. They apparently did not relish mixing with the masses and wanted special treatment. Would Moorefield help?

"Well, there was no question in my mind," Moorefield said later, "that given the importance of their position, we had to make sure the representatives of His Majesty's government were taken care of. So I personally escorted them through the crowds and up to Martin's office. But unfortunately, as we soon discovered, they'd brought a small crisis with them. In the process of squeezing through that door from the French Embassy, they'd dropped their cryptographic gear and left it on the French side. The door had been shut so quickly they couldn't pull it through. Now the communicator, the guy responsible for the equipment, was going absolutely berserk! It was his only function in life to preserve the security of that gear, and the idea of having it fall into the hands of a foreign government—particularly the French—was most unsettling for him. I guess he thought he would be marched before a firing squad once he got back to Tehran. The Iranian Ambassador told Martin about the problem and Martin called Mérillon. No use. We didn't get the equipment back. The Iranians left on the next chopper without it.

"After that little episode I took another breather. I got a chair and sat down on the Embassy's back steps to watch the panorama. It was the first opportunity I'd had in ten days to join the audience and I was trying to take in the scene and its implications. The helo-lift was going full steam by now, though takeoffs continued to be a problem. There wasn't much running room in the courtyard and that meant each pilot had to give his bird full power, then lift it up over the wall at a slight tilt. The CH-53 is a heavy chopper, anyway, and the marines were putting about seventy people on each one, about the max load.

"Couple of times the air currents nearly spelled disaster for us. A chopper would rise up ten feet—back down again—up about ten feet—back down again, while all of us held our breath. Finally the pilot would get enough power and air underneath him to pull off. But we all had nightmare visions of one of those birds crashing into the wall of the Embassy. And if a blade had ever gotten loose in that courtyard, well—there would have been a massacre.

"Those Marine pilots did a fantastic job. That's the only way to describe it—particularly when you consider all they had to contend with. Not only were they running a non-stop shuttle back and forth out of the courtyard, but they soon took over for Air America in handling pickups on the roof as well. The fatigue that set in must have been awful.

"And, of course, the Marine and Army guys on the ground did a magnificent job too. The marshaling had to be carried out quickly and efficiently so none of the choppers spent any more time on the pad than was absolutely necessary. That meant as soon as the wheels touched down, people had to be running for the rear door. Plus, you probably know the prop blast from one of those things is like ninety miles an hour, so there was a real danger that some of the women and children would simply be blown away.

"From time to time one of the Ambassador's emissaries—Wolf Lehmann, George Jacobson, Brunson McKinley—would come down to show the flag and offer advice. All of them were acting very important, with their little radios and their worried airs, as if they were in control. But in fact, the military was running the show quite efficiently without any help from them at all.

"Once George McArthur came out on the front steps, with his bifocals on, very cool, very dapper-looking, totally unruffled, you know, having expended no effort whatsoever. He was not taking notes or clicking off pictures. He was just observing.

"I knew they were drinking upstairs. There was an open bar in the Ambassador's office and I guess in Polgar's too. Given my experiences in the last ten days, this kind of embittered me. Here were these people who had not been responsible for the progress we'd made trying to nurture the illusion they had been—that they were in control—even as they were up there in the Ambassador's suite having a social hour. I'm not saying the Ambassador was. I imagine he never had a drop. You know his mentality. But for the rest . . .

"Anyway, here I was, just an observer for the first time in days, sitting on the steps, picking at this experience, thinking I had no role to play. Again it crossed my mind that I should leave. But I'd promised myself a week before I'd stay till the end, and as far as I could see, the end hadn't come yet.

"I recall thinking how lucky we were. The North Vietnamese obviously had decided to let us continue this evacuation, because it would have been the simplest thing in the world for a terrorist to lob a satchel charge over the wall, or for a lone rifleman in one of those buildings across the street to bring down a chopper. I was still carrying my M-16 and my .38 Smith and Wesson, but I knew none of us could have defended the compound if the VC had wanted to put us out of business."

Actually, Moorefield gave the North Vietnamese more credit than was due. Since daybreak three or four South Vietnamese aircraft had been downed by Communist ground fire on the very outskirts of Saigon, and only an hour and a half before, NVA forces ten nautical miles northeast of the city had opened up on two U.S. Phantom jets with a salvo of SA-7 missiles. The war planes had responded by blasting the launch positions with missiles of their own, heat-seeking "Wild Weasels." Fires from the secondary explosions were still raging. In effect, the Americans were back in the war.

Evening

The hands of the wall clock in the anteroom formed a near-perfect vertical —almost six o'clock. I sat down at the receptionist's desk and toyed absently with the straps of a discarded flak jacket. Had the Communists received Timmes' message in time? Or were we only minutes away from a massive NVA artillery barrage? None of the four or five other CIA officers across the room from me knew anything about the intelligence report foreshadowing the attack. Their nonchalance was almost as unnerving as the prospect of the battering itself.

At exactly six a large hollow explosion echoed through the building, and instinctively I slipped several inches lower in my chair, as if I could somehow tunnel in against the shattering barrage I was sure would follow. But moments passed—long, excruciating moments—and the reverberation died away without so much as an isolated burst of gunfire to punctuate it. Polgar walked out of his office and glanced at me. Apparently, in all the confusion of the afternoon, he had forgotten the intelligence report. Only that single explosion had brought it back to him.

Ken Moorefield was even at that moment stumbling across the Embassy lawn with his M-16 at the ready. "I thought a grenade or a satchel charge had gone off," he recalled, "but when I reached the front gate I saw a Volkswagen camper, full blaze, across the street. Some fool Vietnamese had dropped a match down the gas tank. Then—wham! Several people had been wounded, but I wasn't too eager to go over and find out how many. Two or three of the marines at the gate wanted to offer first aid, but I told them to forget it. They'd be sitting ducks for any sniper in the crowd."

Meanwhile, three miles away at Tan Son Nhut, fighting had broken out in the DAO annex. Don Hays, two other American civilians and several marines were busily rounding up another load of passengers when the trouble erupted. All at once Vietnamese paratroopers who had filtered in through holes in the fence on the far side of the compound began pumping rounds at them. The marines reacted quickly and effectively, first returning the fire, then subduing the snipers in a wild, stumbling chase through the crowds. When General Smith at the headquarters building learned what had happened he ordered his staff to move all evacuees at once to the more secure confines of the DAO compound itself. The annex was to be closed out altogether.

A Marine colonel alerted Hays to the shift and told him buses would be arriving momentarily, to haul the remaining 1,000 evacuees to the main compound. Hays and the two other civilians immediately began rounding up passengers. But no sooner had they pulled together their first busload of fifty than a radio message crackled in from the DAO control center. Vietnamese paratroopers had just overrun the patch of highway between the annex and the compound. The buses would be unable to get through.

Only one practical alternative was now open to Hays and his companions. A row of Quonset huts stood along the southern perimeter of the annex, and beyond it lay the DAO baseball field and one of the landing zones. If the evacuees were beaded out through the buildings, they might be able to jog undetected the short distance to the pad. Minutes later the first of the evacuees were sent on their way.

Within a half-hour the annex had been emptied and the marines began withdrawing toward the buildings adjacent to the baseball field. But as their lines collapsed and the last of them retreated across the parking lot, a group of Vietnamese paratroopers suddenly burst through the fence on the other side of the compound and charged after them. One of the marines hurled a torch on the nearest of the tinderbox barracks that had once served as a home for the American army. Instantly it was washed with flame, walling the paratroopers off from the Americans as they slipped out of the annex and headed for the landing zone.

Inside the DAO compound itself, a few hundred yards away, Nelson Kief, the DAO staffer from Pleiku, was even then calmly destroying his remaining classified files. He had just dipped into his last drawerful when he spotted two Army officers outside his window, pouring gasoline into two tin drums. That's a break, he thought to himself, and began bundling up the refuse. By the time he had lugged it outside, the officers had disappeared and the two drums stood unattended. Kief sidled over to one of them and opened the lid—and nearly fainted at what he saw. Stuffed in the bottom, in neat little bundles, were millions of dollars in cash. The gasoline had soaked a few of the bills, but the rest seemed as good as new.

Kief stared at the treasure a moment, not quite able to believe his eyes. He knew that earlier in the day General Smith had ordered the last of DAO's cash stocks destroyed. Evidently, what lay in the bottom of the drums was the bonanza itself, over three and a half million dollars in small bills. Only one thing was missing: the single match that would set them all ablaze. As far as DAO's records were concerned, Kief figured, that match had already been applied; the money had already been written off. He therefore could have reached in and pulled out a handful without anyone being the wiser.

He put his hands in his pockets and wandered around and around the drums. Would it really be dishonest, he wondered, to take just a few hundred dollars? Officially the money no longer existed, after all. And didn't he deserve a little recompense for all his losses and sacrifices of the past few weeks? In the two evacuations he had already been through—in Pleiku and Nha Trang —he had been forced to abandon everything he owned, even his last stitch of underwear. Now he could make good on it all. But the more he mulled over the possibility, the more uncomfortable he felt with it. "So many other things, more basic, seemed far more important at that moment," he said later. "The life I'd known for the past three years was disintegrating around me. Many of my Vietnamese friends had been lost. What the hell did I need money for, anyway?" He put the lid back on the drums and walked away.

Up in Polgar's reception room I was still trying to convince myself that the NVA had called off their shelling attack when the phone on the desk in front of me rang. Over the din in the streets outside I could just barely make out the voice on the other end. It was Ut, Polgar's driver.

"Harry," I shouted, holding the receiver out to Linden, who was leaning on a desk across from me. "Ut's on the line. See if you can make out what he's saying! He's yelling his head off in Vietnamese."

Linden barked a few words into the mouthpiece, listened, then looked over at me. "Says the stairs to the roof over on Gia Long are jammed with people. Can't move his thirty Vietnamese to the pad. What should he do?" Polgar overheard the exchange from the door of his office. "Tell him to come to the front of the Embassy itself, goddamnit!" he shouted. "I'll pull him and all of them over the wall even if it causes a riot."

As Linden repeated the message over the line, Polgar motioned to Phil Custer, Bill Johnson and several of the younger officers gathered in the ante-room. "You're all coming with me down to the wall," he said. I stood up to join the group, but Polgar shook his head. Pittman and I were to stay in the office, he indicated, to handle what was left of business.

Several of the anointed immediately began stuffing revolvers and billy clubs into their belts. One of Custer's trusted subordinates strapped a white sweatband around his head. Within minutes they were all elbowing their way out through the crowds in the corridor. Harry Linden stared at me, as if expecting some kind of guidance, then turned and followed them out.

A half-hour later Polgar and his colleagues were still heaving Vietnamese over the wall, with the help of a few reluctant marines. Throughout it all, Polgar himself stood pressed against the front gate, pointing out friends in the crowd. Bill Johnson, meanwhile, climbed up on the parapet itself to hoist the women and children over. He was as vulnerable and conspicuous as a silhou-ette target on a firing range. But miraculously no one took a shot at him. Instead, the Vietnamese on the sidewalks just below him began jostling and clubbing each other in a mad scramble to reach this last of the American saviors. From time to time an unwanted Vietnamese would grasp his hand or sleeve and try to heft himself up—only to be booted back by one of the CIA men or the marines.

By the time Polgar and the rest finally slumped back into the anteroom on the sixth floor, they all seemed a little dazed. There were scores of bloodied knuckles and torn fingernails among them, and several members of the group, who apparently had had their fill of heroics, quickly gathered up their belongings and stumbled into the hall to await an outbound chopper. When Polgar himself limped in, he had a clutch of suitcases underarm and four or five Vietnamese women and children trailing behind, and as he bundled them all into a side office, tears and sweat glistened on his cheeks like small glass seams.

A quick head count told the reason for his gloom. Despite all their exertions, Polgar and his colleagues had managed to pull only a few of the chosen thirty over the wall. And among those they had missed were some of the most favored, including Ut, the brave chauffeur who had engineered the rescue from the start. Polgar wandered to a window and stared out into the darkness. "I think I saw him in the crowd," he kept murmuring to himself, "but I could not reach him. I simply could not."

As he repeated these words over and over, Harry Linden shuffled up to the receptionist's desk and tried to steady himself on the edge of it. He gazed at me with terrible expressionless eyes. "None of them," he whispered. "I saw none of our translators down there. They're still outside. Lost."

Ten or fifteen minutes later T. D. Latz pushed into the anteroom. "Goddamn Viets," he growled as he nursed a bleeding right hand. "Rushed me on the roof over there at Gia Long. I had to slug one or two to get them to line up, nicelike. Hell of a lot of 'em, though. Some trips, I couldn't even squeeze myself onto the chopper. Had to ride the skids."

He looked at Polgar and frowned. "I don't know if I got any of your fellows," he added. Polgar gave a shrug of resignation and dragged himself into his office. Latz and I followed him. "The translators haven't been heard from," I said. "Maybe we ought to try another rooftop pickup."

Polgar said nothing. He was standing at his desk with his head bowed. Latz impatiently thrust himself into the silence. "No way I can go out again," he asserted. "Ain't easy landing a chopper on an unfamiliar pad even in broad daylight. After nightfall it's suicide."

In Washington, meanwhile, Kissinger had just called President Ford in his sleeping quarters to tell him the evacuation was moving along smoothly —though perhaps more slowly than planned.

It was around six-thirty when Air America ended its rooftop "extraction" operations in downtown Saigon. Most of its helicopters were now running dangerously low on fuel, and as T. D. Latz emphasized to Polgar, the onset of darkness made further rooftop landings a deadly gamble.

For some of the Embassy officers who had been laboring on the rooftop pads throughout the day, however, the shutdown came all too soon. Walt Martindale, for one, had been insisting for the past hour and a half that additional choppers be dispatched to pull the Vietnamese out of his own apartment complex, not far from Tan Son Nhut. From his vantage point atop the building he could now see thousands of Vietnamese jammed in the streets below. At one point, a half-hour before, two drunken American contractors had punched their way to the gate, and Martindale and several Vietnamese friends had been obliged to go downstairs and pull them over. This select act of charity had whipped the crowds outside into a frenzy, and one Vietnamese woman, in an effort to climb over the surrounding fence herself, had become pinioned on a metal upright. Now she hung there like a speared fish, blood oozing slowly across the front of her white *ao dai.*

As Martindale gazed off toward the twinkling fires of Tan Son Nhut, he glimpsed the frail silhouette of an Air America Huey bearing down toward the building. Almost in the same instant a loud crash resounded up from the courtyard, and suddenly hundreds of fear-stricken Vietnamese were pouring through the broken gate toward the entrance of the building.

Two Vietnamese army lieutenants who had been helping Martindale load choppers since early afternoon pulled pistols from beneath their shirts. "We'll hold off the crowds for you," they promised him, "if you'll make sure we get out of here."

Martindale nodded, and the three of them bounded into the building's interior stairwell to try to lock the steel shutters near the top. But they were too late. Scores of Vietnamese were already snaking up the stairs toward them. Martindale backed up onto the roof as his two companions held the crowds at gunpoint. At that moment the Air America Huey shuddered to a landing on the pad. "Come on! Come on!" the pilot yelled to Martindale. But the young Embassy officer shook his head. He called to the two ARVN troopers in the dimness of the stairwell. "Start organizing a chopper load. We'll put all we can aboard!"

Within a few minutes ten Vietnamese clutching bags and children stumbled onto the roof and Martindale quickly ushered them toward the chopper. The pilot continued to protest: "We want you! Not more Vietnamese." But Martindale and the pair of army officers ignored him. They were already counting off another load.

Finally the Air America Huey lumbered off, packed to twice its normal capacity. Martindale watched it fade away in the distance, and then resumed his count. But even as he did, the enforced discipline of the Vietnamese on the stairwell gave way. Someone screamed, the crowd lurched and then plunged up toward the roof as Martindale's two Vietnamese companions vainly waved their pistols at them. Martindale was driven nearly to the edge of the pad by the human flood. An old woman, a mama-san, struck him on the side of the head, and in a burst of light the world went silent. Everyone and everything in it seemed to lapse into slow motion. Out of the corner of his eye he saw another Air America Huey dropping in out of the darkness. The hordes around him rippled away from it, clearing a space, as it settled down. The pilot was now beckoning to him, all seemingly in slow motion, mouthing the words "Come on! Come on!" Someone else in the cockpit was holding an M-16 on the masses. The urgency of the moment seemed abruptly to slip away. Martindale straightened up, motioned to the two army lieutenants to follow him, and walked leisurely toward the chopper. As he and his two friends were yanked through the hatchway, the sounds and horror of the scene around him came slamming back into his consciousness like a revelation. He was weeping uncontrollably as the chopper zoomed skyward, the Vietnamese abandoned on the roof below hurling pleas and insults after him.

But Martindale's adventure was not quite over. The pilot, out of concern for his dwindling fuel supply, decided to try to set down at Tan Son Nhut, at the Air America terminal which had been abandoned to rampaging Vietnamese troops earlier in the day. When the chopper spun into the loading area, there were no troops to be seen, and one of the Air America mechanics on board jumped out and began fumbling with the fuel pumps. Another, a Filipino, dashed off toward the nearby barracks that had housed the company's office. When the airline's management had pulled out of the compound that morning it had neglected to dispose of $50,000 tucked away in a small office safe. The crew of Martindale's chopper was now determined to make up for that oversight. But as the Filipino was desperately tinkering with the combination lock, several Vietnamese army stragglers appeared on the far side of the runway and began firing at the idling chopper. In an instant all the passengers were back on board—without the money. Forty minutes later they were clambering out onto the deck of the USS *Midway* in the South China Sea.

The Huey that carried Martindale and his companions to safety was one of the last Air America choppers to leave Saigon that evening. Since midmorning, when the rooftop pickups began, the company's daring and heroic pilots had hauled over 1,000 passengers to the Embassy, DAO or the fleet. That was no small accomplishment, to be sure, particularly in view of the fact that the maximum capacity of each Huey was barely twelve people.

Down the street from the Embassy, at the Presidential Palace, Minh was now pacing nervously around his empty office. There still had been no word from the PRG delegation at Tan Son Nhut, and several of his closest aides were urging him to declare an unconditional surrender. But he could not bring himself to do it. Too many of his countrymen would think ill of him, he said. He would postpone any such decision until he had formed his cabinet. At least, then, others would be forced to share the humiliation.

At the Embassy itself other erstwhile stalwarts were not so reluctant to give up the ghost. Shep Lowman caught a helicopter off the roof at 7 P.M., and was followed by a number of his colleagues. Another of those who decided time had run out was my own old friend and fellow analyst, Joe Kingsley. Since midafternoon he had been helping the marines in the courtyard ram passengers aboard the helicopters, but by now his twelve-hour hangover had got the best of him. The last straw, it turned out, was an American newsman.

Each military chopper was now taking on sixty to eighty passengers, far beyond capacity, and an hour or so before, the marines had decided to load without luggage to assure maximum seat-space. But several of the news photographers in the courtyard had failed to get the word, or had chosen to ignore it, and were now demanding that they be allowed to haul all of their gear aboard.

They had failed to reckon with Joe Kingsley, however. As one of them tried to elbow aside an old Vietnamese woman and push his cameras and tripods into the cabin, Kingsley tapped him on the shoulder, flattened him with a roundhouse in the jaw, and threw his cameras into the bushes. With that, Joe figured he had done his good deed for the day and pulled himself aboard the next outborne CH-53. Close on his heels was his Green Beret chum, who had resolved, after all, not to "go down with the ship."

On the third floor of the Embassy, in the Ambassador's suite, Lacy Wright was still helping Eva Kim with the telephones. Shortly after 7 P.M. a Frenchman, who had taken refuge in the abandoned New Zealand Embassy across the street from Martin's own private residence, called to ask for help in evacuating several Vietnamese with him. "Just keep them there," Wright advised him. "I suspect the North Vietnamese will respect foreign legations."

The Frenchman paused, than asked Wright to pass a personal message to Martin. Vietnamese looters, he reported, had just broken into the Ambassador's villa. In the confusion he himself had managed to salvage at least one item and would mail it to Martin at the State Department. It was an autographed picture of former President Nixon.

In the corridor outside Polgar's anteroom the queue of evacuees had turned almost exclusively Vietnamese. There were few Americans among them, and even fewer of us in Polgar's front office, maybe no more than fifteen in all, including Polgar himself, Pittman, Timmes, Custer, Bill Johnson, some communication men and several chosen underlings like myself. Aside from the claque of hangers-on in the Ambassador's office, possibly a dozen State Department officers were still in the Embassy, helping the marines herd passengers up to the rooftop pad.

The hordes of Vietnamese now jammed into every corner of the building were a collage of wasted hopes. Many were carrying all they owned in small brown paper bags. Some had dogs and cats underarm. The children stared in bewilderment at the chaos around them, and as the Embassy's air-conditioning system broke down, the stench and heat in the corridors became unbearable. From time to time I walked down the lines, handing out cups of water or C-rations from the Station's emergency stocks, none of which (thankfully) had been locked away. Occasionally Polgar emerged from his office to read the cable traffic still trickling in over our communications net or to check on the group of Vietnamese he had brought with him up from the wall. One of them, an extraordinarily beautiful woman of mixed Vietnamese-French parentage, sat weeping throughout the evening at a desk in a side office with a small child in her arms. In the crush at the wall she had become separated from her Vietnamese army husband and two older children. They had been left in the crowds outside.

The marines on each floor continued to work quickly and efficiently, funneling the assembled Vietnamese up toward the roof. Most of the troopers, in their late teens or early twenties, were too young to have fought in the war or to have marched with the protesters seven or eight years before, and from my vantage point in the anteroom I watched them with admiration and a little envy. For them this was merely a job. They would finally be able to walk away from it with a furlough or a few extra medals and no sense of loss.

One of them caught sight of a colleague of mine in the anteroom drawing hard on a cognac bottle. "What the hell is going on here?" he demanded, striding up to my desk. "Don't you guys know there's a war on? You'd better get out of here." I gently guided him back to the door, explaining we were involved in evacuating "agents." He looked at me with a certain awe. "You guys spooks?" he asked conspiratorially. I nodded. "Well, in that case, it's all right if you stay," he said, and walked back to the masses in the hall.

General Smith had intended to remain at his post as long as Martin wanted him. Although he had already received orders from Gayler to evacuate, he felt his first responsibility was still to the Ambassador. But even as the marines at the nearby landing zone in the DAO baseball field sent the last of their evacuees on their way, Smith was obliged to change his plans.

The deciding factor was a loss of power—electrical power. Around 7:15 P.M. the lights in the operations center deep in the bowels of the DAO headquarters building itself suddenly blinked out. One of Smith's staffers soon discovered that a Vietnamese saboteur had shorted out an incoming power line with a long wooden pole. An emergency generator was immediately cranked up, but DAO technicians, on surveying the damage, found that the surge of current on the circuits had knocked out the satellite terminal that supported DAO's communications with Washington and the rest of the world. Smith was told it would take about forty minutes to put the station back on the air. With only thirty staffers still at his side, he decided it wasn't worth the effort.

At 8 P.M., Saigon time, Smith led his staff out to the landing zone in the tennis court. As they were lining up to board a waiting chopper, a bus packed with Vietnamese pulled up outside the gate. Smith stood aside and let these late arrivals take his place. He and his few remaining staffers caught the next helicopter out. They were airborne by 8:15.

Among those who flew out with the general and his group was a very weary Don Hays. As the big CH-53 lunged up over the edge of the compound the young Embassy officer took one final look at Tan Son Nhut. As far as he could see, the airfield was littered with fireballs, each going from blue to green to brilliant white as it rolled its way through rows of parked aircraft. He stared out at these Disneyesque images for a few moments, unable to believe that they, and everything else he had witnessed this day, were now part of the irretrievable past. Finally he bowed his head and slept, for the first time in four days.

From this point on, the DAO compound belonged to General Carey and his Marine security force, and for the next hour they continued to lift last-minute Vietnamese evacuees aboard the diminishing supply of choppers bound for the fleet. Only one of Smith's own subordinates, a contract engineer from the Federal Electric Company, had remained behind to lend assistance. It was his job to ensure that DAO's sophisticated communications gear was all properly destroyed.

From the moment the first military chopper had landed in the Embassy courtyard around midafternoon, Martin had insisted that the evacuation be carried out on a first-come, first-served basis; the Americans were to receive no preferential treatment. But as with practically every aspect of the airlift, the Ambassador's dictates finally counted for little against the pressure of events. Throughout the late afternoon and early evening well-meaning Embassy officers had persisted in helping whomever they chose in whatever manner they could. Some slipped Vietnamese friends to the head of the waiting lines; others, like Polgar, shadowed the gates, demanding that the marines open up whenever they spotted a friend or colleague in the crowds outside.

Finally, one of the Mission Warden officers had all he could tolerate, and stormed up to the third floor of the Embassy to register his concerns with Jacobson. In the midst of his harangue Martin walked in. "I'm not aware that anyone is being given priority in terms of seat space," the Ambassador declared serenely. "Everybody is supposed to be an equal here." The Mission Warden officer was so stunned by the remark he could not restrain himself. "Well, sir," he said, "obviously you don't know what's happening out there. Every rule is breaking down." Then, without waiting for a reply, he stalked out. Martin clearly was out of touch, he thought angrily to himself as he waded back into the crowds in the courtyard. The evacuation had become a free-for-all.

By 8:45 Moorefield was prowling the Embassy grounds, looking for some new challenge to justify his continued presence. The marines and Colonel Madison seemed to have the landing and the loading under control, and the crowds in the recreation compound, though still expanding, were as orderly as could be expected, so he was not needed there. He turned and ambled back toward the Embassy's main gate, and it was then he spied several Mission Warden officers on the wall at the far end of the compound. He watched for a few moments as they reached down in the darkness on the other side and began hefting excited Vietnamese policemen up and over the top. By the time the third policeman had been lifted out of the gloom Moorefield was up on the wall himself, straining with the rest. "Several days before," he recounted, "the Mission Warden had promised the officers in the adjacent police compound that we'd take care of them if they would help keep law and order around the Embassy. Now we were paying off."

Everything ran smoothly at first. A ninth, then a tenth police official was pulled into the compound without incident or confusion. But even as Moorefield and his companions were leaning over to grasp another outstretched hand, there was a commotion in the anxious crowd below them. Several of the police officers suddenly became very agitated and tried to climb up on the wall themselves, and within seconds countless hands and groping fingers were locked over the parapet. Some of the stronger Vietnamese managed to wriggle over by themselves, bumping and jostling the Americans up top. Moorefield himself almost lost his balance. "Give us a hand here!" he screamed to a group of marines in the courtyard. "Give us a hand!" Four of the marines were at his side in an instant. They went to work with appropriate military precision, cracking heads with rifle butts, stomping on hands and fingers as wave upon wave of humanity broke on the wall below them like a storm tide. It took them less than three or four minutes to restore calm, but to Moorefield those minutes seemed like eons. At last he straightened and stood shoulder to shoulder with the marines as they waved their M-16s at the police who had not been able to scramble over. "They were just standing back, staring up at us," Moorefield recalled. "I don't know if it was with hostility, disdain, disinterest or what. Their faces were blank, like death masks."

Shortly after 9 P.M. Jim Devine swept through the Ambassador's suite. "Time for most of you non-essentials to leave," he said, half jokingly, gesturing to several of his colleagues. With the Embassy locked up, the barges gone and General Smith on his way, there was not much more for any of them to do.

Lacy Wright and Dan Ellerman, the economic counselor, picked up their attaché cases and walked to the stairwell. Alan Carter, exhausted and embittered after his many futile attempts to muster out help for his stranded USIA employees, was not far behind, and Eva Kim, Martin's secretary, soon joined them at the lip of the rooftop pad. For once in her career Eva looked just a little rumpled, the hair slightly out of place, the easy, confident manner gone. But there was little else about her demeanor to betray the fact that she was preparing to turn her back on her home and haven of the past eleven years. Secretary to three ambassadors before Martin, she probably knew more of the Embassy's secrets than anyone else alive, and was less likely to tell, for in the end as in the beginning she remained the utterly loyal subordinate, discreet, self-disciplined, if not entirely unquestioning.

As she walked across the pad to the idling chopper George McArthur, the *Los Angeles Times* man, stumbled after her, leaning into the prop blast to steady himself. He was almost at the hatchway when a small bundle under his arm assumed a life of its own, squirming, twisting, and finally letting out a few pitiful yelps. "Now, now, it'll be over in a few minutes," he said soothingly to the nervous black dog tucked away in the folds of his coat. He then handed Nit Noy, the Ambassador's poodle, to Eva and lifted both of them into the cabin. As a personal favor to Martin, McArthur had agreed to serve as the dog's chaperone on this last, short ride out of the country.

The CH-47 lifted off almost immediately and circled once to gain altitude. Gazing out of a porthole at the city he knew so well, Lacy Wright felt no personal regrets. He had done his best for his Vietnamese friends and for American policy these past few weeks. Still, he could not help wondering about those Vietnamese he had not been able to track down during this last turbulent day. How terrible it must be for them now, the horror of knowing they would not get out even as the big military choppers continued to drone across the night sky above them.

He tried to conjure up out of the bleary memories of the day the faces he had seen on the streets, the noises, smells and the sense of apprehension. He attempted to fix all of them in his mind, indelibly for all time, for he knew they were unique for an American, the legacy and the shame of total defeat.

At 9:30 A.M., Washington time, the bureaucrats at the State Department, CIA headquarters and the Pentagon were struggling with their first cups of coffee of the morning and trying to focus on the priorities of the new workday. At the White House, Kissinger told Ford the evacuation out of DAO had been completed. Over 4,500 people, including 450 Americans, had been lifted out of Saigon since the initiation of Option IV. That in itself was a spectacular achievement—though it had not been without cost: only a short while before, according to a report from the fleet, one of the CH-53s had been lost at sea, just off the bow of a naval transport. There had been no evacuees on board, but the pilot and co-pilot were missing, and presumed dead. Pilot fatigue was believed responsible for the accident. The airlift had been running for nearly six hours; the weather was now deteriorating, with visibility diminishing as well. Apparently, in his weariness, the pilot had simply miscalculated the remaining distance to the flight deck.

Ford questioned Kissinger about the wisdom of suspending the airlift till the morning. That was what the military wanted, wasn't it? Kissinger said yes, but there were other considerations to be taken into account. The tacit "understanding" with the North Vietnamese, guaranteeing safe transit for the choppers, was tenuous at best. If the evacuation was shut down and then resumed later, Hanoi might well misinterpret the intent behind it. And if that happened, pilot fatigue and navigational error would be the least of anybody's worries.

Kissinger called Martin long distance to solicit his opinion, but for once Martin was not available. The Ambassador was even then roaming the recreation compound, making a head count of his own.

As I walked past the door of Polgar's office I saw him kneeling on a suitcase, trying to press it closed. "We're near the end," he said softly as he struggled with the latch. I asked him if I could help. He said no; he could manage. He was ready to leave.

I went back to the anteroom and began gathering up the scraps of classified cable traffic on the receptionist's desk. I was about to put a match to them when an old acquaintance sauntered in. It was Moorefield, whom I had not seen for days. He came striding out of the crowds in the hallway like a diminutive god of war, his face and blond hair smudged with gunpowder, the M-16 cradled idly on his right arm. His blue jumpsuit was cut to resemble a uniform and he wore it with a kind of dash, like the military man he once was. "I thought you'd already left from Tan Son Nhut," I said as we shook hands. "No, I decided to come back to the Embassy to see how the other half lives," he replied humorlessly, raising a critical eyebrow at my remaining colleagues, many of whom were slouched nonchalantly in chairs and sofas around the anteroom, glasses in hand. "What's with you guys? Looks like a cocktail party up here."

"That's the way we spooks work—through clever illusions," I said as I nudged him back toward the door. I was, in fact, ashamed of the spectacle around me and had no desire to share it with an outsider, even such a good friend as Moorefield. "Look, I'll see you on the outside," I said to him. "We're busy here." He smiled, and nodded as if he understood. Then he wheeled and sidled off down the hall, the rifle still nestled in the crook of his arm. As I looked after him I had the feeling I was glimpsing the last of a long line. Moorefield was, after all, the quintessence of what had once been a stock character in this place—the professional American warrior seeking some proof and satisfaction for himself from the last of the available wars. And now he was an anachronism, like the rest of us.

Polgar sat down at his typewriter a few minutes later and pounded out a message to Washington, explaining he was ready to close shop, since there was no longer any role for intelligence officers here. He then took the message down to the third floor to clear it with the Ambassador. When he returned he said nothing, but merely picked up his suitcase. That served as a cue for the rest of us. I reached under the receptionist's desk for two small attaché cases I had managed to liberate from the litter of my own office earlier in the day. T. D. Latz walked in with two Zenith transoceanic radios under his arm. "Want one?" he said to me. "It's a shame to leave them for the Commies "

"Yes, take everything you can," Polgar murmured as he booted a small $700 General Electric two-way radio across the floor. "The agency has already lost over five million dollars' worth of equipment in this place over the past two months." That jolted even the most anesthetized among the dozen of us still in the anteroom—the last of the CIA's once proud 300-man contingent in South Vietnam.

Polgar pushed through the Vietnamese in the hallway to collect his own special group. I walked back to my own office for a last look. A copy of Don Oberdorfer's book, *Tet!,* was lying on my desk. I started to pick it up, then decided to leave it for the next tenant. He might be somewhat amused to learn what the Americans had thought of that last great offensive. For a moment I could envision him there—black hair slicked back, rumpled green uniform without insignia, his ballpoint pen flicking across a single sheet of Embassy bond on an otherwise bare desk top. The poster-size calendar girl would be gone. It would all be very drab and efficient: spoils befitting the victor.

The twelve of us lined up at the door leading to the roof as the marines in the hall shoved the waiting Vietnamese out of our way. I dared not look at their faces. One of the marines asked if we had any weapons. If so, we would have to leave them here. There was much grumbling among us as we handed over our arsenals.

Polgar pulled his own Browning automatic out of his hip holster and stared down at it for a moment. At last he let out a forlorn sigh. "I've gotta stay," he said. "The Ambassador insists on holding on a bit longer to make sure the military pulls out all the Vietnamese in the compound. I'd better wait and come out with him. And I think you should too." He was looking at his deputy, Pittman, who merely nodded and put down his suitcase. Polgar then turned to me. "Make sure these Vietnamese of mine get on board," he said.

"Want me to stay?" I asked.

"No," he replied. "Headquarters has ordered all of us out. I'll keep only [Pittman] and a commo man to handle communications with Washington."

The last I saw of Polgar that night, he was ambling back down the hall toward his office with one of the marines at his side. He was pleading with the young officer to help him liberate a carton of Heineken beer that was locked in one of the storerooms downstairs.

The roof of the Embassy was a vision out of a nightmare. In the center of the dimly lit helo-pad a CH-47 was already waiting for us, its engines setting up a roar like a primeval scream. The crew and controllers all wore what looked like oversized football helmets, and in the blinking under-light of the landing signals they reminded me of grotesque insects rearing on their hind-quarters. Out beyond the edge of the building a Phantom jet streaked across the horizon as tracers darted up here and there into the night sky.

I stumbled up the stubby ladder to the cabin of the helicopter, reaching back to help Polgar's Vietnamese friends. General Timmes sat down next to me on the starboard side, along with Bob Kantor, the administrative officer. Bill Johnson, the old experienced CIA hand who had spent his morning chauffeuring the Hungarians and the Poles to safety, slumped down in a sling bunk opposite us, his flop-brimmed fishing hat still shading his eyes.

Almost imperceptibly the chopper began rising straight up. Through the open exterior door, where the tail gunner was now crouching over his weapon, I watched numbly as the edge of the pad sank slowly out of sight. Then the cabin lights dimmed, and the chopper banked and arched up over the center of the city. For one brief moment I saw, framed in the porthole over my shoulder, the old Kim Do Hotel on Nguyen Hue Boulevard, my first home in Vietnam, across the street from Mimi's Flamboyant. The streetlamps cast splotches of light along the deserted sidewalks.

The chopper set a course along the highway I had so often driven on those Sunday trips to Vung Tau. As we veered eastward, past Bien Hoa City, the ammunition dump at nearby Long Binh was going up in a succession of miniature atomic explosions, and along the spiderweb of highways leading in from Xuan Loc, I could see literally thousands of trucks and tanks, presumably North Vietnamese, inching their way forward, their headlights blazing.

The Vietnamese woman seated across from me pulled her child closer, wrapping her arms around his head to muffle the ear-splitting whine of the engines. Out of the rear door of the cabin, the lights of Saigon became flickering ciphers as the city receded in the distance.

Just outside the small town of Ba Ria, north of Vung Tau, they opened up on us. At first I thought the fiery stitching in the plastic window across from me was merely the reflection of some interior cabin light, but as I watched, the scattering of yellow and red semaphore formed itself into a perfect replica of a radar screen. I elbowed Timmes. "We're taking ground fire!" I screamed in his ear over the engine. He fairly bolted out of his seat. "Why, it's almost like Normandy!" he bellowed back at me, his eyes glistening. Timmes had been a distinguished Airborne commander at Normandy in 1944, one of the first of the paratroopers to drop in behind the lines, and the old soldier stared at the tattoo outside the port window as if it were some fond acquaintance out of his past. The chopper groped for altitude as the motors wailed in protest. A small radar screen behind the pilot's seat began pulsing with a pale-green glow, converting the navigator's face into a ghoulish mask.

For three or four minutes the tracers continued reaching up for us, slowly burning out as they fell short. Then there was another burst off to the right, and I thought to myself, How absurd. To be shot down on the way out. I tried to divert myself by harking back to a little game I used to play as a kid while waiting in the doctor's office for a hypodermic needle. It will be all over in a few minutes, I repeated to myself again and again, and then you'll be so relieved, the fear and pain won't make any difference at all.

Sometime after 10 P.M. the chopper began its descent toward the fleet in the South China Sea. There was a stirring in the cabin as several of my fellow passengers strained at the windows for a glimpse of the ships. Suddenly one swung into full view, frozen in the open exterior doorway. The landing lights were brightly lit and I could see choppers hovering to the port and starboard. Gradually we were enveloped by the light, the dull-gray superstructure of the USS *Denver* folding in around us like a metallic cocoon. A wave of sadness swept over me. I did not even feel the shudder of the touchdown.

By 10 A.M., Washington time, James Schlesinger had worked himself up into one of his legendary furies. The evacuation out of the Embassy in Saigon was now threatening to become a round-the-clock fiasco. The weather off Vung

Tau had turned treacherous and unpredictable; nearly half the choppers were already down for maintenance; and the pilots obviously were succumbing to fatigue. The ditching of the CH-53 an hour earlier merely underscored the danger of pursuing the operation through the night. Worst of all, Martin himself did not seem to grasp the priorities. The vast number of evacuees in the past ten hours had been Vietnamese. The American community still had not been trimmed down to a manageable chopper load.

Schlesinger registered his complaints in an acerbic phone call to the Embassy, followed by a written message relayed through the Pentagon's National Command Center and the radio room of Admiral Whitmire's flagship. Expressing his own displeasure, and the President's, at the continuation of the helo-lift, Schlesinger insisted on placing a deadline on it. The entire operation, he said, would be brought to a halt at midnight, Saigon time, two hours away, and resumed the following morning. In the meantime, nineteen choppers would be sent to the Embassy to pick up the remaining Americans there, including the Ambassador himself.

Martin's response was resoundingly negative. "We had the Embassy compound full of Vietnamese locals," he later explained to a Congressional committee. "Regarding the situation in Saigon itself, since our operation had been under way for many hours, it was completely well known that we were leaving. The element of panic again was always present and we had hundreds of Vietnamese outside trying to get in the Embassy . . . It simply would not have been safe or feasible to have suspended the evacuation at midnight and to have resumed the following morning."

Martin so informed Kissinger in a direct call to the White House. "I said, and there was concurrence from Washington," he later told Congress, "that we should proceed with the evacuation until it was completed." In fact, the substance of his request was somewhat more specific: he demanded that thirty more choppers be sent to the Embassy. By his estimate, that would be sufficient to clear the compound. It was to this proposal that Washington gave its "concurrence."

At 10:50 P.M., local time, the last of the marines at DAO began boarding their choppers as the rattle of tank fire shimmered along the northern perimeters of Tan Son Nhut. The Marine commander, General Carey, flew out to the fleet to coordinate the pullout. His second-in-command, Colonel A. M. Gray, remained behind to supervise the demolition of the compound itself.

As one chopper after another was diverted to DAO to haul out Carey's men, the helo-lift out of the Embassy sputtered to a halt. Many of the Vietnamese crammed inside in the courtyard and the recreation compound immediately assumed the worst, murmuring apprehensively among themselves that the Americans were preparing to abandon them.

For the past hour and a half Master Sergeant Juan Valdez and several other nervous marines had been holding a cordon just inside the recreation compound, trying to keep the milling crowds away from the chain-link gate that led into the courtyard of the Embassy itself. But now, as tensions rose and rumors and tales of woe swirled among the masses huddled alongside the swimming pool in front of them, the marines were obliged steadily to give ground. All at once a terrified Vietnamese grabbed out at one of them, another marine swung his rifle butt, and within seconds the tight little clutch of Americans and Vietnamese now pressed against the gate exploded into a mélange of flailing fists and arms. The rest of the crowd surged back toward the pool and for a few terrible moments seemed to teeter on the brink of riot. Finally, with the help of reinforcements, Valdez and his men managed to clear the area immediately in front of the gate. But the order and discipline they enforced was at best illusory. Bitterness and tension continued to smolder beneath the surface calm, like an ember whipped by the wind.

At approximately 11:30 P.M. Colonel Gray and the handful of marines still at DAO began the final, systematic destruction of the headquarters building and its vitals. Nothing of value was to fall into communist hands. The sophisticated communications satellite terminal that had carried so many of General Smith's top-secret messages, and alarms, to Washington was among the first items to be "neutralized." Demolition teams had placed high-powered explosives around the base of the antenna dish, and once the destruct order was given, the entire structure, with its magnesium coating, burst into flame and was consumed instantly in a white-hot heat that reminded one of the marines of the fiery interior of a Bessemer furnace.

Several minutes later Colonel Gray and his men triggered delayed-action fuses on thermite bombs scattered around the bottom floor of the headquarters building itself. Then they dashed out to the helo-pad in the tennis courts and climbed aboard their choppers. Only moments after they were airborne, sheets of flame swept through the complex as the bombs went to work. The heat from the explosions was so intense that the roof of this fabled bastion of American power in Vietnam crumpled and collapsed like a ribbon of cheap tin.

Slightly before midnight Graham Martin, his face chalk-white, strode out into the Embassy courtyard, and with several of his aides, began hustling the remaining Americans into the chancery. No one gave any explanation for the move, but rumor had it among the marines that a Communist radio message foreshadowing a massive NVA thrust into the city had been intercepted a few minutes before.

Thirty miles to the north, at his headquarters at Ben Cat, General Dung and his field commanders were, in fact, just finishing a review of their latest achievements. "After a one-day general offensive on all fronts," Dung later wrote in his memoirs, "we realized that the situation had developed very favorably, as we had anticipated. . . . By midnight 29 April the whole of our striking force was fully prepared for the push into Saigon. The air was tense, as though at the raising of a magic hatchet."

With total victory now at his very fingertips, Dung telephoned his superiors in Hanoi to ask for instructions. The Politburo, after listening to his progress report, issued the order he had been awaiting impatiently all day: The Americans had taken long enough to complete their evacuation. The time had come for the army to fulfill its own mission. Attack!

Hanging up the phone, Dung immediately sent a radio alert to his battery commanders east of Saigon. The bombardment of Tan Son Nhut was to be suspended at once so the army could advance on the city without hazard from its own artillery. He also directed his field commanders "to make deep thrusts, to advance to predetermined points" in the city, and if necessary, to bypass any secondary objectives that might slow them down.

The command post was soon humming with activity. "Flashlights, hurricane lamps and searchlights lit the alleyways leading to it," Dung recalled. "Electric lights illuminated the war room. Gray-haired and black-haired officers carefully studied a map, tracing red arrows which pointed directly at the pre-selected major objectives in Saigon. Behind the war room, a row of improved telephone sets were operating non-stop." Dung's chief of operations, General Le Ngoc Hien, the man who had actually blueprinted the offensive, "was on command duty, receiving messages from all units," watching his handiwork finally brought to fruition.

As Dung launched his final attack Kissinger was meeting with reporters at the State Department to emphasize that the evacuation was proceeding satisfactorily. At the end of the press conference he promised another one at 2 P.M. that afternoon, by which time he hoped to be able to announce that all Americans were out of Saigon.

When Kissinger returned to the White House operations center it was already forty-five minutes past midnight in Saigon and the handful of Americans in the Embassy lobby were beginning to filter back into the courtyard. "Nobody told us to go back to work," Moorefield recalled, "but after a few minutes it became obvious that the rumors of an impending ground or shelling attack were false. So we figured we might as well get the evacuation cranked up again."

Up in the Ambassador's office the sense of relief was much shorter-lived, for another sobering message had just flashed in from the fleet: a second chopper, a Cobra gunship, had gone down in the South China Sea. This time all crew members had been rescued. But Whitmire and Gayler were now desperate to bring the helo-lift to a close. How many evacuees were still at the Embassy? they demanded.

Martin actually had no clear idea. But in hopes of keeping the admirals pacified, he began pulling figures out of thin air. Five hundred Vietnamese, 75 Americans and 181 marines still remained to be evacuated, he told Whitmire. Using these statistics, analysts at USSAG headquarters in Thailand quickly drew up a new flight schedule. Nine more CH-53s, they figured, would be sufficient to clear the Embassy of all civilians. When Martin was notified of this he saw he had backed himself into a corner. In direct calls to the White

House he began revising his figures upward. The number of Vietnamese still in the compound, he said, was perhaps twice what he had estimated.

Outside in the recreation area Colonel Madison and four other officers from the Joint Military Team waded into the crowds. The helo-lift had yet to regain its momentum, and despite the ministrations of Sergeant Valdez and the marines, some of the Vietnamese were again edging toward the gate that opened onto the parking lot in the Embassy courtyard.

Colonel Summers, Madison's deputy, picked up a bullhorn. "Don't worry!" he shouted to the crowds. "We're with you. We won't leave until you do!" As he repeated this promise over and over, Captain Herrington and Master Sergeant William Herron moved from one knot of frightened Vietnamese to another, calming them, reassuring them, slowly but surely maneuvering them into two large groups, one on either side of the swimming pool, so they could be more easily controlled.

For all their deftness and sensitivity, however, Madison and his men could not compete with the attraction of the choppers themselves, and minutes later when a CH-53 abruptly materialized over the treetops and began its descent into the courtyard the masses around them began stirring again. Hemmed in by the throng, an old American contract worker suddenly fell to the ground clutching at his chest. Soon afterward, on board a chopper en route to the fleet, he succumbed to a massive heart attack and died in the arms of a colleague.

"We also had some trouble with a group of Korean diplomats in the courtyard," recalled Moorefield, who was now working with Madison's team. "They were under the impression they could board up before anyone else, and at one point the top Korean official tried to push his way to the head of the line. One of the marines saw what was happening, grabbed him and told him essentially he was going to beat him to a pulp if he tried it again. That apparently did the trick. The Koreans meekly slipped back into place."

Although Moorefield did not know it at the time, the Korean official who was causing all the trouble was Brigadier General Rhee Dai Yong, formerly deputy commander of Korean forces in Vietnam and once deputy head of the KCIA. Abandoned by his own Ambassador earlier in the day, he and his colleagues had been obliged, somewhat belatedly, to seek help from the American Embassy, and were now understandably concerned that they might be left behind.

While Moorefield, Madison and the marines tried to wring some order out of the chaos in the Embassy courtyard, another evacuation operation was just drawing to a close. Over a hundred miles south of Saigon, at the mouth of the Bassac River, Consul General MacNamara's small flotilla of boats from Can Tho was at last within hailing distance of salvation.

During the past thirteen hours MacNamara, his crew and passengers had weathered countless hazards as they made their way down the Bassac River to the sea. They had been repeatedly sniped at from the riverbanks, buffeted by heavy storms, and finally forgotten by Admiral Whitmire's task force. Having reached the mouth of the Bassac shortly after nightfall, they had been drifting helpless and ignored ever since, sending out one Mayday call after another, without response. But now, shortly after midnight, they finally hove into view of the American freighter *Pioneer Contender.*

When MacNamara first sighted the lights of the vessel through the blackness he put in a radio call to the skipper, announcing that he intended, after unloading his passengers, to head back upriver to Can Tho on another rescue mission. But a U.S. Navy officer listening in on the conversation would have none of it. "Mr. MacNamara, sir," he said, his voice breaking into the channel, "if you don't get off that boat at once, I'll have to blow you out of the water." He had hardly finished speaking before several small launches were scooting across the whitecaps toward MacNamara's mike boat. As they pulled alongside, the Consul General, still wearing his black helmet with the single star in front, was seen arguing vigorously with one of his subordinates over who would have the honor of carrying the consulate's furled American flag on board. On this almost comic note, MacNamara's daring downriver escape from Can Tho came to an end.

As the first hour of the morning sifted away, the senior Embassy staffers who had chosen to keep Ambassador Martin company during Saigon's final agonies literally had to scratch about for something to do. Pittman went in search of a jar of peanut butter to fortify himself and his comrades; Polgar prowled the halls while Boudreau, Lehmann and others took turns answering the telephones. One of the more poignant calls was from a group of sixty Vietnamese employees of USIA still waiting at Carter's house. The Ambassador himself listened to their pleadings for a few moments as Boudreau tried to reassure them. A short while later a message arrived from IBM executives in Bangkok. They, too, were pleading, but Martin could do no more for their stranded employees than he could for Carter's.

"At one point I went up to the Ambassador's office," Moorefield remembered. "I don't know why. I guess I was just curious. When I walked in, Boudreau was on the phone with a Vietnamese girl who said she had a U.S. passport and three kids by an American. She wanted to know when to show at the Embassy for the evacuation. You knew there was no way she was ever gonna make it now, with or without a passport. Boudreau told her to come at daylight.

"I saw the Ambassador briefly and was startled at how hoarse he was, how barely able to speak. The pneumonia had all but wiped him out.

"I thought about staying around to try to help him, but quickly realized there was really nothing I could do. So I decided to make a brief tour of the Embassy. I figured it would be my last one."

As Moorefield wandered on, Martin, sick as he was, continued playing for time, angling for a continuation of the helo-lift until the compound had been cleared. No one in authority aboard the naval task force or in Washington was under any illusions about what he was doing—or was in favor of it. Admiral Steele, commander of the 7th Fleet, who was overseeing the operation from Whitmire's flagship, continued to press for an early end to it. So did Whitmire. Kissinger himself remained impatient for a definitive cutoff around 2:30 P.M., Washington time, since he had already scheduled a press conference for that hour. Every few minutes he would call Habib at the State Department operations center for a progress report. Is the evacuation nearing completion? Any messages from Graham? Some of the younger officers with Habib began joking among themselves: "Old Man Martin has just evacuated the last six hundred of his last four hundred evacuees."

Finally, Gayler gave up trying to change the Ambassador's mind. At 1:41 A.M. he alerted subordinate elements in his command that the evacuation was to be carried to completion, regardless of pilot fatigue or anything else. Choppers were to begin landing at the Embassy at ten-minute intervals.

Kissinger, meanwhile, again queried Martin about the number of people still waiting at the Embassy to be evacuated. Again Martin sucked figures out of his thumb: roughly 726, he indicated.

On the basis of these figures, the White House and the Pentagon settled on a new plan of action. A chopper sortie sufficient to haul out all 726 evacuees would be sent to Saigon. But after that, no more. The evacuation was to be wrapped up by 3:45 A.M., Saigon time. The Ambassador himself was to be on the next-to-last chopper. Kissinger told Martin directly: "I want you heroes to come home."

At 2:22 A.M. Gayler relayed appropriate instructions to the fleet. In the meantime, an Administration spokesman advised reporters in Washington that Kissinger's press conference was to be pushed back to 5 P.M. that afternoon. Several journalists expressed surprise at the postponement. Had a snag developed in the evacuation? None at all, an official spokesman replied. Everything was running according to plan.

Over the walkie-talkie in his office Martin could eavesdrop on the radio chatter between the marines in the recreation compound and those in the courtyard.

"Hey, there's another gook climbing over the wall. Shoot him!" a caller exclaimed at one point.

"I can't shoot him," came the reply. "For chrissakes, let him over."

Given the growing impatience in Washington, Martin knew he would have to put a stop to such generosity. If the airlift was to end within any reasonable time frame, the steady trickle of additional bodies into the Embassy complex could not continue. He therefore instructed Major Kean to seal off the recreation compound and move all remaining evacuees into the Embassy courtyard itself. That, at least, would make it easier for the marines to keep other Vietnamese from coming in over the walls.

When Colonel Madison and his team were advised of this, they immediately began funneling the assembled evacuees out of the recreation area into the courtyard. It was a laborious process. There was little room around the chopper pad itself for all the passengers they counted off—a total of 1,200, far more than Martin had reported to Washington. Some of the Vietnamese had to be crowded onto the roof of the small firehouse on one side of the courtyard. Others were stuffed into the vest-pocket parking lot alongside the Mission Wardens' office. Only after much pushing and tussling was the recreation compound emptied and sealed off. And all the while Madison, Summers and Herrington circulated through the crowds, trying to reassure them, promising over and over: "You will not be abandoned."

After leaving the Ambassador's office Moorefield spent fifteen or twenty minutes simply roaming the halls of the Embassy, indulging his curiosity at what was obviously a historic moment. On the sixth floor he ran into Jay Blowers, a bearded State Department colleague who was responsible for watching over the Vietnamese in the corridors as they waited for a flight off the roof. For a few minutes he helped Blowers with his task, shepherding a chopper load into the interior stairwell, but because the rooftop pickups were now moving so slowly, he realized he really wasn't needed. So he moved on, drifting down to the second floor, to the offices of the political section where he had once been assigned. "The place had become a tombstone, a ramshackle museum piece," he recalled. Equipment was strewn all over the floor. Wreckage and refuse were everywhere. And it was so quiet, so eerie quiet, except for the rumble of the helicopters as they came in and departed.

"I was curious to see what people had left behind, what a man didn't consider important enough to take with him on his last ride out. One of my friends had abandoned a half-tin of pipe tobacco. I commandeered it, since I figured the VC would have less use for it than I would. Others had left books, all kinds of things.

"As I made the rounds of the offices I had a strange sensation, a feeling of being disembodied. In the confusion of the past few weeks I'd never had time to pack up. I'd lost everything, even the getaway bag I'd put together that morning. And I thought, Here I was, age thirty-one, with literally no material possessions to my name. Suddenly I was overcome with a strange desire to own something, to leave Vietnam with something other than the shirt on my back. And so, as I was going through the litter I picked up a book called *The Principles of War* and tucked it in my pocket. I thought it might be amusing reading on shipboard. I carried it with me for the rest of the journey. It was the only thing I salvaged from Vietnam, this book on the principles of war."

By the time Moorefield trudged back upstairs toward the roof, he had reconciled himself to the prospect of leaving. Now he seemed merely to be in the way.

But despite this new-found resolve, he was not to make his exit so easily. At around 2:30 A.M. one of the Marine controllers on the roof fell asleep on the job. Dozing on his feet, he stumbled over the edge of the helicopter pad and fell one story to the parapet around the roof of the building. He suffered several broken bones and was medevacked out at once. As Moorefield wandered up to the sixth floor one of the marines collared him and asked him to stand in for the injured trooper. Moorefield wearily agreed.

"It really wasn't much of a job," he later explained. "As each little group of evacuees got to the door leading up to the roof, I'd brief them, then escort them up to the pad itself and help them onto the chopper.

"My most vivid memory is of how tired I was, so very tired. I hadn't slept in over two days, except for that one hour I'd caught at home the night before. But I knew I couldn't fall asleep. There was no one to take my place.

"It was all business up there on the roof. No one spoke and we all went about our work with extreme care and attention. The prop blast from the choppers was, of course, gale force, and since there were no guard rails around the pad, you had to be careful you didn't stumble and get blown over the side like the marine.

"At the edge of the roof the smokestacks from incinerators on the floor below were still going full blast, belching flames and smoke high into the air. And on takeoff the chopper pilots had to veer sharply away from them to avoid being blinded. The scene kinda reminded me of a funeral pyre, the roof of the Embassy flaming away into the night.

"Soon after I took up station on the roof, the marines severed the Embassy grounds from the recreation compound out back and sealed the door. But the lights stayed on over there, and from my airy perch I could see the looters gleefully picking through the ruins. The atmosphere was almost carnival-like. The mama-sans were carrying away everything that wasn't bolted down—curtains, chairs, silverware, literally everything! The swimming pool was filled with junk, and in the parking lot beside the restaurant all the abandoned automobiles were running. The looters were playing bumper cars with them.

"On the other side of the Embassy, out front in the street, I could see what I believed to be VC political cadres haranguing the crowds. There'd be a long oration—five to ten minutes—periodically interrupted by a round of applause. I couldn't catch what was being said, but the irony was impressive nonetheless. Just imagine it: to the rear, part of the citadel was being looted by old women and young boys, and out front, heresy of heresies, political cadres were doing their deed on the Embassy's own doorstep.

"In the distance I could see fires still burning in the Tan Son Nhut–Bien Hoa area, and tracer rounds sporadically reaching up after our jets. Over the trees I caught glimpses of the city itself—so dead, so quiet. It was as if we were in an interlude between the changing of the guard, the old regime, the old way of life giving way to the new."

Below the helicopter pad, in his abandoned office on the sixth floor of the Embassy, Tom Polgar had just finished beating out a cable to Washington on his old manual typewriter. It was something of a historic communication, as he pointed out in the first few lines: "With receipt presidential message advising that evacuation American Embassy must be completed before 0345 local time 30 April, wish to advise that this will be final message from Saigon Station. It will take us about twenty minutes to destroy equipment. Accordingly, approximately 0320 hours local time we must terminate classified transmission."

In the next paragraph he turned eloquently philosophical, as if he knew he was writing for posterity. But like so many other messages he had sent to Washington in recent weeks, what he said revealed more about his own illusions than about the circumstances and realities of the moment. For now, as at the beginning of the Communist offensive three months before, Polgar remained convinced that Congressional parsimony—"niggardly half measures" was his catch phrase—was the cause of Saigon's undoing. "It has been a long and hard fight and we have lost," he wrote. "This experience unique in the history of the United States does not signal necessarily the demise of the United States as a world power. The severity of the defeat and the circumstances of it, however, would seem to call for a reassessment of the policies of niggardly half measures which have characterized much of our participation here despite the commitment of manpower and resources which were certainly generous. Those who fail to learn from history are forced to repeat it. Let us hope that we will not have another Vietnam experience and that we have learned our lesson.

"Saigon signing off."

In Washington, almost at the same moment, CIA Director Colby was completing his own final message to Polgar, which in its way was equally memorable. "As we approach end of communication with Saigon," he asserted, "I would like to record Agency's pride and satisfaction with the job that its representatives did there, and at no time during its twenty-odd-year history is this more true than in these past few weeks. The courage, integrity, dedication and high competence the Agency displayed in a variety of situations over these years has been fully matched and even surpassed by your performance during this difficult final phase. Thousands of Vietnamese owe their lives and future hopes to your efforts, your Government has profited immensely from the accuracy and breadth of your reporting and your country will one day learn with admiration of the way you represented its best instincts and ideals. Good luck and many thanks."

Shortly before 3 A.M. there was another brief lull in the helo-lift from the courtyard. Martin, fearful that the U.S. military had finally reached the end of its tether, pleaded for at least six more big CH-53s—a number which, he insisted, would finally accommodate all the civilians in the compound. Reluctantly Whitmire agreed. Within the next forty minutes the half-dozen choppers landed in quick succession. In the meantime, the Embassy's remaining communications officers smashed what was left of their radio gear and joined the diminishing passenger lines on the sixth floor.

At 3:45 A.M., on the stroke of the White House deadline for the evacuation, Martin walked out into the Embassy courtyard, scanned the crowds, then motioned to Colonel Madison. All remaining Vietnamese, he told the army officer, would be lifted out by CH-53. Those still waiting inside the Embassy were to be herded out into the courtyard. The helo-lift off the roof was now to be reserved for Americans only.

Boudreau, who had accompanied Martin into the parking lot, took a brief look at the crowds and was satisfied that the evacuation could soon be brought to an end. "Didn't see any white faces out there," he later told me.

With the Embassy's radio transmitter now off the air, Martin's only link to the outside world was the walkie-talkie system which the marines were using to communicate with the helicopters. By relaying messages through the pilots, he could still communicate with the fleet, and vice versa. But it was a long, roundabout process, and Martin reasoned that by the time Whitmire or Kissinger could get word to him, protesting his failure to end the evacuation on schedule, the last of the evacuees at the Embassy would be airborne.

As the remaining Vietnamese in the chancery building stumbled into the courtyard, Madison and the marines were already breaking the crowd down into chopper-sized loads. Minutes later Madison sent word to Lehmann in the Ambassador's office: Six *more* CH-53s would be sufficient to evacuate everybody. The entire operation could be completed within twenty minutes.

In that case, Lehmann replied, the necessary lift would be provided.

At 4:20 A.M. another CH-53 came in. Madison and his team flung passengers aboard and quickly sent it off, then waited anxiously for the next scheduled chopper.

They waited in vain. On the other end of the chain of command, Gayler and Whitmire had finally decided to call Martin's bluff. Convinced that he was still trying to stall off a shutdown, they refused to accept his protestations that there were only a few more Vietnamese still to be evacuated. In accordance with White House instructions, the helo-lift was to be terminated forthwith, as soon as Martin himself could be pulled out.

"There was a period when no helicopters landed, not in the courtyard, not on the roof," Moorefield noted. "I remember looking down at the courtyard and counting the people left—a little over four hundred, just a few more chopper loads. Not all were Vietnamese. There were a few Koreans and some others—Filipinos, I think—in the group.

"During this hiatus I went down to the sixth floor. Major Kean had just received a message from the fleet through his tactical net. There were a few of us standing there, and the major said to us, very dramatically, that the message was from the White House: 'I've just received an order from the President. Only Embassy staffers are to be evacuated from this point on. Don't panic!' He was very dramatic about it. 'Don't panic,' he said, as if any of us had the mind or the strength to panic at this point. And I remember turning to Jay Blowers and saying sardonically, 'Don't panic! Only Americans will be evacuated from here on. We're not evacuating anyone else!'

"I then went back to the roof and made another eyeball estimate of the bodies in the courtyard: just over four hundred. I knew now that none of them would ever get out."

At that moment Brunson McKinley, the Ambassador's aide, oblivious of Whitmire's decision to shut off the flow, strode out into the courtyard and promised Madison and Summers more choppers would be coming in. The two U.S. Army officers turned to the crowds and repeated the assurance.

In the Ambassador's office John Pittman was jolted out of a light snooze when Major Kean came roaring in. Bellowing at the top of his voice, the young Marine officer reeled off his message from the White House. President Ford had directed that the Ambassador leave by the next chopper from the roof!

Martin merely nodded and picked up his suitcase. "Looks like this is it," he said to the others, and walked out to the elevators. Several of his remaining staffers clambered after him—Polgar, Pittman, Jacobson, John Bennett of USAID, Joe Bennett, the political counselor, and Brunson McKinley. Lehmann, Boudreau and Jim Devine lingered behind for a while longer to watch over what was left of the evacuation.

"I was lying down on the roof near the stairwell, waiting for the next chopper," Moorefield explained. "And all at once I caught a glimpse of people moving on the stairs. It was very dark, but I could see Polgar, McKinley and the Ambassador.

"I crouched down at the entrance and counted off twenty-five passengers. Unfortunately, as luck would have it, the Ambassador was not among them. A few minutes later, as a chopper set down, I rushed that first group across the roof to begin boarding. But then there was one hell of a row, the marines and the pilots shouting at each other over the prop blast. Apparently the White House had directed that the Ambassador be on this very chopper, and I had screwed things up by leaving him out of the passenger load. I went back to the stairwell to talk to him. I don't think he understood me. He looked at me quizzically—you know, the way he could look at you—and then nodded his head. He didn't understand, but I guess he was deferring to me.

"The helicopter stayed put for several minutes as the pilot talked to the fleet. Finally somebody said to me, 'Orders are orders. The Ambassador will have to get aboard—and as soon as possible, since there's a chance the ARVN down in the streets may get pissed off and start taking shots at us if this chopper sits up here too long.' At that point I went back to the stairwell and escorted the Ambassador to the ramp. As I lifted him through the door of the helicopter, he seemed . . . frail, so terribly frail.

"Once the helicopter flew off I walked back to the stairs and told Polgar and the rest they'd be going out soon. Finally another chopper came in and I put them aboard. Then I went back to the edge of the pad and looked down in the courtyard at those people waiting there. Colonel Summers and Madison and the other Joint Military Team people were still with them. And I thought to myself there was nothing left I could do. That it had all been done . . ."

Out in the courtyard Summers was puzzled. Where were those promised choppers? At last Major Kean walked out and gave him an answer: there were to be no more, he said, except for the ones for the marines and the few remaining Embassy and Army personnel. When Madison heard that, he could scarcely restrain himself. There were six more passenger loads, he rasped. He would not leave without them. Where was the Ambassador? He would take the matter up with him.

Kean shook his head. "The Ambassador just left," he sighed. All the Americans were leaving.

Madison could hardly believe it. Less than half an hour ago both Lehmann and McKinley had assured him the necessary lift would be provided for the Vietnamese. Now, abruptly, all plans were changed.

Madison, shocked and incredulous, looked Kean square in the eye. *Neither he nor his team,* he said carefully, *would leave until the rest of the Vietnamese had been evacuated. Kean and his men were to hold the perimeters until that was accomplished.*

But again Kean shook his head. The President had ordered the Ambassador's departure and an end to the airlift, he insisted. He would not defy the President. Nor would he put his own men in any further jeopardy. With that, he turned and directed his marines to begin pulling back into the Embassy.

Madison had only four Army officers with him, far too few to secure even a fraction of the Embassy grounds without Kean's help. He therefore had no choice but to withdraw. He quietly alerted his men, and in the next few minutes they all slipped away into the Embassy. "Remaining in the parking-lot landing zone," Madison declared in his final report, "were six marshaled organized lifts of approximately 420 personnel, including members of the Korean Embassy [Brigadier General Rhee Dai Yong and colleagues], the American Embassy, fire department employees who had volunteered to stay on duty until the final lift in case of fire in the compound, a German priest who had been working with refugee groups and who had been of great assistance in organizing the CRA [recreation] compound, and other American Embassy local national employees and their dependents. All these personnel had abandoned their luggage on our orders so they could be more easily extracted. It was evident at this point that the moral commitment to these evacuees and the obligation of the U.S. personnel to honor the commitment of their government was not widely shared outside the U.S. [Joint Military Team] delegation."*

When Madison, Colonel Summers and the rest of the Army team reached

*The group left behind in the courtyard also included several prominent South Vietnamese politicians—among them, a former minister of finance in the Thieu government who later escaped Saigon on his own. Korean General Yong was not so lucky. Detained by NVA forces when they entered the city, he was still in a Communist prison two years later.

the top of the Embassy stairwell, Moorefield was waiting at the pad to help them board. "Marv Garrett and a couple of Mission Warden officers also came up the stairs toward me," Moorefield noted. "They'd been sitting down in the Embassy someplace and had been given the word to leave too. There was an American girl with them and I remember how astounded I was there was still a girl in the Embassy. As it turned out, Summers had been trying all day to persuade her to leave. She was married to a Vietnamese official of some sort who hadn't gotten out. Finally Summers had convinced her.

"After putting them all on the chopper I went back to the stairwell. No one else was coming. I turned around and walked back to the helicopter and got on. As the chopper spiraled up off the roof I looked at my watch: 5:24 in the morning, 30 April. From the cabin window I could see those Vietnamese evacuees still waiting in the courtyard below.

"We flew out over Saigon and I strained to capture a last impression of the city in my mind's eye. I remember thinking it could have been a surburban community in the United States. All was calm and peaceful, except for the fires burning in the distance.

"By the time we landed on the fleet forty-five minutes later, dawn was breaking over the edge of the water, and an armada of fishing boats, laden with refugees, stretched away toward the coast as far as you could see. When we stepped out onto the deck, Marine security officers immediately disarmed us. Since I had no identification on me, they wanted to know who I was. Someone vouched for me, saying I was a member of the Embassy staff. The marines then walked to the railing of the ship and threw our weapons into the sea."

Once on board the USS *Okinawa,* Colonel Madison tried to persuade the commander of a helicopter squadron to mount six more flights to the Embassy. He was unsuccessful. No one on the Ambassador's staff had seen fit to advise the fleet of the small crowd still in the courtyard, and flight commanders assumed the numbers they would have to evacuate if they went back in were infinite. So they decided to make no further effort at all.

At approximately 5:30 A.M., local time, NVA Tank Brigade 203 crossed the Newport bridge and inched its way into Saigon, as the squadron commander pored over his maps, trying to locate his primary objective, the Presidential Palace. A short while later Admiral Gayler, monitoring the progress of the invasion force from Honolulu, ordered that a specially armed helicopter be dispatched to Saigon to provide protective cover at the Embassy as the remaining marines destroyed the last of the office equipment.

In Washington, Henry Kissinger had just opened his long-scheduled afternoon press conference. The evacuation of all Americans in Saigon had been completed, he announced triumphantly. A few minutes later one of his aides slipped him a note: in fact, there were still marines in the Embassy. Kissinger chose not to mention this detail to the press, but as soon as the klieg lights were shut down he rushed to his staff headquarters in the Executive Office Building and flew into a rage. Get those marines out of Saigon at once!

he screamed. If even one was lost after he had so articulately proclaimed the operation a success, he would have somebody's head!

At 7:30 A.M., Saigon time, Major Kean's men slammed the Embassy's huge oaken doors, barred them and ran into the stairwells. On the first and fourth floors they threw gas grenades into the elevator shafts and pulled the steel shutters closed behind them on the landings. But even as they leaped up the last few steps to the rooftop pad, the panic-stricken Vietnamese from the courtyard were smashing through the doors on the ground floor and surging up after them.

At the top of the stairwell the marines managed to lock and bar the small door leading to the pad, buying themselves a few precious moments to clamber aboard the waiting chopper. But by the time the last of them shinnied into the cabin, several Vietnamese were already scrambling up over the edge of the pad. Just as those in the lead dove for the wheels, the helicopter pulled off. It was 7:53 A.M., Saigon time, 30 April.

On the USS *Denver,* I had just climbed into a hard sling bunk. I had been up all night, sitting at a steel table in the galley, drinking coffee and watching the weary helicopter pilots parade in and out. The ship was so jammed with evacuees, there was not even enough room in the hatchways to lie down. We all had to sleep in staggered three- or four-hour shifts, doubling up on bunk space. My turn came well after daybreak. I lay down and dropped off immediately, despite a leaky pipe overhead. But I did not sleep long. An hour or so later one of my colleagues came stumbling through the crews' quarters. "We've just picked it up on the BBC," he said. "The NVA are in Saigon. They've renamed it 'Ho Chi Minh City.' "

Postscript: Internal Hemorrhaging

As even General Dung acknowledged in his memoirs, the airlift of 29 and 30 April 1975 was a spectacular achievement, "the largest evacuation operation by helicopter in U.S. history." By final count, the rescue force of 70 choppers and 865 marines flew over 630 "sorties" during those last eighteen hours and evacuated 1,373 Americans, 5,595 South Vietnamese and 85 "third country nationals." Of these, nearly 2,100, including 978 Americans, were helo-lifted out of the Embassy courtyard alone.

The day after the airlift was completed, President Ford spelled out the particulars in a letter to Congress and admitted that the evacuation force had "on occasion" exchanged fire with NVA units. Lest these actions be seen as a violation of the War Powers Act, he was careful to point out that the entire operation had been conducted pursuant to his own authority as Commander in Chief of U.S. Forces. It was the same argument he had used earlier in the month to try to justify committing American forces to an evacuation without Congressional approval, and now as before, many legislators found it unsatisfactory. While there was no debate over the President's right to protect American lives abroad, the legality of his using ships, warplanes and fighting men to evacuate foreigners remained very much in dispute. Had the President in fact broken the law by rescuing those 5,595 Vietnamese without a clear Congressional mandate? Ultimately, Ford wearied of the debate. His press spokesman declared testily that the President had acted on "moral, not legalistic grounds" and quoted the Chief Executive as saying, "I did it because the people would have been killed and I'm proud of it."

The President's self-congratulatory mood extended to other members of the Administration. Ambassador Martin and his closest aides were only too ready to embrace it. In conversations with me in the months following the evacuation, Lehmann, Boudreau, Jazynka, McKinley and Shep Lowman all described it as a "great success." Martin himself, in later Congressional testimony, made the same point with typical eloquence and attention to detail. All told, he remarked, over 51,888 people—6,763 Americans and 45,125 Vietnamese and other foreigners—had been lifted out of Saigon during April on American military aircraft. Furthermore, he noted, if one included the Americans who had departed by commercial carrier, the Vietnamese who had left on "black" flights, and the 6,000 others who came out by barge on the final day, the total number of evacuees for whom the Embassy was somehow responsible would exceed 65,000.*

"When the whole story gets on the record," Martin told Congress in summing up his own role, "it will undoubtedly prove what the American people already sense—that it was a hell of a good job."

Some legislators, however, were not so sure. Although none disputed the difficulties the Ambassador had faced, there lingered widespread suspicion that he had brought a great many of them on himself. Far from expediting the evacuation during the first weeks of April, he had, it seemed, helped to stall it off—partly by fostering the notion (with Kissinger and Weyand's help) that one more aid appropriation might avert disaster. Only when the Administration belatedly changed its mind and forced him to act on 19 April did he move to set the evacuation in gear.

Even then it was less Martin's ingenuity than the imagination and initiative of subordinate staffers that kept the operation rolling along. Without General Smith's "inspirations" there probably would have been no evacuation at all. And had Moorefield, Joe McBride and the handful of consular officers working with them at DAO waited on directives from the Embassy, the airlift would surely have ground to a halt. By Moorefield's own estimate, he and his colleagues were personally responsible for evacuating over 20,000 Vietnamese who might otherwise have become hung up in red tape.

Accident and a kind of perverse good fortune also helped immeasurably. If General Dung had chosen to attack Saigon head-on, rather than to strip away its outer defenses beforehand, the city would have become a battleground, and an airlift rendered impossible. Equally crucial was the decision of CIA officers, including Ted Shackley, in early April to cordon Saigon off from the rampaging refugee population in the countryside.

The layout of the city and the location of Tan Son Nhut itself also played a part in what transpired, and what did not. Unlike the airfield at Danang, Tan Son Nhut was some distance from the downtown area, and surrounded by military compounds that could be sealed off to limit access. Behind its fences and checkpoints General Smith was able to set up his evacuation center and move thousands out through it without the population of the city becoming fully aware.

Of all the factors that accounted for our salvation, however, perhaps the

---

*Another 65,000 escaped on their own, just before the Communist takeover and in the two years that followed, bringing the total evacuee count to over 140,000.

most decisive was the attitude of the Vietnamese themselves. In Danang and Nha Trang our Vietnamese friends and co-workers knew that there were still other places to escape to, and that a little initiative might get them there, even without our help. But by the time Saigon came under attack such options had disappeared, and those who wanted to save themselves had no choice but to stand back and defer to us.

The improvisatory and haphazard nature of the evacuation of course had its cost. Working under terrible pressure, without proper guidance, Moorefield, Lacy Wright, Rosenblatt and the scores of others like them were unable to screen the evacuees as Washington intended. Consequently, bar girls and maids often got seats that should have been reserved for "high risk" individuals. Even the "black" flights, especially arranged for "priority" evacuees, were misused. As Colonel Legro admitted after the fall of Saigon, only twenty percent of the 2,000 Vietnamese he and his immediate staff had ushered out secretly could truly be considered "high risk."

Ambassador Martin tried to minimize these problems in his testimony to Congress, claiming that some 22,294 Vietnamese employed by American agencies or related to those who were had been evacuated as of 30 April 1975. On the surface, this seemed a respectable number, but in fact it was distressingly small, particularly in view of the total number of past and present employees of the Embassy and their families—over 90,000 by the final State Department estimate. To judge from Martin's figures, less than one-third of these actually benefited from the airlift. The rest were left behind, or were obliged to escape on their own.

Predictably, the Defense Attaché's Office was the only agency in the Mission that came close to evacuating all of the locals on its payroll—about 1,500 out of 3,800. The scorecard for the rest of us was far less impressive. As of the summer of 1977, the breakdown was as follows:

AGENCY	TOTAL DIRECT-HIRE EMPLOYEES, INCLUDING CONSULATE STAFFS*	PRESENT IN THE U.S. (EVACUEES & ESCAPEES)	STILL IN VIETNAM
State Department	900	225	675
SAFFO (formerly CORDS, under George Jacobson)	1,122	218	904
USIA	167	55	112
USAID	924	362	562
Mission Wardens' Office (under Marv Garrett)	3,500	200	3,300†

* Totals do not include the thousands of Vietnamese who worked for the various agencies under contract
† The evacuation from Can Tho, mounted independently of the Saigon airlift, yielded roughly the

Since George Jacobson, the Ambassador's Special Assistant for Field Operations (SAFFO) was technically in charge of the latter phases of the evacuation, it is noteworthy that such a large number of his own evacuees (904) failed to get out. That in itself provides a telling commentary on the kind of leadership the Ambassador imposed on us in Saigon's final days.

Among those on Jacobson's own evacuee rolls who were left behind was a highly knowledgeable Communist defector who had provided us over the years with our most comprehensive data on COSVN and its personalities. In late April, Jacobson had offered to evacuate him, but not his two sons, since they were of draft age. The defector, needless to say, had refused to leave without them.

Jacobson also bungled the evacuation of Nay Luette, the montagnard leader, for whom he had assumed responsibility. Luette went to a designated rendezvous point on the final day of the war, but was never picked up. The Communists later jailed him.*

Because of the sensitivity of their jobs, the list of CIA locals who were evacuated, or left behind, remained hidden away in agency vaults in the months following the Communist victory. Yet several of my former colleagues, who were outraged at what had taken place, saw to it that some basic statistics were made available to me. According to these tabulations, only about 537 of the Station's 1,900 "indigenous employees" were finally evacuated, together with 2,000 others—including family members—who had enjoyed privileged contacts with the agency over the years.

As was true of other elements of the Mission, individual initiative accounted for the Station's most successful rescue efforts. By defying Consul General MacNamara and orders from Saigon, "Larry Downs" of the CIA base in Can Tho managed to evacuate by helicopter all 300 Vietnamese on his roster. Similarly, by ignoring Polgar and operating in secret, Bill Johnson succeeded in moving the employees of the radio station House 7 and their families (roughly 1,000 people) to Phu Quoc Island, from which they were later rescued. Countless other CIA men, often working on their own or with minimal guidance, also made certain that Vietnamese friends and co-workers got aboard an evacuation flight.

Unfortunately, however, the imagination and perseverence of such individuals could not compensate for the ineptitude of Station management as a whole. Consequently, large categories of Vietnamese who faced untold dan-

same kind of results. Of the 573 locals on the consulate's evacuee lists (excluding those who worked for the CIA), only 47 were among the 200 people who sailed with MacNamara down the Bassac River to the sea.
*Luette's fellow montagnard tribesmen fared no better, though Jacobson certainly does not bear sole responsibility for this. Of the estimated 5,000 montagnards who had escaped from the highlands in mid- and late-March, only around eighty had been logged in at the Guamian reception center as of 8 July 1975. As for Vietnam's other ethnic minorities: only about seventy Chinese Nungs and forty northern "black Thais" had turned up on Guam by the same date. Since then, an unknown number have escaped from Vietnam on their own.

ger from the Communists or whose capture could prejudice American intelligence interests were left behind. Among them: the 400 members of the Special Police Branch, whose training the CIA had financed and supervised; 400 working echelon members of the Central Intelligence Organization, also our protégés; a large staff of clerks and computer operators which the Station had set up to keep book on PRG personalities; the young Vietnamese who served as our clandestine radio operators at the Embassy; the staff which maintained our special radio links with Vietnamese police headquarters; the hundred or more Vietnamese, including maids, waitresses and agents, who had collected at the Duc Hotel on the final day; several agents from Bien Hoa; the 70 translators whom "Harry Linden" had tried to rescue; literally hundreds of high-level defectors who had worked closely with the Station over the years to pinpoint and hunt down their former Communist comrades; and countless counterterrorist agents—perhaps numbering as high as 30,000—specially trained to operate with the Phoenix Program.

Then too, to compound our errors and their costs, we committed that unpardonable mistake of failing to ensure the destruction of the personnel files and intelligence dossiers we had helped the government assemble—and which identified so many of those left on the tarmac or outside the gates of the Embassy. Equally unfortunate, the capture and interrogation of the young CIA officer "Lew James," led to the exposure of information that struck directly at our own operations.

Although the Station bore no immediate responsibility, another authority on agency activities also was lost to the Communists at the time of the collapse. During the last week in April a retired CIA officer named Tucker Gougelmann, who had previously worked in Saigon, returned to look for Vietnamese friends, somehow missed the final helo-lift, and was later captured by the North Vietnamese. Interrogated by the Soviet KGB and other intelligence organizations, he died in captivity a year later. What he disclosed under questioning has not been determined. His knowledge of CIA operations and personnel both in Vietnam and elsewhere in Asia was considerable.

The full impact of CIA losses and failures in Vietnam will probably never be known. There are too many unanswered questions. But based on what can be ascertained, it is not too much to say that in terms of squandered lives, blown secrets and the betrayal of agents, friends and collaborators, our handling of the evacuation was an institutional disgrace. Not since the abortive Bay of Pigs invasion of 1961 had the agency put so much on the line, and lost it through stupidity and mismanagement.

But lives and secrets were not the only items of value forfeited to poor American planning. Despite Erich Von Marbod's last-minute salvage efforts, equipment losses resulting from Saigon's defeat were massive. NVA forces, according to Pentagon estimates, captured over $5 billion in U.S.-supplied military hardware, including 550 tanks, 73 F-5 jet fighters, 1,300 artillery pieces, 1,600,000 rifles and enough other matériel to field an entire army, air force and navy. Although the Pentagon claimed that much of this equipment would soon become unserviceable without American spare parts, even a fraction of it would keep insurgent or terrorist movements in Asia or the Middle East in business for some time.

In the months immediately following the Communist victory, those of us who had been involved in the evacuation and who knew of its failings anxiously scanned the refugee reports from Vietnam for some clue to how the Communists meant to dispose of the friends and the country we had left behind. From all signs, the blood bath the White House had predicted never materialized. Yet few of us could take any comfort from what actually did take place. For if the Communists refrained from the most extreme "solutions," there was ample evidence that they intended to crush every vestige of independent thought and action in the south.

The NVA 324th Division was the first major Communist unit to enter Saigon on the morning of 30 April. At 12:15 P.M., local time, the flag of the National Liberation Front was hoisted over the Presidential Palace and "Big" Minh was placed under arrest. Soon afterward the American Embassy was ransacked. An American journalist, who had stayed behind to cover the takeover, managed to save the metal plaque that had hung in the downstairs foyer to commemorate the five servicemen killed in the Communist attack on the Embassy in 1968.

The following day General Dung drove to Saigon from his headquarters at Ben Cat. No doubt he treated himself to a cigarette or two to celebrate his extraordinary victory. Within the next few days Le Duan and various other North Vietnamese notables also showed up to survey the spoils. In practical terms their arrival marked the beginning of the absorption process that would produce a formally unified Vietnam a year later.

At the time of the Communist victory the party apparatus in the south was in shambles, thanks in part to the depredations of the Phoenix Program. The army thus remained the primary instrument of control. Although one or two NVA divisions would be withdrawn in the next two years, over 150,000 troops stayed on to ensure the loyalty of Hanoi's new subjects. There was also an influx of secret police and some 30,000 administrative cadres from the north to help buttress the party structure and reorganize the economy.

During the first nine months General Tran Van Tra, Dung's principal deputy, served as Hanoi's front man in Saigon, although Pham Hung and Le Duc Tho remained the actual formulators of policy. When a civilian administrative apparatus was finally set up in the city in early 1976, the three top posts all went to former COSVN officials.

The PRG meanwhile was swept into the dustbin of history. In March 1976 the entire population of Vietnam went to the polls to elect a new national assembly, but only a scattering of PRG or "third force neutralists" were on the ballots, and the lists of candidates had all been carefully screened by the party beforehand. A few weeks later, on 2 July, the eclipse of the southern "revolution" and its spokesmen became complete. Hanoi formally declared the country unified under its control. The president of the National Liberation Front was reduced to a ceremonial vice-presidential post in Hanoi and the PRG's well-known Foreign Minister, Nguyen Thi Binh, likewise found herself in a position of minor consequence. Eventually the National Liberation Front was dissolved.

Within a year of their victory the Communists also moved decisively to crush all potential or actual opposition. Organized religion was among their first targets. The leaders of the bitterly anti-Communist Hoa Hao Buddhist sect in the delta were jailed; the An Quang Buddhist Pagoda, once the center of militant opposition to the Saigon regime, was closed down; religious publications were stopped and over 200 Catholic prelates were arrested and imprisoned, including the Bishops of Danang and Nha Trang and the Reverend Tran Huu Thanh, the fire-breathing priest who had led the anti-corruption drive against Thieu in the fall of 1974. Ironically, the Communists arrested Thanh on charges of being a "CIA agent."

The most draconian of Hanoi's security measures, however, were directed at former government officials and military personnel. By Hanoi's own admission, over 200,000 of them were sent to reeducation camps in the first year. Located in remote areas, often close to former Communist bases, the camps resembled something out of Solzhenitsyn. In one, near Tay Ninh, inmates were obliged to perform every manner of demeaning and dangerous task, from cleaning out the toilets of party cadres to deactivating minefields, often with no training or proper equipment. In another, outside Nha Trang, over fifty people were assigned to each cell. The daily food ration amounted to no more than 200 grams of rice, barely enough for subsistence, with seldom any meat or even fish sauce to provide needed protein. Malnutrition and attendant diseases like beriberi thus became widespread. Every six months each inmate received a change of pajamas, and once a week a bucket of water to cleanse himself. Every two months he and his family were allowed to exchange short letters, the format of which was dictated by authorities.

Occasionally torture and even execution were meted out to intransigents. According to one widely repeated refugee account, a camp near Saigon, which had been given over to former police officials, was burned to the ground with the inmates inside after the authorities discovered that privation alone could not break their spirit. It was also reported that NVA forces systematically eliminated many of those who had "rallied" to the government from their ranks during the war.

In June 1976 Hanoi announced that twelve categories of people still under detention (unofficially a Communist official in Saigon acknowledged that the number still approximated 200,000) were to be tried by people's courts and "severely punished." Among those singled out were "lackeys of imperialism" and veterans of Thieu's puppet regime who refused "to repent their crimes" or who "owed blood debts to the people." The list read like a roster of those the CIA Station and the Embassy had left behind. In fact, some of the names that surfaced in subsequent refugee reports were not unfamiliar to CIA management. One of them was that of Tran Ngoc Chau—the opposition leader whom the CIA had helped frame as a Communist in the early 1970s and whom it had refused to evacuate in the final days of the war.

In addition to cracking down on real or imagined opponents, the Communists attempted in the two years following their takeover to revamp the society and the economy of the south according to their ideological lights. The problems they faced were staggering. Over 3,500,000 people had been left unemployed by the dissolution of Thieu's government and army, and despite the massive foreign aid that had been lavished on Hanoi and Saigon during the war, unified Vietnam was among the twenty-five poorest countries in the world.

One of the Communists' first (unspoken) objectives was to try to equalize the poverty. In June 1975 all bank accounts in the south were frozen, and four months later all citizens were given exactly twelve hours to exchange old currency for new. The conversion effectively reduced most people's life savings to less than forty dollars. At the same time the south's middle class, long the staunchest anti-Communist force in the country, was effectively disenfranchised, stripped of jobs, pensions and state housing, and denied access to hospitals and universities.

Meanwhile, as the new authorities moved to take over the rationing and marketing of vital commodities, inflation jumped by fifty percent. By the summer of 1977 one chicken, at ten dollars, cost half of a southerner's average monthly wage, and a shirt roughly double.

To meet the awesome problems of the cities the Communists also attempted to pare the urban population down to manageable size. Over 1,500,000 city dwellers—including 200,000 from Saigon—were forcibly moved to so-called "new economic zones" in the countryside, with over 5,000,000 more to be resettled by 1980. In spite of official claims, these wilderness redoubts were a far cry from any Communist utopia. Housing, food and medical facilities were almost nonexistent, and diseases like malaria, which had been contained by the Americans, quickly revived.

The policies of the Communist regime did not go totally unnoticed in the United States. In December 1976 a group of former anti-war activists issued a public appeal calling on Hanoi "to honor the concern for human rights which you have expressed both in formal agreements and in countless conversations with peace activists." The Politburo, however, ignored these pleas and rejected all charges of wrongdoing. As Hanoi's army newspaper later declared defiantly, the regime would continue to "deprive all rights of freedom to those who look at socialism with a grudging eye or who describe all aspects of socialism in a passive manner."

•   •   •

The trends that emerged during the first two years of Communist rule were not passing aberrations. In the winter of 1976 a party Congress, the first since 1960, was convened in Hanoi to ratify a five-year development program that preserved and elaborated on the policies that had already been set out. The Politburo and the party Central Committee also were expanded to include allies and protégés of hard-liners like Le Duan. One of the newly appointed Politburo members, a man named Le Van Luong, was of special interest to me. An old-line Stalinist who had engineered the bloody land-reform program in North Vietnam in the mid-1950s, Luong happened to be the uncle of someone I had known well at the time of the cease-fire—Nguyen Van Tai, the man in the snow-white cell who had been executed just hours before Communist forces rolled into Saigon.

Although the rulers of the new Vietnam continued in the wake of their victory to pay lip service to the ideal of Communist solidarity, they soon discovered that they could not count on the kind of support from their allies they had enjoyed in the past. Indeed, once the war had been won and the humiliation of the United States was complete, the Soviets and the Chinese began cutting back their aid to Hanoi, canceling non-refundable grants altogether, and it quickly became apparent to Le Duan and his colleagues that they would have to look elsewhere for benefactors. The prospect of seeking assistance even from the United States itself became a very real consideration.

The Americans themselves made the first overtures. A select Congressional delegation visited Hanoi in December 1975 to seek information on the 2,700 American servicemen still missing in action, and several weeks later Senator Edward Kennedy asked the Communists to repatriate the remains of the two young marines who had been killed in the shelling of Tan Son Nhut on the last day of the war. In March 1976 Kissinger himself initiated a secret exchange of diplomatic notes. "The interests of peace and security," he wrote to Hanoi, "will benefit from placing the past behind us and developing the basis for a new relationship between the two countries." For the next few months the dialogue continued sporadically as Hanoi insisted on $4.2 billion in aid from the United States—a figure Nixon had mentioned secretly at the time of the cease-fire—as the price for further dealings. By August, however, it was apparent that Washington would not bend to this demand, and Hanoi in a dramatic turnabout released the names of twelve missing American pilots as a gesture of good will.

That opened the door. When the Carter Administration took office several months later, it chose to overlook the human-rights problems in Vietnam and soon sent a presidential commission to Hanoi to explore new avenues of conciliation. In May 1977 American and Vietnamese negotiators met around an oval table in Paris to begin concrete discussions.

The bargaining was bound to be difficult, particularly since a majority in Congress remained opposed to Hanoi's aid demands, and Le Duan was determined to hold out for maximum concessions. Yet a beginning had been made, and that was invaluable, for once Hanoi could be made to believe it had been accepted in the West, and could expect some measure of assistance, its temptation to seek retribution against those tens of thousands the Americans had left behind might well be allayed.

COVER-UP

While official Washington labored quietly in the two years following Hanoi's victory to establish a new relationship with the Vietnamese, most Americans tried to forget about Vietnam altogether. The amnesia was understandable. After all the bloodshed and bitterness of the war, who could be blamed for wanting to put it out of mind?

Yet there was also, behind the silence and public indifference, a bit of official conjuring. Those who had made cease-fire policy in Vietnam wanted us to forget how it had ended—or at least to remember only what best suited their versions of the truth.

The cover-up and the cosmeticizing of events began almost immediately. Meeting with newsmen in the final hours of the airlift, Kissinger insisted that there had been a chance for a negotiated settlement up until 27 April, whereupon, he maintained, the North Vietnamese had shifted course and opted for a military solution. He did not choose to acknowledge that the intelligence told a different story. Nor was he candid enough to admit that the Soviets, with the help of the Hungarians, Poles and the French, had played him and so many others for fools. By his lights (as he put it later, in another press conference) the Soviets had played "a moderately constructive role in enabling us to understand the possibilities there were for the evacuation, both of Americans and South Vietnamese, and the possibilities that might exist for a political solution."

While still on board the USS *Blueridge,* Polgar gave an elaborate press briefing of his own which essentially corroborated Kissinger's story. There was in fact only one significant difference between their separate accounts. Polgar could not resist taking verbal swipes at the Ambassador, intimating that Martin had never appreciated the gravity of the military situation, as he had. This was true, of course, as far as it went. But what Polgar failed to mention was that he himself had contributed mightily to Martin and Kissinger's second illusion: the notion that there was a chance for a Vichy-type peace.

Once the Administration had established its own slant on reality, Kissinger acted promptly to forestall contradictions. He cabled Martin on shipboard, ordering him to say nothing to the press. He also made it clear to former President Thieu in Taiwan that he could expect no entry visa to the United States (where his daughter was in school) until after the American presidential elections.

In the meantime, other Vietnamese notables were given a devastating lesson in humility. Shortly after arriving in Guam several of the defeated

ARVN generals were brought together in one of the old metal barracks. An exhausted General Toan, the former MR 3 commander, was pushed into the meeting in a wheelchair, and General Truong, the defender of Danang, was suffering from such an acute case of conjunctivitis he could not find his way to a chair. Moments later an American naval officer marched in and demanded that the generals remove their uniforms. "Can't we at least keep our shoulder stars?" one of them asked. "No," the American replied. "You have no army, no country any more." It was as if the Republic of Vietnam had never existed at all.

When the U.S. naval task force docked in Manila on 5 May, I was flown immediately to Thailand on "special assignment," to debrief journalists and refugees still trickling out of Vietnam.*

From my interviews I produced the first intelligence on the Communist takeover, and was instrumental in setting up a kind of underground railway back into Vietnam to ferret out other refugees. My diligence, however, was not appreciated at CIA headquarters. Some of the information I gathered only served to highlight the failures of agency management. After a month I was called home.

I reached CIA headquarters in August after a brief vacation (my first in two and a half years) and was "processed in" through Ted Shackley's East Asia Division. Like all returnees, I was directed to fill out an affidavit which in effect attributed the breakdown of the evacuation to "local enemy action." I refused to sign it. Instead I went from office to office, asking for permission to do a real "damage assessment" so that the agency could learn from its mistakes. I was told no one was interested in anything so "controversial."

Polgar, meanwhile, was quickly shunted off into a new assignment. Not one ranking official in Shackley's division ever bothered to question him on the evacuation or on the personalities or documents left behind.

Having spent so much time overseas, I was virtually unknown to my fellow CIA "analysts" when I returned to Langley and could find no job in my own old "home" office. Out of sympathy for my predicament, Polgar invited me to accompany him to his own next posting abroad. I agreed and was immediately placed in special language training.

But soon several things happened to cause me to reconsider. In mid-August the Foreign Service Institute invited Polgar to deliver a lecture on the evacuation to a "cleared" audience of State Department officers. He was unable to oblige, but asked me to stand in for him. I did so, turning the briefing into a full-fledged commentary on what had taken place during Saigon's final days. When Shackley learned of it he was furious.

---

*My reassignment was not without complications. So confused had the evacuation been, the CIA lost track of me between Manila and Bangkok. Before thinking to consult the cable traffic to pinpoint my whereabouts, agency officials contacted my parents to tell them I was missing in action. The error was not corrected for several days.

Soon afterward, at a cocktail party for old "Vietnam hands," I ran into Wolfgang Lehmann and was treated to another shock. After a few minutes of polite chitchat Lehmann pulled me aside and began questioning me on several aspects of Hanoi's military strategy. He confided he was in the process of briefing two journalists, both Kissinger favorites, on the evacuation and the collapse, and he wanted to refresh his memory. I was appalled at what he told me. His version of the truth, as he spun it out that evening, bore little relation to what I remembered. Nor could I understand why Administration officials were "leaking" to the press before either the CIA or the State Department had completed an assessment of its own.

I soon discovered that Lehmann's briefing was only the beginning. In the next week or so Vietnam specialists in the State Department and the Pentagon were directed to open their files (selectively) to the two newsmen. The CIA did likewise. Colby and two top assistants met with one of them, attempted to dress up the agency's role in the evacuation, and provided the journalist with a compilation of our top-secret reporting from Vietnam, a document which dealt explicitly with both our intelligence "sources" and "methods." In its zeal to protect its image, the CIA in effect was jeopardizing the few secrets that had survived the collapse.

In early fall my confidence in my colleagues and superiors suffered a mortal blow. Several former Saigon Station officers, myself included, were called in by the CIA's Inspector General and asked to provide "background" on Polgar's reporting habits and biases. Despite my personal feelings for Polgar, I felt I had no choice but to be candid, particularly since I had been pressing for a thorough review of what had gone wrong. I acknowledged that Polgar had at times blocked reports—on the grounds of poor sourcing or quality—that might have put the South Vietnamese government in an unfavorable light.

As my interview drew to a close, I asked to be allowed to file a full accounting of the Station's performance in the final days so that the "blame" could be spread around, as it should be. But my interviewer rejected the project as "too complicated." He explained that his own inquiry was meant simply to give Colby "ammunition" with which to fend off any Congressional probes into CIA activities in Vietnam.

His remarks confirmed all of my grimmest suspicions. I resolved then to write a damage assessment on my own, whether the agency liked it or not, even if I had to go "outside" to do so.

Throughout the fall and winter of 1975 the Administration continued to do what it could to blank Vietnam out of the public memory. The Pentagon contracted several former Saigon generals to write a history of the final campaign, then promptly slapped a classified label on the project so that none of the participants could talk to newsmen without authorization. In the meantime, the White House and the State Department parceled out honors and choice jobs to members of Martin's immediate entourage to keep them content

—and silent. Martin himself, briefly hospitalized as the result of complications stemming from his pneumonia, was given a presidential citation. Lehmann was designated Consul General in Frankfurt, and Boudreau and Jazynka were assigned to plush administrative posts in Paris.

Several Kissinger associates suggested that the young State Department officers whose diligence and imagination had actually saved the evacuation be rewarded as well. But Martin and Lehmann (with Kissinger's support) balked at this, claiming that there were simply "too many." As a result, prior to Gerald Ford's defeat in the 1976 presidential elections, only two of the middle-level State Department officers who had taken part in the evacuation were given any recognition at all. The Foreign Service Association, in effect the State Department union, cited both Lionel Rosenblatt and Craig Johnstone, organizers of the luncheon group "conspirators," for their services during the crisis.

The CIA, to its credit, was more generous in honoring its Vietnam "heroes," though at times it gave less than due attention to matching rewards with deserts. "Howard Archer," the former Base Chief in Nha Trang who had abandoned both employees and documents, was elevated to the staff Colby created to defend the agency against Congressional inquiries, and "Custer," his counterpart from Danang, was named Chief of an important CIA Station in Asia. In late December 1975 agency management called other Vietnam veterans together in the CIA's bubble-shaped auditorium and handed out a variety of classified medals—secret awards for secret accomplishments. The citation which accompanied my own Medal of Merit applauded my analytical acuity during the final month of the war.

In his remarks at the ceremony Colby commended us all for our sacrifice and service and vigorously defended American policies in Vietnam, particularly the Phoenix and pacification programs, which he suggested would have won the war had it not been for the North Vietnamese army. I sat there, listening to this nonsense and wondering what had happened to the CIA I had thought I was serving.

A few days later I advised George Carver, co-author of the Weyand Report, that I would like to write a book on the cease-fire period, with the agency's blessings and help. Carver gave me no encouragement. Not long afterward I was summoned to the office of the CIA's chief legal counsel and put through a classic interrogation, one interviewer playing the sympathetic listener, the other the accuser. My motives and my integrity were impugned. I was ordered to submit to a lie-detector test to "ensure" I had leaked no classified information to the press, and to turn over any personal notes or diaries I might have kept while in Vietnam. That evening, three weeks after the CIA had given me one of its highest awards, I announced to my immediate superior that I was resigning in protest.

Once I had severed my ties, CIA officials tried to discredit me with former colleagues. Memos advising everyone not to talk with me were circulated around the headquarters building, as if I were on the verge of betraying national secrets. CIA officials who had known or worked with me, including a former girl friend, were called in, interrogated and threatened with firing if they did not inform on me.

Meanwhile, public discussion of Saigon's demise flared briefly. On 27 January 1976 Ambassador Martin appeared before members of the House International Relations Committee to offer his first extended public comment on the fiasco. It was a masterful performance. Without pointing an accusatory finger at anyone, he said just enough to obscure his own mistakes and to convey the impression that Kissinger, Polgar and Congress had all been responsible for Saigon's collapse and for the problems surrounding the evacuation.

As Martin later explained to me, his testimony was carefully calculated. Despite the presidential citation, and the awards for his top subordinates, he felt the Administration had ignored and even slighted him in recent months, letting him take all the blame for what had gone sour in Vietnam. Kissinger, by his account, had even spread rumors around Washington that Martin was a little "insane." Now the Ambassador was determined to have his revenge. His testimony to Congress, so subtle yet pointed in its insinuations, was his opening shot.

The maneuver paid off. Soon afterward Kissinger appointed him "special assistant," as if to subdue him through kindness. But Martin would not be so easily appeased. He began talking with me and various journalists at length, always embellishing on the notion that he had done "one hell of a job" in Saigon. He also quietly squirreled away secret papers to buttress his case.

While Martin jockeyed for advantage, my own problems with the CIA came to a head. In the spring of 1976 the NVA commander, General Dung, published his memoirs, indirectly confirming many of the Embassy's mistakes and misjudgments in Saigon's final days. A journalist for the *Washington Post,* who had long known me, called and asked if I would comment on the disclosures, particularly Dung's assertion that NVA forces had captured many intelligence files intact. Since the CIA had been unwilling to give me a hearing, I agreed. The resulting newspaper story, headlined "Saigon's Secrets Lost," marked the first time any former Embassy officer had openly and for the record challenged the Administration's line on the collapse.

From that point on I was a public enemy in the eyes of some Administration officials. Assistant Secretary Habib, in a memo to Kissinger, described my comments to the press as "tendentious," and George Carver went so far as to suggest that the CIA assign a "case officer" to look over my shoulder, as if I were a foreign spy. The action was not only an insult to me, it was of questionable legality, since the National Security Acts rule out any domestic police activities by the CIA.

Finally, in the summer of 1976, Polgar was called home to lecture and threaten me. During our meeting my old mentor accused me of a lack of patriotism for daring to criticize the agency and intimated that I was "a little crazy." He also attempted to put a favorable gloss on his own performance during the evacuation, even to the point of claiming credit for the rescue of the 1,000 Vietnamese employees of House 7, the clandestine radio station, whom in fact Bill Johnson had evacuated over Polgar's objections. On this somewhat melancholy note, our conversation ended. I never saw Polgar again.

Several weeks later I traveled to Paris to seek background material for my book. Among others, I talked with officials of the Vietnamese Communist Embassy. I asked them to convey a list of questions from me to General Dung in Hanoi and requested that as a gesture of good will they arrange for the return of some of Ambassador Martin's household belongings, which he had abandoned in Saigon. In a more general vein I urged them to be more forthcoming with the United States on the issue of American servicemen missing in action and provided them with some information on current public attitudes in the United States, particularly the apathy toward Vietnam, about which they knew nothing. Soon afterward, whether by coincidence or not, Hanoi provided Washington with the list of twelve missing servicemen that was to open the way to more candid dealings.

When I returned home I informed both the CIA and the State Department of my activities and pleaded with friends in the Administration to accelerate official contacts with Hanoi, if only to provide the Communists with an incentive to ease up on their treatment of those we had left behind. For my trouble the CIA stepped up its harassment tactics against me.

Because of its continued assaults on my integrity, and its reluctance to deal candidly with the Vietnam issue, I eventually stopped meeting with the case officer the agency had assigned to me. I also resolved not to submit my manuscript to the agency for clearance and censorship, as all former employees-turned-author are required to do. In my view, if the CIA could officially leak to the press to whitewash its role in Vietnam, it had forfeited the right to censor me in the name of security or national interest.

While I struggled over draft after draft of my book, Graham Martin continued his quest for public vindication. At his insistence, the White House nominated him in the fall of 1976, just prior to the presidential elections, for the post of ambassador-at-large. Once the proposal was submitted to Congress, however, some of Martin's old enemies managed to tie it up in committee, where it languished.

The presidential elections wrote an end to Martin's hopes, and from then on he could only reconcile himself to the prospect of retirement.* He made one last effort, however, to refurbish his image. In the final days of the Ford Administration he recommended to Kissinger that some of the young State Department officers from Saigon be finally recognized for their services. Yet even in this moment of magnanimity Martin could not quite divest himself of the prejudices and parochialism that had so marred his management of the Embassy. Many of those he recommended for citation were old protégés.

---

*Two of Martin's severest critics rose to top posts in the Carter Administration. Habib was appointed Undersecretary of State—the second highest position in the State Department—and Dick Moose, co-author of the Moose-Miessner report for the Senate Foreign Relations Committee, became an Assistant Secretary.

Brunson McKinley, Al Francis and several of Francis' own subordinates from Danang were given the State Department's highest award for valor. Moorefield, Don Hays and countless others who were equally deserving did not receive even a note of thanks.

Several State Department officers, encouraged and aided by outsiders like myself, immediately set to work to rectify this injustice. Eventually, the list of awardees was expanded to include Moorefield, Hays and many others.

My own Vietnam adventure effectively came to an end on a Friday afternoon in late February 1977—appropriately, in the presence of Martin himself. He had called me that morning and asked me to visit him in his office on the top floor of the State Department.

The specter who greeted me at the door was merely a shadow of the swashbuckling diplomat I remembered from those exciting first encounters in Saigon in the summer of 1973. Weary, his face parched and old, Martin motioned me to the couch facing his desk. It was his last day in the Department, he told me, and he wanted to make sure that I had the facts "straight" for my book. He then proceeded to review much of what we had discussed in our many previous interviews, attempting as usual to put a favorable construction on all his actions and decisions in Saigon's final days. By the time he had finished, an hour and a half had passed—but I had hardly written a note. After sitting at the man's elbow for over four years, I knew all his arguments and rationalizations by heart.

As he stood up to usher me out, the intensity he had always displayed during our interviews suddenly vanished, and a look of sadness flickered momentarily in the tired, dull eyes. "You know," he said, "I'm going out of here almost as I came in. I was sworn into government service by an old country preacher over forty years ago, and today I'm leaving it without any more ceremony. After all my years here in the Department, my colleagues didn't even give me a farewell luncheon."

I stared at him a moment, not quite sure whether to smile or sympathize. Was he still the consummate actor, playing for effect? Before I could make up my mind, the face became a mask again. I shook his hand and left.

I remembered as I walked to the elevator what one of my former colleagues had said about Martin. It seemed only too apropos, a kind of final tribute to him. "He was a lot like American policy in Vietnam," my friend had said. "He saw himself as an old swamp fox, able through wit and cunning to alter anything he wanted. But in fact he was much more akin to swamp fire, an illusory if brilliant light, darting from point to point but altering very little at all."

There are some who say that the Vietnam the Americans nurtured and supported was destined to end as it did, that our policies were so flawed and ill-advised from the very beginning, they could only have produced a Communist victory.

While I cannot in conscience defend those policies, I reject such logic. As a former intelligence officer I must believe, perhaps naïvely, that right decisions taken at appropriate moments on the basis of accurate information might have averted the outcome, or at least have modified it. This view would undoubtedly find favor among many Vietnamese, both North and South. For it is one of the ancient tenets of their culture that while there may be a predisposition toward certain events, nothing is predetermined and men who understand the forces at work can alter their direction.

Clearly, Henry Kissinger was the American who most directly affected the forces at work in Vietnam as it emerged from the cease-fire. He negotiated the "peace" and shaped American policies in the aftermath. In both instances his handiwork was faulty and too hastily done. But was he to be blamed for that? The American people wanted out of Vietnam under any circumstances, as quickly as possible, and if Kissinger erred in obliging them, he did so in deference to sensitivities and frustrations that traced back to the mistakes of the Kennedy and Johnson Administrations before him.

Following the cease-fire, Kissinger erred again by placing his trust in Soviet and Chinese cooperation and in the efficacy—and continued availability —of American aid to Saigon as a shield against North Vietnamese aggressiveness. But he could not have known at the time that the very underpinnings of these policies and premises would be destroyed by Watergate.

Of all of Kissinger's mistakes in the realm of Vietnam policy, perhaps only two fit clearly into the category of "all his own." One of them stemmed from his way of doing business, his penchant for the virtuoso performance. Determined to do just about everything himself, he failed to delegate any real oversight responsibility for Vietnam to his subordinates. Consequently, as his own attention became diverted by the Middle East and other problems, Washington lost sight, and control, of its most enduring crisis. By the time the crisis boiled over, there was only one perspective on it—Graham Martin's.

Then, too, Kissinger, with his addiction to secrecy, never quite leveled with Congress or the American people about what was essential to preserving his imperfect peace. Martin once remarked to me that the greatest tragedy of the cease-fire period was that the Paris agreement had never been submitted to Congress for approval, like the peace treaty it was supposed to be. If it had been, Congress at least would have known what was at stake in Vietnam as it moved to circumscribe the President's war-making powers in reaction to Watergate.

Next to Kissinger, Martin must of course bear primary responsibility for what occurred in the end. The Administration's stalking horse, he was sent to Saigon in the wake of the cease-fire to make sure that Kissinger's peace did not become the ticket for a Communist takeover. His "mistake" was that he did his job too well—and too long. His hard-line views, a reflection of Nixon's, strengthened the South Vietnamese in their own intransigence and in their dependence on the United States, and when finally the bombing was halted and Nixon succumbed to his own excesses, neither the protégés nor the Ambassador was able to shift course in time, in the direction of compromise. On the contrary, Martin through manipulation and force of will tried to create an illusion of continued support in Washington to stiffen Thieu's back, only to drive him further into his stubbornness and misapprehension. Martin erred in this, to be sure. But was he to blame? If he continued to try to remold reality in the image of what he thought it should be, it was because Kissinger and eventually President Ford were only too willing to share his illusions.

Beyond the phalanx of known names and reputations, there are others who must answer for Saigon's demise and for the way it happened. Not the least of these are the American people themselves. True, the sense of revulsion that spread through the country in the late 1960s and early '70s helped to bring the Vietnam war to its first tentative conclusion and forced an end to the barbarity of the American involvement. But once the boys had come home, that "gone-with-the-wind" syndrome that eventually afflicted much of the foreign policy establishment itself also took its toll on the population at large, sweeping Vietnam from our collective consciousness and giving rise to a complacency and indifference among us that enabled a few very powerful men to continue pursuing policies and tactics that had already been brought into question. The consequences of our forgetfulness should be a warning, for by the time General Dung's forces moved on Saigon in April 1975 many of the mistakes and omissions that had plunged us into Vietnam in the first place had been replayed in miniature. Two Presidents had misled Congress; the Ambassador had overdrawn the prospects for success; and our protégés in Saigon had been tolerated in their most self-defeating policies. It was as if the lessons of the past had already been forgotten at the top levels of our government.

Hopefully, with the passage of time and healing of the national trauma inflicted by the war, we will be able to give history its due, a complete and unflinching retrospective, extending beyond the platitudes and recriminations that till now have blinded so many of us to what actually happened to Vietnam, and to ourselves, in the two years following the Paris peace agreement. If we fail to seize the opportunity, and continue to treat Vietnam as an aberration, painfully remembered and best forgotten, particularly in its death throes, then we cannot hope to escape the kind of leadership both in the intelligence field and in the policy-making arena that made Saigon's "decent interval" such an indecent end to this American tragedy.

Index

About the Author

A native North Carolinian, FRANK SNEPP was born in Kinston and reared in Charlotte. Following family tradition, he attended Columbia College in New York, where he majored in Elizabethan literature and graduated in 1965. After a brief stint as a researcher and promotion copywriter for CBS News, he returned to Columbia in 1966 to earn a master's in International Affairs. His specialization, nuclear strategy and NATO, attracted the attention of CIA recruiters, and following his graduation in 1968 he was invited to "sign on." During his eight years in the CIA, Snepp worked both "sides" of the espionage arena, serving as operative as well as analyst, contrary to standard agency practice. Initially a resident specialist on European security matters, he later became the agency's principal analyst of North Vietnamese political affairs and did two "tours" of duty at the U.S. Embassy in Saigon, 1969–1971 and 1972–1975, where he was responsible for preparing strategic estimates and briefings and handling interrogations and informant networks, including one of the CIA's best in Vietnam. A year after Saigon's collapse he resigned from the agency, following several futile attempts to generate interest in an official after-action report.